Preface
to
Quantitative
Economics
&
Econometrics

Michael J. Brennan

Professor of Economics
Wesleyan University

Thomas M. Carroll

Professor of Economics
University of Nevada, Las Vegas

Fourth Edition

Published by
H23 **SOUTH-WESTERN PUBLISHING CO.**

CINCINNATI   WEST CHICAGO, IL   DALLAS   LIVERMORE, CA

Preface to Fourth Edition

It has been twenty-four years since the first edition of Michael Brennan's *Preface to Econometrics* and thirteen years since the third edition. In that time there has been considerable advancement in the techniques and technology of econometrics. Professor Brennan's book has continued to be a mainstay in the instruction of quantitative economics and econometrics because he addresses himself directly to the student, communicating clearly the concepts of quantitative economics and econometrics.

In collaborating with Professor Brennan on a fourth edition of his text, I have tried to remain true to those qualities that made earlier editions of this text classics. Where there have been changes, the goal has been to enhance the original Brennan concept. First, we have changed the name to more clearly reflect the content of the text. Unlike many texts that divorce the principles of mathematical economics from those of econometrics, we have emphasized that both quantitative economics and econometrics are critical to economic research. Second, we have blended the economic examples more directly into the text, showing in every chapter real-world applications of the mathematical and statistical concepts. Third, we have extended the discussions of matrix algebra (Chapter 5) and statistical estimation (Part III) to incorporate major advancements in computer software. No longer do we treat matrix inversion and multiple regression as the tedious processes they were even a decade ago.

I wish to thank Michael Brennan for the confidence he showed by agreeing to this collaboration. Second, I would like to thank my former colleagues at Memphis State University, particularly Professor Karen Pickerill, for constructive comments over a period of eighteen months. Finally, I thank my undergraduate and graduate students at Memphis State, who read and criticized early drafts of this text as the book was classroom tested.

Thomas M. Carroll
University of Nevada, Las Vegas

Contents

Part II   From Mathematics to Statistics

Part III   Econometrics

Introduction

This text addresses two topics: *quantitative economics* and *econometrics*. Quantitative economics deals with the use of mathematical concepts and techniques in the analysis of economic phenomena. Econometrics involves the use of statistical methods to estimate the equations that describe economic events. Quantitative economics and econometrics are two closely related, but distinct aspects of economic science. They are related in the sense that the econometrician uses mathematical methods to generate economic models to be subjected to empirical testing. Furthermore, the procedures of econometrics provide estimates of the unknowns in mathematical models. It would not be exaggerating to say that mathematical economics is the foundation of econometrics, and that econometrics adds realism to abstract mathematical models. Hence, it is natural for a text to treat both quantitative economics and econometrics. But it is also reasonable to address these topics separately.

Despite the intimate relation between mathematical economics and econometrics, they both lead lives of their own. Many theoretical economics texts and articles are written in general mathematical terms without concern for the precise values of economic variables. Mathematics, by itself, lends precision to economic concepts that are more difficult to grasp with non-mathematical language. For instance, a mathematical economist may use a particular symbol to stand for the price and another to stand for the marginal cost of production. The principles of calculus can be employed to show that profit maximization by a competitive firm requires that marginal cost equal price.

While mathematical economics can stand without econometrics, it is less clear that econometrics can be used or understood without a basic understanding of mathematical concepts. It is true that modern electronic computers have taken much of the drudgery out of mathematical computation. But computers, even loaded with sophisticated econometric software, only do what they are told. We must have a pretty good idea of what we want the computer to do, or we will have a difficult time interpreting the computer output. That is why this book devotes half of its contents to mathematical economics. Chapters 1 through 11 develop the major mathematical tools necessary for understanding econometrics. These chapters can stand alone in a course in quantitative or mathematical economics, or they can serve as background in a course in econometrics.

Econometrics might simply be defined as a bridge between economic theory and reality. Obviously some elaboration is in order. Life is rich in experience, vast in complexity, and intimidating in importance. Theory is simple, precise, and elegant. Theory cuts away irrelevant detail and organizes what remains into a model of an ideal system. Some people are put off by the lack of realism of theory; they fail to appreciate that it is precisely its abstraction that gives theory its ability to predict. Ironically, some theorists lose patience with the sloppiness of the real world; they fail to appreciate the fact that the ultimate test of a theory is its ability to predict and/or explain actual events.

The problem of testing theory—any theory—rests in reconciling observed events and theoretical explanations. In the physical sciences, theories are tested in controlled experiments. The chemist or the physicist literally creates an imaginary world in the laboratory so that "causes" and "effects" can be clearly isolated and identified. In the behavioral sciences the researcher contrasts an experimental group with a control group. Since factors influencing human (and even animal) behavior are too complex to control directly, researchers rely on the rules of probability to isolate the influence of a stipulated stimulus (e.g., stress) on the subject population. In economics, we use published data on past events to estimate the mathematical structure of theories, comparing the statistical relationship between "causes" and "effects" with those predicted by theory. The greater the probability that the observations could have been generated by chance, the less credence is given to the theory.

Econometrics essentially follows a four-step process, commonly known as the *scientific method*: (1) the assembly of facts and similar information, (2) the formation of a hypothesis or hypotheses about the behavior of economic variables or the causes of events, (3) the derivation of testable assertions or predictions that are logically derived from the hypotheses, and (4) the testing of predictions by the reference to observed facts. We might refer to step (1) as *experience*, step (2) as *theorizing*, step (3) as *mathematical reasoning* and step (4) as *statistical inference*.

Each step can be self-contained, practiced and studied in isolation from the others. Many practitioners of the business arts are sometimes bored by theory, terrified of mathematics, and confused by statistics. Yet it is amazing how frequently they rely on "rules of thumb" that are little else but *ad hoc* theories. They also survive by "seat of the pants" calculations and playing their hunches. When we think about it, most businesspersons are actually amateur econometricians!

Similarly, the economics profession, and indeed the world, is full of "pure" theorists, thinkers who so admire the elegance of a theoretical system that they disdain the real world, or perhaps more dangerously, mistake the real world for their ideal type. Having a nearly religious commitment to the principles of their theories, they see no need to test their beliefs. If "the real world" fails to conform to the predictions of their theories, so much the worse for the real world! Alas, when reality is seen as the servant of theory, rather than the other way around, hostile camps of conflicting theories coalesce around conflicting interest groups. The reputations and careers that are destroyed in the name of preserving the purity of theory are legion. If different theoretical propositions are but put to the test, much of the disagreement could be resolved.

Mathematics is a language that facilitates the communication of economic concepts. Most economic concepts are quantitative; prices, income, saving, amounts of commodities produced and consumed, and many other economic magnitudes are, at least in principle, measurable. The use of mathematical symbols is perfectly natural in economics. There is no fundamental difference between mathematical economic theory and economic theory that does not use mathematics. Although the same conclusions can be reached whether the theory is stated verbally or mathematically, there are definite advantages to mathematical formulation: (1) it introduces rigor into the definitions and relationships, (2) it makes the assumptions explicit at each stage of the reasoning process and thereby avoids hidden assumptions not easily discovered, (3) it brings out clearly the limitations of the theory, and (4) it identifies implications that might be overlooked in purely verbal presentations.

Econometrics differs somewhat from mathematical economics, however. It differs in that its mathematical formulations are designed with a view to statistical measurement and testing. Statistics is also an important aspect of econometrics, yet we must distinguish econometrics from what we may call statistical economics. The latter is a form of quantitative economics that avoids economic theory and claims to provide a statistical summary of the economic data themselves. The recording and charting of the gross national product of the total United States is an example of statistical economics. Another example is the tabulation of the consumer price index. But the mere accumulation and ordering of data seldom provide solutions to important economic questions. Some theory is required to interpret the behavior of items in the data; explanations do not come ready-made. Since some theory is unavoidable, it is usually best to state the theory explicitly. Econometrics, unlike statistical economics, synthesizes theoretical ideas, mathematical form, and quantitative evidence.

Econometrics, when it is done well, blends the elements of experience, theory, mathematics, and statistical inference to provide a unified picture of economics. A practicing econometrician is a generalist, a practical theorist with a working understanding of both mathematics and statistics. This book is designed to be the first step in the training of an econometrician. No doubt you already possess, in varying degrees, the various talents and aptitudes necessary to master the subject matter of this text. You certainly have had some experiences. You have also taken previous courses in mathematics, statistics, and economics. Yet if your experience is like that of most students (including that of the authors of this book), these four facets of econometrics have been learned in isolation from each other. So this book is designed to put the pieces together.

Part I covers the essentials of mathematical economics, with the goal of understanding how to translate verbal economic arguments into their mathematical equivalents. Many economic examples are used to develop these topics. You may discover that your knowledge of economics will help you understand mathematical concepts that heretofore seemed like so many abstractions. Alternatively your deepening understanding of mathematics will reveal insights into economics you previously missed with a "verbal" orientation to the subject.

Part II presents a transition from quantitative economics to econometrics, reviewing how risk and uncertainty play a crucial role in the estimation of economic models. Part III deals with the problem of statistical inference as it relates to the testing of economic theories. These chapters are rich in economic applications, including many tests of controversial theories. It is likely that you will not agree with all the conclusions we make. But that is the point of econometrics. Disagreements should be resolved by recourse to the data. Accordingly, the data for most of the examples in the text are provided on a microcomputer disk that accompanies your professor's instructor's manual. You should find that by retracing our steps, and trying a few twists of your own, many disagreements can be resolved.

Many students find that the easiest way through a course is to psyche out the professor, memorize the relevant concepts, and forget the material after the final exam. But that is not the best approach to econometrics. Econometrics is "hands-on" economics, designed to subject our most closely held convictions to objective tests. Econometrics must be understood in order to be applied, and it must be applied in order to be understood. This book is a preface to econometrics, a first step to understanding the interaction between economic theory and the real world.

PART I

Mathematical

Analysis

1

Variables and

Functions

As shown in the preceding introductory sketch of econometrics, there are two aspects to the empirical science of economics: (1) theoretical explanations of events in the economy are phrased in terms of mathematics; and (2) the mathematical equations that describe economic behavior are subjected to statistical analysis. In the early chapters we will focus on the former aspect. We shall see how familiar notions of economic theory can be phrased in mathematical terms. Mathematics is a language for the expression of theoretical propositions. For the most part, you will already be familiar with the economic ideas we will use to introduce some elementary mathematical terms. We shall see how these terms, once understood, provide deeper insights into economic concepts by adding both rigor and clarity.

VARIABLES

Before we can formulate economic theory in mathematical terms, it is necessary to understand the mathematical elements that make up that formulation. The most basic of these is the variable. A *variable* may be defined as a quantity that can assume any value from a given set of numbers. A variable is usually symbolized by a letter, such as x, y, or z, or a terse group of letters used to describe its meaning (e.g., *CON* for consumption, *MC* for marginal cost, or *MR* for marginal revenue). Suppose that the variable under consideration is called x and that x can take on any positive value from zero to one million. We represent the potential values of x as a set, called the *domain* of the variable. Individual values of the domain, such as the numbers 0, 0.5, 1, 2, 15.125, 27, and 1,000, are each elements of that set. We show that 2 is an element of the set of numbers between zero and one million in the following way: $2 \in \{0 < x < 1,000,000\}$, where "$\epsilon$" (the Greek letter "epsilon") means "is an element of."

The domain of a variable may be either finite or infinite. A *finite* set has a specified number of elements; the number of elements can be counted. The set of integers between 0 and 10 is a finite set; the entire set can be enumerated: $\{1, 2, 3, 4, 5, 6, 7, 8, 9\}$. It follows that an infinite set cannot be listed explicitly because the number of elements cannot be counted. The set of positive integers is an infinite set. The entire set can only be listed by stipulation of the rule for inclusion: $\{x$ is an integer and $x > 0\}$.

You are no doubt familiar with a number of mathematical operations that can be performed on variables. For instance, if we are concerned with the set of positive integers, the operations addition, multiplication, and exponentiation performed between two or more elements in the set of positive integers generates a result (value for x) that is also an element of that domain. In other words, the sum of two or more positive integers is also a positive integer; the product of two or more positive integers is also a positive integer; and a positive integer raised to a power that is also a positive integer produces an answer that is a positive integer. By contrast, the operations subtraction and division, when performed between two or more members of the set of positive integers, do not always yield results that are positive integers. If we take two values of x, say x_1 and x_2, such that both are positive integers and $x_2 > x_1$, then $(x_2 - x_1) \in \{$positive integers$\}$ while $(x_1 - x_2) \notin \{$positive integers$\}$. (The epsilon with a slash through it is read "is not an element of.") If x_1 is a prime number, there is no positive integer, aside from x_1 itself and the number "1" which, when divided into x_1, will yield another positive integer.

The set of *real numbers* is used frequently in economics. This set is composed of all *rational numbers* (numbers that can be expressed as the *ratio* of two integers) and the set of *irrational numbers* (which cannot be expressed as the ratio of two integers). An attractive feature of the set of *real numbers* is that the five common mathematical operations—addition, subtraction, multiplication, division, and exponentiation—are all defined over the domain of real numbers. If we add any two real numbers, our result is a real number; if we multiply any two real numbers, our result is a real number. The set of real numbers includes negative as well as positive integers. Hence, if we subtract a larger integer from a smaller integer, our result is a negative integer, which is, of course a real number. When one integer is divided by another, the result is a rational number, although not necessarily an integer. All rational numbers are included in the set of real numbers.

Recall that an integer raised to an integral power generates an integer; but an integer raised to a power that is not an integer will not normally produce an integer. A variable raised to an exponent that is a negative number is equivalent to taking the reciprocal of that variable raised to the absolute value of that power; e.g., $x^{-2} = 1/(x^2)$. A variable raised to a fractional power yields a result that is equivalent to raising the variable to the power indicated by the numerator of the fraction, then taking the root indicated by the denominator of the fraction; e.g., $x^{1/2} = \sqrt{x}$; $x^{2/3} = \sqrt[3]{x^2}$.

It should be clear why economists and other scientists usually specify the set of real numbers as the domain for the variables of their theories; specification of a more restricted domain constricts the freedom of investigators to employ mathematical operations on those variables. Nevertheless, there are some instances when relevance dictates a limit to the set of values a variable can assume. In this universe, mass and energy cannot assume negative numbers. When economists speak of technology, their subject is bound by the rules of known science. Therefore, we cannot speak of negative outputs or negative inputs, although changes of inputs or outputs could be positive, negative, or zero. By similar logic, it usually makes better sense to constrain prices and costs to the set of positive real numbers.

FUNCTIONS

As you can see, many diverse phenomena can be treated as variables in economics: rates of input and output; flows of income, cost, and revenue; stocks of machinery and inventories. But not even the pure mathematician is interested in variables for their own sake. The mathematician attempts to relate one or more variables to others. In economics the theorist tries to determine the connection among relevant concepts (variables). A *relation* is formally defined as *a set of ordered pairs*. This means that the relationship between two variables, say x and y, defines a set of paired values, in which the first element in each pair is a value for x, and the second element of that pair is a corresponding value of y. We can let the letter R denote some *relation* between them. For instance, let $R(x, y)$ stand for the relationship "y is greater than x": $R(x, y) = \{(x, y)$ such that $y > x\}$. The pair of numbers $(2, 4)$ belongs to the relation, whereas the pair $(4, 2)$ does not.

A *function* is a special kind of relation with the property that each value of the first element (drawn from a set called the *domain*) of the ordered pair is associated with a unique value of the second element (drawn from a set called the *range*). The relation defined in the previous paragraph is not a function; we can find two pairs, say $(2, 4)$ and $(2, 5)$, which both satisfy the relation. For a specified value of x, there is more than one admissible value of y. By contrast, the relation $y = x^2$ is a function; whatever real number we specify as the value of x, there is only one value of y that is admissible: namely, the result of x multiplied by itself. The variable y is said to be a function of x if, once the value of x has been specified, the value of y is uniquely determined. The variable x, whose value may be arbitrarily assigned, is called the *independent* variable. The variable y, whose numerical value is stipulated by the selection of x, is called the *dependent* variable.

To this point we have defined functions as relations between only two variables. These are the types of functions with which you are most familiar, given the prevalence of two-dimensional diagrams in economics. However, we will learn presently that a dependent variable can also be defined for combinations of two or more independent variables.

The standard notation for defining a functional relation between the dependent variable y and the independent variable x is: $y = f(x)$ (although nearly any letter or symbol could be used in place of "f"). This notation means that the value of y depends on the value of x in some unspecified way.

To appreciate the usefulness of this mathematical symbolism, consider an example from economics. Let p represent the price of a commodity and q the quantity of that commodity that a household will buy, given values for the prices of complements, substitutes, the household's real income, and the tastes of family members. The demand function can be written $q = D(p)$; the quantity demanded is unique for each price, although the relation is as yet unspecified. Estimation of the demand equation could yield explicit mathematical functions, such as $q = 100 - 2p$ or $q = 20p^{-2}$. Likewise, the consumption function might be written as $C = C(Y_d)$, where the dependent variable is aggregate consumption and the independent variable is aggregate disposable income. Statistical techniques could be employed to determine a specific mathematical relation between the two variables. No doubt you can think of many more examples from economics.

We can now discuss the specification of functional form in more detail. As we will see in Part III, before we attempt an empirical estimation of a function, it is necessary to specify a general mathematical form the equation will take. An *equation* is a statement of equality between two mathematical entities. It stipulates the value of one variable, once the value of the other has been specified. The convention is to place the dependent variable on the left side of the equal sign and the independent variable on the right side. This notation is referred to as the *explicit form* of the function. The familiar "intercept-slope" form of the linear equation, e.g., $y = 6 + 3x$, is an example of the explicit form. This equation says that the value of y is determined by taking the value of x, multiplying it by 3, and adding 6. The value of y is unique for each value of x because each time the value of x changes, the value of y changes by three times that amount.

In contrast to the explicit form of an equation, the *implicit* form depicts a mutual relation between variables. The function $f(x, y) = 3y - 9x - 18 = 0$ is equivalent to the explicit function in the previous paragraph, i.e., $y = 6 + 3x$. Note that by adding "$9x + 18$" to (or subtracting "$-9x - 18$" from) each side of the equation, then dividing through by 3, we obtain our implicit equation from the explicit one. Indeed, this is what we mean when we say we have "solved" an equation: we have translated an implicit functional form into an explicit form. Note that we could have solved the implicit form to make x a function of y: $3y - 9x - 18 = 0$ becomes $x = (1/3)y - 2$ by adding $9x$ to both sides of the equation, dividing through by 9, and then transposing. An implicit linear equation has the property that either variable can be assigned the role of dependent variable. This is not always the case with nonlinear functions. The implicit function $y - x^2 - 9 = 0$ can be solved for y to yield the function $y = x^2 + 9$, since each value for x is associated with only one value of y. However, if we solved this equation for x, we would generate the relation $x = \pm\sqrt{y - 9}$, which is not a function. For instance, if we set $y = 13$, there are two values of x implied, namely $x = 2$ and $x = -2$.

Let us return to our demand function example: $q = D(p)$, where p is the price of the commodity and q is the quantity demanded. We might write this demand function explicitly as:

(1) $q = 100 - 2p$

We could also write it implicitly as:

(2) $q + 2p - 100 = 0$

By expressing the demand function explicitly as in (1), we not only state that q depends on p, but go further and state the exact way in which q depends on p: q is determined by multiplying p by 2 and subtracting that product from 100. For any value of p, q is uniquely determined. You have probably already recognized equation (1) as a specific example of the "law of demand."

However, if we solved the implicit equation for p, we would obtain the function $p = 50 - 0.5q$, which could represent the average revenue function for an imperfectly competitive seller. As we will see in Part III, the specification of which variable is independent and which is dependent has a profound influence on the nature of the model being tested. Many controversies in economics involve disagreements about the assignment of independent and dependent variables. For example, in his classic article, A. W. Phillips[1] hypothesized that wage changes are a function of the unemployment rate. In his attack on the "inflation-unemployment trade-off," Milton Friedman[2] disputed the argument that the unemployment rate is a function of the rate of inflation (which presumably reflects money wage changes). In the debate, the unemployment variable was transformed from the independent variable to the dependent variable.

---

[1] A. W. Phillips, "The Relation Between Unemployment and the Rate of Change of Money Wage Rates in the United Kingdom, 1861-1957," *Economica* (November 1958), pp. 283-299.

[2] Milton Friedman, "Nobel Lecture: Inflation and Unemployment," *Journal of Political Economy*, (June 1977), pp. 451-472.

Functions of One Variable

The notation $y = f(x)$ signifies no more than the proposition that we are taking y as some explicit function of x. More specifically, it states that y is a function of one variable only, x. Both y and x enter the equation, but there is only one independent variable. Hence, we say that this is a function of one variable. There are several types of explicit functions of one variable, and we shall discuss some types that are commonly used in economics.

Linear Functions

A *linear function* is one in which only the first power of the independent variable appears in the equation. The reason for the name "linear" will become clear when we discuss graphs of functions. The equation for this function is sometimes called a first-degree equation. The following equations all represent linear functions:

(1) $y = x$
(2) $y = 2 - x$
(3) $y = 4 + 3x$
(4) $y = a + bx$

Equation (4) is a general statement of a linear function. The letters a and b refer to constants whose values are unspecified. This general form would take on the configuration of (1) if $a = 0$ and $b = 1$; it would take form (2) if $a = 2$ and $b = -1$; and so forth. Equation (4) is called the general form of the equation because a and b represent unknowns rather than stipulated constants.

Polynomial Functions

When the single independent variable is raised to powers that are nonnegative integers, we have a *polynomial function*. A linear function is a polynomial function whose greatest exponent equals 1. A quadratic function is a polynomial function wherein the independent variable is raised to the second power. The following set of equations all represent quadratic functions:

(1) $y = x^2$
(2) $y = 10 + 3x^2$
(3) $y = 2 - 3x + 4x^2$
(4) $y = a + bx + cx^2$

Equation (4) is the general quadratic form with a, b, and c as unspecified constants.

Higher powers of the independent variable may also be encountered in a polynomial function. The cubic function includes at most the third power of the independent variable: $y = a + bx + cx^2 + dx^3$. Fourth powers or higher might well be used to describe the function $y = f(x)$, although such functions are infrequently encountered in economics.

Other Types of Functions

Several other types of functions are often encountered in econometric work. *Exponential functions* are those in which the independent variable is contained in an exponent on some specified base, and the dependent variable is the result of that operation. For instance, $y = 10^x$ is an exponential function with base 10; y is the value obtained when 10 is raised to the x power. The number "e," whose approximate value is 2.71828, is frequently encountered in econometrics. The function $y = 3e^{0.05t}$ might express the value of some variable y, with the independent variable t being time.

Logarithmic functions are functions in which the dependent variable is expressed as the exponent of some specified base. For instance, if we are told $x = 10^y$, we can express y as the logarithm of x to the base 10: $y = \log_{10} x$, which means y is the exponent on 10 necessary to obtain the specified value of x. As in the case of exponential functions, logarithms of base e are frequently encountered in econometric work. The function $y = 2 \log_e x$ is an equivalent way of expressing $x = e^{y/2}$.

It can easily be seen that when we write $y = f(x)$, we mean that y depends on x in any one of an indefinite number of ways. Any one of the above equations—or another equation involving x and y—could be the equation that specifies this function.

Functions of Two or More Variables

Not all explicit functions relate one dependent variable to only one independent variable. There is little difficulty extending the concept and notation to include explicit functions of two or more variables. When we specified the demand function as $q = f(p)$, we stated that other factors (e.g., prices of related goods, income, and tastes) were held constant. If we allow the price of a good (p), the prices of substitutes (p_s), the prices of complements (p_c), real income (y), and tastes (T) to vary simultaneously, we generate a demand function with five independent variables: $q = f(p, p_s, p_c, y, T)$. In econometrics, the designation of independent means something quite specific: that variable influences the value of the dependent variable, but it is not influenced by the value of the dependent variable. Whether those variables are truly independent is critical to the reliability of statistical estimates.

As with functions of one variable, functions of multiple variables come in many different mathematical forms. One functional form not encountered in the two-variable case is the *multivariate power function,* a function in which the independent variables are raised to some specified exponents and multiplied together. Let us consider some alternative forms our four-variable demand functions could take (making the assumption that tastes remain constant):

(1) $q = 20 - 0.5p + 0.2p_s - p_c + 0.75y$ Linear Function

(2) $q = 2p^{-0.5}p_s^{0.2}p_c^{-1}y^{0.75}$ Power Function

(3) $\log_e q = 0.693 - 0.5 \log_e(p) + 0.2 \log_e(p_s) - \log_e(p_c)$
       $+ 0.75 \log_e(y)$ Logarithmic Function

Notice that the logarithmic specification of the demand function has multiplicative constants (called *coefficients*) which are identical to the exponents in the power function. Also note that $\log_e 2 = 0.693$. By transforming a power function into its logarithmic equivalent, a function with constant exponents whose terms are multiplied together becomes a function with multiplicative constants whose terms are added together.

SUMMARY

Several definitions have been introduced in this chapter. Since the concepts will be used in later work, it is necessary that they be understood fully at the outset. It will help to establish these concepts if the most important ones are reviewed.

- **Variables** are magnitudes that may assume any value specified by a set called the domain.
  - *Finite domain:* the variable may take on a countable number of values.
  - *Infinite domain:* the variable may take on an infinite number of values.
- **Functions** are relations among variables such that values assigned to the independent variable(s) determine unique values of the dependent variable.
  - *Implicit function:* variables are treated as mutually dependent.
  - *Explicit function:* one variable (dependent) is assumed to depend on one or more others (the independent variables).
  - *Functions of one variable:* one dependent variable and one independent variable.
  - *Functions of two or more variables:* one dependent variable and two or more independent variables.

APPENDIX

REVIEW OF MATHEMATICAL

OPERATIONS

Addition and Subtraction

1. The number "0" is the *additive identity*. Zero added to any real number yields that number.

2. The *additive inverse* of any real number is that number preceded by a "minus" sign $(-)$. When a number is added to its additive inverse, the sum is zero (0), the additive identity.

3. Subtraction is equivalent to adding the inverse of a number; e.g., $3 - 2$ is the same as $3 + (-2)$. Subtraction of a negative number is equivalent to adding a positive number; e.g., $3 - (-2) = 3 + 2 = 5$.

4. Addition can occur in any order; e.g., $3 + 2 = 2 + 3$. In subtraction, order is critical; e.g., $3 - 2 \neq 2 - 3$.

Multiplication and Division

1. The number "1" is the *multiplicative identity*. One multiplied times any number yields that number.

2. The *multiplicative inverse* (also called the *reciprocal*) of a number is one divided by that number. When a number is multiplied by its inverse, the result is the multiplicative identity; e.g., $2 \times (1/2) = 1$.

3. Division by a number is the same as multiplying by its reciprocal; e.g., $3/2 = 3 \times (1/2)$. Dividing by the reciprocal of a number is the same as multiplying by that number; e.g., $2/(2/3) = 2 \times (3/2) = 3$.

4. Multiplication can occur in any order; e.g., $3 \times 2 = 2 \times 3$. In division, order is important; e.g., $3/2 \neq 2/3$.

Exponentiation

1. When the exponent of a real number is a positive integer, the real number is multiplied by itself the number of times indicated by the exponent; e.g., $2^2 = 2 \times 2 = 4$, $6^4 = 6 \times 6 \times 6 \times 6 = 1,296$.

2. When the exponent of a real number is the reciprocal of a positive integer, the root corresponding to the denominator of the exponent is taken; e.g., $4^{1/2} = \sqrt{4} = 2$, $27^{1/3} = \sqrt[3]{27} = 3$.

3. When the exponent of a real number is a fraction, the real number is raised to the power indicated by the numerator of the exponent, then the root indicated by the denominator of the exponent is taken; e.g., $16^{3/4} = \sqrt[4]{16^3} = \sqrt[4]{4,096} = 8$.

4. When the exponent of a real number is a negative number, the multiplicative inverse of the real number is raised to the absolute value of the exponent; e.g., $3^{-2} = 1/3^2 = 1/9$.

5. When multiplying two numbers with the same base, add their exponents; e.g., $10^2 \times 10^3 = 10^{2+3} = 10^5 = 100,000$.

6. When dividing numbers with the same base, subtract the exponent of the denominator from the exponent of the numerator; e.g., $10^3/10^2 = 10^{3-2} = 10^1 = 10$. (Note this implies that a number raised to the zero power must equal one: $10^3/10^3 = 10^{3-3} = 10^0 = 1$.)

7. When raising a number to a power, multiply the exponents; e.g., $(10^3)^2 = 10^{2\times3} = 10^6 = 1,000,000$.

8. When taking roots, change the root to a fractional exponent and multiply exponents; e.g., $\sqrt{4^8} = (4^8)^{1/2} = 4^4 = 256$.

Logarithms

1. Logarithmic operations allow us to simplify some mathematical operations by using the rules of exponents. Any nonnegative real number can be expressed as the result of taking one number (called the base) to some power (the logarithm). For instance, $4 = 2^2$ and $4 = 10^{0.602}$; the logarithm of 4 to the base 2 (written $\log_2 4$) is 2; the logarithm of 4 to the base 10 ($\log_{10} 4$) is 0.602.

2. The two most frequently used bases in economics are 10, the base of "common" logarithms, and e, an irrational number approximately equal to 2.71828, which is the base of the "natural" logarithms. The latter base is particularly important in calculus and will be discussed in more detail in Chapter 6.

3. By first translating variables or numbers to a common base, we can change a multiplication problem into an addition problem. For example, if $y = e^u$ and $x = e^v$, we have $xy = (e^u)(e^v) = e^{u+v}$. Therefore, since $\log_e y = u$ (also written as $\ln y = u$), and $\ln x = v$, it follows that $\ln yx = \ln y + \ln x = u + v$.

4. The logarithm of a ratio of two numbers is equal to the difference in their logarithms; e.g., $\log(x/y) = \log x - \log y$.

5. The logarithm of a number raised to a power is equal to the logarithm of that number multiplied by the exponent; e.g., $\log(x^b) = b \log x$.

PROBLEMS

Group I

1. Let $y = f(x) = 2x$.
    Find $f(3)$, $f(6)$, $f(16)$, $f(40)$.

2.   Let $y = f(x) = 18$.
     Find $f(0)$, $f(18)$, $f(20)$, $f(-100)$.

3.   Let $y = f(x) = 4 + 3x$.
     Find $f(0)$, $f(3)$, $f(12)$, $f(-2)$, $f(-5)$.

4.   Let $y = f(x) = 0.5x$.
     Find $f(0)$, $f(1)$, $f(10)$, $f(-3)$, $f(-6)$.

5.   Let $y = f(x) = 6 + 4x + 2x^2$.
     Find $f(0)$, $f(1)$, $f(5)$, $f(-2)$.

Group II

6.   Let $y = f(x) = -4 + x - 0.5x^2$.
     Find $f(0)$, $f(1)$, $f(3)$, $f(-100)$.

7.   Let $y = f(x) = 3^x$.
     Find $f(0)$, $f(1)$, $f(4)$, $f(-1)$, $f(-3)$.

8.   Let $y = f(x) = \log_{10} x$.
     Find $f(1)$, $f(10)$, $f(100)$, $f(150)$.

9.   Let $y = f(x) = (8 - x)/2x^2$.
     Find $f(0)$, $f(2)$, $f(4)$, $f(-3)$.

10. Let $y = f(x) = 1 - 2x^{-2}$.
     Find $f(-2)$, $f(1)$, $f(-1)$, $f(10)$.

11. Let $y = f(x, z) = 8x^2 + 2z$.
     Find $f(0, 1)$, $f(1, 0)$, $f(2, 2)$, $f(3, 10)$.

12. Let $y = f(x, z, u) = 3 + 10x - 4z + u^2$.
     Find $f(1, 1, 1)$, $f(0, 2, 2)$, $f(3, 4, 3)$, $f(0, 0, 0)$.

2

Graphs of

Functions

One of the great discoveries in the history of mathematics was made by Rene Descartes. He found that there is a one-to-one correspondence between the points on a two-dimensional plane and the combinations of two mathematical variables. Diagrams are the visual counterparts of equations; they are pictorial representations of mathematical statements. Supply curves, demand curves, cost curves, and IS and LM curves are familiar from the study of economic theory. Whenever a demand schedule is depicted by a curve, this diagrammatic representation implies the existence of an equivalent mathematical statement of demand. A verbal statement of a relation between quantity demanded and price or between quantity produced and marginal cost (or any relation between economic magnitudes) can in principle be reduced to a mathematical expression. This in turn can be expresed as a diagram.

RECTANGULAR COORDINATES

Graphical representations or pictures of relations between two variables are very prominent in economics. The first step in diagramming a function is the choice of units of measurement for the variables. These units need not be the same, since the two variables may represent entirely different types of quantities. For instance, if the independent variable is the rate of output, to be measured in "tons per month," the unit for that variable may be "one ton per month." If the dependent variable is average cost, each unit might be "one dollar per ton." The domain and range of the function being depicted determine the units of measurement.

The values of two variables, which may be negative or positive, are measured on two axes, one vertical and one horizontal. The two axes intersect at a right angle where both values equal zero. This point is labeled zero and is called the *origin*. The horizontal axis is called the *x*-axis and the vertical axis is the *y*-axis. (See Figure 2.1). The two-dimensional plane (called the *xy*-plane) is divided into four parts by the two axes. On the *x*-axis all points to the right of the origin depict positive values of *x* and all points to the left of the origin depict negative values of *x*. As we move to the right along the *x*-axis, the value of the independent variable increases. Above the origin, points on the *y*-axis indicate positive values for *y*; points below the origin on the *y*-axis represent negative values for *y*. As we move upward along the *y*-axis, the value of *y* increases.

Figure 2.1

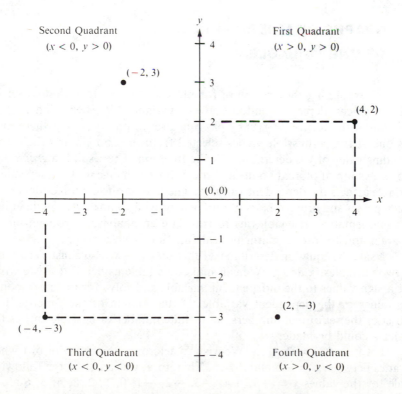

The two axes divide the plane representing combinations of x and y into four parts, or *quadrants*. These are labeled in Figure 2.1. In the first quadrant, the values of both x and y are positive at all points. In the second quadrant, the value of x is negative and the value of y is positive. In the third quadrant, the values of x and y are both negative. In the fourth quadrant, the value of x is positive and the value of y is negative. Most diagrams in economics are restricted to the first quadrant because the domain and range of most economic functions are limited to nonnegative real numbers.

A specific value of x and the related value of y are represented on the xy-plane by a point. Each point on the plane corresponds to a unique pair of values for x and y, and is denoted by the ordered pair (x, y). The point $(4, 2)$ is plotted by moving four units to the right on the x-axis, then moving up two units parallel to the y-axis. This point indicates that $x = 4$ and $y = 2$. The point $(-4, -3)$ is plotted by moving four units to the left of the origin on the x-axis then down three units. Two other points have been depicted in Figure 2.1, and you may wish to trace the procedure of locating these points yourself. Note that the origin depicts the point $(0, 0)$. Here $x = 0$ and $y = 0$.

GRAPHS OF LINEAR FUNCTIONS
OF ONE VARIABLE

By expanding the procedure for plotting a point to include a set of points, we can depict a relation between variables. We depict an explicit function of the form $y = f(x)$ by plotting a set of points (x, y), where each x is one of the permissible values selected from the domain and the corresponding value of y is determined by the function. The result is a *graph* that shows a group of plotted points and traces how a change in the independent variable affects the dependent variable. The one-to-one correspondence between points and ordered pairs of numbers provides a link between diagrams and mathematics. It enables us to translate an analytical problem into a diagram and to infer a mathematical function from a graph.

Using the equation describing a function, $f(x)$, we can construct a table of two variables, x and y. We can make this table as detailed as we wish. We assign values to the independent variable and solve for the corresponding values of the dependent variable. If the domain of the function is a subset of the set of real numbers, an infinite number of possible entries for x and y could be made.

Let $y = f(x) = 2 + 3x$. We wish to determine the behavior of y when x varies between $x = -5$ and $x = 6$. Therefore, we construct the following table for the values $x = -5, -4, -3, -2, -1, 0, 1, 2, 3, 4, 5, 6$ along with the corresponding values of y.

x	y
-5	-13
-4	-10
-3	-7
-2	-4
-1	-1
0	2
1	5
2	8
3	11
4	14
5	17
6	20

The Nature of a Linear Function Graph

The related values of x and y from this table, namely $(-5, -13)$, $(-4, -10)$, and so forth, determine a set of points that are plotted on the same xy-plane. If we chose our x values at smaller intervals (say -5, -4.9, -4.8, ...) more points would result and they would lie closer to one another. Our function is defined for the set of real numbers, which means that we could choose values of x at such small intervals that the plotted points would touch each other, generating an unbroken straight line. The points and the line are shown in Figure 2.2.

Just as the variables are related in an ordered way by the function, so the corresponding points on a graph must be uniquely identified by position and direction of the line. The direction of a line is indicated by its *slope*. The position of the line can be identified by where the line crosses the y-axis. Recall from our earlier discussion that the position or the direction of a graph can be changed by choosing different units of measurement along the axes.

We can see why functions that use only the first power of the variables are called linear functions. They generate a straight line when those variables are plotted on coordinate axes. Any function of the general form $y = a + bx$, where a and b are constants, is said to be a linear function. The graph corresponding to a linear function shows a straight line.

The Slope of a Line

Consider now a straight line that goes through two specific points. These two points imply a unique location for that line. The line that passes through the points $(2, 2)$ and $(4, 8)$ has a *slope* equal to $(8 - 2)/(4 - 2) = 6/2 = 3$. The slope is measured by dividing the change in the dependent variable (the "rise") by the change in the independent variable (the "run"). Since the

Figure 2.2

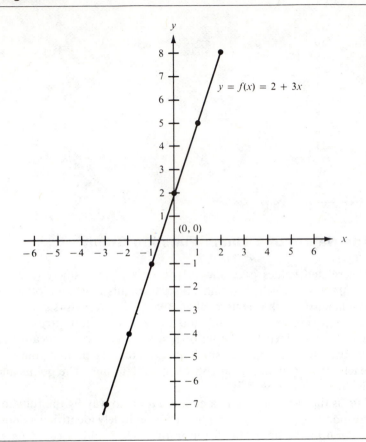

$y = f(x) = 2 + 3x$

$(0, 0)$

line has the same slope between any two points, we can substitute the unknowns x and y for the numbers 8 and 4 respectively, and obtain the equation for the line:

$$\frac{y - 2}{x - 2} = 3$$

or

$$y - 2 = 3(x - 2)$$

Simplifying we get:

$$y = 3x - 6 + 2$$

or

$$y = -4 + 3x$$

Figure 2.3

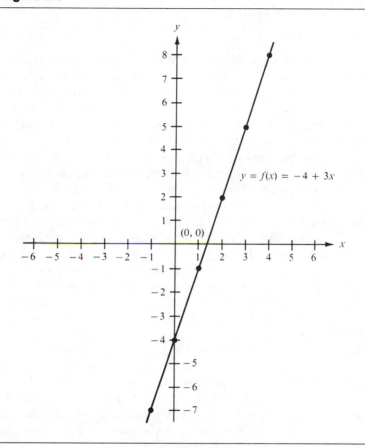

$$y = f(x) = -4 + 3x$$

This is the equation of the straight line shown in Figure 2.3. It is easy to show that such a line passes through the two points (2, 2) and (4, 8) by merely substituting each pair of values of x and y into the equation. For $x = 2$ and $y = 2$ we have $2 = -4 + 3(2) = -4 + 6 = 2$. For $x = 4$ and $y = 8$, $8 = -4 + 3(4) = -4 + 12 = 8$. If we tried to use a pair of numbers not on the line, a contradiction would result. Hence, for $x = 0$ and $y = 0$, we get $0 = -4 + 3(0) = -4 \neq 0$. The origin does not lie on the same line as the points (2, 2) and (4, 8).

The expression

$$b = \frac{y_2 - y_1}{x_2 - x_1}$$

is the general formula for the slope of a line, where (x_1, y_1) and (x_2, y_2) are any two different points on the line. As before, we substitute the variables

x and y for the specific values x_2 and y_2 and the general equation for a straight line can be written:

$$y - y_1 = b(x - x_1)$$

As we have seen, the slope is the ratio of the change in the dependent variable to the change in the independent variable. If we move to the right by one unit from any point on the line, then move vertically by b units, we will arrive at another point on that line. In Figure 2.3 we can arbitrarily pick the starting point at (2, 2). Move horizontally one unit to the point (3, 2). Since the equation of the line is $y = -4 + 3x$, the slope, $b = 3$, is positive. We move upward three units from (3, 2) to the point (3, 5), which is also on the line in Figure 2.3. Had we moved two units to the right, to point (4, 2), we would have moved 3(2) = 6 units upward to the point (4, 8). And had we moved to the *left* by two units (-2 units to the right) to the point (0, 2), we would move downward 6 units (upward 3(-2) = -6 units) to the point (0, -4). This is the y-intercept, the point where the line crosses the y-axis.

If our equation had been $y - 2 = -3(x - 2)$, which simplifies to $y = 8 - 3x$, a movement to the right of one unit implies a *downward* movement of three units. The line corresponding to the equation $y = 8 - 3x$, whose slope is -3, is shown in Figure 2.4. Picking an arbitrary starting point at (1, 5) and moving one unit to the right followed by a movement downward of three units, we reach the point (2, 2), which is also on the line.

The equation $y - y_1 = b(x - x_1)$ is called the *point-slope* form of the equation for a straight line. Given the point (x_1, y_1) and the slope b, the line can be plotted over any permissible range of x and y. It goes through the point (x_1, y_1) with a slope of b. If b is positive, the line goes upward as the value of x increases. As in Figure 2.3, y is an increasing function of x. If b is negative, the line goes downward as the value of x increases, and y is a decreasing function of x, as in Figure 2.4.

We can write $y - y_1 = b(x - x_1)$ as $y = (y_1 - bx_1) + bx$. Since y_1, x_1, and b are constants, this equation can be expressed as $y = f(x) = a + bx$, where $a = (y_1 - bx_1)$. In this general linear form, b is the slope of the function. By setting $x = 0$ we find that $f(0) = a + b(0) = a$. Thus, a is the value of y when x equals 0, and is the y-intercept of the line. In Figure 2.4 the y-intercept is 8. This format of the general equation $y = a + bx$ is called the *slope-intercept* form of a linear equation. It is encountered often in statistical estimation.

GRAPHS OF NONLINEAR FUNCTIONS
OF ONE VARIABLE

The notion of a graph is readily extended to nonlinear functions. The distinguishing characteristic of a *linear* function is its constant slope. A

Figure 2.4

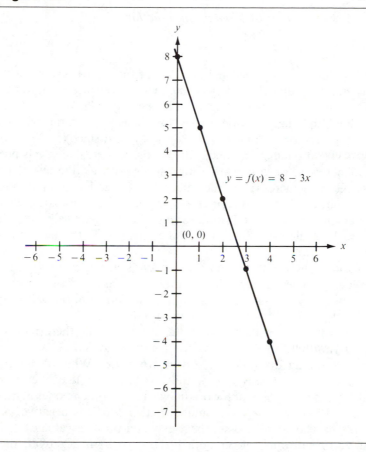

$y = f(x) = 8 - 3x$

change in the independent variable always implies a proportionate change in the dependent variable. It follows that *nonlinear* functions change direction from one point to another; their slopes are not always constant. The change in the dependent variable implied by a one-unit change in the independent variable varies along the graph of the function.

Polynomial Functions

In Chapter 1 we discussed polynomial functions, functions whose terms contain a single independent variable raised to exponents that are nonnegative integers. Indeed, a linear function is a polynomial function in which the greatest power attained by x is one. When a polynomial function contains exponents greater than one, the graph generated by the polynomial will be nonlinear. We will discuss two nonlinear polynomial functions most often encountered in economics: quadratic functions and cubic functions.

Quadratic Functions

The general form of a *quadratic function* is:

$$y = a + bx + cx^2$$

where $c \neq 0$. (If $c = 0$, then we have a linear function.) A quadratic function generates a graph called a *parabola*. The values of the constants a, b, and c determine the shape and position of the parabola. When $a = b = 0$, the quadratic equation simplifies to $y = cx^2$. Since $0^2 = 0$, the parabola will pass through the origin (when $x = 0$, $y = 0$), and since $(-x)^2 = x^2$, the parabola will be symmetrical about the y-axis. If the value of c is positive, the parabola will "open upward." In other words, as (the absolute value of) x increases, y increases. If the value of c is negative, the parabola will "open downward," and as x increases, y decreases. Comparing different parabolas, the greater the (absolute) value of c, the narrower the parabola becomes. As x increases, the greater the value of c, the more rapidly y increases.

If $a \neq 0$ and $b = 0$, the parabola remains symmetrical about the y-axis, but no longer passes through the origin. Given the function $y = a + cx^2$, $x = 0$ implies $y = a$. As in the case of a linear function, the value of a determines where the parabola crosses the y-axis.

If $a = 0$ and $b \neq 0$, the parabola passes through the origin, but no longer is symmetric about the y-axis. Given $y = bx + cx^2$, we can factor out an x, restating the function as $y = x(b + cx)$. When $x = -b/c$ the term inside the parentheses is zero, and $y = 0$. Hence, the function would cross the x-axis twice, once at the origin (where $x = 0$), and once at the point $x = -b/c$. If b/c is a negative number (either b or c is negative, but not both), the parabola also crosses the x-axis at a positive value of x. If b/c is positive (b and c are either both positive or both negative), then the parabola crosses the x-axis at the origin and at a negative value of x.

Finally, when all three constants are nonzero (a, b, $c \neq 0$), we have $y = a + bx + cx^2$. The parabola no longer passes through the origin. It may cross the axis twice, once (a point of tangency), or not at all. In Chapter 4 we will see that the number of times a parabola crosses the x-axis determines the number of *solutions* to the quadratic equation.

Figure 2.5 presents the diagrams of three different quadratic equations. Figure 2.5a shows the diagram of the simple equation $y = x^2$. As indicated, the parabola passes through the origin, is symmetric to the y-axis, and opens upward. Figure 2.5b shows the diagram of the quadratic equation $y = -2x^2 + 2x$. In this case the coefficient attached to x^2 is negative, so the parabola opens downward. Also the parabola crosses the x-axis at two points, the origin (0, 0) and the point (1, 0). Figure 2.5c is a plot of the function $y = 10 - 12x + 2x^2$. This parabola opens upward, does not pass through the origin, and crosses the x-axis at two positive values of x, $x = 1$ and $x = 6$.

Figure 2.5a

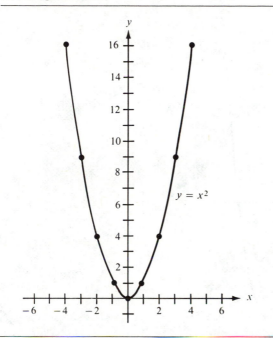

$y = x^2$

Figure 2.5b

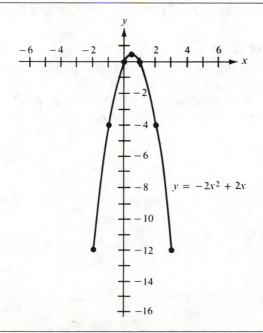

$y = -2x^2 + 2x$

Figure 2.5c

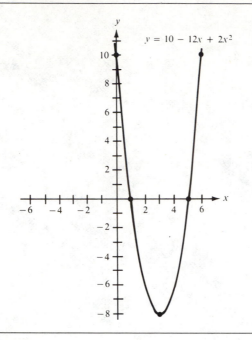

$y = 10 - 12x + 2x^2$

Cubic Functions

The general form of a *cubic function*, or third-degree polynomial function, is:

$$y = a + bx + cx^2 + dx^3$$

Suppose we make a graph indicating the behavior of a specific cubic function over a particular set of values for x. Suppose $y = 8 - 6x - 3x^2 + x^3$, and we wish to plot the diagram of this function over the range $x = -3$ to $x = 5$. We construct the following table, then plot the points as the curve in Figure 2.6.

x	y
-3	-28
-2	0
-1	10
0	8
1	0
2	-8
3	-10
4	0
5	28

Figure 2.6

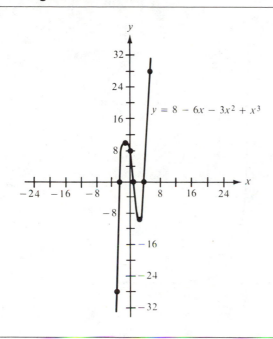

$$y = 8 - 6x - 3x^2 + x^3$$

We notice that this function crosses the x-axis at three points: $(-2, 0)$, $(1, 0)$, and $(4, 0)$. The function begins in the third quadrant (both x and y are negative), crosses briefly into the second, first, and fourth quadrants, then remains in the first quadrant. We can generalize on the diagrams of quadratic and cubic functions to obtain the following rules for graphs of polynomial functions.

First, the degree of the polynomial (the largest exponent appearing in a term with a nonzero coefficient) determines the *maximum* number of times the graph of that function can cross the x-axis. In Chapter 4 we will see that this rule features prominently in determining the number of *solutions* the function has when it is set equal to zero. Second, if the a term equals zero, the graph of the function passes through the origin. If $a > 0$, the value of y is positive when $x = 0$. If $a < 0$, the value of y is negative when $x = 0$.

Nonpolynomial Functions

Besides polynomial functions, there are several other types of nonlinear functions that occur frequently in economics. Examples of these are presented in Figures 2.7, 2.8, and 2.9. Figure 2.7 is a diagram of the exponential function $y = 2^{-x}$. Since any number raised to the power 0 equals 1, the function crosses the y-axis at the point $(0, 1)$; when $x = 0$, $y = 1$. Since the sign

Figure 2.7

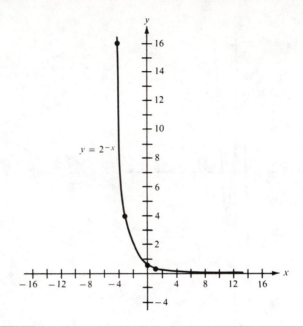

$y = 2^{-x}$

Figure 2.8

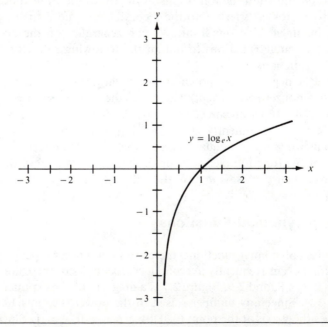

$y = \log_e x$

Figure 2.9

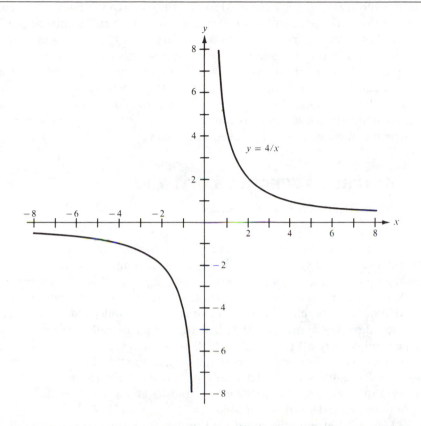

$y = 4/x$

of the exponent is negative, large values of y appear for negative values of x and small values of y for positive values of x. Since 2^{-x} comes progressively closer to zero as x becomes larger, we see that the function is *asymptotic* to the x-axis. This means that as the value of x increases, the value of y gets closer and closer to zero, but never actually reaches that value.

Figure 2.8 is a plot of the logarithmic function $y = \log_e x$. Since the natural logarithm can be defined only for positive real numbers, the graph of the function is restricted to the first and fourth quadrants. For values of x close to zero, the natural logarithm is negative and the function is asymptotic to the y-axis. The function crosses the x-axis when $x = 1$; the natural logarithm of 1 is zero. For $x > 1$, the natural logarithm of x is positive and increasing.

Figure 2.9 is a plot of the hyperbolic function $y = 4/x$. Hyperbolic functions are so called because the graphs of these functions generate hyperbolas. If we multiply both sides of the explicit function $y = 4/x$ by the independent variable x, we get the implicit function $xy = 4$. The points in the hyperbolic function are arranged so that the two variables have the same product. Since the product, 4, is positive, either both x and y must be positive, or both must be negative. Hence, the graph of the hyperbola shows mirror images in the first and third quadrants. Furthermore, since neither x nor y can be zero (since zero times any number must equal zero, not a positive constant such as 4), the two parts of the hyperbola are asymptotic to both the x-axis and the y-axis. Finally, we see that both parts of the hyperbola involve an *inverse* relationship between x and y; as the value of x increases, the value of y decreases, and vice versa.

GRAPHS OF FUNCTIONS OF TWO INDEPENDENT VARIABLES

Chapter 1 explained that a dependent variable may be a function of several independent variables. The limits of normal human perception constrain graphs to three or fewer dimensions. A page of a book has two dimensions: length and width. The book itself has three dimensions: length, width, and depth. It is possible to depict functions with two independent variables by three-dimensional models. Alas, true three-dimensional diagrams would make a book difficult to close. Authors of economics texts must content themselves to depicting three-dimensional diagrams in two dimensions. However, the difficulty of drawing and interpreting three-dimensional diagrams deters most economists from achieving virtuosity at graphing functions with more than one independent variable.

Figure 2.10 shows the coordinate system for a three-dimensional diagram represented in two dimensions. We simulate a system of three mutually perpendicular axes: the lines measuring x, y, and z are made to look perpendicular. In a three-dimensional diagram, a point is represented by (x, y, z) rather than (x, y) as in the two-dimensional case. If we wish to plot the point $(2, 1, 2)$ corresponding to the x, y, and z axes, respectively, we proceed as shown in Figure 2.10. We move two units from the origin in the positive x direction, one unit in the positive y direction, then two units in the positive z direction. A *parallelepiped* (a three-dimensional figure with six sides joined at right angles) is generated in the process of plotting a point in three dimensions.

Consider an explicit function with two independent variables and which takes the form of a simple linear equation: $z = f(x, y) = 1 + x - y$. Each pair of values for x and y identifies a point on the xy-plane, which in turn implies a value for z in the third dimension. For the values of $x = -1$ and $y = 0$, the value of $z = 1 + (-1) - (0) = 0$. The distance along the z-axis is zero and the point $(-1, 0, 0)$ lies in the xy-plane. For the values $x = 1$ and $y = 1$, the value of $z = 1 + 1 - 1 = 1$. The value of z is one unit

Figure 2.10

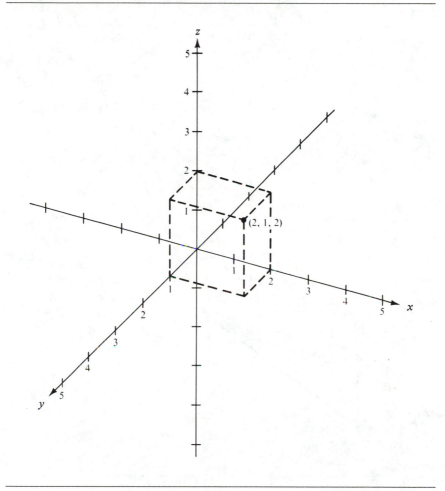

"above" the xy-plane. When we plot all admissible values of x, y, and z, we generate a *plane*, the three-dimensional plot of a linear equation. Such a plane is illustrated in Figure 2.11.

It now becomes clear that the two-dimensional representation is a special case of three-dimensional geometry. If we let $z = 4$, the equation becomes $4 = 1 + x - y$ or $x - y = 3$, which is also an implicit function involving only x and y. An implicit function can be transformed to make either variable dependent on the other. Solving for y, $x - y = 3$ becomes $y = -3 + x$. This explicit function is a particular case of the general form $y = a + bx$, where $a = -3$ and $b = 1$. By assigning a different value to z, we obtain a different value for a. As a simple exercise, determine what happens to the value of a when $z = 8$ and when $z = 12$.

Figure 2.11

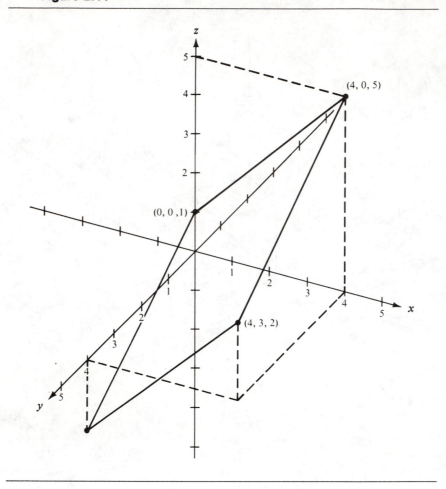

When an equation with two independent variables involves a nonlinear function, the surface described by the function is no longer flat; it is rounded, just as the graph of the two-dimensional case is curved rather than a straight line. Figure 2.12 shows one type of curved surface for positive values of x, y, and z. (Notice that unless we restrict z to nonnegative values, this equation would not describe a function.) The general equation for this surface is $x^2/a^2 + y^2/b^2 + z^2/c^2 = 1$. The surface itself is called an ellipsoid.

Notice in Figure 2.12 that setting $z = z_0$ generates a two-dimensional function between x and y. There are many diverse kinds of rounded surfaces resulting from nonlinear functions with two independent variables, just as there are many types of nonlinear functions with one independent variable.

Figure 2.12

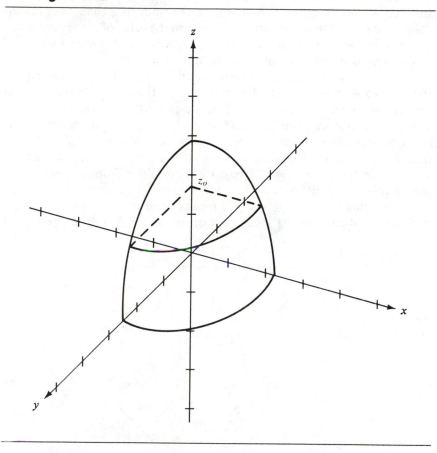

PARAMETERS AND CURVES

As mentioned, few economists are as adept at drawing three-dimensional diagrams as they are at constructing two-dimensional ones. There are easier ways of analyzing functions involving three or more variables than drawing three-dimensional diagrams. One is to use mathematics, particularly calculus, in place of graphs. Indeed, this approach will concern us through most of the rest of this book. A second alternative is to use the third variable in a function to change the location or the shape of a function depicted in two dimensions. In the last section we saw that a three-variable function such as $z = 1 + x - y$ would define a linear function between x and y for each unique value of z. When $z = 4$, the function $x - y = 3$ is described; when $z = 8$, we have $x - y = 7$, and so forth. This approach involves treating the value of z as a *parameter* that affects the position of the curve described by the function between x and y. Fixing the value of z traces a function in two dimensions. A change in the value of z changes either the shape or the location of the curve. A change in the value of z, the parameter, changes the value of the intercept term, a, when a function between y and x is expressed in the intercept-slope form $y = a + bx$.

Suppose we introduce a fourth variable, w, and define an implicit function $wx + y - z = -1$. We can solve this function to make y the dependent variable: $y = z - 1 - wx$. If we project this function into two dimensions, treating x and y as variables and w and z as parameters, we see that changing the value of z changes the intercept of the line $y = a + bx$ (i.e., $a = z - 1$) and changing the value of w changes the slope of the line $y = a + bx$ (i.e., $b = -w$). Different lines resulting from different parametric values of z and w (a and b) are presented in Figure 2.13.

Note that the line $y = -1 + x$ results when $w = -1$ and $z = 0$. Increasing z to 4 and holding w constant causes the linear relation between y

Figure 2.13

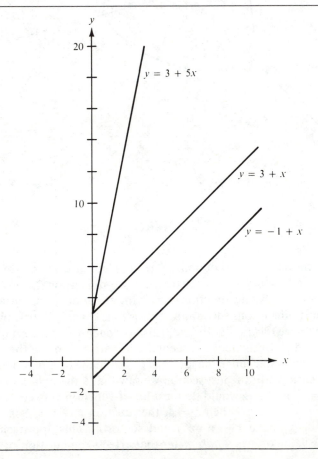

$y = 3 + 5x$

$y = 3 + x$

$y = -1 + x$

and x to shift upward. The line $y = 3 + x$ is parallel to the line $y = -1 + x$. If we hold z constant at 4 and imagine that w changes to -5, the line becomes $y = 3 + 5x$. An increase in the slope of a line (with the intercept constant) rotates the line in a counterclockwise direction and a decrease in slope rotates it in a clockwise direction.

Many economic theories simplify the relationship among variables by focusing on two-dimensional functions. In explicit functions, changes in the dependent variable are wholly attributed to changes in the independent variable *assuming that other relevant variables remain constant*. The variables that are assumed to remain constant are designated as *exogenous* variables, while the variables assumed to change are designated as *endogenous* variables. Economists use the concept of *ceteris paribus* (Latin for "other things constant") to concentrate on the relationship between two variables at a time. For the slope-intercept form of a linear function, $y = a + bx$, the economist treats a and b as parameters whose values may be determined by exogneous variables held constant by *ceteris paribus* assumptions. In econometrics, the values of a and b must be estimated from observations on x and y and any other variables covered by *ceteris paribus* assumptions.

The concept of a parameter is also encountered in nonlinear functions of two or more independent variables. If the function has the form $y = az + bx + cx^2$, a change in the value of z would change the y-intercept of the parabola relating y to x, but would have no effect on its shape. If the equation took a form such as $y = a + bzx + c(zx)^2$, a change in the value of z would change the shape of the parabola generated by the quadratic function relating y to x.

SUMMARY

This chapter has explored the graphical representation of mathematical functions. The one-to-one correspondence between points in two-dimensional space and ordered pairs of real numbers allows us to generate pictures of functions. We saw that two points are sufficient to identify a linear function. In a function of the form $y = a + bx$, a is the intercept term (the value of y when x equals zero) and b is the slope (the change in the dependent variable due to a one-unit change in the independent variable). It is also possible to graph nonlinear functions. For such functions, the direction of the function (its slope) changes from one point on the curve to another.

We also saw that functions with two independent variables can be plotted in three-dimensional space, and that three-dimensional diagrams can be represented in two-dimensional space. However, most economists prefer to use mathematics instead of three-dimensional diagrams, given the difficulty of drawing and interpreting those graphs. Another way to depict functions with more than one independent variable is to treat all but one of the independent variables as exogenous variables or shift parameters. A change in an exogenous variable can cause a change in either the position or the slope of a two-variable function.

In the next chapter we will apply the concepts of functions and graphs to specific economic examples. We will see how economic theories imply either linear or nonlinear diagrams, and how the concept of *ceteris paribus* can be interpreted as a two-dimensional relation between endogenous variables for a specified combination of exogenous variables.

PROBLEMS

Group I

1. Let (x, y) represent a point in the xy-plane. Draw rectangular coordinates and plot the following points: $(9, 2)$, $(3, -3)$, $(0, 0)$, $(-5, -8)$.

2. Plot the function $y = f(x) = 3 + 2x$ for the range $x = -2$ to $x = 6$.

3. Plot the function $y = f(x) = -3 - 2x$ for the range $x = -2$ to $x = 6$. Compute the slope of the line.

4. Graph the function $y = f(x) = 10 - 0.3x$ for the range $x = -10$ to $x = -2$.

5. Graph the function $y = f(x) = -8 + 4x$ for the range $x = -6$ to $x = 0$. Compute the slope of the line.

6. Plot a smooth curve corresponding to the function $y = f(x) = x^2 - 4$ for the range $x = -4$ to $x = 4$.

Group II

7. Plot a smooth curve corresponding to the function $y = f(x) = 100 - x^2$ for the range $x = 0$ to $x = 10$.

8. Plot a smooth curve corresponding to the function $y = f(x) = 100/x$ for the range $x = -1$ to $x = -100$.

9. Plot a smooth curve corresponding to the function $y = f(x) = 2 - 2^x$ for the range $x = 0$ to $x = 8$.

10. Plot a smooth curve corresponding to the function $y = f(x) = 20 - 2x + 3^x$ for the range $x = -4$ to $x = 4$.

11. Let (x, y, z) represent a point in three-dimensional space. Draw three mutually perpendicular axes and plot the points $(1, 8, 2)$, $(4, 2, 4)$, and $(3, 1, 10)$.

12. Graph the function $z = f(x, y) = 2 - 2x + 3y$ from $x = 0$, $y = 0$ to $x = 4$, $y = 4$.

13. Graph the function $z = f(x, y) = x/y$ from $x = 1$, $y = 1$ to $x = 4$, $y = 4$.

14. a. Graph the function $y = f(x) = 6 + 2x$ for the range $x = -3$ to $x = 3$. The constants 6 and 2 are parameters of this function. Label this line I.
    b. Allow the parameter 6 to change to 9, while the parameter 2 is unchanged. Plot the resulting function for the same range on the same diagram. Label this line II.
    c. Allow the parameter 2 to change to 1, while the parameter 6 remains unchanged. Plot the resulting function for the same range on the same diagram and label this line III.

15. a. Graph the function $y = f(x) = 100/x^2$ for the range $x = 1$ to $x = 10$. The constant 100 is a parameter of this function. Label this curve I.
    b. Allow the parameter to change to 200. Graph the resulting function for the same range on the same diagram. Label this curve II.
    c. Allow the parameter to change to 50. Graph this function for the same range on the same diagram and label the curve III.

3

Economic
Applications of
Functions and
Graphs

Most propositions in economic theory can be stated in mathematical terms, and most mathematical models of economic phenomena can be stipulated as functions of one independent variable, with other variables assuming the role of parameters. Any economic proposition that can be specified as a function of one or two independent variables can be illustrated with the aid of a graph. Corresponding to each function there is a graph that we can use to interpret the relationship among economic variables. There are demand and supply curves as well as demand and supply functions. These curves can be represented on a set of axes, and the relationship among several curves can be displayed on one diagram. Diagrams clarify and highlight the relationships stated in an analytical exposition. In this chapter we shall illustrate how several familiar economic concepts are translated into mathematical and graphical forms.

DEMAND FUNCTIONS

The amount of a commodity consumers wish to buy (the quantity demanded) can be expressed as a function of several variables: the price of the good, the prices of substitute and complementary goods, real income, population (the size of the market), tastes, and expectations. The law of demand states that quantity demanded varies inversely with the price of a good, other factors remaining constant. To construct a two-dimensional demand curve, we treat all of these other influences on demand as *exogenous variables*, imagining that these variables do not change when the price of the good changes. All other influences on quantity demanded are *parameters* of the demand function. A change in these variables will affect the position or the shape of the demand curve, but the law of demand states that whatever happens to the other influences on quantity demanded, the demand curve itself will always be negatively sloped with respect to price.

You are probably aware from your previous studies in economics that demand curves violate the usual practice of plotting the independent variable on the horizontal axis and the dependent variable on the vertical axis. The primary reason for this break with mathematical convention has its roots in the early development of microeconomic theory. The relationship between price and quantity demanded involves an implicit function which can be made into an explicit function of either variable. That is, we can solve the implicit function for quantity and obtain the demand function. But we can also solve that implicit function for price and obtain the average revenue function. When Alfred Marshall introduced demand curves nearly a century ago, he plotted the price against the quantity purchased. So even after economists conceived of demand as a function with price as the "cause" and quantity demanded as the "effect," they continued the practice of drawing Marshallian demand curves with price on the vertical axis and quantity on the horizontal axis.

Figure 3.1 is a *linear* demand curve, a graphical representation of a demand equation of the form $Q_d = a + bp$, where $a > 0$ and $b < 0$, indicating the horizontal *intercept* and the inverse *slope*, respectively. As we saw in the previous chapter, the values of these parameters are influenced by the values of the exogenous variables. For instance, a linear demand equation may have been specified as:

$$Q_d = a_0 + a_1 y + a_2 p_s + a_3 p_c + bp$$

where y is real income, p_s is the price of a substitute good, and p_c is the price of a complementary good. According to economic theory, $a_1 > 0$ (for normal goods), $a_2 > 0$, $a_3 < 0$, and $b < 0$, while a_0 could be either positive, negative, or zero. In the case of the multivariate linear demand equation, the intercept of the two-variable equation, $Q_d = a + bp$, is given by:

$$a = a_0 + a_1 y + a_2 p_s + a_3 p_c$$

That is, changes of the exogenous variables (y, p_c, p_s) change the intercept of the two-variable equation in a predictable way.

In Figure 3.1 we assume that econometric techniques have been used to estimate a specific demand equation:

$$Q_d = 25 + 0.5y + 2p_s - 7.5p_c - 2.5p$$

When we specify values of three exogenous variables, we obtain different two-variable demand functions. If $y = 150$, $p_s = 40$, and $p_c = 16$, the demand equation becomes:

$$Q_d = 25 + 0.5(150) + 2(40) - 7.5(16) - 2.5p$$
$$= 60 - 2.5p$$

That set of exogenous variables generates demand curve D_1 in Figure 3.1. If income y were to increase to 200 while the other exogenous variables retained their values, the demand equation would become:

$$Q_d = 25 + 0.5(200) + 2(40) - 7.5(16) - 2.5p$$
$$= 85 - 2.5p$$

This is depicted as D_2 in Figure 3.1. Note that an increase in y causes a parallel shift in the demand function. At each price, the quantity demanded along D_2 exceeds the quantity demanded along D_1 by 25 units. However, as the price increases, quantity demanded decreases, along both D_1 and D_2.

Figure 3.1

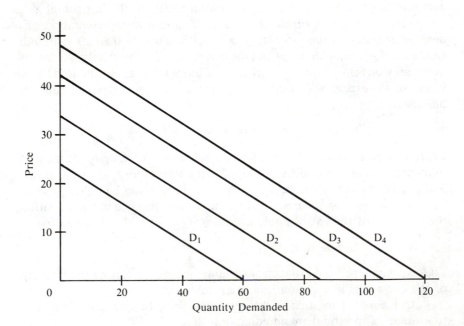

Quantity Demanded

Next suppose that p_s increases from 40 to 50. The two-variable demand function becomes:

$$Q_d = 25 + 0.5(200) + 2(50) - 7.5(16) - 2.5p$$
$$= 105 - 2.5p$$

This is the formula for demand curve D_3 in Figure 3.1. Again, an increase in an exogenous variable (in this case $\Delta p_s = 10$, where the symbol ''Δ'' means *change*) caused quantity demanded at each price to increase by the coefficient on the affected variable times the change in that variable (i.e., $\Delta Q_d = 2(10) = 20$). Finally, if the price of the complement, p_c, were to decrease by \$2 (i.e., from \$16 to \$14), the demand curve would shift from D_3 to D_4 in Figure 3.1, reflecting the new two-variable equation:

$$Q_d = 25 + 0.5(200) + 2(50) - 7.5(14) - 2.5p$$
$$= 120 - 2.5p$$

From Figure 3.1 we learn that a demand equation that is linear in all variables (both endogenous and exogenous) generates a linear function of the endogenous variables, and that a change in any of the exogenous variables generates a parallel shift in the demand curve. In other words, *the slope of a linear demand function is preserved when exogenous variables change.*

Of course, not every demand curve is linear. If the demand equation is nonlinear, the demand curve will truly be a curve instead of a straight line. For instance, the equation describing the relationship between price and quantity might be a hyperbolic equation, with the form:

$$Q_d = \frac{R}{p}$$

where Q_d is quantity demanded, p is price, and R is the total expenditure on the good, here assumed to be a constant. Figure 3.2 is a plot of the demand curve D_1 for the equation:

$$Q_d = \frac{100}{p}$$

That is, total expenditure is assumed to be 100 for each price/quantity combination. When price is very high, quantity demanded is very low; as price falls, quantity demanded increases. Hence, a hyperbolic demand function generates a demand curve showing an inverse relationship between price and quantity.

In our hyperbolic demand equation we have suppressed the influence of exogenous variables on quantity demanded. Nevertheless, it is possible to illustrate how a change in income, the prices of related goods, or even tastes could displace the demand curve. For instance, an increase in demand (e.g., caused by a change in income) might increase the value of the constant R. In Figure 3.2 the demand curve D_2 is drawn for the equation $Q_d = 160/p$. It is conceivable that an increase in income could change the amount of

Figure 3.2

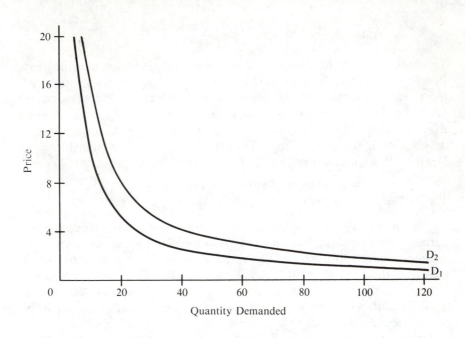

money households budget for a commodity, thereby implying that the quantity demanded of a commodity would increase by 60 percent at each price. Instead of the demand curve shifting by a constant distance, this demand curve shifts by a constant percentage of the original quantity demanded. Hence, the horizontal distance between demand curves D_1 and D_2 is relatively small for high prices, and the horizontal distance between these curves increases as price falls. In a later chapter we will see that hyperbolic demand curves have the characteristic of *constant price elasticity of demand*. For the two curves depicted in Figure 3.2, the price elasticity of demand is everywhere unitary.

SUPPLY FUNCTIONS

The relationships between mathematical functions and the shapes of diagrams developed for demand functions also apply to supply functions. Economic theory tells us that short-run market supply functions are generated by the horizontal summation of the supply curves for all the firms in a competitive industry. There are accordingly two ways that market supply curves could be estimated. First, we could take observations on price and market quantity supplied over a short period of time (say over a three-year period using monthly data) and estimate a market supply curve directly. Second, we may obtain the equation for the supply curve of a representative firm, then multiply quantity supplied at each price by the number of firms in the industry to obtain the market supply curve.

Like the demand curve, the supply curve also violates the mathematical convention of plotting the independent variable on the horizontal axis and the dependent variable on the vertical axis. In the theory of the competitive firm, we begin with the marginal cost function, which shows the cost of producing an extra unit at each rate of output. In this case, marginal cost, the dependent variable, is plotted on the vertical axis and the rate of output, the independent variable, is plotted on the horizontal axis. The optimal rate of output is then determined where marginal cost equals price (which is a horizontal line). Solving the marginal cost equals price rule for quantity yields the supply equation. Therefore, since the supply curve is derived from the marginal cost curve, the practice of plotting quantity on the horizontal axis is continued.

If we use the former approach, we might obtain a supply equation with the general form:

$$Q_s = a_0 + a_1 w_L + a_2 w_k + a_3 n + bp$$

where Q_s is the quantity per year, in thousands, p is the price of the product, w_L is the hourly wage rate, w_k is the hourly cost of capital, and n is the number of firms in the industry. As in the case of the demand curve, the variables Q_s and p are *endogenous* variables used to plot the supply diagram, while w_L, w_k, and n are *exogenous* variables that determine the intercept of the supply curve whose equation is:

$$Q_s = a + bp$$

where

$$a = a_0 + a_1 w_L + a_2 w_k + a_3 n$$

Econometric techniques discussed in Part III are used to provide specific numerical values for a_0, a_1, a_2, a_3, and b. Let us suppose that the estimated equation is:

$$Q_s = 120 - 25 w_L - 50 w_k + 5n + 2p$$

We then assign specific values of w_L, w_k, and n in the supply equation. Suppose $w_L = 10$, $w_k = 5$, and $n = 80$. Then the intercept of the supply equation becomes:

$$a = 120 - 25(10) - 50(5) + 5(80)$$
$$= 120 - 250 - 250 + 400 = 20$$

The *ceteris paribus* supply curve is given by the equation:

$$Q_s = 20 + 2p$$

Like the demand curve, the dependent variable (quantity) is plotted on the horizontal axis and the independent variable (price) is plotted on the vertical axis. The actual slope is the change in price divided by the change in quantity, which is the reciprocal of the change in quantity divided by the change in price. This supply curve has a positive quantity intercept and a slope of 0.5; it is labeled S_0 in Figure 3.3.

Now suppose that the wage rate increases from 10 to 10.80. The new intercept of the supply curve becomes:

$$a = 120 - 25(10.80) - 50(5) + 5(80)$$
$$= 120 - 270 - 250 + 400 = 0$$

In Figure 3.3 supply curve S_1 passes through the origin but has the same slope as supply curve S_0. An increase in the wage rate would cause a parallel

Figure 3.3

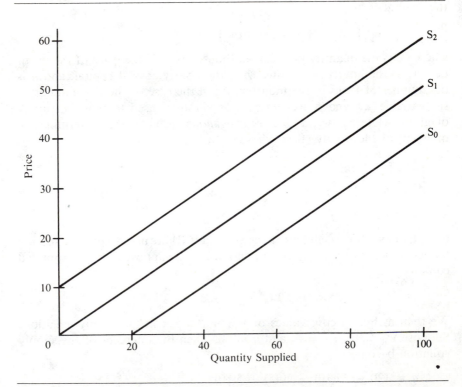

leftward shift in the supply curve. Finally, if the number of firms declined from 80 to 76, the constant term would change in a predictable manner:

$$a = 120 - 25(10.80) - 50(5) + 5(76)$$
$$= 120 - 270 - 250 + 380 = -20$$

Subtracting the previous value of a from the new intercept term, we find:

$$\Delta a = 5(\Delta n) = 5(-4) = -20$$

The quantity intercept of the supply curve becomes -20. This supply curve is labeled S_2 in Figure 3.3.

We may decide that a supply equation that is linear in all variables does not conform well to the predictions of economic theory. For instance, a change in the number of firms should have a greater impact on the quantity supplied at higher prices than it would at lower prices, since we assume that each firm produces more output at higher prices than at lower prices. Rather than forcing the supply curve to have a constant slope, which would result from estimating a multivariate linear equation, a more satisfactory result might be obtained from "aggregating" the supply curve of an individual firm.

Suppose the supply curve for an individual firm were given by the equation $q_s = (5/w)p$,[1] where q_s is the quantity supplied by the "representative firm," w is the wage rate, and p is price. In this case the firm's supply curve passes through the origin and has a slope that depends on the prevailing wage rate. An increase in w would reduce quantity supplied at each price, while a decline in w would increase quantity supplied at each price.

Given the observation that market quantity supplied is the sum of the quantity supplied by all firms in the industry, we can obtain the market supply equation by multiplying individual quantity supplied by n, the number of firms in the market. But since individual quantity supplied is a function of p and w, market quantity supplied is a function of p, w, and n:

$$Q_s = nq_s = n\left[\left(\frac{5}{w}\right)p\right] = 5\left(\frac{n}{w}\right)p$$

In Figure 3.4 we plot three supply curves corresponding to different values of the *exogenous* variables n and w. For supply curve S_0 we assume that $w = 10$ and $n = 80$, yielding the market supply function in one variable:

$$Q_s = 40p$$

Again, because price is plotted on the vertical axis, the actual equation depicted in Figure 3.4 is $p = (1/40)Q_s = 0.025Q_s$. If the number of firms were

---

[1]We know from microeconomic theory that marginal cost is equal to the price of the variable input(s) divided by the marginal product of that input. If labor were the only variable input, and its marginal product were given by the formula $MP_L = 5/q$, we would have the profit maximizing condition: $MC = w/(5/q) = wq/5 = p$, implying $q = (5/w)p$.

Figure 3.4

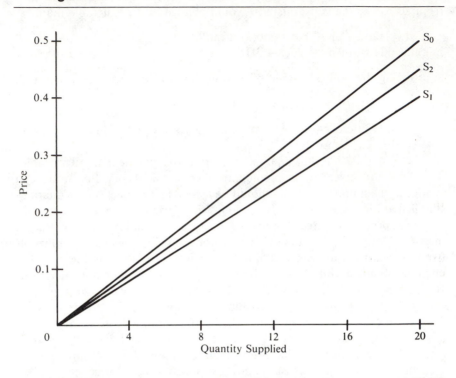

to increase to 100 (while the wage rate remained constant at 10), the supply curve would *rotate* to the right, corresponding to the equation:

$$Q_s = 5\left(\frac{100}{10}\right)p = 50p$$

The intercept of the market supply curve remains the same, but the impact of a one-unit increase in price on quantity is now greater. Note that this implies a decrease in the slope measured as the change in price divided by the change in quantity; the slope of S_1 is $1/50 = 0.02$.

Finally, if the wage rate increased from 10 to 11.11, the supply curve would rotate to the left from S_1 to S_2 in Figure 3.4. The market supply function would become:

$$Q_s = 5\left(\frac{100}{11.11}\right)p \approx 5(9)p = 45p$$

In this case the observed supply curve (with p plotted against Q_s) would appear to become steeper.

PRODUCTION FUNCTIONS

Typically a production function relates the rate of output, q, to the amount of two or more factors of production that are employed in a production process. A three-variable production function relates output to combinations of labor (L) and capital (K) services:

$$q = F(L, K)$$

There are two ways of depicting a production function with three variables (the rate of output and two inputs) in two-dimensional space. A *short-run* production function may be generated by holding one of the inputs (e.g., capital) constant, then plotting the output associated with each amount of the other input (e.g., labor):

$$q = F(L, \overline{K_1}) = f(L)$$

One of the most popular formulas for production functions used in empirical work is the *Cobb-Douglas* production function[2], whose general form is:

$$q = AL^\alpha K^\beta$$

where q is the rate of output, L and K are the quantity of labor and capital services, respectively, and A, α, and β are all positive constants, with $\alpha < 1$ and $\beta < 1$. In Figure 3.5 we plot three short-run production functions for the Cobb-Douglas production function:

$$q = L^{1/2} K^{1/2}$$

that is, with the specific values of $A = 1$ and $\alpha = \beta = 1/2$.

The curve labeled $f(L, 4)$ is generated by fixing the value of capital at $K = 4$, and allowing the value of labor to vary from $L = 0$ to $L = 16$. Note that this curve starts at the origin and increases as L increases. The curve labeled $f(L, 8)$ is generated by fixing the value of capital at $K = 8$, and again allowing the amount of labor to vary from $L = 0$ to $L = 16$. The curve labeled $f(L, 16)$ is generated by setting $K = 16$. Note that increasing the amount of capital causes the rate of output to be larger for each positive amount of labor. In the short-run production function the amount of the "fixed" input serves as a parameter that changes the location of the curve.

An alternative method of presenting a production function with two independent variables and one dependent variable is to treat the rate of output as a shift parameter and allow the combinations of inputs to vary.

[2]C. W. Cobb and P. H. Douglas, "A Theory of Production," *American Economic Review*, Vol. XVIII (Supplement, 1938), pp. 139-156.

Figure 3.5

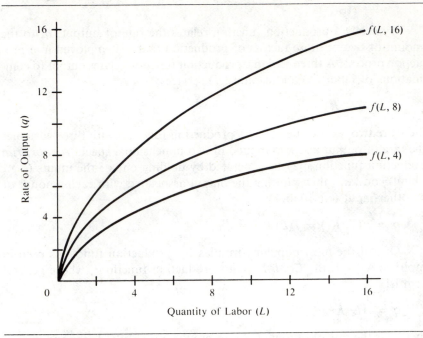

Figure 3.6

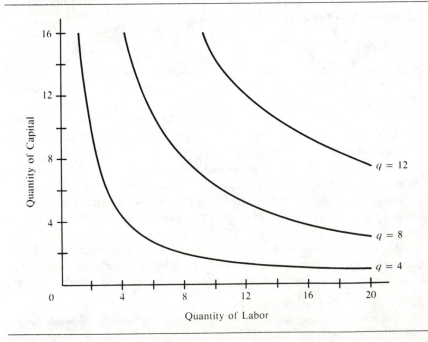

Hence, if we stipulate that $q = 4$ and restate our production function so that capital is a function of labor, we obtain:

$$q = 4 = L^{1/2}K^{1/2}$$

implies

$$K^{1/2} = \frac{4}{L^{1/2}}$$

or

$$K = \frac{16}{L}$$

From our earlier discussions, you may recognize this equation as a hyperbolic function.

In economic theory, an *isoquant* is generated by holding output constant and allowing labor and capital to vary. Figure 3.6 presents an *isoquant map* for three rates of output: $q = 4$, $q = 8$, and $q = 12$. Note that as the rate of output is increased (that is, as we move to isoquants depicting greater rates of output), more capital is required for each amount of labor used, and vice versa.

THE CONSUMPTION FUNCTION

Now we pass through that mystical veil that separates macroeconomics from microeconomics and encounter the aggregate consumption function. An econometrician would typically assume that aggregate consumption increases as disposable income increases. There are two approaches to estimating the relation between consumption and disposable income. By employing cross-sectional data, the econometrician relates the spending, C, to the net income, y, of each of a number of households during a particular time, typically a year. Since many other factors besides income influence household consumption, the econometrician would also estimate the influence of the size of the households, n, their wealth, W, and the ages of their members, A, to obtain a multivariate function of the form:

$$C = f(y, n, W, A)$$

The econometrician might specify a linear, quadratic, or other functional form for the cross-sectional consumption function. As with the supply and demand functions, variations in the exogenous variables (n, W, A) would shift or rotate the two-variable consumption function.

Time-series data—data recorded at equal time intervals—could be used to relate aggregate household consumption to total disposable income. When estimating an aggregate consumption function, the econometrician need include only variables that influence all households in a systematic way. Figure 3.7 depicts an aggregate consumption function for the United States for the

Figure 3.7

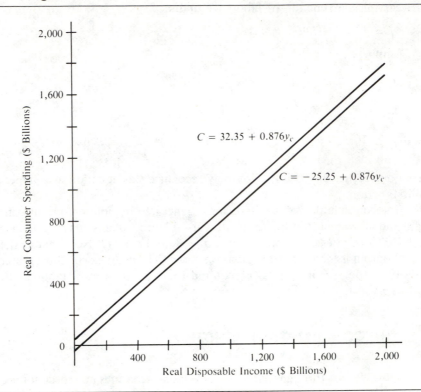

years 1931 to 1983. To make income and consumption comparable from year to year, both variables were translated into constant 1972 dollars. It is well known that during World War II households consumed a smaller share of disposable income than during other years. Hence, two equations were estimated: $C_t = 32.35 + 0.876y_t$ for 1931-1940 and 1946-1983, and $C_t = -25.25 + 0.876y_t$ for 1941-1945. Hence, the greater average propensity to save during World War II caused a parallel shift in the consumption function for those years.

THE PHILLIPS CURVE

The alleged trade-off between employment and price stability, often associated with the Phillips curve[3], continues to be a controversial topic in macroeconomic theory. But controversial theories are just as amenable to mathematical and graphical treatment as uncontroversial ones. In fact,

[3]A. W. Phillips, "The Relation Between Unemployment and the Rate of Change of Money Wage Rates in the United Kingdom, 1861-1957," *Economica*, Vol. XXV (1958), pp. 283-300.

controversies are often better understood, if not resolved, by mathematical formulations that contain less ambiguity than verbal descriptions of an idea.

A. W. Phillips argued that there was an inverse, nonlinear relation between nominal wage changes and the unemployment rate in Great Britain between 1861 and 1957. Although his data were limited and his econometric techniques were crude by today's standards, Phillips did estimate a simple two-variable function of the form:

$$\frac{\Delta w}{w} + a = b(UE)^c, \, b > 0 \text{ and } c < 0$$

where $\Delta w/w$ is the rate of change in the average money wage rate, and UE is the unemployment rate. A more complete specification of the Phillips model relates price inflation, productivity changes, and the unemployment rate to money wage changes. Using data for the U.S. economy for 1949 to 1983, we estimated the equation:[4]

$$\frac{\Delta w}{w} = -1.53 + 10.28\left(\frac{1}{UE}\right) + 0.55\left(\frac{\Delta PROD}{PROD}\right) + 0.86\left(\frac{\Delta p}{p}\right)$$

According to these results, the nominal wage rate increases with the rate of price inflation ($\Delta p/p$), the rate of increase in productivity ($\Delta PROD/PROD$), and the *inverse* of the unemployment rate (i.e., as the unemployment rate increases, nominal wages decrease, *ceteris paribus*). For instance, suppose that the rate of inflation is 6 percent and that labor productivity is increasing at the rate of 3 percent per year. Then the equation becomes:

$$\frac{\Delta w}{w} = 5.28 + \frac{10.28}{UE}$$

This relation is plotted in Figure 3.8 as $f(UE)_0$.

According to the function $f(UE)_0$, an unemployment rate of slightly less than 3 percent (2.76 percent) would result in a wage increase of 9 percent. This nominal wage increase is consistent with a real wage increase equal to the assumed 3 percent increase in productivity. As the rate of unemployment increases, the rate of increase in the nominal wage rate decreases. At 3.78 percent unemployment, the wage increase is only 8 percent; at 6 percent, the wage increase is only 7 percent. In fact, at an unemployment rate of 14 percent, nominal wages would keep up with inflation ($\Delta w/w = 6$), but productivity increases would go unrewarded.

Figure 3.8 shows that more modest inflation would improve the ability of workers to bargain for real wage increases. Assuming $\Delta p/p = 3$ percent and $\Delta PROD/PROD = 3$ percent generates the equation:

$$\frac{\Delta w}{w} = 2.7 + \frac{10.28}{UE}$$

[4]Statistical aspects of this estimation are discussed in Chapter 19.

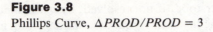

Figure 3.8

Phillips Curve, $\Delta PROD/PROD = 3$

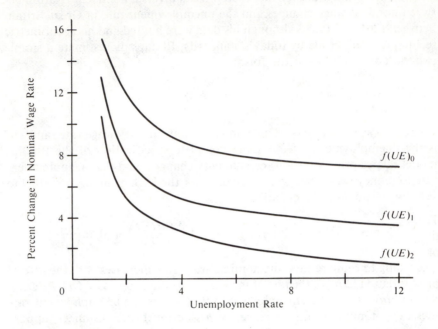

This equation is shown in Figure 3.8 as $f(UE)_1$. At $UE = 3.1$ percent, $\Delta w/w = 6$ percent, and wage increases would equal the sum of price and productivity increases. At $UE = 4.5$ percent, $\Delta w/w = 5$ percent; at $UE = 7.9$ percent, $\Delta w/w = 4$ percent; and at $UE = 34.3$ percent, $\Delta w/w = 3$ percent.

Finally, if the rate of inflation is zero, while $\Delta PROD/PROD$ is 3 percent, the Phillips curve becomes:

$$\frac{\Delta w}{w} = 0.12 + \frac{10.28}{UE}$$

This equation is shown in Figure 3.8 as $f(UE)_2$. At a 3.47 percent unemployment rate, percentage change in the nominal wage rate would equal the percentage change in productivity. Note how closely this parallels the notion of a "natural rate of unemployment": the rate at which changes in labor productivity translate into changes in real wages. When the rate of unemployment is greater than 3.47 percent, nominal wage changes would not keep pace with productivity, and real wage rates would fall. At lower rates of unemployment, nominal wage changes would exceed productivity increases, implying either increasing unemployment or price inflation, depending on what happens to the money supply.

HOMOGENEOUS FUNCTIONS

A special type of function—the homogeneous function—is important in several areas of economics. It has particular properties that are extremely useful in many economic problems. We shall explore the features of homogeneous functions and then discuss some of the applications of this function in economics.

Consider a function with two independent variables:

$$z = f(x, y)$$

This function is said to be homogeneous of degree n in x and y if the following relationship holds:

$$f(ax, ay) = a^n f(x, y)$$

That is, if when each of the independent variables is multiplied by a positive constant a, the new value of the function is a^n times the value of the original function.

Let's look at a simple example. Let dependent variable z be the sum of the squares of the independent variables:

$$z = f(x, y) = x^2 + y^2$$

Multiply each of the independent variables by an arbitrary constant a:

$$
\begin{aligned}
f(ax, ay) &= (ax)^2 + (ay)^2 \\
&= a^2 x^2 + a^2 y^2 \\
&= a^2 (x^2 + y^2) \\
&= a^2 f(x, y)
\end{aligned}
$$

Since $f(ax, ay) = a^2 f(x, y)$, this function is homogeneous of degree two; that is, $n = 2$. Homogeneous functions may be homogeneous of any degree and can be generalized for any number of independent variables.

In economic theory, production functions are often assumed to exhibit *constant returns to scale*. This is equivalent to assuming that the mathematical function describing the relation between input services and the rate of output is homogeneous of degree one, often called a *linear homogeneous function*.[5] Let q represent the rate of output, with L and K representing labor and capital services, respectively:

$$q = f(L, K)$$

[5]This should not be confused with a linear function since the independent variables need not enter linearly for a linear homogeneous function; it is the constant a that enters linearly.

If this function is homogeneous of the first degree, then:

$$n = 1$$

and

$$f(aL, aK) = af(L, K) = aq$$

By multiplying each of the inputs by an arbitrary positive constant,[6] output is multiplied by the same constant. For example, if all input services were doubled, output would double; if all input services were reduced by one-half, output would decline proportionally.

A *Cobb-Douglas* production function was introduced earlier. This homogeneous production function is popular in econometric work because of the relative ease with which it can be estimated. Its general form is:

$$q = AL^\alpha K^\beta$$

where q represents production, L is the quantity of labor, K is the quantity of capital, and A, α, and β are constants. The degree of homogeneity is given by the sum of α and β, which are the *output elasticities* for labor and capital, respectively. If, as is usually assumed, $\beta = 1 - \alpha$, the production function will be homogeneous of first degree.[7]

Suppose we are given that $q_0 = A(L_0)^\alpha (K_0)^{1-\alpha}$. If we multiply both labor and capital by any positive constant a, we obtain:

$$\begin{aligned} A(aL_0)^\alpha (aK_0)^{1-\alpha} &= a^{(\alpha + 1 - \alpha)} A(L_0)^\alpha (K_0)^{1-\alpha} \\ &= aA(L_0)^\alpha (K_0)^{1-\alpha} \\ &= aq_0 \end{aligned}$$

Economic theory also predicts that, in the absence of a money illusion, demand functions will be *homogeneous of degree zero*. According to the theory of consumer choice, the combination of commodities chosen (say q_1 and q_2) depends on *real* income and the *relative* prices of those commodities. Let the demand function for commodity q_1 be given by:

$$q_{1d} = D(p_1, p_2, Y) = 40\left(\frac{Y}{p_2}\right) - 10\left(\frac{p_1}{p_2}\right)$$

where p_1 and p_2 are the prices of q_1 and q_2, respectively, and Y is money income. Imagine a "pure" inflation raises all prices and money income to

---

[6]We restrict the constant here to be positive; otherwise total output would turn out to be negative. To discuss decreases in output when all inputs are reduced we merely let $0 < a < 1$. That is, we restrict the positive a to values less than one.

[7]The econometrician could test this hypothesis when estimating a Cobb-Douglas production function.

a percent of their previous levels. The quantity of q_1 demanded should not be affected:

$$q_{1d} = D(ap_1, ap_2, aY) = 40\left(\frac{aY}{ap_2}\right) - 10\left(\frac{ap_1}{ap_2}\right)$$

$$= \left(\frac{a}{a}\right)\left[40\left(\frac{Y}{p_2}\right) - 10\left(\frac{p_1}{p_2}\right)\right]$$

$$= a^0 D(p_1, p_2, Y)$$

$$= D(p_1, p_2, Y)$$

since any number to the zero power equals one. Once again, econometrics allows economists who *believe* that demand functions *ought* to be homogeneous of degree zero to check whether their beliefs conform to reality (or whether reality conforms to their beliefs).

SUMMARY

This chapter has been an excursion into the use of functions and graphs in economics. The convention of drawing two-dimensional diagrams rests on the designation of variables as *exogenous* and *endogenous*. Using *ceteris paribus* logic, the economist incorporates exogenous variables into the *parameters* of the function. When these parameters change, the graph depicting a relation between endogenous variables will shift, depending on the mathematical form chosen to express the function. When a function is linear in all variables, a change in one or more of the exogenous variables will change the intercept of the two-variable graph, leaving the slope unchanged. When a power (or log-linear) function is chosen, a change in one or more exogenous variables changes the slope of the two-variable graph.

We saw many applications of two-variable functions: demand, supply, production, and consumption functions, and the Phillips curve. In each case, the shape of the two-variable diagram reflected the functional form assumed or estimated. The chapter concluded with a discussion of homogeneous functions that have the special characteristic that proportionate changes in all independent variables change the dependent variables in a consistent manner. Two applications of homogeneous functions involved production functions, often assumed to be homogeneous of degree one (*linear homogeneous*), and demand functions, often assumed to be homogeneous of degree zero.

PROBLEMS

Group I

1.   Assume the market demand function for a college education in the United States is given as:

$$e = f(y, p) = 500 + 0.3y - 50p$$

where e is measured in thousands of college entrants per year, y represents national income in the United States in billions of constant dollars, and p denotes the average price per year of a college education in thousands of dollars (tuition plus fees, foregone income, etc.). It is known that y is equal to $2,000 billion per year.

   a. Construct the demand schedule for college education for the range $p = 1$ to $p = 5$, inclusive, at unit intervals, assuming that $y = \$2,000$.

   b. Plot a smooth demand curve for college education for the same price range. Label this curve D_1.

   c. Assume that national income increases to $2,200 billion. Plot the new demand curve and label it D_2.

   d. Assume national income decreases to $1,800 billion. Plot the new demand curve and label it D_3.

2.   Assume the market supply function for beer in the United States is given as:

$$Q_b = f(p) = 100p^{0.5}$$

where Q_b denotes the quantity of beer supplied measured in thousands of gallons per year and p signifies the price of beer in dollars per gallon.

   a. Construct the supply schedule for beer for the price range $p = 1$ to $p = 5$, inclusive, at $1 intervals.

   b. Plot a smooth supply curve for beer for the same price range.

3.   Aggregate consumption for the American economy is assumed to be given as:

$$C = C(Y, T, A) = 20 + 0.7(Y - T) + 0.1A$$

where C represents aggregate consumption by households in the U.S., Y is personal income, T signifies total tax payments to the government, and A denotes the asset holdings of households. All variables are measured in billions of constant dollars. Assume it is known that total tax payments equal $200 billion and total asset holdings equal $2,000 billion.

   a. Graph the consumption function of income for the range $Y = 0$ to $Y = 1,500$, inclusive, assuming $T = \$200$ and $A = \$2,000$. Label this curve C_1.

   b. Assume that taxes are increased to $300 billion, while asset holdings do not change. Graph the new consumption curve for the same income range and label it C_2.

   c. Assume asset holdings increase to $2,400 billion, while taxes remain at $200 billion. Graph the new consumption function and label it C_3.

   d. Suppose that both taxes and assets are assumed to be increasing functions of income, such that $T = tY = 0.2Y$ and $A = aY = 2Y$. What is the equation for the new consumption function? Plot this function and label it C_4.

4. A production function is given for the rate of output, q, in terms of labor, L, and capital, K, according to the equation:

$$q = F(L, K) = 16L^{0.75}K^{0.25}$$

   a. Assume that capital is fixed at $K = 16$. Plot a short-run production function, relating q to L over the range $L = 0$ to $L = 16$. Label this curve $f(L, 16)$.
   b. Assume that capital increases to $K = 32$. Plot the new short-run production function over the same range and label it $f(L, 32)$.

Group II

5. Assume the market demand function for electric guitars in the United States is given by:

$$g = f(p) = 400 - 10p^{0.5}$$

   where g represents the quantity demanded per year (in thousands of guitars) and p denotes the price (in dollars per guitar).
   a. Construct the market demand schedule for electric guitars for values of p equal to 100, 225, 400, 625, and 900.
   b. Plot the demand curve for electric guitars over the price range $p = 100$ to $p = 900$.

6. The total-cost-of-production function for a firm producing q units of output per month is:

$$c = f(q) = 100 + 5q - 4q^2 + 2q^3$$

   where c represents total cost in thousands of dollars and q represents output in hundreds of units per month.
   a. Construct the total cost schedule for the range $q = 0$ to $q = 12$ units, inclusive.
   b. Plot the smooth total cost curve over the same range.

7. Assume that the market demand function for unskilled labor in a certain city is given by:

$$l = f(w) = \frac{1,600}{w^2}$$

   where l represents thousands of workers per month and w signifies the wage rate in dollars. Construct the demand schedule for unskilled labor for the range $w = \$1$ to $w = \$10$, inclusive, at $\$1$ intervals.

8. The demand function for a commodity X is given as:

$$x = f(p_x, p_y) = 100\left(\frac{p_y}{p_x}\right)$$

   where x denotes the quantity of X per unit of time and p_x and p_y denote, respectively, the price of X and the price of Y, a substitute commodity. Is this demand function homogeneous? If so, of what degree is it homogeneous? How would you give a common-sense explanation of this characteristic of the demand function?

9.   The production function for a firm is given as:

$$q = f(L, K) = 10(L + K)$$

where q measures the firm's output in thousands of units per year, L denotes the amount of labor used by the firm in hours per year, and K denotes the capital input of the firm measured in thousands of machine hours per year. Prove that this production function is homogeneous of degree one.

4

Systems of

Equations

Defining the behavior of economic agents by a single equation is usually only a first step in economic theory. The second (and often more challenging) step is the specification of equilibrium conditions that link the actions of different agents. One of the basic principles of economic theory is that market price is determined by the interaction of supply and demand: the equilibrium price occurs where the quantity demanded equals the quantity supplied. The equilibrium rate of output for the profit maximizing firm occurs where marginal cost equals marginal revenue. In general, knowing one function will not enable the economist to predict economic events. In order to account for the countervailing forces that generate stable outcomes, the economist constructs a system of equations. In this chapter we will consider simple techniques for solving a system of two or more equations. If you have studied college algebra, the procedures reviewed in this chapter will no doubt be familiar to you. In the next chapter we will see how the techniques of matrix algebra can streamline the solutions to systems of equations.

SYSTEMS OF TWO LINEAR EQUATIONS

Assume that the market demand schedule for a commodity is known and can be described by the equation $Q_d = 2,000 - 100p$, where Q_d is the quantity demanded (measured in thousands of pounds per month) and p is the price (measured in cents per pound). Also assume that the supply schedule is known to be described by the equation $Q_s = -100 + 50p$, where Q_s is the quantity supplied (also measured in thousands of pounds per month). As mentioned, a market is in equilibrium when the quantity demanded by buyers equals the quantity supplied by sellers; that is, when both quantity demanded and quantity supplied equal the quantity exchanged: $Q_d = Q_s = Q$. Substituting Q for both Q_d and Q_s, we obtain a system of two equations in two unknowns:

$$Q = 2{,}000 - 100p$$
$$Q = -100 + 50p$$

To solve this system for the two unknowns, we must find the values of Q and p that will satisfy both of the equations. Indeed, this system is a set of *simultaneous equations*, meaning that both equations must be true for the same set of values of Q and p. We arrive at the solution by first eliminating one of the two variables. In this system it would be easiest to eliminate Q, since both the demand and supply equations are explicit functions expressing Q in terms of p. Since $2{,}000 - 100p$ equals Q, and $-100 + 50p$ equals Q, it follows that:

$$-100 + 50p = 2{,}000 - 100p$$

Adding $100 + 100p$ to both sides of the equation isolates the unknown p on the left side and the constant(s) on the right side:

$$50p + 100p = 2{,}000 + 100$$
$$150p = 2{,}100$$

Solving for p is a simple matter of dividing both sides of the equation by 150:

$$\frac{150p}{150} = \frac{2{,}100}{150}$$
$$p = 14$$

Obtaining the value of Q is also straightforward. Substituting 14 for p in either equation, we generate the associated value of Q. Using the demand equation:

$$Q = Q_d = 2{,}000 - 100(14) = 2{,}100 - 1{,}400 = 600$$

Since we did not use the supply equation to find the value of Q, we can substitute $p = 14$ into that equation to check our results:

$$Q = Q_s = -100 + 50(14) = -100 + 700 = 600$$

The solution to the system, then, is $p = 14$ and $Q = 600$.

SYSTEMS OF MORE THAN
TWO LINEAR EQUATIONS

The demand for a commodity often depends both on its own price and on the price of another commodity. It is also possible that the supply equation for one commodity may contain the prices of that commodity and of a related commodity. For example, wheat and corn can be considered substitutes in consumption (i.e., if the price of corn increases relative to the price of wheat, households will substitute wheat for corn) and substitutes in production (farmers who expect the price of wheat to increase relative to that of corn will plant wheat instead of corn).

Denote p_w as the price of wheat and p_c as the price of corn. Let D_w and D_c be the quantities demanded of wheat and corn, respectively, and let S_w and S_c be the quantities supplied. The demand functions for wheat and corn are given as:

$$D_w = 26 - p_w + p_c$$
$$D_c = 8 + p_w - p_c$$

The respective supply functions are:

$$S_w = -4 + 3p_w - p_c$$
$$S_c = -2 - p_w + 5p_c$$

As in the case of one price and one equilibrium quantity, the first step in solving these equations involves substituting the *equilibrium quantities* Q_w and Q_c for the quantities demanded and supplied in both equations. Then we set the right side of the demand equation equal to the right side of the supply equation. The equations for the wheat market,

$$Q_w = 26 - p_w + p_c$$
$$Q_w = -4 + 3p_w - p_c$$

yield:

$$26 - p_w + p_c = -4 + 3p_w - p_c$$
$$4p_w - 2p_c = 30$$

Notice that the demand and supply equations for the wheat market yield an equation with two variables, p_w and p_c. Obviously, one equation is insufficient to generate unique values for both unknowns. Technically, we say that the equation $4p_w - 2p_c = 30$ has *one degree of freedom*, meaning we can specify a value for either p_w or p_c and the value of the other variable will be uniquely determined.

In order to find unique values for p_w *and* p_c we must combine the demand and supply equations for corn:

$$Q_c = 8 + p_w - p_c$$
$$Q_c = -2 - p_w + 5p_c$$

These equations yield:

$$8 + p_w - p_c = -2 - p_w + 5p_c$$
$$-2p_w + 6p_c = 10$$

Combining the resulting equations for the two markets, we get a system of two equations in two unknowns which, in this case, yield unique values of those unknowns:

$$4p_w - 2p_c = 30$$
$$-2p_w + 6p_c = 10$$

These two equations are in implicit form; i.e., both unknowns are on the same side of the equal sign in the two equations. We can eliminate one of the variables by transforming one of the equations so that the coefficients of one variable are the same (in absolute value) in both equations. If we multiply the first equation by 3, the coefficient of p_c becomes -6. Adding the transformed first equation to the second equation eliminates p_c, allowing us to solve for p_w. Alternatively, we could multiply the second equation by 2 and add the result to the first equation, eliminating the p_w term. Choosing the latter approach:

$$
\begin{array}{lll}
4p_w - 2p_c = 30 & \text{becomes} & 4p_w - 2p_c = 30 \\
2(-2p_w + 6p_c = 10) & \text{becomes} & -4p_w + 12p_c = 20 \\
& \text{adding} & \overline{10p_c = 50} \\
& & p_c = 5
\end{array}
$$

By substituting the solution for p_c into either equation, we obtain the solution for p_w. Using the first equation:

$$4p_w - 2(5) = 30$$
$$4p_w = 30 + 10 = 40$$
$$p_w = 10$$

Using the second equation to check our results:

$$-2(10) + 6(5) = -20 + 30 = 10$$

We still have to find the equilibrium values of Q_w and Q_c. Since we have a demand equation and a supply equation for each quantity, we can use one to determine the equilibrium quantity and the other to check our results. Substituting the equilibrium values for p_w and p_c into the demand equation for wheat, we obtain:

$$Q_w = D_w = 26 - 10 + 5 = 21$$

Checking:

$$Q_w = S_w = -4 + 3(10) - 5 = 21$$

Finally, substituting the solutions for p_w and p_c into the demand equation for corn, we obtain the equilibrium value for Q_c:

$$Q_c = D_c = 8 + 10 - 5 = 13$$

We use the supply equation for corn to check our result:

$$Q_c = S_c = -2 - 10 + 5(5) = 13$$

If we had information about the demand and supply functions for every commodity in the economy, we could compute the *Walrasian general equilibrium* prices and quantities. For n commodities we would have n demand functions and n supply functions. By combining the equations two-by-two and successively eliminating variables, the equilibrium prices and quantities traded of each of the n commodities could be determined.

SYSTEMS INVOLVING
QUADRATIC EQUATIONS

A quadratic equation is an equation with the independent variable raised to the second power. For instance, suppose we have a competitive firm with a total cost function given by:

$$C = 100 + 5q + q^2$$

where C is total cost and q is the rate of output. Suppose the owner wishes to determine the rate of output that will allow all costs to be covered. This problem is often referred to as the *break-even* problem. For the competitive firm, total revenue per unit of time, R, equals price, p, times quantity, q: $R = pq$.

For each price there will be a different solution to the break-even problem. Assume that $p = 30$. The firm will break even when total revenue, R, equals total cost, C, that is, when:

$$30q = 100 + 5q + q^2$$

or

$$q^2 - 25q + 100 = 0$$

You may recall that to solve a quadratic equation, you factor the equation into two multiplicative terms, each of which implies an acceptable value of q when set equal to zero. In this case:

$$q^2 - 25q + 100 = (q - 5)(q - 20) = 0$$

Factoring gives us a product of two expressions which equals zero. It follows that one of the terms must equal zero. Hence, if $(q - 5) = 0$, $q = 5$; if $(q - 20) = 0$, $q = 20$. The firm would exactly cover its costs if it produced 5 units of output or if it produced 20 units of output.

A linear equation with one independent variable has at most one solution, but a quadratic equation with one independent variable can have two solutions. However, it is *possible* that a quadratic equation may have only one solution, or even no solution at all. Continuing with our example, assume that $p = 25$, so that the break-even problem becomes:

$$25q = 100 + 5q + q^2$$
$$q^2 - 20q + 100 = 0$$
$$(q - 10)^2 = 0$$
$$q = 10$$

Most quadratic equations cannot be easily factored into a form that makes their solution(s) obvious. Economists and mathematicians find it much more efficient to employ the *quadratic formula* to solve quadratic equations.

To develop the quadratic formula, consider a general quadratic equation of the form:

$$aq^2 + bq + c = 0$$

where a, b, and c are constants. Of course, when $a = 0$, the equation is linear. Hence, for a quadratic equation, $a \neq 0$, we can divide both sides of the equation by a:

$$q^2 + \left(\frac{b}{a}\right)q + \frac{c}{a} = 0$$

The first two terms of the transformed equation are part of the square: $(q + b/2a)^2 = q^2 + (b/a)q + b^2/4a^2$. By subtracting c/a from both sides of the equation and adding $b^2/4a^2$ to both sides of the equation we obtain:

$$q^2 + \left(\frac{b}{a}\right)q + \frac{b^2}{4a^2} = \frac{b^2}{4a^2} - \frac{c}{c}$$

After multiplying c/a by $4a/4a$, we can combine the terms to the right of the equal sign:

$$\left(q + \frac{b}{2a}\right)^2 = \frac{b^2 - 4ac}{4a^2}$$

Taking the square root of both sides of the equation:

$$q + \frac{b}{2a} = \pm\sqrt{\frac{b^2 - 4ac}{4a^2}}$$

Finally by subtracting $b/2a$ from both sides, we have the solution(s) for q (or any independent variable) in terms of the general coefficients of a quadratic equation:

$$q = \frac{-b \pm \sqrt{b^2 - 4ac}}{2a}$$

Let's see how the quadratic formula works in our break-even analysis. If $p = 27$, the break-even condition becomes:

$$27q = 100 + 5q + q^2$$
$$q^2 - 22q + 100 = 0$$

The factors for this quadratic equation are not as obvious. Using the quadratic formula (with $a = 1$, $b = -22$, and $c = 100$) provides a straightforward solution:

$$q = \frac{-(-22) \pm \sqrt{(-22)^2 - 4(100)}}{2}$$

$$= \frac{22 \pm \sqrt{484 - 400}}{2} = \frac{22 \pm \sqrt{84}}{2}$$

or $q \approx (22 - 9.17)/2$, $(22 + 9.17)/2$; $q = 6.42, 15.58$.

We hinted earlier that a quadratic equation might have no *real* solutions. Let's squeeze one more example from our break-even problem. Suppose $p = 20$, which yields the break-even equation:

$$20q = 100 + 5q + q^2$$
$$q^2 - 15q + 100 = 0$$

We use the quadratic formula, with $a = 1$, $b = -15$, and $c = 100$:

$$q = \frac{-(-15) \pm \sqrt{225 - 400}}{2} = \frac{7.5 \pm \sqrt{-150}}{2}$$

In the world of real numbers (the domain of the output variable), $\sqrt{-150}$ is undefined. There is no rate of output that would allow this firm to recover its total costs with a price of only $20.

GRAPHICAL INTERPRETATIONS
OF THE SOLUTIONS

In Chapter 2, each function with one or two independent variables corresponds to a graph in two or three dimensions. By using diagrams we can depict the solution for a system of two equations.

Systems of Linear Equations

In Figure 4.1 we view the supply and demand example introduced earlier in this chapter:

$$Q_d = 2{,}000 - 100p$$
$$Q_s = -100 + 50p$$

As we saw in Chapter 3, economists generally switch the independent and dependent variable axes for demand and supply curves, plotting price on the vertical axis and quantity on the horizontal axis. Nevertheless, the most important feature of both curves—the positive slope of the supply curve and the negative slope of the demand curve—is preserved when price is plotted against quantity. The fact that these curves have *different* slopes guarantees that they intersect somewhere, yielding a solution to the system of equations. That they intersect at a point corresponding to positive values for price and quantity guarantees an *economically relevant* solution to the equation system.

Figures 4.2 and 4.3 show two examples of demand and supply curves that intersect outside the first quadrant of the price-quantity plane. (Recall from Chapter 2 that both variables are positive in the first quadrant.) In Figure 4.2, the intercept of the supply curve is greater than the intercept of the demand curve; the highest price a consumer would pay for the commodity is less than the minimum price a supplier would accept. (Figure 4.2 might describe the 1986 market for business trips to the moon aboard a space shuttle.) In fact, the equations used to generate Figure 4.2 are:

$$Q_d = 2,000 - 4p$$
$$Q_s = -2,400 + 4p$$

Figure 4.1

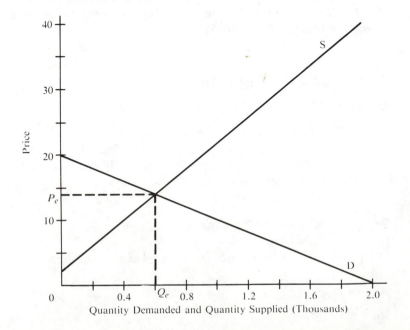

Figure 4.2

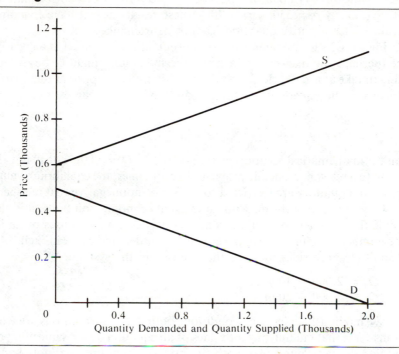

Figure 4.3

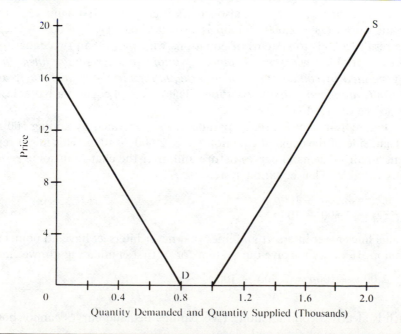

Hence, while there is a pair of values for Q and p for which both equations are true (namely $p = 550$, $q = -200$), these results do not have economic relevance since negative quantities cannot be exchanged.

Figure 4.3 shows demand and supply curves that intersect at a negative price (perhaps the market for garbage: the maximum quantity buyers are willing to take at a zero price is less than the quantity supplied at that price). In this case, the equations for the demand and supply curves are:

$$Q_d = 800 - 50p$$
$$Q_s = 1,000 + 50p$$

Again, a mathematical solution exists ($p = -2$, $Q = 900$), but is not the solution to a relevant economic problem. In economics, the equilibrium values of price and quantity are restricted to the set of nonnegative real numbers.

In addition to problems with no relevant economic solutions, it is also possible that a system of equations may either have no solutions or an infinite number of solutions. Suppose we take our demand curve in Figure 4.1 and multiply both sides by 2, so that we obtain the system:

$$Q_d = 2,000 - 100p$$
$$2Q_d = 4,000 - 200p$$

We might ask under what conditions both demand equations are true. The answer is that multiplying both sides of an equation by the same number, or adding the same number to both sides of the equation, does not change the graph of the equation. The graph of $2Q_d = 4,000 - 200p$ is identical to the graph of $Q_d = 2,000 - 100p$. Hence, any combination of p and Q that satisfies one equation will also satisfy the second. In Figure 4.4a, the demand curve $Q_d = 2,000 - 100p$ is also labeled $2Q_d = 4,000 - 200p$. This result extends to systems of equations with more than two equations and two variables: *when one or more equations in a system are linear and are generated by combinations of other equations in the system, there are an infinite number of possible solutions.* The system of equations has at least one degree of freedom.

Figure 4.4b shows a set of parallel lines, generated by adding 500 to the right side of the demand equation $Q_d = 2,000 - 100p$. This might represent a pair of demand curves before and after the change in some exogenous variable. That equation system is:

$$Q_d = 2,000 - 100p$$
$$Q_d = 2,500 - 100p$$

Parallel lines never intersect and lines that never intersect have no points in common. If we try to solve our system for p (first eliminating Q), we find:

$$2,000 - 100p = 2,500 - 100p$$
$$0 = 500$$

which is clearly a contradiction. Two parallel demand curves cannot both be true at the same time and place.

Figure 4.4a

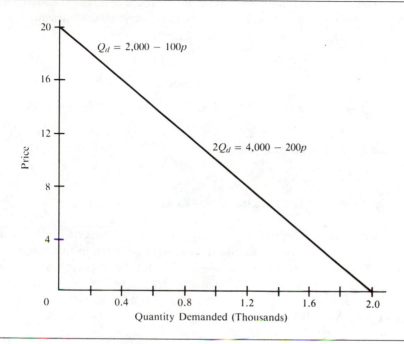

$Q_d = 2,000 - 100p$

$2Q_d = 4,000 - 200p$

Quantity Demanded (Thousands)

Figure 4.4b

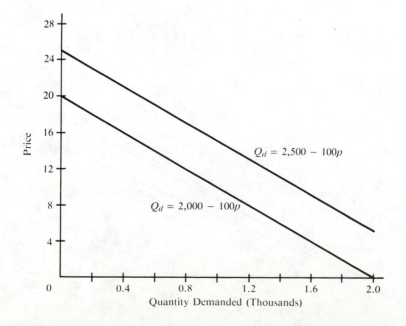

$Q_d = 2,500 - 100p$

$Q_d = 2,000 - 100p$

Quantity Demanded (Thousands)

By constrast, if we solve a system of redundant equations (that is, where one equation is a linear combination of one or more of the other equations in the system) we would find obvious, but not very useful information:

$$Q_d = 2,000 - 100p$$
$$2Q_d = 4,000 - 200p$$

implies

$$2,000 - 100p = 0.5(4,000 - 200p)$$
$$0 = 0$$

Not exactly earth shattering, but true.

Systems of Quadratic Equations

We now turn our attention to the graphs of systems of one or more quadratic equations. Again, we use the example of break-even analysis. In Figure 4.5 we assume that the firm confronts a total cost curve given by the equation $TC = 100 + 5q + q^2$. This cost curve is shown as the right half of a parabola. (The left half is missing since output is restricted to positive values of q.) Also shown in Figure 4.5 are three total revenue lines, corresponding to three different prices.

Figure 4.5

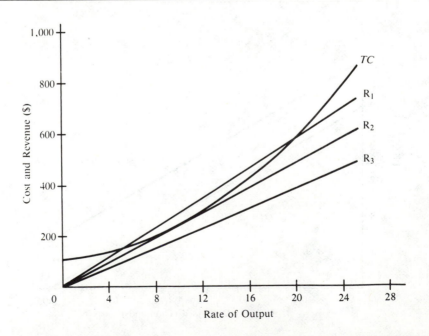

Revenue line R_1 is associated with the price $p = 30$. The equation for line R_1 is $TR = 30q$. To find the break-even rates of output, we subtract the cost function from the total revenue function, set the result equal to zero, and solve for q:

$$TR - TC = 30q - (100 + 5q + q^2) = 0$$
$$-q^2 + 25q - 100 = 0$$

Employing the quadratic formula:

$$q = \frac{-25 \pm \sqrt{625 - 4(-1)(-100)}}{-2}$$

$$= \frac{-25 \pm \sqrt{625 - 400}}{-2} = \frac{-25 \pm \sqrt{225}}{-2} = \frac{-25 \pm 15}{-2}$$

$$q = \frac{-10}{-2} = 5 \text{ and } q = \frac{-40}{-2} = 20$$

We see in Figure 4.5 that the parabola representing total cost intersects the total revenue line R_1 at two rates of output, $q = 5$ and $q = 20$. The two points of intersection correspond to the two solutions to the relevant quadratic equation.

Just as a quadratic equation may have only one solution, it follows that the curves of two functions that make up the quadratic equation may only have one point in common. In Figure 4.5, the revenue line R_2 corresponds to the function $TR = 25q$. With the same total cost function (curve), this generates the break-even problem:

$$25q - (100 + 5q + q^2) = 0$$
$$-q^2 + 20q - 100 = 0$$

Again using the quadratic formula:

$$q = \frac{-20 \pm \sqrt{400 - 4(-1)(-100)}}{-2}$$

$$= \frac{-20 \pm \sqrt{400 - 400}}{-2} = \frac{-20 \pm 0}{-2} = 10$$

When the quadratic equation describing the intersection of a parabola and a line has only one solution, the parabola touches the line at one point. We will see in Chapter 6 that this situation corresponds to a point of *tangency* between the curve and the line.

Finally, if the total revenue line in Figure 4.5 corresponds to R_3, whose formula is $TR = 20q$ (i.e., $p = 20$), there is no point of intersection. This situation corresponds to a quadratic equation that has no solution. Inserting the value of the total revenue function into the break-even problem we have:

$$20q - (100 + 5q + q^2) = 0$$
$$-q^2 + 15q - 100 = 0$$

Using the quadratic formula:

$$q = \frac{-15 \pm \sqrt{225 - 400}}{-2} = \frac{-15 \pm \sqrt{-175}}{-2}$$

which has no *real* solution.

THE EFFECTS OF CHANGES
IN PARAMETERS

We saw in Chapter 2 that a set of supply and demand curves represents relationships between quantity and price for a given set of exogenous variables. The *ceteris paribus* assumption is invoked to specify a set of curves (two equations with two unknowns) for exogenous variables whose values are treated as constants for the context of the problem. For instance, assume a demand function that includes per capita income, y, and a supply function that includes the average wage rate, w, as shift parameters, with quantity measured in thousands of units per month:

$$Q_d = 50 + 0.1y - 2p$$
$$Q_s = 60 - 4w + 0.8p$$

If we are given specific values for the exogenous variables y and w, for example, $y = \$5,000$ and $w = \$5.00$, we obtain a system of two equations with two unknowns:

$$Q_d = 50 + 0.1(5,000) - 2p = 550 - 2p$$
$$Q_s = 60 - 4(5) + 0.8p = 40 + 0.8p$$

This system of equations is represented by lines D_1 and S_1 in Figure 4.6. To solve, we equate the right sides of the two equations by making use of the equilibrium condition: $Q = Q_d = Q_s$.

$$550 - 2p = 40 + 0.8p$$
$$2.8p = 510$$
$$p = \frac{510}{2.8} = 182.14$$

Substituting the value for p into the demand equation:

$$Q = Q_d = 550 - 2(182.14) = 185.71$$

Using the supply function to check:

$$Q = Q_s = 40 + 0.8(182.14) = 185.71$$

Now suppose that per capita income increased by $500 (say due to a tax cut) while the average wage rate remained the same. In this case, the new demand equation would generate a new equation system that translates into a new equilibrium price and quantity:

$$Q_d = 50 + 0.1(5,500) - 2p = 600 - 2p$$
$$Q_s = 60 - 4(5) + 0.8p = 40 + 0.8p$$

The equilibrium price changes to:

$$600 - 2p = 40 + 0.8p$$
$$2.8p = 560$$
$$p = \frac{560}{2.8} = 200$$

Substituting the equilibrium price into the supply equation:

$$Q = Q_d = 40 + 0.8(200) = 200$$

and checking:

$$Q = Q_d = 600 - 2(200) = 200$$

In Figure 4.6, the shift in the demand curve from D_1 to D_2 causes an increase in both equilibrium price and equilibrium quantity. When the demand

Figure 4.6

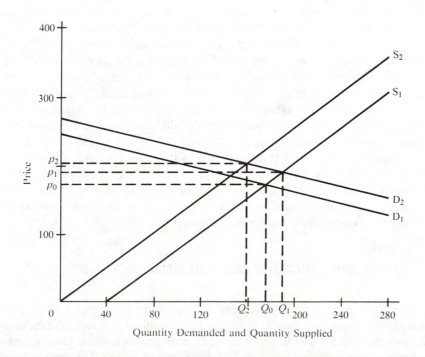

Quantity Demanded and Quantity Supplied

curve shifts and the supply curve remains stationary, the new equilibrium price and quantity will lie on the original supply curve. Alternatively, if the supply curve shifts from S_1 to S_2, while the demand curve remains stationary at D_2, the new equilibrium price and quantity will lie on the stationary demand curve.

We could continue to pick arbitrary values for the exogenous variables and solve for the associated equilibrium price and quantity, but there is a more efficient approach. Given the original demand and supply equations, we can solve for the equilibrium values of p and q as functions of the exogenous variables y and w:

$$Q_d = 50 + 0.1y - 2p$$
$$Q_s = 60 - 4w + 0.8p$$

$Q = Q_d = Q_s$ implies $50 + 0.1y - 2p = 60 - 4w + 0.8p$, or:

$$2.8p = -10 + 0.1y + 4w$$
$$p = -3.571 + 0.036y + 1.429w$$

Substituting the formula for p into either equation, we obtain equilibrium quantity as a function of y and w:

$$Q = Q_d = 50 + 0.1y - 2(-3.571 + 0.036y + 1.429w)$$
$$= 57.142 + 0.028y - 2.858w$$

Economic analysis would predict that the equilibrium price increases when demand increases or when supply decreases. Since an increase in y shifts the demand curve to the right, the price increases as income increases, *ceteris paribus*. Since an increase in w shifts the supply curve to the left, an increase in w causes the equilibrium value of p to increase. Since an increase in demand causes quantity exchanged to increase, equilibrium Q increases as y increases. On the other hand, a decrease in supply causes quantity exchanged to decrease, and equilibrium Q falls as w increases. Equilibrium price changes in the same direction as y and w, while the equilibrium quantity changes in the same direction as y and in the opposite direction as w, *ceteris paribus*. Incidentally, the two equations that express the equilibrium values of p and q as functions of the exogenous variables y and w are called *reduced form equations*. These are very important in the estimation of simultaneous equations models in econometrics.

NATIONAL INCOME EQUILIBRIUM

So far our examples have been restricted to microeconomics. Let us now discuss a macroeconomic example. It is a familiar proposition that total consumption of goods and services for an economy as a whole is an increasing function of national income. The definition of national income as total consumption plus total investment plus government purchases is also familiar. We shall combine these two propositions by specifying values for the exogenous variables, investment and government spending, in order to derive the equilibrium national income for the economy.

We have a system of four equations and four unknowns, which reduces to a system of two equations and two unknowns when the values of the exogenous variables are substituted:

$$C = 50 + 0.6Y$$
$$I = 150$$
$$G = 200$$
$$Y = C + I + G$$

where C denotes consumption as a linear function of income, I denotes investment, and G denotes government purchases. Each is plausibly measured in billions of constant dollars. Substituting the values of the exogenous variables and the consumption function into the last equation, we solve for the equilibrium national income:

$$Y = 50 + 0.6Y + 150 + 200$$
$$(1 - 0.6)Y = 400$$
$$Y = \frac{400}{0.4} = 1,000$$

With the equilibrium value of Y determined, the equilibrium value of C can be inferred by substituting 1,000 for Y in the consumption function:

$$C = 50 + 0.6(1,000) = 650$$

Of course, the values of I and G are already known to be 150 and 200, respectively. Adding $C + I + G = 650 + 150 + 200 = 1,000$, gives the equilibrium value of Y. It always pays to check.

The graphical presentation of this example is shown in Figure 4.7. The equilibrium value of income is determined at the point where the curve labeled $C + I + G$ crosses the 45-degree line. A 45-degree line has the property that at every point on it, the value of the variable measured on the vertical axis is exactly equal to the value of the variable measured on the horizontal axis, as long as both axes are scaled in the same units. In the simple Keynesian model of national income determination, the 45-degree line is a very useful device. It does not describe the behavior of consumers, firms, or the government, but it is convenient for depicting the solution to the Keynesian model.

A careful examination of the line reveals that when the value on the horizontal axis is 1,000, the value on the vertical axis corresponding to the same point on the line is also 1,000. Notice that the $C + I + G$ line cuts the 45-degree line when $C + I + G$, measured on the vertical axis, is 1,000. It follows that Y, measured on the horizontal axis, is also 1,000. At that point,

Figure 4.7

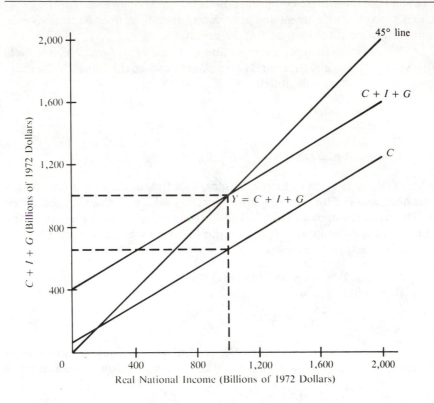

and only at that point where the $C + I + G$ line intersects the 45-degree line is the equilibrium condition, $Y = C + I + G$, satisfied. At lower levels of income, intended spending exceeds national income ($C + I + G > Y$). At higher levels of income, intended spending falls short of national income ($C + I + G < Y$).

The method used to arrive at equilibrium national income is essentially the same as that used to arrive at the equilibrium price and quantity in microeconomic theory. Once the equilibrium is defined by an equation, the problem reduces to one of solving all the equations in the system simultaneously. The solution of the system of equations yields the equilibrium values of the variables that the theory is intended to predict. Corresponding to the analytical solution is the geometric solution, visualized by the intersection of the curves plotted from the equations after the values of the exogenous variables have been specified. The point of intersection of the curves corresponds to the equilibrium values of the endogenous variables.

SUMMARY

If you have had previous courses in algebra and economic theory, you are probably familiar with most of the concepts presented in this chapter. If this ground is unfamiliar, be sure to review it until you have mastered the material in these early chapters. You will need the help of some reliable friends as we begin our trek through the jungles of matrix algebra and calculus.

We have seen that simple systems of two equations and two unknowns are solved by using linear transformations (multiplication and addition) on one or more equations to eliminate all but one of the unknowns, then substituting into one of the equations to find the other unknown. The process for solving a system with more than two equations and two unknowns is similar to the process used for the simple system, although sometimes that process can be quite involved. We also developed the quadratic formula for solving an equation of the form $ax^2 + bx + c = 0$. The formula is given by:

$$q = \frac{-b \pm \sqrt{b^2 - 4ac}}{2a}$$

We saw graphically that a system of linear equations has a solution if the two lines describing the system have different slopes, although this solution will not be relevant to economic theory if the intersection of those lines occurs outside the domain or range of the function. If two equations describe the same line (there is one degree of freedom in the system), there are an infinite number of possible solutions. When the two lines are parallel, there is no solution to the system. A system of quadratic equations will have two solutions if the parabola intersects the other function at two points, one solution if there is one common (tangency) point, and no solution if the two curves do not intersect. We also saw that changes in exogenous variables would generally change the equilibrium values of the endogenous variables, and that it is generally possible to obtain reduced form equations. These are equations that specify the equilibrium values of the endogenous variables as functions of the exogenous variables.

PROBLEMS

1. Solve each of the following systems of equations and check your answers. Give a graphic interpretation of each solution.
   a. $2x + y = 100$
      $-4x + 2y = 40$
   b. $x - y = 20$
      $\frac{1}{3}x - y = 0$

   c. $x^2 - y = 20$
      $x^2 + y = 10$
   d. $2x - y^2 = 4$
      $-x + y^2 = 16$

2. Solve each of the following systems of equations and check your answers. Give a graphic interpretation of each solution.
   a. $10x + 10y = 30$
      $4x + 8y = 12$
   b. $x - y = 16$
      $x - y = 20$
   c. $x^2 - y = 0$
      $x^2 + y = 10$
   d. $x^2 - 2y = 3$
      $x - y = 2$

3. Solve each of the following systems of equations and check your answers. Give a graphic interpretation of each solution.
   a. $y = x^2 - 10x + 16$
      $y = 0$
   b. $y = x^2 - 10x + 16$
      $y = x$

4. Solve the following:

$$x + y + z = 1$$
$$-x - \tfrac{1}{2}y - \tfrac{2}{3}z = 4$$
$$2x + 2y - z = 5$$

5. Assume United States aggregate consumption and investment are both
   increasing functions of national income given by:

$$C = 60 + 0.6Y$$
$$I = 24 + 0.2Y$$

   while government purchases are constant at $100 billion (i.e., $G = 100$).
   a. Find equilibrium national income ($Y = C + I + G$).
   b. Show the equilibrium graphically.

6. Let q denote the quantity of a commodity demanded or supplied and
   p its price. Find the equilibrium price and quantity traded for each of
   the following demand and supply functions. Give a graphic interpretation of each solution.
   a. $q = 150 - 30p$ (demand equation)
      $q = -10 + 20p$ (supply equation)
   b. $q = 80 - 10p$ (demand equation)
      $q = 10p$ (supply equation)
   c. $400 - 2q - 10p = 0$ (demand equation)
      $150 - 3q + 30p = 0$ (supply equation)

7. With q denoting quantity and p denoting price, find the equilibrium for each of the following demand and supply functions.

    a. $q = 180 - 2p^2$ (demand equation)

       $q = -12 + p^2$ (supply equation)

    b. $q = 20 - p$ (demand equation)

       $q = 0.10p^2$ (supply equation)

8. Let D_x and S_x represent the quantities demanded and supplied, respectively, of the commodity X. Let D_y and S_y denote the quantities demanded and supplied of the commodity Y. Let p_x and p_y denote the prices of X and Y, respectively. The demand and supply functions for the two commodities are interrelated:

$$D_x = 100 - 10p_x - 20p_y$$
$$S_x = -30 + 10p_x + 10p_y$$
$$D_y = 60 - 10p_x - 10p_y$$
$$S_y = -20 + 10p_y$$

    a. Find the equilibrium prices of X and Y.

    b. Find the equilibrium quantity exchanged.

9. Let D_w and S_w represent the quantities of wheat demanded and supplied, respectively. Let D_c and S_c represent the quantities of corn demanded and supplied. Let p_w and p_c be the prices of wheat and corn, respectively. Solve for the equilibrium price and quantity for each commodity in the following system:

$$D_w = 325 - 100p_w + 80p_c$$
$$S_w = -35 + 60p_w - 40p_c$$
$$D_c = 185 + 90p_w - 125p_c$$
$$S_c = -30 - 20p_w + 50p_c$$

10. A monopolist's total cost curve is given by $TC = 100 + 5q + q^2$, and the total revenue curve is given by $TR = 50q - 0.2q^2$. Find the break-even rate(s) of output (i.e., where $TR = TC$).

5

Fundamentals of

Matrix Algebra

Imagine the simplest type of equation system—a system with one equation and one unknown, of the form:

$$4x = 24$$

The solution to that system is trivial. Multiply both sides of the equation by 0.25, the multiplicative inverse of 4, and the value of x become obvious:

$$0.25(4x) = 0.25(24)$$
$$x = 6$$

This chapter will introduce matrix algebra techniques that emulate the solution to one-variable, one-equation systems for systems with many equations and many unknowns. Furthermore, the matrix techniques outlined here will be used in the latter half of this book when we analyze econometric operations.

SOME DEFINITIONS AND NOTATION

A *matrix* is defined as a rectangular array of numbers. Each element of a matrix is identified by its position within the matrix.

Suppose we define matrix **A** as follows:

$$A = \begin{bmatrix} 4 & 8.6 \\ 9 & 0.5 \\ 6 & 19 \end{bmatrix}$$

The number "9" is an element of matrix **A**, and it appears in the second row and the first column. Using a_{ij} to denote the element of matrix **A** that appears in the ith row and the jth column, it follows that $a_{21} = 9$, $a_{12} = 8.6$, $a_{32} = 19$, and so on. When a matrix has the same number of rows and columns, it is called a *square matrix*. Matrix **A** is *not* a square matrix, since the number of rows exceeds the number of columns. The following matrices are square matrices; matrix **B** is a 2 × 2 (read "two-by-two") matrix and matrix **C** is a 3 × 3 ("three-by-three") matrix.

$$B = \begin{bmatrix} 2 & 4 \\ 6 & 5 \end{bmatrix} \qquad\qquad C = \begin{bmatrix} 17 & 8 & 45 \\ 6 & 14 & 12 \\ -9 & 0 & 12 \end{bmatrix}$$

A special kind of matrix, which contains only one row or only one column is called a *vector*. The terminology is simple: a matrix with a single column is called a *column vector*; a matrix with only one row is called a *row vector*. Below, vector v_1 is a column vector and vector v_2 is a row vector.

$$v_1 = \begin{bmatrix} 8 \\ 5 \\ 3 \end{bmatrix} \qquad\qquad v_2 = \begin{bmatrix} 8 & 5 & 3 \end{bmatrix}$$

To review, a matrix is a rectangular array of numbers, and the position of each element is designated by its row and column. In general form, a matrix with m rows and n columns is represented as:

$$A = \begin{bmatrix} a_{11} & a_{12} & . & . & . & a_{1n} \\ a_{21} & a_{22} & . & . & . & a_{2n} \\ . & . & . & . & . & . \\ . & . & . & . & . & . \\ a_{m1} & a_{m2} & . & . & . & a_{mn} \end{bmatrix}$$

If $m = n$ (the number of rows equals the number of columns), matrix **A** is a *square matrix*. If $m = 1$, **A** is a *row vector*; if $n = 1$, **A** is a *column vector*.

MATRIX ADDITION AND

MULTIPLICATION

You may be thinking: "Fine, but what can you do with a matrix?" Obviously, you can array numbers in a matrix; but what good is that? We might wish to array numbers in two or more matrices so that we can compare those numbers, add them, subtract them, or multiply them by a constant. Such operations can be performed on numbers one at a time, of course, but matrix addition, subtraction, and scalar multiplication are often much more efficient.

One matrix is said to be equal to another matrix if and only if each element in the first matrix is identical to the corresponding element in the second matrix. That is, $a_{ij} = b_{ij}$, for all i's and all j's; each element in matrix **B** must be the same as the element in matrix **A** in the corresponding row and column. Obviously, two matrices can be equal only if they have the same number of rows and the same number of columns; that is, they must have the same dimensions. Consider the following matrices:

$$A = \begin{bmatrix} 1 & 2 & 3 \\ 4 & 5 & 6 \\ 7 & 8 & 9 \end{bmatrix} \qquad B = \begin{bmatrix} 1 & 2 & 3 \\ 4 & 5 & 6 \\ 7 & 8 & 9 \end{bmatrix}$$

$$C = \begin{bmatrix} 1 & 2 & 2 \\ 4 & 5 & 6 \\ 7 & 8 & 9 \end{bmatrix} \qquad D = \begin{bmatrix} 1 & 4 & 7 \\ 2 & 5 & 8 \\ 3 & 6 & 9 \end{bmatrix}$$

Matrix **A** *equals* matrix **B** (**A** = **B**) because each element of matrix **B** contains exactly the same number as the corresponding row and column of matrix **A** (and vice-versa); $a_{ij} = b_{ij}$ for $i = 1, 2, 3$ and $j = 1, 2, 3$. Matrix **A** *does not* equal matrix **C** (**A** ≠ **C**) because $a_{13} \neq c_{13}$; even though all other elements in the two matrices are identical. Inequality between just two corresponding elements in two matrices is sufficient to make those matrices unequal. By similar logic, matrix **D** does not equal matrix **A** (**D** ≠ **A**) because the rows of matrix **D** are the columns of matrix **A** (and vice-versa). In fact, as we will see later, matrix **D** is called the *transpose* of matrix **A**, and matrix **A** is the transpose of matrix **D**. A transpose of a matrix is the matrix obtained by interchanging the rows and columns of the original matrix.

Now that we are able to compare matrices, we can introduce operations that transform and combine matrices. *Scalar multiplication* is the simplest matrix operation, by which every element in a matrix is multiplied by the same constant. Scalar multiplication is depicted by placing some constant, (e.g., k) in front of the matrix being "scaled": k**A** means that every element in matrix **A** is multiplied by the constant k. To take specific examples:

$$A = \begin{bmatrix} 3 & 5 & 9 \\ 2 & 6 & 1 \\ 4 & 2 & 2 \end{bmatrix}$$

$$kA = \begin{bmatrix} k3 & k5 & k9 \\ k2 & k6 & k1 \\ k4 & k2 & k2 \end{bmatrix} \qquad 3A = \begin{bmatrix} 9 & 15 & 27 \\ 6 & 18 & 3 \\ 12 & 6 & 6 \end{bmatrix}$$

Because scalar multiplication involves a constant and one matrix, there are no restrictions on the dimensions of the matrix on which scalar multiplication is performed.

Another fairly simple operation on matrices is *matrix addition*. Two matrices can be added if and only if they have the same dimensions. They must have the same number of rows and the same number of columns (although they need not be square matrices). The element in the ith row and the jth column of matrix **A** is added to the corresponding element in matrix **B**. Hence, if we add matrix **A** and matrix **B**, both of which have m rows and n columns, the resulting matrix, matrix **C**, will also be an $m \times n$ matrix, each of whose elements is the sum of the corresponding elements in matrix **A** and matrix **B**. Here's an example to illustrate:

$$\mathbf{A} = \begin{bmatrix} 1 & 2 \\ 5 & 10 \end{bmatrix} \qquad\qquad \mathbf{B} = \begin{bmatrix} 2 & 8 \\ 9 & -2 \end{bmatrix}$$

$$\mathbf{C} = \mathbf{A} + \mathbf{B} = \begin{bmatrix} 1+2 & 2+8 \\ 5+9 & 10-2 \end{bmatrix} = \begin{bmatrix} 3 & 10 \\ 14 & 8 \end{bmatrix}$$

Matrix subtraction is simply a combination of matrix addition and scalar multiplication. To subtract matrix **B** from matrix **A**, we first multiply matrix **B** by -1, then add the resulting matrix to **A**. In our example:

$$\mathbf{D} = \mathbf{A} - \mathbf{B} = \begin{bmatrix} 1 & 2 \\ 5 & 10 \end{bmatrix} - \begin{bmatrix} 2 & 8 \\ 9 & -2 \end{bmatrix}$$

$$= \begin{bmatrix} 1-2 & 2-8 \\ 5-9 & 10+2 \end{bmatrix} = \begin{bmatrix} -1 & -6 \\ -4 & 12 \end{bmatrix}$$

Once you become adept at working with arrays of numbers instead of working with them one at a time, the similarities between these matrix operations and more conventional operations are easy to spot. Scalar multiplication is similar to conventional multiplication: the multiplicand (*scalar*) changes each element in the affected matrix by the same proportion. It follows that identity operations for matrix addition and scalar multiplication are very similar to the identity operations for conventional addition and multiplication. If we have an $m \times n$ matrix, and we add it to an $m \times n$ matrix containing only zeros, the solution matrix equals the original matrix. Suppose we take a matrix and multiply every element by -1. We get the *additive inverse* of that matrix. When we add the original matrix and its additive inverse, we get a matrix containing only zeros, the additive identity. It should be obvious that the number "1" is the *identity element* for scalar multiplication. If we multiply every element in a matrix by 1, the result is the original matrix. However, since a matrix cannot be transformed into a scalar, there is no inverse for scalar multiplication.

MATRIX MULTIPLICATION

Once mastered, matrix addition, subtraction, and scalar multiplication are uncomplicated. *Matrix multiplication*, which is necessary to transform a system of equations into matrix notation, is a more complicated matrix operation. Sometimes it is less frightening to know the outcome of an operation before a step-by-step description of a complex process. Consider an equation system as it is expressed in conventional and matrix form:

$$a_1x + a_2y = c_1 \qquad \begin{bmatrix} a_1 & a_2 \\ b_1 & b_2 \end{bmatrix} \begin{bmatrix} x \\ y \end{bmatrix} = \begin{bmatrix} c_1 \\ c_2 \end{bmatrix}$$
$$b_1x + b_2y = c_2$$

Matrix notation allows us to separate the coefficients of a system of equations into a matrix and the variables and constants into vectors. (Recall that a vector is a special matrix with only one column or only one row.) Later we will see how such notation facilitates the solution to a system of equations. Now we will unravel the role of matrix multiplication in this scheme. The elements in the first row of the coefficient matrix are multiplied times the two elements in the unknown column vector to obtain the first element, c_1, in the constant vector. Similarly, the elements in the second row of the coefficient matrix are multiplied times the respective elements in the unknown vector to obtain the second element, c_2, in the constant vector. After we separate the coefficients into a matrix and the variables and constants into vectors, matrix multiplication performs those steps necessary to reintegrate the matrix and vectors into a set of equations.

To multiply two matrices, we combine the rows of the first matrix and the columns of the second matrix. Two matrices can be multiplied together only if the number of rows of the second matrix (called the *multiplicand*) is equal to the number of columns of the first matrix (called the *multiplier*). Square matrices with an equal number of rows (and columns) can always be multiplied together, in either order. But matrices do not have to be square in order to be multiplied. In our system of equations example, we *multiplied* a coefficient matrix (2 × 2) times an unknown vector (2 × 1) to get a constant vector (2 × 1). The product matrix (constant vector) has the same number of columns as the multiplicand and the same number of rows as the multiplier.

When first encountered, the process of matrix multiplication seems quite complex. But with practice, you will find that the advantages of this powerful tool justify the effort of learning it. To multiply matrix **B** by matrix **A**, take the element in the first row and first column in the multiplier matrix (**A**) times the element in the first row and first column in the mulitplicand (**B**). Then add the product of the element in the first row second column of matrix **A** and the second row first column of matrix **B**. Continue along the first row of the multiplier matrix and the first column of the multiplicand until each product has been taken and summed. When the number of elements in the first row of matrix **A** (which equals the number of elements in the first column of matrix **B**) have been exhausted, we have the first element of the product matrix. We continue this process for each row of the multiplier matrix (**A**) and each column of the multiplicand matrix (**B**).

Let's trace through the process in general terms. Let:

$$A = \begin{bmatrix} a_{11} & a_{12} \\ a_{21} & a_{22} \end{bmatrix} \qquad B = \begin{bmatrix} b_{11} & b_{12} & b_{13} \\ b_{21} & b_{22} & b_{23} \end{bmatrix}$$

$$AB = \begin{bmatrix} a_{11}b_{11} + a_{12}b_{21} & a_{11}b_{12} + a_{12}b_{22} & a_{11}b_{13} + a_{12}b_{23} \\ a_{21}b_{11} + a_{22}b_{21} & a_{21}b_{12} + a_{22}b_{22} & a_{21}b_{13} + a_{22}b_{23} \end{bmatrix}$$

$$= \begin{bmatrix} c_{11} & c_{12} & c_{13} \\ c_{21} & c_{22} & c_{23} \end{bmatrix}$$

In general notation, **AB** = **C**. By examining the elements of matrix **C**, we may yet come to grips with the intricacies of matrix multiplication. Element c_{ij} of the product matrix is the result of summing the products of each entry in the ith row of the multiplier with the corresponding element in the jth column of the multiplicand. We can make the process more concrete by using actual numbers. Let:

$$A = \begin{bmatrix} 2 & 3 & 4 \\ 5 & 7 & 8 \end{bmatrix} \qquad B = \begin{bmatrix} 6 & 4 \\ 8 & 10 \\ 2 & 1 \end{bmatrix}$$

$$AB = \begin{bmatrix} 2(6) + 3(8) + 4(2) & 2(4) + 3(10) + 4(1) \\ 5(6) + 7(8) + 8(2) & 5(4) + 7(10) + 8(1) \end{bmatrix}$$

$$= \begin{bmatrix} 12 + 24 + 8 & 8 + 30 + 4 \\ 30 + 56 + 16 & 20 + 70 + 8 \end{bmatrix} = \begin{bmatrix} 44 & 42 \\ 102 & 98 \end{bmatrix}$$

When we multiply a 2 × 3 matrix (**A**) times a 3 × 2 matrix (**B**) the solution matrix is a 2 × 2. Had we reversed the order and multiplied a 3 × 2 matrix times a 2 × 3 matrix, the resulting matrix would have different dimensions (3 × 3). Unlike conventional multiplication, for which the order of the numbers does not affect the product, order is crucial in matrix multiplication.

Now consider the nature of the identity operation for matrix multiplication. We want to find a matrix which, when used to multiply another matrix, will return the multiplicand as the product matrix. Multiplication by the *identity matrix* must change neither the position nor the magnitude of any element of the multiplicand. Since one is the multiplicative identity and zero is the additive identity for the set of real numbers, a little reflection should reveal that the identity matrix is a square matrix with a "1" in the first row, first column, and "1's" along the diagonal emanating from that first element (called the *principal diagonal*), and zeros in all other positions.

In the trivial case of a 1×1 matrix, $[a]$, the identity matrix is $[1]$. For 2×2 matrices,

$$\begin{bmatrix} a_{11} & a_{12} \\ a_{21} & a_{22} \end{bmatrix}$$

the identity matrix is,

$$\mathbf{I} = \begin{bmatrix} 1 & 0 \\ 0 & 1 \end{bmatrix}$$

and so forth. Although all matrices have identity matrices, matrices have inverses only if that matrix is square and has independent rows (no row is a linear combination of any other row(s)).

MATRIX ALGEBRA AND SYSTEMS OF EQUATIONS

One of the major advantages of matrix algebra is streamlining the solution of systems of equations, providing procedures that lie at the heart of econometric estimation. But we have already seen that matrix algebra can become complicated. Before proceeding with more material, let's apply matrix concepts to some examples from Chapter 4. First, let's take a simple two-equation supply and demand model and restate it in matrix terms. Given that:

$$Q_d = 2,000 - 100p$$
$$Q_s = -100 + 50p$$

$Q_d = Q_s = Q$ implies:

$$Q + 100p = 2,000$$
$$Q - 50p = -100$$

Using what we have learned in this chapter, this supply and demand system can be expressed in matrix form as:

$$\begin{bmatrix} 1 & 100 \\ 1 & -50 \end{bmatrix} \begin{bmatrix} Q \\ p \end{bmatrix} = \begin{bmatrix} 2,000 \\ -100 \end{bmatrix}$$

The algebraic method of solving systems of equations (using algebraic transformations of both sides of different equations) can be performed on the coefficient matrix and the constant vector; no transformations of variables themselves occur. If we can transform the coefficient matrix into the identity matrix and use the same transformations on the constant vector, we will obtain a transparently obvious solution to our equation system.

We begin by eliminating elements not on the principal diagonal by replacing those elements with zeros. The coefficient of p is negative in the second equation and positive in the first equation, suggesting that we can eliminate this variable in one equation by multiplying the second equation by 2 and adding it to the first equation. Performing this operation on the rows of the coefficient matrix and the elements of the constant vector, we have:

$$\begin{bmatrix} 1 & 100 \\ 1 & -50 \end{bmatrix} \quad \text{becomes} \quad \begin{bmatrix} 3 & 0 \\ 1 & -50 \end{bmatrix}$$

and

$$\begin{bmatrix} 2{,}000 \\ -100 \end{bmatrix} \quad \text{becomes} \quad \begin{bmatrix} 1{,}800 \\ -100 \end{bmatrix}$$

Next, to obtain a "1" in the first column of the first row of the coefficient matrix, we divide that row, and the first element of the constant vector by 3:

$$\begin{bmatrix} 3 & 0 \\ 1 & -50 \end{bmatrix} \quad \text{becomes} \quad \begin{bmatrix} 1 & 0 \\ 1 & -50 \end{bmatrix}$$

and

$$\begin{bmatrix} 1{,}800 \\ -100 \end{bmatrix} \quad \text{becomes} \quad \begin{bmatrix} 600 \\ -100 \end{bmatrix}$$

Continuing, we can eliminate the coefficient of Q in the second equation by subtracting the first row from the second and replacing the second row:

$$\begin{bmatrix} 1 & 0 \\ 1 & -50 \end{bmatrix} \quad \text{becomes} \quad \begin{bmatrix} 1 & 0 \\ 0 & -50 \end{bmatrix}$$

and

$$\begin{bmatrix} 600 \\ -100 \end{bmatrix} \quad \text{becomes} \quad \begin{bmatrix} 600 \\ -700 \end{bmatrix}$$

Dividing the second row by -50 completes the transformation of the coefficient matrix into the 2×2 identity matrix. The parallel transformation on the constant vector produces the solution to the equation system:

$$\begin{bmatrix} 1 & 0 \\ 0 & -50 \end{bmatrix} \quad \text{becomes} \quad \begin{bmatrix} 1 & 0 \\ 0 & 1 \end{bmatrix}$$

and

$$\begin{bmatrix} 600 \\ -700 \end{bmatrix} \quad \text{becomes} \quad \begin{bmatrix} 600 \\ 14 \end{bmatrix}$$

Let's review. We started with a system of two equations and two unknowns, expressed in matrix notation. By performing a series of algebraic transformations on the rows of the coefficient matrix and on the corresponding elements in the constant vector, we obtained a simple matrix multiplication problem that yields the solution to the system of equations. Given:

$$\begin{bmatrix} 1 & 100 \\ 1 & -50 \end{bmatrix} \begin{bmatrix} Q \\ p \end{bmatrix} = \begin{bmatrix} 2,000 \\ -100 \end{bmatrix}$$

we obtained

$$\begin{bmatrix} 1 & 0 \\ 0 & 1 \end{bmatrix} \begin{bmatrix} Q \\ p \end{bmatrix} = \begin{bmatrix} 600 \\ 14 \end{bmatrix}$$

Perhaps this exercise seems a waste of effort. Matrix manipulation of an equation system with two equations and two unknowns did not save any effort over the procedures used in Chapter 4. However, there is a more efficient approach that is particularly useful when solving systems of equations with more than two variables.

The streamlined version of the process we just completed involves using the inverse of the coefficient matrix, which turns our iterative method into a matrix multiplication problem. Designate the coefficient matrix as $\mathbf{A}$, the vector of unknowns as $\mathbf{x}$ and the constant vector as $\mathbf{c}$. The standard notation for the inverse of matrix $\mathbf{A}$ is $\mathbf{A}^{-1}$. $\mathbf{A}^{-1}$ has the property that $\mathbf{AA}^{-1} = \mathbf{A}^{-1}\mathbf{A} = \mathbf{I}$, the relevant identity matrix. If we multiply both the coefficient matrix and the constant vector by $\mathbf{A}^{-1}$, we solve for the values of Q and p:

$$\mathbf{Ax} = \mathbf{c}$$

implies

$$\mathbf{A}^{-1}\mathbf{Ax} = \mathbf{A}^{-1}\mathbf{c}$$
$$\mathbf{Ix} = \mathbf{A}^{-1}\mathbf{c}$$
$$\mathbf{x} = \mathbf{A}^{-1}\mathbf{c}$$

To demonstrate, we will rework our example, using the inverse of the coefficient matrix. Since we have yet to discuss how the inverse matrix is discovered, you will have to take our word that:

$$\mathbf{A}^{-1} = \begin{bmatrix} 1/3 & 2/3 \\ 1/150 & -1/150 \end{bmatrix}$$

Multiplying the coefficient matrix by its inverse, we obtain:

$$\begin{bmatrix} 1/3 & 2/3 \\ 1/150 & -1/150 \end{bmatrix} \begin{bmatrix} 1 & 100 \\ 1 & -50 \end{bmatrix}$$

$$= \begin{bmatrix} (1/3)(1) + (2/3)(1) & (1/3)(100) + (2/3)(-50) \\ (1/150)(1) + (-1/150)(1) & (1/150)(100) + (-1/150)(-50) \end{bmatrix}$$

$$= \begin{bmatrix} 1 & 0 \\ 0 & 1 \end{bmatrix}$$

Transforming the constant vector:

$$\begin{bmatrix} 1/3 & 2/3 \\ 1/150 & -1/150 \end{bmatrix} \begin{bmatrix} 2,000 \\ -100 \end{bmatrix}$$

$$= \begin{bmatrix} (1/3)(2,000) + (2/3)(-100) \\ (1/150)(2,000) + (-1/150)(-100) \end{bmatrix} = \begin{bmatrix} 600 \\ 14 \end{bmatrix}$$

Once we have discovered the inverse of the coefficient matrix, we can easily handle parallel shifts (changes in the constants) for the set of equations. For instance, suppose that the demand curve shifted to the right by 500 units at each price, so that the equation system becomes:

$$Q_d = 2,500 - 100p$$
$$Q_s = -100 + 50p$$

or

$$Q + 100p = 2,500$$
$$Q - 50p = -100$$

or

$$\begin{bmatrix} 1 & 100 \\ 1 & -50 \end{bmatrix} \begin{bmatrix} Q \\ p \end{bmatrix} = \begin{bmatrix} 2,500 \\ -100 \end{bmatrix}$$

We could transform rows or columns to eliminate variables or to transform the coefficient matrix into the 2×2 identity matrix. However, armed with the knowledge of the identity matrix, we merely multiply the constant vector by the known inverse and obtain the new solution vector:

$$\begin{bmatrix} 1/3 & 2/3 \\ 1/150 & -1/150 \end{bmatrix} \begin{bmatrix} 2,500 \\ -100 \end{bmatrix} = \begin{bmatrix} 833.333 - 66.667 \\ 16.667 + 0.6667 \end{bmatrix}$$

$$= \begin{bmatrix} 766.67 \\ 17.33 \end{bmatrix}$$

Since we have already transformed the coefficient matrix into the identity matrix by multiplying by its inverse, there is no need to repeat this process. Even for simple systems with two equations and two unknowns, finding the inverse matrix is a definite time-saver in repetitious matrix operations:

$$\begin{bmatrix} 1 & 0 \\ 0 & 1 \end{bmatrix} \begin{bmatrix} Q \\ p \end{bmatrix} = \begin{bmatrix} 766.67 \\ 17.33 \end{bmatrix}$$

or $Q = 766.67$ and $p = 17.33$.

What works for a 2×2 matrix works for a larger system. Recall from Chapter 4 that two or more markets may be linked together through a general equilibrium system. For example, we introduced a four-equation system linking the equilibrium price and quantities of wheat and corn as follows:

$$D_w = 26 - p_w + p_c$$
$$D_c = 8 + p_w - p_c$$
$$S_w = -4 + 3p_w - p_c$$
$$S_c = -2 - p_w + p_c$$

This system can be written:

$$
\begin{aligned}
Q_w && + \; p_w - p_c &= 26 \\
Q_c && - \; p_w + p_c &= 8 \\
Q_w && - \; 3p_w + p_c &= -4 \\
Q_c && + \; p_w - p_c &= -2
\end{aligned}
$$

You may have felt that solving this system by conventional techniques is rather tedious. However, by translating the system into matrix notation and multiplying both the coefficient matrix and the constant vector by the inverse matrix, the process is much sleeker.

Rewriting this system into matrix notation:

$$
\begin{bmatrix}
1 & 0 & 1 & -1 \\
0 & 1 & -1 & 1 \\
1 & 0 & -3 & 1 \\
0 & 1 & 1 & -1
\end{bmatrix}
\begin{bmatrix}
Q_w \\ Q_c \\ p_w \\ p_c
\end{bmatrix}
=
\begin{bmatrix}
26 \\ 8 \\ -4 \\ -2
\end{bmatrix}
$$

Once again, the reader will have to accept on faith that the identity matrix is:

$$
\mathbf{A}^{-1} =
\begin{bmatrix}
1 & 0.5 & 0 & -0.5 \\
0 & 0.5 & 0 & 0.5 \\
0.25 & 0 & -0.25 & 0 \\
0.25 & 0.5 & -0.25 & -0.5
\end{bmatrix}
$$

Multiplying both the coefficient matrix and the constant vector by the inverse of the coefficient matrix, we find:

$$
\begin{bmatrix}
1 & 0.5 & 0 & -0.5 \\
0 & 0.5 & 0 & 0.5 \\
0.25 & 0 & -0.25 & 0 \\
0.25 & 0.5 & -0.25 & -0.5
\end{bmatrix}
\begin{bmatrix}
1 & 0 & 1 & -1 \\
0 & 1 & -1 & 1 \\
1 & 0 & -3 & 1 \\
0 & 1 & 1 & -1
\end{bmatrix}
\begin{bmatrix}
Q_w \\ Q_c \\ p_w \\ p_c
\end{bmatrix}
$$

$$
=
\begin{bmatrix}
1 & 0.5 & 0 & -0.5 \\
0 & 0.5 & 0 & 0.5 \\
0.25 & 0 & -0.25 & 0 \\
0.25 & 0.5 & -0.25 & -0.5
\end{bmatrix}
\begin{bmatrix}
26 \\ 8 \\ -4 \\ -2
\end{bmatrix}
$$

or

$$
\begin{bmatrix}
1 & 0 & 0 & 0 \\
0 & 1 & 0 & 0 \\
0 & 0 & 1 & 0 \\
0 & 0 & 0 & 1
\end{bmatrix}
\begin{bmatrix}
Q_w \\ Q_c \\ p_w \\ p_c
\end{bmatrix}
=
\begin{bmatrix}
26 + 4 - 0 + 1 \\
0 + 4 - 0 - 1 \\
6.5 + 0 + 1 + 0 \\
6.5 + 4 + 1 + 1
\end{bmatrix}
=
\begin{bmatrix}
31 \\ 3 \\ 7.5 \\ 12.5
\end{bmatrix}
$$

that is,

$$
\begin{aligned}
Q_w &= 31 \\
Q_c &= 3 \\
p_w &= 7.5 \\
p_c &= 12.5
\end{aligned}
$$

Both microcomputers and mainframe computers use matrix techniques when performing many calculations. This means that we can rely on computers to grind through both matrix inversion and matrix multiplication procedures. However, computers cannot find solutions that do not exist. When the *determinant* of the coefficient matrix is zero, there is no unique solution to a system of equations. Our next task, therefore, is to investigate determinants.

DETERMINANTS AND INVERSES

In the last section we solved systems of equations by combining matrix notation with linear transformations of the coefficient matrix and the constant vector to derive the unique values of unknowns. We then showed how this process can be streamlined by multiplying both the coefficient matrix and the constant vector by the inverse of the coefficient matrix. In this section we develop the notion of the *determinant* of the coefficient matrix. The determinant will tell us whether the coefficient matrix actually *has* an inverse. In the next section, we will use the determinant along with transformations of the coefficient matrix to calculate the inverse of the coefficient matrix. At the end of the chapter we will see that determinants alone can be used to solve systems of linear equations.

Determinants of Simple Matrices

The *determinant* of a matrix is a single number that serves as the "value" for the matrix. The process of calculating a determinant depends on the size of the matrix. The simplest case is the 1×1 matrix: the determinant of a 1×1 matrix equals the value of the single element of that matrix. The notation for a determinant is the symbol (or elements) of the matrix enclosed by parallel vertical lines. Given $\mathbf{A} = [a_{11}]$, the determinant of $\mathbf{A}$ (or det $\mathbf{A}$) $= |\mathbf{A}| = a_{11}$. Other examples of 1×1 matrices are:

$\mathbf{B} = [-8]$, det $\mathbf{B} = |\mathbf{B}| = -8$
$\mathbf{I} = [1]$, $|\mathbf{I}| = 1$

For a 2×2 matrix, the determinant is the product of the elements of the left-to-right diagonal (called the *major* diagonal), minus the product of the right-to-left diagonal (called the *minor* diagonal):

$$\mathbf{A} = \begin{bmatrix} a_{11} & a_{12} \\ a_{21} & a_{22} \end{bmatrix}$$

$$|\mathbf{A}| = a_{11}a_{22} - a_{21}a_{12}$$
$$\quad\;\; \text{(major)} \quad\; \text{(minor)}$$

Given the 2 × 2 matrices, **B**, **C**, and **I**, we calculate their determinants as follows:

$$\mathbf{B} = \begin{bmatrix} 3 & -4 \\ 1 & 2 \end{bmatrix} \qquad \mathbf{C} = \begin{bmatrix} 3 & 4 \\ 6 & 8 \end{bmatrix} \qquad \mathbf{I} = \begin{bmatrix} 1 & 0 \\ 0 & 1 \end{bmatrix}$$

$|\mathbf{B}| = (3 \times 2) - (1 \times -4) = 6 + 4 = 10$
$|\mathbf{C}| = (3 \times 8) - (6 \times 4) = 24 - 24 = 0$
$|\mathbf{I}| = (1 \times 1) - (0 \times 0) = 1 - 0 = 1$

Matrix **C**, whose determinant is zero, is called a singular matrix. Note that the determinant of **I**, the 2 × 2 identity matrix, is one.

For a 3 × 3 matrix, the determinant is the sum of the products of the three left-to-right diagonals (imagining the rows "wrap around") minus the sum of the products of the three right-to-left diagonals. Given the general 3 × 3 matrix **A**:

$$\mathbf{A} = \begin{bmatrix} a_{11} & a_{12} & a_{13} \\ a_{21} & a_{22} & a_{23} \\ a_{31} & a_{32} & a_{33} \end{bmatrix}$$

$$|\mathbf{A}| = a_{11}a_{22}a_{33} + a_{12}a_{23}a_{31} + a_{13}a_{21}a_{32} - (a_{31}a_{22}a_{13} + a_{32}a_{23}a_{11} + a_{33}a_{21}a_{12})$$

Let's try some additional examples:

$$\mathbf{I} = \begin{bmatrix} 1 & 0 & 0 \\ 0 & 1 & 0 \\ 0 & 0 & 1 \end{bmatrix}$$

$|\mathbf{I}| = (1 \times 1 \times 1) + (0 \times 0 \times 0) + (0 \times 0 \times 0)$
$\qquad - [(0 \times 1 \times 0) + (0 \times 0 \times 1) + (1 \times 0 \times 0)]$
$\quad = (1 + 0 + 0) - (0 + 0 + 0) = 1 - 0 = 1$

$$\mathbf{B} = \begin{bmatrix} 6 & 9 & 1 \\ 4 & -2 & 6 \\ 3 & 1 & 5 \end{bmatrix}$$

$|\mathbf{B}| = (6 \times -2 \times 5) + (4 \times 1 \times 1) + (3 \times 9 \times 6)$
$\qquad - [(3 \times -2 \times 1) + (4 \times 9 \times 5) + (6 \times 1 \times 6)]$
$\quad = (-60 + 4 + 162) - (-6 + 180 + 36)$
$\quad = 106 - 210 = -104$

$$\mathbf{C} = \begin{bmatrix} 4 & 9 & 2 \\ 6 & 1 & 5 \\ 2 & 17 & -1 \end{bmatrix}$$

$|\mathbf{C}| = (4 \times 1 \times -1) + (6 \times 17 \times 2) + (2 \times 9 \times 5)$
$\qquad - [(2 \times 1 \times 2) + (17 \times 5 \times 4) + (-1 \times 6 \times 9)]$
$\quad = (-4 + 204 + 90) - (4 + 340 - 54) = 290 - 290 = 0$

We find that the determinant of the identity matrix is 1, while matrix **C** is a singular matrix, since its determinant is zero.

Most economists and mathematicians today use electronic computers to calculate the determinants of matrices with dimensions greater than 3×3. However, it is prudent to know what the computer is doing when you ask for a calculation. A computer is merely a machine for doing routine calculations very quickly. The calculations are routine only if we have made a few passing attempts at them ourselves.

Higher-Order Determinants

We can find the value of any determinant by a process known as *expansion* along any row or column of the matrix. The *minor* of any element of a matrix is the determinant of the submatrix obtained by striking out the row and the column containing that element. In the general three-dimensional matrix, we get the minor of a_{11} by deleting the first row and the first column:

$$\begin{bmatrix} a_{11} & a_{12} & a_{13} \\ a_{21} & a_{22} & a_{23} \\ a_{31} & a_{32} & a_{33} \end{bmatrix}$$

yields

$$\begin{vmatrix} a_{22} & a_{23} \\ a_{32} & a_{33} \end{vmatrix}$$

as the minor of element a_{11}. The minor of elements a_{12} and a_{13} are found by striking out their respective rows and columns, yielding the respective minors:

$$\begin{vmatrix} a_{21} & a_{23} \\ a_{31} & a_{33} \end{vmatrix} \quad \text{and} \quad \begin{vmatrix} a_{21} & a_{22} \\ a_{31} & a_{33} \end{vmatrix}$$

We now have the minors of each of the elements of the first row. The determinant of the general 3×3 matrix can be calculated as:

$$\begin{vmatrix} a_{11} & a_{12} & a_{13} \\ a_{21} & a_{22} & a_{23} \\ a_{31} & a_{32} & a_{33} \end{vmatrix} = a_{11}\begin{vmatrix} a_{22} & a_{32} \\ a_{32} & a_{33} \end{vmatrix} - a_{12}\begin{vmatrix} a_{21} & a_{23} \\ a_{31} & a_{33} \end{vmatrix} + a_{13}\begin{vmatrix} a_{21} & a_{31} \\ a_{31} & a_{32} \end{vmatrix}$$

That is, each element in the first row is multiplied by its minor. Note carefully the alternating signs in the development of minors.

Substituting the determinants for each minor, the determinant of the general 3×3 matrix is:

$$|\mathbf{A}| = a_{11}(a_{22}a_{33} - a_{32}a_{23}) - a_{12}(a_{21}a_{33} - a_{31}a_{23}) + a_{13}(a_{21}a_{32} - a_{31}a_{22})$$

Rearranging the elements, we find the formula for the determinant of a 3×3 matrix developed in the previous section:

$$|\mathbf{A}| = a_{11}a_{22}a_{33} + a_{12}a_{23}a_{31} + a_{13}a_{21}a_{32}$$
$$- a_{31}a_{22}a_{13} - a_{32}a_{23}a_{11} - a_{33}a_{21}a_{12}$$

Remembering whether to add or subtract a minor from an element can be tricky without a general rule. We provide such a rule by defining the *cofactor* of element a_{ij} as $(-1)^{i+j}|\mathbf{M_{ij}}|$. That is, the cofactor of an element is the minor of that element times (-1) raised to the power given by the sum of the row and column of that element. When $i + j$ is even, the cofactor is equal to the minor; when $i + j$ is odd, the cofactor is equal to the minor multiplied by -1.

Any row or column can be selected as the basis of the expansion approach to determinant calculation, since all elements in the matrix will be used in the calculations in each row or column. The practical benefit of this general rule is that we can select the row or column that implies the least amount of number crunching as our basis of expansion. For instance, using rows or columns with one or more zeros allows us to avoid calculating the cofactor for those elements, since multiplying a cofactor by zero will result in zero, regardless of the value of the cofactor. Here are several other properties of matrices that simplify the calculation of determinants:

1. Adding or subtracting any nonzero multiple of one row (or column) will have no effect on the determinant.
2. Interchanging any two rows or columns of a matrix will change the sign, but not the absolute value of the determinant.
3. Multiplying the elements of any row or column by a constant will cause the determinant to be multiplied by the constant.
4. The determinant of a *triangular matrix*, i.e., a matrix with zero elements everywhere above or below the principal diagonal, is equal to the product of the elements of the principal diagonal.
5. The determinant of a matrix equals the determinant of its *transpose*: $|\mathbf{A}| = |\mathbf{A}'|$. (Remember, the transpose is the matrix whose rows are the corresponding columns of the original matrix.)
6. If all the elements in any row or any column are zero, the determinant of the matrix is zero.
7. If two rows or two columns are identical or proportional, the matrix is singular and its determinant is zero.

Let's use some of these rules to simplify the calculation of determinants for some matrices of otherwise intimidating size:

$$|\mathbf{B}| = \begin{vmatrix} 1 & 0 & 1 & -1 \\ 0 & 1 & -1 & 1 \\ 1 & 0 & -3 & -1 \\ 0 & 1 & 1 & -1 \end{vmatrix} = \begin{vmatrix} 1 & -1 & 1 \\ 0 & -3 & -1 \\ 1 & 1 & -1 \end{vmatrix} + \begin{vmatrix} 0 & 1 & -1 \\ 1 & -1 & 1 \\ 1 & 1 & -1 \end{vmatrix}$$

$$= (3 + 1 + 0) - (-3 + 0 - 1) + [(0 + 1 - 1) - (1 + 0 - 1)]$$
$$= (4 + 4) + (0 - 0) = 8$$

Beginning with a 4 × 4 matrix, we note that all but two of the elements in the first column are zero. Expanding on the first column means that the determinant of **B** is simply the sum of the nonzero cofactors in that column. (Note that **B** is the coefficient matrix for our four-equation model discussed in the previous section. It is comforting to verify the nonzero determinant for that matrix.)

Consider a 5 × 5 matrix that looks frightful:

$$\mathbf{C} = \begin{bmatrix} 0 & 99 & 4.75 & 96 & -432 \\ 0 & 86 & 3.95 & 14 & 1{,}671 \\ 0 & 75 & 1.06 & -4 & 7.93 \\ 0 & -6 & 1{,}914 & 60 & 0.541 \\ 0 & 18 & 7{,}598 & 13 & 62.7 \end{bmatrix}$$

The first column of matrix **C** contains only zeros; therefore $|\mathbf{C}| = 0$. The 6 × 6 matrix that follows is a triangular matrix; its determinant is the product of the elements of the principal diagonal.

$$\mathbf{D} = \begin{bmatrix} 28 & 34 & 19 & 76 & 42 & 1 \\ 0 & 16 & 91 & 14 & 9 & 64 \\ 0 & 0 & 6 & 9 & 42 & 38 \\ 0 & 0 & 0 & 18 & 14 & 91 \\ 0 & 0 & 0 & 0 & 4 & 47 \\ 0 & 0 & 0 & 0 & 0 & 1 \end{bmatrix}$$

$$|\mathbf{D}| = 28 \times 16 \times 6 \times 18 \times 4 \times 1 = 193{,}536$$

Inverse Matrices

This discussion of determinants is predicated on the calculation of inverse matrices, which streamlines the solution of systems of equations. To review, an inverse matrix, $\mathbf{A}^{-1}$, must be a square matrix satisfying the relationship,

$$\mathbf{A}\mathbf{A}^{-1} = \mathbf{I} = \mathbf{A}^{-1}\mathbf{A}$$

Multiplying a square matrix by its inverse transforms that matrix into the identity matrix. This is precisely the operation we had in mind when translating a system of equations into matrix notation. The inverse matrix performs the same function as the multiplicative inverse in conventional algebra. The formula for deriving an inverse is:

$$\mathbf{A}^{-1} = \frac{1}{|\mathbf{A}|}(\text{Adj } \mathbf{A})$$

where (Adj **A**) stands for the *adjoint matrix* of **A**. The adjoint matrix is given by the transpose of the cofactor matrix. The *cofactor matrix* is the matrix whose elements are the corresponding cofactors of the original matrix.

Since each cofactor is a determinant of a minor matrix multiplied by $(-1)^{i+j}$, the elements of the cofactor matrix are simply numbers. The transpose of any matrix is obtained by making the first row of the original matrix into the first column of the transpose, the second row of the original matrix into the second column of the transpose, and so on.

Consider the general 3×3 matrix,

$$\mathbf{A} = \begin{bmatrix} a_{11} & a_{12} & a_{13} \\ a_{21} & a_{22} & a_{23} \\ a_{31} & a_{32} & a_{33} \end{bmatrix}$$

The cofactor matrix is:

$$\text{Cof }(\mathbf{A}) = \begin{bmatrix} +\begin{vmatrix} a_{22} & a_{23} \\ a_{32} & a_{33} \end{vmatrix} & -\begin{vmatrix} a_{21} & a_{23} \\ a_{31} & a_{33} \end{vmatrix} & +\begin{vmatrix} a_{21} & a_{22} \\ a_{31} & a_{32} \end{vmatrix} \\ -\begin{vmatrix} a_{12} & a_{13} \\ a_{32} & a_{33} \end{vmatrix} & +\begin{vmatrix} a_{11} & a_{13} \\ a_{31} & a_{33} \end{vmatrix} & -\begin{vmatrix} a_{11} & a_{12} \\ a_{31} & a_{32} \end{vmatrix} \\ +\begin{vmatrix} a_{12} & a_{13} \\ a_{22} & a_{23} \end{vmatrix} & -\begin{vmatrix} a_{11} & a_{13} \\ a_{21} & a_{23} \end{vmatrix} & +\begin{vmatrix} a_{11} & a_{12} \\ a_{21} & a_{22} \end{vmatrix} \end{bmatrix}$$

And the transpose of the cofactor matrix is the adjoint matrix of $\mathbf{A}$:

$$\text{Adj }(\mathbf{A}) = \begin{bmatrix} +\begin{vmatrix} a_{22} & a_{23} \\ a_{32} & a_{33} \end{vmatrix} & -\begin{vmatrix} a_{12} & a_{13} \\ a_{32} & a_{33} \end{vmatrix} & +\begin{vmatrix} a_{12} & a_{13} \\ a_{22} & a_{23} \end{vmatrix} \\ -\begin{vmatrix} a_{21} & a_{23} \\ a_{31} & a_{33} \end{vmatrix} & +\begin{vmatrix} a_{11} & a_{13} \\ a_{31} & a_{33} \end{vmatrix} & -\begin{vmatrix} a_{11} & a_{13} \\ a_{21} & a_{23} \end{vmatrix} \\ +\begin{vmatrix} a_{21} & a_{22} \\ a_{31} & a_{32} \end{vmatrix} & -\begin{vmatrix} a_{11} & a_{12} \\ a_{31} & a_{32} \end{vmatrix} & +\begin{vmatrix} a_{11} & a_{12} \\ a_{21} & a_{22} \end{vmatrix} \end{bmatrix}$$

Comparing, we see that the rows of Cof $(\mathbf{A})$ are the columns of Adj $(\mathbf{A})$, and vice versa. Finally, using scalar multiplication, we multiply the adjoint matrix of $\mathbf{A}$ by the reciprocal of the determinant of $\mathbf{A}$ to get the inverse of matrix $\mathbf{A}$.

$$\mathbf{A}^{-1} = \frac{1}{|\mathbf{A}|} \begin{bmatrix} +\begin{vmatrix} a_{22} & a_{23} \\ a_{32} & a_{33} \end{vmatrix} & -\begin{vmatrix} a_{12} & a_{13} \\ a_{32} & a_{33} \end{vmatrix} & +\begin{vmatrix} a_{12} & a_{13} \\ a_{22} & a_{23} \end{vmatrix} \\ -\begin{vmatrix} a_{21} & a_{23} \\ a_{31} & a_{33} \end{vmatrix} & +\begin{vmatrix} a_{11} & a_{13} \\ a_{31} & a_{33} \end{vmatrix} & -\begin{vmatrix} a_{11} & a_{13} \\ a_{21} & a_{23} \end{vmatrix} \\ +\begin{vmatrix} a_{21} & a_{22} \\ a_{31} & a_{32} \end{vmatrix} & -\begin{vmatrix} a_{11} & a_{12} \\ a_{31} & a_{32} \end{vmatrix} & +\begin{vmatrix} a_{11} & a_{12} \\ a_{21} & a_{22} \end{vmatrix} \end{bmatrix}$$

If the determinant of a matrix is zero, the inverse of that matrix does not exist, since scalar multiplication by $1/0$ is undefined.

Let's pause to check our heading. We started by translating a system of equations into a matrix multiplication problem as a way of separating the coefficients and the constants of the equations from the unknowns (which are never transformed in the solution process). We discovered that the system of equations could indeed be solved by means of simultaneous linear transformations of the coefficient matrix and constant vector. We then argued that finding the inverse of the coefficient matrix would reach the same outcome in one operation: the coefficient matrix would be transformed into the identity matrix, and the constant vector would be transformed into the solution vector. We then defined the determinant of the coefficient matrix as a way of discerning whether or not an inverse exists. Finally, we found that the inverse is calculated as the adjoint matrix (the transpose of the cofactor matrix) multiplied by the reciprocal of the determinant of the coefficient matrix.

Let's return to our two-equation supply and demand model:

$$Q_d = 2,000 - 100p \qquad \begin{bmatrix} 1 & 100 \\ 1 & -50 \end{bmatrix} \begin{bmatrix} Q \\ p \end{bmatrix} = \begin{bmatrix} 2,000 \\ -100 \end{bmatrix}$$
$$Q_s = -100 + 50p$$

First, we calculate the determinant of the coefficient matrix:

$$\begin{vmatrix} 1 & 100 \\ 1 & -50 \end{vmatrix} = -50 - 100 = -150$$

Since $|\mathbf{A}|$ does not equal zero, matrix $\mathbf{A}$ has an inverse. Next we generate the cofactor matrix and transpose it:

$$\text{Cof } (\mathbf{A}) = \begin{bmatrix} -50 & -1 \\ -100 & 1 \end{bmatrix} \qquad \text{Adj } (\mathbf{A}) = \begin{bmatrix} -50 & -100 \\ -1 & 1 \end{bmatrix}$$

$$\mathbf{A}^{-1} = \begin{bmatrix} 1/3 & 2/3 \\ 1/150 & -1/150 \end{bmatrix}$$

As we demonstrated earlier, solving the system of equations becomes a straightforward application of matrix multiplication.

$$\begin{bmatrix} 1/3 & 2/3 \\ 1/150 & -1/150 \end{bmatrix} \begin{bmatrix} 1 & 100 \\ 1 & -50 \end{bmatrix} \begin{bmatrix} Q \\ p \end{bmatrix} = \begin{bmatrix} 1/3 & 2/3 \\ 1/150 & -1/150 \end{bmatrix} \begin{bmatrix} 2,000 \\ -100 \end{bmatrix}$$

$$\begin{bmatrix} 1 & 0 \\ 0 & 1 \end{bmatrix} \begin{bmatrix} Q \\ p \end{bmatrix} = \begin{bmatrix} 1,800/3 \\ 42/3 \end{bmatrix} = \begin{bmatrix} 600 \\ 14 \end{bmatrix}$$

Now let's try an example from macroeconomic theory. Imagine a simple economy wherein consumption and investment are the only sources of income, and each are given as linear functions of income:

$$Y = C + I$$
$$C = 50 + 0.8Y$$
$$I = 10 + 0.1Y$$

This system has three equations and three unknowns, and hence will have a unique solution if the coefficient matrix has a nonzero determinant. First, we write the equation system as:

$$C + I - \quad Y = 0$$
$$C \qquad - 0.8Y = 50$$
$$I - 0.1Y = 10$$

The system can be written in matrix notation as:

$$\begin{bmatrix} 1 & 1 & -1 \\ 1 & 0 & -0.8 \\ 0 & 1 & -0.1 \end{bmatrix} \begin{bmatrix} C \\ I \\ Y \end{bmatrix} = \begin{bmatrix} 0 \\ 50 \\ 10 \end{bmatrix}$$

Next, we calculate the determinant of the coefficient matrix:

$$\begin{vmatrix} 1 & 1 & -1 \\ 1 & 0 & -0.8 \\ 0 & 1 & -0.1 \end{vmatrix} = [(1 \times 0 \times -0.1) + (1 \times 1 \times -1) + (0 \times -0.8 \times 1)]$$
$$- [(0 \times 0 \times -1) + (1 \times -0.8 \times 1) + (-0.1 \times 1 \times 1)]$$
$$= (0 - 1 + 0) - (0 - 0.8 - 0.1) = -1 + 0.9 = -0.1$$

Since the determinant of the coefficient matrix is nonzero, we can proceed to calculate its inverse. The matrix of cofactors is:

$$\text{Cof (A)} = \begin{bmatrix} \begin{vmatrix} 0 & -0.8 \\ 1 & -0.1 \end{vmatrix} & -\begin{vmatrix} 1 & -0.8 \\ 0 & -0.1 \end{vmatrix} & \begin{vmatrix} 1 & 0 \\ 0 & 1 \end{vmatrix} \\ -\begin{vmatrix} 1 & -1 \\ 1 & -0.1 \end{vmatrix} & \begin{vmatrix} 1 & -1 \\ 0 & -0.1 \end{vmatrix} & -\begin{vmatrix} 1 & 1 \\ 0 & 1 \end{vmatrix} \\ \begin{vmatrix} 1 & -1 \\ 1 & -0.8 \end{vmatrix} & -\begin{vmatrix} 1 & -1 \\ 0 & -0.8 \end{vmatrix} & \begin{vmatrix} 1 & 1 \\ 1 & 0 \end{vmatrix} \end{bmatrix}$$

$$= \begin{bmatrix} -0.8 & -0.1 & -1 \\ 0.9 & 0.1 & 1 \\ 0.8 & 0.2 & 1 \end{bmatrix}$$

The inverse is calculated by scaling the adjoint matrix (the transpose of the cofactor matrix) by the reciprocal of the determinant:

$$A^{-1} = \frac{1}{0.1} \begin{bmatrix} -0.8 & 0.9 & 0.8 \\ -0.1 & 0.1 & 0.2 \\ -1 & 1 & 1 \end{bmatrix} = \begin{bmatrix} -8 & 9 & 8 \\ -1 & 1 & 2 \\ -10 & 10 & 10 \end{bmatrix}$$

Finally, we multiply the coefficient matrix and the constant vector by A^{-1} and arrive at the solution for this equation system:

$$\begin{bmatrix} -8 & 9 & 8 \\ -1 & 1 & 2 \\ -10 & 10 & 10 \end{bmatrix} \begin{bmatrix} 1 & 1 & -1 \\ 1 & 0 & -0.8 \\ 0 & 1 & -0.1 \end{bmatrix} \begin{bmatrix} C \\ I \\ Y \end{bmatrix} = \begin{bmatrix} -8 & 9 & 8 \\ -1 & 1 & 2 \\ -10 & 10 & 10 \end{bmatrix} \begin{bmatrix} 0 \\ 50 \\ 10 \end{bmatrix}$$

$$\begin{bmatrix} -8+9 & -8+8 & 8-7.2-0.8 \\ -1+1 & -1+2 & 1-0.8-0.2 \\ -10+10 & -10+10 & 10-8-1 \end{bmatrix} \begin{bmatrix} C \\ I \\ Y \end{bmatrix} = \begin{bmatrix} 450+80 \\ 50+20 \\ 500+100 \end{bmatrix}$$

$$\begin{bmatrix} 1 & 0 & 0 \\ 0 & 1 & 0 \\ 0 & 0 & 1 \end{bmatrix} \begin{bmatrix} C \\ I \\ Y \end{bmatrix} = \begin{bmatrix} 530 \\ 70 \\ 600 \end{bmatrix}$$

CRAMER'S RULE

In the last section we saw that given the system of equations, $\mathbf{Ax} = \mathbf{c}$, of the form:

$$\begin{bmatrix} a_{11} & a_{12} & a_{13} \\ a_{21} & a_{22} & a_{23} \\ a_{31} & a_{32} & a_{33} \end{bmatrix} \begin{bmatrix} x_1 \\ x_2 \\ x_3 \end{bmatrix} = \begin{bmatrix} c_1 \\ c_2 \\ c_3 \end{bmatrix}$$

the solution is found as: $\mathbf{A}^{-1}\mathbf{Ax} = \mathbf{A}^{-1}\mathbf{c}$, or $\mathbf{Ix} = \mathbf{A}^{-1}\mathbf{c}$. We also found that $\mathbf{A}^{-1}$, the inverse matrix of $\mathbf{A}$, is derived from the adjoint matrix (composed of elements $\mathbf{A}_{ij}$, which are cofactors of the coefficient matrix $\mathbf{A}$) and $|\mathbf{A}|$, the determinant of matrix $\mathbf{A}$. It follows that:

$$\begin{bmatrix} x_1 \\ x_2 \\ x_3 \end{bmatrix} = \frac{1}{|\mathbf{A}|} \begin{bmatrix} A_{11} & A_{21} & A_{31} \\ A_{12} & A_{22} & A_{32} \\ A_{13} & A_{23} & A_{33} \end{bmatrix} \begin{bmatrix} c_1 \\ c_2 \\ c_3 \end{bmatrix}$$

For each x_i, $i = 1, 2, 3$,

$$x_i = \frac{1}{|\mathbf{A}|}(A_{1i}c_1 + A_{2i}c_2 + A_{3i}c_3)$$

When the constant matrix is changed repeatedly, as might be the case in a simulation of a system of equations using different constant vectors to indicate different targets or contingencies, there is a definite advantage to calculating the inverse matrix. Once the inverse matrix has been calculated, the solution to the equation system implied by each new set of constants requires only matrix multiplication. However, when the equation system is relatively simple and only one set of constant terms is required, it may be simpler to solve the system by limiting calculations to determinants. This procedure is known as *Cramer's rule*.

In the above system, the parenthetical expression, $(A_{1i}c_1 + A_{2i}c_2 + A_{3i}c_3)$, is equivalent to the determinant of an *augmented matrix*. The augmented matrix is formed by substituting the constant vector for the vector of coefficients. That is, the numerator of each of the three solutions in a three-equation system is:

$$|\mathbf{B_1}| = \begin{vmatrix} c_1 & a_{12} & a_{13} \\ c_2 & a_{22} & a_{23} \\ c_3 & a_{32} & a_{33} \end{vmatrix} \qquad |\mathbf{B_2}| = \begin{vmatrix} a_{11} & c_1 & a_{13} \\ a_{21} & c_2 & a_{23} \\ a_{31} & c_3 & a_{33} \end{vmatrix}$$

$$|\mathbf{B_3}| = \begin{vmatrix} a_{11} & a_{12} & c_1 \\ a_{21} & a_{22} & c_2 \\ a_{31} & a_{32} & c_3 \end{vmatrix}$$

Furthermore, the denominator of each of the solutions is $|\mathbf{A}|$, the determinant of the coefficient matrix. Cramer's rule is as follows: the solution to a system of equations of the form $\mathbf{Ax} = \mathbf{b}$, where $\mathbf{A}$ is the coefficient matrix, $\mathbf{x}$ is the vector of unknowns and $\mathbf{b}$ is the vector of (right-side) constants, is given by:

$$x_i = \frac{|\mathbf{B_i}|}{|\mathbf{A}|}$$

where $|\mathbf{A}|$ is the determinant of the coefficient matrix, and $|\mathbf{B_i}|$ is the determinant of a matrix formed by substituting the constant vector for the column of coefficients corresponding to x_i in the coefficient matrix.

Let's see how Cramer's rule works for the two-equation supply and demand model discussed earlier:

$$\begin{bmatrix} 1 & 100 \\ 1 & -50 \end{bmatrix} \begin{bmatrix} Q \\ p \end{bmatrix} = \begin{bmatrix} 2{,}000 \\ -100 \end{bmatrix}$$

Substituting the constant vector into the appropriate columns, we get the following matrices, whose determinants are the numerators for the solutions to the respective unknowns:

$$\mathbf{B_1} = \begin{bmatrix} 2{,}000 & 100 \\ -100 & -50 \end{bmatrix} \qquad \mathbf{B_2} = \begin{bmatrix} 1 & 2{,}000 \\ 1 & -100 \end{bmatrix}$$

Now we calculate the determinant of the coefficient matrix and the determinants of $\mathbf{B_1}$ and $\mathbf{B_2}$:

$$|\mathbf{A}| = \begin{vmatrix} 1 & 100 \\ 1 & -50 \end{vmatrix} = -50 - 100 = -150$$

$$|\mathbf{B_1}| = \begin{vmatrix} 2{,}000 & 100 \\ -100 & -50 \end{vmatrix} = -100{,}000 + 10{,}000 = -90{,}000$$

$$|\mathbf{B_2}| = \begin{vmatrix} 1 & 2{,}000 \\ 1 & -100 \end{vmatrix} = -100 - 2{,}000 = -2{,}100$$

We obtain the solutions:

$$Q = \frac{|\mathbf{B_1}|}{|\mathbf{A}|} = \frac{-90{,}000}{-150} = 180$$

$$p = \frac{|\mathbf{B_2}|}{|\mathbf{A}|} = \frac{-2{,}100}{-150} = 14$$

Similarly, our three-equation macroeconomic model:

$$\begin{bmatrix} 1 & 1 & -1 \\ 1 & 0 & -0.8 \\ 0 & 1 & -0.1 \end{bmatrix} \begin{bmatrix} C \\ I \\ Y \end{bmatrix} = \begin{bmatrix} 0 \\ 50 \\ 10 \end{bmatrix}$$

can also be solved by Cramer's rule.

First, we find the determinants of the coefficient matrix and the three augmented matrices from the system:

$$|\mathbf{A}| = \begin{vmatrix} 1 & 1 & -1 \\ 1 & 0 & -0.8 \\ 0 & 1 & -1 \end{vmatrix} = -0.1 \qquad |\mathbf{B}_1| = \begin{vmatrix} 0 & 1 & -1 \\ 50 & 0 & -0.8 \\ 10 & 1 & -0.1 \end{vmatrix} = -53$$

$$|\mathbf{B}_2| = \begin{vmatrix} 1 & 0 & -1 \\ 1 & 50 & -0.8 \\ 0 & 10 & -0.1 \end{vmatrix} = -7 \qquad |\mathbf{B}_3| = \begin{vmatrix} 1 & 1 & 0 \\ 1 & 0 & 50 \\ 0 & 1 & 10 \end{vmatrix} = -60$$

Then, by dividing the determinant of each augmented matrix by the determinant of the coefficient matrix, the system is solved:

$$C = \frac{|\mathbf{B}_1|}{|\mathbf{A}|} = \frac{-53}{-0.1} = 530$$

$$I = \frac{|\mathbf{B}_2|}{|\mathbf{A}|} = \frac{-7}{-0.1} = 70$$

$$Y = \frac{|\mathbf{B}_3|}{|\mathbf{A}|} = \frac{-60}{-0.1} = 600$$

SUMMARY

We have seen how systems of equations can be streamlined in matrix form, and can be solved by linear transformation, matrix inversion, or Cramer's rule. Perhaps you feel that having more than one way to solve a problem is redundant, requiring extra effort to tote that excess intellectual baggage. However, knowing multiple ways of solving a system of equations allows us to pick the easiest approach for a given problem. In all likelihood you will continue to solve equation systems with one or two unknowns by the old linear transformation approach, perhaps not even bothering to translate the equations into matrix form. Nevertheless, you will find that systems of equations with three unknowns can often be solved most efficiently by using Cramer's rule. For systems of more than three equations (variables), calculating determinants is tedious; it may be easier to use matrix inversion techniques, particularly if you have a computer do the inversion for you.

To help with your review, here is a brief glossary of terms:

1. A *matrix* is a rectangular array of numbers.
2. A *vector* is a matrix containing only one row or one column.
3. *Scalar multiplication:* an operation in which every element of a matrix is changed by the same proportion, given by the *scalar*.
4. *Matrix addition:* an operation performed on matrices of equal dimension, whereby the elements in the same row and column in each matrix are added, yielding the element in the answer matrix.

5. *Matrix subtraction:* an operation where the second matrix is multiplied by -1, then the two matrices are added.
6. *Matrix multiplication:* an operation performed on matrices for which the number of rows in the first matrix equals the number of columns in the second matrix. Each element in the product matrix equals the sum of the products of the elements in that row of the first (multiplier) matrix and of that column in the second (multiplicand) matrix.
7. The *identity matrix* is a matrix with ones along the principal diagonal and zeros everywhere else. When multiplied by the appropriate matrix, a matrix retains the same elements in the same places.
8. The *inverse matrix* is a matrix which, when multiplied by the matrix in question, yields the identity matrix.
9. The *transpose* of a matrix is that matrix whose columns are rows of the original matrix, and whose rows are the corresponding columns of the original matrix.
10. The *determinant* of a matrix is the "value" of that matrix, obtained (for a 2×2 matrix) as the product of the major diagonal minus the product of the minor diagonal.
11. *Cramer's rule:* a method of solving systems of equations based on determinants.

PROBLEMS

Use matrices **A**, **B**, and **C** to answer the questions that follow:

$$\mathbf{A} = \begin{bmatrix} 5 & 19 & 3 \\ 4 & 9 & 3 \\ 1 & 2 & 3 \end{bmatrix} \quad \mathbf{B} = \begin{bmatrix} 5 & 4 & 1 \\ 19 & 9 & 2 \\ 3 & 3 & 3 \end{bmatrix} \quad \mathbf{C} = \begin{bmatrix} 17 & 9 & 14 \\ 8 & 2 & -7 \\ 0 & 9 & 0 \end{bmatrix}$$

1. Calculate the following:
   a. **A + B**   d. **AB**
   b. **A + B − C**   e. **BA**
   c. **3A − 7B + 0.5C**   f. **CA**

2. Explain the relationship between matrix **A** and matrix **B**.

3. Calculate the determinant and the inverse of **A**, **B**, and **C** (if possible).

4. Write the following systems of equations in matrix notation:
   a. $6x - 7y = 16$
      $x + 3y = 4$
   b. $a_{11}x_1 + a_{12}x_2 + a_{13}x_3 + \cdots + a_{1n}x_n = b_1$
      $a_{21}x_1 + a_{22}x_2 + a_{23}x_3 + \cdots + a_{2n}x_n = b_2$
      $$\vdots \qquad \vdots \qquad \vdots \qquad \cdots \qquad \vdots \qquad \vdots$$
      $a_{n1}x_1 + a_{n2}x_2 + a_{n3}x_3 + \cdots + a_{nn}x_n = b_n$

5. Express each of the following equation systems in matrix form and solve by Cramer's rule or matrix inversion (show your work):
   a. $10x + 4y = 20$
      $2x + y = 5$
   b. $2x - y = 13$
      $x + 2y = 24$
   c. $-18 + 8x + 24y = 0$
      $6 + 4x - 8y = 0$
   d. $D_x = 100 - 10p_x - 20p_y$
      $S_x = -30 + 10p_x + 10p_y$
      $D_y = 60 - 10p_x - 10p_y$
      $S_y = -20 + 10p_y$

6. Find the values of the following determinants:

   a. $\begin{vmatrix} 1 & 2 & 3 \\ 3 & 2 & 4 \\ 0 & 1 & 2 \end{vmatrix}$ b. $\begin{vmatrix} 6 & 3 & 5 \\ 2 & 1 & -4 \\ 1 & 0 & 1 \end{vmatrix}$

   Solve the following systems of equations by determinants. Check your answers.

7. Let q denote the quantity of a commodity demanded or supplied and p its price.
   a. $q = 150 - 30p$ (demand equation)
      $q = -10 + 20p$ (supply equation)
   b. $q = 80 - 10p$ (demand equation)
      $q = 10p$ (supply equation)
   c. $400 - 2q - 10p = 0$ (demand equation)
      $150 - 3q + 30p = 0$ (supply equation)

8. $x + y + z = 1$
   $-x - \frac{1}{2}y - \frac{2}{3}z = 4$
   $2x + 2y - z = 5$

9. Let D_w and S_w represent the quantities of wheat demanded and supplied, respectively. Let D_c and S_c represent the quantities of corn demanded and supplied. Let p_w and p_c be the prices of wheat and corn, respectively.

   $D_w = 325 - 100p_w + 80p_c$
   $S_w = -35 + 60p_w - 40p_c$
   $D_c = 185 + 90p_w - 125p_c$
   $S_c = -30 - 20p_w + 50p_c$

10. $x + 3y - z = 0$
    $3x + 4y - 2z = 10$
    $y + z = -6$

6

Limits and

Derivatives

What do the concepts "marginal cost," "marginal utility," and "marginal propensity to consume" have in common? Obviously, they all contain the term "marginal." Economists use the term "marginal" to measure how the *change* in an independent variable produces a *change* in the dependent variable. Hence, *marginal revenue* is defined as the increase (or decrease) in revenue generated by selling one more unit of output. That is, a change in the rate of output (the independent variable) changes revenue (the dependent variable). In economics we learn that optimal decisions are based on marginal considerations: revenue is maximized where marginal revenue is zero; profit is maximized at that rate of output where marginal revenue equals marginal cost.

In mathematics, and therefore in economics, differential calculus is used to *derive* a function that relates the change in the dependent variable to change(s) in the independent variable(s). Calculus makes marginal relationships precise, allowing unambiguous definitions of optimal outcomes. Consider an example similar to ones you probably encountered in your introductory economics course. We assume that a monopolist faces an average revenue (inverse demand) function given by the equation $p = 10 - 0.5q$. The price starts at \$10, and falls by fifty cents for each unit increase in output. The average revenue and total revenue functions for this monopoly are shown in Table 6.1.

Table 6.1

q	$p = 10 - 0.5q$	$TR = pq$	$\Delta TR/\Delta q$	dTR/dq
0	10.00	0.00		10.00
1	9.50	9.50	9.50	9.00
2	9.00	18.00	8.50	8.00
3	8.50	25.50	7.50	7.00
4	8.00	32.00	6.50	6.00
5	7.50	37.50	5.50	5.00
6	7.00	42.00	4.50	4.00
7	6.50	45.50	3.50	3.00
8	6.00	48.00	2.50	2.00
9	5.50	49.50	1.50	1.00
10	5.00	50.00	0.50	0.00
11	4.50	49.50	−0.50	−1.00
12	4.00	48.00	−1.50	−2.00
13	3.50	45.50	−2.50	−3.00
14	3.00	42.00	−3.50	−4.00
15	2.50	37.50	−4.50	−5.00
16	2.00	32.00	−5.50	−6.00
17	1.50	25.50	−6.50	−7.00
18	1.00	18.00	−7.50	−8.00
19	0.50	9.50	−8.50	−9.00
20	0.00	0.00	−9.50	−10.00

The first column in Table 6.1 shows alternative rates of output, q, the independent variable. The monopolist can influence revenue by varying the rate of output. The second column gives price (average revenue), which commences at $10 and declines by $0.50 each time output increases by one unit. The third column gives total revenue, which equals price times output.

The fourth column, labeled "$\Delta TR/\Delta q$," is constructed arithmetically, as is typically done in principles of economics texts. It shows that the change in revenue attributed to the last unit of output equals the change in total revenue divided by the change in output. According to theory, we should find the revenue maximizing rate of output by setting $\Delta TR/\Delta q$ equal to zero. However, there is something a tad wrong with Column 4. Perusing that column shows that 10 units of output are associated with $50 revenue, while both 9 and 11 units of output are associated with revenue of $49.50. It appears that 10 units of output maximizes revenue, yet $\Delta TR/\Delta q = \$0.50$, rather than zero. Why?

The problem with Column 4 is that the discreteness of the data for output and price gives an imprecise measure of the *rate of change* of the revenue function with respect to output. Between $q = 9$ and $q = 10$, revenue increases by $0.50; between $q = 10$ and $q = 11$, revenue decreases by $0.50. Since revenue increases with the production of the tenth unit and falls with the production of the eleventh unit it follows that revenue is maximized by producing 10 units. The only shortcoming of this logic is that it lacks precision.

Now consider Column 5, which presents the *derivative* (dTR/dq) of the total revenue function with respect to output. The derivative of a function measures the rate at which the function is changing at different values of the dependent variable. For $q < 10$, $dTR/dq > 0$ and revenue is increasing with output. For $q > 10$, $dTR/dq < 0$ and revenue declines as output increases. Finally, at $q = 10$, $dTR/dq = 0$, and revenue is maximum (i.e., is neither increasing nor decreasing at that rate of output).

If a production manager is unaware of the firm's average revenue function, the revenue maximizing rate of output must be estimated by trial-and-error. Using trial-and-error, the firm must produce a particular rate of output, determine its market clearing price, and compare the change in revenue with the change in output. Even if the changes in output are very small (which implies a large number of trials), the revenue maximizing output can be identified only after revenue begins to fall. Knowledge of the rate of change of the revenue function allows the production manager to pick the revenue maximizing output immediately, without the "error" of "trial-and-error." But before we go off on a tangent, let's talk about tangents.

TANGENTS

Figure 6.1 presents a simple diagram of the average revenue function introduced in Table 6.1. In earlier chapters we learned that the slope of a line is the geometric representation of the change of the dependent variable divided by the change of the independent variable. We also learned that the slope of a linear function is everywhere the same. Between any two points on the diagram of a linear function, the change in the dependent variable (the "rise") is proportional to the change in the independent variable ("the run"). The line passing through points (q_1, p_1) and (q_2, p_2) has slope b, where:

$$b = \frac{p_2 - p_1}{q_2 - q_1}$$

as long as $q_2 \neq q_1$. We let the symbol Δp represent the finite change in p. Hence, $\Delta p = p_2 - p_1$. Equivalently, the symbol Δq denotes the change in q: $\Delta q = q_2 - q_1$.

Suppose we let $q_1 = 4$ and $q_2 = 8$. The associated values of price are $p_1 = 8$ and $p_2 = 6$. Using our formula for slope, we find that:

$$b = \frac{(6 - 8)}{(8 - 4)} = \frac{-2}{4} = -0.50$$

Since the slope of the average revenue curve in Figure 6.1 is negative, the change in price is depicted as $-\Delta p$. Negative distances are difficult to

Figure 6.1

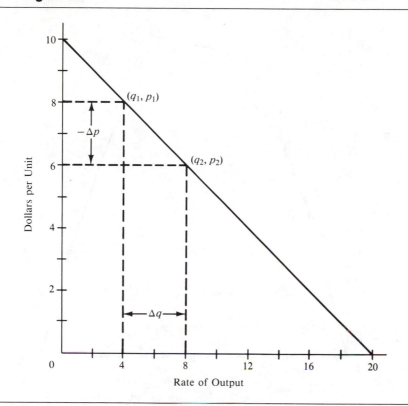

perceive geometrically. If we measured the slope between two other points along the line, namely (8, 6) and (10, 5), we find the same value:

$$b = \frac{(5 - 6)}{(10 - 8)} = \frac{-1}{2} = -0.5$$

Indeed, we could pick any two different points to generate the same ratio of the change in the dependent variable to the change in the independent variable.

What is true for the graph of a linear function is not true for the graph of a nonlinear function. Along a curve, the slope changes from one point to the next. Consequently, we need a method of measuring the slope of a curve at particular points on that curve. Geometrically, this can be done by finding the slope of a line that is *tangent* to the curve at the point of interest. The tangent line is a line that touches the curve at the point in question and has the same slope as the curve at their common point.

Figure 6.2 depicts the parabola that is generated by the revenue function $R = (10 - 0.5q)q = 10q - 0.5q^2$. This function corresponds to Column 3 in Table 6.1. The solid line that touches the parabola at point (4, 32) has

Figure 6.2

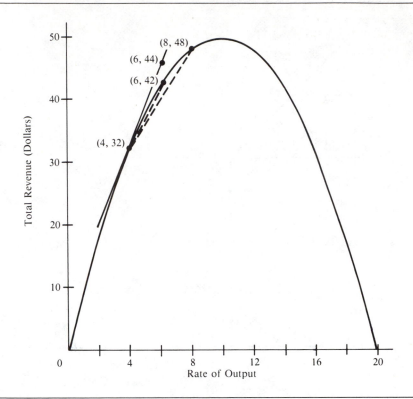

the same slope as the curve at that point. Assume we know that the solid line also goes through the point (6, 44). Applying the formula for the slope of a line, we find:

$$b = \frac{(44 - 32)}{(6 - 4)} = \frac{12}{2} = 6$$

At the point (4, 32) revenue increases at the rate of $6.00 per unit of output.

The problem is that we have no way of identifying the point (6, 44) from knowledge of the function alone, since that point is not contained in the graph of the function $R = 10q - 0.5q^2$. However, if we take points on the parabola we can construct *secant lines* (lines connecting two points on the curve) whose slopes will approximate the slope of the tangent line as we get progressively closer to the point of interest, in this case (4, 32).

If we pick a point on the parabola, say (8, 48), we can calculate the slope of the secant line that connects this point and (4, 32):

$$b = \frac{\Delta TR}{\Delta q} = \frac{(48 - 32)}{(8 - 4)} = \frac{16}{4} = 4$$

Between $q = 4$ and $q = 8$, revenue increases by an *average* of \$4.00 each time output increases by one unit. This is not the same slope as that of the tangent line at (4, 32). However, as we select points closer to (4, 32), our estimates of that slope become more accurate.

Now let us choose a point that lies closer to (4, 32), namely (6, 42). The slope of the line passing through (4, 32) and (6, 42) is given by:

$$b = \frac{\Delta TR}{\Delta q} = \frac{(42 - 32)}{(6 - 4)} = \frac{10}{2} = 5$$

Between $q = 4$ and $q = 6$, revenue increases by an average of \$5.00 for each unit increase in output. If we let $q = 5$ and $R = 37.50$, we find $b = (37.50 - 32)/(5 - 4) = 5.50/1 = 5.50$. The closer we get to the point of interest, namely (4, 32), the more closely the slope of a line segment connecting those points approximates the slope of the tangent line. In fact, since the parabola, $R = 10q - q^2$ is *continuous* (i.e., it has no breaks or gaps and its slope changes gradually), we can make the two points on the curve as close together as we want, thereby getting closer and closer to the tangent line we desire. No matter how close we place our two points, however, we will never be able to obtain the *exact* tangent line, because the tangent line touches the curve at only one point. However, using the concept of a *limit*, we will be able to find the precise slope of a nonlinear function.

LIMITS

A precise definition of the rate of change of the dependent variable due to an infinitesimal change in the independent variable makes use of the concept of a *limit*. To arrive at the slope of the tangent to the parabola given by $R = 10q - 0.5q^2$, we first chose a specific point (4, 32) on the parabola. We then considered points in the neighborhood of this point, approaching closer and closer to (4, 32). We found that the slope of the tangent line at (4, 32) is $m = 6$, which is also the slope of the parabola at this point.

We shall now restate the process in general terms. Let the point in question be denoted by (q, R)—for which $R = f(q)$. In this example, we have $R = 10q - 0.5q^2$. Next, we pick any specific point, such as (4, 32); when $q = 4$, $R = 32$. A point in the neighborhood of (q, R) is denoted by $(q + \Delta q, R + \Delta R)$, where Δq and ΔR represent small (positive or negative) increments of q and R, respectively. If we let $\Delta q = 1$, then $\Delta R = f(5) - f(4) = 37.50 - 32 = 5.50$. We join (4, 32) with (5, 37.5). In the previous section, we let other points on the parabola approach the fixed point (4, 32). Consequently, what we did, stated in more general terms, was to let Δq approach zero. As Δq approached zero, $q + \Delta q$ approached q. Furthermore, as Δq approached zero, so did ΔR; hence $R + \Delta R$ approached R.

Using this notation, the ratio of the change in R to the change in q can be given as:

$$\frac{\Delta R}{\Delta q} = \frac{(R + \Delta R) - R}{(q + \Delta q) - q}$$

This notation can be used for any function. Following the mathematical convention that x is an unspecified independent variable and y is a dependent variable given by $y = f(x)$, the change in the dependent variable along a function can be written as:

$$\Delta y = f(x + \Delta x) - f(x)$$

Hence, the change in the dependent variable divided by the change in the independent variable can be written as:

$$\frac{\Delta y}{\Delta x} = \frac{f(x + \Delta x) - f(x)}{(x + \Delta x) - x} = \frac{f(x + \Delta x) - f(x)}{\Delta x}$$

But we have seen that to approximate the slope of the tangent line (which touches the function at one point), the change in the independent variable must approach zero. It is the convention in mathematics to use a horizontal arrow to indicate that one magnitude approaches another. Thus, we can say "Δx approaches zero" by writing:

$$\Delta x \rightarrow 0$$

There is also a mathematical notion called a *limit*. In this context, we mean that Δx, which cannot actually take on the value of zero, is allowed to take on such infinitesimally small values that the difference between Δx and zero is negligible. That is, the value of Δx is limited, since it cannot actually take on the value of zero, but we can define Δx to be as close to that "limit" as we desire. Since the slope of the curve is equal to the slope of the tangent line, we define the slope of the curve as the limit of the ratio of the change in the dependent variable to the change in the independent variable as the latter approaches zero:

$$\lim_{\Delta x \rightarrow 0} \frac{f(x + \Delta x) - f(x)}{\Delta x}$$

We shall return to the relationship between the slope of a tangent and a limit in a moment. We must first explore the concept of a limit in more detail. Let k be some number, and let $y = f(x)$ be a function whose permissible values of x include all numbers close to k and may or may not include k. If there is a number L such that $f(x)$ may be as close to L as we please merely by choosing for x any number whatsoever close enough to k, but different from k, we write the following:

$$\lim_{x \rightarrow k} f(x) = L$$

We read this symbolic statement as: "the limit of $f(x)$ as x approaches k is L." If no such number L exists, the function does not have a limit at the value of x in question.

For example, suppose that we define:

$$f(x) = \frac{(x - 1)(2 - x)}{(x - 1)}$$

You are no doubt tempted to factor $(x - 1)$ out of the numerator and the denominator to simplify this function to $f(x) = 2 - x$. A moment's reflection should indicate that we cannot perform that operation if $x = 1$, since division by zero is not defined. This innocuous little function has a "hole" in it at $x = 1$ and the function is not defined when $x = 1$. Nevertheless, the *limit* of the function is defined when $x = 1$. We can verify this by calculating the value of $f(x)$ at points close to $x = 1$, and showing the function *converges* on a particular value.

Approaching $x = 1$ from greater values of x, we let $x = 2$ and discover $f(x) = (2 - 1)(2 - 2)/(2 - 1) = 0/1 = 0$. When $x = 1.5$, $f(x) = (1.5 - 1)(2 - 1.5)/(1.5 - 1) = (0.5)(0.5)/(0.5) = 0.5$. When $x = 1.1$, $f(x) = (1.1 - 1)(2 - 1.1)/(1.1 - 1) = (0.1)(0.9)/(0.1) = 0.9$. When $x = 1.001$, $f(x) = (1.001 - 1)(2 - 1.001)/(1.001 - 1) = (0.001)(0.999)/(0.001) = 0.999$. As x gets closer and closer to 1 from the greater values of x, $f(x)$ gets progressively closer to 1. A similar result occurs when we allow x to approach 1 from smaller values of x:

$$f(0) = \frac{(0 - 1)(2 - 0)}{(0 - 1)} = \frac{-2}{-1} = 2$$

$$f(0.5) = \frac{(0.5 - 1)(2 - 0.5)}{(0.5 - 1)} = \frac{-0.75}{-0.5} = 1.5$$

$$f(0.9) = \frac{(0.9 - 1)(2 - 0.9)}{(0.9 - 1)} = \frac{-0.11}{-0.1} = 1.1$$

$$f(0.999) = \frac{(0.999 - 1)(2 - 0.999)}{(0.999 - 1)} = \frac{-0.001001}{-0.001} = 1.001$$

The function

$$f(x) = \frac{(x - 1)(2 - x)}{(x - 1)}$$

is not defined for $x = 1$. Nevertheless $f(x)$ has a limit as x approaches 1, since, as x is allowed to get closer and closer to 1, $f(x)$ gets closer and closer to 1, whether we approach $x = 1$ from greater or smaller values of x.

By contrast, consider the function $f(x) = 1/(x - 1)$. This function is also undefined when $x = 1$, again because division by zero is undefined. However, as the following equations show, the function has no limit for two reasons. As x approaches 1 from a positive direction, $f(x)$ approaches positive infinity $(+\infty)$; as x approaches 1 from a negative direction, $f(x)$ approaches negative infinity $(-\infty)$. Hence, the function does not converge on a single value as x approaches 1 from opposite directions.

$$f(2) = \frac{1}{(2-1)} = \frac{1}{1} = 1$$

$$f(1.5) = \frac{1}{(1.5-1)} = \frac{1}{0.5} = 2$$

$$f(1.1) = \frac{1}{(1.1-1)} = \frac{1}{0.1} = 10$$

$$f(1.001) = \frac{1}{(1.001-1)} = \frac{1}{0.001} = 1{,}000$$

$$f(0) = \frac{1}{(0-1)} = \frac{1}{-1} = -1$$

$$f(0.5) = \frac{1}{(0.5-1)} = \frac{1}{-0.5} = -2$$

$$f(0.9) = \frac{1}{(0.9-1)} = \frac{1}{-0.1} = -10$$

$$f(0.999) = \frac{1}{(0.999-1)} = \frac{1}{-0.001} = -1{,}000$$

Having defined the limit, let us return to the relationship between tangents and limits. The slope of the tangent to a curve can be approximated by calculating the slope of a line connecting two points on the curve. As those points are brought closer together, the change in the independent variable approaches zero. In our revenue function example, the slope at $R(4)$ is given by:

$$\lim_{\Delta q \to 0} \frac{[10(4 + \Delta q) - 0.5(4 + \Delta q)^2] - [10(4) - 0.5(4)^2]}{\Delta q}$$

$$= \lim_{\Delta q \to 0} \frac{40 + 10\Delta q - 8 - 4\Delta q - 0.5(\Delta q)^2 - 32}{\Delta q}$$

$$= \lim_{\Delta q \to 0} \frac{6\Delta q - 0.5(\Delta q)^2}{\Delta q} = \lim_{\Delta q \to 0} 6 - 0.5\Delta q = 6$$

Although Δq approaches zero it is not equal to zero. This allows us to factor Δq out of the numerator and the denominator. Once we eliminate Δq from the denominator, we no longer worry about division by zero. We can therefore imagine Δq going all the way to zero, eliminating the Δq terms from the remaining expression. The slope of the tangent line when $q = 4$ is 6.

DERIVATIVES

By using the concept of a limit, the slope of a tangent line can be computed from the equation of a function. In this way, we *derive* a function that relates the *rate of change* of the dependent variable at each value of the independent variable. Returning to our revenue function, $R(q) = 10q - 0.5q^2$, we define:

$$\frac{dR}{dq} = \lim_{\Delta q \to 0} \frac{R(q + \Delta q) - R(q)}{\Delta q}$$

$$= \lim_{\Delta q \to 0} \frac{10(q + \Delta q) - 0.5(q + \Delta q)^2 - 10q + 0.5q^2}{\Delta q}$$

$$= \lim_{\Delta q \to 0} \frac{10q + 10\Delta q - 0.5q^2 - q\Delta q - 0.5(\Delta q)^2 - 10q + 0.5q^2}{\Delta q}$$

All terms in $R(q + \Delta q)$ that do not contain Δq also appear in $R(q)$. These terms can be subtracted from the numerator, leaving an expression that contains Δq in each term in the numerator and the denominator:

$$\frac{dR}{dq} = \lim_{\Delta q \to 0} \frac{10\Delta q - q\Delta q - 0.5(\Delta q)^2}{\Delta q}$$

By factoring Δq out of the numerator and the denominator (since Δq does not equal zero), we eliminate the denominator:

$$\frac{dR}{dq} = \lim_{\Delta q \to 0} \frac{10\Delta q - q\Delta q - 0.5(\Delta q)^2}{\Delta q} = \lim_{\Delta q \to 0} (10 - q - 0.5\Delta q)$$

Without the troublesome Δq in the denominator, we can imagine that Δq goes all the way to zero, thereby eliminating all terms that contain it:

$$\frac{dR}{dq} = \frac{d(10 - 0.5q^2)}{dq} = \lim_{\Delta q \to 0} (10 - q - 0.5\Delta q) = 10 - q$$

Once we have obtained the general formula for dR/dq, we can obtain the slope of the original function at any point by substituting the appropriate value of q. Hence, if $q = 4$, we have:

$$\frac{dR}{dq} = 10 - q = 10 - 4 = 6$$

One of the most fundamental definitions in calculus is that of the derivative of a function. The process of calculating the derivative is called *differentiating a function*. Much work in calculus (and in its application to economics) centers around this notion. We define a *derivative* of a function as another function that relates the change in the dependent variable (due to infinitely small changes in the independent variable) to the change in the independent variable as the latter change approaches zero. The term "derivative" stems from the fact that it is a function derived from another function. For a general function, $y = f(x)$:

$$\frac{dy}{dx} = \lim_{\Delta x \to 0} \frac{f(x + \Delta x) - f(x)}{\Delta x}$$

Other symbols which are commonly used for a derivative include:

$$\frac{dy}{dx} = \frac{df(x)}{dx} = f'(x)$$

Regardless of the notation used, the derivative allows us to calculate the slope of a function at each value of the independent variable. This leads to two viewpoints on terminology. The first is that the derivative is a specific value for a given x (rather than an entire function of x)—the slope of the tangent at a specific point. The second perspective is that the derivative may be taken as a function of x—the formula for the slope of the tangent at any point. When the former terminology is adopted, the "derived function" is distinguished from the "derivative" and is the term applied to the general formula for the slope of the tangent line for any value of the dependent variable. However, the latter approach is most prevalent in mathematics and economics, and we will follow this convention.

For us "derivative" and "derived function" refer to the same thing. When we want to know the rate of change of the original function at one chosen point, we will speak of the *value* of the *derivative* at that point. We will use the notation dy/dx or $df(x)/dx$ or $f'(x)$ to indicate the derivative, and we will use the notation $df(3)/dx$ or $f'(3)$ to denote the value of the derivative at the point on the function $f(x)$ when $x = 3$, a chosen fixed value.

RULES OF DIFFERENTIATION

Having established the definition of a derivative as the limit of the ratio of the change in the dependent variable to the change in the independent variable, we now proceed to develop some general rules of differentiation. These rules will not be rigorously proven, but will be linked to the definition of a derivative whenever possible. As you work with derivatives throughout the rest of this book, and throughout your work in mathematics and economics, these rules will become second nature to you. However, if you should forget these rules, it will often be possible to jog your memory by beginning with the definition of a derivative and working from there.

Power Functions

A function of the form $y = ax^n$ is called a *power* function. When the exponent, n, equals zero, the power function becomes a constant function: $y = ax^0 = a$. A good example of a constant function is the average revenue function facing a single perfectly competitive firm: regardless of the rate of output, the seller receives the market price as the revenue for an additional unit of output. Since the price does not change with the firm's output, it follows that $dp/dq = 0$. In general, the derivative of a constant function with respect to a variable is zero.

If the exponent on a power function is 1, we have a linear function that passes through the origin: $y = ax$. In our previous example, we have the average revenue function for a competitive firm as $p = p_0$, where p_0 is a constant. The total revenue function is $R = p_0 q$. Each time output increases by one unit, total revenue increases by a constant p_0 units. That is, if the average revenue function is constant, the total revenue function is linear. The *marginal revenue function*, which is the derivative of the total revenue function with respect to output, turns out to be a constant function:

$$\frac{dR}{dq} = \frac{d(p_0 q)}{dq} = \lim_{\Delta q \to 0} \frac{p_0(q + \Delta q) - p_0 q}{\Delta q} = \lim_{\Delta q \to 0} \frac{p_0(\Delta q)}{\Delta q} = p_0$$

Now, suppose that the power function were quadratic, with the form $y = f(x) = x^2$. In this case, the derivative of the dependent variable, y, with respect to the independent variable, x, is:

$$\frac{dy}{dx} = \lim_{\Delta x \to 0} \frac{f(x + \Delta x) - f(x)}{\Delta x} = \lim_{\Delta x \to 0} \frac{(x + \Delta x)^2 - x^2}{\Delta x}$$

Expanding the numerator and subtracting the last term, we have:

$$\frac{dy}{dx} = \lim_{\Delta x \to 0} \frac{x^2 + 2x\Delta x + (\Delta x)^2 - x^2}{\Delta x} = \lim_{\Delta x \to 0} \frac{2x(\Delta x) + (\Delta x)^2}{\Delta x}$$

Since $\Delta x \neq 0$, we can divide it out of the numerator and the denominator, yielding:

$$\frac{dy}{dx} = \lim_{\Delta x \to 0} (2x + \Delta x) = 2x + \lim_{\Delta x \to 0} \Delta x = 2x$$

Again, once we have eliminated Δx from the denominator, we can imagine Δx becoming zero, eliminating the term containing Δx from the expression. Put simply:

$$\frac{d(x^2)}{dx} = 2x$$

If the power function is cubic ($n = 3$), its derivative is given as:

$$\frac{dx^3}{dx} = 3x^2$$

This also can be demonstrated from the definition of the derivative. First, we set up the problem as:

$$\frac{dx^3}{dx} = \frac{d(x^3)}{dx} = \lim_{\Delta x \to 0} \frac{(x + \Delta x)^3 - x^3}{\Delta x}$$

$$= \lim_{\Delta x \to 0} \frac{x^3 + 3x^2(\Delta x) + 3x(\Delta x)^2 + (\Delta x)^3 - x^3}{\Delta x}$$

Again, we subtract the x^3 term, which allows us to cancel the Δx term from the numerator and the denominator, leaving:

$$\frac{dx^3}{dx} = \lim_{\Delta x \to 0} [3x^2 + 3x(\Delta x) + (\Delta x)^2]$$

$$= 3x^2 + \lim_{\Delta x \to 0} [3x(\Delta x) + (\Delta x)^2]$$

Imagining that Δx shrinks to zero, we have:

$$\frac{d(x^3)}{dx} = 3x^2$$

We can generalize on the derivative of the power function. When $y = x^n$, the derivative of y with respect to x is:

$$\frac{dy}{dx} = \frac{dx^n}{dx} = nx^{n-1}$$

To take the derivative of a power function, we bring the exponent down to the front of the expression, then reduce the value of the exponent by 1.

An extension of the power function rule involves the effect of multiplying a function by a constant. The derivative of a function obtained by multiplying a function by a constant equals the derivative of the original function multiplied by the same constant.

Consider the function $y = f(x) = x^n$. Now multiply $f(x)$ by a constant c: $cf(x) = cx^n$. It follows that $d(cf(x))/dx = ncx^{n-1}$. This rule is valid for any function, not just power functions. The derivative of a function generated by multiplying a function by a constant is that constant times the derivative of the original function.

So far we have considered power functions for which the exponent is a nonnegative integer. However, the power function rule is more general than this. For instance, suppose $n = -1$, so that $cx^n = cx^{-1} = c/x$. Applying the power function rule,

$$\frac{d(cx^{-1})}{dx} = -1(cx^{-2}) = -\frac{c}{x^2}$$

The behavior of average fixed cost as output increases is a good illustration of the power function rule applied to reciprocals of functions. Average fixed cost can be written as $AFC = FC/q = FCq^{-1}$, where FC is, of course, a constant. The change in average fixed cost with respect to output is the derivative of AFC with respect to q:

$$\frac{d(AFC)}{dq} = \frac{d(FCq^{-1})}{dq} = \frac{-FC}{q^2}$$

As output increases, average fixed cost falls at a rate proportional to the square of the inverse of output. We can show this using the definition of the derivative:

$$\frac{d(FC/q)}{dq} = \lim_{\Delta q \to 0} \frac{FC/(q + \Delta q) - FC/q}{\Delta q}$$

$$= \lim_{\Delta q \to 0} \frac{qFC/q(q + \Delta q) - FC(q + \Delta q)/q(q + \Delta q)}{\Delta q}$$

$$= \lim_{\Delta q \to 0} \frac{qFC - qFC - \Delta qFC}{q\Delta q(q + \Delta q)} = \lim_{\Delta q \to 0} \frac{-\Delta qFC}{q\Delta q(q + \Delta q)}$$

$$= \lim_{\Delta q \to 0} \frac{-FC}{q(q + \Delta q)} = \frac{-FC}{q^2}$$

The functions given by the following equations have the derivatives shown in the column on the right. As an exercise, you should apply the rule of differentiation to each function to obtain the derivative shown in the right-hand column.

Function	Derivative
$y = 2x^7$	$\dfrac{dy}{dx} = 14x^6$
$y = 3\sqrt{x} = 3x^{0.5}$	$\dfrac{dy}{dx} = 1.5x^{-0.5} = \dfrac{3}{2\sqrt{x}}$
$y = \dfrac{4}{x^2} = 4x^{-2}$	$\dfrac{dy}{dx} = -8x^{-3} = \dfrac{-8}{x^3}$

Derivatives of Sums and Differences of Functions

Many functions in economics are generated by combining two or more related functions. For instance, short-run total cost equals the sum of fixed cost and variable cost. Profit equals the difference between total revenue and total cost, both of which are functions of output. More generally, polynomial functions have multiple terms, each of which contain the independent variable, raised to a power that is a nonnegative integer. It is convenient to know the derivative of a function that is the sum of two other functions.

Let g and h be given functions of x. Define f as:

$$f(x) = g(x) + h(x)$$

As long as the two derivatives, $dg(x)/dx$ and $dh(x)/dx$ both exist over the domain of x, the sum of functions rule for derivatives states that:

$$\frac{df(x)}{dx} = f'(x) = \frac{dg(x)}{dx} + \frac{dh(x)}{dx} = g'(x) + h'(x)$$

This simple rule has important applications in microeconomic theory. As stated, short-run total cost is defined as the sum of fixed cost and variable cost: $TC = FC + VC$. We can define marginal cost as the rate of change of total cost with respect to output. We could also define marginal cost as the rate of change of variable cost with respect to output. Can these two definitions be reconciled? Applying the sum of functions rule:

$$\frac{dTC}{dq} = \frac{dFC}{dq} + \frac{dVC}{dq}$$

But fixed cost is a constant, so that $dFC/dq = 0$. It follows that $dTC/dq = dVC/dq$, and our two definitions of marginal cost are equivalent.

Recall from the previous section that the derivative of a function generated by multiplying another function by a constant equals the constant times the derivative of the original function. Let's define function $H(x)$ as $-1[h(x)]$ and $F(x)$ as:

$$F(x) = g(x) + H(x)$$

so that

$$F'(x) = g'(x) + H'(x)$$

However, since $H(x) = -1[h(x)]$, $H'(x) = -h'(x)$. Hence:

$$F'(x) = \frac{d[g(x) - h(x)]}{dx} = g'(x) - h'(x)$$

The derivative of a function that is the difference between two other functions is equal to the difference in their derivatives.

We have seen that economic profit is defined as the difference between total revenue and total cost, both of which are functions of output:

$$\pi(q) = R(q) - C(q)$$

The change in profit with respect to output equals the difference between the change in revenue and the change in cost:

$$\frac{d\pi(q)}{dq} = \frac{dR(q)}{dq} - \frac{dC(q)}{dq}$$

As output changes, the change in profit equals the change in revenue (marginal revenue) minus the change in cost (marginal cost).

One final application involves the use of polynomial functions in the theory of cost. A typical short-run cost function for a producer might have the form:

$$C(q) = a_0 + a_1 q + a_2 q^2 + a_3 q^3$$

Here the parameters, a_0, a_1, a_2, and a_3, may be estimated by statistical techniques. The firm's marginal cost function is the derivative of C with respect to q. This derivative can be determined by applying the power function rule to each of the terms of the function and adding the results:

$$\frac{dC(q)}{dq} = \frac{da_0}{dq} + \frac{d(a_1 q)}{dq} + \frac{d(a_2 q^2)}{dq} + \frac{d(a_3 q^3)}{dq}$$

$$= 0 + a_1 + 2a_2 q + 3a_3 q^2$$

If $a_3 > 0$, the cost function is a cubic function and the marginal cost function is a quadratic function. If $a_3 = 0$ and $a_2 > 0$, then the cost function is a quadratic function and the marginal cost function is a linear function. If $a_3 = a_2 = 0$, the cost function is linear and $MC = a_1$. The marginal cost function is a constant function.

The Chain Rule

There are many instances in economics when a variable is dependent in one function and independent in another function. For instance, output is the dependent variable in a short-run production function (which we will assume has only one independent variable, labor). At the same time, output is the causal variable in the firm's revenue function. In factor market theory, we learn that the demand for labor services is based on labor's *marginal revenue product*, defined as the rate of change in revenue with respect to labor. We require a technique for taking the derivative of one function whose independent variable is the dependent variable of another function. Literally, we must take the derivative of a *function of a function*. To do so, we make use of the *chain rule*.

While we still have a chance, it is prudent to make use of intuition: the derivative of revenue with respect to labor is obtained by first taking the derivative of revenue with respect to output, then multiplying by the derivative or output with respect to labor. Imagine a competitive firm that faces a constant price of \$5 per unit, $R(q) = 5q$. Further imagine a short-run production function given by $q = 20L - L^2$. There are two ways of solving for dR/dq. One is to substitute the formula $20L - L^2$ for q, then take the derivative directly:

$$R(L) = 5(20L - L^2) = 100L - 5L^2$$

$$\frac{dR}{dL} = 100 - 10L$$

When $L = 0$, $q = 0$. When $L = 1$, $q = 20(1) - 1 = 19$ and $R = 19(5) = 95$. When $L = 1$, the revenue function is *changing* at the rate of $100 - 10 = 90$ (per additional worker). For the second worker, marginal revenue is $100 - 20 = 80$, for the third it is 70, and so forth. It follows that the firm would not hire more than 10 workers in the short run, since the tenth worker would generate zero additional revenue.

A second method is to use the chain rule: take the derivative of $R(q)$ with respect to q, then multiply the result by the derivative of q with respect to L. The advantage of this approach is that we can generalize for all revenue and production functions, something that is not possible when we must first substitute the production function into the revenue function. Letting $R = R(q)$ and $q = f(L)$:

$$\frac{dR}{dL} = \frac{dR}{dq} \cdot \frac{dq}{dL}$$

In our specific example, $dR/dq = 5$ and $dq/dL = 20 - 2L$, which yields:

$$\frac{dR}{dL} = 5(20 - 2L) = 100 - 10L$$

This is the same result that we obtained with the substitution approach. However, the chain rule also shows us that the marginal product of labor is zero when $L = 10$. Regardless of the price of the output, the firm would not wish to hire more than ten workers.

Derivative of the Product of Functions

There are many problems in economics in which we must find the derivative of a function which is itself the product of two other functions. In our example that began this chapter, the revenue function for a monopolist was defined as the product of price (which is a function of output) times output (which is a function of itself). Marginal revenue is the limit of the change in revenue with respect to output as the change in output approaches zero. That is, marginal revenue is the derivative of price times quantity with respect to quantity. But how do we take the derivative of a function that is the product of two other functions? Intuition may hint that the derivative of the product of two functions ought to be the product of their derivatives. Alas, intuition would lead us astray in this case. We have already encountered the chain rule: the derivative of a function whose independent variable is itself a dependent variable of another function is the product of the derivatives of those two functions. The rule we seek is different.

While not exactly intuitive, a diagram may help clarify the product rule. In Figure 6.3 we have the average revenue (inverse demand) function, similar to the one in Figure 6.1. Recall that the area of a rectangle equals the width (q_0) times the height (p_0). In Figure 6.3, price (average revenue) equals p_0 when quantity equals q_0, so that total revenue is given by the area of rectangle $0p_0Aq_0$. Now suppose output increases to q_1. A *nondiscriminating monopolist* would have to reduce price to p_1, not just for the extra output ($\Delta q = q_1 - q_0$), but for all the output ($q_0 + \Delta q$). Hence, there are two components to the change in revenue: the increase in revenue because

Figure 6.3

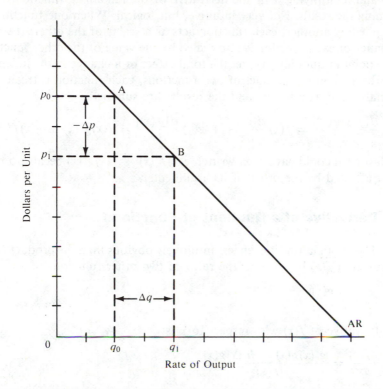

Rate of Output

additional units are sold ($p_1 \Delta q$), and the loss of *inframarginal* revenue because price must be reduced on the first q_0 units ($q_0 \Delta p$):

$$\Delta R = p_1 \Delta q - q_0(-\Delta p) \qquad \text{(since } \Delta p < 0\text{)}$$
$$= p_1 \Delta q + q_0 \Delta p$$

To determine the ratio of the change in revenue to the change in output, we divide through by the change in quantity, Δq.

$$\frac{\Delta R}{\Delta q} = \frac{p_1 \Delta q}{\Delta q} + \frac{q_0 \Delta p}{\Delta q}$$

Finally, to calculate the derivative of R with respect to q, we take the limit of $\Delta R/\Delta q$ as Δq approaches zero. (Note, since points A and B more closer together, we drop the subscripts on p and q.)

$$\frac{dR}{dq} = \lim_{\Delta q \to 0} p \frac{(\Delta q)}{\Delta q} + \lim_{\Delta q \to 0} q \frac{(\Delta p)}{\Delta q} = p \frac{dq}{dq} + q \frac{dp}{dq}$$

The derivative of a function that is the product of two other functions is given by treating one function as a constant and multiplying it by the derivative of the other function, then treating the other function as a constant and multiplying it by the derivative of the remaining function, then summing the result. Not very intuitive, but logical. When one function is multiplied by another, each function acts as a scalar of the other: the rate of change of each function is also scaled by the value of the other function at the point in question. To get the total effect of a change in the independent variable on the product of two functions, each function is treated as a variable and as a scalar, and the results are summed.

$$\frac{d[f(x)g(x)]}{dx} = f(x)\frac{d[g(x)]}{dx} + g(x)\frac{d[f(x)]}{dx} = f(x)g'(x) + g(x)f'(x)$$

The last term could have been written $g(x)f'(x) + f(x)g'(x)$ because a sum is not affected by the order of its arguments.

Derivative of a Quotient of Functions

The quotient rule is even less intuitively obvious than the product rule. Let function $f(x)$ be given as the ratio of two other functions of x:

$$f(x) = \frac{g(x)}{h(x)}$$

The derivative of $f(x)$ with respect to x is:

$$\frac{df(x)}{dx} = \frac{g'(x)h(x) - h'(x)g(x)}{[h(x)]^2}$$

To take the derivative of a ratio of two functions, we take the derivative of the numerator multiplied by the denominator, then subtract the derivative of the denominator times the numerator, then divide the whole thing by the denominator function *squared*. Since this rule is not intuitively obvious, it is difficult to memorize. To insure against forgetting this rule (especially at exam time) it is prudent to learn how to derive the rule with the help of the product rule and the chain rule.

Let's define $H(x)$ as $[h(x)]^{-1}$; that is, $H(x)$ is the reciprocal of the function $h(x)$. Substituting $H(x)$, $f(x)$ becomes the product of two functions, $f(x) = g(x)H(x)$, whose derivative is:

$$f'(x) = g'(x)H(x) + H'(x)g(x)$$

By the chain rule,

$$H'(x) = \frac{d[h(x)]^{-1}}{dh(x)} \cdot \frac{dh(x)}{dx} = -[h(x)]^{-2}h'(x)$$

so by substitution

$$f'(x) = \frac{g'(x)}{h(x)} - \frac{h'(x)g(x)}{[h(x)]^2} = \frac{g'(x)h(x) - h'(x)g(x)}{[h(x)]^2}$$

There are many economic applications of the quotient rule of differentiation. For instance, in cost theory, we wish to know how average variable cost changes as the rate of output changes. Since $AVC = VC/q$, we take the derivative of this ratio with respect to q and obtain:

$$\frac{d(AVC)}{dq} = \frac{d(VC/q)}{dq} = \frac{q(dVC/dq) - VC(dq/dq)}{q^2}$$

$$= \frac{1}{q}\left(\frac{dVC}{dq} - \frac{VC}{q}\right)$$

We have already shown that marginal cost is the change in variable cost with respect to output ($MC = dVC/dq$). The change in average variable cost due to a change in output is equal to the difference between marginal cost and average variable cost, divided by the rate of output. When marginal cost is less than average variable cost (VC/q), average variable cost is decreasing. When $dVC/dq > VC/q$, average variable cost is increasing.

Derivatives of Logarithmic and Exponential Functions

We now consider the derivatives of two important functions, the exponential function and the logarithmic function. The number e, which is the base of the *natural exponential function*, $y = e^x$, and the natural logarithmic function, $y = \log_e x = \ln x$, is itself generated as the limit to an interesting series:

$$e = \lim_{n \to \infty}\left[1 + \frac{1}{n}\right]^n$$

Suppose you deposited \$1 in a savings account that paid an interest rate of r percent. If your interest were *not* compounded, at the end of a year you would have $(1 + r)$ dollars. If interest were compounded twice a year, at the end of one year you would have $(1 + r/2)^2$ dollars; if interest were compounded twelve times a year, you would have $(1 + r/12)^{12}$ dollars; and so forth. If the number of times interest were compounded approached infinity, we would approach *continuous compounding* and the value of your dollar at the end of a year would be:

$$\lim_{n \to \infty}\left[1 + \frac{r}{n}\right]^n = e^r$$

Now suppose you deposited V_o dollars and left it accumulating interest that was continuously compounded for t years. At the end of t years your deposit would be worth:

$$\lim_{n \to \infty}\left[V_o\left(1 + \frac{r}{n}\right)^{nt}\right] = V_o\left[\lim_{n \to \infty}\left(1 + \frac{r}{n}\right)^n\right]^t = V_o e^{rt}$$

But (you object), banks don't always compound continuously. However, nature often does. The rate of growth of population, the rate of innovation, and even the rate of economic growth can all be approximated by exponential functions, as can some important probability distributions encountered in statistics.

Derivative of a Logarithmic Function

The natural logarithmic function, $y = \log_e x$, has many applications in both mathematical economics and econometrics. The derivative of the natural logarithm of a variable with respect to that variable equals the reciprocal of that variable:

$$\frac{d(\log_e x)}{dx} = \frac{d \ln x}{dx} = \frac{1}{x}$$

The proof of this rule involves a little sleight of hand, but is nevertheless informative. By the definition of the derivative and the rule of logarithms introduced in Chapter 2, we have:

$$\frac{d(\log_e x)}{dx} = \lim_{\Delta x \to 0} \frac{\log_e(x + \Delta x) - \log_e x}{\Delta x}$$

$$= \lim_{\Delta x \to 0} \frac{\log_e[(x + \Delta x)/x]}{\Delta x}$$

Next, we define $m = x/\Delta x$, so that m approaches infinity as Δx approaches zero. Making the appropriate substitutions, we have:

$$\frac{d \log_e x}{dx} = \lim_{m \to \infty} \frac{\log_e[1 + 1/m]}{x/m}$$

$$= \lim_{m \to \infty} \frac{m \log_e[1 + 1/m]}{x}$$

Since the value of x is not affected by what happens to m, we can factor out the $1/x$. Next, we bring the limit into the logarithmic function:

$$\frac{d \log_e x}{dx} = \frac{1}{x} \log_e \left[\lim_{m \to \infty} \left(1 + \frac{1}{m} \right)^m \right]$$

Notice that the bracketed expression is simply the definition of the base of the natural logarithms, e, whose natural logarithm is, of course, 1. Hence, the expression immediately simplifies to the logarithm function rule we seek:

$$\frac{d \log_e x}{dx} = \frac{1}{x} \log_e e = \frac{1}{x}(1) = \frac{1}{x}$$

When more complicated functions are involved, we can invoke the chain rule. For instance, suppose that $y = \log_e u$, and that u in turn is a function of x. The derivative of y with respect to x is the derivative of y with respect to u times the derivative of u with respect to x. For instance, suppose that $y = \log_e x^2$. It follows that:

$$\frac{dy}{dx} = \frac{d\log_e x^2}{dx} = \frac{d\log_e x^2}{dx^2} \cdot \frac{dx^2}{dx} = \frac{1}{x^2}(2x) = \frac{2}{x}$$

The same result could have been obtained through the laws of logarithms. The $\log_e x^2$ is equal to $2\log_e x$. It follows that:

$$\frac{d\log_e x^2}{dx} = \frac{d(2\log_e x)}{dx} = 2\left(\frac{d\log_e x}{dx}\right) = \frac{2}{x}$$

Sometimes we have occasion to use a logarithmic function whose base is not the "natural number" e. We can still take the derivative of y with respect to x by means of a simple transformation. Suppose that $y = \log_a x$, which is equivalent to saying that $x = a^y$. We can translate the base from a to e by simply noting that $a = e^{\ln a}$, so that $x = [e^{\ln a}]^y$. Taking the natural logarithm for both sides, we have $y = \ln x/\ln a$, where $\ln a$ is a constant. Hence we have:

$$\frac{d\log_a x}{dx} = \frac{d(\ln x/\ln a)}{dx} = \frac{1}{\log_e a} \cdot \frac{1}{x}$$

For example, suppose we wish to find the derivative of $\log_{10} x$ with respect to x. From Table A in the back of the book we find that $\log_e 10 = 2.3026$. Therefore, it follows that:

$$\frac{d\log_{10} x}{dx} = \frac{1}{\log_e 10(x)} = \frac{1}{2.3026x}$$

Derivatives of Exponential Functions

The logarithmic and exponential functions are related in a special way: if we "solve" one function (reverse the role of the indepenent and dependent variables), we generate another function called the *inverse function*. The logarithmic function is the *inverse* of the exponential function, and vice-versa. That is, if we are given that $x = e^y$, it follows that $y = \log_e x$, and if $x = \log_e y$, it follows that $y = e^x$. When two functions are related in this way, their derivatives are also related: $dy/dx = 1/(dx/dy)$. Making use of this rule gives us a straightforward proof of the exponential function rule:

$$\frac{de^x}{dx} = \frac{dy}{dx} = \frac{1}{dx/dy} = \frac{1}{d\ln y/dy} = \frac{1}{1/y} = y = e^x$$

The derivative of the exponential function is the exponential function itself.

Let y be given as a function of e raised to the power u, where u, in turn, is a function of x. Then according to the chain rule and the exponential function rule:

$$\frac{dy}{dx} = \frac{de^u}{dx} = \frac{de^u}{du} \cdot \frac{du}{dx} = e^u \cdot \frac{du}{dx}$$

To return to our continuous compounding example, suppose the value of an asset is given by $V(t) = V_o e^{rt}$, where r is the rate of interest, t is time, and V_o is the initial value of the asset. The rate of change in the value of the asset with respect to time is:

$$\frac{d(V_o e^{rt})}{dt} = rV_o e^{rt}$$

That is, the rate of change is the rate of interest times the value of the asset at time t. The longer the asset is held, the faster its value increases.

IMPLICIT DIFFERENTIATION

So far we have been working with explicit functions—the dependent variable is isolated on the left side of the equal sign and all arguments containing the independent variable appear on the right side. However, there are many cases in economics when we wish to find the derivative of an implicit function. This often occurs when two variables are simultaneously determined by some equilibrium mechanism, and which variable is perceived as the "causal" variable is largely a matter of expository convenience. For instance, in macroeconomic theory, aggregate consumption is a function of national income, while national income is the sum of consumption, net investment, government purchases, and net exports.

$$Y = C(Y) + I + G + (X - M)$$

Since the variable Y appears on both sides of this equation, the effect of a change of I on equilibrium Y, with G and $(X - M)$ constant, is not immediately obvious. If we knew the consumption function in explicit form, we could solve for an explicit function for Y, and then take the derivative. However, we may not know the explicit form of the consumption function. We can still obtain the derivative dY/dI by implicit differentiation. First, we introduce a variation in notation. The letter d preceding a variable will stand for the (very small) change in that variable. Hence, imagine that I changes set up a chain reaction, whereby Y and C also change, since Y is a function of I and C is a function of Y. Assuming that G and $(X - M)$ are independent of I, C, and Y, means that these variables do not respond to a change in I ($dG = d(X - M) = 0$). In terms of our new notation, we have:

$$dY = \left(\frac{dC}{dY}\right)dY + dI$$

We isolate all terms containing dY on the left side of the equation:

$$\left(1 - \frac{dC}{dY}\right)dY = dI$$

Then dividing through by $1 - (dC/dY)$ and dI, we have:

$$\frac{dY}{dI} = \frac{1}{1 - (dC/dY)}$$

This is the famous investment multiplier of Keynesian theory.

To implicitly differentiate a function, we treat the changes in the two variables, dY and dI, as unknowns, then solve for the ratio of the change in the dependent variable to the change in the independent variable, which is the derivative in explicit form.

HIGHER DERIVATIVES

We have seen that a derivative is a function that is *derived* from another function. Since a derivative is also a function, it too should have a derivative. By using the derivative rules on a derivative function, we can produce the *second derivative* of the function. Literally, we find the derivative of a derivative. For example, in our discussion of cost functions, we specified a short-run total cost function as a third-degree polynomial, $C = a_0 + a_1 q + a_2 q^2 + a_3 q^3$, whose derivative is:

$$\frac{dC}{dq} = a_1 + 2a_2 q + 3a_3 q^2$$

As we have seen, the derivative of the cost function is *marginal cost*, which measures the *rate of change* of cost with respect to output. The derivative of the marginal cost function measures the *rate of change* of marginal cost with respect to output:

$$\frac{dMC}{dq} = \frac{d^2 C}{dq^2} = 2a_2 + 6a_3 q$$

If $c < 0$ and $d > 0$, the slope of the marginal cost function is negative over the range $q < a_2/3a_3$ and positive over the range $q > a_2/3a_3$. By taking the derivative of a function a second time, we determine the rate of change of the slope of that function. As shown in the example above, the symbolism of the second derivative involves a superscript 2 before the dependent variable and after the independent variable. In some cases this convention leads to confusion between the second derivative and a quadratic function. In such cases it is prudent to use an alternative notation:

$$\frac{d^2[f(x)]}{dx^2} = \frac{d[f'(x)]}{dx} = f''(x)$$

Having taken the second derivative of a function, we can proceed to the third derivative:

$$\frac{d^3(a + bq + cq^2 + dq^3)}{dq^3} = \frac{d^2(b + 2cq + 3dq^2)}{dq^2}$$

$$= \frac{d(2c + 6dq)}{dq} = 6d$$

The third derivative indicates that the value of the second derivative changes at a constant rate, $6d$. In economics the second derivative plays a prominent role in the identification of minimum and maximum points of functions. (See Chapters 8 and 10.) However, applications of third and higher order derivatives are rare.

SUMMARY

We have covered a great deal of material in this chapter. We began by discussing tangent lines to nonlinear curves. The slopes of these tangent lines can be approximated by calculating the slopes of lines connecting points along the curve which converge on the point in question. We then formalized the definition of a limit as the value on which a function converges when the independent variable approaches some specified value. Next we combined the concept of a tangent with that of the limit to define the *derivative* of a function, such as $y = f(x)$, as:

$$\frac{dy}{dx} = f'(x) = \lim_{\Delta x \to 0} \frac{f(x + \Delta x) - f(x)}{\Delta x}$$

We next developed some useful rules for *differentiating* functions:

1. The *power function rule:* If $f(x) = cx^n$, where c and n are con-stants, then

   $$\frac{df(x)}{dx} = f'(x) = ncx^{n-1}$$

2. The *sum or difference of two functions:* If $f(x) = g(x) + h(x)$, then $f'(x) = g'(x) + h'(x)$. If $f(x) = g(x) - h(x)$, then $f'(x) = g'(x) - h'(x)$.

3. The *chain rule:* If $y = f(x)$, and $x = g(w)$, then

$$\frac{dy}{dw} = \frac{dy}{dx} \cdot \frac{dx}{dw} = f'(x)g'(w)$$

4. The *product rule:* If $f(x) = g(x)h(x)$, then

$$f'(x) = g(x)h'(x) + h(x)g'(x)$$

5. The *quotient rule:* If $f(x) = g(x)/h(x)$, then

$$\frac{df(x)}{dx} = \frac{g'(x)h(x) - h'(x)g(x)}{[h(x)]^2}$$

6. The *derivative of a logarithmic function:* If $y = f(x) = \log_e x = \ln x$, then

$$\frac{d \log_e x}{dx} = \frac{d \ln x}{dx} = \frac{1}{x}$$

For logarithmic functions with bases other than e:

$$\frac{d \log_a x}{dx} = \frac{1}{x \log_e a}$$

7. The *derivative of an exponential function:* If $y = f(x) = e^x$, then

$$\frac{dy}{dx} = \frac{de^x}{dx} = e^x$$

After developing the general rules of differentiation, we learned how to differentiate implicit functions. This involves treating the changes in variables as unknowns and designating these unknowns by inserting the letter d before the relevant variables. Then the derivative in question is obtained by solving for the change in the dependent variable with respect to the independent variable. For instance, if we have the implicit linear function $ax + by = c$, we implicitly differentiate this function by substituting dx for x and dy for y. Since the derivative of a constant is zero, we substitute 0 for c to obtain:

$$adx + bdy = 0$$

If we wish to obtain the derivative of y with respect to x (which is equivalent to stipulating x as the independent variable), we "solve" for dy/dx as:

$$\frac{dy}{dx} = \frac{-a}{b}$$

On the other hand, we could determine the impact of a change of y on x by solving for dx/dy:

$$\frac{dx}{dy} = \frac{-b}{a}$$

This symmetry in the derivatives of an implicit function points out one more characteristic of derivatives: when the inverse of a function is also a function, the derivative of that inverse function is the reciprocal of the derivative of the original function:

$$\frac{dx}{dy} = \frac{1}{dy/dx}$$

The chapter ended with a discussion of higher order derivatives. Since the derivative of a function is itself a function, it usually has a derivative itself. This second derivative has a standard notation:

$$\frac{d^2y}{dx^2} = \frac{df'(x)}{dx} = f''(x)$$

While it is possible to define *third* derivatives and even higher order derivatives, there are few economic applications of derivatives beyond the second order.

Although several economic examples were used in this chapter, we have by no means exhausted the relevance of differential calculus to economic discourse. The next chapter will provide more economic applications of derivatives.

PROBLEMS

Group I

1. Graph the function $y = \sqrt{x}$ from $x = 0$ to $x = 25$. Use straight lines to connect the point (9, 3) with the point (16, 4), and (9, 3) with (25, 5). Draw a tangent to the curve at point (9, 3).

2. Find the limit of $y = \sqrt{x}$ as x approaches 9. Explain your answer using the information from Problem 1 above.

3. Let $y = 100 - x^2$.
    a. Graph the function from $x = 0$ to $x = 10$.
    b. Use straight lines to connect the point (8, 36) with each of the following points: (4, 84), (5, 75), (7, 51).
    c. By computing $f(6)$, $f(7)$, $f(7.5)$, and $f(7.9)$, show that:

    $$\lim_{x \to 8} f(x) = 36$$

4. Let $y = \frac{x + 3}{x - 1}$.
    a. Graph the function from $x = 0$ to $x = 10$.
    b. By computing $f(2), f(1.5), f(1.1), f(0.9), f(0.5)$, and $f(0)$, verify that the $\lim_{x \to 1} f(x)$ does not exist.

5. Find each of the following limits.
   a. $\lim\limits_{x\to 2} (2 - x)$

   b. $\lim\limits_{x\to 2} (8 + \sqrt{8x})$

   c. $\lim\limits_{x\to 1} \dfrac{x^2 - 1}{x - 1}$

   d. $\lim\limits_{\Delta x\to 0} \dfrac{(x + \Delta x)^2 - x^2}{\Delta x}$

Group II

Find the first derivatives and the indicated values of the derivatives.

6. $y = f(x) = 9 + 6x$.
   Find $f'(0)$, $f'(2)$, $f'(12)$.

7. $y = f(x) = x^4$.
   Find $f'(-2)$, $f'(0)$, $f'(2)$, $f'(4)$.

8. $y = f(x) = 3 + 3x^2$.
   Find $f'(-3)$, $f'(1)$, $3f'(2)$, $6f'(3)$.

9. $y = f(x) = 12 + 0.8x - 0.2x^2 - x^3$.
   Find $f'(-1)$, $f'(2)$, $2f'(3)$.

10. $y = f(x) = \dfrac{2}{x^2}$.

11. $y = f(x) = 5\sqrt[3]{x}$.

12. $y = f(x) = 2x^2 - \dfrac{4}{x} + \sqrt{4x} - \sqrt[3]{x}$.

13. $y = f(x) = (2 + x)(3 - x)$.

14. $y = f(x) = (3x + 2)(2x^2 - 2x)$.
    Find $f'(-4)$, $f'(0)$, $f'(1)$, $f'(3)$.

15. $y = f(x) = \dfrac{x - 2}{x^2 + 4}$.
    Find $f'(-3)$, $f'(0)$, $f'(2)$.

16. $y = f(x) = 3(x^2 - 8x + 3)^2$.

17. $y = f(x) = \sqrt{x + 7}$.

18. $y = f(x) = \left(\dfrac{x - 1}{x + 4}\right)^3$.
    Find $f'(-2)$, $f'(0)$, $f'(2)$.

19. $y = f(x) = 326 \log_e x$.

20. $y = f(x) = 3 \log_e x - \tfrac{3}{4} \log_e x$.

21. $y = f(x) = 2 \log_e(2x^2 - 3x + 4)$.

22. $y = f(x) = 6e^x$.
     Find $f'(-1), f'(0), f'(1), f'(2)$.

23. $y = f(x) = (x^2 - 2e^x)^{1/2}$.

Find the second derivatives.

24. $y = f(x) = 8x + 3x^2 - 13$.
     Plot the graphs of the functions $f(x), f'(x)$, and $f''(x)$ from $x = -3$
     to $x = 3$.

25. $y = f(x) = e^x + x^2 - (2x - 4)^2$.

26. $y = f(x) = \frac{x}{3} + 4\sqrt{x} - (x - 3)^2(x^2 + 2)$.

27. $y = f(x) = 2 \log_e(x^2 + 4x) - \left(\frac{x - 2}{x + 3}\right)^2$.

Group III

Find the first derivatives and indicated values of the derivatives.

28. $y = f(x) = x^4 - 2x^3 + 3x^2 - 5x + x^{-1} - x^{-2} + 24$.
     Find $f'(-3), f'(0), f'(3)$.

29. $y = f(x) = (3x + 2\sqrt{x})(x^2 + 4)$.
     Find $f'(-2), f'(2)$.

30. $y = f(x) = (x^2 + 6x)^{-1/2}$.

31. $y = f(x) = \frac{x^2 + x - 10}{3x^3 + 2x^2 - 10}$.

32. $y = f(x) = \frac{(x^2 + 7)}{\sqrt{x} + \sqrt[3]{x}}$.

33. $y = f(x) = 4\left(\frac{x^2 + 3x}{3x + 1}\right)^2 - 2(3x^2 + x - 9)^3$.

34. $y = f)x) = (2x - x^2)^{-2} + 4(\sqrt{x} - 9)^2$.

35. $y = f(x) = 3 \log_e\left(\frac{x + 1}{x - 3}\right) + 2 \log_e(x^2 + 2)^2$.

36. $y = f(x) = 2e^x - \log_e(2 - x^2)^2 + \left(\frac{2x - 4e^x}{e^x + 1}\right)^2$.

Find the second derivatives and the indicated values of the derivatives.

37. $y = f(x) = 2x^3 - 4x^2 + 3x - 8$.
     Plot the graphs of the functions $f(x), f'(x)$, and $f''(x)$ from $x = 0$ to
     $x = 5$.

38. $y = f(x) = 3x^2 + 8x - 14$.

Plot the graphs of the functions $f(x)$, $f'(x)$, and $f''(x)$ from $x = -3$ to $x = 4$.

39. $y = f(x) = \log_e(5x^3 + x^2 - 4x + 7)^2$.

40. $22 + y^2 - 4x^2 - 2x = 0$.

41. $x - \sqrt[3]{y} - 7 = 0$.

42. $xy + 4y - 2x - 3 = 0$.

Find the third derivatives of the following functions.

43. $y = f(x) = (x^3 - 9x^2 + 8x - 6)^2$.

44. $y = f(x) = 2x^3 - 3x^2 + 3x + 4$.

7

Economic

Applications of

Derivatives

In Chapter 6 we encountered several economic applications of derivatives. How changes in the rate of output affect profit, cost, and revenue are some examples. Practically all decisions in economics involve marginal considerations. How does a change in a variable under our control (or the control of economic agents being studied) influence the variable representing our (or someone else's) goal? Should the firm's rate of output be increased and would profit increase or decrease as a result? How does a change in the relative price of labor affect the optimal combination of labor and capital? As real income rises, what happens to consumer spending?

Chapter 3 shows how a relationship between two or more economic variables can be expressed as a function given by some equation. In this chapter, we shall show that differentiating a function of one variable with respect to the independent variable yields a *marginal* function. In Chapter 10 we will extend the concept of the derivative to functions with two or more independent variables.

ELASTICITY OF DEMAND AND SUPPLY

There are a few notions in economic theory that are expressed as *laws*. Laws are theories that are believed so strongly that few, if any, exceptions are acknowledged. One of these is the *law of demand*: when the price of a good changes, the quantity of that good consumers wish to purchase will change in the opposite direction, *ceteris paribus*. Yet while the law of demand is clear about how a change in price influences quantity demanded, it is ambiguous about how a change in price affects *expenditure* on a good. If price rises (declines) and quantity purchased falls (rises), the product of price times quantity might increase, decrease, or remain unchanged. The concept of *price elasticity of demand* is used by economists to explain how a change in price influences expenditure.

Elasticity of Demand

With our knowledge of derivatives, we can directly relate the change in price to a change in *price times quantity*, that is, expenditure. Recall that the derivative of a product of two functions with respect to the independent variables in those functions equals the sum of each function times the derivative of the other function. Hence, letting $q = f(p)$, we define the expenditure function as $E = p \cdot q = p[f(p)]$. The change in the expenditure, E, with respect to price, p, is given by:

$$\frac{dE}{dp} = \frac{d(qp)}{dp} = q\frac{dp}{dp} + p\frac{dq}{dp}$$

Since $dp/dp = 1$, the derivative simplifies to:

$$\frac{dE}{dp} = q + p\frac{dq}{dp}$$

By factoring q out of both expressions, we obtain the relationship we seek:

$$\frac{dE}{dp} = \frac{d(qp)}{dp} = q\left(1 + \frac{dq/q}{dp/p}\right) = q(1 + \eta)$$

where the Greek letter η ("eta") is the price elasticity of demand. That is, η = percent change in quantity divided by percent change in price:

$$\eta = \frac{dq/q}{dp/p}$$

where dq/q is the percentage change in quantity demanded and dp/p is the percentage change in price.

The change in expenditure due to a price change is equal to quantity times 1 plus eta, the price elasticity of demand. If $q = 0$, a price increase would have no effect on expenditure. The household wasn't buying the product at a lower price, so it does not spend anything on the commodity at the higher price. If $q > 0$, the impact of a price change on expenditure depends on the value of η. Because of the law of demand, we know that

η is a negative number[1], since $\eta = (dq/dp)(p/q)$. If $\eta < -1$ ($|\eta| > 1$), the percentage change in quantity demanded outweighs the percentage change in price, and expenditure moves in the opposite direction of price. That is, $\eta < -1$ implies $d(pq)/dq < 0$ and demand is *price elastic*. If $0 > \eta > -1$ ($|\eta| < 1$), the percentage change in price outweighs the precentage change in quantity, and expenditure moves in the same direction as price. That is, $0 > \eta > -1$ implies $d(pq)/dp > 0$ and demand is *price inelastic*. Finally, when $\eta = -1$ ($|\eta| = 1$), the percentage change in price is exactly balanced by the change in quantity, and expenditure does not change. That is, $\eta = -1$ implies $d(pq)/dp = 0$ and demand is *unit elastic*.

We have noted that the *mathematical form* of a function usually must be chosen by an econometrician prior to its estimation. Hence, it is important to note how alternative specifications of the demand function affect the elasticity of demand. The simplest demand curve to draw and to estimate is the *linear* demand function with the form:

$$q_d = a - bp$$

As we saw in Chapter 3, changes in the exogenous variables for a linear demand function change the intercept term, a, but not the slope term, b, of the *ceteris paribus* demand curve. As we learned in Chapter 6, the derivative of a linear function is a constant, in this case, $dq/dp = -b$. Multiplying this slope term by the ratio of price to quantity demanded, we find the formula for the price elasticity of demand:

$$\eta = \frac{dq}{dp} \cdot \frac{p}{q} = -b \cdot \frac{p}{q} = \frac{-bp}{a - bp}$$

Note that a linear demand curve has a constant slope ($dq/dp = -b$) and has an elasticity that ranges from $-\infty$, (when $p = a/b$) to 0 (when $p = 0$). Indeed, at the midpoint of the demand curve (where $p = a/2b$, $q = a/2$), price elasticity is unity:

$$\eta = -b \cdot \frac{a/2b}{a/2} = -b \cdot \frac{1}{b} = -1$$

The ranges for the elasticity of demand along a linear demand curve are shown in Figure 7.1.

An alternate specification of the demand function often encountered in empirical work is the *power function* of the form $q_d = ap^{-b}$, where a and b are estimated parameters. Unlike the linear demand function whose graph is a straight line, the graph of the power demand function has a different slope at each price.

$$\frac{dq_d}{dp} = \frac{d(ap^{-b})}{dp} = -bap^{-b-1}$$

[1]A number of economics texts define price elasticity as a positive number by multiplying $(dq/q)/(dp/p)$ by -1. Letting $\epsilon = -(dq/q)/(dp/p)$, we have $d(pq)/dp = q(1 - \epsilon)$.

Figure 7.1

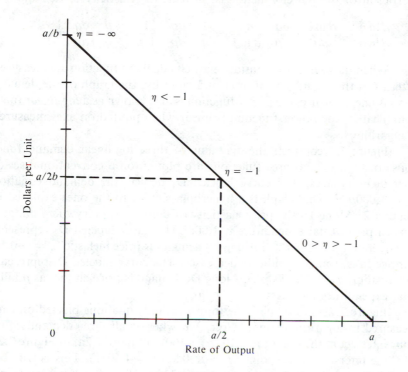

Although a power demand function has a different derivative at each price, it has a constant elasticity. This can be verified by substituting the formula for the derivative into the formula for price elasticity:

$$\eta = \frac{dq}{dp} \cdot \frac{p}{q} = -bap^{-b-1} \cdot \frac{p}{q} = -b \cdot \frac{ap^{-b}p^{-1}p}{ap^{-b}} = -b$$

For this reason the power demand function is also called a *constant elasticity demand function*.

If we transform the constant elasticity demand function into natural logarithms, we have:

$$\log_e(q_d) = \log_e(ap^{-b}) = \log_e a - b(\log_e p)$$

Treating the natural logarithm of q_d as the dependent variable and the natural logarithm of price as the independent variable, we have:

$$\frac{d\ln q}{d\ln p} = -b$$

By applying the chain rule to the left side of this equation, we find that the coefficient of the power function is, in fact, the elasticity of demand:

$$\frac{d\ln q}{d\ln p} = \frac{d\ln q}{dq} \cdot \frac{dq}{dp} \cdot \frac{dp}{d\ln p} = \frac{1}{q} \cdot \frac{dq}{dp} \cdot \frac{1}{1/p} = \frac{p}{q} \cdot \frac{dq}{dp} = \eta$$

When the axes of the constant elasticity demand function are measured in terms of the logarithms of price and quantity, the graph of the demand curve is linear. Hence, the power function is also known as a *log-linear* function. That is, the power function is linear when plotted on axes measured in logarithms.

Figure 7.2 contrasts the diagrams of three log-linear demand functions. In Figure 7.2a three functions are plotted on a conventional set of price-quantity axes. The curve labeled D_1 depicts the demand equation $q_d = 1,000p^{-1}$. This graph is a hyperbola similar to the ones explored in Chapter 2. Along D_1 the price elasticity of demand is everywhere unitary; at each price, total expenditure is 1,000. The curve labeled D_2 represents the equation $q_d = 100p^{-0.5}$. Along D_2 demand is price inelastic ($\eta = -0.5$); as price falls, total expenditure decreases. The curve labeled D_3 represents the equation $q_d = 100,000p^{-2}$. Along D_3 demand is price elastic; as p falls, total expenditure increases.

Figure 7.2b shows the same three demand equations plotted on axes measured in logarithmic units. Note that whereas all three demand equations intersect at the point ($q = 10$, $p = 100$) in Figure 7.2a, in Figure 7.2b all three intersect at the point ($q = 2.3026$, $p = 4.6051$). This is true because $2.3026 = \log_e(10)$ and $\log_e(100) = 2\log_e(10) = 4.6051$. Line D_1 reflects the equation $\log_e q_d = 6.908 - \log_e p$, line D_2 reflects the equation $\log_e q_d = 4.605 - 0.5\log_e p$, and line D_3 is generated by the equation $\log_e q_d = 9.210 - 2\log_e p$. As expected, all three graphs of the log-linear demand functions are indeed straight lines.

Elasticity of Supply

The concept of the elasticity of supply is analogous to the concept of the elasticity of demand. Elasticity of supply measures the percentage change in *quantity supplied* due to a one percent increase in the price, *exogenous variables remaining constant*. The procedure of generating the elasticity of supply using the derivative is quite similar to the procedure we used to derive the elasticity of demand. However, while the elasticity of demand is a *negative* number, the elasticity of supply is a *positive* number. Unlike the ambiguity that surrounds the impact of a price change on consumer expenditure along the same demand curve, there is no ambiguity about the relationship between a price change and revenue change along a given supply curve. Quantity *supplied* changes in the *same* direction as price, so price times quantity supplied moves in the same direction as price.

Figure 7.2a

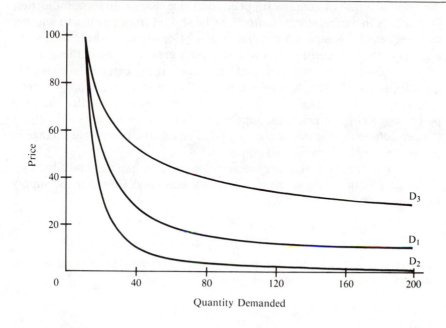

Figure 7.2b

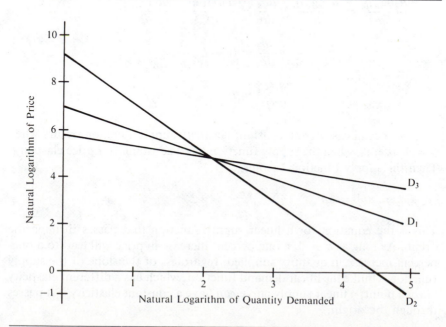

Price elasticity of supply is generally used by economists to measure the responsiveness of quantity supplied to a price change. In some industries, particularly in agriculture, resources can be shifted from one use to another relatively easily. Hence, an increase in the price of, say, wheat relative to another crop (e.g., corn) will cause a relatively great increase in the quantity of wheat planted and later delivered to market. If the percentage change in quantity supplied exceeds the percentage change in price, supply is *price elastic*. If the percentage change in quantity supplied is smaller than the percentage change in price, the supply function is *price inelastic*. Finally, if the percentage change in quantity supplied equals the percentage change in price, the supply curve is *unit elastic*.

Supply functions that are linear in logarithms, like demand functions with that functional form, have a constant elasticity. Consider the supply function:

$$q_s = ap^b$$

where q_s is quantity supplied, p is price, and a and b are positive constants. The function can be written:

$$\log_e q_s = \log_e a + b \log_e p$$

Differentiating both sides of this equation with respect to p:

$$\frac{d \log_e q_s}{dp} = \frac{d \log_e q_s}{dq_s} \cdot \frac{dq_s}{dp} = \frac{d \log_e a}{dp} + \frac{bd \log_e p}{dp}$$

$$\frac{1}{q_s} \cdot \frac{dq_s}{dp} = 0 + b \cdot \frac{1}{p}$$

$$\frac{dq_s/q_s}{dp/p} = b$$

A special case of the constant elasticity supply function occurs when $b = 1$; that is, when the supply function has a constant *unit* price elasticity. Then the supply function becomes:

$$q_s = ap^1 = ap$$

This is the equation for a linear supply function that passes through the origin. As long as $a > 0$, a one-percent increase in price will lead to a one-percent increase in quantity supplied, regardless of the slope of the supply function. Unlike the linear demand function, which has a different elasticity at each point, a linear supply curve *can* have a constant elasticity if it passes through the origin.

More generally, a linear supply function has an equation of the form $q_s = a + bp$, where $b > 0$ and a can be positive, negative, or, of course, zero. Since $dq_s/dp = b$, the elasticity of supply, ϵ, is given by:

$$\epsilon = b \cdot \frac{p}{q_s} = \frac{bp}{a + bp}$$

When $a > 0$ (the supply function intersects the quantity axis to the right of the origin), the linear supply function is everywhere *price inelastic*. When $a < 0$ (the supply function intersects the price axis above the origin), the linear supply function is everywhere *price elastic*. And, as we have already demonstrated, when $a = 0$, $\epsilon = (bp/bp) = 1$ and the supply function is everywhere *unit elastic*.

Figure 7.3 contrasts the elasticity characteristics of linear and power specifications of supply functions. Three linear supply functions are depicted in Figure 7.3a. Supply function S_1, which passes through the origin, has a unit supply elasticity. Supply function S_2, which intersects the quantity axis ($a > 0$), is price inelastic. Supply curve S_3, which intersects the price axis ($a < 0$), is price elastic.

Figure 7.3a

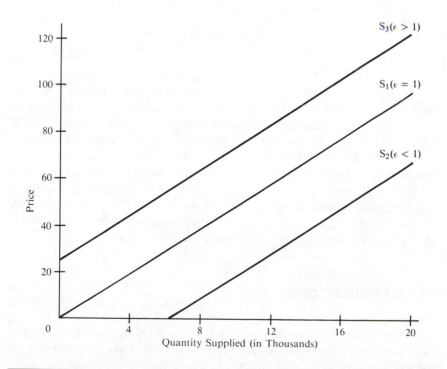

Figure 7.3b

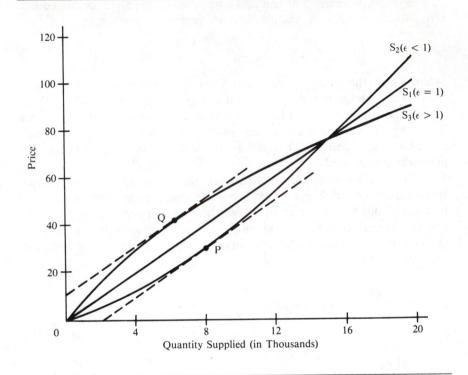

Figure 7.3b presents three power functions. Supply curve S_1 is a linear function passing through the origin. As in Figure 7.3a, this function has a constant unit price elasticity. Supply curve S_2 is everywhere price inelastic. Note that the tangent line drawn at any point (such as P on S_2) intersects the quantity axis to the right of the origin. Since the tangent and the curve have the same slope at their common point (P), they have the same elasticity at that point. Supply curve S_2 exhibits an inelastic response of quantity supplied to price. Supply curve S_3 is everywhere price elastic. Any tangent line (such as at point Q on S_3) intersects the price axis above the origin, indicating the supply curve is everywhere price elastic.

MARGINAL COST

The total cost of production for a single firm can be expressed as a function of output. We introduced marginal cost in the previous chapter when demonstrating the addition rule of the derivative. Expressing total cost as the sum of fixed cost and variable cost, it follows that marginal cost, which is the derivative of total cost with respect to output, equals the sum of the derivative of fixed cost with respect to output plus the derivative of variable cost with respect to output:

$$MC = \frac{dTC}{dq} = \frac{dFC}{dq} + \frac{dVC}{dq} = \frac{dVC}{dq}$$

Often econometricians estimate total cost as a polynomial function of the form:

$$C = a_0 + a_1 q + a_2 q^2 + a_3 q^3$$

It is possible that the total cost function could be a polynomial of degree greater than three, but a cubic equation captures the interesting theoretical and econometric features of a short-run total cost. (A long-run total cost function could be generated by specifying that $a_0 = 0$.) If $a_2 = 0$ and $a_3 = 0$, then the short-run cost function is linear, so that marginal cost is a constant function parallel to the quantity axis:

$$MC = \frac{d(a_0 + a_1 q)}{dq} = a_1$$

Since marginal cost cannot be negative, the econometrician must check that $a_1 > 0$.

If $a_3 = 0$ but $a_2 \neq 0$, the total cost function is a quadratic equation, $C = a_0 + a_1 q + a_2 q^2$. Since the derivative of a quadratic function is linear, we have:

$$MC = \frac{dC}{dq} = a_1 + 2a_2 q$$

The coefficient a_1 is the intercept of the marginal cost curve and must be positive. Unless we are dealing with the unlikely case of a *natural monopoly*, the *law of diminishing returns* implies that marginal cost increases as output increases. Hence, a_2 must also be greater than zero.

Finally, if $a_3 > 0$, then it is possible that a_2 is a negative number, allowing the *slope* of the marginal cost curve to decrease at low rates of output. This phenomenon is known as *increasing returns to the variable factor* or *increasing marginal productivity* in microeconomics. First we have the marginal cost function, which is obtained by differentiating C with respect to q:

$$MC = \frac{d(a_0 + a_1 q + a_2 q^2 + a_3 q^3)}{dq} = a_1 + 2a_2 q + 3a_3 q^2$$

If marginal cost decreases (although remaining positive) over part of its range, the *second derivative* of the total cost function will be negative. We find the rate of change in marginal cost with respect to output as:

$$\frac{dMC}{dq} = 2a_2 + 6a_3 q$$

$dMC/dq < 0$ if $q < -a_2/3a_3$ and $dMC/dq > 0$ if $q > -a_2/3a_3$.

Another perspective on marginal cost involves the relationship between the price of a variable input and its marginal product. In Chapter 3 we showed how the supply curve of the competitive firm, derived from the firm's marginal cost curve, would shift with changes in the price of the variable input. Using the concept of the derivative, this relationship can be shown more directly by relating both the change in cost and the change in output to the variable input, say labor:

$$MC = \frac{dC}{dq} = \frac{dC/dL}{dq/dL} = \frac{w}{MP_L}$$

where w is the wage rate (the price of labor services) and MP_L is the marginal product of labor. It follows that the change in marginal cost due to a change in output is equal to the derivative of w/MP_L with respect to output. Making use of the chain rule:

$$\frac{dMC}{dq} = \frac{d(w/MP_L)}{dq} = \frac{d(w/MP_L)}{dL} \cdot \frac{dL}{dq}$$

$$= \frac{MP_L(dw/dL) - w(dMP_L/dL)}{[MP_L]^2} \cdot \frac{dL}{dq}$$

Economic efficiency requires that $dL/dq > 0$. If output is to increase, variable factor services must increase (otherwise, productive potential had been wasted at the lower rate of output). Since $[MP_L]^2$ must be positive, the sign of dMC/dq is determined by the numerator of the first term. When labor is hired under contract or through a competitive market, $dw/dL = 0$, so that the change in the marginal cost with respect to output is governed by the change in the marginal product of labor with respect to the amount of labor hired. Once fixed inputs are used to capacity, the marginal product of labor decreases as output increases. Over this same range of output, marginal cost increases as output increases.

MARGINAL REVENUE

In Chapter 6 we developed several rules of differentiation with the use of marginal revenue as an example. Nevertheless, it is useful to review the various features of the marginal revenue function now that you have gained more familiarity with derivatives. Recall that the firm's *average revenue* function is generated as an *inverse demand* function. That is, quantity is the causal variable and price is the dependent variable:

$$R(Q) = pQ$$

To obtain marginal revenue we take the derivative of $R(Q)$ with respect to Q. Because R is a function generated as the product of two other functions, the marginal revenue function is generated by the product rule of differentiation:

$$\frac{dR}{dQ} = p\frac{dQ}{dQ} + Q\frac{dp}{dQ}$$

For the perfectly competitive firm, price is invariant with respect to output ($dp/dQ = 0$), and since $dQ/dQ = 1$, marginal revenue equals price: $d(pQ)/dQ = p$. The marginal revenue curve of the purely competitive firm is a horizontal line. If the firm were imperfectly competitive, it is assumed to charge the market-clearing price for each rate of output it produces. In order to sell additional output, price must be reduced: $dp/dQ < 0$. In this case, the firm deducts revenue lost from inframarginal sales ($Q[dp/dQ]$) from the revenue received for the last unit (p). Under imperfect competition, $MR < p$.

Now consider another insight: the greater the responsiveness of quantity demanded to a price change, the smaller would be the required price decrease necessary to sell an extra unit of output. Intuitively, marginal revenue should be inversely related to the elasticity of demand. Considering the beating our intuition took developing the rules of differentiation, let us verify our hunch mathematically. Given the marginal revenue function, we can factor the p out of the expression and obtain:

$$MR = p\left(1 + \frac{Q}{p} \cdot \frac{dp}{dQ}\right) = p\left(1 + \frac{1}{\eta}\right)$$

where η is the *price elasticity of demand*. If $\eta < -1$, $1/\eta > -1$ and $dR/dQ > 0$. Thus, when demand is price elastic, marginal revenue is positive. If $0 > \eta > -1$, then $1/\eta < -1$ and $dR/dQ < 0$. Thus, when demand is price inelastic, marginal revenue is negative. Finally, when $\eta = -1$, $1/\eta = -1$ and $dR/dQ = 0$. Thus, when demand is unit elastic, marginal revenue is zero.

If the average revenue (inverse demand) function is linear, the marginal revenue function is also linear, having twice the slope as the former. For instance, if the demand function for a monopolist's product is $Q_d = a - bp$, we solve for p in terms of Q to get the monopolist's average revenue function:

$$p = \frac{a}{b} - \frac{1}{b} \cdot Q = \alpha - \beta Q$$

The monopolist's total revenue function is given as:

$$R = pQ = (\alpha - \beta Q)Q = \alpha Q - \beta Q^2$$

Taking the derivative of R with respect to Q, we have:

$$MR = \frac{dR}{dQ} = \alpha - 2\beta Q$$

In Figure 7.4a we see that the marginal revenue function has the same intercept as the linear average revenue function, with MR declining at twice the rate at which AR declines. The rate of output where MR crosses the quantity axis corresponds to the midpoint of the linear average revenue curve. When $\eta = -1$ (at $Q = \alpha/2\beta = a/2$), the value of marginal revenue is zero.

Figure 7.4b shows the average revenue function corresponding to the constant elasticity demand function $Q = 64p^{-2}$. Solving for p in terms of Q to obtain the average revenue function, we have:

$$p^2 = \frac{64}{Q}$$

implying

$$p = \frac{8}{\sqrt{Q}}$$

Multiplying through by Q to get the total revenue function:

$$R = 8Q^{0.5}$$

implying

$$MR = 8(0.5)Q^{-0.5} = 4Q^{-0.5}$$

At each rate of output, the ratio of marginal revenue to price is a constant:

$$\frac{MR}{p} = \frac{4Q^{-0.5}}{8Q^{-0.5}} = \frac{1}{2}$$

This could have also been determined by noting that $\eta = -2$ at every quantity:

$$MR = p\left(1 + \frac{1}{\eta}\right) = p\left(1 - \frac{1}{2}\right) = \frac{p}{2}$$

THE MARGINAL PROPENSITIES
TO CONSUME AND SAVE

When studying the determination of aggregate variables in macroeconomics, an important relationship is encountered between total consumer spending and national income, given by the *consumption function*. The law of consumption says that as income increases (or decreases), a typical household's consumption spending tends to increase (or decrease), but by a slightly smaller magnitude. The *marginal propensity to consume*, which is the derivative of the consumption function with respect to income, is greater than zero but less than one. Empirical estimates, which are explored in more detail in Part III of this book, place the aggregate marginal propensity to consume at about 0.92 in terms of *disposable personal income* and equal to about 0.75 in terms of *national income*.

Figure 7.4a

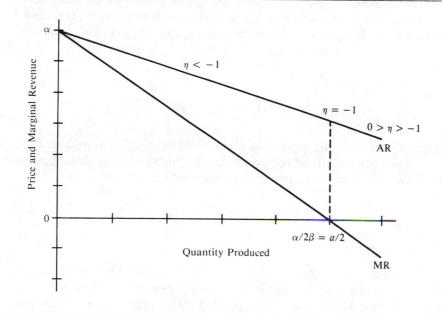

Figure 7.4b

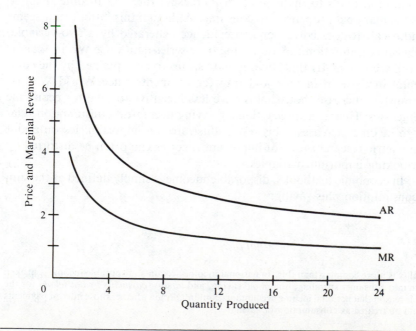

As we have said, the results of empirical estimates are often the predictable consequence of the type of functional form chosen by the econometrician doing the estimation. Hence, if aggregate consumption, C, is assumed to be a linear function of national income, Y, then the marginal propensity to consume will be a constant:

$$C = a + bY$$

$$\frac{dC}{dY} = b, \text{ where } 0 < b < 1$$

Alternatively, the consumption function might be specified as a power function, again because of the relative ease with which *log-linear* equations can be estimated empirically. In this case we would have:

$$C = aY^b$$

$$\frac{dC}{dY} = baY^{b-1}$$

In the case of the *log-linear* consumption function, the econometrician could test the hypothesis of a constant marginal propensity to consume directly. If $b \approx 1$, then the hypothesis of a constant marginal propensity to consume would be sustained, and the marginal propensity to consume would be approximately equal to the coefficient, a. However, if $b < 1$, then consumption tends to increase at a decreasing rate with income. As income increases, the marginal propensity to consume decreases. Alternatively, if $b > 1$, then consumption tends to increase at an increasing rate. As income rises, so does the marginal propensity to consume. Although this latter result seems paradoxical, it does correspond to evidence generated by a two-variable, log-linear consumption function using time-series data since World War II. We will see in Part III that this anomaly seems to be explained by the coincidental increase in income and transfer payments since World War II. As transfers increase, households have less incentive to save for economic emergencies. Hence, as precautionary saving decreases, consumption relative to income increases. This result illustrates an important lesson about econometric research: tests of important theories can often be distorted by overlooking important variables.

In economic textbooks, disposable income is simply defined as the sum of consumption plus saving:[2]

$$Y_d = C + S$$

---

[2]Reality is more complex than this. In national income accounts, disposable income is broken down into consumer spending, household saving, and *interest payments by household* for the simple reason that national income accountants couldn't decide whether those interest payments should be treated as consumption or saving!

Taking the derivative of this equation with respect to Y_d, we find:

$$\frac{dY_d}{dY_d} = \frac{dC}{dY_d} + \frac{dS}{dY_d}$$

or

$$\text{MPC} + \text{MPS} = 1$$

where MPC is the *marginal propensity to consume* and MPS is the *marginal propensity to save*. If econometric evidence has already shown that the marginal propensity to consume is 0.92, we infer that the marginal propensity to save is 0.08.

If the consumption function is nonlinear, the saving function will also be nonlinear. Suppose that:

$$C = 10 + 5\sqrt{Y} = 10 + 5Y^{1/2}$$

The marginal propensity to consume is the derivative of C with respect to Y:

$$\frac{dC}{dY} = \tfrac{5}{2}Y^{-1/2} = \frac{5}{2\sqrt{Y}}$$

Since the marginal propensity to save is $1 - \text{MPC}$, it follows that:

$$\frac{dS}{dY} = 1 - \frac{5}{2\sqrt{Y}}$$

We can verify this by first calculating the saving function from the definition, then taking the derivative of S with respect to Y:

$$S = Y - C = Y - (10 + 5\sqrt{Y}) = -10 + Y - 5\sqrt{Y}$$

$$\frac{dS}{dY} = \frac{d(-10)}{dY} + \frac{dY}{dY} - \frac{d(5\sqrt{Y})}{dY}$$

$$\frac{dS}{dY} = 0 + 1 - \tfrac{5}{2}Y^{-1/2} = 1 - \frac{5}{2\sqrt{Y}}$$

SUMMARY

This chapter has presented additional applications of the derivative in economic analysis. This mathematical tool has much wider use than we have presented here. Many of the functions that economists study are derivatives, and estimates of the rate of change of one economic variable with respect to another may be obtained either through direct estimation of those functions or by applying the rules of differentiation to other econometric functions. In the next chapter we will study another important use of the calculus of functions of one independent variable: the solution to optimization problems.

PROBLEMS

Group I

1. Assume that the aggregate consumption function for the economy as a whole is given as:

$$C = 30 + 16\sqrt{Y}$$

where C denotes total consumption and Y denotes national income.
   a. Find the marginal propensity to consume.
   b. Find the marginal propensity to save.
   c. Find the values of the marginal propensities to consume and save for $Y = 100$, $Y = 144$, $Y = 256$, and $Y = 400$.

2. The aggregate investment function for the economy as a whole is given as:

$$I = 200 - 10,000r^3$$

where I denotes total investment and r denotes the rate of interest. Compute the rate of change of investment with respect to the interest rate when $r = 0.03$, $r = 0.05$, and $r = 0.10$.

   Let q denote quantity demanded or supplied and let p denote the price of the commodity. Compute the price elasticity of demand or supply as indicated at the prices and quantities specified in Problems 3-6.

3. Demand equation: $q = 330 - 28p$. Compute elasticity when
   a. $p = 10$
   b. $p = 6$
   c. $p = 2$

4. Demand equation: $q = \dfrac{400}{p}$. Compute elasticity when
   a. $p = 10$
   b. $p = 5$

5. Supply equation: $q = 40 + 0.15p + p^{1/2}$. Compute elasticity when
   a. $p = 4$
   b. $p = 16$
   c. $p = 100$

6. Supply equation: $q = 5 + e^p$. Compute elasticity when
   a. $p = 1$
   b. $p = 2$
   c. $p = 3$

Group II

7. Using p and q to designate price and quantity, respectively, let the demand function for a commodity be:

$$q = a - b \log_e p$$

where a and b are positive constants. Find the price elasticity equation.

8. Again using p and q for price and quantity, respectively, let the supply function for a commodity be:

$$q = \frac{(10 + p)^2}{4 + p}$$

Find the price elasticity equation.

9. In the production function of a firm, a given (constant) output can be produced with varying amounts of labor and capital. The possible combinations of labor and capital (represented by l and c) that will produce the same output are specified by the equation:

$$\sqrt{l}\sqrt{c} - 100 = 0$$

Find the marginal rate of substitution of capital for labor (dc/dl) when $l = 100$, $l = 200$, and $l = 300$.

10. The total cost function of a firm is given as:

$$c = 800 + 12x + 0.018x^2$$

where c denotes total cost and x denotes the quantity produced per unit of time.
a. Graph the total cost function from $x = 0$ to $x = 100$.
b. Find the marginal cost function.
c. Find the marginal cost of production from $x = 0$ to $x = 100$.

11. The total cost of production of a firm is given as:

$$c = 2{,}000 + 10x - 0.02x^2 + 0.001x^3$$

where c denotes total cost and x denotes the quantity produced per unit of time.
a. Graph the total cost function from $x = 0$ to $x = 200$.
b. Find the marginal cost function.
c. Find the average cost function.
d. Graph in the same diagram the average and marginal costs of production from $x = 0$ to $x = 200$.

12.   The market demand function for a commodity X is given as:

$$x = 300 - 30\sqrt{p}$$

where x denotes the quantity of X demanded and p its price.

a. Find the average revenue function (i.e., price as a function of quantity).

b. Find the marginal revenue function for a monopolist who produces x.

c. Graph the average revenue curve and the marginal revenue curve from $x = 1$ to $x = 100$.

8

Maxima and

Minima of

Functions of

One Variable

One of the most fundamental assumptions of economic theory is the assumption of optimizing behavior—that economic agents attempt to maximize benefits and minimize opportunity cost. Since the optimization assumption provides insights into more complex motives, most economists do not worry if the assumption is not literally true. Once models based on optimizing assumptions have been constructed, departures from such behavior can be diagnosed and, where appropriate, recommendations can be made. Many practicing economists earn their livings advising business firms and government agencies. They apply theories of efficiency to bring the "real world" closer to the ideal hypothesized in economic theory. Hence, our theories of maximizing profit or minimizing costs help us earn a living precisely because these goals are only partly achieved without the economist's help.

If you have completed a course in microeconomics, you are already familiar with a number of maximization or minimization theories. The typical household is assumed to pick that combination of commodities which maximizes utility, consistent with the limitations of available income and wealth. The theory of market demand is then derived from the model of utility maximization. The producer is assumed to pick that combination of input services which minimizes the cost of producing a given rate of output, or equivalently, maximizes the rate of output for a specified cost. The economist assumes that managers attempt to produce the target rate of output at minimum opportunity cost. The firm's cost function is defined by relating the cost of the efficient combination of inputs to each respective rate of output. A competitive firm is depicted as maximizing its profit, the difference between total revenue and the opportunity cost of inputs. The assumption of profit maximization gives rise to the market supply curve. In short, economic models based on assumptions of optimizing behavior enable the economist to make testable predictions about economic events.

When objectives to be maximized or minimized can be expressed as mathematical functions, theories of optimizing behavior involve mathematical techniques for discovering maxima or minima for those functions. For theories involving two variables, economic relationships can be easily graphed. In these cases, the maximum or the minimum point on a curve can be found by investigating the *slope* of the function. A positive slope means the function is still increasing at the point in question. The maximum value of the function would exist at a greater value of the independent variable, and a minimum would exist at a smaller value of the independent variable. If the slope of the function is negative, the function is getting smaller as the independent variable gets larger. A maximum value of the function would be found by reducing the value of the independent variable, and a minimum by increasing the value of the independent variable. If the function has a maximum or a minimum, it will occur where the function has a slope (the first derivative) of zero. A maximum occurs when the slope of the function is positive to the left of the point, zero at the point, and negative to the right of the point. This is equivalent to saying that at a maximum the *first derivative* is zero and the *second derivative* is negative. A minimum occurs when the slope of the function goes from negative, to zero, to positive, implying that the *second derivative* is positive at a minimum.

PROFIT MAXIMIZATION UNDER PERFECT COMPETITION

We begin our formal investigation of the mathematics of maxima and minima with a familiar example from economics. A competitive producer has a profit function given by:

$$\pi(q) = pq - C(q)$$

This is the mathematical expression of the definition of economic profit as total revenue minus total cost. Since output is the only variable under the firm's control, profit is depicted as a function of one variable. When the rate of output is determined, so are total revenue (price times quantity) and total cost. Hence, the *change* in profit equals the change in revenue minus the change in cost:

$$\frac{d\pi}{dq} = \frac{d(pq)}{dq} - \frac{dC}{dq} = p - MC$$

The competitive firm's profit increases as long as $d\pi/dq > 0$. In that case, another unit of output adds more to revenue than to cost ($dTR/dq > dC/dq$; $p > MC$). Profit decreases as output increases if price (marginal revenue) is less than marginal cost. Therefore, the optimal rate of output occurs where marginal cost equals marginal revenue. *Maximizing* profit requires expanding output as long as profit is increasing, cutting output if profit is decreasing, and maintaining that rate of output where profit is neither increasing nor decreasing. Profit is maximized at the rate of output where the profit function has a slope of zero.

The Graphical Approach to
Maxima and Minima

Figure 8.1 presents the total revenue and total cost functions for a competitive firm, along with the profit function. The profit function is generated by plotting the distance between the total revenue function, TR, and the total cost function, TC. Since the firm faces fixed costs in the short run, the total

Figure 8.1

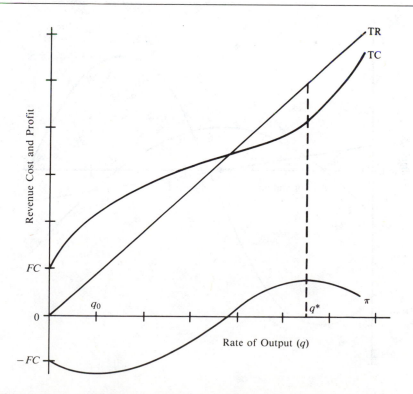

cost curve emanates from *FC* on the vertical axis. The profit function begins below the horizontal axis; if nothing is produced, the firm loses fixed costs and $\pi(0) = -FC$. If total cost initially rises faster than total revenue, losses actually increase (profit declines) for the first few units of output. However, after reaching its minimum (at q_0 in Figure 8.1), profit increases with output until it achieves its maximum at q^*. For $q > q^*$, profit declines with output, since the total cost curve is rising faster than the total revenue line.

Figure 8.2 presents the profit function shown in Figure 8.1, along with the first and second derivatives of that profit function. As in Figure 8.1, the profit function in Figure 8.2 begins at the point $\pi = -FC$ when $q = 0$. For the first few units of output, profit falls with output. The slope of the profit function is negative. At q_0, the profit function "bottoms out." For $q < q_0$, profit falls as output increases. For $q > q_0$, profit rises with output. At q_0, profit is neither increasing nor decreasing; the function is at a *local minimum*. We refer to profit at q_0 as a *local* minimum. Profit reaches a minimum for points in the neighborhood of q_0, but that *local* minimum may not be a *global* minimum—the smallest value the function ever achieves.

Figure 8.2

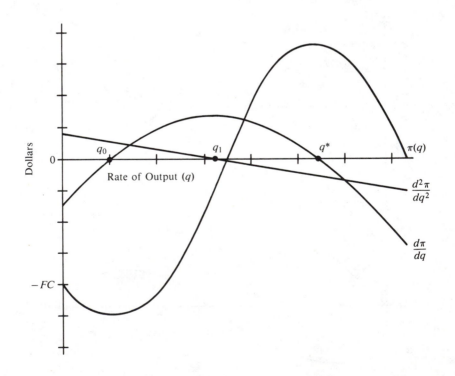

Note that the curve labeled $d\pi/dq$ intersects the quantity axis at q_0, implying $d\pi/dq = 0$. When a function is at a local minimum, its slope must be zero, because the function is neither increasing nor decreasing at that point. Also note that the line labeled $d^2\pi/dq^2$ lies above the quantity axis at q_0. To the left of q_0, profit decreases as output increases. At q_0, profit does not change with respect to output. To the right of q_0, profit increases as output increases. Because the slope goes from negative to zero to positive in the neighborhood of q_0, the second derivative of the profit function is positive.

Between q_0 and q_1, profit increases at an increasing rate. For this output range, both the first and second derivative functions lie above the quantity axis ($d\pi/dq > 0$ and $d^2\pi/dq^2 > 0$). At q_1, the second derivative equals zero, becoming negative for $q > q_1$. Between q_1 and q^*, the profit function increases at a decreasing rate ($d\pi/dq > 0$ and $d^2\pi/dq^2 < 0$). When $q = q^*$, the diagram of $\pi(q)$ achieves a point of zero slope and $\pi(q)$ decreases to the right of q^*. Note that the derivative $d\pi/dq$ is also equal to zero at q^* and that $d^2\pi/dq^2$ lies *below* the quantity axis ($d^2\pi/dq^2 < 0$). This point constitutes a *local maximum*. At q^*, the function attains its highest value in that neighborhood of points. Because the slope of the function is negative for all $q > q^*$, and because $\pi(q^*) > \pi(0)$, the *local maximum* at q^* is also the *global maximum*. At q^*, profit reaches its highest value for all possible rates of output.

Let's review. Geometrically, the local maximum and the local minimum of a function occur where the slope of the curve representing that function is zero. Whether the function is at a local maximum or a local minimum is determined by the *second* derivative. If the second derivative is positive, the function achieves a local minimum and if the second derivative is negative the function achieves a local maximum. We determine if a local minimum (or maximum) is a global minimum (or maximum) by comparing the value of the function at that critical point with the value of the function at the end points of its domain.

In Figure 8.3 we encounter a total revenue function that lies everywhere below the total cost function, generating a total profit function which lies everywhere below the quantity axis. This firm would experience economic losses at every conceivable rate of output. Furthermore, the local maximum at q^*, identified where $d\pi(q)/dq = 0$, and $d^2\pi(q)/dq^2 < 0$, is below the rate of profit associated with a zero rate of output. That is, $\pi(q^*) < \pi(0) = -FC$. Profit falls (losses increase) by such a great amount between $q = 0$ and $q = q_0$ that profit never returns to its initial value of negative fixed costs. In this case the function $\pi(q)$ has its *global maximum* at the "corner" of its domain, namely where $q = 0$ and $\pi = -FC$. This outcome is appropriately called a *corner solution* to the maximization problem.

Figure 8.4 provides a close-up view of the corner solution. Note that the local minimum at q_0 and the local maximum at q^* are again identified

Figure 8.3

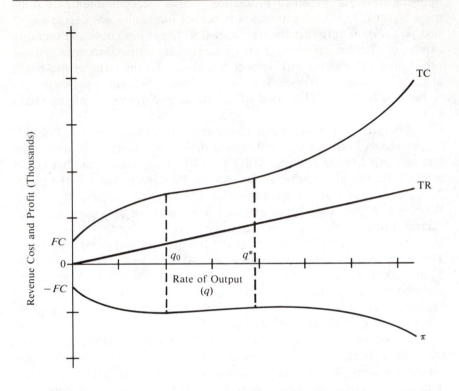

by the intersection of the first derivative function and the quantity axis. Furthermore, we note that the value of the second derivative function is positive at q_0 (implying a local minimum) and negative at q^* (implying a local maximum). As in Figure 8.2, the local minimum is not a global minimum because the profit function achieves lower values at higher rates of output. Furthermore, the local profit maximum at q^* is *not* a *global* maximum because $\pi(q^*) < -FC$. The function achieves its highest value at the *corner* $q = 0$.

A Numerical Illustration

Let's make this discussion more concrete by introducing a specific cost function:

$$C(q) = 200 + 160q - 20q^2 + q^3$$

Assume that $p = \$95$, making the profit function:

$$\pi(q) = 95q - (200 + 160q - 20q^2 + q^3)$$
$$= -200 - 65q + 20q^2 - q^3$$

Figure 8.4

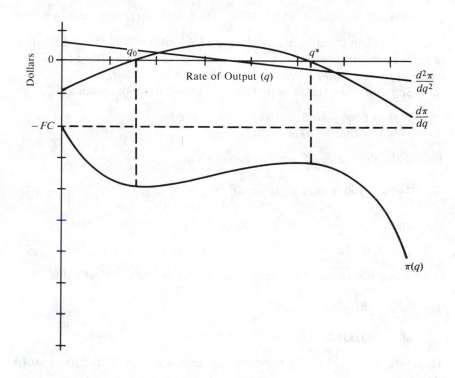

To identify the critical values of q we take the derivative of π with respect to q, set the result equal to zero and solve for q:

$$\frac{d\pi}{dq} = -65 + 40q - 3q^2 = 0$$

Using the quadratic formula (see Chapter 4), we find the critical values of q as:

$$q = \frac{-40 \pm \sqrt{1,600 - 780}}{-6} = 1.89, \ 11.44$$

Calculating the second derivative of π with respect to q at the two critical values yields:

$$\frac{d^2\pi}{dq^2} = 40 - 6q$$

$$40 - 6(1.89) > 0 \text{ and } 40 - 6(11.44) < 0$$

Hence, $q = 1.89$ is the profit minimum (loss maximum) and $q = 11.44$ is the profit maximum.

Substituting the rate of output associated with the *local maximum* into the profit function, we discover:

$$\pi(11.44) = -200 - 65(11.44) + 20(11.44)^2 - (11.44)^3 = 176.7 > 0$$

Clearly this firm is better off producing 11.44 units of output and earning positive economic profits than shutting down and losing its fixed costs. The *local profit maximum* is also the *global profit maximum*.

Suppose price fell to $60. Then the profit function becomes:

$$\pi(q) = 60q - (200 + 160q - 20q^2 + q^3)$$
$$= -200 - 100q + 20q^2 - q^3$$

Taking the derivative of π with respect to q:

$$\frac{d\pi}{dq} = -100 + 40q - 3q^2 = 0$$

implies

$$q = 3.33, 10$$

Calculating the value of the second derivative at each critical value of q:

$$\frac{d^2\pi}{dq^2} = 40 - 6q$$

$$40 - 6(3.33) > 0 \text{ and } 40 - 6(10) < 0$$

Therefore, $q = 3.33$ is a local profit minimum and $q = 10$ is a local profit maximum.

To determine whether $q = 10$ is a global maximum, we substitute for q in the profit function:

$$\pi(10) = -200 - 100(10) + 20(10)^2 - (10)^3 = -200$$

In this case the profit (loss) at the local maximum would be identical to the profit (loss) at the corner. It would make no difference for the firm's profit whether zero or ten units of output were produced. However, any other rate of output would result in losses greater than fixed costs.

Finally, suppose price fell to $50. Then the profit function becomes:

$$\pi(q) = 50q - (200 + 160q - 20q^2 + q^3)$$
$$= -200 - 110q + 20q^2 - q^3$$

Taking the derivative of π with respect to q:

$$\frac{d\pi}{dq} = -110 + 40q - 3q^2 = 0$$

implies

$$q = 3.86, 9.46$$

Calculating the second derivative at the critical values of q:

$$\frac{d^2\pi}{dq^2} = 40 - 6q$$

$$40 - 6(3.86) = 16.84 > 0 \text{ and } 40 - 6(9.46) = -16.76 < 0$$

So $q = 3.86$ is a local profit minimum ($\pi(3.86) = -384.12$), while $q = 9.46$ is a *local* profit maximum. However, $\pi(9.46) = -297.36$ is less than the profit associated with producing zero output. When $p = 50$, we encounter a corner solution; losses are minimized (profit is maximized) by producing nothing.

Let us review one more time. Although a function in one variable can be plotted in two dimensions, the most expedient means of identifying the maxima or minima of a function is to take the first derivative of the function, set the first derivative equal to zero, and solve for the critical values of the independent variable. Local minima are distinguished from local maxima by calculating the value of the second derivative of the function at those critical values. If the second derivative is negative, the function is at a maximum at that point and if the second derivative is positive, the function is at a local minimum at that value of the independent variable. Finally, to determine if the local maximum (minimum) is a global maximum (minimum), the value of the function at the critical values must be compared to the value of the function at the "corners" of its domain.

Theoretical Generalization

We can now generalize on the insights obtained from our graphical and numerical examples. The revenue function for a perfectly competitive firm is given by multiplying price, an exogenously determined variable, by quantity, the variable under the firm's control: $R(q) = p_0 q$. Total cost is equal to the sum of fixed cost, a constant, and variable cost, which, like revenue, varies with the rate of output: $TC = FC + VC(q)$. The profit function is generated as the difference between the total revenue and the total cost functions:

$$\pi(q) = p_0 q - [FC + VC(q)]$$

As we have seen, the critical values of the profit function are identified by taking the first derivative of $\pi(q)$ with respect to q, then setting the results equal to zero and solving for q:

$$\frac{d\pi}{dq} = \frac{d(p_0 q)}{dq} - \frac{dFC}{dq} - \frac{dVC}{dq} = 0$$

Since

$$\frac{dFC}{dq} = 0$$

this equation implies

$$MC = p_0$$

This is the well-known result that the price-taking firm maximizes profit by setting the rate of output where marginal cost equals market determined price. However, as Figure 8.5 shows, this is not quite the whole story. In Figure 8.5, $MC = p_0$ at two rates of output, q_0 and q^*. One of these critical values of q is the profit minimum while the other is a local profit maximum. The second derivative test discriminates between these critical values of q. Taking the second derivative of π with respect to q:

$$\frac{d^2\pi}{dq^2} = \frac{d^2R}{dq^2} - \frac{d^2TC}{dq^2} = \frac{dp_0}{dq} - \frac{dMC}{dq} = \frac{-dMC}{dq}$$

At q_0, marginal cost is declining as output increases ($dMC/dq < 0$). Thus, output q_0 is a *profit minimizing* (loss maximizing) rate of output. At q^*, marginal cost is increasing as output increases ($dMC/dq > 0$). Thus, output q^* is a *local profit maximizing* rate of output. Output q^* will be a global maximum if and only if $\pi(q^*) > \pi(0)$.

Figure 8.5

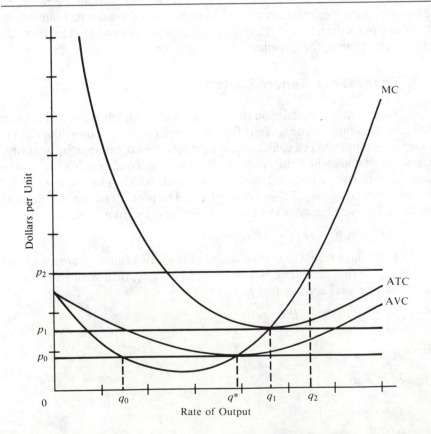

To eliminate the possibility of a corner solution, we must compare the rate of profit at the *local* profit maximum with the "corner" at $q = 0$. We know that $\pi(0) = -FC$, since $TR = 0$ and $TC = FC$ when $q = 0$. To be a global maximum, the rate of profit at q^* must exceed $-FC$. Therefore:

$$\pi(q^*) = p_0 q^* - (FC + VC) > -FC$$

Adding $FC + VC$ to both sides of the "greater than" sign, we have:

$$p_0 q^* > VC$$

This is another familiar rule from the theory of the competitive firm: revenue must exceed variable cost in order for output to be produced. Finally, if we divide through by q, we derive the shutdown condition for the firm. The firm should produce output only if price exceeds average variable cost:

$$p_0 > AVC$$

Figure 8.5 is drawn so that $MC = p_0$ at the minimum point on the average variable cost curve. (See the next section.) It follows that p_0 is the lowest price at which the firm would produce. For any price less than p_0, $AVC > p$ at that rate of output where $MC = p$. For all prices greater than p_0, (e.g., p_1 and p_2 in Figure 8.5), output is determined by the positive sloped portion of the short-run marginal cost curve. Hence, the supply curve of the price-taker is that portion of its marginal cost curve that lies above the firm's average cost curve.

MINIMIZING AVERAGE COST

We have just seen that the supply curve of the price-taking firm commences where price equals *minimum* average variable cost. In this section we will show how the first and second derivative rules can be used to locate the rate of output that minimizes average cost. Recall that average variable cost is generated by dividing variable cost by output: $AVC = VC/q$. To find the minimum point on the average variable cost curve, we take the first derivative of AVC with respect to q, set the derivative equal to zero, and solve for q:

$$\frac{d(AVC)}{dq} = \frac{d(VC/q)}{dq} = \frac{q(dVC/dq) - VC(dq/dq)}{q^2}$$

$$= \frac{1}{q}\left(\frac{dVC}{dq} - \frac{VC}{q}\right)$$

$d(AVC)/dq = 0$ implies

$$\frac{1}{q}(MC - AVC) = 0$$

or

$$AVC = MC$$

To verify that we have a local minimum, rather than a local maximum, we take the second derivative of AVC with respect to q and determine its algebraic sign:

$$\frac{d^2(AVC)}{dq^2} = \frac{d[(1/q)(MC - AVC)]}{dq}$$

$$= \frac{-1}{q^2}(MC - AVC) + \frac{1}{q}\left(\frac{dMC}{dq} - \frac{dAVC}{dq}\right)$$

We have already established that $dAVC/dq = (MC - AVC)/q$. Making this substitution and factoring out $1/q^2$, we have:

$$\frac{d^2(AVC)}{dq^2} = \frac{1}{q^2}\left[-(MC - AVC) + q\left(\frac{dMC}{dq}\right) - (MC - AVC)\right]$$

Since we know $MC = AVC$ at the critical value of q, the terms containing $(MC - AVC)$ drop out, leaving:

$$\frac{d^2(AVC)}{dq^2} = q\left(\frac{dMC}{dq}\right)$$

Since q is always positive, $d^2(AVC)/dq^2$ is positive (implying a local minimum) as long as marginal cost is increasing.

In Figure 8.5, the average variable cost and marginal cost curves emanate from the vertical axis and marginal cost declines as output increases; $q = 0$ implies a *local maximum* to the average variable cost curve. (Can you explain why this is not a global maximum?) At q^*, the marginal cost curve intersects the average variable cost curve from below ($dMC/dq > 0$). This is the minimum point on the average variable cost curve.

Similar logic locates the minimum point on the average total cost curve. Given that average total cost equals total cost divided by output, the critical value of q is identified by taking the derivative of TC/q with respect to zero, setting the result equal to zero and solving for q:

$$\frac{d(ATC)}{dq} = \frac{d(TC/q)}{dq} = \frac{q(dTC/dq) - TC(dq/dq)}{q^2}$$

$$= \frac{1}{q}\left(\frac{dTC}{dq} - \frac{TC}{q}\right)$$

$d(ATC)/dq = 0$ implies

$$\frac{1}{q}(MC - ATC) = 0$$

or

$$ATC = MC$$

This result invokes strong feelings of *deja vu*; the critical value of q occurs where average total cost equals marginal cost. Once again, we verify that this point represents a local minimum rather than a local maximum by taking the second derivative of the ATC function and checking its sign.

$$\frac{d^2(ATC)}{dq^2} = \frac{d[(1/q)(MC - ATC)]}{dq}$$

$$= \frac{-1}{q^2}(MC - ATC) + \frac{1}{q}\left(\frac{dMC}{dq} - \frac{dATC}{dq}\right)$$

$$= q\left(\frac{dMC}{dq}\right) > 0 \text{ if } \frac{dMC}{dq} > 0$$

An alert student may wonder about the possibility of a corner solution. For $q = 0$, $ATC = \infty$, since $FC > 0$ even when $q = 0$. At all other points, $ATC < \infty$, implying that the *local minimum* on the ATC curve is also the *global minimum*.

Looking at Figure 8.5 one more time, we observe that the marginal cost curve intersects the horizontal line p_1 at q_1, the same rate of output which minimizes total cost. When $p = p_1$, the firm earns *zero economic profit*, which is the long-run outcome in the theory of perfect competition. For prices below p_0, the firm ceases production in the short run, causing output to be zero. For prices greater than p_0 but less than p_1, output is given by the rising portion of the marginal cost curve, even though the firm makes negative economic profit. If the price persisted below p_1, the firm would exit the industry in the long run. For prices greater than p_1, new firms would be attracted to the industry, increasing total output (market supply) until price fell back to p_1.

PROFIT MAXIMIZATION
UNDER MONOPOLY

We saw in the first section of this chapter that a competitive firm maximizes profit by setting the rate of output where marginal cost equals price, as long as price exceeds minimum average variable cost. Because the competitive firm is a price-taker, that is, its price does not change with its rate of output, marginal revenue is identical to price. The "marginal cost equals price" rule for maximizing profit under competition is a special case of the more general rule: "maximize profit by producing where marginal cost equals marginal revenue." The only substantive difference between the profit maximizing monopolist and the profit maximizing competitive firm is that marginal revenue of the former changes as output varies.

As in the case of perfect competition, we define profit under monopoly as total revenue minus total cost:

$$\pi(Q) = R(Q) - C(Q)$$

The critical values of Q are determined by taking the derivative of π with respect to Q, setting the result equal to zero and solving for Q:

$$\frac{d\pi}{dQ} = \frac{dR}{dQ} - \frac{dC}{dQ} = 0$$

implying

$$MR = MC$$

The second-order condition for a monopoly is also obtained by taking the second derivative of π with respect to Q and checking its sign:

$$\frac{d^2\pi}{dQ^2} = \frac{dMR}{dQ} - \frac{dMC}{dQ} < 0$$

implying

$$\frac{dMC}{dQ} > \frac{dMR}{dQ}$$

Because $dMR/dQ = 0$ for the competitive firm, the second derivative condition can be simplified to $dMC/dQ > 0$. By contrast, $dMR/dQ < 0$ for a monopolist. If $dMC/dQ > 0$, then we know that $dMC/dQ > dMR/dQ$. We will refer to this type of monopoly as a *conventional monopoly*, since the marginal cost curve of the monopoly is similar to the marginal cost curve of a competitive firm. Also, $dMC/dQ > 0$ is said to be a *sufficient* condition for a local profit maximum. However, in the case of a natural monopoly, it is possible that the firm's marginal cost curve is declining when it intersects the marginal revenue curve. If the marginal revenue curve is declining faster than the marginal cost curve, we would still have a local profit maximum; $dMC/dQ > dMR/dQ$ is a *necessary* condition *for a local maximum.*

The Conventional Monopolist

To contrast the theories of monopoly and competition, we imagine a monopoly firm with a total cost function given by:

$$TC = 200 + 160Q - 20Q^2 + Q^3$$

where Q is total output. For instance, the monopoly might be a *cartel* composed of 1,000 plants, each identical to the competitive firm in our example in the first section of this chapter.

Next we imagine that the market demand curve facing the monopoly is:

$$Q_d = 15 - 0.05p$$

where Q_d is quantity demanded in thousands and p is the price. This demand function is constructed so that it intersects the marginal cost function (which generates the *competitive supply curve*) at the minimum point on the average total cost curve. This outcome simulates a long-run competitive equilibrium. The market demand function can be translated into the monopoly's *average revenue* function by reversing the roles of price and quantity; that is, by solving the demand function for p in terms of Q:

$$\frac{R}{q} = p = 300 - 20Q$$

The total revenue function is the average revenue function multiplied times quantity:

$$R = pQ = (300 - 20Q)Q = 300Q - 20Q^2$$

To obtain the marginal revenue function we calculate the first derivative of R with respect to Q:

$$MR = \frac{dR}{dQ} = 300 - 40Q$$

Now we pause to compare the average revenue function with the marginal revenue function. When output is zero, both are equal to 300. The marginal revenue curve has the same vertical intercept as the average revenue function. The slope of the average revenue curve is -20, while the slope of the marginal revenue curve is -40. That is, the marginal revenue curve lies below the average revenue curve for all positive rates of output and declines at a faster rate than the average revenue curve. (For a linear demand equation, the slope of the marginal revenue function is twice the slope of the average revenue function.)

There are two ways of identifying the critical output level(s) for the monopolist. One is to calculate the profit function by subtracting the cost function from the revenue function, take the derivative of profit with respect to output, then solve for quantity. The alternative way is to take the derivative of the cost function with respect to output, then equate the marginal revenue and marginal cost functions, and solve for output.

Following the former approach, we define profit as:

$$\begin{aligned}
\pi(Q) &= R(Q) - C(Q) \\
&= (300Q - 20Q^2) - (200 + 160Q - 20Q^2 + Q^3) \\
&= -200 + 140Q - Q^3
\end{aligned}$$

Setting the derivative of $\pi(Q)$ equal to zero and solving for Q:

$$\frac{d\pi(Q)}{dQ} = 140 - 3Q^2 = 0$$

$$Q = \sqrt{46.67} \approx 6.83 \text{ thousand units}$$

Taking the second derivative of π with respect to Q verifies that we have a local maximum:

$$\frac{d^2\pi(Q)}{dQ^2} = -6Q = -6(6.83) = -40.98 < 0$$

Finally, we calculate the value of $\pi(6.83)$ to eliminate the possibility of a corner solution.

$$\pi(6.83) = -200 + 140(6.83) - (6.83)^3 = 437.59$$

Since $\pi(0) = -200$, this monopolist is better off producing 6.83 thousand units of output than producing nothing.

Next we try the marginal cost equals marginal revenue approach to verify that we do obtain equivalent solutions. We have seen that $MR = 300 - 40Q$. Taking the derivative of $C(Q)$ with respect to Q we obtain the marginal cost function:

$$MC = \frac{dC}{dQ} = 160 - 40Q + 3Q^2$$

Setting $MC = MR$, we find:

$$300 - 40Q = 160 - 40Q + 3Q^2$$
$$3Q^2 = 140$$
$$Q = \sqrt{46.67} \approx 6.83 \text{ (thousand) units}$$

Figure 8.6

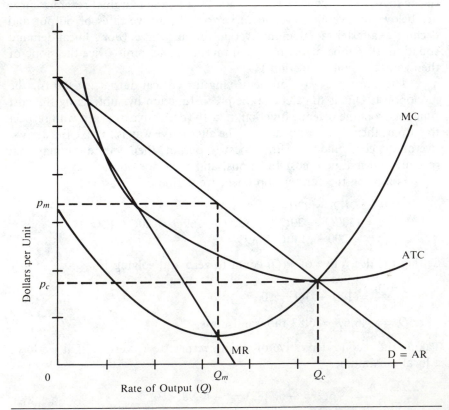

Checking for the second-order condition and eliminating the possibility of
a corner solution are straightforward.

In Figure 8.6 the monopoly price and output equilibrium is compared to
the long-run competitive outcome. Instead of producing at Q_c (where $MC =$
p_c and $dMC/dQ > 0$), the monopoly reduces output until $MC = MR$.
A competitive outcome with zero economic profit is transformed into a
monopoly outcome with positive economic (monopoly) profit. We thus see
how important precepts of economic theory can be revealed through the use
of optimization techniques.

Natural Monopoly

A natural monopoly is said to occur when the long-run average cost
curve of one firm intersects the market demand curve before the former has
reached its minimum point. (See Figure 8.7.) Because even one firm would be
unable to realize all potential *economies of scale*, the condition of monopoly
is said to be a *natural* consequence of the limited market size. Hence, the
term *natural monopoly*.

Figure 8.7

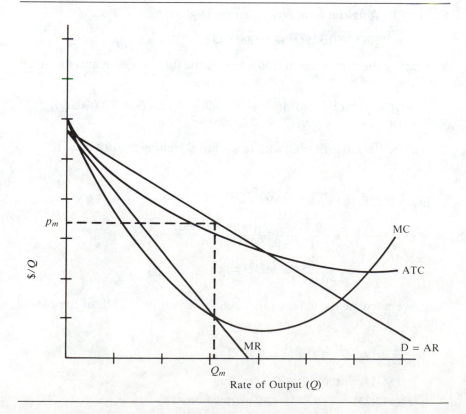

If, as depicted in Figure 8.7, the long-run average cost (LAC) curve is *declining* in the relevant output range, market competition would be an unstable situation. Firms with larger plants would incur lower average costs than firms with smaller plants, leading to an economic "survival of the fittest."

In Figure 8.7, $MC = MR$ at Q_0 and Q_m units of output. At Q_0, marginal cost is falling faster than marginal revenue ($dMR/dQ > dMC/dQ$), implying that Q_0 is a *local profit minimum*. By contrast, marginal revenue is falling faster than marginal cost at output Q_m ($dMC/dQ > dMR/dQ$), even though marginal cost itself is decreasing. Finally, in Figure 8.7, the market clearing price for output Q_m, namely p_m, exceeds $LAC(Q_m)$, implying that the local profit maximum is also the global profit maximum (recall that all costs are variable in the long run).

Yet Another Numerical Illustration

Assume that the average revenue curve facing a natural monopoly is given by:

$$p = 115 - 0.075Q$$

and that its *long-run* total cost function is given as:

$$C = 120Q - 0.125Q^2 + 0.00005Q^3$$

Subtracting the cost function from the revenue function generates the profit function:

$$\pi(Q) = (115Q - 0.075Q^2) - (120Q - 0.125Q^2 + 0.00005Q^3)$$
$$= -5Q + 0.05Q^2 - 0.00005Q^3$$

Taking the derivative of $\pi(Q)$ with respect to Q, setting $d\pi/dQ$ equal to zero, and solving:

$$\frac{d\pi}{dQ} = -5 + 0.1Q - 0.00015Q^2 = 0$$

$$Q = \frac{-0.1 \pm \sqrt{(0.1)^2 - (4)(-5)(-0.00015)}}{(2)(-0.00015)}$$

$$Q = \frac{-0.1 \pm \sqrt{0.01 - 0.003}}{-0.0003} = 54.45, \ 612.23$$

Next, we calculate the value of the second derivative at each of the critical values of Q:

$$\frac{d^2\pi}{dQ^2} = \pi''(Q) = 0.1 - 0.0003Q$$

$$\pi''(54.45) = 0.0837 > 0 \quad \text{(minimum)}$$
$$\pi''(612.23) = -0.0837 < 0 \quad \text{(maximum)}$$

Finally, we check for the possibility of a corner solution. Since all costs are variable in the long run, the monopoly would abandon the market if $\pi < 0$. Calculating the level of profit at the local maximum, we find:

$$\pi(612.23) = -5(612.23) + 0.05(612.23)^2 - 0.00005(612.23)^3$$
$$= 4,206.16 > 0$$

The local maximum is also a global maximum.

To review, a monopoly firm is distinguished from a competitive firm because its price varies with the rate of output, causing the monopoly's marginal revenue curve to lie below its average revenue (demand) curve. The monopoly maximizes profit by producing where marginal cost equals marginal revenue, if the change in marginal cost exceeds the change in marginal revenue and if total revenue exceeds variable cost. The marginal cost curve of a *conventional monopoly* is increasing where $MR = MC$, causing $dMC/dq > 0$ to be a *sufficient condition* for a profit maximum. By contrast, the *natural monopoly's* marginal cost curve may be declining where $MC = MR$. A *necessary condition* for a local profit maximum is that $dMC/dq > dMR/dq$, even if $dMC/dq < 0$.

SUMMARY

This chapter has introduced one of the most important uses of differential calculus in economic theory: the identification of maxima and minima of economic *objective* functions. The theory of the firm is virtually unique in economics, in that objective functions (e.g., minimizing average variable cost, maximizing profit) can be defined in terms of a single causal variable. Indeed, one important purpose of the theory of cost—that links each rate of output to a single *efficient* cost level—is that profit can be defined solely in terms of output. The analytical advantage is that the profit maximization problem can be easily graphed in two dimensions, allowing us to present the calculus of profit maximization against the background of those simple diagrams.

Unfortunately for pedagogy, but fortunately for realism sake, most economic problems involve functions of more than one independent variable. Generally, economic optimization problems require techniques for isolating the influence of each independent variable. This is the technique of *partial* differentiation, which we discuss in the next chapter.

PROBLEMS

Find the maxima and/or minima, if any, of the following functions for the ranges of the independent variables specified.

1. $y = f(x) = 24 + x^2$

2. $y = f(x) = 12 - 4(x - 3)^2$

3. $y = f(x) = \sqrt{x} - 10x,\ 0 < x < 5$

4. $y = f(x) = 6 - 4x + 3x^3,\ 0 < x < 2$

5.   The total cost function for a firm in a purely competitive industry is given as:

$$C = 200 + 25q - 2q^2 + 0.1q^3$$

where C denotes total cost and q denotes output. Calculate the profit maximizing rate of output when:
a. $p = 10$
b. $p = 30$
c. $p = 40$
d. $p = 50$

6.   Given the cost function in Problem 5,
a. At what rate of output is marginal cost at a minimum?
b. What is the lowest price necessary for this firm to produce a positive rate of output? (Hint: What is the value of minimum average variable cost?)
c. What is the formula for this firm's supply curve? (Hint: Solve the profit maximization requirement, $MC = p$ as a function with p as the independent variable and q as the dependent variable. Don't forget the role of minimum average variable cost in defining the domain of this function.)

7.   The market demand function for a commodity Q is given by:

$$Q_d = 200 - 2p$$

where p is the product's price. The commodity is produced by a monopolist whose total cost of production is given as:

$$C = 1,000 + 12Q + 0.75Q^2$$

a. Find the profit maximizing output for the monopoly.
b. Find the price and total cost of that output.
c. Find the total profit for the monopoly.
d. Graph on the same diagram the average revenue, the marginal revenue, the average variable cost, the marginal cost, and the average total cost functions. Indicate the profit maximizing output, the product price, and the total profit of the monopoly.

8.   Redo Problem 7 assuming the same demand curve, but a new total cost function:

$$C = 50Q - Q^2 + 0.0075Q^3$$

Does this firm constitute a natural monopoly? Explain.

9

Partial

Derivatives and

Their Applications

To this point our explorations of derivatives and their applications to economics have dealt solely with functions of one independent variable. We have been measuring the rate of change of y with respect to x when no variables, other than x, have influenced the value of y. This approach has simplified our understanding of derivatives and allowed us to present maxima and minima against the background of two-dimensional diagrams. However, because most economic problems involve functions with more than one independent variable, limiting derivatives to functions of one variable has restricted economic applications of derivatives. In this chapter we introduce the *partial derivative* to cover cases that involve functions of two or more independent variables. In the next chapter we use partial derivatives in the maximization and minimization of functions of two or more variables.

Suppose a demand function is given by:

$$Q_d = D(p, p_c, p_s, y)$$

Where Q_d is quantity demanded, p is market price, p_c is the price of a complementary good, p_s is the price of a substitute good, and y is real income. According to the law of demand, a change in price will change quantity demanded in the opposite direction, other factors remaining constant. But in the real world, one variable seldom changes without coincidental changes in other variables. We need a method of isolating the influence of each independent variable. A *partial derivative* measures the rate of change of the dependent variable with respect to one of the independent variables with all other independent variables conceptually held constant. Another way of restating the law of demand is: "the partial derivative of quantity demanded with respect to price is negative." The mathematical concept of the *partial derivative* parallels the concept of *ceteris paribus*: independent variables other than the one being discussed are assumed to remain constant.

Aside from demand theory there are many other economic applications of partial derivatives. Production functions relate output to the services of several inputs; the *marginal product* of each factor represents the partial derivative of output with respect to that factor. Total cost is the sum of each factor's price times the quantity of that factor used; marginal cost can be measured as the common ratio of each variable factor's price to its marginal product. In macroeconomics there are many applications of partial derivatives. For instance, the marginal propensities to save and consume are partial derivatives of the saving and consumption functions, respectively, with respect to disposable income. And as we will see in Part III of this text, econometrics largely involves the estimation of multiple regression equations whose coefficients are estimates of partial derivatives.

PARTIAL DERIVATIVES

If a variable z is stated as a function of two other variables x and y, we write:

$$z = f(x, y)$$

This formulation means that for each permissible pair of values of the independent variables x and y, we can find exactly one value of z corresponding to that pair. Ideally, variables x and y are independent in the sense that the value of x has no influence on the value of y and vice versa.[1]

Now we inquire about the rate of change of z with respect to one or the other of the two independent variables. To do this, we introduce the operator "∂" which is the symbol used to designate the partial derivative. Another symbol commonly used to designate the partial derivative of the function with respect to, say, x is $f_x(x, y)$. The partial derivative of z with respect to x is defined as:

$$\frac{\partial z}{\partial x} = f_x(x, y) = \lim_{\Delta x \to 0} \frac{\Delta z}{\Delta x} = \lim_{\Delta x \to 0} \frac{f(x + \Delta x, y) - f(x, y)}{\Delta x}$$

The variable x takes on an increment, Δx, but the variable y is kept constant. The partial derivative of z with respect to x is computed by taking

[1] When we study econometrics, we will see that empirical variables do not always behave in an ideal fashion, which creates the statistical problem called *multicollinearity*.

the derivative of z with respect to x, treating y as if it were a constant. Likewise, the partial derivative of z with respect to y is computed by taking the derivative of z with respect to y and treating x as if it were a constant. The rules of differentiation presented in Chapter 6 also apply when computing the derivative of z with respect to either x or y. The only difference is that the other independent variable is treated like any other constant in the equation.

Partial Derivatives of a Demand Function

To make our discussion more concrete, let's return to our example of a demand equation. Imagine that an econometrician has estimated the following demand equation:

$$Q_d = 25p^{-2}p_s p_c^{-0.5} y^2$$

where Q_d is quantity demanded per time period, p is the price of that commodity, p_s is the price of a substitute good, p_c is the price of a complementary good, and y is real per-capita income. According to our definition, the impact of a change in p on Q_d is given as the *partial derivative* of Q_d with respect to p:

$$\frac{\partial Q_d}{\partial p} = \lim_{\Delta p \to 0} \frac{25(p + \Delta p)^{-2}p_s p_c^{-0.5}y^2 - 25p^{-2}p_s p_c^{-0.5}y^2}{\Delta p}$$

We can then factor out all terms not containing p or Δp:

$$\frac{\partial Q_d}{\partial p} = \lim_{\Delta p \to 0} \frac{25 p_s p_c^{-0.5} y^2 [(p + \Delta p)^{-2} - p^{-2}]}{\Delta p}$$

Since the value of $25 p_s p_c^{-0.5} y^2$ is independent of what happens to Δp, we can move this term outside the limit operator:

$$\frac{\partial Q_d}{\partial p} = (25 p_s p_c^{-0.5} y^2) \lim_{\Delta p \to 0} \frac{(p + \Delta p)^{-2} - p^{-2}}{\Delta p}$$

$$= (25 p_s p_c^{-0.5} y^2) \lim_{\Delta p \to 0} \left(\frac{1}{\Delta p (p + \Delta p)^2} - \frac{1}{\Delta p (p^2)} \right)$$

Finding a common denominator:

$$\frac{\partial Q_d}{\partial p} = (25 p_s p_c^{-0.5} y^2) \lim_{\Delta p \to 0} \frac{p^2 - [p^2 + 2p\Delta p + (\Delta p)^2]}{(p^2 \Delta p)[p^2 + 2p\Delta p + (\Delta p)^2]}$$

$$= (25 p_s p_c^{-0.5} y^2) \lim_{\Delta p \to 0} \frac{-2p\Delta p - (\Delta p)^2}{p^4 \Delta p + 2p^3 (\Delta p)^2 + p^2 (\Delta p)^3}$$

Factoring Δp from the numerator and the denominator:

$$\frac{\partial Q_d}{\partial p} = (25 p_s p_c^{-0.5} y^2) \lim_{\Delta p \to 0} \frac{-2p - \Delta p}{p^4 + 2p^3 \Delta p + p^2 (\Delta p)^2}$$

Finally, letting Δp go all the way to zero, we have:

$$\frac{\partial Q_d}{\partial p} = 25 p_s p_c^{-0.5} y^2 \cdot \frac{-2p}{p^4} = -50 p^{-3} p_s p_c^{-0.5} y^2$$

The mathematical gymnastics of the previous example probably struck you as tedious and unnecessary. Yet it is instructive to follow the procedures for one long-winded example to better appreciate the advantages of the general rules of partial differentiation. The first step of the above derivation involves the simple definition of a derivative we developed in Chapter 6: the partial derivative of the demand function with respect to p is defined as the limit, as Δp approaches zero, of $D(p + \Delta p)$ minus $D(p)$, divided by Δp. The second step is the crucial step: we factored out the "constant," $25 p_s p_c^{-0.5} y^2$, then proceeded to take the limit of $[(p + \Delta p)^{-2} - p^{-2}]$ divided by Δp as the latter approached zero. We then found a common denominator for the expression $[1/\Delta p(p + \Delta p) - 1/\Delta p(p^2)]$, and found a way of eliminating Δp from the denominator. But this is all old hat. Once the "constant term" had been factored out of the expression, we merely had to apply the power rule to determine:

$$\frac{\partial Q_d}{\partial p} = 25 p_s p_c^{-0.5} y^2 \cdot \frac{\partial (p^{-2})}{\partial p} = (25 p_s p_c^{-0.5} y^2)(-2p^{-3})$$

$$\frac{\partial Q_d}{\partial p} = -50 p^{-3} p_s p_c^{-0.5} y^2$$

The "secret" of partial derivatives is simple and straightforward. One merely treats all the other variables in the equation as if they were constants and applies the rules of differentiation to the independent variable of interest. Because a change in one independent variable does not *cause* the other independent variables to change, we can take a "snapshot" of the equation to isolate the impact of the variable in question on the dependent variable. In a power function, as in our example, the values of the other independent variables do influence the formula for the derivative. Nevertheless, the values of those other variables do not change *because* the value of p changed.

Before proceeding, let's compute the other partial derivatives of our demand function. The partial derivative of Q_d with respect to p_s shows the effect of a change in the price of the substitute good while other influences on quantity remain constant. We could churn through the derivation of $\partial Q_d / \partial p_s$, using the definition of a limit, but surely we have had enough unnecessary complications already. Instead, we can factor out the "constant," $25p^{-2}p_c^{-0.5}y^2$ and apply a simple derivative formula:

$$\frac{\partial Q_d}{\partial p_s} = \frac{\partial(25p^{-2}p_s p_c^{-0.5}y^2)}{\partial p_s} = 25p^{-2}p_c^{-0.5}y^2 \cdot \frac{\partial p_s}{\partial p_s}$$

$$= 25p^{-2}p_c^{-0.5}y^2$$

Similarly, the partial derivative of Q_d with respect to p_c shows the impact of a change in the price of a complement on quantity demanded:

$$\frac{\partial Q_d}{\partial p_c} = 25p^{-2}p_s y^2 \cdot \frac{\partial p_c^{-0.5}}{\partial p_c} = -12.5p^{-2}p_s p_c^{-1.5}y^2$$

The impact of a change in real income on quantity demanded, in this example, becomes a simple application of the derivative of a quadratic equation:

$$\frac{\partial Q_d}{\partial y} = 25p^{-2}p_s p_c^{-0.5} \cdot \frac{\partial y^2}{\partial y} = 50p^{-2}p_s p_c^{-0.5}y$$

A Numerical Illustration

Let's work through a numerical illustration to visualize partial derivatives even more clearly. Staying with the same demand equation,

$$Q_d = 25p^{-2}p_s p_c^{-0.5}y^2$$

assume that $p = 25$, $p_s = 16$, $p_c = 4$, and $y = 100$. Substituting these values, the quantity of this good demanded is:

$$Q_d = 25(25)^{-2}(16)(4)^{-0.5}(100)^2 = 3{,}200$$

Imagine small changes in p. Their effects on the value of Q_d are presented in Table 9.1.

Table 9.1

Δp	$D(p + \Delta p)$	$D(p + \Delta p) - D(p)$	$\dfrac{D(p + \Delta p) - D(p)}{\Delta p}$
2.0	2,743.48	−456.52	−228.26
1.0	2,958.58	−241.42	−241.42
0.5	3,075.74	−124.26	−248.52
0.1	3,174.55	−25.45	−254.47
0.01	3,197.44	−2.5584	−255.84
−0.01	3,202.56	+2.5615	−256.15
−0.1	3,225.75	+25.75	−257.54
−0.5	3,331.95	+131.95	−263.89
−1.0	3,472.22	+272.22	−272.22
−2.0	3,780.72	+580.72	−290.36

We saw in the previous section that the partial derivative of Q_d with respect to p is:

$$\frac{\partial Q_d}{\partial p} = -50p^{-3}p_sp_c^{-0.5}y^2 = -50(25)^{-3}(16)(4)^{-0.5}(100)^2 = -256$$

We also note that as the change in p approaches zero from either a positive or negative direction, $\Delta Q_d/\Delta p$ approaches -256. You may want to verify the other partial derivative formulas with numerical examples of your own.

HIGHER-ORDER PARTIAL DERIVATIVES

Since derivatives of functions of one variable are themselves functions of one variable, we have seen that such functions have second, third, and still higher-order derivatives. By the same logic, partial derivatives of multivariate functions are themselves multivariate functions, and we can define partial derivatives of order higher than one. The second partial derivative of a continuous function,

$$z = f(x, y)$$

with respect to x is computed by differentiating the first partial derivative $\partial z/\partial x$ partially with respect to x. That is, we take the derivative of the function $f_x(x, y)$ with respect to x, holding y constant. The symbols used to denote this second partial derivative are:

$$\frac{\partial^2 z}{\partial x^2} \text{ or } f_{xx}(x, y)$$

Similarly, the second partial derivative with respect to y is obtained by differentiating the first partial derivative $\partial z/\partial y$ partially with respect to y, holding x constant. The symbols used to denote the second partial with respect to y are analogous to those used to denote the second partial with respect to x:

$$\frac{\partial^2 z}{\partial y^2} \text{ or } f_{yy}(x, y)$$

There is another way of taking higher-order partial derivatives. Since partial derivatives are multivariate functions, we are not restricted to the same independent variable when taking higher-order partial derivatives. For the function $z = f(x, y)$, we can define two *cross-partial derivatives*:

$$\frac{\partial^2 z}{\partial x \partial y} = f_{xy}(x, y) = \frac{\partial f_y(x, y)}{\partial x}$$

and

$$\frac{\partial^2 z}{\partial y \partial x} = f_{yx}(x, y) = \frac{\partial f_x(x, y)}{\partial y}$$

We can differentiate the function $z = f(x, y)$ first with respect to y, and then differentiate this partial derivative with respect to x, and vice versa. In this case, the first partial derivative of the function with respect to, say, y is computed; then this partial derivative is in turn differentiated partially, but this time with respect to x.

Under certain conditions of continuity that are possessed by most commonly encountered functions, these two cross-partial derivatives are equal. That is:

$$\frac{\partial^2 z}{\partial x \partial y} = \frac{\partial^2 z}{\partial y \partial x}$$

Production Functions, Marginal
Products, and Diminishing Returns

One aspect of economic theory where second-order partial derivatives feature prominently is production theory. A production function relates the rate of output to the services of two or more factors of production. A simple case relates the rate of output, q, to the services of labor, L, and capital, K:

$$q = f(L, K)$$

One of the most popular types of production functions is the Cobb-Douglas production function whose general form is:

$$q = AL^{\alpha}K^{\beta}$$

where A is a positive constant $(A > 0)$ and α and β are both positive fractions $(0 < \alpha < 1$ and $0 < \beta < 1)$.

The first feature of the Cobb-Douglas production function that makes it attractive to researchers is that the marginal products of labor and capital are always positive. Since the partial derivative of output with respect to labor (capital) is the marginal product of labor (capital), we have:

$$MP_L = \frac{\partial(AL^{\alpha}K^{\beta})}{\partial L} = \alpha AL^{\alpha-1}K^{\beta} = \alpha \cdot \frac{q}{L} > 0$$

and

$$MP_K = \frac{\partial(AL^{\alpha}K^{\beta})}{\partial K} = \beta AL^{\alpha}K^{\beta-1} = \beta \cdot \frac{q}{K} > 0$$

According to production theory, efficiency requires that both factors of production have positive marginal products. The Cobb-Douglas production function generates the types of marginal products that are likely to be observed.

Another lesson of production theory is the principle of *diminishing returns*, or *diminishing marginal productivity*: if one factor's services are increased, while other factors' services are held constant, that factor's marginal product eventually must decrease. This is equivalent to saying that the second partial derivative of the production function with respect to each factor must be negative. We find this feature is also built into the formula for the Cobb-Douglas production function:

$$\frac{\partial^2 q}{\partial L^2} = \frac{\partial(\alpha AL^{\alpha-1}K^\beta)}{\partial L} = \alpha(\alpha - 1)AL^{\alpha-2}K^\beta < 0 \quad \text{(since } \alpha - 1 < 0)$$

and

$$\frac{\partial^2 q}{\partial K^2} = \frac{\partial(\beta AL^\alpha K^{\beta-1})}{\partial K} = \beta(\beta - 1)AL^\alpha K^{\beta-2} < 0 \quad \text{(since } \beta - 1 < 0)$$

THE TOTAL DIFFERENTIAL

We have just seen that partial derivatives allow us to isolate the influence of a change of one independent variable on the change of the dependent variable. As we stated, this can be very handy when attempting to concentrate on one of the many influences on a dependent variable. However, another question goes begging: precisely how do we interpret the effect of simultaneous changes of many independent variables on the dependent variable? As a case in point, how would coincidental changes in a good's own price, the price of a substitute, the price of a complement, and real income affect the change in quantity demanded? The answer involves the *total differential* of the demand equation.

We have seen that the process of *deriving* the derivative of a function is called the *differentiation* of that function. When we compute a partial derivative of a function with respect to one independent variable, we treat all the other independent variables as constants, then proceed to differentiate the function with respect to the variable in question. The *total differential* of a function is the function that relates the *total* change of the dependent variable to the change of *each* independent variable in the equation. The total differential is computed as the sum of the partial derivatives of the dependent variable with respect to each independent variable times the change of that independent variable. For instance, the total differential of a demand function of the form:

$$Q_d = D(p, p_s, p_c, y)$$

is

$$dQ_d = \left(\frac{\partial Q_d}{\partial p}\right)dp + \left(\frac{\partial Q_d}{\partial p_s}\right)dp_s + \left(\frac{\partial Q_d}{\partial p_c}\right)dp_c + \left(\frac{\partial Q_d}{\partial y}\right)dy$$

Partial Elasticities

For the power function of our ongoing demand function example, the total differential at first seems quite complex:

$$dQ_d = (-50p^{-3}p_s p_c^{-0.5} y^2)dp + (25p^{-2}p_c^{-0.5}y^2)dp_s$$
$$+ (-12.5p^{-2}p_s p_c^{-1.5}y^2)dp_c + (50p^{-2}p_s p_c^{-0.5}y)dy$$

By multiplying each term by the ratio of the relevant independent variable to itself (i.e., $p/p = p_s/p_s = p_c/p_c = y/y = 1$), each term of the total differential can be translated into a constant times the ratio of Q_d to the independent variable featured in the partial derivative.

$$dQ_d = (-50p^{-2}p_s p_c^{-0.5}y^2)\frac{dp}{p} + (25p^{-2}p_s p_c^{-0.5}y^2)\frac{dp_s}{p_s}$$
$$+ (-12.5p^{-2}p_s p_c^{-0.5}y^2)\frac{dp_c}{p_c} + (50p^{-2}p_s p_c^{-0.5}y^2)\frac{dy}{y}$$

Factoring $Q_d = 25p^{-2}p_s p_c^{-0.5}y^2$ from each term simplifies the total differential to:

$$dQ_d = (25p^{-2}p_s p_c^{-0.5}y^2)[(-2p^{-1})dp + (p_s^{-1})dp_s + (-0.5p_c^{-1})dp_c + (2y^{-1})dy]$$

Dividing both sides by Q_d, we transform each expression so that it ends with the ratio of the *change* in the respective independent variable to the level of that variable, which is identical to the *percentage change* in that variable. Finally, dividing through the equation by Q_d, we get an expression for the total *percentage change* in the dependent variable due to percentage changes in the independent variables (called the *partial elasticity*):

$$\frac{dQ_d}{Q_d} = (-2)\frac{dp}{p} + (1)\frac{dp_s}{p_s} + (-0.5)\frac{dp_c}{p_c} + (2)\frac{dy}{y}$$

You may have noticed that the constant term preceding the percentage change in each independent variable is the exponent on that variable in the original demand function. In fact, each exponent is the elasticity of demand with respect to that particular variable; i.e., the price elasticity of demand is -2, the cross-elasticity of demand with respect to the substitute is $+1$, the cross-elasticity of demand with respect to the complement is -0.5, and the income elasticity of demand is $+2$. When a demand function is expressed as a power function, demand for that product has a constant elasticity with respect to each of the right-side variables.

Output Elasticities and
Economies of Scale

Another theoretical insight involves the total differentiation of the production function. Assume that output, q, is a function of the quantities of labor, L, capital, K, and land, T, employed:

$$q = f(L, K, T)$$

We have seen that the partial derivative of output with respect to each of the factors of production is the marginal product of that factor. If all factor services are changing at the same time, as is the case with long-run production planning, the total change in output equals the sum of each partial derivative times the change in that factor:

$$dq = \left(\frac{\partial q}{\partial L}\right)dL + \left(\frac{\partial q}{\partial K}\right)dK + \left(\frac{\partial q}{\partial T}\right)dT$$
$$= MP_L\,dL + MP_K\,dK + MP_T\,dT$$

By dividing dq, the change in output, by q, the rate of output, we obtain dq/q, the percentage change in output. Then, by inserting the ratio of each factor to itself (e.g., L/L, K/K, T/T) into each right-side term, we get an interesting result:

$$\frac{dq}{q} = \frac{\partial q}{\partial L} \cdot \frac{L}{q} \cdot \frac{dL}{L} + \frac{\partial q}{\partial K} \cdot \frac{K}{q} \cdot \frac{dK}{K} + \frac{\partial q}{\partial T} \cdot \frac{T}{q} \cdot \frac{dT}{T}$$
$$\frac{dq}{q} = \frac{MP_L}{AP_L} \cdot \frac{dL}{L} + \frac{MP_K}{AP_K} \cdot \frac{dK}{K} + \frac{MP_T}{AP_T} \cdot \frac{dT}{T}$$

The ratio of each factor's marginal product to its average product is the *output elasticity* of that factor (e.g., labor's output elasticity, ϵ_L, is the percentage change in output due to a one percent increase in the amount of labor used, other factor services remaining constant). Hence, the percentage change in output is equal to the sum of each output's elasticity times the percentage change of that factor's services:

$$\frac{dq}{q} = \epsilon_L \cdot \frac{dL}{L} + \epsilon_K \cdot \frac{dK}{K} + \epsilon_T \cdot \frac{dT}{T}$$

Now suppose the firm *planned* to increase all factor services by the same proportion. We could set the percentage change of each factor's services equal to some positive constant, λ. That is:

$$\frac{dL}{L} = \frac{dK}{K} = \frac{dT}{T} = \lambda$$

Dividing both sides of the equation by λ, we obtain an interesting result:

$$\frac{dq/q}{\lambda} = \epsilon_L + \epsilon_K + \epsilon_T$$

The percentage change in output divided by the *equal percentage change* in all input services is equal to the sum of the output elasticities. From production theory we know that the *returns to scale* of a production function measure the ratio of the percent change in output to the proportional change in all inputs. We have just proven that the returns to scale for a production function equal the sum of the output elasticities for that production function.

Marginal Utility

Even when we are dealing in economics with nonmeasurable magnitudes, the notations of calculus are still very useful. The theory that lies behind consumer choice is the theory of utility. The negative slope of the demand curve is "rationalized" by the assumption that each consumer maximizes total utility, given his or her income. We cannot observe people's utility, or rather their scales of preference, and so we cannot measure utility. Though we cannot measure it, we can derive from utility theory certain propositions about economic magnitudes that are measurable—particularly consumer response to price and income changes. It is demonstrated in economic theory that if consumers maximize total utility, they will consume those quantities of any two commodities X and Y such that the ratio of the marginal utility of X to the marginal utility of Y is equal to the ratio of the given price of X to the given price of Y. From this proposition, the negatively-sloped demand curve for, say, X is inferred.

In terms of calculus, let us now ask what is meant by marginal utility. In general, each household will consume many commodities, and from this "bundle" of commodities, members of the household will receive a certain (nonmeasurable) total utility. For the sake of simplicity, let us assume a household composed of one individual who consumes only two commodities, X and Y, and spends his or her entire income on them. Let the amounts of the two commodities be denoted by x and y, respectively. Then we can write the consumer's total utility as a function of x and y:

$$u = u(x, y)$$

where u signifies total utility as a continuous function of the amounts of X and Y. We cannot write a specific mathematical equation for the utility function (or estimate the function from empirical data) because the dependent variable is not observable. We can, however, give a precise meaning to marginal utility. We define the marginal utility of a commodity X as the partial derivative of the utility function with respect to x. That is:

$$MU_x = \lim_{\Delta x \to 0} \frac{u(x + \Delta x, y) - u(x, y)}{\Delta x} = \frac{\partial u}{\partial x}$$

The marginal utility of x is the limit of the change in total utility divided by the change in the consumption of x, as the change in x approaches zero, with the consumption of all other goods remaining constant. Similarly, the marginal utility of y is defined as:

$$MU_y = \frac{\partial u}{\partial y}$$

Now let's proceed to one of the ironic results of the theory of consumer choice: Although total utility is not a measurable magnitude, the *relative marginal utility* a consumer receives from a commodity can be inferred from his or her willingness to substitute one commodity or another. First, we take the total derivative of u with respect to the quantities of X and Y:

$$du = \left(\frac{\partial u}{\partial x}\right)dx + \left(\frac{\partial u}{\partial y}\right)dy$$

Then we define the consumer's *marginal rate of substitution* as the maximum amount of Y the consumer would be willing to sacrifice in order to obtain another unit of X. The maximum amount of y a consumer would exchange for another unit of x would be that amount that left total utility unchanged. Setting du equal to zero, we solve for dy/dx, the marginal rate of substitution:

$$du = \frac{\partial u}{\partial x}dx + \frac{\partial u}{\partial y}dy = 0$$

implies

$$\frac{\partial u}{\partial x}dx = -\frac{\partial u}{\partial y}dy$$

or

$$\frac{dy}{dx} = -\frac{MU_x}{MU_y}$$

The maximum amount of Y that a consumer would give up to obtain another unit of X is equal to (minus) the ratio of the marginal utility of X to the marginal utility of Y. Hence, if we know the maximum amount of one good a consumer would sacrifice to obtain another unit of another good, we have a measure of the marginal utility of the latter good relative to the marginal utility of the former good.

Implicit Differentiation: The
Product Transformation Function

As in the case of implicit functions with two variables, implicit functions with more than two variables can be differentiated directly, that is, without first translating the function into an explicit one. For instance, suppose we are given a relationship among three products, x, y, and z, such that:

$$x^2 + 0.8y^2 + 0.6z^2 = 1,600$$

This relationship, called a *transformation function*, relates the amounts of three products that could be produced, either by a firm or an economy. It is a function because only nonnegative values of the three variables are allowed.

Once *any two* outputs have been specified, the value of the other product is given by the equation. It might be possible to solve this function for any of the three variables, making that variable the dependent variable. Then we could determine the impact of changing one product on the (designated) dependent variable, holding the third output constant. However, we may wish to determine the influence of one variable on another, holding the third variable constant, without first transforming the function into explicit form. After all, it may not always be possible to solve the equation for one variable. In this case we merely apply the concept of the total differential, setting the result equal to zero (since the value of the right-side constant does not change).

$$2xdx + 1.6ydy + 1.2zdz = 0$$

If we wish to hold the output of good z constant and determine the impact of the change in x on y, then the third term drops out (because we stipulate that $dz = 0$), and we have:

$$2xdx + 1.6ydy = 0$$

or

$$\frac{dy}{dx} = -\frac{2x}{1.6y} = -1.25\left(\frac{x}{y}\right)$$

Similarly, we could stipulate that the change in x is zero and inquire about the impact of a change in y on z. In this case we have:

$$1.6ydy + 1.2zdz = 0$$

or

$$\frac{dz}{dy} = -\frac{1.6y}{1.2z} = -1.33\left(\frac{y}{z}\right)$$

These derivatives are called *marginal rates of transformation*. They measure how a change in the production of one good influences the rate of output of another good when other rates of output are held constant. The marginal rate of transformation is encountered frequently in both theoretical and applied economics.

SUMMARY

In this chapter we learned how to apply the rules of differentiation to functions of more than one independent variable. The *partial derivative* of the dependent variable with respect to one independent variable is obtained by using the rules of differentiation on the function in question, treating the other right-side variables as constants. We then defined the total differential as the total change in the dependent variable, which is equal to the sum of the partial derivative of the function with respect to each independent variable, times the change in that variable. We also saw that the percentage change in the dependent variable could be measured as the sum of the *partial elasticity* of the function with respect to each independent variable times the percentage change in that variable.

PROBLEMS

Group I

Find the first partial derivatives $\partial z/\partial x$ and $\partial z/\partial y$ for the following functions and the indicated values of the derivatives.

1. $z = f(x, y) = 3x^3 - x^2 + 3y^3 - y^2$.
    Find $f_x(2, 1), f_y(2, 1)$.

2. $z = f(x, y) = 3x^3 - y^2 + 2x^2y - 2y^3x + y$.
    Find $f_x(1, 2), f_x(3, 4), f_y(1, 2), f_y(3, 4)$.

3. $z = f(x, y) = (x^2y + 3y^3x)^2$.

4. $z = f(x, y) = \sqrt{x^2y^2 + 2xy}$.

5. $z = f(x, y) = \log_e(x^2 + 4y^2)$.

6. $z = f(x, y) = \log_e(2x^2y + 3xy + xy^2)$.
    Find $f_x(2, 4), f_y(1, 1)$.

7. $z = f(x, y) = e^x + (e^y)^2$.

Find the second partial derivatives $\partial^2 z/\partial x^2, \partial^2 z/\partial y^2, \partial^2 z/\partial x \partial y$. and $\partial^2 z/\partial y \partial x$ for the following functions and the indicated values of the derivatives.

8. $z = f(x, y) = xy$.
    Find $f_{xx}(-8, 4), f_{yy}(0, 0), f_{xy}(2, 10), f_{yx}(6, 3)$.

9. $z = f(x, y) = x^3 + x^2y^2 + 2xy$.
    Find $f_{xx}(3, 2), f_{yy}(4, 1), f_{xy}(1, 3), f_{yx}(1, 3)$.

10. $z = f(x, y) = \log_e(2x + y)$.

11. You are given the following aggregate consumption function for the economy as a whole:

$$C = 10 + 0.7Y + 0.13A^2$$

where C denotes total consumption, Y national income, and A total asset holdings by households.

a. Find the marginal propensity to consume out of income.
b. Find the marginal propensity to consume out of assets.

12. You are given the production function:

$$x = j(l, k, r, v)$$
$$= 10l + 50k + 20r + 12v - 0.5l^2 - 0.25k^2 - 0.2r^2 - 0.125v^2$$

where x represents total output and l, k, r, and v are amounts of factor inputs L, K, R, and V.

a. Find the marginal productivity functions for each of the factors of production.
b. Are there diminishing marginal returns to each of the factors? How do you know?
c. Compute the marginal products of each of the factors for $l = 10$, $k = 5$, $r = 20$, and $v = 14$.

13. You are given the following demand function for the commodity X:

$$x = 300 - 0.5p_x^2 + 0.02p_o + 0.05y$$

where x denotes the quantity demanded of X, p_x the price of X, p_o the price of a related commodity, and y consumer income.

a. Compute the price elasticity of demand when $p_x = 12$, $p_o = 10$, and $y = 200$.
b. Compute the cross-elasticity of demand for X with respect to p_o when $p_x = 12$, $p_o = 10$, and $y = 200$.
c. Compute the income elasticity of demand for X when $p_x = 12$, $p_o = 10$, and $y = 200$.

Group II

Find the first partial derivatives of the following functions.

14. $z = f(x, y) = 2x^4 - 7x^2y^2 + 5y^2 - 3y^4$.

15. $z = f(x, y) = \log_e(3x^2 - xy + 2y^2)^{1/2}$.

16. $z = f(x, y) = \left(\dfrac{x^2 + 3y}{x + 2y} \right)^3$.

17. $f(x, y, z) = 2x^2z - 3xyz - 0.5x^2y^2z^2 = 0$.

18. $f(x, y, z) = (4x - 3x^2z + yz^3 - 7)^2 = 0$.

19. $f(x, y, z) = \sqrt{x^2 + y^2 + z^2}$.

Find the second partial derivatives of the following functions.

20. $z = f(x, y) = \log_e xy + e^x + e^y$.

21. $z = f(x, y) = 2x^4 - 7x^2y^2 + 5y^2 - 3y^4$.

22. Let the production function for a commodity be given as:

$$x = a\sqrt{l}\sqrt{c}$$

where x denotes the commodity output, a is a positive constant, l represents the input of labor, and c represents the input of capital.

a. Show that the marginal physical product of each factor input is diminishing.

b. Show that doubling both inputs results in a doubling of output.

23. You are given the following supply function for a commodity X:

$$x = 100 + 0.10p^2 + e^p - 0.12w - 0.007m^2$$

where x denotes the quantity of X supplied, p the price of X, w the wage rate of labor employed in the production of X, and m the price of raw materials used in X. Find the equations for:

a. The price elasticity of supply

b. The wage elasticity of supply

c. The elasticity of supply with respect to the price of raw materials.

10

Maxima and

Minima of

Functions of

Several Variables

In Chapter 8 we applied the techniques of differentiation to identify the minimum and maximum values of functions with one independent variable. The advantage of investigating such functions is the ease with which they can be graphed, providing a visual depiction of the optimization procedures. However, functions of one independent variable are often unrealistic depictions of economic relationships. In this chapter we will explore how the tools of partial differentiation developed in Chapter 9 are used to locate maxima and minima of functions with two or more independent variables.

UNCONSTRAINED MAXIMIZATION
AND MINIMIZATION

Assume that a commodity is produced with a production function of the form:

$$q = f(L, K)$$

where q is the rate of output, L is the amount of labor services used, and K is the amount of capital services used. According to this function, q is given by the values of L and K. If we hold one input constant, we can attribute all variation in the rate of output to changes in the other input. In Figure 10.1, we set the amount of capital equal to K^*, a constant, and trace the short-run production function:

$$q = f(L, K^*)$$

This is a function of one independent variable, L. As demonstrated in Chapter 8, the necessary condition for a maximum or minimum of this function is that the first derivative with respect to L be zero:

$$\frac{\partial q}{\partial L} = f_L(L, K^*) = 0$$

In Figure 10.1 we see that the maximum value of q occurs at L^*, where the *first derivative function*, $\partial q/\partial L$, crosses the quantity axis. We verify that this is a local maximum because the value of the second derivative function, $\partial^2 q/\partial L^2$ is negative at L^*.

Figure 10.1

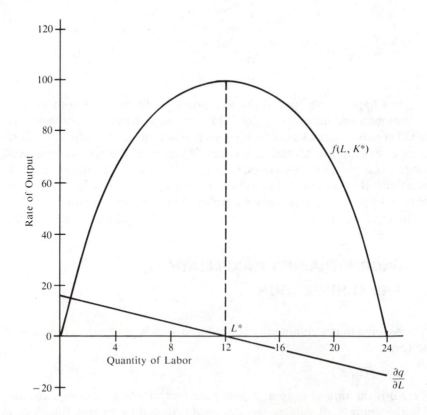

Having found a critical value for L, we proceed to search for critical values of K. Hence, we substitute $L = L^*$ into the two-variable production function, defining a short-run production function for capital. The function becomes:

$$q = f(L^*, K)$$

This is a function of one variable, K, which is plotted in Figure 10.2. We find that the short-run production function (of capital) reaches a local maximum at $K = K^*$, where the value of the first derivative is zero and the second derivative is negative. Now, *if the critical value of labor does not change*, we should find the global maximum of this function at the point $L = L^*$ and $K = K^*$.

From our investigation of Figures 10.1 and 10.2, we see that a local maximum should occur where the values of both *partial derivatives* are zero and both *second partial derivatives* are negative. However, these *necessary*

Figure 10.2

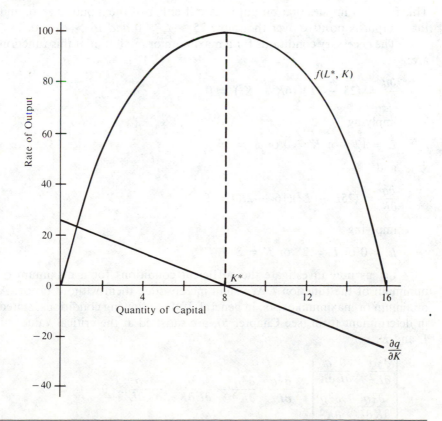

conditions only guarantee a maximum of the function *viewed from the axes of the independent variables*. In order to guarantee a maximum when the function is viewed from all directions, there is an additional requirement. The product of the cross-partial derivatives must be smaller than the product of the *second partial* derivatives:

$$\frac{\partial^2 q}{\partial L^2} \cdot \frac{\partial^2 q}{\partial K^2} - \frac{\partial^2 q}{\partial L \partial K} \cdot \frac{\partial^2 q}{\partial K \partial L} > 0$$

In our example, it is conceivable that the marginal product of one factor increases with increases in the use of the other factor. Therefore, while we may be able to define a maximum rate of output when either factor is held constant, we cannot define such a maximum when both inputs are allowed to vary. Indeed, this is a feature of many mathematical production functions. But let's proceed with an example that does have a global maximum.

For example, consider the production function given by the equation:

$$q = (25L - L^2)(16K - K^2)$$

This function implies that output is zero if either of the inputs is zero, and that output is positive over the range $25 > L > 0$ *and* $16 > K > 0$.

The necessary conditions for a maximum or minimum of this function are:

$$\frac{\partial q}{\partial L} = (25 - 2L)(16K - K^2) = 0$$

implying

$$L = 12.5 \text{ or } K = 0 \text{ or } K = 16$$

and

$$\frac{\partial q}{\partial K} = (25L - L^2)(16 - 2K) = 0$$

implying

$$L = 0 \text{ or } L = 25 \text{ or } K = 8$$

Let us now investigate the sufficient conditions for a maximum or minimum of the function f. We shall merely state them without proof. A minimum or maximum exists, in general, if the following conditions, stated in determinant form (see Chapter 5), are satisfied at the critical values of L and K:

$$\begin{vmatrix} \dfrac{\partial^2 q}{\partial L^2} & \dfrac{\partial^2 q}{\partial L \partial K} \\ \dfrac{\partial^2 q}{\partial K \partial L} & \dfrac{\partial^2 q}{\partial K^2} \end{vmatrix} = \frac{\partial^2 q}{\partial L^2} \cdot \frac{\partial^2 q}{\partial K^2} - \frac{\partial^2 q}{\partial L \partial K} \cdot \frac{\partial^2 q}{\partial K \partial L} > 0$$

This determinant must be positive in order to have a maximum or a minimum at the critical values of L and K.[1] Furthermore, we can state the conditions that will assure our having a maximum:

$$\frac{\partial^2 q}{\partial L^2} < 0 \text{ and } \frac{\partial^2 q}{\partial K^2} < 0$$

and the conditions that will assure our having a minimum:

$$\frac{\partial^2 q}{\partial L^2} > 0 \text{ and } \frac{\partial^2 q}{\partial K^2} > 0$$

Either one of these conditions will yield a positive value for the principal diagonal of the determinant. Therefore, we know that when the determinant is positive, and the signs of both second partial derivatives are negative, then the function is at a (local) maximum. Moreover, when the determinant is positive and the signs of both second partial derivatives are positive, the function is at a local minimum.

Let us return to our production function example. The solutions to the first-order conditions imply that $L = 12.5$ or $K = 0$ or $K = 16$, and $L = 0$ or $L = 25$ or $K = 8$. This gives us nine points to consider in the L-K plane: (0, 0), (0, 8), (0, 16), (12.5, 0), (12.5, 8), (12.5, 16), (25, 0), (25, 8), and (25, 16). We do not know whether a local minimum or maximum occurs at any of these points. Therefore, we compute the second partial derivatives:

$$\frac{\partial^2 q}{\partial L^2} = \frac{\partial[(25 - 2L)(16K - K^2)]}{\partial L} = -2(16K - K^2)$$

$$\frac{\partial^2 q}{\partial L^2} < 0 \text{ if } K = 8$$

$$\frac{\partial^2 q}{\partial L^2} = 0 \text{ if } K = 0 \text{ or if } K = 16$$

$$\frac{\partial^2 q}{\partial K^2} = \frac{\partial[(25L - L^2)(16 - 2K)]}{\partial K} = -2(25L - L^2)$$

$$\frac{\partial^2 q}{\partial K^2} < 0 \text{ if } L = 12.5$$

$$\frac{\partial^2 q}{\partial K^2} = 0 \text{ if } L = 0 \text{ or if } L = 25$$

[1] A maximum or minimum may occur when the value of the determinant is zero. As in the case of explicit functions of one variable, however, we shall ignore this possibility as being unimportant for our purposes.

We also compute the cross-partial derivatives:

$$\frac{\partial^2 q}{\partial K \partial L} = \frac{\partial[(25L - L^2)(16 - 2K)]}{\partial L} = (25 - 2L)(16 - 2K)$$

$$\frac{\partial^2 q}{\partial L \partial K} = \frac{\partial[(25 - 2L)(16K - K^2)]}{\partial K} = (25 - 2L)(16 - 2K)$$

$$\frac{\partial^2 q}{\partial L \partial K} = \frac{\partial^2 q}{\partial K \partial L} = 0 \text{ if } L = 12.5 \text{ or if } K = 8$$

$$\frac{\partial^2 q}{\partial L \partial K} > 0 \text{ and } \frac{\partial^2 q}{\partial K \partial L} > 0 \text{ if } L = 0 \text{ and } K = 0$$

Because the second partial derivatives are zero when $L = 0$ or 25 and when $K = 0$ or 16, we can eliminate eight of our possible nine points identified by the first derivative condition. That leaves us with only one candidate, the point (12.5, 8) on the L-K plane. We form the determinant of these derivatives for $L = 12.5$ and $K = 8$:

$$\begin{vmatrix} \dfrac{\partial^2 q}{\partial L^2} & \dfrac{\partial^2 q}{\partial L \partial K} \\ \dfrac{\partial^2 q}{\partial K \partial L} & \dfrac{\partial^2 q}{\partial K^2} \end{vmatrix} = \begin{vmatrix} -128 & 0 \\ 0 & -312.5 \end{vmatrix} = 40{,}000 > 0$$

Hence, we have either a maximum or a minimum when $L = 12.5$ and $K = 8$. We notice that both second partial derivatives are negative:

$$\frac{\partial^2 q}{\partial L^2} = -2(16K - K^2) = -128 < 0$$

$$\frac{\partial^2 q}{\partial K^2} = -2(25L - L^2) = -312.5 < 0$$

The value of q at this point is a relative maximum. To find the value of q at this point (the maximum value of $f(L, K)$), we merely substitute 12.5 for L and 8 for K into the function. Thus:

$$q_{max} = [25(12.5) - (12.5)^2][16(8) - 8^2] = (156.25)(64) = 10{,}000$$

Since the function is defined over the range $0 < L < 25$ and $0 < K < 16$, we check for the possibility of a corner solution. Output is zero at both "corners," i.e., when either $L = 0$ or 25 or $K = 0$ or 16. Thus, the local maximum at point (12.5, 8, 10,000) is also a global maximum.

In this particular example, the determinant turned out to be positive for one pair of independent variables and negative for the eight other pairs of independent variables. Hence, the function had only one critical point, a maximum. Had the second partial derivatives both been positive, the function would have taken a minimum value at that point. If more than one point had a positive value for the determinant, then there would have been multiple local maxima or minima, depending on the signs of the second partial derivatives.

This example used an explicit function of *two* independent variables, but we can extend the conclusion to include a function of any number of independent variables. The necessary condition for the existence of a maximum or a minimum of an explicit function of several variables is that all the first partial derivatives be equal to zero. For the function,

$$y = f(x_1, x_2, x_3, \ldots, x_n)$$

where the subscripts on the x's refer to different variables, we can write the necessary condition for a maximum or minimum as:

$$\frac{\partial y}{\partial x_i} = 0, \; i = 1, 2, 3, \ldots, n$$

The partial derivative of y with respect to each independent variable must be equal to zero. The sufficient conditions for a maximum or a minimum of a function of several variables involve mathematical techniques that are beyond the scope of this book.

CONSTRAINED OPTIMIZATION:
THE SUBSTITUTION APPROACH

The previous section involved a problem rarely encountered in economics, the search for a global maximum or minimum. In the case of the two-factor production function, the marginal products (first partial derivatives) of labor and capital both achieved the value of zero at a particular point: $L = 12.5$, $K = 8$, and $q = 10,000$. Increasing either labor or capital would have caused output to decrease. While such a circumstance is possible, the more typical optimization problem involves a limit or *constraint* on the values the independent variables can have, rather than a physical limit on the value of the dependent variable. The economic agent confronts an objective function (e.g., output maximization, utility maximization, cost minimization) for which no global maximum or minimum is defined, yet there are definite limits placed on the values of the independent variables that can be chosen. A *constraint function*, analytically distinct from the *objective function*, implies one or more optimal value(s) of the objective.

For example, suppose a production manager produces a commodity with a Cobb-Douglas production function of the form:

$$q = 2.5L^{2/3}K^{1/3}$$

where q is the rate of output, L is the quantity of labor services used, and K is the quantity of capital services used. Inspection of this equation reveals that there is no *global* maximum. The two first partial derivatives, namely:

$$\frac{\partial q}{\partial L} = \tfrac{5}{3}L^{-1/3}K^{1/3} = 1.67\left(\frac{K}{L}\right)^{1/3}$$

$$\frac{\partial q}{\partial K} = \tfrac{5}{6}L^{2/3}K^{-2/3} = 0.833\left(\frac{L}{K}\right)^{2/3}$$

are both positive for all positive values of L and K. A production manager who set out to maximize output would merely drive his firm into bankruptcy incurring exorbitant input costs trying to produce an infinite rate of output!

Output Maximization with a
Cost Constraint

It is reasonable to imagine that a production manager has been given a budget for factors of production, say $C = \$60,000$ per month, with which to purchase labor services (say at $w_L = \$10$/hour) and capital services (say at $w_K = \$5$/hour). His job is to *maximize the rate of output without exceeding his input cost constraint*. Expressed as a mathematical problem, the manager wishes to:

Maximize: $q = f(L, K) = 2.5L^{2/3}K^{1/3}$
Subject to: $C = 10L + 5K \leq 60{,}000$

The inequality in the constraint equation allows for the possibility of a *global* maximum existing for some combination of inputs whose cost falls short of the maximum allowable cost. However, in this problem we have already assured ourselves that no such global maximum exists. In this context, the cost constraint could be stated as an equation:

$$C = 10L + 5K = 60{,}000$$

How is such a problem solved?

Figure 10.3 is an isoquant/isocost diagram that illustrates the mathematical solution to our constrained output maximization problem. Recall from Chapter 3 that an isoquant represents all combinations of two inputs that produce the same rate of output. An isocost line shows all combinations of inputs that generate the same cost. The set of isoquants, labeled q_0, q_1, q_2, etc., represent alternative values of the objective (production) function. The isocost line, labeled C_2, depicts the cost constraint. According to microeconomic theory, the maximum rate of output consistent with this cost constraint is identified as q_2, whose isoquant is tangent to the isocost line at point R. Indeed, isoquant q_2 is the highest *attainable* isoquant. While isoquants for greater rates of output (e.g., q_3, q_4) are shown in Figure 10.3, these are unattainable—the cost associated with these combinations of labor and capital exceed the level of cost allowed.

Figure 10.3

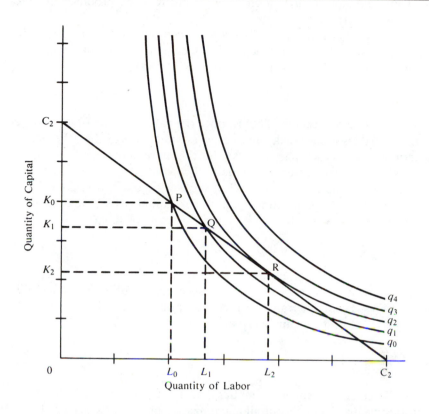

The isocost (constraint) line can be considered the search path for locating the optimal rate of output. The search begins at an arbitrary point, say point P, which is identified by the intersection of isoquant q_0 and the isocost line. The production manager (perhaps using a computer) calculates the cost of L_0 hours of labor and K_0 hours of capital, notes that the total cost equals the allowable cost, and then calculates and records the rate of output. Using an iterative method, the plant manager calculates the rate of output for other points lying along the isocost line. Points above and to the left of point P generate lower rates of output, while points to the immediate right of point P along the isocost line produce higher rates of output. By substituting labor for capital along the isocost line, the rate of output increases. Since q_1, produced at point Q (which also satisfies the cost constraint), exceeds q_0, point P is not the optimal point on the isocost line. Similarly, q_2, produced at point R (which also satisfies the cost constraint), exceeds q_1, and point Q is not the optimal point. However, there is no other point along the isocost line that generates a higher rate of output than point R. Thus, the input combination $L = L_2$ and $K = K_2$ produces the *maximum possible* rate of output, q_2.

One approach to solving this constrained output maximization problem is the "substitution approach," which emulates the graphical approach presented above. The constraint equation:

$$C = 10L + 5K = 60{,}000$$

has one degree of freedom. That is, once the value of one of the "independent" variables is specified, say as $L = L_0$, the value of the other input is determined: $L = L_0$ implies $K = K_0$. Furthermore, any time the amount of labor services are increased, the amount of capital services must be decreased in order to maintain the same level of cost. We make this relationship explicit by solving the constraint equation for capital (which we designate as the dependent variable for convenience) in terms of labor:

$$K = \frac{C - 10L}{5} = \frac{60{,}000}{5} - \frac{10L}{5} = 12{,}000 - 2L$$

Taking the derivative of K with respect to L, we find the slope of the isocost line. This is the rate at which capital must be reduced when labor is increased if cost remains constant:[2]

$$\frac{dK}{dL} = -2$$

The constraint equation implies that K is dependent on L. Adding the constraint equation to the output maximization problem means the objective function has only one independent variable. Therefore, the objective function can be maximized for L, under the condition that K decreases as L decreases according to the rule $dK/dL = -2$. Using the chain rule, we differentiate q with respect to L:

$$\frac{dq}{dL} = \frac{\partial q}{\partial L} + \frac{\partial q}{\partial K} \cdot \frac{dK}{dL}$$

$$= \tfrac{5}{3}L^{-2/3}K^{1/3} + \tfrac{5}{6}L^{2/3}K^{-2/3}(-2)$$

Notice that the value for dK/dL was substituted into the second expression. Setting this result equal to zero, we solve for the optimal values of L and K:

$$\frac{dq}{dL} = 0 \text{ implies } 1.67\left(\frac{K}{L}\right)^{1/3} = 1.67\left(\frac{L}{K}\right)^{2/3}$$

---

[2]An equivalent method of attaining the slope of the isocost line is to take the total differential of C with respect to L and K: $dC = (\partial C/\partial L)dL + (\partial C/\partial K)dK = 10dL + 5dK$. Setting $dC = 0$, we solve for dK/dL: $10dL + 5dK = 0$ implies $dK/dL = -10/5 = -2$.

Multiplying both sides of this expression by $(K/L)^{2/3}$ (the reciprocal of $(L/K)^{2/3}$), we obtain:

$$1.67\left(\frac{K}{L}\right) = 1.67 \text{ or } K = L$$

What we have is the formula for the optimal ratio, i.e., $K/L = 1$, of capital to labor for producing *any* rate of output. However, the maximum rate of output that can be produced in this context is *constrained* by the isocost equation, $C = 10L + 5K = 60,000$. To obtain the optimal quantities of L and K, we substitute L for K in the constraint equation:

$$C = 10L + 5K = 10L + 5(L) = 60,000$$
$$15L = 60,000$$
$$L = \frac{60,000}{15} = 4,000$$

$$K = L = 4,000$$

Finally, substituting the values for L and K into the production function, we discover the maximum output consistent with the cost constraint:

$$q = 2.5L^{2/3}K^{1/3} = 2.5(4,000)^{0.67}(4,000)^{0.33}$$
$$= 2.5(251.98)(15.87) = 10,000$$

Because the substitution approach generates only one independent variable (L), the second-order condition simplifies to verifying that the second derivative of q with respect to L is negative:

$$\frac{d^2q}{dL^2} = \frac{d(dq/dL)}{dL} = \frac{d(1.67L^{-1/3}K^{1/3} - 1.67L^{2/3}K^{-2/3})}{dL}$$
$$= \frac{d(dq/dL)}{dL} + \frac{d(dq/dL)}{dK} \cdot \frac{dK}{dL}$$
$$= -0.56L^{-4/3}K^{1/3} - 1.11L^{2/3}K^{-5/3} - 1.11L^{-1/3}K^{-2/3}$$
$$\quad - 1.11L^{-1/3}K^{-2/3}$$
$$= -0.56L^{-4/3}K^{1/3} - 1.11L^{2/3}K^{-5/3} - 2.22L^{-1/3}K^{-2/3} < 0$$

Finally, since the constraint equation is defined for the domain, $6,000 \geq L \geq 0$ (i.e., the range $12,000 \geq K \geq 0$), we check for corner solutions at the points $(0, 12,000)$ and $(6,000, 0)$ on the L-K plane. However, since $2.5(0)^{2/3}(12,000)^{1/3} = 2.5(6,000)^{2/3}(0)^{1/3} = 0$, we are assured that the optimal point on the constraint line ($L = 4,000$, $K = 4,000$) is also the global maximum *along the constraint line*.

Cost Minimization with an Output Constraint

One of the more important notions in production and cost theory is that there are equivalent solutions to maximizing output under a cost constraint and minimizing cost under an output constraint. Imagine that a production manager, confronting the production function of the previous example, was told to produce 10,000 units of output at minimum cost. Formally, this objective function would be stated as:

Minimize: $C = 10L + 5K$

Subject to: $f(L, K) = 2.5L^{2/3}K^{1/3} \geq 10,000$

In this case, the isoquant for $q = 10,000$ is the search path for the lowest available isocost line. In Figure 10.4, the search begins at point P, where isoquant $q = 10,000$ intersects the isocost line C_4. By substituting labor for capital, production is switched from point P to point Q, where the same isoquant intersects a lower isocost line (C_3). Since part of isoquant $q = 10,000$ still lies below isocost line C_3 at point Q, the search continues until point R is reached. At point R, isoquant $q = 10,000$ is tangent to isocost line C_2. It is impossible to reduce cost any further (e.g., to C_1 or C_0) unless output also is reduced.

Figure 10.4

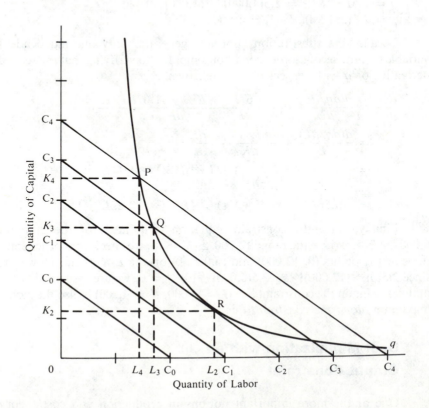

To solve this problem by substitution, we transform the objective function into a function with one independent variable. Since we are trying to reduce cost as far as permissible, we must be *constrained* to augment capital when labor is reduced (or vice-versa) so that output remains constant. This can be done by solving the production function for capital and substituting that expression into the cost function:

$$2.5L^{2/3}K^{1/3} = 10,000 \text{ implies } L^{2/3}K^{1/3} = 4,000$$

implying

$$K^{1/3} = \frac{4,000}{L^{2/3}}$$

or

$$K = \left(\frac{4,000}{L^{2/3}}\right)^3 = \frac{640,000,000}{L^2}$$

With the augmented cost function now given by:

$$C = 10L + 5\left(\frac{64,000,000,000}{L^2}\right)$$

we simply set dC/dL equal to zero and solve for L. We obtain the corresponding value of K by substitution:

$$\frac{dC}{dL} = 10 - \frac{640,000,000,000}{L^3} = 0$$

$$10L^3 = 640,000,000,000$$
$$L = (64,000,000,000)^{1/3} = 4,000$$

$$K = \frac{64,000,000,000}{(4,000)^2} = 4,000$$

The resulting cost is given by:

$$C = 10(4,000) + 5(4,000) = 40,000 + 20,000 = 60,000$$

Finally we can verify that we have a cost minimum, rather than a maximum, by taking the second derivative of the augmented cost function with respect to L:

$$\frac{d^2C}{dL^2} = \frac{d(10 - 640,000,000,000/L^3)}{dL}$$

$$= -3(-640,000,000,000)L^{-4} > 0$$

Since isoquant $q = 10,000$ is asymptotic to both axes (q cannot equal 10,000 when either $K = 0$ or $L = 0$), we do not have any corners to check. In this case, the local minimum is also the global minimum (for points satisfying the output constraint).

In this section we have seen that a *constrained* optimization problem, wherein both the objective function and the constraint have two independent variables, can be turned into an objective function involving only one variable. First, we employed the chain rule, whereby the objective function was differentiated with respect to one of the independent variables, and the derivative of the other independent variable with respect to the first was obtained by differentiating the constraint equation. As an alternative approach, we solved the constraint equation for one of the choice variables, then substituted that expression for that variable in the objective function. In the process we verified the dual nature of the cost minimization/output maximization problem: equivalent solutions are obtained when the cost (output) function is used as the constraint and the output (cost) function serves as the objective. When the objective and constraint equations are interchangeable, the practicing economist can solve either specification of the problem and obtain an equivalent result.

THE LAGRANGE MULTIPLIER
TECHNIQUE

Despite its apparent simplicity, there are two drawbacks to the substitution approach to optimization problems outlined above. First, these problems are limited to functions with two independent variables, which in many contexts is little improvement over the limitations imposed by techniques employing functions of one independent variable. Second, there are many contexts wherein the explicit form of the constraint equation is unknown, making direct substitution through solving the constraint equation impossible.

To illustrate, let's add a third factor of production, E for energy, to the production function. Let the new production function be given by:

$$q = f(L, K, E) = 2.5L^{1/2}K^{1/3}E^{1/6}$$

We imagine that our production manager has been given the task of maximizing the rate of output, subject to a cost constraint of \$60,000 to spend on the three factors (the unit price of energy being \$2):

$$C = 10L + 5K + 2E \leq 60,000$$

Because there are three independent variables in both the constraint equation and the objective function, we cannot create an augmented function with just one independent variable. Nevertheless, there is a way of introducing the constraint into the objective function making use of *Lagrange multipliers*. First, we write the constraint equation so that it equals zero when the constraint is satisfied:

$$g(L, K, E) = 60,000 - 10L - 5K - 2L = 0$$

Then we write an augmented function of the form:

$$h(L, K, E) = f(L, K, E) + \lambda g(L, K, E)$$
$$= 2.5L^{1/2}K^{1/3}E^{1/6} + \lambda(60{,}000 - 10L - 5K - 2E)$$

Now there are *four* unknowns: L, K, E, and λ. The symbol λ is an unknown constant called the *Lagrange multiplier*. In this maximization problem, the danger is picking values of L, K, and E whose total cost exceeds the allowed expenditure of \$60,000. By imagining λ to be a large positive number, we build "negative feedback" into the augmented function. If the combination of L, K, and E violates the constraint, the constraint term becomes negative, offsetting the increase in output. However, when the constraint is satisfied, the value of the term multiplied by λ becomes zero, and the values of L, K, and E that maximize q will also maximize $h(L, K, E)$.

The necessary conditions for a maximum of $h(L, K, E)$ are:

$$\frac{\partial h}{\partial L} = \frac{\partial f}{\partial L} + \lambda \frac{\partial g}{\partial L} = 1.25L^{-1/2}K^{1/3}E^{1/6} - 10\lambda = 0$$

$$\frac{\partial h}{\partial K} = \frac{\partial f}{\partial K} + \lambda \frac{\partial g}{\partial K} = 0.833L^{1/2}K^{-2/3}E^{1/6} - 5\lambda = 0$$

$$\frac{\partial h}{\partial E} = \frac{\partial f}{\partial E} + \lambda \frac{\partial g}{\partial E} = 0.417L^{1/2}K^{1/3}E^{-5/6} - 2\lambda = 0$$

$$\frac{\partial h}{\partial \lambda} = \frac{\partial f}{\partial \lambda} + \lambda \frac{\partial g}{\partial \lambda} = 60{,}000 - 10L - 5K - 2E = 0$$

The necessary conditions give us a system of four equations in four unknowns. The first three equations can be solved for any of the factors of production in terms of the other two (the λ disappears).

Taking the first two equations, solving for λ and setting the resulting expressions equal to each other, we have:

$$\lambda = 0.125L^{-1/2}K^{1/3}E^{1/6} = 0.167L^{1/2}K^{-2/3}E^{1/3}$$

Multiplying both expressions by $L^{1/2}K^{2/3}$, we have:

$$0.125KE^{1/6} = 0.167LE^{1/6} \rightarrow K = \tfrac{4}{3}L$$

Taking the first and third equations, solving for λ and setting the resulting expressions equal to each other, we have:

$$\lambda = 0.125L^{-1/2}K^{1/3}E^{1/6} = 0.208L^{1/2}K^{1/3}E^{-5/6}$$

This time we multiply both sides of the expression by $K^{2/3}E^{5/6}$ and we obtain:

$$0.125K^{1/3}E = 0.208K^{1/3}L \rightarrow E = 1.67L = \tfrac{5}{3}L$$

With the formula for the optimal ratio of capital to labor ($K = \frac{4}{3}L$) and the optimal ratio of energy to labor ($E = \frac{5}{3}L$), we can substitute for those inputs in the fourth (constraint) equation and solve for L:

$$60,000 - 10L - 5(\tfrac{4}{3}L) - 2(\tfrac{5}{3}L) = 0$$
$$\tfrac{60}{3}L = 60,000$$
$$20L = 60,000$$
$$L = 3,000$$

It follows that $K = \frac{4}{3}(3,000) = 4,000$ and $E = \frac{5}{3}(3,000) = 5,000$. Substituting these three input levels into the production function, we have the maximum rate of output:

$$q_{max} = 2.5(3,000)^{1/2}(4,000)^{1/3}(5,000)^{1/6}$$
$$= 2.5(54.772)(15.874)(4.135) = 8,988.398$$

Substituting the optimal values of L, K, and E in any of the three expressions for λ, we have:

$$\lambda = 0.125(3,000)^{-1/2}(4,000)^{1/3}(5,000)^{1/6}$$
$$= 0.167(3,000)^{1/2}(4,000)^{-2/3}(5,000)^{1/6}$$
$$= 0.208(3,000)^{1/2}(4,000)^{1/3}(5,000)^{-5/6} = 0.150$$

Note that λ is the common ratio of the marginal product of each input to its price; λ can be interpreted as the marginal productivity of the last dollar spent on each input when all inputs are used efficiently.

We can verify the equivalence of the output maximization problem (with a cost constraint) and the cost minimization problem (with an output constraint) by switching the objective and constraint equations in the augmented function. Hence, we define:

$$\pounds = 10L + 5K + 2E + \lambda(8,988.398 - 2.5L^{1/2}K^{1/3}E^{1/6})$$

When the expression inside the parentheses is zero, the constraint is satisfied and the combination of inputs which minimizes ($10L + 5K + 2E$) will also minimize function $\pounds$.

As before, the necessary conditions for a minimum are obtained by taking the partial derivative of $\pounds$ with respect to L, K, E, and λ, setting each partial derivative equal to zero and solving:

$$\frac{\partial \pounds}{\partial L} = 10 - \lambda(1.25L^{-1/2}K^{1/3}E^{1/6}) = 0 \text{ implies } \lambda = \frac{8}{L^{-1/2}K^{1/3}E^{1/6}}$$

$$\frac{\partial \pounds}{\partial K} = 5 - \lambda(0.833L^{1/2}K^{-2/3}E^{1/6}) = 0 \text{ implies } \lambda = \frac{6}{L^{1/2}K^{-2/3}E^{1/6}}$$

$$\frac{\partial \pounds}{\partial E} = 2 - \lambda(0.417L^{1/2}K^{1/3}E^{-5/6}) = 0 \text{ implies } \lambda = \frac{4.8}{L^{1/2}K^{1/3}E^{-5/6}}$$

$$\frac{\partial \pounds}{\partial \lambda} = 8,988.398 - 2.5L^{1/2}K^{1/3}E^{1/6} = 0 \text{ implies } 2.5L^{1/2}K^{1/3}E^{1/6} = 8,988.398$$

Again we have four equations in four unknowns. These can be solved by eliminating the λ from the first three equations, solving for one of the inputs in terms of the other two, and substituting in the fourth (constraint) equation:

$$\lambda = \frac{8}{L^{-1/2}K^{1/3}E^{1/6}} = \frac{6}{L^{1/2}K^{-2/3}E^{1/6}}$$

implies

$$8L^{1/2}K^{-1/3}E^{-1/6} = 6L^{-1/2}K^{2/3}E^{-1/6}$$
$$L = 0.75K$$

From the second and third equations:

$$\lambda = \frac{6}{L^{1/2}K^{-2/3}E^{1/6}} = \frac{4.8}{L^{1/2}K^{1/3}E^{-5/6}}$$

implies

$$6L^{-1/2}K^{2/3}E^{-1/6} = 4.8L^{-1/2}K^{-1/3}E^{5/6}$$
$$E = 1.25K$$

Substituting into the fourth (constraint) equation, we have:

$$2.5(0.75K)^{1/2}K^{1/3}(1.25K)^{1/6} = 2.5(0.866)(1.031)K = 8,988.398$$
$$2.232K = 8,988.398$$
$$K = 4,000$$

Substituting the optimal ratios of labor and capital, we have:

$$L = 0.75K = (0.75)(4,000) = 3,000$$
$$E = 1.25K = (1.25)(4,000) = 5,000$$

Inserting these quantities into the cost equation, we have:

$$C = 10(3,000) + 5(4,000) + 2(5,000) = 60,000$$

This is the minimum cost of producing the target rate of output. Finally, we insert the appropriate values for L, K, and E in the formulas for λ, and we have:

$$\lambda = \frac{8}{L^{-1/2}K^{1/3}E^{1/6}} = \frac{8}{1.198} = 6.676$$

$$= \frac{6}{L^{1/2}K^{-2/3}E^{1/6}} = \frac{6}{0.899} = 6.676$$

$$= \frac{4.8}{L^{1/2}K^{1/3}E^{-5/6}} = \frac{4.8}{7.19} = 6.676$$

In this case the Lagrange multiplier, λ, is equal to the ratio of each factor's price to its marginal product and λ can be interpreted as long-run marginal cost.

APPLICATIONS OF THE
LAGRANGE MULTIPLIER TECHNIQUE

The Lagrange multiplier approach to constrained optimization has many economic applications. Indeed, all problems that can be handled with the substitution approach to constrained maxima and minima can also be handled with the Lagrange multiplier approach. However, the reverse is not the case. There are many problems that can be solved with the Lagrange multiplier method that cannot be solved by the substitution approach.

Utility Maximization with an
Income Constraint

We turn to the economic theory of consumer choice. In economics each consumer is assumed to maximize the total utility he or she derives from the goods consumed, subject to a budget constraint (that is, given household income and the prices of commodities). For the sake of simplicity we shall assume the individual consumes three goods, X, Y, and Z. Let the quantities of these goods be denoted by x, y, and z, respectively. We assume, in addition, that the consumer spends his or her entire (given) income on these three goods. The unobservable and unmeasurable utility function is given symbolically as:

$$u = f(x, y, z)$$

where u designates total utility. The budget equation of the consumer is:

$$p_x x + p_y y + p_z z = I$$

where p_x is the price of good X, p_y is the price of good Y, p_z is the price of good Z, and I is given money income. The constants of this equation are p_x, p_y, p_z, and I. The budget equation states that all income is spent on X, Y, and Z, since $p_x x$ is expenditure on X, $p_y y$ is expenditure on Y, and $p_z z$ is expenditure on Z.

The basic assumption of consumer choice theory is that the consumer will maximize u, subject to the side conditions imposed by the budget constraint. The individual maximizes u by choosing the appropriate amounts of X, Y, and Z, taking into consideration the market prices of those goods and money income. This is a problem of constrained maximization.

Because there are three independent variables in both the constraint equation and the objective function, we cannot create an augmented function with just one independent variable. Again, we solve this problem by introducing *Lagrange multipliers*. First we write the constraint so that the function equals zero when the constraint is met:

$$g(x, y, z) = I - p_x x - p_y y - p_z z = 0$$

Then we write an augmented function of the form:

$$h(x, y, z) = f(x, y, z) + \lambda g(x, y, z)$$

Again we have *four* unknowns: $x, y, z,$ *and* λ. The necessary conditions for a maximum of $h(x, y, z)$ are:

$$\frac{\partial h}{\partial x} = \frac{\partial f}{\partial x} + \lambda \frac{\partial g}{\partial x} = 0$$

$$\frac{\partial h}{\partial y} = \frac{\partial f}{\partial y} + \lambda \frac{\partial g}{\partial y} = 0$$

$$\frac{\partial h}{\partial z} = \frac{\partial f}{\partial z} + \lambda \frac{\partial g}{\partial z} = 0$$

$$\frac{\partial h}{\partial \lambda} = g(x, y, z) = 0$$

However,

$$\frac{\partial g}{\partial x} = \frac{\partial (I - p_x x - p_y y - p_z z)}{\partial x} = -p_x$$

$$\frac{\partial g}{\partial y} = \frac{\partial (I - p_x x - p_y y - p_z z)}{\partial y} = -p_y$$

$$\frac{\partial g}{\partial z} = \frac{\partial (I - p_x x - p_y y - p_z z)}{\partial z} = -p_z$$

and

$$g(x, y, z) = 0 \text{ implies } I = p_x x + p_y y + p_z z$$

Consequently, we can write the necessary conditions for a maximum of h (i.e., the *constrained* maximum of u) as:

$$\frac{\partial f}{\partial x} - \lambda p_x = 0, \text{ implying } \lambda = \frac{\partial f/\partial x}{p_x}$$

$$\frac{\partial f}{\partial y} - \lambda p_y = 0, \text{ implying } \lambda = \frac{\partial f/\partial y}{p_y}$$

$$\frac{\partial f}{\partial z} - \lambda p_z = 0, \text{ implying } \lambda = \frac{\partial f/\partial z}{p_z}$$

and

$$I = p_x x + p_y y + p_z z$$

We have three expressions for λ. Hence, each of these expressions is equal to each other one:

$$\lambda = \frac{\partial u/\partial x}{p_x} = \frac{\partial u/\partial y}{p_y} = \frac{\partial u/\partial z}{p_z}$$

The final equation implies that the total expenditure on goods X, Y, and Z exactly equals money income, which is the constraint requirement.

Furthermore, the unknown λ is equal to the ratio of the marginal utility of each good purchased to its price; another name for λ is the *marginal utility of income*.

The Allocation of Time Between
Work and Leisure

One of the assumptions we made in developing the simple consumer choice theory was that money income is constant. In reality, of course, people can influence their money income by the types of jobs they choose and the number of hours they devote to work as opposed to leisure. Let us pursue the second issue, imagining that an individual has accepted a job that pays a wage rate of w_o dollars per hour, and that this same person has nonlabor income equal to π_o dollars per month. This makes the person's monthly income equal to:

$$y = \pi_o + w_o t_w$$

where y is real income per month and t_w is the total hours of work per month. We can simplify matters by imagining the month is February, with twenty typical working days, eight weekend days, and $28(24) = 672$ potential hours of work, which we will designate as T.

Of course, no one works 24 hours a day, 28 days a month. Human physiology, let alone human psychology, is not made to maintain such a strain. Hence, individuals do not maximize income, but are assumed to maximize utility, which is a function of real income and nonlabor (leisure) time, $t_l = T - t_w$:

$$u = u(y, t_l)$$

In this case we could use either the substitution or the Lagrange multiplier approach, given the simple *time* constraint:[3]

$$T = t_w + t_l$$

We will use the Lagrange multiplier approach.

First, we define the function:

$$\pounds = u(y, t_l) + \lambda(T - t_w - t_l)$$

The two independent variables are t_w and t_l which are linked by the time constraint. The necessary condition for a maximum of the function $\pounds$ is

---

[3]We are making the *simplifying* assumption that all time not spent earning a money income is spent in leisure. This is clearly not the case, since much "household time" is actually spent in "household production." For a further elaboration of this point, see Gary S. Becker, "A Theory of the Allocation of Time," *Economic Journal*, (September 1965), pp. 493-517.

obtained by taking the partial derivative of this function with respect to the choice variables, t_w and t_l, and the unknown Lagrangian multiplier, λ:

$$\frac{\partial \pounds}{\partial t_w} = \frac{\partial u}{\partial y} \cdot \frac{\partial y}{\partial t_w} - \lambda = 0 \text{ implies } \lambda = \frac{\partial u}{\partial y} \cdot \frac{\partial y}{\partial t_w} = \frac{\partial u}{\partial y} \cdot w_o$$

$$\frac{\partial \pounds}{\partial t_l} = \frac{\partial u}{\partial t_l} - \lambda = 0 \text{ implies } \lambda = \frac{\partial u}{\partial t_l}$$

$$\frac{\partial \pounds}{\partial \lambda} = \frac{\partial \lambda(T - t_l - t_w)}{\partial \lambda} = 0 \text{ implies } T = t_w + t_l$$

Again we have a system of equations with three unknowns (t_w, t_l, and λ). A utility maximum implies that time is allocated between work and leisure so that the marginal utility of income generated by the last hour's work equals the marginal utility generated by the last hour's leisure. Furthermore, since $\partial y / \partial t_w = w_o$, this result simplifies to:

$$\lambda = w_o \cdot \frac{\partial u}{\partial y} = \frac{\partial u}{\partial t_l} \qquad or \qquad \frac{\partial u / \partial t_l}{\partial u / \partial y} = w_o$$

By allocating time so that the relative marginal utility of leisure time is equal to its opportunity cost (the foregone wage rate), the individual maximizes utility under his or her time constraint.

The Allocation of Consumption Over Time

Another assumption that is made in the simple model of consumer choice is that the consumer must spend all income in the period it is earned. In reality, of course, people save and borrow, spending either less or more than their current income, respectively. Economic theory can take saving and borrowing into account by imagining that consumers maximize utility in the present while confronting a *multiperiod income constraint*. Imagine that the person's utility function takes the form:

$$u_t = u(C_t, C_{t+1})$$

where u_t is the utility experienced in the present, C_t is present consumption, and C_{t+1} is consumption *expected* for next year. In other words, the satisfaction resulting today reflects the satisfaction from current consumption and the prospect of future consumption. But how do they know what their future consumption will be?

This question concerns *risk and uncertainty*, which will be discussed in greater detail in Part II of this text. At this stage of the analysis we simply note that people realize that their current consumption decisions influence their future consumption prospects. If we consume less than our current income, we save; the increase in our wealth (or reduction in our debt) enhances our future consumption prospects. If we consume more than our current income, we borrow; the reduction in our wealth (or increase in our debt) reduces our future consumption prospects. Hence, we face a multiperiod budget constraint. We do not have to restrict our consumption to our present income, but our future consumption possibilities will reflect our present consumption decisions.

For simplicity, we will assume that consumption occurs in two periods, today (t) and tomorrow ($t + 1$). Consumption tomorrow equals next year's *expected* income, y_{t+1}, plus savings (or debt) resulting from today's consumption decision. If the household consumes less than current income ($C_t < y_t$), it can augment future consumption by that saving plus accumulated interest earnings: $(1 + r)(y_t - C_t)$. If consumption today exceeds current income, then future consumption is reduced by the principal and interest payments on that debt: $(1 + r)(C_t - y_t)$. In either case, next year's consumption is given by y_{t+1} plus the deviation of present consumption from present income, times $(1 + r)$ where r is the market rate of interest:

$$C_{t+1} = y_{t+1} + (1 + r)(y_t - C_t)$$

Subtracting C_{t+1} from both sides of the equation transforms it into constraint form.

The consumer is assumed to maximize the utility function,

$$u_t = u(C_t, C_{t+1})$$

subject to the budget constraint,

$$y_{t+1} - C_{t+1} + (1 + r)(y_t - C_t) = 0$$

This problem can be expressed in the Lagrange multiplier form as:

$$\pounds = u(C_t, C_{t+1}) + \lambda[y_{t+1} - C_{t+1} + (1 + r)(y_t - C_t)]$$

The necessary condition for a maximum value of $\pounds$ is that the first partial derivatives of $\pounds$ with respect to C_t, C_{t+1}, and λ equal zero:

$$\frac{\partial \pounds}{\partial C_t} = \frac{\partial u}{\partial C_t} - \lambda(1 + r) = 0 \text{ implies } \lambda = \frac{\partial u/\partial C_t}{1 + r}$$

$$\frac{\partial \pounds}{\partial C_{t+1}} = \frac{\partial u}{\partial C_{t+1}} - \lambda = 0 \text{ implies } \lambda = \frac{\partial u}{\partial C_{t+1}}$$

$$\frac{\partial \pounds}{\partial \lambda} = y_{t+1} - C_{t+1} + (1 + r)(y_t - C_t) = 0$$

The first two equations imply:

$$\lambda = \frac{\partial u/\partial C_t}{1 + r} = \frac{\partial u}{\partial C_{t+1}}$$

or

$$\frac{MU_t}{MU_{t-1}} = 1 + r$$

That is, income is allocated in the current period so that the marginal rate of substitution equals the market rate of interest plus one. The last equation implies:

$$C_{t+1} = y_{t+1} + (1 + r)(y_t - C_t)$$

This assures that future consumption is restricted by the present consumption decision.

SUMMARY

This chapter has explored the process by which maxima and minima of multivariate functions are identified. Although there are few cases in economics wherein unconstrained maxima and minima are relevant, we found that a necessary condition for such maxima or minima is that the first partial derivatives of the function with respect to each of the independent variables be zero. A sufficient condition for either a maximum or a minimum is that the product of the second partial derivatives minus the product of the cross-partial derivatives be positive (for functions with two independent variables). If this condition is satisfied and the second partial derivatives are both negative, a maximum exists. If the second partial derivatives are both positive, a minimum exists.

We then investigated the case of *constrained* maxima and minima. In such cases the economic agent attempts to minimize or maximize a function subject to side conditions that limit the values of the choice (independent) variables. Two approaches to constrained optimization were presented. The substitution approach involves first solving the constraint equation for one of the variables, substituting into the objective function, then using the chain rule to maximize the objective function with respect to the other variable. The substitution approach is limited to functions of two independent variables. The Lagrange multiplier approach involves optimizing a function which is composed of the objective function plus the constraint equation (specified to equal zero when the constraint is satisfied) multiplied by the Lagrange multiplier. Then the hybrid function is differentiated with respect to the choice variables and the Lagrange multiplier, and the results are set equal to zero.

PROBLEMS

Find the maxima and/or minima, if any, of the following functions for the ranges of the independent variables specified.

1. $z = f(x, y) = (x^2 - 1)(y^2 - 1)$.
     $-\frac{1}{2} < x < \frac{1}{2}, \ -\frac{1}{2} < y < \frac{1}{2}$

2. $z = f(x, y) = 10 + 3x^2 - x + 2y^3 - y.$
     $-3 < x < 3, -3 < y < 3$

3. $z = f(x, y) = x^2 y.$
     $-10 < x < 10, -10 < y < 10$

4. $z = f(x, y) = 2 + x^2 + y^2.$
     $-3 < x < 3, -3 < y < 3$

5.   A firm produces an output with two inputs, v_1 and v_2, according to
     the function:

     $$q = 10\sqrt{v_1}\sqrt{v_2}$$

     Each unit of V_1 costs \$10 and each unit of V_2 costs \$5. The manager
     has a budget of \$10,000 for inputs. What is the maximum rate of out-
     put the manager can produce and what are the optimal quantities of
     the two inputs?

6.   The production function of a firm (in the short run) is given as:

     $$x = j(l, k) = 3l^2 - 0.01l^3 + 0.4k^2 - 0.02k^3$$

     where x denotes the amount of the commodity X produced and l and
     k denote the amounts of the factors of production L and K. Find the
     maximum value of x and the associated values of l and k.

7.   Assume the total net investment function for the economy as a whole
     is given as:

     $$I = f(i, Y) = 50 + 8i - 40i^2 + 0.6Y - 0.003Y^2$$

     where I denotes total investment, i denotes the interest rate, and Y
     denotes national income. Find the values of i and Y that would pro-
     duce the maximum value of I, and find the value of maximum I.

8.   A firm attempts to maximize output given by the production function
     $q = 2.5L^{2/3}K^{1/3}$, subject to the cost constraint $C = 10L + 5K =$
     60,000. Compare this answer to the example in the second section of
     this chapter (see page 192). What happens to the optimal quantity of
     inputs when the price of one input increases? Does this result carry over
     to the cost minimization problem with an output constraint?

9.   Redo the example in the third section of this chapter (page 198), chang-
     ing the production function to $q = 2.5L^{2/3}K^{1/6}E^{1/6}$, and keeping the
     cost constraint $C = 10L + 5K + 2E$. Compare the results of the output
     maximization problem with those in the example. How does a change
     in the output elasticities of inputs affect the optimal combination of
     inputs?

11

Elements of

Integral

Calculus

The concept of an *integral*, which completes our discussion of calculus, is encountered in economic analysis, and plays an important role in the development of statistical techniques. We may look at this concept from two different angles. From one viewpoint, an integral is the limit of a certain summation or addition process. In geometric terms, this interpretation corresponds to the area enclosed by a curve or by a set of curves. Regarded in this way, the integral is called the *definite integral*.

From another viewpoint, an integral is the result of reversing the process of differentiation. When y is a function of x and its derivative exists, then the derivative of y is also a function of x. The reverse problem is that of finding from a given derivative, the function from which the derivative was derived. If it can be found, this second function is called the *indefinite integral* of the given function. Let us consider each of these viewpoints separately, and then turn to additional economic applications of these perspectives on the integral.

THE DEFINITE INTEGRAL

Suppose we have a marginal revenue curve for a monopolist given by the equation:

$$MR = f(Q) = 100Q^{-1/2}$$

Also suppose we wish to find the area under this curve above the quantity axis from $Q = 4$ to $Q = 9$. (This area would correspond to the additional revenue the monopolist would receive by increasing output from 4 to 9 units.) We can obtain an approximation of the total area under the curve by first considering the approximate area of one part of the total area. We can next consider another part of the total area, and so on until we have considered all parts. For example, we can first consider the part from $Q = 4$ to $Q = 5$. The approximate area under this section of the curve is the area of the rectangle whose width is one and whose height is $f(5) = 100/\sqrt{5} \approx 100/2.236 \approx 44.72$. The curve corresponding to $p = 100Q^{-1/2}$ and the rectangle described above are shown in Figure 11.1.

Figure 11.1

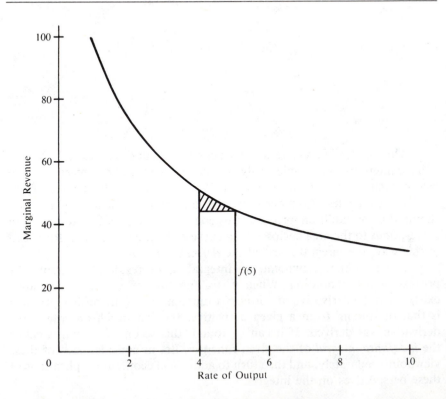

The area of the rectangle is $44.72 \cdot 1 = 44.72$. We say the area of this rectangle is an *approximation* of the area under the curve (and above the Q-axis) between $Q = 4$ and $Q = 5$, because it involves an error equal to the shaded portion between the rectangle and the curve.

Next, we treat the area under the curve between $Q = 5$ and $Q = 6$. This area is approximated by the area of the rectangle whose width is $6 - 5 = 1$ and whose height is $f(6) = 100/\sqrt{6} \approx 100/2.45 \approx 40.82$. This rectangle also involves an error equal to that portion that lies between the rectangle and the curve. Proceeding in this way, we compute the areas of the rectangles up to and including $Q = 9$. Now the approximate total area under the curve and above the Q-axis from $Q = 4$ to $Q = 9$ is the sum of the areas of the five rectangles so computed. Figure 11.2 shows the curve and the five rectangles. The total error committed in estimating the area under the curve is equal to the sum of the five shaded portions between the rectangles and the curve.

We can calculate the sum of the areas of the five rectangles. It is:

$$f(5) \cdot 1 + f(6) \cdot 1 + f(7) \cdot 1 + f(8) \cdot 1 + f(9) \cdot 1$$
$$= 44.72 + 40.82 + 37.80 + 35.36 + 33.33 = 192.03$$

Figure 11.2

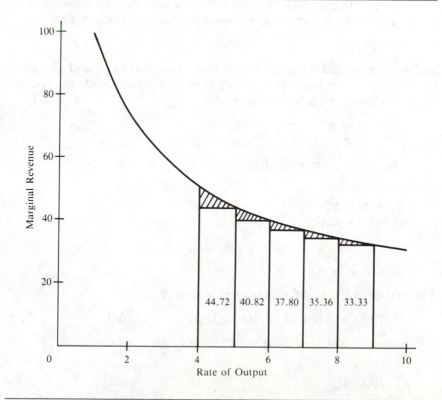

We conclude that 192.03 is the approximate area under the curve and above the Q-axis from $Q = 4$ to $Q = 9$. To write this more conveniently, we introduce the operator Σ. This Greek letter, sigma, means "the summation of." Hence, we write:

$$\sum_{Q=5}^{9} f(Q)(\Delta Q) = 192.03$$

The symbol

$$\sum_{Q=5}^{9}$$

means that we let Q increase by finite increments from $Q = 5$ to $Q = 9$. Since in our example $\Delta Q = 1$, we would expand the preceding expression as follows:

$$\sum_{Q=5}^{9} f(Q)(\Delta Q) = f(5) \cdot 1 + f(6) \cdot 1 + f(7) \cdot 1 + f(8) \cdot 1 + f(9) \cdot 1$$
$$= 192.03$$

It is easy to generalize this procedure for obtaining an approximation of the area under a curve. Assume we know the equation of a curve,

$$R = f(Q)$$

and we wish to find the approximate area under this curve and above the Q-axis between the limits $Q = a$ and $Q = b$. We first divide the interval from a to b into n parts of equal width:

$$\Delta Q = \frac{a - b}{n}$$

The subdivisions (including $Q = a$ and $Q = b$) are:

$Q_0 = a$
$Q_1 = a + \Delta Q$
$Q_2 = a + 2\Delta Q$
.   .
.   .
.   .
$Q_n = a + n(\Delta Q) = b$

The sum of the areas of n rectangles is given by:

$$f(Q_1)\Delta Q + f(Q_2)\Delta Q + f(Q_3)\Delta Q + \ldots + f(Q_n)\Delta Q$$

Using the operator Σ, we can write this sum more concisely as:

$$\sum_{i=1}^{n} f(Q_i)(\Delta Q)$$

Up to this point, we still have only an approximate measure of the area under a curve, but we require an exact measure. Looking at Figure 11.2, we can see that if we let ΔQ get smaller, the error involved in using the sum of the areas of the rectangles also becomes smaller. For instance, if we let $\Delta Q = 1/2$ instead of 1, we get twice as many rectangles from $Q = 4$ to $Q = 9$ and the sum of the shaded areas becomes smaller. If we set $\Delta Q = 1/4$, the sum of the shaded areas would become even smaller. Finally, if we let ΔQ approach zero, the sum of the errors also approaches zero. Stating this another way, if we let n approach infinity (let the number of rectangles approach infinity), the error disappears. Hence, we have as the exact measure of the area under a curve given by $f(Q)$ and above the Q-axis between the limits $Q = a$ and $Q = b$:

$$\lim_{n \to \infty} \sum_{i=1}^{n} f(Q_i)(\Delta Q) = \int_{a}^{b} f(Q) \, dQ$$

The last expression is called the *definite integral*, and the symbol $\int$ is an operator meaning "sum" similar to the Σ operator. The Σ operator is used to indicate the sum of a finite series of discrete elements; the operator $\int$ is used to indicate the limit of the sum of an infinite number of elements in a continuous function. When the number of values on Q in the interval between $Q = a$ and $Q = b$ approaches infinity, the change in Q from one value of Q to the next approaches zero. Thus, the ΔQ in the first expression becomes dQ in the second, just as in the case of a derivative. The definite integral is a limiting sum that gives the area under the curve. It is a limit, just as the derivative is a limit, except in this case it is the limit of a sum.

So much for the meaning of the definite integral. The process of computing the integral is called *integration*, and is the reverse of the process of differentiation. There are rules similar to those presented for the differentiation of a function. These we develop in the next section.

RULES OF INTEGRATION

Because integration involves reversing the process of differentiation, there are rules for indefinite integration that parallel those of differentiation. The first one parallels the power function rule for derivatives.

1. The *power rule:* Given a function of the form $y = f(x) = x^n$, where n is a real number and $n \neq -1$, then

$$\int f(x) \, dx = \int x^n \, dx = \frac{1}{n + 1}(x)^{n+1} + k$$

For example:

$$\int x \, dx = \tfrac{1}{2}x^2 + k$$

$$\int x^2 \, dx = \tfrac{1}{3}x^3 + k$$

$$\int x^{-17} \, dx = \frac{1}{-16}x^{-16} + k = -\frac{1}{16}x^{-16} + k$$

Note the addition of the unknown constant k in each of the above examples. That is because the derivative of any constant term in a function is zero. The constant k is added to the integral for the purpose of generality. Since the derivative of a constant is zero, the result of differentiation is not affected if an arbitrary constant is added to the function. Hence:

$$\frac{d}{dx}\int (n + 1)x^n \, dx = \frac{d}{dx}(x^{n+1}) = dx(x^{n+1} + k) = (n + 1)x^n$$

As mentioned, the power function rule of integration works for all values of n *except* $n = -1$. However, in Chapter 6 we learned that the derivative of the *natural logarithm* of a variable (plus or minus an arbitrary constant) is the reciprocal of that variable. That is:

$$\frac{d(\log_e x)}{dx} = \frac{1}{x} = x^{-1}$$

From this information we can derive rule 2.

2. The integral of the reciprocal of a variable is equal to the natural logarithm of that variable, plus an arbitrary constant.

$$\int x^{-1} \, dx = \log_e x + k$$

Another fact about derivatives that has many useful applications in integral calculus involves the exponential function of the form $y = e^x$. Since:

$$\frac{d(e^x)}{dx} = e^x$$

it follows that:

3. The integral of an exponential function of the form $y = e^x$ equals the exponential function plus a constant.

$$\int e^x \, dx = e^x + k$$

In Chapter 6 we saw that the derivative of the sum (or difference) of two functions is equal to the sum (or difference) of their derivatives, and that the derivative of a constant times a function equals that constant times the derivative of that function. The next three rules are straightforward extensions of those rules for derivatives.

4. The integral of the sum of functions is the sum of the integrals of those functions.

$$\int (f(x) + g(x)) \, dx = \int f(x) \, dx + \int g(x) \, dx$$

5. The integral of the difference of functions is the difference in their integrals.

$$\int (f(x) - g(x)) \, dx = \int f(x) \, dx - \int g(x) \, dx$$

6. The integral of a constant times a function is the constant times the integral of the function.

$$\int k f(x) \, dx = k \int f(x) \, dx$$

Suppose we have a variable y, which is a function of u, while u is a function of x. According to the chain rule of differentiation:

$$\frac{dy}{dx} = \frac{dy}{du} \cdot \frac{du}{dx}$$

There are many problems in integration that require a reversal of the chain rule. For example, suppose we have a problem of the form:

$$F(x) = \int 2e^{2x} \, dx$$

How do we determine the form of the function $F(x)$?

First we note that the integral of $e^u \, du = \int e^u \, du = e^u + k$. However, the integral of $e^u \, dx = (1/du/dx) e^u + k$. If we designate u as $2x$, we have $du/dx = 2$. Therefore, by *substitution*, we have:

$$\int 2e^{2x} \, dx = \int (e^{2x}) 2 \, dx = \int e^u \, du = e^u + k$$

7. The substitution rule: the integral of a function of the form:

$$\int f(u) \cdot \frac{du}{dx} \cdot dx = \int f(u) \, du$$

Consider the following example:

$$\int (2x^3 + 8x)\, dx = \int (x^2 + 4)\, 2x\, dx = \int u\, du$$

where $u = (x^2 + 4)$ and $du = 2x\, dx$. Since $\int u\, du = \frac{1}{2}u^2$:

$$\int (x^2 + 4)\, 2x\, dx = \frac{1}{2}(x^2 + 4)^2 + k$$

As another example:

$$\int \frac{2x}{(x^2 + 2)^2}\, dx = \int \frac{1}{u^2}\, du = (-1)u^{-1} + k = -\frac{1}{x^2 + 2} + k$$

where $u = x^2 + 2$.

Textbooks on calculus customarily give tables of indefinite integrals for more complicated functions, and this greatly facilitates the procedure of integration.

THE INDEFINITE INTEGRAL

Indefinite integration is the reverse of differentiation. It consists of finding a function whose derivative is given. If $f(Q)$ is a given function and $F(Q)$ is an unknown function with the characteristic that $F'(Q) = f(Q)$, we write for the indefinite integral:

$$\int f(Q)\, dQ = F(Q) + k$$

where k is some arbitrary constant.

In the first section of this chapter, we were given a marginal revenue function:

$$MR = \frac{dR}{dQ} = 100Q^{-1/2}$$

This time we have expressed the function $f(Q)$ as a "differential equation" involving the derivative dR/dQ of a function R, so far unknown. We know:

$$\frac{d}{dQ}(200Q^{1/2}) = 100Q^{-1/2}$$

Therefore, one possible function we seek is:

$$R = 200Q^{1/2}$$

But if we were to add any constant whatsoever to this function, we would get the same derivative. Consequently, this is not a unique solution to the differential equation. If we were to add an arbitrary constant k (where k may also be zero), then

$$R = 200Q^{1/2} + k$$

is the function required. We may write this result as follows:

$$\int (100Q^{-1/2}) \, dQ = 200Q^{1/2} + k$$

Notice that the additive constant, which disappears on differentiation, reappears in the reverse process. Given the *total revenue function* $R = F(Q) = 200Q^{1/2} + k$, we have:

$$\frac{dR}{dQ} = \frac{d(200Q^{1/2} + k)}{dQ} = \tfrac{1}{2}(200Q^{-1/2}) = 100Q^{-1/2}$$

as desired. Reversing the process:

$$\int (100Q^{-1/2}) \, dQ = 200Q^{1/2} + k$$

Sometimes, we can use other information to determine the value of k. For example, we know from economic theory that total revenue is zero when output (quantity sold) equals zero. Substituting:

$$R(0) = 200(0)^{1/2} + k = 0 \text{ implying } 0 + k = 0 \text{ or } k = 0$$

With this additional information, we can write the indefinite integral as:

$$R = \int (100Q^{-1/2}) \, dQ = 200Q^{1/2}$$

Application: Maximum Profit
for the Competitive Firm

Suppose a competitive firm produces with a *marginal cost* function given by:

$$MC = \frac{dC}{dq} = q^2 - 6q + 10$$

where q is the rate of output and the (unknown) function $C(q)$ is the total cost function. If the prevailing price of the output is $p = 10$, we know from Chapter 8 that the derivative of profit (π) with respect to output is:

$$\frac{d\pi}{dq} = p - MC = 10 - (q^2 - 6q + 10) = 6q - q^2$$

Setting $d\pi/dq$ equal to zero, and solving for q, we find the critical values of q:

$$6q - q^2 = 0 \text{ implies } q = 0 \text{ or } q = 6$$

Taking the derivative of $d\pi/dq$ with respect to q gives us the second derivative of the profit function, which separates the local maximum from the local minimum:

$$\frac{d^2\pi}{dq^2} = \frac{d(6q - q^2)}{dq} = 6 - 2q$$

$$6 - 2(0) > 0 \text{ and } 6 - 2(6) < 0$$

Hence, $q = 0$ is the local *minimum* (where the firm loses its fixed costs), and $q = 6$ is the profit *maximum* (where the firm covers at least a portion of fixed costs).

Without knowledge of the total cost function, we are apparently unable to determine exactly what the firm's maximum profits are. However, we can take the integral of the *marginal profit* function, which was used to determine the optimal rate of output, to estimate the profit function:

$$\pi(q) = \int \frac{d\pi}{dq} dq = \int (6q - q^2) dq = 3q^2 - \tfrac{1}{3}q^3 + k$$

$$\pi(6) = 3(6)^2 - \frac{1}{3}(6)^3 + k = 3(36) - \frac{216}{3} + k = 36 + k$$

In this case, $k = \pi(0) = -FC$, where FC is the firm's fixed cost. Hence, the maximum profit that can be earned when the price is $10 is $36 *minus fixed cost*. In other words, knowledge of the marginal profit function (price minus marginal cost) allows us to calculate *gross profit*, that is, total revenue minus variable cost. Calculation of net profit requires the additional knowledge of fixed cost.

COMPUTATION OF THE DEFINITE INTEGRAL

With knowledge of indefinite integration as the reverse of differentiation, we can answer the question: How does one compute the definite integral? The answer is given in what is known as the fundamental theorem of the integral calculus. We merely assert it here without proof.

If f is a given continuous function, if a and b are numbers, and if F is any function such that $F'(x) = f(x)$, then

$$\int_a^b f(x) \, dx = F(b) - F(a)$$

Let us see how this theorem is used to obtain the definite integral illustrated in the first section of this chapter. We were given there a marginal revenue function:

$$MR = f(Q) = 100Q^{-1/2}$$

We wish to find the definite integral from $Q = 4$ to $Q = 9$. From our knowledge of indefinite integration, we know:

$$R(Q) = \int (100Q^{-1/2})\, dQ = 200Q^{1/2} + k$$

Therefore, by the fundamental theorem:

$$\int_4^9 (100Q^{1/2})\, dQ = R(9) - R(4) = [200(9)^{1/2} + k] - [200(4)^{1/2} + k]$$
$$= 600 - 400 = 200$$

We interpret this result geometrically in the following way. The area under the marginal revenue curve given by $MR = 100Q^{1/2}$ and above the quantity axis from $Q = 4$ to $Q = 9$ is 200. Recall that our approximation of this area was 192.03. The total error involved in using the sum of the areas of the rectangles with $\Delta Q = 1$ amounts to 7.97. This is the total area of the shaded portions between the rectangles and the curve in Figure 11.2.

Suppose our problem is to find the area under the marginal cost curve:

$$MC = q^2 - 6q + 10$$

from $q = 0$ to $q = 6$. The indefinite integral is:

$$C(q) = \int (q^2 - 6q + 10)\, dq = \int q^2\, dq - \int 6q\, dq + \int 10\, dq$$
$$= \tfrac{1}{3}q^3 - 3q^2 + 10q + k$$

We check this by seeing if the reverse process of differentiation of the function $C(q)$ gives MC:

$$\frac{d}{dq} C(q) = \frac{d}{dq}(\tfrac{1}{3}q^3 - 3q^2 + 10q + k)$$
$$= q^2 - 6q + 10 = MC$$

The definite integral is evaluated as:

$$\int_0^6 (q^2 - 6q + 10)\, dq = C(6) - C(0)$$
$$= [\tfrac{1}{3}(6)^3 - 3(6)^2 + 10(6) + k]$$
$$- [\tfrac{1}{3}(0)^3 - 3(0)^2 + 10(0) + k]$$
$$= 72 - 108 + 60 + k - 0 + 0 - 0 - k$$
$$= 24$$

The area under the marginal cost curve corresponding to:

$$MC = q^2 - 6q + 10$$

and above the axis from $q = 0$ to $q = 6$ is 24.

APPLICATIONS OF INTEGRATION

Some of the most important applications of integration in economic problems must await discussion of probability theory in a later part of this book. We will mention a few additional applications at this time. These applications are designed to emphasize the relationship of integration to differentiation and to familiarize you with the basic value of integral calculus in economic analysis.

Consumer Surplus

We have already seen that the definite integral of a firm's marginal revenue function over some range of output provides a measure of total revenue generated by a specified increase in output. Now we investigate a related concept in demand theory, the concept of consumer surplus. Suppose we have an income compensated demand curve[1] with the equation:

$$Q_d = 100 - 10p$$

Furthermore, suppose $p = 5$, so that $Q_d = 50$. It is easy to see that total consumer expenditure is $5 \times 50 = 250$. However, economic theory tells us that the benefits that consumers receive from the 50 units they purchase exceeds their expenditure of $250. The difference between total consumer benefits and consumer expenditure is known as *consumer surplus* and can be measured as the difference between the area under the demand curve and the total expenditure rectangle given by price times quantity.

Since demand curves are plotted with quantity on the horizontal axis and price on the vertical axis, we begin by solving the demand equation for price:

$$Q_d = 100 - 10p \text{ implies } p = 10 - 0.1Q$$

In this case p can be interpreted as the *maximum* price consumers would pay for the last unit, given the quantity already consumed. Hence, the maximum price consumers would pay for the fiftieth unit is determined by substituting $Q = 50$ into the reverse demand equation: $p = 10 - 0.1(50) = 5$, which is the price that gave us $Q_d = 50$ in the first place. However, if $Q < 50$, the price consumers are willing to pay exceeds $5. The fact that consumers can also buy these units at a price of $5 generates a *consumer surplus*, which we seek to measure. (See Figure 11.3.)

---

[1] An income compensated demand curve is a demand curve along which real income is held constant (by varying money income at different prices) so that the change in quantity demanded due to changes in price reflects only the substitution effect. The area under an income compensated demand curve measures the *maximum* expenditure a group of consumers would spend in order to obtain each quantity of the commodity in question.

Figure 11.3

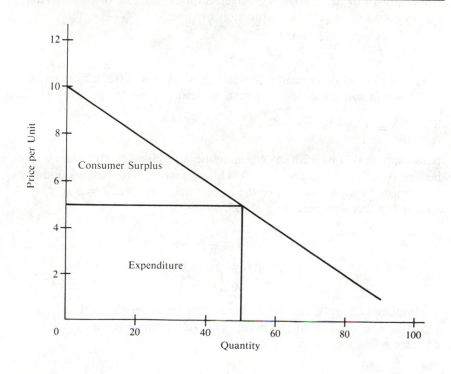

The area under the demand curve between $Q = 0$ and $Q = 50$ is given by the definite integral:

$$\int_0^{50} (10 - 0.1Q)\, dQ = [10(50) - 0.05(50)^2] - [10(0) - 0.05(0)^2]$$
$$= 500 - 125 = 375$$

Given that the area under the (inverse) demand curve between $Q = 0$ and $Q = 50$ is 375, we find the consumer surplus by subtracting total expenditure, which we have already calculated as 250. Hence, the consumer surplus for 50 units is $375 - 250 = 125$. By purchasing 50 units of the good at a price of $5 each, consumers obtain benefits worth $125 more to them than the $250 of purchasing power they must sacrifice to consume that commodity.

Investment and the Capital Stock

Now we turn our attention to an application from macroeconomic theory, specifically "steady state" growth theory that assumes the economy is approaching a stable equilibrium through time (unless "jolted" by population growth or technological change). Suppose the rate of net investment for an economy is given as a function of time:

$$I_t = f(t) = \frac{250}{t}$$

We know that net investment is the change in the capital stock from one year to the next (assuming a one-year gestation period for new equipment). Hence:

$$\frac{dK}{dt} = I_t = \frac{250}{t}$$

Now suppose that we wish to determine the total change in the capital stock between the time $t = 5$ and $t = 10$. This corresponds to the area under the investment function and above the horizontal axis from $t = 5$ to $t = 10$. Expressing this as a definite integral:

$$K = \int_5^{10} \frac{250}{t} dt = 250(\log_e 10) - 250(\log_e 5)$$

$$= 250(2.303) - 250(1.609)$$

$$= 575.65 - 402.36 = 173.29$$

The values of $\log_e 10$ and $\log_e 5$ were obtained from the table of natural logarithms at the end of the book. The area under the investment curve corresponding to:

$$I = \frac{250}{t}$$

and above the horizontal axis from $t = 5$ to $t = 10$ is 173.29.

SUMMARY

In this chapter we have briefly reviewed the elements of integral calculus. The *indefinite integral* is obtained by reversing the process of differentiation. Given $f(x) = F'(x)$, the indefinite integral is given by:

$$\int f(x)\, dx = F(x) + k$$

Because the derivative of a constant is zero, in reversing the process of differentiation, we cannot determine (without additional information) what additive constant was in the original function. Hence, the indefinite integral always includes an arbitrary constant term, here designated as k.

Since the indefinite integral involves reversing the process of differentiation, the *rules* of integral calculus closely parallel the rules of differential calculus.

The rules introduced in this chapter were:

1. For derivatives of the form $dy/dx = x^n$, the original function y is obtained as:

$$y = \int x^n \, dx = \frac{1}{n+1} x^{n+1} + k$$

   as long as $n \neq -1$.

2. For derivatives of the form $dy/dx = 1/x$, the integral is the natural logarithm of x, plus an arbitrary constant:

$$y = \int \frac{1}{x} \, dx = \log_e x + k$$

3. The indefinite integral of the exponential function with base e is the exponential function plus an arbitrary constant:

$$\int e^x \, dx = e^x + k$$

4. The integral of the sum of functions equals the sum of the integrals of those functions.

5. The integral of the difference of functions equals the difference in their integrals.

6. The integral of a constant times a function is that constant times the integral of the function.

7. Sometimes complicated integrals can be simplified by reversing the chain rule of differentiation. Hence, an integration problem of the form:

$$\int \frac{df(u)}{du} \cdot \frac{du}{dx} \, dx$$

   Can more easily be solved in the form:

$$\int f'(u) \, du$$

Next we turned to the calculation of the definite integral, which is used to measure the area beneath a curve. Given a function of the form $y = f(x)$, the area under the curve between two values of x, say $x = a$ and $x = b$, is given by calculating the indefinite integral at $x = b$, then subtracting the value of the indefinite integral at $x = a$. Since the arbitrary constants cancel, the definite integral is written as:

$$\int_a^b f(x) \, dx = F(b) - F(a)$$

where $f(x) = dF(x)/dx$.

PROBLEMS

Group I

Find the indefinite integrals, $f(x)$, of the following functions.

1. $f'(x) = 7 + 4x - 9x^2$.

2. $f'(x) = \frac{1}{2}x^2 + \frac{1}{2}x^{-2}$.

3. $f'(x) = \sqrt{x} + \sqrt[3]{x}$.

4. $f'(x) = a + bx - cx^2 - dx^3 + e^x$.

5. $f'(x) = 6(2x + 5)^2$.

Find the following definite integrals.

6. $\displaystyle\int_1^6 (6x + 8)\, dx$

7. $\displaystyle\int_1^4 \frac{1}{x}\, dx$

8. $\displaystyle\int_4^9 \frac{2}{\sqrt{x}}\, dx$

9. The marginal cost of production function of a firm is given as:

    $$C'(x) = 14 - 0.3x^2 + 0.08x^3$$

    where C' denotes marginal cost and x denotes the quantity produced. Find the total cost function if total cost is known to be $3,000.

10. The marginal revenue function of a monopolist is given as:

    $$R'(x) = 50 - 0.0002x^2$$

    where R' denotes marginal revenue and x denotes the quantity produced and sold. It is known that total revenue is zero when $x = 0$. Find the market demand function for the commodity. (Hint: First find price as a function of x, then solve for x as a function of p).

Group II

Find the indefinite integrals, $f(x)$, of the following functions.

11. $f'(x) = x^{-2} + x^{-1} + 8x - 1$.

12. $f'(x) = \frac{1}{x^3} - \frac{1}{x} + \frac{1}{4}$.

13. $f'(x) = \sqrt{a + bx}$.

14. $f'(x) = \dfrac{1}{x} - e^x - \dfrac{1}{x^2} + \dfrac{1}{2\sqrt{x}}$.

Find the following definite integrals.

15. $\displaystyle\int_{2}^{10} 5\,dx$

16. $\displaystyle\int_{1}^{7} (2x^3 - 2x^2 - 2x + 2)\,dx$

17. $\displaystyle\int_{-3}^{3} \left(\dfrac{1}{x^2} + x^2 - \dfrac{1}{5}x \right) dx$

18. $\displaystyle\int_{2}^{23} \dfrac{1}{\sqrt{3 + 2x}}\,dx$

19.   When national income is zero, total consumption equals $20 billion. The marginal propensity to consume is 0.85. Find the consumption function and the saving function.

20.   The market demand function for a commodity X is given as:

$$x = \dfrac{20}{p}$$

where x denotes the quantity demanded per unit of time and p denotes the price of x. Find the area under the demand curve and above the quantity axis from $x = 2$ to $x = 10$.

PART II

From

Mathematics

to Statistics

12

Static

Models

We have now reached a transition point in this book. Part I presents the basic tools for mathematical analysis and demonstrates how these tools are used in economic models. In Part I we saw that relationships among economic magnitudes can be formulated in mathematical terms. A set of economic relationships can be expressed by a set of one or more equations, such as cost equations, profit equations, or supply and demand equations. We explored how a system of equations can be solved using either standard algebra or matrix algebra techniques. We also examined the operations of differential and integral calculus, exploring how these tools are used to describe the optimizing behavior of economic agents. In Part III we will investigate the statistical techniques that allow us to estimate the mathematical parameters of the equations that describe actual economic events. We will discover that the econometrician must specify the form an equation is to have and the variables that will be involved in the estimation of an economic relationship. It follows that we need to know how to express economic concepts in mathematical form, a topic only partly developed so far in the text.

Throughout Part I you encountered economic illustrations of mathematical techniques. The validity of these economic examples was rarely questioned. Nor was the logic behind various theories exhaustively explored. Such explorations are the purview of microeconomic and macroeconomic theory courses. Yet we have reached a stage in this text when we are being asked to participate more directly in the process of model construction. In the five chapters of Part II, we will address such issues as: How are hypotheses about economic relationships stated in mathematical terms? What are the *types* of equations that economists use? Why and how do we distinguish between economic variables that are predicted by the equation system and those that are taken as given or *predetermined*? How is time handled in an economic equation, and how does this treatment influence the way in which a relationship is tested? What kinds of information are economic agents assumed to possess? How does the assumption about information correspond to the ability of the investigator to analyze the underlying equations that describe the behavior of such agents? How can we estimate the probability of different economic events, and how does this information assist in the testing of competing hypotheses?

HYPOTHESES, MODELS, AND THEORIES

An economist, like any scientist, strives to communicate in clear and precise language. At the same time, an economist strives to be unique, to be different from other economists. The tension between these two goals frequently shows up as a confusion of terminology. While most economists use the same terms, they frequently have slightly different meanings for those terms. One source of confusion involves the terms *hypothesis*, *model*, and *theory*. Many times these terms are used interchangeably. Yet there are subtle and important distinctions among these terms. We will pause briefly to establish the distinctions, as we will use the three terms throughout the rest of the book.

By a *hypothesis* we mean a declaration of fact that may or may not be true. Hypotheses tend to be very simple statements, and as such, they often lack precision. For instance, we may hypothesize that an increase in investment spending increases real consumption. This statement might be true for an economy with excess capacity, but incorrect for an economy operating at full employment. Or we may hypothesize that an increase in the price of a commodity will reduce consumption. This would be true if the demand curve does not shift, but may be false if another influence on consumer behavior, such as income or the prices of related goods, changes. In order to test a hypothesis, the researcher must stipulate the conditions under which it is expected to be true. In order to incorporate these conditions into the test of the hypothesis, the econometrician constructs a *model*.

An *econometric model* is an abstract representation of the operation of economic forces in the "real world," just as an architect's blueprint is an abstract depiction of a real building. From the viewpoint of the model, we regard economic life as explainable by a system of equations, and the model is a complete system of such equations. One or more of the equations may represent the hypothesis the researcher wishes to test. Other equations are added to make the system capable of solution. If the equations can be solved for the values of the endogenous variables, a prediction has been made. For a stipulated set of values for exogenous variables, specific values of endogenous variables are inferred. More important, *changes* in the value(s) of one or more exogenous variables predict changes in the values of endogenous variables. For example, we might solve simultaneously a demand equation and a supply equation to determine the equilibrium values of market price and quantity traded (the variables observed using actual market data). Of even greater interest will be predictions about how changes in income or prices of other goods (which shift the demand curve), or changes in the number of sellers or the prices of inputs (which shift the supply curve), change price and quantity exchanged.

In the process of model construction, the hypothesis often precedes the model. The researcher has an idea he or she wishes to test, and constructs a model to provide a mathematical framework to test the hypothesis. When we encounter someone else's work, however, we are first presented with a model, from which hypothetical propositions are deduced. In this case, the model comes before the hypothesis. In point of fact, there is a continuous interaction between models and hypotheses. Interest in a hypothesis motivates the original design of the model, but as the model is refined, the hypothesis itself is modified.

If a hypothesis survives repeated tests (i.e., it is not contradicted by empirical evidence), it ultimately can achieve the status of a *theory*. If a hypothesis is contradicted by empirical evidence, either the model through which the hypothesis is expressed must be modified or the hypothesis may be abandoned entirely. Once a hypothesis achieves the status of a theory, it continues to be expressed in the framework of its model. Hence, the terms *hypothesis*, *model*, and *theory* are sometimes used interchangeably. Actually, all theories are models, and all models are (or contain) hypotheses. However, there are hypotheses that are not models, since they have not been specified as a system of equations. And there are models that are not theories, since the relevance of the model has not been demonstrated empirically.

Mathematical and Econometric Models

Part I of this book deals almost exclusively with mathematical models of economic relationships. Relationships between economic variables are assumed to hold exactly and every system of equations is assumed to have a unique solution. Part III of this book explores the estimation of econometric models. Before proceeding further we should elaborate on the connection between mathematical models and econometric ones.

Actually, *econometric* models are special cases of mathematical models. As we have seen, a mathematical model is used to express an economic hypothesis as a system of equations (including the simple case of a system with one equation). As such, mathematical models are not constrained by empirical concerns such as data availability. One can construct mathematical models stipulating relationships between utility, tastes, or expectations—variables that are difficult to measure or observe. An econometric model is a mathematical model that is specified to conform to the constraints of data availability; i.e., which variables can be observed and in what form is the data collected? An econometric model must conform to the general requirements of a mathematical model in that the number of endogenous variables to be found must be no greater than the number of equations in the system. In addition, econometric models are also governed by the rules of statistical inference, which we will study in Part III.

Static and Dynamic Models

Another distinction between economic models involves the role of time in the process of generating solutions. *Dynamic models* involve considerations of time, and these models will be discussed in the next chapter. In this chapter we treat *static models*. Static models abstract from time, just as other models abstract from details considered irrelevant in testing a particular hypothesis. In static models, economic relationships are viewed as occurring at an instant of time. It is as if we froze time by taking a snapshot of economic relationships (equations) at a single moment. Indeed this is precisely what the econometrician does when using data that reflect observations on events occurring at discrete intervals of time (*time-series data*) or that reflect the behavior of different agents at roughly the same time (*cross-section data*).

How then do we account for changes? When we are working with a static model, we assume that each observation constitutes a set of equilibrium values of the variables in the system. Obviously the values of those variables change from one observation to the next, but we do not concern ourselves with the process by which the adjustment took place. Our data do not allow that process to be observed anyway. For instance, if there is a shift in the supply curve (the value of one or more exogenous variables in the supply equation changes), the equilibrium values of price and quantity demanded are assumed to correspond to the price and quantity observed in the later data. However, the data hide the process by which the new equilibria are attained. Consider the case of the adjustment of households' aggregate consumption to a change in national income. If we have annual observations on income and consumption, we assume that the change in consumption from one year to the next reacts to the change in income over that same period; consumers are assumed to spend their additional income in the year they receive it.

When viewing the world through a static model, we are concerned only with comparisons of equilibrium values of the variables in question. In a supply and demand model the supply and demand equations represent different contingencies at the same time and place; the equilibrium values of price and quantity reconcile the forces represented by supply and demand. In a mathematical model, if either the supply curve or the demand curve shifts (an exogenous variable in either the supply or demand equation changes), the old equilibrium immediately becomes irrelevant, and the new equilibrium (the new solution to the system of equations) can be calculated. Econometricians use static models when they believe that the speed of the adjustment process is sufficiently short that each subsequent observation of variables can be treated as an observation of equilibrium variables.

The static view of economic activity may seem to be a great distortion of reality. It involves a timeless world. The gain in convenience and simplicity, however, may outweigh the cost of the distortions. If we keep in mind the purpose of a model, namely to make predictions and to facilitate the testing of hypotheses, we cannot make unreasonable demands on the model. Hence, if the available data do not allow us to trace the process by which a system moves from one equilibrium to another, we can hardly fault the model for not doing that which the data already make impossible. However, there are some problems in which time lags in the adjustment process are crucial to the predictions of the model. For the solution of these problems, a static model may not be adequate. For other problems or other purposes, the time lags may be small enough to be ignored without serious harm to the predictions.

THE EQUATIONS OF THE MODEL

Before actually demonstrating the construction of static models, we must examine more closely the equations that make up the system. Not all of the equations in an econometric model are of the same nature. The equations of a model are called *structural equations*, because they show the basic structure of the firm, industry, economy, etc., that is being studied. Depending on the complexity of the problem and the particular interests of the economist, the number of structural equations will vary, that is, the "size" of the model will vary. A simple model designed to predict United States national income may contain single structural equations describing total consumer spending, total investment spending, total government spending, net exports, and the rate of interest, with additional equations linking the equilibrium values of these variables. On the other hand, large-scale econometric models may contain literally hundreds of equations depicting the output of individual components of consumption, investment, government spending, foreign trade, and the term structure of interest rates. The number of equations in the model will depend in part on the number of variables the econometrician is trying to explain or the number of hypotheses being tested. It will also depend on the number of other variables required to explain or predict changes in any one variable of interest.

A requirement of good model construction is insuring that all the variables an econometrician seeks to explain are consistent with an underlying model. A specialist in macroeconomics might wish to discover why the inverse relationship between price changes and unemployment rates, which seemed to be strong until the late 1960s, became so weak during the 1970s. Simply relating the rate of inflation to the unemployment rate might confirm or contradict the relationship between those two variables, but would not provide insights into the link between those factors. However, by linking wage rate changes to unemployment, productivity changes, and the rate of inflation, while connecting the rate of inflation to wage rate changes, money supply changes, and changes in fuel prices, a more complete model is generated. Hence, although the hypothesis being tested may be very simple, the econometric model necessary to adequately test that hypothesis might be considerably more complex.

Behavioral Equations

In general, the structural equations of a model are of two kinds: *behavioral equations* and *definitional equations*. Let us treat behavioral equations first. These equations describe the actions of individuals or groups in the economy. They contain theoretical or hypothetical statements in mathematical form and are capable of disproof or *disverification*. The behavioral equations may describe the response of consumption to changes in income, the reaction of purchases of a product to changes in its price, the change in the crime rate due to a change in police expenditures, and so forth. Demand equations, supply equations, cost equations, investment equations, consumption equations, and equations of exchange are all examples of behavioral equations.

A behavioral equation may express a function of one independent variable or several independent variables. An equation that states that the total household consumption depends on total disposable income is a behavioral equation. It describes the response of households (reflected in total consumer expenditure) to various levels of disposable income. The equation that states that household consumption depends on household income, the cost of consumer credit, the marginal tax rate, and the number of members of the household and their age distribution is, likewise, a behavioral equation. The latter equation defines a function of four independent variables. The first "explains" the behavior of households with only one variable, disposable personal income. The second differs only in that explicit account is taken of other variables that influence the decisions of households with respect to total expenditure. Both are behavioral equations.

One type of behavioral equation deserves special mention. This is the behavioral equation that states that some economic magnitude is given. For instance, a supply equation might stipulate that quantity supplied is equal to one thousand units. This equation implies that quantity does not vary when price (or any other economic magnitude) varies. The supply has zero price elasticity, and the supply curve is a vertical straight line. It must be remembered that this is as genuine and important a behavioral equation as one that states that quantity supplied varies with price. Consider an analogy of describing a person's movements. If we describe the person as running at ten miles per hour in a northeast direction, we describe one aspect of behavior. We would also be describing behavior if we describe the person as standing still on the front porch. Our supply equation, which states that the number of new houses for sale in a one-month period is fixed at one thousand units, states that homebuilders do not vary housing completions in response to price changes *in less than a month's time*. It is a behavioral equation that fixes quantity supplied for the purpose of a particular model. As we shall see in a moment, such behavioral equations involve exogenous variables.

Definitional Equations

Definitional equations require little elaboration. As the name implies, such equations introduce into the model certain relevant definitions. The following equation is a definition: $Y_d = C + S$, where Y_d denotes current disposable income, C designates current consumption, and S signifies current savings. The equation asserts that out of any current net income, the only options open to a household are consumption and saving. *Saving* is defined as disposable income not consumed. Hence, a household may consume all or part of its income and, therefore, must save the remainder (which may be zero or negative). Such an equation really tells us nothing about how consumption and saving vary when income varies. It does not tell us whether consumption increases, decreases, or remains constant when income increases. We say that it is not a behavioral equation, although it is a structural equation. It is merely a definition of the income disposal alternatives open to the household. Such alternatives are nevertheless an important part of the structure of the income-consumption-saving relation.

Another example of a definitional equation is the mathematical statement that the price of a commodity times the quantity purchased is equal to total expenditures on the commodity. This equation does not describe the behavior of any unit or group in the economy. It merely states an important mathematical necessity. It actually does not explain anything about the workings of the economic system, but it may be necessary for the econometrician to state it explicitly for purposes of logical completeness.

Included also in the category of definitional equations are statements of equilibrium conditions. The mathematical assertion that quantity demanded equals quantity supplied is a definition of market equilibrium, and it is an essential part of a complete model. Likewise, in an aggregate model for the economy as a whole, the statement that national income equals intended consumption plus investment plus government purchases plus net exports is a definition of equilibrium. It merely states that national income is stable when all income received is voluntarily returned to the economy in one form of spending or another. But again, this equilibrium condition should be stated explicitly in order that the model be complete.

Summarizing the role of equations in the theoretical structure, we say that a model is a complete system or set of structural equations. The equations of the model are of two types: behavioral equations (which describe the behavior of units or groups in the economic system and which are capable of disproof) and definitional equations (which are identities or equilibrium conditions and which cannot be contradicted by evidence).

VARIABLES OF THE MODEL

An equation is a statement of equality between two mathematical arguments. In general, an equation contains one or more variables, the coefficients and exponents associated with these variables, and a constant term giving the "value" of the equation. Consequently, we shall want to examine the variables that comprise the structural equations in an econometric model. The variables may be divided into endogenous and exogenous variables. *Endogenous variables* are those that are explained by the model; *exogenous variables* are not explained by the model, but rather are determined by forces outside the scope of the model. How comprehensive or broad the model is depends on how many variables one wishes to include in the category of endogenous variables. The more variables that are endogenous to the model—the more variables that are explained by the model—the greater the scope or inclusiveness of the model.

In the study of any economic problem, it is unavoidable that some factors be taken as given for purposes of analysis. It is utterly impossible to take into account and explain all of the forces that influence the variable or variables being studied. Because of the limitations of the human mind, and because economic data are scarce and often unavailable, some simplifications are unavoidable. It is the recognition of this fact that has led economists to classify economic variables as endogenous or exogenous.

Endogenous Variables

Endogenous variables are determined by other variables in a model and may, in turn, determine other variables. They are the variables that are explained by the model. Their values are not assumed to be specified for a model, but rather their values are obtained by the solution of the system of equations that comprise the model. For example, in a simple national income model we might write consumption as a function of income. Here consumption is determined by income, another variable in the model. But income may also be determined by the introduction of additional functional relationships, particularly by an investment function, a government spending function, a net export function, and an equilibrium condition that consumption plus investment plus government spending plus net exports equals national income. In this model then, both consumption and income are endogenous variables. Consumption is determined by income in the consumption function. Furthermore, income is determined by consumption (and investment, government spending, and net exports) in the equilibrium condition. There is a mutual dependence between income and consumption. Both play the role of determinants and the role of being determined.

A dependent variable is always an endogenous variable; the impact of independent variables on the dependent variable is explicitly specified by the equation itself. However, a variable may be an independent variable in one equation and a dependent variable in another equation. Such a variable is endogenous in every equation, even if it performs the *role* of an independent variable in particular equations. In fact, whether a variable is endogenous often depends on the level of *aggregation* of the economic model or the data being used to test that model. On the household level, consumption expenditures clearly reflect the level of income, as well as other variables. However, households do not usually purchase consumer goods from themselves. Hence, at the household level, income does not depend on consumption. Using disaggregated data would allow the investigator to treat income as an *exogenous* (predetermined) variable. The problem is that the investigator may not have access to reliable data at the household level that is representative of the economy as a whole. If only aggregate data are available, then the dependence of income on consumption must also be taken into account. As we will see later in the text, such a distinction is very important for the reliability of statistical estimates.

Consider a model that consists of three structural equations: a demand equation, a supply equation, and an equilibrium equation that states that quantity demanded equals quantity supplied. In a competitive market, both buyers and sellers are *price takers*. That is, the quantity that an individual buys or sells has no effect on the market price, which is assumed to prevail everywhere. Clearly, then, both quantity demanded and quantity supplied are endogenous variables; these variables are the dependent variables in their respective equations. If it were possible to obtain data on the purchases of individual households or the sales of firms at different prices, it would be appropriate to treat price as a predetermined variable. However, it is likely that only market data are available, and the equilibrium equation implies that market price adjusts to equate quantity demanded and quantity supplied. Hence, in the model of a competitive market, there are three endogenous variables: quantity demanded, quantity supplied, and price, which reconciles the other two. It is this *mutual dependence* that characterizes the endogenous variables.

Exogenous Variables

We have already mentioned that exogenous variables are those whose values are not determined by the model. Their values are taken as given for the particular model being used. This is not to say that the value of an exogenous variable is not explainable. We merely say that it is not explained or determined by this model. Its value can, in principle, be determined by a different model of broader scope. In this particular model, the exogenous variable determines the value of at least one endogenous variable, but its value is not determined by other variables in the model.

In the previous example of the consumption function, both consumption and income were endogenous variables in the national income model, but only consumption was endogenous when the consumption of individual households was predicted. Because income is determined in *factor markets* that are outside the scope of a model explaining individual consumption, income constitutes an exogenous variable when explaining individual consumption. In the national income model, both consumption and income are endogenous variables, the latter depending on consumption, investment, government spending, and net exports. If investment is assumed exogenous, we imply that investment is determined outside the context of the model by variables other than consumption and income. Investment determines income (in the equilibrium equation), but it is influenced by neither income nor consumption. It determines other variables in the model, but it is not determined by them.

As an alternative to this formulation, we might express investment as a function of the interest rate. Then investment becomes an endogenous variable; it is determined by the interest rate. But we must now make a decision about how we shall handle the interest rate. We might assume it is exogenous, although that assumption is dubious in light of economic theory that states that the interest rate is determined by the interaction of the supply of loanable funds (e.g., savings and tax collections, equal to income minus consumption) and the demand for loanable funds (e.g., investment and government spending). In mathematical models, the distinction between endogenous and exogenous variables is frequently a matter of analytical convenience. In econometric models, the determination of which variables are exogenous is usually a reflection of the consensus of economic opinion and previous empirical evidence.

There must, of course, be some stopping place. If we continue to push back the frontiers of the exogenous variables, we eventually come to the boundary between economics and other disciplines (although the location of that boundary is subject to change in light of advances in econometric and theoretical research). We come to the point where exogenous variables are noneconomic in nature. Exogenous variables are determined ultimately by technological, political, natural, or institutional forces. They may also be determined by the past, or higher levels of aggregation. In Part III we will see that there must always be some exogenous variables in a model if that model is to be estimated empirically. Hence, an attempt to develop an econometric model so encompassing that all variables are determined within the context of that model has a rather dubious payoff. It is an elegant mathematical model that may have a determinate solution in principle, but whose validity cannot be tested empirically.

SOLUTION OF THE MODEL:
REDUCED FORM EQUATIONS

In solving systems of equations, the number of *endogenous* variables must equal the number of equations. If all the variables in a system are endogenous, and the number of equations equals the number of unknowns, there is a unique solution to that set of equations.[1] The structural equations imply exactly one set of values for the variables that make all the equations true. When the system of equations contains exogenous variables, the solution will involve a new set of equations called *reduced form equations*. Each reduced form equation will be composed of one endogenous variable, on the left side of the equal sign, and *all* the exogenous variables, plus their coefficients and a constant term, on the right side of the equal sign. Technically, if there are no exogenous variables in the system, each reduced form equation will be composed of one endogenous variable on the left side and a constant term (equal to the equilibrium value of that variable) on the right side.

In a mathematical model the exogenous variables may be assigned specific numerical values or may be treated as unknown constants. On the basis of (known or unknown) values of the exogenous variables, the values of endogenous variables in the model are determined. These are the equilibrium values of the variables. In an econometric model, the values of the exogenous variables (like those of the endogenous variables) are generated by empirical data. Econometric techniques can then be used to estimate the parameters of the reduced form equations. Then, if certain conditions are met, the econometrician may also be able to estimate the coefficients of the structural equations from the estimates of the reduced form equations.

---

[1] An additional requirement is that the determinant of the coefficient matrix of the system of equations be nonzero.

ILLUSTRATIONS OF STATIC MODELS

Market Equilibrium for One Commodity

Let us take as our first illustration a simple demand-supply model for a particular commodity. We shall first present the mathematical model in purely formal notation, without specifying the forms of the functions involved. Then we shall present the model in terms of equations as an econometrician might. Let x_d signify the quantity demanded of the commodity X. It may be measured in, say, pounds per unit of time. Depending on the nature of the commodity, we would use whatever units are convenient, for example, yards, tons, or single items. Let x_s designate the quantity supplied of the commodity X, measured in the same units as quantity demanded. Finally, let p represent the price of commodity X measured in, say, dollars per pound. We write the demand and supply functions as:

(1) $x_d = f(p)$
(2) $x_s = g(p)$

Let us pause for a moment and ask whether the model at this point has a solution. Functional notations (1) and (2) imply two equations. Both of these equations, incidentally, will be behavioral equations. But we also note that there are three variables in the model: x_d, x_s, and p. Therefore, we need a third equation to make the model complete. The third equation is a definitional equation—the equilibrium condition:

(3) $x_d = x_s$

The third equation does not add a variable. Thus, the number of variables is equal to the number of equations. This is a necessary condition for the system to have a solution.

Let us proceed to solve the system. To do this we rewrite the model in equation form. Assume we know the equations and that they are:

(1) $x_d = 100 - 10p$
(2) $x_s = 25 + 15p$
(3) $x_d = x_s$

We have three variables, each of which is an endogenous variable: x_d is determined by p in equation (1); x_s is determined by p in equation (2); p is determined by the interaction of x_d and x_s in equation (3). We can specify the system in matrix form as:

$$\begin{bmatrix} 1 & 0 & 10 \\ 0 & 1 & -15 \\ 1 & -1 & 0 \end{bmatrix} \begin{bmatrix} x_d \\ x_s \\ p \end{bmatrix} = \begin{bmatrix} 100 \\ 25 \\ 0 \end{bmatrix}$$

The determinant of the coefficient matrix is -25, so the system has a unique solution. Using Cramer's rule, the solution is given as:

$$x_d = \frac{\begin{vmatrix} 100 & 0 & 10 \\ 25 & 1 & -15 \\ 0 & -1 & 0 \end{vmatrix}}{\begin{vmatrix} 1 & 0 & 10 \\ 0 & 1 & -15 \\ 1 & -1 & 0 \end{vmatrix}} = \frac{-1,750}{-25} = 70$$

$$x_s = \frac{\begin{vmatrix} 1 & 100 & 10 \\ 0 & 25 & -15 \\ 1 & 0 & 0 \end{vmatrix}}{\begin{vmatrix} 1 & 0 & 10 \\ 0 & 1 & -15 \\ 1 & -1 & 0 \end{vmatrix}} = \frac{-1,750}{-25} = 70$$

$$p = \frac{\begin{vmatrix} 1 & 0 & 100 \\ 0 & 1 & 25 \\ 1 & -1 & 0 \end{vmatrix}}{\begin{vmatrix} 1 & 0 & 10 \\ 0 & 1 & -15 \\ 1 & -1 & 0 \end{vmatrix}} = \frac{-75}{-25} = 3$$

The equilibrium price, $p = 3$, is the price at which quantity demanded equals quantity supplied. The equilibrium quantity traded is $x_d = x_s = 70$.

To illustrate the way in which endogenous variables are treated, let us now consider a variation on this theme. We present the following model in formal notation:

(1) $x_d = f(p_x, p_o, y)$
(2) $x_s = g(p_x)$
(3) $p_o = \bar{p}_o$
(4) $y = \bar{y}$
(5) $x_d = x_s$

Again, x_d represents the quantity demanded of commodity X, and x_s represents the quantity supplied. The price of commodity X is denoted by p_x, and p_o is the price of another commodity (say a close substitute for X in consumption). Finally, y designates consumer income. The symbol $\bar{p}_o$ indicates a constant—the given value of p_o. Likewise $\bar{y}$ designates the known value of y.

At this formal stage, we can already tell that the necessary condition has been met for the model to have a unique solution. We note that there are five variables in the model: x_d, x_s, p_x, p_o, and y. There are five equations consisting of the five variables. Equations (1) through (4) are behavioral and equation (5) is definitional.

Again we assume that the equations in the system are known:

(1) $x_d = 109 - 5p_x + 2p_o + 0.6y$
(2) $x_s = 25 + 10p_x$
(3) $p_o = 3$
(4) $y = 200$
(5) $x_d = x_s$

Suppose that p_x and p_o are measured in dollars per unit, y in billions of dollars, and x_d and x_s in millions of units per year. Equations (3) and (4) give us the values of p_o and y. Technically we could determine whether the sufficient condition for a unique solution was satisfied by expressing the equation system in matrix form and calculating the determinant of the co-efficient matrix. However, using standard algebra is more straightforward. We first substitute equations (3) and (4) into equation (1). This reduces the model to:

(1′) $x_d = 109 - 5p_x + 6 + 120 = 235 - 5p_x$
(2) $x_s = 25 + 10p_x$
(5) $x_d = x_s$

As in the previous example, we have three endogenous variables and three equations. Substitute (1′) and (2) into (5) to obtain the equilibrium value of p_x:

$$235 - 5p_x = 25 + 10p_x$$
$$15p_x = 210$$
$$p_x = 14$$

The values of the variables x_d and x_s are obtained by substitution of the value of p_x into either (1′) or (2). Using equation (2), we find:

$$x_d = x_s = 25 + 10(14) = 165$$

To check our result, we use equation (1′):

$$x_d = x_s = 235 - 5(14) = 165$$

The equilibrium price of X is \$14, and the equilibrium quantity traded is 165 million units per year.

It may not be immediately obvious why economists bother to specify exogenous variables explicitly in mathematical models, since the exogenous variables were simply eliminated when generating the solution. But in econo-metric work, the values of the exogenous variables change from one observa-tion to the next. So while those variables are still "predetermined," they are not "known" until an observation is made and recorded. Then all the observations are used to generate estimates of the reduced form equations, which, under certain circumstances, may yield estimates of the structural equations. Recall that the reduced form equations specify each endogenous variable as an explicit function of the exogenous variables. We will now trace how those equations are generated from the structural equations.

The idea behind statistical estimation is to translate a general model of an equation system into a set of structural equations with specific numerical parameters. For purposes of illustration, suppose the econometrician believes the equation in our demand and supply system, even though the numerical values of the coefficients are unknown:[2]

(1) $x_d = a_0 + a_1 p_x + a_2 p_o + a_3 y$
(2) $x_s = b_0 + b_1 p_x$
(3) $p_o = \bar{p}_o$
(4) $y = \bar{y}$
(5) $x_d = x_s$

Note the similarity between the above model and the previous model. The only difference is that the intercept and slope coefficients in equations (1) and (2) are given by letters rather than specific numbers. In an econometric model, the parameters of the equation are unknown until they have been estimated. Similarly, the values of the exogenous variables are unknown until they are observed.

To obtain the reduced form equations from the general linear structural equations, we proceed as before. First, we substitute equations (3) and (4) into equation (1). In this case, this is equivalent to specifying p_o and y as exogenous variables. Next, we substitute equations (1) and (2) into equation (5), and solve for p_x:

$$(5) \quad a_0 + a_1 p_x + a_2 \bar{p}_o + a_3 \bar{y} = b_0 + b_1 p_x$$

$$(b_1 - a_1) p_x = a_0 - b_0 + a_2 \bar{p}_o + a_3 \bar{y}$$

$$p_x = \frac{a_0 - b_0}{b_1 - a_1} + \frac{a_2}{b_1 - a_1} \bar{p}_o + \frac{a_3}{b_1 - a_1} \bar{y}$$

As before, the values of the variables x_d and x_s are obtained by substitution of the expression for p_x into equation (1) or equation (2). Substituting into equation (2), we have:

$$x_s = b_0 + b_1 p_x$$

$$= b_0 + \left[\frac{b_1}{b_1 - a_1} (a_0 - b_0 + a_2 \bar{p}_o + a_3 \bar{y}) \right]$$

$$= \frac{b_1 a_0 - a_1 b_0}{b_1 - a_1} + \frac{b_1 a_2}{b_1 - a_1} \bar{p}_o + \frac{b_1 a_3}{b_1 - a_1} \bar{y}$$

---

[2] Another difference between econometric models and mathematical models is the inclusion of an "error term" in each behavioral equation of the econometric model. Since the error term will not be discussed until a later chapter, it is being suppressed in this discussion.

Similarly, we can substitute the expression for p_x into equation (1):

$$x_d = a_0 + a_1 p_x + a_2 \overline{p}_o + a_3 \overline{y}$$

$$= a_0 + \left[\frac{a_1}{b_1 - a_1}(a_0 - b_0 + a_2\overline{p}_o + a_3\overline{y}) \right] + a_2\overline{p}_o + a_3\overline{y}$$

$$= \frac{b_1 a_0 - a_1 b_0}{b_1 - a_1} + \frac{b_1 a_2}{b_1 - a_1}\overline{p}_o + \frac{b_1 a_3}{b_1 - a_1}\overline{y}$$

In the process of estimating an econometric model, the endogenous variables are treated as dependent and the exogenous variables are treated as independent. If the structural equations contain endogenous variables on the right side of the equal sign, those equations are first transformed into reduced form, and the reduced form equations are used to generate equilibrium values of the endogenous variables. In principle, then, solving a system of structural equations to obtain their reduced form is equivalent to obtaining the equilibrium values of endogenous variables in a mathematical model.

Theory of the Firm

In this section we present the economic theory of the competitive firm as a mathematical model. Assuming pure competition makes the individual firm a price taker, price is an exogenous variable at the individual firm level of aggregation. The problem is to determine the equilibrium output; that is, the output that maximizes total profit for the firm. Our model consists of five structural equations in five variables:

(1) $C = 80 + 2q + 0.04q^2$
(2) $R = pq$
(3) $p = 10$
(4) $\pi = R - C$
(5) $\pi = \text{Max.}[\pi]$

Equation (1) shows the total cost function of the firm, where C denotes total cost (in dollars) and q represents total output (in thousands of units per year). Equation (2) gives the total revenue of the firm, where R designates total revenue and p the price of the product (in dollars per unit). Equation (3) indicates that the market is purely competitive; the price of the product is given to the firm as \$10. Therefore, p is an exogenous variable in this model. Equation (4) is the definition of total profit, and π is consequently measured in total dollars. Equation (5) states the equilibrium condition for the firm, namely that total profit must be a maximum. Without this fifth equation, the number of variables would exceed the number of equations. This last equation requires us to select from among the *possible* values of π the one that is maximum.

We solve the system of equations for the value of q that maximizes π. From this condition we can also determine the values of C, π, and R, given that p is already known. We first substitute (1) and (2) into (4) to obtain total profit as a function of output. Finally, we maximize π with respect to q. The total profit is given by the equation:

(4') $\pi = 10q - 80 - 2q - 0.04q^2$

Equation (5) states that π must be a maximum. We found in our discussion in Chapter 8 that the necessary condition for maximum π is that $d\pi/dq = 0$. We perform this operation on (4') and solve the resulting equation for the value of q:

$$\frac{d\pi}{dq} = 10 - 2 - 0.08q = 0$$

$$q = \frac{8}{0.08} = 100$$

We can check to see whether this value of q does indeed yield a maximum π by considering the sufficient condition for π to be a maximum. Recall that this condition is $d^2\pi/dq^2 < 0$. Thus:

$$\frac{d^2\pi}{dq^2} = \frac{d}{dq}(10 - 2 - 0.08q) = -0.08$$

This value is less than zero, so we can conclude that total profit is a maximum when output is 100,000 units a year. This is the equilibrium value of the firm. With the value of q known, the values of C, R, and π can now be determined:

$C = 80 + 2(100) + 0.04(100)^2 = 80 + 200 + 400 = 680$
$R = 10(100) = 1,000$
$\pi = 1,000 - 680 = 320$

Since the value of p is known exogenously, the five structural equations have determined the values of the five variables in the model. The entire system is determined.

Once again a parallel can be drawn between the specific solution of a mathematical model and the specification of an econometric model in preparation for empirical estimation. Let's specify the model of the competitive firm, only this time in more general terms:

(1) $C = a_0 + a_1 q + a_2 q^2$
(2) $R = pq$
(3) $p = \bar{p}$
(4) $\pi = R - C$
(5) $\pi = \text{Max.}[\pi]$

The only differences between this model and the previous one are in equation (1), where a general quadratic equation replaces one with specific coefficients, and in equation (3), where the value of p is specified as an (unknown) constant.

Furthermore, the procedure for determining the econometric model parallels the solution of the mathematical model. First, equation (3) is substituted into equation (2). This is done by merely noting that p is an exogenous variable. Next, equations (1) and (2) are substituted for C and R, respectively, in equation (4):

$$(4') \quad \pi = \bar{p}q - (a_0 + a_1 q + a_2 q^2)$$

Taking the derivative of π with respect to q, setting the result equal to zero, and solving for q, we find:

$$\frac{d\pi}{dq} = \bar{p} - a_1 - 2a_2 q = 0$$

implies

$$q = \frac{-a_1}{2a_2} + \frac{1}{2a_2}\bar{p}$$

In this case, the optimal rate of output is a linear function of the market determined price. The econometrician could then *estimate* that function by relating observations of the output of a firm to the corresponding price for each observation. Once that equation is estimated, the optimal rate of output can then be *predicted*, based either on hypothetical or observed prices.

National Income Model

Let us examine the following national income model, presented first in formal notation:

(1) $C = f(Y)$
(2) $I = I_o$
(3) $G = G_o$
(4) $Y = C + I + G$

In this model C designates total consumption, Y is total national income, I is total net investment, and G is government spending (all measured in, say, billions of dollars). There are four variables: C and Y are endogenous and I and G are exogenous. There are also four equations. In equation (1), C is determined by Y; in (2), I is given as some known value I_o; in (3), G is given as some known value G_o; and in (4), Y is determined by C, I, and G. Note that C and Y are determining and determined, while I and G are determining but not determined within the model. The model is complete since there are the necessary number of equations to determine all values of the four variables.

Let us now present the four equations, all assumed known to us:

(1) $C = 10 + 0.75Y$
(2) $I = 30$
(3) $G = 50$
(4) $Y = C + I + G$

Equations (1), (2), and (3) are behavioral equations, and equation (4) is a definitional equation of equilibrium. To solve the system we substitute (1), (2), and (3) into (4) and solve for the value of Y:

(4')
$$Y = 10 + 0.75Y + 30 + 50$$
$$(1 - 0.75)Y = 90$$
$$Y = \frac{90}{0.25} = 360$$

Substituting this value of Y in (1) yields the value of C:

(1') $C = 10 + 0.75(360) = 10 + 270 = 280$

The values of I and G are known, so the entire system is determined.

Our assumption that investment and government spending are exogenous is a convenient simplification in a mathematical model. Suppose we now wish to explain the value of I. We therefore make investment an endogenous variable by assuming that the level of investment depends on the interest rate, r. We rewrite the model as:

(1) $C = 10 + 0.75Y$
(2) $I = 90 - 1,200r$
(3) $G = G_o$
(4) $Y = C + I + G$

Now I is determined as well as determining. But our model is now incomplete; we have five variables and only four equations. For a complete model, we need another equation, which must involve the interest rate, r. If we assume that the interest rate is exogenous and known to be equal to 5 percent, the model becomes:

(1) $C = 10 + 0.75Y$
(2) $I = 90 - 1,200r$
(3) $G = 50$
(4) $r = 0.05$
(5) $Y = C + I + G$

Equations (1) through (4) are behavioral equations and (5) is a definitional equation. To solve the system, we substitute (4) into (2) to get the value of I:

(2') $I = 90 - 1,200(0.05) = 30$

Substituting the value of I and the value of G along with (1) into (5) gives:

(5′) $Y = 10 + 0.75Y + 30 + 50$

  $Y = \dfrac{90}{0.25} = 360$

Note that we have the same values of I and C and Y in this model as we had in the previous one. The difference is that in this model we have explained why investment is equal to $30 billion. In the previous model, we merely assumed that this value was given without attempting to explain what determined the level of investment.

We can also make the interest rate endogenous to our model. To do this, however, we need additional variables to explain the interest rate. In turn, we then need one or more equations to describe the behavior of these determinants of the interest rate. In particular, we need a theory of the money market, which might be the liquidity-preference theory. The interest rate can also be determined through a demand and supply framework, with investment and government spending serving as variables in the demand equation and with saving, taxation, and the change in the money supply serving as variables in the supply equation.

A mathematical model is essentially speculative or introspective in nature, and the theorist has considerable latitude about the assumptions of the model. The only requirement is logical consistency; there can be no internal contradictions among the functions, and the number of equations should at least equal the number of endogenous variables. As we will see in Part III of this book, economists have less latitude in the construction of econometric models. In a mathematical model, a theorist can make as many simplifying assumptions as are consistent with the problem at hand. More care must be taken so that the econometric model being tested is consistent with the data used to test that model. Hence, economists who wish to explain the influence of investment on national income may find it convenient to assume away a government sector. However, if they then use empirical data generated in an economy where government spending is positive, they will have to adjust their econometric model to take that sector into account.

COMPARATIVE STATICS

Every economic phenomenon is characterized by change. How shall we account for change in our static view of the economy? *Comparative statics* is a term used to describe change within the context of a static model. Essentially, it amounts to tracing through the consequences of changes in the parameters of the structural equations. Each equation contains parameters or constant numbers. But we have seen in Chapter 2 that parameters are "variable" constants—constant for the purpose of a solution but permitted to vary as the conditions of the model change. When one or more of the parameters of a system change, the equilibrium values of the variables in the model will change. The problem of comparative statics is that of finding the new equilibrium values of the variables when the parameters of the model change.

As we have already pointed out, our interest centers on the old equilibrium and the new equilibrium, not on the time required for the change or the path of movement through time from the old equilibrium to the new equilibrium. Suppose we consider our first illustrative static model presented in the preceding section. It is a model of behavior in the market for a single commodity:

(1) $x_d = 100 - 10p$
(2) $x_s = 25 + 15p$
(3) $x_d = x_s$

As we have seen, the solution of this model is $p = 3$, $x_d = x_s = 70$. Now suppose we have a change in a parameter of the demand function. Let us assume the quantity intercept increases from 100 to 125. In diagrammatic terms, this is equivalent to a shift to the right in the demand curve. What is the new equilibrium? In terms of the diagram, what is the new point of intersection of the demand and supply curves? Our new model is written:

(1) $x_d = 125 - 10p$
(2) $x_s = 25 + 15p$
(3) $x_d = x_s$

We now solve this system to find that $p = 4$ and $x_d = x_s = 85$. Price rises by $1, and total output of the industry increases by 15 million pounds per unit of time. This static model predicts new equilibrium values of the variables.

The previous model does not explain what caused the shift in the demand curve. If the model were expanded to accommodate exogenous variables, a change in the equilibrium values of the endogenous variables could be traced to changes in one or more exogenous variables. Consider our alternative model of the market for one good (also presented in the preceding section):

(1) $x_d = 109 - 5p_x + 2p_o + 0.6y$
(2) $x_s = 25 + 10p_x$
(3) $p_o = 3$
(4) $y = 200$
(5) $x_d = x_s$

The exogenous variables, p_o and y, are parameters of the demand equation. If the price of the substitute good, p_o, should rise (because of a change in supply in that market), one condition of the model changes. If the price of the substitute doubles, equation (3) becomes:

(3') $\quad p_o = 6$

Then equation (1') for this model becomes:

(1') $\quad x_d = 109 - 5p_x + 2(6) + 0.6(200)$
$\qquad = 241 - 5p_x$

Solving this new system of equations yields the solution $p_x = 14.4$, $x_d = x_s = 169$. The former solution gave $p_x = 14$ and $x_d = x_s = 165$.

For an econometric model, the impact of a change in an exogenous variable on an endogenous variable would be determined from the values of the coefficients in the reduced form equation. In our econometric model of the market for one commodity, we found:

$$p = \frac{a_0 - b_0}{b_1 - a_1} + \frac{a_2}{b_1 - a_1}p_o + \frac{a_3}{b_1 - a_1}y$$

$$x_s = x_d = \frac{b_1 a_0 - a_1 b_0}{b_1 - a_1} + \frac{b_1 a_2}{b_1 - a_1}p_o + \frac{b_1 a_3}{b_1 - a_1}y$$

Taking the derivative of p and x_s with respect to y, we find:

$$\frac{dp}{dy} = \frac{a_3}{b_1 - a_1} \text{ and } \frac{dx_s}{dy} = \frac{b_1 a_3}{b_1 - a_1}$$

where the a's and b's are the (estimated) parameters for the structural equations. By hypothesis (subject to econometric test), $a_3 > 0$, $a_1 < 0$, and $b_1 > 0$. Hence, a change in y is predicted to increase *equilibrium* price and quantity in the same direction.

In econometrics, what we observe has a decisive influence on the parameters we are able to estimate. If income increased, we would observe a change in price and a change in *equilibrium* quantity. Since both equilibrium price and quantity increase in the wake of an increase in y, the change in observed quantity with respect to price must have been along the *supply* curve. We can verify this by the chain rule:

$$\frac{dx}{dp} = \frac{dx}{dy} \cdot \frac{dy}{dp} = \frac{b_1 a_3}{b_1 - a_1} \cdot \frac{b_1 - a_1}{a_3} = b_1$$

A change in income (y) would shift the *demand* curve generating a new equilibrium price and quantity *along the supply curve*.

In the theory of the firm (the second illustration in the preceding section), we have a problem of comparative statics if a parameter of the cost function or the exogenous variable in the cost function should change. For example, a rise in the price of one or more factors of production will raise total cost for each level of output. A shift to the right in the market demand curve will raise the price of the product (taken as given by the firm) and so raise total revenue for each level of output. Comparative static analysis of the firm will attempt to answer the question, "What will be the new equilibrium output of the firm and new equilibrium levels of total cost, revenue, and profit if a change occurs in a parameter of the system?"

In the econometric model of the firm, price was treated as an exogenous variable: the effect of a change in price on equilibrium quantity would be predicted by the reduced form equation for quantity. However, the econometric model was specified as if the cost equation were given as a quadratic function of output, namely:

$$C = a_0 + a_1 q + a_2 q^2$$

where the *parameters* a_0, a_1, and a_2 are estimated statistically from market data. A change in the price of a variable input would change the parameters a_1 and a_2; a change in fixed cost would change the parameter a_0. In the former case, the identity of the profit maximizing rate of output would change, although the person using the econometric model would not discover the change until he or she noticed that the model failed to predict accurately. Hence, when possible, it is desirable to specify the econometric model so that changes in exogenous variables, such as factor prices, are explicitly taken into account in the estimation process.

Finally, let us turn to the comparative static properties of the simple national income model:

(1) $C = 10 + 0.75Y$
(2) $I = 30$
(3) $G = 50$
(4) $Y = C + I + G$

Assume that there is a given change in the level of investment: I increases from \$30 billion to \$40 billion, a \$10 billion increase, while G remains constant at \$50 billion. Equation (2) becomes:

(2′) $I = 40$

We solve the system and obtain the values $Y = 400$, $C = 310$, $I = 40$, and $G = 50$. A \$10 billion increase in investment produces a \$40 billion increase in income. This is the familiar principle of the investment multiplier. The investment multiplier is defined as:

$$k = \frac{dY}{dI}$$

In this case we have:

$$k = \frac{40}{10} = 4$$

A given increment in investment increases income by an amount equal to four times the increase in investment.

The investment multiplier operates through "rounds" of expenditure. The investment expenditure is paid to the owners of factors of production as income. Part of this income is spent on consumption and the remainder is saved or absorbed as tax collections. Some persons receive these consumption expenditures as income and they, in turn, consume part of it and save part of it in the second "round." This process is continued until all the original increase in investment has gone into saving and tax collections. At the end of the process, income has risen by some multiple of the increase in investment. These "rounds" of expenditure obviously take time to work themselves out, and the new equilibrium level of income does not occur immediately. In the static model, however, we do not concern ourselves with the time required to achieve the new, higher level of income. We are interested in the final result only, and this is all that the static mathematical model shows. However, if the econometric model is tested using time-series data, the time required for adjustment must be shorter than the time between one observation and another, otherwise the empirical estimates of the multiplier could be seriously mistaken.

CONCLUSION

Before passing on to the examination of other models, it is essential to emphasize the flexibility of mathematical construction, and the somewhat more stringent requirements for econometric model specification. A mathematical model is a means of presenting an economic hypothesis so that crucial elements of the economic process being described are clear, and so that all endogenous variables are explained within the context of the model. If one wanted to focus on the role of particular exogenous variables, it is a simple matter to omit other exogenous variables from the mathematical model. Indeed, such omissions are often covered explicitly by the economist's *ceteris paribus* assumptions. Mathematical models are tools of analysis, capable of handling variations in assumptions and conditions of exogenous variables.

At some point, however, the econometrician may wish to test the *relevance* of a mathematical model by subjecting the predictions of that model to empirical test. In this context it is important that econometric models are in reasonable conformity to the data that will be used to test them. In a mathematical model of national income analysis, one may assume that an economy's exports always equal its imports, or even that government spending (and taxation) is zero to focus the impact of a change of investment on equilibrium national income. However, if real world data were generated by an economic system where foreign trade was sometimes out of balance, and where government spending is a major portion of national income, these factors must be taken into account if the test of the hypothesis is to be given any credibility.

PROBLEMS

You are given the following behavioral equations and values of the exogenous variables. Complete the models and find the equilibrium solutions for the values of the endogenous variables.

1. $x_d = 100 - 15p$ (market demand equation)
    $x_s = 20 + 5p$ (market supply equation)

    where x_d and x_s are the quantities demanded and supplied of the commodity X, respectively, and p denotes its price.

2. $x_d = 317 - 60p$ (market demand equation)
    $x_s = 100 + 2p$ (market supply equation)

    where x_d and x_s are the quantities demanded and supplied of the commodity X, respectively, and p denotes its price.

3. $x_d = 310 - 20p_x - 2p_o + 0.2y$ (market demand equation)
    $x_s = 25 + 10p_x - 0.1w$ (market supply equation)

    where x_d and x_s are the quantities demanded and supplied of X, p_x is the price of X, p_o is the price of another commodity, y is consumer income, and w is the wage rate of labor used to produce the commodity X. You are given that $w = 10$, $y = 200$, and $p_o = 4$.

4. $C = 20 + 0.65Y + 0.06M$ (consumption function)
    $I = 100 - 900r$ (investment function)

    where C denotes consumption, Y is income, M is total monetary assets of households, I is investment, and r is the rate of interest. You are given that $M = 200$ and $r = 0.07$.

5. $c = 100 + 1.5x + 0.03x^2$ (total cost function of a firm)

    where c denotes the total cost and x denotes the output of the commodity X produced by a firm that operates in a purely competitive market. You are given that the price of the commodity X is 30.

6. Assume the demand for money, M, is a function of the interest rate, r, and national income, Y, and is given by the equation:

    $$M_d = 325 - 2{,}000r + 0.25Y$$

    Assume the supply of money is a function of the interest rate and is given by the equation:

    $$M_s = -80 + 6{,}000r$$

    Complete the model and find the equilibrium interest rate and stock of money in the economy.

7. Suppose the level of consumer income in Problem 3 decreases from 200 to 100. Find the new equilibrium values of the endogenous variables.

8. Suppose the interest rate in Problem 4 changes from 0.07 to 0.08, and monetary asset holdings increase from 200 to 300. Find the new equilibrium values of the endogenous variables.

9. Suppose the price of the product in Problem 5 decreases from 30 to 20. Find the new equilibrium values of the endogenous variables. Suppose the total cost function changes to:

$$c = 200 + 2x + 0.05x^2$$

while price remains at 20. Find the new equilibrium values of the endogenous variables.

13

Dynamic

Models

Time plays no explicit or essential part in the static models of the preceding chapter. This is because the designer of such a mathematical model is not interested in the path variables take in reaching a new equilibrium, or because the econometric model is designed for data that are inadequate for tracing the path of adjustment. Nevertheless, when a variable is measured as a *flow*, time does enter into the definition of the variables in the sense that we define a period relevant to the quantities measured. A *flow* is a variable that can only be understood in the context of the period over which the variable is measured. To learn that a person "earns $100" doesn't tell us whether to congratulate or pity: $100 per hour is an income to be envied; $100 a week is below the poverty level; $100 per year is below the starvation level. Net national product measures productive activity; the convention is to report net national product on an annual basis (e.g., during the third quarter of 1983, net national product was $3,001.9 billion *per year*). When told that a firm's output is one million tons, we must inquire whether output is measured per hour, per week, per month, or per year. The time *dimension* is crucial when reporting variables measured on a flow basis.

By contrast, a *stock* variable does not have a time dimension. The variable is imagined or measured at a point in time, rather than taking place over time. The *stock* of money held by the public does not have a time dimension. For example, M2 averaged $2,136.2 billion during the third quarter of 1983. In 1983, the total value of manufacturing equipment was estimated at \$1,269.6 billion dollars. No time dimension is implied.

It is also true that empirical data may be reported in time increments. Such data are called *time-series* data. An econometrician may test a static model by using data that are changing through time. However, if the investigator believes that the duration of time required for market adjustment is less than the time interval between observations, then the econometric model will not simulate the adjustment process. It will merely compare equilibrium values of endogenous variables.

Dynamic models are those in which time does enter explicitly. The variables are understood as existing at some point in time or during some interval of time. For instance, instead of merely specifying that aggregate consumption is a function of current aggregate income, consumption in year t may be stipulated as a function of income in year $t - 1$. This latter relationship is called a lagged relationship, because the change in the dependent variable responds to a change in the independent variable only after a time lag.

As a result of the explicit role played by time, the information content of a dynamic model is greater than that of a static model. Comparative statics deals only with the attainment of a new equilibrium, once a parameter of the system has changed. It contains no information about the movement of the variables over time or the rate at which the variables approach their new equilibrium values. A dynamic model traces the values of variables through time. The *path* of endogenous variables is traced to changes in exogenous variables.

The classification of models as mathematical or econometric, the classification of equations as behavioral or definitional (and as structural or reduced form), and the classification of variables as endogenous or exogenous apply in dynamic models just as in static models. The only difference involves the role of lagged endogenous variables. A variable may be endogenous in the current period, although the value of that variable from a previous period serves as an exogenous variable. Both exogenous variables and lagged endogenous variables are known as *predetermined* variables. Neither is determined within the system itself, and both are determinants of other variables; i.e., the model describes the state of the system in period t—it takes the lagged endogenous variables as given during that time period.

In general, there are two types of dynamic models. In one type we deal with quantities that are relevant to specified time intervals. For instance, quantity demanded is interpreted as quantity that consumers are willing to purchase during one year or one month. The units of time are viewed as discrete. In the second type, the variables are viewed as changing continuously through time rather than in finite steps or jumps from one period to the next. Each value of a variable exists at a point in time. Some dynamic models may be a mixture of the two. Econometric models are invariably estimated with data taken at discrete intervals. In this case, discrete models are used to simulate the behavior of continuous variables.

DISCRETE DYNAMIC MODELS

The best way to understand the difference between static and dynamic models is to work some specific examples. For purposes of comparison, we shall consider dynamic illustrations in which the economic problems are similar to those covered in Chapter 12.

The Cobweb Model

The famous cobweb theorem is a relatively simple model of the market for a particular commodity. It is an excellent example of a dynamic model involving discrete time units, and it may be used to analyze the market for a perishable farm crop. Furthermore, it lends itself readily to diagrammatic representation.

Let the quantity demanded of a perishable good X be denoted by x_{dt} (measured in millions of bushels per year), and let its price be denoted by p_t (in dollars per bushel). The quantity demanded during any period of time is assumed to depend on the current price. Thus, if we know the parameters of the demand equation (which reflect the values of the exogenous variables, here suppressed for simplicity), we can write:

(1) $x_{dt} = 200 - 5p_t$

The subscript t on the variables refers to the date that variable is measured. In general, the data may be measured in any time period that is convenient. We assume it is a year to correspond to the growing season for a crop, so t refers to the *current year*. The demand equation is interpreted as follows: the quantity demanded of a good X during year t is a decreasing linear function of the price of X in year t.

In the cobweb model, it is assumed that the quantity supplied in year t is a function of the price in the previous year. There are plausible grounds for this assumption. The crop must be planted well before the date of harvest and sale.[1] It follows that the output decisions of farmers are based on the prevailing market price at the time of planting. Again, assuming that the supply equation is known, this hypothesis leads to the supply formulation:

(2) $x_{st} = -10 + 2p_{t-1}$

where x and p are measured in millions of bushels per year and dollars per year, respectively. The subscript t on x signifies the quantity supplied in

---

[1] Of course farmers might sign a *futures contract* with a speculator, agreeing to deliver a specified quantity at a predetermined price. However, by understanding the fluctuations in price and quantity generated by a cobweb adjustment model, we are able to appreciate why futures markets exist. Furthermore, speculators themselves may be using an ad hoc variation of a cobweb model to *predict* what the actual future price will be. Finally, not all crops are covered by futures markets, nor do all farmers sign futures contracts for crops where futures markets exist.

year t, and the subscript $t - 1$ on p denotes the price in the previous year. The lagged variable p_{t-1}, is predetermined and so is treated like an exogenous variable—it is known in year t.

If this were a static model, we would have no lagged prices. More precisely, the question of lags would not arise at all. We would abstract from time by omitting time subscripts on all of the variables. In the static model, we would add another equation, the definition of equilibrium, $x_d = x_s$, and the model would be determinate. The equilibrium values of all the variables would be determined by the simultaneous solution of the three equations.

Can we do the same in this dynamic model? The time subscripts force us to use a somewhat different procedure. Since the price in the supply equation is predetermined, we can assign some value to it. Suppose we know the initial value of the lagged price, and we call our first relevant period year one. Then $t = 1$ and p_{t-1} is labeled p_0. Assume this initial lagged price is \$20 per bushel. From the supply equation, we know that 30 million bushels are supplied in year one (i.e., $x_{s1} = -10 + 2(20) = 30$). Setting quantity demanded equal to (the predetermined) quantity supplied, we determine the current price. In this case we do not have an equilibrium because buyers are willing to pay $40 - 0.2(30) = \$34$ per bushel for the 30 million bushels supplied. This change in price changes quantity supplied during the next period. When the market price is \$34, suppliers will produce $x_{s2} = -10 + 2(34) = 58$ million bushels in year two. When the 58 million bushels hit the market in year two, the market price drops to $p_2 = 40 - 0.2(58) = \$28.40$. Hence, suppliers again change their output for year three, and so on. When the values of price or quantity change from one period to another, equilibrium has not been established. However, price and quantity may be *converging* on equilibrium.

Table 13.1 shows what happens to output and price as we proceed through time. With a known initial price, $p_0 = 20$, the initial quantity traded in year one is 30 million bushels. In general, the quantity traded each year is read from the supply equation, and the price in each year is obtained by solving the demand equation for price, after substituting the quantity produced in that year.

With each successive time period, the change in quantity (and price) is smaller in absolute value than in the previous period. Quantity exchanged approaches 50 million bushels and price approaches \$30 per bushel. If equilibrium were achieved, price would remain equal to \$30 and quantity would remain at 50 million bushels until either the demand curve or the supply curve shifted. Since equilibrium implies that $p_t = p_{t-1}$ and that $x_{dt} = x_{st}$, we could obtain this same result by solving the equations as if all the variables referred to the same period of time (as in the static model). By removing the time subscripts, the price variable is the same variable in both the demand and supply equations. By adding the equilibrium definition, we can simultaneously solve the equations. The solution turns out to be $p = 30$ and $x_d = x_s = 50$.

Table 13.1

t	x_t	p_t	$p_0 = 20$
1	30.00	34.00	
2	58.00	28.40	
3	48.60	30.28	
4	50.56	29.89	
5	49.78	30.04	
6	50.09	29.98	
7	49.96	30.01	
.	.	.	
.	.	.	
.	.	.	
∞	50.00	30.00	

It might seem, then, that the dynamic model has not given us any more information than the static one. However, we must remember that in addition to the equilibrium solution we have also determined the movement of the variables over time. We have also determined the rate at which they approach their equilibrium values. Such information is not imparted by the static model. Ths fact is clearly demonstrated in Figures 13.1, 13.2, and 13.3. In Figure 13.1 the demand and supply curves are depicted. Notice that the figure drops the time subscripts on the variables. This is necessary in order to relate both quantity supplied and demanded to the same variable, price. This is a procedure comparable to the analytic solution when the model is treated as if it were static. The broken line in the figure traces the movement to the equilibrium point ($x = 50$, $p = 30$).

Figures 13.2 and 13.3 show the movements of the market price and the quantity exchanged through time. These are called the *time paths* of the variables. The observations are plotted in the center of each time period and are assumed to remain unchanged during that period. The variables move by steps from one year to the next, which is a necessary consequence of defining them in discrete terms. Note that these two variables approach the equilibrium solution: $p = 30$, $x = 50$. These values are the equilibrium values because once obtained there is no tendency to move elsewhere as long as the demand and/or supply curves do not shift. The variables oscillate around their equilibrium values, but these oscillations are *dampened*. That is, they get smaller and smaller through time and approach the equilibrium. For this reason, the model is called a *stable equilibrium model*. The equilibrium is said to be stable because regardless of the initial value of the lagged endogenous variable (in this case, $p_0 = 20$), the endogenous variables approach their equilibrium values.

The complete dynamic model contains equations (1) and (2). Equation (3) gives the initial value of the lagged price:

(3) $p_0 = 20$

Figure 13.1

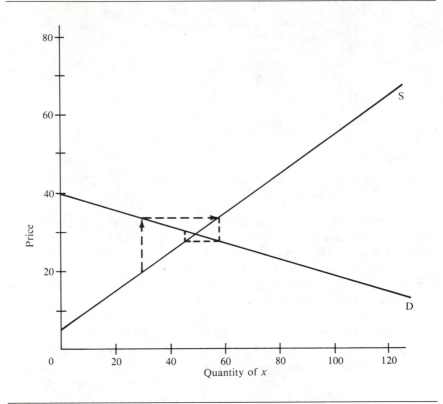

The stable equilibrium is given by equation (4):

(4) $x_{dt} = x_{st}$

The model is complete. For different values of p_0, we would obtain different time paths for the variables, but they would approach the same equilibrium. These time paths of the variables distinguish the stable dynamic model from the static model.

An econometric model could be constructed to estimate the parameters of the mathematical model just discussed. However, the exogenous variables that determine the positions of the demand and supply curves, which were suppressed in the previous discussion, would have to be made explicit. For instance, a measure of the weather, say the the average rainfall during the growing season, R, could be added to the supply equation, while per capita income, y, could be added to the demand equation. If, as the system is approaching a new equilibrium , a change in per capita income shifts the demand curve, the disturbance generates a new equilibrium and the time paths of price and quantity converge on a new equilibrium. In Figure 13.4,

Figure 13.2

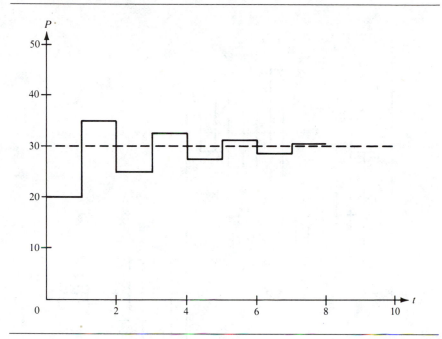

Figure 13.3

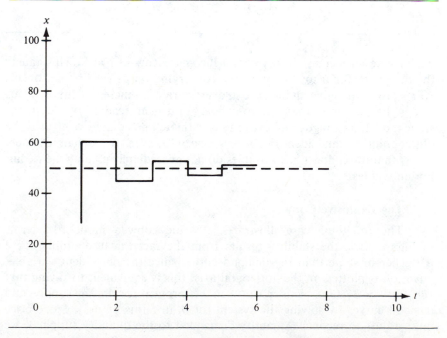

Figure 13.4

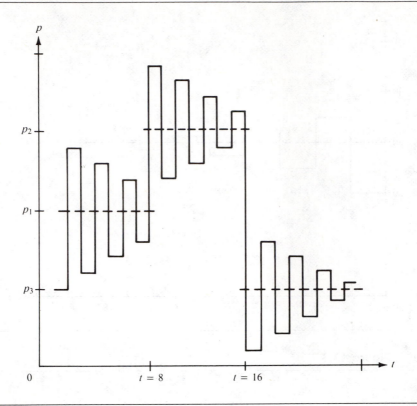

we imagine an increase in per capita income occurs at $t = 8$. This causes the time path for p to shift upward, converging on p_2 rather than on p_1. At $t = 16$ we imagine an increase in average rainfall increases supply. This causes the time path for price to converge on p_3 instead of p_2. As in the static model, a change in an exogenous variable immediately overturns the old equilibrium and identifies a new one. However, the dynamic model allows that the endogenous variables do not immediately assume their equilibrium values.

The Explosive Cobweb

The foregoing case illustrates a stable cobweb model. In terms of Figure 13.1, the stability results from the fact that the supply curve is steeper in slope than the demand curve (since the dependent variable, quantity, is plotted on the horizontal axis, this is equivalent to saying that $|\partial q_d/\partial p| > \partial q_s/\partial p$). This result can be proven for linear supply and demand curves by solving the system for p_t in terms of p_{t-1}. Since price must adjust to reconcile quantity demanded to the quantity supplied, we set x_{dt} equal to x_{st} and solve for p_t. In terms of a general linear equation, we have:

(1) $x_{dt} = a_0 - a_1 p_t$
(2) $x_{st} = b_0 + b_1 p_{t-1}$
(3) $x_{dt} = x_{st}$ implies $a_0 - a_1 p_t = b_0 + b_1 p_{t-1}$

Derivatives are not exactly appropriate for a discrete dynamic model. Hence, we will specify a *difference equation* for the change in p_t in terms of the change in p_{t-1}:

$$-a_1 \Delta p_t = b_1 \Delta p_{t-1}$$
$$\frac{\Delta p_t}{\Delta p_{t-1}} = -\frac{b_1}{a_1}$$

The minus sign indicates that the change in the current price with respect to the previous price alternates between negative and positive. If b_1 (the slope of the supply curve) is smaller than a_1 (the absolute value of the slope of the demand curve), then the change in price becomes progressively smaller, and the system converges on equilibrium. However, if consumers are less responsive to a price change than producers are (i.e., if $a_1 < b_1$), the changes in price become progressively greater in absolute value. The system does not approach equilibrium and the model is said to be explosive.

Consider the following demand and supply equations:

(1) $x_{dt} = 200 - 3p_t$
(2) $x_{st} = -10 + 4p_{t-1}$

The lines corresponding to these equations are plotted in Figure 13.5, where the intersection is shown to be at the point (110, 30). That is, if the system is solved as if it were static, the solution is $p = 30$, $x_d = x_s = 110$.

Let us now repeat the process of choosing a lagged price less than or greater than the equilibrium price. Assume that $p_0 = 28$. We get the behavior of price and quantity traded over time shown in Table 13.2. The time paths of the variables are shown in Figures 13.6 and 13.7.

We can fully appreciate why this model is called explosive. Any disturbance from equilibrium (because of a shift in either of the curves) sets in motion forces that carry the system farther and farther away from equilibrium. In contrast to the stable dynamic model, it does not approach a new equilibrium when a change in one or more of the parameters occurs. Few markets with exploding cobwebs have been verified using actual market data. This is because of the existence of futures markets and other institutions assumed away in the simple mathematical model. However, it is precisely by understanding the patterns markets might take in the absence of arbitrage or speculative behavior by economic agents that we come to understand the role of those institutions in facilitating the attainment of market equilibrium. Furthermore, speculators themselves have a strong interest in the estimation of econometric models of price and quantity movements to assist them in their activities.

Table 13.2

t	x_t	p_t	$p_0 = 28$
1	102.00	32.67	
2	120.68	26.44	
3	95.76	34.75	
4	129.00	23.67	
5	84.68	38.44	
6	143.76	18.75	
7	65.00	45.00	
8	170.00	10.00	
9	30.00	56.67	
.	.	.	
.	.	.	
.	.	.	
.	.	.	

Figure 13.5

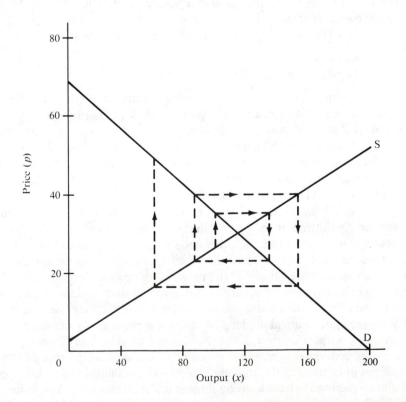

Output (x)

Figure 13.6

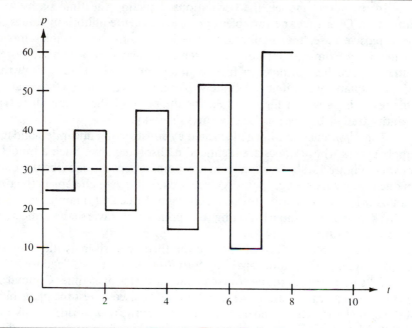

Figure 13.7

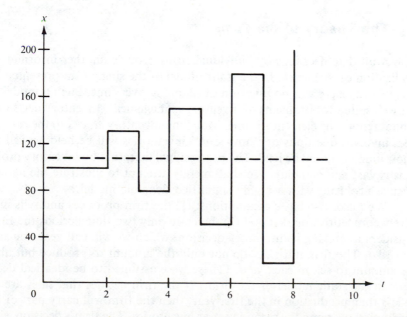

The Nondampened Oscillating Cobweb

In the stable model, the oscillations depicting the time paths were dampened. Over time the variables approached their equilibrium values. In the explosive case, the oscillations grew larger and the variables moved farther away from equilibrium. There remains the case in which the system neither approaches nor diverges from equilibrium. The time paths show that price and quantity continue indefinitely to oscillate between two fixed values. This result is shown in Figure 13.8a for the price of the commodity. The quantity traded behaves in exactly the same way.

This phenomenon can be illustrated by constructing linear demand and supply curves whose slopes are identical in absolute value. Such a model is shown in Figure 13.8b. Starting from any point except the equilibrium point on one of the curves (e.g., point A), the broken line, which depicts the time path of price and quantity, forms a rectangle. Price and quantity move on the broken line continuously among four points and traverse the same route again and again.

These three variations on the cobweb theorem strikingly illustrate the purpose and use of dynamic analysis. Variations in the model lead to different results with respect to the course of the variables over time. Comparing the predictions of the path of the variables can be used to test the plausibility of the model and help us understand more about the real world. In this context, it is the predictions of the dynamic model which help us understand the origin and functioning of futures markets. These insights are not as easily gleaned from static models.

The Theory of the Firm

Multidate decisions by individual firms provide another informative application of dynamics. In the static model of the single firm presented in Chapter 12, there was no question of planning over time. Such a model is not well suited for problems of inventory management. Inventory decisions cannot ignore the element of time. Matching inventory *stocks* to the *rate* of sales involves questions of "how long" inventories will be held as well as "how much" should be held. The professional literature on inventory problems is vast and complex. We shall merely attempt to illustrate the nature of such problems with a highly simplified dynamic model.

We make two basic assumptions: (1) the firm produces and sells in a purely competitive market and (2) there are only two time periods the firm considers in making its inventory decision, which we will call year one and year two. The firm must decide not only the amount to produce but also the amount to sell in each year. (These were assumed to be identical decisions in the static model of the firm.) If the firm decides that sales are to be less than production in the first year, then the firm will carry part of its production over into the second year as inventories. The firm's decision with

Figure 13.8a

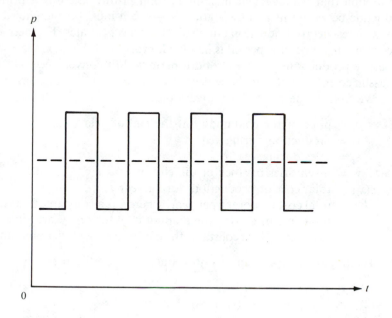

Figure 13.8b

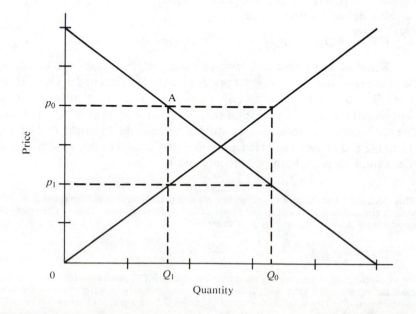

respect to production and sales (hence, inventories) is based on the usual assumption that management maximizes total profit. There is a primary distinction between this and the static case—profit must be maximized not only with respect to production but also with respect to sales. Furthermore, since more than one time period is involved, profit must be maximized with respect to production and sales in both periods. For convenience, all sales are assumed to be made at the end of the year.

We first define the following variables:

p_t = price of the commodity at the end of year t
x_t = production during year t
s_t = sales during year t
y_t = inventories in stock at the end of year t
$c(x_t)$ = total cost of production during year t
ky_t = total cost of storage per year, where k is a constant; that is, the total cost of storing the amount of y for one year. Since k is assumed to be a constant, the cost of storage function is linear.

To simplify the problem, we introduce two conditions:

(1) $y_1 = x_1 - s_1 \geq 0$
(2) $y_2 = (x_1 + x_2) - (s_1 + s_2) = 0$

The first condition merely states that inventories at the end of the first year can be zero but cannot be negative. The firm cannot carry less than zero inventories. Equation (2) states that inventories at the end of the second year are zero—none are carried over into a third year.

We define total profit, π, as:[2]

(3) $\pi = p_1 s_1 + p_2 s_2 - c(x_1) - c(x_2) - ky_1$

Since we have assumed pure competition, p_1 and p_2 are constants. These are spot and future market prices given to the firm and are unaffected by its decisions. Also, k is a known constant. The first two terms on the right side of the equation are total revenue from sales in years one and two. The last term is the total cost of storing inventories from the end of year one to the end of year two. Hence, total profit is total revenue from all sales minus total costs of both production and storage.

---

[2]This specification of the profit function implies that management is indifferent as to whether profit is realized in the present or the future. This simplifying assumption can be relaxed by introducing a discount factor, $1 + r$, where r is the rate of interest. Equation (3) becomes:

(3') $\pi = p_1 s_1 + \dfrac{p_2 s_2}{1 + r} - c(x_1) - \dfrac{c(x_2)}{1 + r} - \dfrac{ky_1}{1 + r}$

For a constant rate of interest, the maximum for equation (3') closely approximates the maximum for equation (3). Of course, if the market rate of interest changes, so does the firm's optimal inventory. This is the advantage of including the market rate of interest in the multi-period profit function.

Profit is to be maximized with respect to x_1, x_2, s_1, s_2, and y_1. By substituting equation (1) for y_1 in the last term and by substituting equation (2) for s_2 in the second term, we can simplify the expression for profit. In particular, we can eliminate s_2 and y_1. Then we maximize:

(4) $\pi = p_1 s_1 + p_2(x_1 + x_2 - s_1) - c(x_1) - c(x_2) - k(x_1 - s_1)$

with respect to only three variables, x_1, x_2, and s_1. We rewrite the expression for π as follows to group the terms with each variable:

(5) $\pi = [s_1(p_1 - p_2 + k) + x_1(p_2 - k) - c(x_1)] + [x_2 p_2 - c(x_2)]$

Note that if $(p_1 - p_2 + k)$ is negative, then π is largest for $s_1 = 0$. That is, store all that is produced. Since s_1 cannot be negative, any positive nonzero value for s_1 makes the first term negative. If, on the other hand, $(p_1 - p_2 + k)$ is positive, then π is largest for s_1 made as large as possible. That is, $s_1 = x_1$ by equation (1); all production is sold in year one, so $y_1 = 0$.

The common sense of this result should be clear. If the price next year, p_2, exceeds the price this year plus the cost of storage per unit, $p_1 + k$, then store all you can and sell it in year two. If the reverse is true, don't store at all. Finally, if the price this year plus storage cost per unit just equals the price next year, that is, if $p_1 - p_2 + k = 0$, the size of s_1 does not affect profit, so it does not matter which decision is made.

Let us take each of these three cases separately, compute the profit, and then maximize it.

CASE 1

$p_2 < p_1 + k$
Therefore, $s_1 = x_1$, so $y_1 = 0$.
And, by equation (2), $s_2 = x_2$. So:

$$\pi = x_1(p_1 - p_2 + k + p_2 - k) - c(x_1) + x_2 p_2 - c(x_2)$$
$$= x_1 p_1 - c(x_1) + x_2 p_2 - c(x_2)$$

For maximum π we have:

$$\frac{\partial \pi}{\partial x_1} = p_1 - c'(x_1) = 0$$

$$\frac{\partial \pi}{\partial x_2} = p_2 - c'(x_2) = 0$$

With $c(x_1)$ and $c(x_2)$ known, these equations can be solved for the values of x_1 and x_2. (See Chapter 10.) In this case we have the familiar condition that the amount of production in each year is chosen so as to equate the marginal cost of production to the price in that year.

CASE 2

$p_2 > p_1 + k$
Therefore, $s_1 = 0$, so $y_1 = x_1$.
And, by equation (2), $s_2 = x_1 + x_2$. So:

$$\pi = x_1(p_2 - k) - c(x_1) + x_2 p_2 - c(x_2)$$

For maximum π:

$$\frac{\partial \pi}{\partial x_1} = p_2 - k - c'(x_1) = 0$$

$$\frac{\partial \pi}{\partial x_2} = p_2 - c'(x_2) = 0$$

Production in the first year, x_1, is chosen so as to make the marginal cost of production equal to the price in the second year minus the marginal storage cost. Production in the second year, x_2, is chosen, as in Case 1, so that the marginal cost equals the price in the second year.

CASE 3

$p_2 = p_1 + k$
Therefore, s_1 is arbitrary; π and, therefore, the solutions for x_1 and x_2 are the same as in Case 1 and Case 2.

In actual applications, one most often deals with more than two time periods, and management discounts the revenue and cost *expected* in future periods using the appropriate rate of interest. Hence, the decisions of actual firms rarely, if ever, correspond to the type derived here, namely, store all production or sell all of it. More developed inventory problems lead to decisions with respect to how much shall be produced in each of several years and what proportion of this production should be stored. They also derive a rule for determining how long, on average, each unit of production should be stored. Nevertheless, this simplified model serves to illustrate the general nature of the inventory problem and the way in which dynamic models can be used to solve the problem.

National Income Models

Dynamic models are useful in studying the determinants of national income, which in turn influence business cycles of recession and/or inflation. One approach to discrete dynamic analysis is the *difference equation*. Let us consider a variation on a national income model presented by R. F. Harrod.[3] It clearly demonstrates how difference equations comprise an integral part of the solution of a dynamic system. The theory is presented in terms

[3]R. F. Harrod, "An Essay in Dynamic Theory," *Economic Journal*, Vol. XLIX (1939), pp. 14-33.

of saving and investment. This, of course, is an alternative to stating the theory in terms of consumption and investment (as in the static model on page 246). If consumption is a function of income, then saving is a function of income, and in equilibrium, intended saving equals intended investment (suppressing the government and foreign trade sectors).

Assuming the structural equations are known, we have the following complete model:

(1) $S_t = 0.1 Y_t$
(2) $I_t = 0.5(Y_t - Y_{t-1})$
(3) $Y_0 = 200$
(4) $I_t = S_t$

The symbols S, I, and Y designate saving, investment, and income, respectively (all measured in billions of dollars per year). Y_0 denotes the value of income in the initial year, that is, when $t = 0$. Equation (2) is a *difference equation*, an equation that involves finite differences in one or more of the variables.

We combine equations (1), (2), and (4) to get:

$$0.1 Y_t = 0.5 Y_t - 0.5 Y_{t-1}$$

which implies:

(5) $Y_t = 1.25 Y_{t-1}$

Equation (5) is called a *linear homogeneous difference equation of the first order*. To find its solution, we must know the value of this function at one point. Equation (3) tells us that national income is \$200 billion when $t = 0$, so we proceed step by step:

$$Y_1 = 1.25 Y_0$$
$$Y_2 = 1.25 Y_1 = (1.25)^2 Y_0$$
$$Y_3 = 1.25 Y_2 = (1.25)^3 Y_0$$
and so on.

The general solution to the difference equation will express Y_t in terms of the parameter and the initial value of Y given by equation (3). By extrapolating our example, we find:

(6) $Y_t = (1.25)^t Y_0 = 200(1.25)^t$

Equation (6) describes the time path of national income, which is shown in Figure 13.9.

The model leads to a nonoscillating increase in national income over time for the given coefficient of 1.25. This increase is due to the fact that the coefficient 1.25 is greater than one. It is interesting to note that if this coefficient had been positive but less than one, national income would show a nonoscillating decrease over time. If it had been equal to one, then income

Figure 13.9

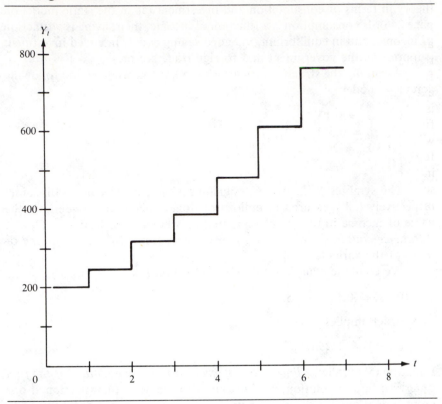

would remain constant at $200 billion and the graph in Figure 13.9 would be a horizontal line.

For purposes of comparison, it is worth noting that if the base of the exponent t were negative, the model would predict an oscillating time path of income. With a coefficient of less than -1 (say -2), the oscillation would be explosive. For values between -1 and 0, the oscillation would be dampened. Finally, if the coefficient in (6) equaled -1, the model would generate nondampened oscillating cycles alternating between $200 billion and $-$200 billion, the latter being impossible. Consequently, restrictions on the coefficients in equations (1) and (2) must be introduced into the mathematical model to insure that only positive values of income are predicted. The plausibility of these restrictions can then be tested with an econometric model.

Both of these conditions are reasonable: (1) saving must increase when income increases and (2) investment must increase when the rate of increase in income increases. These restrictions nevertheless show that requirements for mathematical consistency place limitations on the econometric model in addition to the constraints imposed by nature and frequency of the data used to estimate that model.

CONTINUOUS DYNAMIC MODELS

By shortening the length of the time period, a discrete dynamic model approaches a continuous model. In a continuous model, the variables are regarded as changing continuously through time instead of moving in steps from one period to the next. Changes in income in the discrete model, for example, were denoted by ($\Delta Y_t = Y_t - Y_{t-1}$). When the income variable is treated as continuous with respect to time, changes are indicated by the first derivative of income with respect to time, dY/dt. Such models contain what are called *differential equations*. It is convenient to think of the differential equation as a difference equation in which the differences are infinitesimal—expressed as derivatives rather than finite differences. The solution of a continuous model involves the process of integration discussed in Chapter 11.

The Market for One Commodity

The following dynamic model is given for a particular commodity X:

(1) $x_d(t) = 100 - 10p(t)$

(2) $x_s(t) = 25 + 15p(t)$

(3) $\dfrac{dp}{dt} = 0.10(x_d - x_s)$

where x_d, x_s, and p denote the quantity of X demanded, the quantity supplied, and the price of X, respectively.[4] Each of these variables is assumed to be a continuous function of time, denoted by t. In place of the equilibrium condition of the static model, we have equation (3) which states that the rate of change of price over time depends on the difference between the quantity demanded and the quantity supplied. The change in price is proportional to excess demand. When the quantity demanded exceeds the quantity supplied, the price rises. The price falls whenever the quantity supplied exceeds the quantity demanded. Only when equilibrium is disturbed is there a price change, for in equilibrium $x_d - x_s = 0$ and $dp/dt = 0$. Given a change in a parameter of either the demand or supply equation or both, equation (3) tells us in what direction price will move. Furthermore, it tells us the *rate* at which the price will approach its new equilibrium value, if at all.

The equilibrium price for this continuous dynamic model would be obtained by solving equation (3) for the condition $dp/dt = 0$. This is equivalent

[4]See A. Marshall, *Principles of Economics* (8th ed.; London: Macmillan and Co., Ltd., 1930), p. 374, and G. C. Evans, *Mathematical Introduction to Economics* (New York: McGraw-Hill Book Company, Inc., 1930), p. 48.

to the requirement that $x_d = x_s$. Hence, by substituting the right side of equation (2) for the left side of equation (1), we have:

$$25 + 15p(t) = 100 - 10p(t)$$
$$25p(t) = 75$$
$$p(t) = 3$$

As in the static model, once the equilibrium price is attained, that price and the associated quantity exchanged persist until either of the curves shifts. However, if the market is not in equilibrium, the solution to equation (3) tells how price changes through time. Substituting equations (1) and (2) into equation (3), we have:

$$\frac{dp}{dt} = 0.10(x_d - x_s)$$
$$= 0.10[(100 - 10p(t)) - (25 + 15p(t))]$$
$$(4) \quad \frac{dp}{dt} = 0.10[75 - 25p(t)]$$

If the price is greater than $p(t) = 3$, the bracketed expression in equation (4) is negative; excess supply reduces the price toward equilibrium. If $p(t) < 3$, the change in price through time would be positive; excess demand causes price to rise through time.

The dynamic behavior of this model can be better appreciated by specifying it in general terms, as would be the case of an econometric model prior to estimation. Let us designate the unknown parameters in the demand equation by a's, the unknown parameters of the supply equation by b's, and the unknown rate of change in price due to excess demand as the Greek letter theta, θ:

$$(1) \quad x_d = a_0 - a_1 p(t) + a_2 y$$
$$(2) \quad x_s = -b_0 + b_1 p(t) - b_2 w$$
$$(3) \quad \frac{dp}{dt} = \theta(x_d - x_s)$$

where y is per capita income and w is the wage rate in the industry. Both y and w serve as exogenous variables in the model. The expected signs of the coefficients are stated explicitly, so that all the a's and b's stand for positive (albeit unknown) constants. The reader can verify that the equilibrium price is determined by solving equations (1) and (2) simultaneously as if the model were static. The equilibrium price is:

$$p^* = \frac{a_0 + b_0}{b_1 + a_1} + \frac{a_2}{b_1 + a_1} y + \frac{b_2}{b_1 + a_1} w$$

And the equilibrium quantity is:

$$x^* = \frac{b_1 a_0 - a_1 b_0}{b_1 + a_1} + \frac{b_1 a_2}{b_1 + a_1} y - \frac{a_1 b_2}{b_1 + a_1} w$$

We will see in Part III of this book how the parameters of the structural coefficients can (sometimes) be estimated empirically. In this context, however, we are more interested in how the rate of change of price is related to the parameters of the structural equations. After substituting equations (1) and (2) into equation (3), we find:

$$\frac{dp}{dt} = \theta[a_0 - a_1 p + a_2 y - (-b_0 + b_1 p - b_2 w)]$$

$$= \theta[a_0 + b_0 + a_2 y + b_2 w - (a_1 + b_1)p]$$

(4′) $$\frac{dp}{dt} = \theta[(a_1 + b_1)(p^* - p)]$$

Note that when $p = p^*$, the bracketed expression in equation (4′) is zero, and price does not change through time unless y or w changes (which would set the time path moving toward a new equilibrium). If $p > p^*$ (i.e., because y or w decreased), the bracketed expression would be negative, and price would fall towards equilibrium. If $p < p^*$ (due to an increase in y or w), the bracketed term would be positive and $dp/dt > 0$.

By the solution of the differential equation (4′), moreover, we can find the time path of price and the rate at which it approaches p^*. The solution is given in the footnote below.[5] Had the coefficient of (4′) been positive,

---

[5] We have $dp/dt = \theta[(b_1 + a_1)(p^* - p)] = \lambda(p^* - p) = -\lambda(p - p^*)$, where λ is a constant determined by the slopes of the demand and supply equations and the adjustment factor θ. Introduce a new variable which is also a function of time:

(1) $z(t) = p(t) - p^*$

Differentiating this expression gives:

(2) $\frac{dz}{dt} = \frac{dp}{dt} - 0 = -\lambda[p(t) - p^*]$

Dividing by z we obtain:

(3) $\frac{z'(t)}{z(t)} = \frac{-\lambda[p(t) - p^*]}{p(t) - p^*} = -\lambda$

This can be written as the differential equation:

(4) $\frac{1}{z} \cdot \frac{dz}{dt} = -\lambda$

The integral of (4) by the methods of Chapter 11 is:

(5) $\int \frac{1}{z} \cdot \frac{dz}{dt} = Ae^{-\lambda t} = z(t)$

Hence, from (1) we have:

(6) $p(t) = z(t) + p^* = Ae^{-\lambda t} + p^*$

When $t = 0$, then $A = p_0 - p^*$, where p_0 is the price at time zero (which, in turn, is given by the initial values of y and w, plus a deviation from the initial equilibrium). Therefore:

(7) $p(t) = p^* + (p_0 - p^*)e^{-\lambda t}$

For a known p_0, this equation gives the time path of the price of the commodity.

which is inconsistent with the usual assumptions of economic theory with regard to the slopes of the demand and supply curves, the price would not have approached its equilibrium for any values of p other than its equilibrium values. In this case, a change in the exogenous variables would not lead to a new equilibrium.

National Income Models

The discrete national income model from the first section of this chapter can also be formulated as a continuous model. Let us rewrite that model in terms of continuous variables:

(1) $S(t) = 0.1 Y(t)$

(2) $I(t) = 0.5 \dfrac{dY}{dt}$

(3) $S(t) = I(t)$

where saving, investment, and income, represented by S, I, and Y, are all expressed as continuous functions of time, t. Equation (2) is a differential equation.

As the first step in the solution, we follow the same procedure as that used in the discrete case. Equations (1) and (2) are substituted into equation (3). This substitution yields:

$$0.1 Y(t) = 0.5 \frac{dY}{dt}$$

or

(4) $\dfrac{dY}{dt} = 0.2 Y(t)$

The problem then becomes one of finding the solution of this differential equation for the behavior of income over time. After both sides of the equation have been multiplied by $1/Y$, the equation may be written:

(5) $\dfrac{1}{Y} \cdot \dfrac{dY}{dt} = 0.2$

Integration of both sides of equation (5) yields:

$$\int \frac{1}{Y} \cdot \frac{dY}{dt} \, dt = \int 0.2 \, dt$$

(6) $\displaystyle \int \frac{dY}{Y} = \int 0.2 \, dt$

We know from rule 2 on page 214 that the left side of (6) can be expressed as $\log_e Y + k$, since the derivative of $\log_e Y$ is $1/Y$. Considering the right side, we know from Chapter 11 that the indefinite integration indicated gives $0.2t + k$. Combining the arbitrary constants on the right, we rewrite (6) as:

(7) $\log_e Y = 0.2t + k$

To find the solution that gives Y as a function of t, we merely translate the logarithmic expression into an exponential one:

(8) $Y(t) = e^{(0.2t+k)} = e^{0.2t} \cdot e^k = Ae^{0.2t}$

where $A = e^k$. Now we have an arbitrary constant in the solution. But we may specify a value for A by stating the initial value of Y. The value of Y at time zero will be designated by Y_0. That is, the value of the function $Y(t)$ when $t = 0$ is denoted by Y_0. Then:

(9) $Y(t) = Y_0 e^{0.2t}$

Under the assumption that $Y_0 = \$200$ billion, the time path of national income is shown in Figure 13.10. Note the continuity of the time path as opposed to those shown for discrete dynamic models. The solutions for S and I can also be found. Their time paths can be plotted from equations (1) and (2) when the value of Y at each time point is known.

Figure 13.10

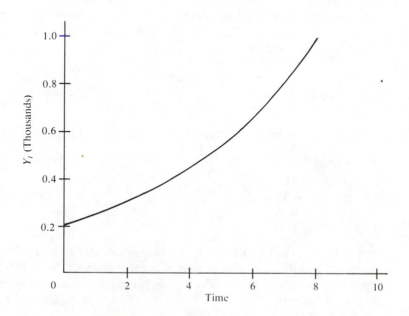

CONCLUSION

It has not been the purpose of this chapter to present an exhaustive set of examples of dynamic models. The foregoing illustrations are designed to show the kind of information that economists can glean from dynamic mathematical and econometric models, and how these models differ from their static counterparts. A careful scrutiny of the illustrations should help you grasp the importance of other applications of dynamic models you may encounter in the rest of this book and in your other work in economics. Many variations of dynamic models appear in professional literature in economics. For a complete understanding of some of these, more sophisticated mathematics than that offered in this text is required.

Despite the limitations of the current discussion, you should gain enough from this introduction to appreciate the importance of dynamic models in analyzing economic fluctuations. Though not regular in amplitude or duration, the so-called business cycles are a kind of economic oscillation with respect to time. Seasonal cycles in production, inventories, and consumption can be better understood with the aid of dynamic analyses. Again it should be emphasized that dynamics, like statics, is a useful set of tools of analysis rather than a codified body of doctrine. Our success in using dynamic mathematical models depends in part on our ingenuity in applying these tools to diverse problems. Our success in estimating dynamic econometric models depends in part on how well the model we construct conforms to the constraints imposed by the availability and quality of data. Both dynamic and static analysis are powerful tools, but even powerful tools will not do the job by themselves. Their ultimate productivity depends on the skill of those who wield them.

PROBLEMS

1. Explain the difference between a static model and a dynamic model.

2. You are given the following dynamic national income model:

    (1) $S_t = aY_t$
    (2) $I_t = b(Y_t - Y_{t-1})$
    (3) $Y_0 = 400$
    (4) $S_t = I_t$

    where S denotes saving, Y is income, I is investment, and a and b are constants. The subscripts refer to time. Compute and plot the time path of national income from $t = 0$ to $t = 5$, inclusive, for the following values of a and b:
    a. $a = 0.2, b = 0.3$
    b. $a = 0.5, b = -0.2$
    c. $a = 0, b = 2$

3.   You are given the following demand and supply equations for a cobweb market model:

(1) $Q_{st} = -a_0 + a_1 p_{t-1}$
(2) $Q_{dt} = b_0 - b_1 p_t$
(3) $Q_{et} = Q_{dt} = Q_{st}$

where Q_{st} and Q_{dt} are the quantity demanded and supplied, respectively, in period t, p_{t-1} is the price in period $t - 1$, and p_t is the price in period t. Determine equilibrium price and quantity for each of the following sets of parameters, and explain whether the model predicts convergence towards that equilibrium through time:

a. $a_0 = 100$, $a_1 = 5$, $b_0 = 500$, $b_1 = 10$
b. $a_0 = 100$, $a_1 = 5$, $b_0 = 500$, $b_1 = 5$
c. $a_0 = 100$, $a_1 = 10$, $b_0 = 500$, $b_1 = 5$

4.   Plot the time paths from $t = 0$ to $t = 4$, inclusive, for saving and investment corresponding to the following continuous dynamic model:

(1) $S(t) = 0.2Y(t)$

(2) $I(t) = 0.5\dfrac{dY}{dt}$

(3) $S(t) = I(t)$

where S denotes saving, I is investment, and Y is income, all as continuous functions of time, t. Assume income in period zero is 200.

5.   You are given the following continuous dynamic model:

(1) $S(t) = 0.1Y(t)$

(2) $I(t) = -1\dfrac{dY}{dt}$

(3) $S(t) = I(t)$

where S denotes saving, I is investment, and Y is income, all as continuous functions of time. Assume income in period zero is 300 and find the general solution for income as a function of time. Plot the time path of income from $t = 0$ to $t = 5$, inclusive.

14

The Problem of

Uncertainty

Up to this point, we have pretended that the parameters of mathematical models were known with certainty and that the parameters of econometric models were capable of precise estimation. Neither assumption is realistic. Most mathematical models are constructed in the most general terms. Usually little is known (or assumed) except which variables are included in specific structural equations and the signs of the first and second derivatives of functions. It is the purpose of econometric models to fill in the gaps of mathematical models, to provide numerical estimates of the parameters in structural or reduced form equations. There is no rigid requirement that mathematical models conform to reality. Indeed, it is the role of mathematical models to focus on the crucial ingredients in an economic problem, abstracting those details that make every event unique. However, since actual data are used to estimate the parameters in an econometric model, there must be a much closer correspondence between reality and the econometric model than between reality and the typical mathematical model. But because this correspondence can never be exact, econometric models are fraught with *uncertainty*.

There are two types of uncertainty in economic models. First, imperfect information may plague the economic agents whose behavior our model is intended to explain. When firms undertake an investment, they incur known costs in the present, but the outcome of the investment depends on demand

and cost conditions that will prevail when the new facility comes "on line." Those conditions cannot be predicted with absolute accuracy; the investment decision is uncertain. Similarly, students undertake different courses of study based (in part) on their *beliefs* or *estimates* of the job prospects in various fields. Yet the student will not embark on that career for several years. By graduation time the demand and supply conditions in that occupation may have changed dramatically. Choosing a career is an uncertain decision. Monetary authorities engage in open market operations on the basis of their *estimates* of the monetary base and the speed at which new bank reserves will be turned into loans. Since monetary authorities do not directly control bank behavior, there is no way the impact of open market operations on money growth or inflation can be predicted with complete accuracy. Monetary policy involves uncertainty.

The second type of uncertainty that permeates economic models involves incomplete information on the part of the investigator about the equations that describe the behavior of economic agents and the data used to estimate those equations. True, economic theory can tell us which variables are relevant to a structural equation. We know that we can write the quantity demanded and the quantity supplied as dependent on the price of the commodity. We also know the direction in which income, other prices, or expectations influence the demand for that commodity. And we know the direction in which factor prices and technological conditions influence the quantity supplied. Furthermore, our theoretical reasoning can tell us that the demand curve cannot be positively sloped and that the supply curve cannot be negatively sloped. These are all predictions of models based on the assumptions of utility maximization by households and profit maximization by firms.

But theoretical reasoning does not reveal the exact *value* of the parameters in the model. The parameters of the price variable in a linear demand equation, for example, can range from zero to minus infinity. Any of these values is consistent with the theoretical requirement that the partial derivative of quantity demanded with respect to price not be positive. In fact, the *estimated* coefficient on price in an econometric demand equation might be positive, indicating the *likely* prospect that an error has been committed in estimating that parameter or the *unlikely* prospect that the theory of demand is untrue, at least for the economic events underlying the data set used to test the model. Likewise, the Keynesian consumption function predicts that a change in disposable income causes consumption to increase in the same direction, but by a smaller magnitude. That is, the first derivative of consumption with respect to income is positive but less than one. Economic reasoning alone does not tell us whether that first derivative is $+0.001$ or $+0.999$ or any other value in the predicted range. Econometric techniques are required to estimate the numerical value of the marginal propensity to consume, thereby providing a test of the accuracy of this theory.

Since economic theory cannot tell us more than the forms of the structural equations, we must turn to empirical data generated by events in the "real world" to approximate the values of parameters in economic models. We must use empirical observations on prices, quantities produced and consumed, income, saving, or whatever economic magnitudes are relevant to the model. In other words, we use empirical observations of the values of the variables of the model to estimate the parameters of the equations that generated the data. It is a tricky business indeed, fraught with pitfalls such as specifying incorrect structural equations, omitting important variables or including spurious ones, and making incorrect assumptions about the direction of causation between right-side and left-side variables in the equations. Furthermore, there are disagreements and controversies raging in economics which imply different models, often containing different sets of variables, to explain the same events. Faced with this environment, the prudent econometrician appreciates the role of uncertainty in the estimation process.

CERTAINTY, RISK, AND UNCERTAINTY

As we have seen repeatedly in this text, much economic theory involves maximizing behavior on the part of economic agents. Households are assumed to maximize utility within the constraints of available income, wealth, and credit. Firms are assumed to maximize profit given demand conditions, the structure of the market, technological conditions, and the supply of factor services. In these and many other cases, the economic agent (e.g., the household or the firm) exercises control over some variables (e.g., the quantity of goods purchased or produced) in order to attain some desired outcome (e.g., utility or profit) measured by other variables. In the mathematical model of an economic hypothesis, it is convenient to assume a *one-to-one correspondence* between the options open to the agent and the outcomes of his or her decision. Picking the appropriate combination of commodities is seen as *causing* the household's level of utility; setting the appropriate rate of output *generates* the firm's profit. In each case the selection of an alternative is associated with a unique, known outcome.

There are two crucial ingredients in the certainty model.[1] First, there must be *complete control*: for each alternative open to the decision-maker, there must be no more than one outcome. Second, there must be *complete information*: the outcome of each option must be known *before* the decision is made. When more than one outcome from a decision is possible, an element of *risk* is encountered. When there is incomplete or inaccurate information about the correspondence between outcomes and alternatives, the element of *uncertainty* is encountered.

---

[1]The discussion in the rest of this section is based on Robert J. Wolfson and Thomas M. Carroll, "Ignorance, Error and Information in the Classic Theory of Decision," *Behavioral Science* (March 1976), pp. 107-115.

Figure 14.1 provides a simplified picture of the decision environments that can confront economic agents. On the vertical axis we are measuring the degree of control the economic agent has over his or her environment. A "1" means complete control over the decision environment: each action has only one outcome. A "0" means complete impotence; regardless of the action the agent undertakes, the outcome he or she will experience is immutable. Ranging between "0" and "1" are the various degrees of imperfect control, where the outcome of a decision is partly influenced by the agent in question, partly influenced by other economic agents (e.g., rivals, government bureaucrats), and partly influenced by random events (e.g., changes in the weather, unexplained changes in tastes, external shocks to the system). Ironically, "control" in the sense that we are using it here does not necessarily translate into "power" or "influence." For instance, the perfectly competitive firm has very little discretion. The only variable management can control is the rate of output. Nevertheless, complete control is assumed by a one-to-one correspondence between alternatives (different rates of output) and outcomes (the corresponding rates of profit). By contrast, firms operating in oligopolistic markets have much more influence over factor prices and product prices. Because this influence is shared with rivals, management has imperfect control over that firm's environment.

Figure 14.1

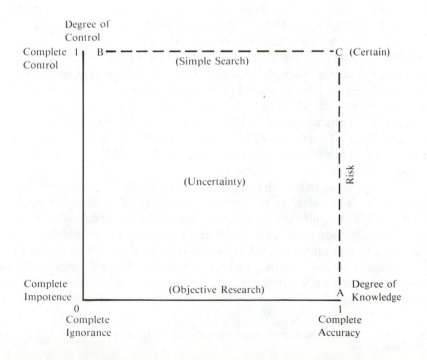

Along the horizontal axis in Figure 14.1 we measure the "degree of information" possessed by the economic agent. Although the measurement is admittedly imprecise, we let "1" stand for perfect information; the agent has accurate information about the connection between alternatives and outcomes. By contrast, point "0" implies complete ignorance; the agent does not know what alternatives are available, what the possible outcomes of various alternatives are, and what the *probability* of any outcome is, given the selection of an alternative. Again, the range of points between "0" and "1" represents incomplete or inaccurate information. Some alternatives or outcomes are known or the agent has made subjective estimates of the likelihood of outcomes for different alternatives.

In Figure 14.1, the condition of certainty corresponds to point (1, 1). At this point the economic agent has complete control over his or her environment and the consequences of decisions are completely predictable. This point is the locus of most basic economic theory. Certainty is the simplest environment to study, since if the outcomes can be ranked, so can the alternatives that "cause" them. Furthermore, when the connection between alternatives and outcomes can be depicted by a continuous function, economic models are easily translated into mathematical models. The convenience of mathematical models need not be restated; that has been the topic of this book to this point!

But economic theory sometimes confronts situations when the assumptions of perfect knowledge or perfect control lead to erroneous predictions of economic events. Consumers do not always know the prices or the characteristics of products they wish to purchase; the economics of imperfect competition in general, and of advertising in particular, must somehow account for the *search* behavior of households and firms. For instance, we can imagine a shopper beginning at point B, knowing none of the prices that different merchants charge for a commodity he or she wishes to purchase. After perusing the advertisements in newspapers and talking to friends, the shopper accumulates additional information. If information were free, which it is not, the search might take the shopper from point B to point C, the certainty point. Actually, even for a simple search problem (wherein there is only one outcome per alternative sampled), decisions will ordinarily be made before information is complete.

On the other hand, we can imagine that control is incomplete while information is as complete as is consistent with the decision environment. That is, there are multiple possible outcomes to individual decisions, but the decision maker possesses accurate information about the *probability distribution* of those outcomes. Such a situation is properly referred to as *risk*. For instance, the rate of return on an investment depends on the conditions prevailing at some point in the future. The entrepreneur may know (or believe[2]) that there is a 70 percent probability of economic prosperity and a

---

[2]As argued in Wolfson and Carroll, erroneous information leads to behavior consistent with individual beliefs.

30 percent chance of a recession. Knowlege of the probability of outcomes allows the agent to calculate an *expected value* for each investment option. That is, the "payoff" in the case of prosperity is multiplied by the probability of prosperity and the payoff in the case of a recession is multiplied by the probability of a recession. The sum of these *weighted outcomes* equals the expected value of the option. By ranking the expected values of the options, we can in turn rank the options themselves. Hence, by assuming that economic agents attempt to maximize *expected* profit or *expected* utility, we may be able to predict the outcomes of decision *as if* a condition of certainty prevailed.

However, there are pitfalls to analyzing behavior under risk that are not as serious in models that assume certainty. We saw in our discussion of utility maximization that (under certainty) it is not necessary that utility be a measurable concept. All that is required is that the individual be able to discern which alternatives (e.g., combinations of commodities) generate the "highest" indifference curve. However, in calculating "expected utility," assigning specific numbers to outcomes themselves is necessary. While techniques have been developed to estimate the values assigned to outcomes by individuals confronting a state of risk,[3] some economists find the assumptions required for these estimates unrealistic. For instance, the individual is assumed to be *risk neutral*, that is, that expected utility is unaffected by the variability of outcomes. A risk neutral person would be indifferent between prospects that offered a 100% chance of winning $100, a 10% chance of winning $1,000 (and a 90% chance of nothing), and a 1% chance of winning $10,000 (and a 99% chance of nothing). If people are risk neutral, then maximizing expected utility is equivalent to maximizing expected wealth. If people are not risk neutral, the degree of *risk aversion* can be diagnosed by the deviation between choices and the rankings of outcomes by expected wealth. However, if the subjective probability that economic agents use is different from the probabilies the investigator assigns to those outcomes, risk preferences can be misinterpreted.

As we have stated, the condition of *uncertainty* exists when the individual has incomplete control over the outcomes of decisions and the probability of outcomes resulting from different actions is imperfectly known. The purpose of statistical analysis in general and econometric analysis in particular is to improve the quality of information consistent with the decision environment, to move from a state of uncertainty to a state of risk. Indeed, the initial situation confronting the objective scientist may be depicted at point 0, where there is no information about the relationship between "causes" and "effects," nor is there any ability to influence the environment. Statistical procedures, along with econometric models, are employed to estimate the probability distribution of outcomes and to estimate an

---

[3]The pathbreaking work on this subject is John Von Neumann and Oskar Morgenstern, *The Theory of Games and Economic Behavior*, 2nd edition, Princeton University Press, 1947.

"expected value" for each alternative. For example, what is the expected impact of a change in investment on equilibrium national income? Ideally the scientist can collect data from published sources without changing the environment. The probability of a change in investment does not change just because we study it, or does it? The economist working for a large firm or advising a government client must contend with the possibility that the influence his or her agency exerts over its environment may influence the nature and reliability of the data that are used to estimate statistical relationships.

UNCERTAINTY AND RISK
IN ECONOMETRICS

Notice that we began the previous section discussing the nature of risk and uncertainty as it confronts the subjects of economic theory and ended by noting that economic investigators not only confront complex decision environments, but may also influence the structure of those environments. Econometrics itself is an economic activity involving the allocation of scarce resources (time, creativity, information, and luck) to achieve alternative ends (truth, prestige, making bosses and clients happy). Like any other economic process, we can develop models describing the crucial ingredients of the econometric process while assuming away more troublesome details. We can also take periodic looks at the "real world" to determine just how well our model conforms to actual events. Hence, throughout the rest of this text we will explore the theoretical underpinnings of the estimation procedures used by econometricians. At the same time we will explore actual examples of the econometric process in operation.

In light of our previous discussion, we may conveniently regard the problem of statistical measurement in the following way: there exists one "true" economic relationship, say the "true" demand equation for tennis shoes in the United States today. If we could identify all potential and actual customers, and determine with perfect accuracy the quantity they would buy at all possible prices, holding incomes, prices of other goods, and tastes constant, we could have a perfect measure of the "true" demand equation. But because of human and technological limitations, we obviously cannot do this. We therefore take a sample of observations on price, quantity consumed, income, and other relevant economic magnitudes. From this sample, we attempt to estimate the parameters of the "true" demand equation. Because we must work with incomplete information about the relevant variables, our estimate of the "true" demand equation will contain error. If the error is relatively large, the estimate will be a poor one. But if the error is small (in terms of criteria established by statistical analysis), our estimate may be considered reliable. There is always an element of *risk* in econometric analysis. There are many sets of parameter estimates that can be made for one "true" econometric model. It is the role of statistical estimation to transform our *uncertainty* about the values of those parameters into reliable *expected values*.

Let us consider the problem of statistical measurement in more general terms. Mathematical models consist of general equations or laws of economics that refer to the entire set of economic events being studied. The consumption function, for example, implies a positive relationship between consumer expenditure and income that holds for different households at the same time, the same households over time, and aggregations of households, both for *cross-section* and for *time-series* data. In fact, the theory is meant to hold for different income levels that *might* prevail at a specified time and place. This set of events is called the *population* in statistics. The population is an abstract term and refers to all conceivable observations of consumption and income by, say, American households. It must be emphasized that it is not the households that are being observed, it is rather combinations of consumption and income. Similarly, in the case of a supply function, the population is the set of all conceivable combinations of price, quantity offered for sale, and the relevant exogenous variables (e.g., prices of factors of production, number of firms in the industry, expected future prices).

It is obviously inconceivable to collect all possible observations on a population covered by an economic theory or hypothesis. Our observations are limited to *recorded events* that have occurred in the past. The data on these observations may be arranged in a *time series*, such as total consumption and total income, reported by year, from 1929 to the present. Or they may be in the form of *cross-sectional* data, such as the consumption and income of 1,000 households in the United States in 1985. For a *statistic* of the sample (e.g., how a variation in income is associated with a variation in consumption), we attempt to infer the value of the parameter in the population. The characteristic of the population is regarded as the "true" parameter, and the sample statistic is interpreted as a (good or poor) estimate of the unknown true parameter.

The statistical theory of random sampling describes the relationship between samples and the population. There will not be an exact correspondence between the population and any one sample from that population, because what we get in the sample depends partly on chance. That is, there are rules of probability that govern the composition of any sample we use. Without knowledge of this underlying probability distribution, the connection between the sample statistics we calculate and the true parameters of the underlying population is uncertain. The purpose of statistical measurement is to move from a state of uncertainty to a state of risk, so that we can make educated estimates of the likelihood of parameters in the population.

RANDOM VARIABLES

We have seen in the two previous chapters that there is something of an inconsistency between mathematical and econometric models. A mathematical model is constructed for the purpose of simplicity, to distill from the confusion of the "real world" those crucial ingredients of an economic event that give it generality. Hence, a mathematical statement of the law of demand is simply: $\partial Q_d / \partial p < 0$. No qualifications, no exceptions. A change in the price of a good (p) changes the quantity demanded (Q_d) in the opposite direction, *ceteris paribus*. This statement is meant to apply to all conceivable commodities at all conceivable times and in all conceivable places. Yet, despite the wide-spread acceptance of the law of demand it still constitutes a hypothesis about economic behavior, to be subjected to repeated empirical scrutiny. In order to test this hypothesis, we must translate the law of demand into an econometric model capable of being tested. Unlike the mathematical model, the econometric model must take into account other factors (e.g., changes in income, changes in the prices of related goods, perhaps even changes in tastes) that cause the *observed* consumption of a commodity to vary from time to time and place to place. We must construct an econometric model designed to conform to the data used to test it.

But we have just argued that empirical data can never contain all possible observations relevant to an economic hypothesis. Nor is it usually possible for a model to include variables that account for all the influences on economic events. There are unavoidable *errors of observation* and *errors of omission*. Because we don't get an exact and orderly variability in our empirical observations—all other things are not in fact constant—we must have some means for explaining the deviations from the exact theoretical predictions of our model. For this reason, we introduce into the behavioral equations (but not the definitions, per se) random variables.

When we think of the word "random" we think of something erratic or "hit-or-miss." There is a certain amount of accuracy in such a conception. More exactly, we may think of a *random variable* as a variable that can assume different values with definite probabilities. A random variable is one that is subject to the laws of probability.

In econometrics, random variables are generated by random errors. If X is the "true" value of some variable or parameter, and we measure its value as $X' \neq X$, then the random error in the measurement of X is $e = X' - X$. It follows that $X' = X + e$ and the observed value is a random variable, even if the true value of X is a constant. When we come to apply the model to empirical data, we find that our systematic relationships do not predict with perfect precision. Suppose we have a demand-supply model for a commodity X, and suppose we have estimated the parameters of the equations. We would find that observed quantity exchanged did not precisely match the quantity *predicted* by the equation, given price and the exogenous variables, even for the data used to estimate that equation. By construction, the deviation between the observed and "predicted" values of quantity are random in nature. But we would also find that the quantity predicted on the basis of "new" data would also deviate from the observed quantity. Are these errors random in nature or is there a systematic "bias" in the model that is unaccounted for by the systematic (nonrandom) variables? If the deviations are random, we can account for their influence on the variable to be explained by adding to the explanatory systematic variables of the equations other variables that are random variables. In general there are two sources of these random errors: errors of observation and errors of omission.

Errors of Observation

We have seen that when an econometrician attempts to estimate the parameters of a model, the estimate is made from a sample of observations on the values of the systematic (nonrandom) variables. Assume the econometrician has a series of published tables on market prices of X and quantities traded on the market. This is a sample. It is, at best a subset of all possible observations that might have been made. Someone had to go out into the "field" and collect this information. The information might have been collected at different places or at different points in time. That is, there was an element of luck or chance that figured into precisely when and where the information was recorded. Furthermore, there may have been clerical or other errors in the way the data were recorded, a number may have been miscopied here or fudged there. Questions asked of traders in the market may have been misunderstood; firms may have been unwilling to relinquish certain exact cost or output data; families may have had to make rough guesses about their consumption, especially if the answer depended on memory. These chance phenomena cause some unavoidable deviation in the sample from the actual or "true" values of the economic magnitudes.

These errors in the observation of the values of the systematic variables will lead to errors in the predictions of the model. If a theoretical relation is stated between aggregate consumption and income in the United States, the (time) series of observations on pairs of values of consumption and income will not exactly satisfy the theoretical consumption equation. If these pairs of values are plotted as points in a diagram, the estimated equation will not pass through all the plotted points. The recognition that observations are likely to deviate from the "true" relationship allows economists to select simple mathematical forms rather than very complex ones. For instance, if we have fifty observations on consumption and income, it would be possible to discover an equation (say a polynomial of the forty-ninth degree) that passed through all the points. Yet such an "exact fit" would still involve errors of observation. To avoid the false security of a "good fit" most economists attempt to take the impact of errors of observation into account when estimating simple equations. The deviations of the observed values from those expected from the equation can, under certain circumstances, be treated as random.

Errors of Omission

When writing a demand equation for a particular commodity X, for example, we may write the quantity demanded as a function of the price of X only. We know from economic theory that other variables, such as income, other prices, population, and tastes, influence the quantity demanded. The question arises whether these other variables ought to be included as additional systematic variables in the demand equation. The answer lies in the *law of large numbers*. It is permissible to attribute the influence of a set of variables to the random variable in an equation if those variables are (1) many in number, (2) individually small in influence, and (3) independent of one another. If these three requirements are met, then the sum of the components will behave as if it were random. Excluded variables will be "absorbed" by the error term in the equation.

Suppose that we wish to estimate the marginal propensity to consume for the United States using annual data from 1929 to 1987. According to theory, the aggregate consumption function, whose parameter we are measuring, is extrapolated from the consumption functions of millions of households. Furthermore, we believe that consumption at the household level will vary according to the family's disposable income, the number of members of the household, their age distribution, their amount of wealth or debt, the market rate of interest, their expectations, and their tastes. At any time there is a roughly stable distribution of households by size and age. If this average does not change appreciably from one time to another, it need not be accounted for in the data. Similar logic can apply to changes in tastes. At any time there will be a fairly stable distribution of households that are frugal and those that are spendthrift, even if there are frequent changes in tastes at the individual level.

Hence, we may relate the aggregate United States consumption to national income and a random variable. Then suppose we suspect that our "random" variable is not really random (there are statistical tests available to judge this). This means that there are other strong influences operating on consumption for which the law of large numbers does not apply. Since all households will tend to face the same rate of interest (after adjusting for default risk), we decide that this variable should be included in the model. We then reformulate the model, making consumption a function of disposable personal income, the interest rate, and a random variable.

Now, if the residual amount of consumption that is not explained by either income or the interest rate behaves as if it were random, we have a statistically reliable estimate of the structural equation. Consequently, there is a continual interaction between the theoretical and empirical stages of economic research. Any given equation may require repeated empirical and theoretical reexamination before it is accepted as a valid structural equation.

RESTATEMENT OF
ECONOMETRIC MODELS

As stated earlier, the feature of uncertainty may be said to exist in two senses. First, there is the uncertainty on the part of the economic topic being studied. Government policymakers do not know all the possible outcomes of their policies, let alone the probability distribution of those outcomes. Entrepreneurs often guess at the demand for a commodity being introduced to the market. Corporations discover that costs actually experienced after the opening of a new plant are quite different from those expected when the plant was being planned. Uncertainty is particularly a factor in dynamic models such as the inventory model of Chapter 13. We cannot adequately treat such decision rules at this point. They must await consideration of probability theory, which we shall discuss in the next chapter.

The second sense in which we may speak about uncertainty is the uncertainty of the research worker. It is this type of uncertainty that we have emphasized in the preceding sections of this chapter—uncertainty about the "true" values of the parameters in a market or social relationship. Though the two kinds of uncertainty are not completely separate, the second type is more important for economists. Economics is a social science that uses theories of individual behavior as a stepping-stone to understanding group behavior. It is ultimately interested in equations that describe the behavior of such social groups as consumers, industries, speculators, workers, and government.

The econometrician's choice between static and dynamic models is governed by theoretical factors and the kind of information he or she desires to know. The characteristic of uncertainty may be appended to either static or dynamic models. Indeed, it must be included if the econometrician is to have meaningful and testable empirical predictions. A model cannot strictly be said to be an econometric model unless it is formulated with a view to its statistical properties. We shall illustrate the formulation of a static and a dynamic econometric model. The characteristics of deductive logical consistency and completeness (discussed in Chapter 12 and 13) are not to be disregarded, but we shall emphasize the preparation of the model for statistical analysis.

Static Models

One of the first steps in an econometric investigation is the formulation of a testable model. As we have seen, economic theory can tell us the general forms of functional relationships. It can tell us, for instance, that quantity demanded is a decreasing function of price, but it cannot tell us whether the demand function is linear, quadratic, cubic, etc. Consequently, the second step is a general review of the data to determine approximately whether the equation is linear or of another type. We shall say more about this in a later chapter.

Let us assume that we have a static model designed to explain the price and quantity traded of commodity X. Furthermore, suppose a preliminary look at the data suggests the equations are linear and are each in two variables. In one equation quantity demanded depends on price and per capita income, and in the other equation quantity supplied depends on price and the average hourly wage rate. The system of equations would be:

(1) $x_d = a_0 + a_1 p + a_2 y + u$, $a_1 < 0$ and $a_2 > 0$

(2) $x_s = b_0 + b_1 p + b_2 w + v$, $b_1 > 0$ and $b_2 < 0$

(3) $x_d = x_s$

where x_d and x_s denote quantity demanded and quantity supplied, respectively, p denotes the price of X, y denotes per capita income, w represents the average hourly wage rate, and the a's and b's are unknown constants. Note that this model differs from our previous static models. In the first place, we have not assumed that we know the values of the parameters. We know from economic theory that quantity demanded decreases with price ($a_1 < 0$) and increases with per capita income ($a_2 > 0$), *ceteris paribus*. We also know that quantity supplied increases with price ($b_1 > 0$) and decreases with the cost of labor ($b_2 < 0$), *ceteris paribus*. But this is as far as economic theory can carry us. The problem remaining is a statistical one, namely to estimate the values of the unknown parameters a_0, a_1, a_2, b_0, b_1, and b_2.

The second main characteristic that distinguishes this model from previous static models is the inclusion of random variables. The variable u is assumed to be a random variable in the demand equation and v is assumed to be a random variable, different from u, in the supply equation. These variables orient the model toward the statistical analysis that will be applied to it in order to estimate the values of the parameters from a sample. These random terms are subject to the laws of probability on which modern statistical estimation is based. The quantities demanded and supplied are linear functions of the errors, so they too may be treated as random variables. We shall not go into the actual statistical analysis at this point. Before discussing the statistical techniques, it is important that we understand the proper formulation of the model.

Dynamic Models

As an illustration of an uncertain dynamic model, let us reconsider the continuous national income model presented in Chapter 13. We add the random variables to get:

(1) $S(t) = aY(t) + u,\ a > 0$

(2) $I(t) = b\dfrac{dY}{dt} + v,\ b > 0$

(3) $S(t) = I(t)$

Here again S, I, and Y represent saving, investment, and income, respectively. The variables u and v are assumed random, while a and b are positive constants. The parameters are unknown. Assuming we do successfully estimate the values of a and b, the systematic relation will predict a steadily increasing level of income over time (see Figure 13.10). The actual values of income over that same period of time will in general differ somewhat from the predicted values. If these errors of measurement are small and in fact random (according to the proper statistical test), the model may be considered a good dynamic predictor of income.

We can see clearly from these two illustrations what the role of random variables is in econometrics. Since random variables are subject to the laws of probability, they put the model into a form that permits the estimation of parameters by statistical inference. It is to these statistical procedures that we now turn our attention. The remaining two chapters in Part II provide an exposition of elementary probability theory and statistical inference. After having become familiar with the meaning and techniques of statistical analysis, we shall reconsider econometric models from a more comprehensive viewpoint in Part III.

15

Elements of

Probability

Theory

Statistical analysis is an integral part of econometrics. Before we can say more about the estimation of econometric models, we must explore the statistical theory on which empirical estimation is based. This statistical theory, in turn, rests on the laws of probability. In this chapter we shall define probability and discuss some of the laws of probability. Since we are primarily interested in the practical application of statistics to economics rather than in the theory of statistics itself, this chapter and the next are summaries. Nevertheless, we shall want to investigate enough details about probability theory to understand and interpret the general implications for econometric research.

Consider an analogy between a laboratory experiment in the physical sciences and statistical measurement in economics. In both cases, we search for predictable relationships between some events and the causes of those events. In a laboratory one attempts to control, to a greater or lesser degree, the exterior conditions that surround an event and the imputed causes of that event. The physical scientist tries to vary the assigned causes and test whether or not the event behaves in the way predicted under the controlled conditions (other factors that are held constant). Even if all the assignable causes have been controlled, however, the outcome of any experiment is still subject to variation from causes the scientist cannot control or does not even know about. It is these unassignable disturbances or influences—these "accidental" or random errors—that create the need for a concept of probability.

Similarly, in economics we hypothesize that certain social phenomena are determinants or causes of other social phenomena. For example, aggregate national consumption is assumed to be determined or "caused" by national income. When dealing with social phenomena as we do in econometrics, we cannot conduct an experiment in the strict sense of the term, because we cannot control the causes and conditions that surround any given event. We can collect data on, say, consumption and income to see if the "cause" and its "effect" move in tandem. Just as in an experiment, when we come to measure or test the relation between the assigned cause (which varies, but not by experimental control) and the result, we find that the result is influenced by unassignable causes. Hence, random errors and the notion of probability play an important part in econometrics too.

THE CONCEPT OF PROBABILITY

A random variable may be called a probability variable. Although we can assign values to a systematic variable with certainty (each "event" has only one value), the values of the random variable are determined by chance. These values are predictable only with a specified degree of probability. The modern analysis of probability is a branch of pure mathematics. The foundations of probability theory are found in the mathematical theory of sets.[1] But we shall not find it necessary to enter into this axiomatic interpretation because a less rigorous treatment will be adequate for purposes of application.

The Classical or *A Priori* Definition

One definition of probability is an imaginative one: probability is defined as the number of times an event is *likely* to occur, given all possible outcomes. To take a simple example, a fair coin has two sides, "heads" and "tails." Of the two possible outcomes, the event "heads" has a probability of 1/2. To take another example, there are 6 sides to a die, so there are 36 possible combinations when a pair of dice are thrown. Of these 36 combinations, there are 6 ways of getting a "seven." The probability of rolling a seven is 6 out of 36, or 1/6. Stated more formally, the *a priori* definition of probability is:

Let there be x possible outcomes that constitute event E and let there be k possible outcomes that constitute "not E." If each outcome is equally likely and all outcomes are mutually exclusive, then the probability of event E, written $P_r(E)$, is the ratio of x to $x + k$:

$$P_r(E) = \frac{\text{number of outcomes that indicate } E}{\text{total number of possible outcomes}} = \frac{x}{x + k}$$

[1] See H. Cramer, *The Elements of Probability Theory and Some of Its Applications* (New York: John Wiley & Sons, Inc., 1955), Chapters 1 and 2.

The Principle of Insufficient Reason

To many economists and mathematicians, the classic *a priori* definition begs as many questions as it answers. How do we know that all possible
events we imagine are equally likely? Once in a while, a coin balances on
its edge when tossed. Does that make the probability of a "head" 1/3?
Of course not. Common sense and our experience tells us that coins do
not balance on their edges very often; the event is so rare that we may treat
its probability as zero. However, among likely outcomes we can invoke the
principle of insufficient reason as a starting point:

> Given a finite (limited number), exhaustive list of possible outcomes
> of a particular experiment, if there is no reason to believe that one
> outcome is more likely than any other, then assume all outcomes are
> equally likely.

The Relative Frequency
Definition of Probability

When *a priori* information provides no hint about the probability of
events, it is prudent to conduct an experiment. So if we do not know the
likelihood of a coin balancing on its edge because the principle of insufficient reason does not apply, we can toss a coin a number of times and record
the outcomes of our experiments. If the coin balances on its edge exactly
once in 1,000 tosses, we would *estimate* that the probability of a coin standing on its edge is 1/1,000 or 0.001.

If a well defined experiment is conducted n times (there are n trials),
and the number of times event E occurs is x (there are x successes),
then the probability of E is the ratio of x to n:

$$P_r(E) = \frac{x}{n}$$

The Limit of Relative Frequency

Anyone who has participated in a game of chance knows that "runs
of luck" sometimes occur. Sometimes we roll nothing but "sevens" at
the crap table or draw nothing but "twenty-one" in blackjack. At other
times "sevens" seem to never occur or there seem to be no aces in the
deck. The problem with the relative frequency definition of probability is
that there may not be enough trials to give an accurate measure of the
actual likelihood of an event. Presumably, however, if we allow the number of trials to become very large, runs of "good luck" and "rotten luck"
will cancel out, and the pattern of outcomes will come to approximate
the "actual" probabilities. Hence, we have the idea of probability as the

limiting value of the relative frequency of an event if the series of trials is a random series:

> If a random experiment is conducted a greater and greater number of times ($n \rightarrow \infty$), then the probability of E is the limit of the ratio of the number of successes, x, to the number of trials, n, as n approaches infinity:

$$P_r(E) = \lim_{n \rightarrow \infty} \frac{x(n)}{n} = p$$

This approach to probability implies precise boundaries to the numbers that p can assume. If an event always occurs ($1 + 1$ always equals 2), then its probability is 1. If an event never occurs in an infinite number of trials ($1 + 1$ never equals 3), then its probability is zero. Hence, for any experiment:

$$0 \leq p \leq 1$$

Furthermore, if the probability of an event happening is p, the probability that it does not happen is $1 - p$. Hence, if the probability of a coin balancing on its edge is zero, the probability of a head or a tail is 1. If the probability of a head is 1/2, the probability of a tail is 1/2. If the probability of a coin balancing on its edge is 1/1,000, the probability of a head or a tail is 999/1,000 or 1,998/2,000. Hence, if the probability of a head is 999/2,000, then the probability of a tail is 999/2,000.

Randomness and Probability

The concept of probability requires that the series of trials be a random series. By a random series, we mean that any arbitrary selection of trials from the n trials gives the same value for p as the original n trials. Suppose that we make the following quite arbitrary selection: we choose every third trial out of the total n trials. Assume this gives us n_3 trials (n_3, of course, is approximately equal to $n/3$). We observe that the event in question occurs x_3 times in the n_3 trials. If the original series of n trials is indeed random, then we must find:

$$P_r(E) = \lim_{n_3 \rightarrow \infty} \frac{x_3}{n_3} = p$$

We could repeat this process for any number of different arbitrary selections. In general, we say:

> A series of n trials showing x occurrences of the event E is a random series, if, when we arbitrarily choose n' of these trials out of the original series of n trials by any arbitrary method and obtain x' occurrences of E, then:

$$P_r(E) = \lim_{n' \rightarrow \infty} \frac{x'}{n'} = \lim_{n \rightarrow \infty} \frac{x}{n} = p$$

Subjective Probability

We have apparently come full circle. We started with an *a priori* definition of probability, that is, a definition abstracted from experience, whereby the probability of an event is defined by the *hypothetical relative frequency* of that event out of all possible events. According to the *principle of insufficient reason*, if there is no reason to believe one outcome of an experiment as more likely than any other, all outcomes are equally likely. Hence, the probability of a "success" is the ratio of the number of outcomes constituting success to the total number of possible outcomes. However, because we *feel* on the basis of actual experience that some outcomes are more likely than others, we revert to the relative frequency definition. The probability of a success is simply the ratio of *observed* successes to the total *observed* outcomes. Yet this definition was found wanting because actual experience can deviate from patterns of probability. Experience is not necessarily random, and even apparently nonrandom *patterns* may sometimes be generated from random events when the number of observations is finite. So we defined probability on the basis of the *limit* of the ratio of successes to the total number of trials, as the number of trials approaches infinity. We also indicated that the pattern would be random if any arbitrary subset of the number of trials gave the same ratio of successes to trials.

But how do we know when the number of trials is sufficiently close to infinity that the ratio of observed successes to observed events constitutes the "true" probability? According to some economists and mathematicians (members of the Bayesian school of probability theory to be discussed in more detail below), there is no such thing as a "true" probability. Probability is a reflection of human experience, not some abstract number that can be measured independently of that experience. In other words, probability is subjective:

The *subjective probability* of an event E is the degree of belief that E will occur:

1. If $P_r(E) = 1$, event E is said to be *certain*.
2. If $P_r(E) = 0$, event E is said to be *impossible*.
3. If $0 < P_r(E) < 1$, $P_r(E)$ is the degree of *certainty* (or *uncertainty*) about the event.

The differences between the *a priori* (non-Bayesian) and the *subjective* (Bayesian) definitions of probability may seem to be irreconcilable. Indeed, when one explores the more complex areas of mathematical probability theory, there are differences which have yet to be resolved to universal satisfaction. However, for practical purposes, these two perspectives can be seen as complementary. Each adds something to the gaps in the other approach. Since subjective probability is based on experience, it is reasonable to use the *a priori* definition when personal experience is missing. If you are approached by a friend with a gambling proposition ("Let's flip a coin to see who pays for lunch''), it is reasonable to *assume* that the coin is fair and that a "heads" is just as likely as a "tails." However, if after you pay the check you casually toss the coin and it winds up heads only once in ten tries, you will have reason to *reassess* your *estimate* of the probability. The *a priori* definition constitutes the *prior* probability estimate and the subjective probability estimate constitutes the *posterior* probability estimate. We will return to these notions.

CALCULATION OF PROBABILITIES

In the previous section, we spoke of the probability p of an event happening, and implied this meant the probability of its happening in one trial chosen at random. The contradiction between defining probability in terms of an infinite number of trials and the fact that experience occurs in finite bundles led to the subjective approach to probability which we seek to reconcile with the *a priori* approach. Another problem that has widespread implications for statistical analysis is the following. Assume that the probability of an event happening is p. The probability that it does not happen is $q = 1 - p$. We plan a total of n trials, believing that the experiment will be conducted randomly. What is the probability that the event will happen x times in n independent trials? For instance, if we have a fair coin, what is the chance of the coin turning up "heads" only one time in ten trials?

To answer this question, we must first introduce the notion of *combinations*. We may regard the problem as one in which we have n distinct trials and we do not care about the arrangement in which the x successes occur (e.g., we do not care whether the one "head" occurs on the first, the fifth, or the tenth toss). The number of possible arrangements is given by a rule. Given n distinct trials, the number of possible ways of obtaining x successes out of n trials is determined by the formula:

$$_nC_x = \frac{n!}{x!(n - x)!}$$

$_nC_x$ is called the *binomial coefficient* and it measures the number of *combinations* of x successes out of n trials. The symbol $n!$ is read "n factorial," $x!$ is read "x factorial," etc. The meaning of $n!$ is that the integer n is multiplied by successively smaller integers until we reach 1:

$$n! = n(n - 1)(n - 2)(n - 3) \cdots (4)(3)(2)(1)$$

The same is true for $x!$ and $(n - x)!$. To get the number of combinations of one "head" from ten trials, we divide ten factorial by the product of one factorial (which is one) and nine factorial:

$$_{10}C_1 = \frac{(10)(9)(8)(7)(6)(5)(4)(3)(2)(1)}{(1)(9)(8)(7)(6)(5)(4)(3)(2)(1)} = \frac{10}{1} = 10$$

This result makes sense. The "head" can occur on any of the ten coin tosses and there are ten combinations of one head and nine tails. It follows that there are ten combinations of nine tails and one head:

$$_{10}C_9 = \frac{(10)(9)(8)(7)(6)(5)(4)(3)(2)(1)}{(9)(8)(7)(6)(5)(4)(3)(2)(1)(1)} = \frac{10}{1} = 10$$

To obtain the probability that the event E will happen x times in n trials, we multiply the binomial coefficient by the probabilities p and q raised to the powers x and $n - x$, respectively:

$$P_r(E_x) = {_nC_x} \cdot p^x \cdot q^{(n-x)}$$

where E_x signifies that event E happens x times out of n trials. This probability is called the binomial formula.

To return to our example of a coin toss to determine who pays for lunch, we began the gamble believing the coin was fair. Thus, according to the principle of insufficient reason, $p = 1/2$. When we called "heads" we knew there was a 50 percent chance of a tail, and so paid for the lunch. However, after checking the coin casually, we found only one "head" in ten tosses. According to our formula, if the coin is fair, the probability of only one "head" in ten tosses is:

$$P_r(E_1) = {_{10}C_1}(\tfrac{1}{2})^1(\tfrac{1}{2})^9 = 10(0.5)^{10} = 10(0.0009765) = 0.009765$$

The chance of getting only one "head" in ten coin tosses is slightly less than 1 in 100. Whether we accuse our friend of cheating would depend on (1) how much we value the friendship, (2) the amount of the meal tab, and (3) how much previous evidence we have of our friend's honesty. In other words, how strongly did we believe our prior probability assessment? Nevertheless, in light of this new evidence, we are less likely to gamble with this friend in the future.

THE LAWS OF PROBABILITY

Sometimes a probability problem may be a bit more complicated than our simple example above. For instance, we may wish to know the probability of two events or even three events. Suppose you are playing poker and hold the 2, 3, 5, and 6 of hearts and the 9 of clubs. You would like to throw the 9 of clubs, but your mother taught you never to draw to an inside straight. But should you draw to an inside straight-flush? What is the probability of drawing both a 4 and a heart? What is the probability of drawing either a 4 or a heart? There are several simple rules for the calculations of separate probabilities.

Addition Rule:

Mutually Exclusive Events

If two events E and F are *mutually exclusive* (cannot occur together), then the probability of either E or F is the sum of their separate probabilities:

$$P_r(E \text{ or } F) = P_r(E) + P_r(F)$$

Suppose you are drawing to an outside straight; that is, you have four cards in sequence, so the straight can be completed at either end of the sequence. For instance, you could hold a 3, 4, 5, 6, and 9 without hope of a flush. If you throw the 9, what is the probability of drawing a 2 or a 7 to make a straight? The two events are mutually exclusive since a card cannot be both a 2 and a 7. You have seen 5 cards so there are 47 cards remaining in the deck and the hands of other players. If the deck was shuffled fairly, the probability of any card being in the deck is the same as the probability of it being in any other player's hand. Four of the unseen cards are 2's and four of them are 7's. The probability of drawing either a 2 or a 7, we find, is:

$$P_r(E \text{ or } F) = \frac{4}{47} + \frac{4}{47} = \frac{8}{47} = 0.1702$$

A similar rule applies to the occurrence of three or more mutually exclusive events. For the three independent events E, F, and G:

$$P_r(E \text{ or } F \text{ or } G) = P_r(E) + P_r(F) + P_r(G)$$

Multiplication Rule:

Independent Events

Let two events be designated by E and F where the occurrence of F does not depend on whether E has occurred or not. With E and F independent, the probability of *both* E and F occurring is the product of their probabilities:

$$P_r(E \text{ and } F) = P_r(E) \cdot P_r(F)$$

In our example of drawing to an inside straight-flush, the probability of getting a heart *is* influenced by whether we get a 4 and vice versa. Hence, this rule does not apply. A simpler example will have to suffice. Out of a deck of playing cards two cards are successively drawn at random, the first being replaced before the second is drawn. What is the probability that the first card is an ace (event E) and that the second is also an ace (event F)? Since the first card is to be replaced before the second is drawn, the chance of the second card being an ace does not depend on whether the first is an ace or not—the two events are independent. There are four aces in the deck of fifty-two cards, so we have:

$$P_r(E) = P_r(F) = \frac{4}{52} = \frac{1}{13}$$

By the multiplication rule of independent events, the probability of obtaining two aces in two draws is:

$$P_r(E \text{ and } F) = \frac{1}{13} \cdot \frac{1}{13} = \frac{1}{169}$$

There is one chance in one hundred sixty-nine that both events will occur.

This rule also applies to the occurrence of three or more independent events. For the three independent events E, F, and G:

$$P_r(E \text{ and } F \text{ and } G) = P_r(E) \cdot P_r(F) \cdot P_r(G)$$

Multiplication Rule:
Dependent Events

When the probability of one event does depend on the occurrence of the other, then the probability of the joint occurrence of those two events is the probability of one multiplied by the probability of the other, given that the first event has occurred:

$$P_r(E \text{ and } F) = P_r(E) \cdot P_r(F \mid E)$$

The symbol $P_r(F \mid E)$ designates the *conditional probability* of F and is interpreted as the probability of F, given the occurrence of E. In our example, you hold the 2, 3, 5, and 6 of hearts and the 9 of clubs. You toss away the 9 and draw one card. There are four 4's remaining in the deck (or other players' hands) and nine hearts. Your chances of picking a 4 (event E) are 4/47, but if you pick a heart your chance of picking a 4 improves to 1 in 9. Your chances of picking a heart (event F) are 9/47, but if you pick a 4, your chances of picking a heart become 1/4. The probability of picking both a 4 and a heart is:

$$P_r(E \text{ and } F) = \frac{4}{47} \cdot \frac{1}{4} = \frac{9}{47} \cdot \frac{1}{9} = \frac{1}{47}$$

For the joint occurrence of three or more dependent events, we merely expand the rule. The probability of the occurrence of E and F and G, all of which are dependent is given as:

$$P_r(E \text{ and } F \text{ and } G) = P_r(E) \cdot P_r(F \mid E) \cdot P_r(G \mid F \text{ and } E)$$

Addition Rule: Events
Not Mutually Exclusive

If E and F are not mutually exclusive, the occurrence of either E or F does not preclude occurrence of the other event, or both of them. The probability of either E or F (or both) is given by the formula:

$$P_r(E \text{ or } F) = P_r(E) + P_r(F) - P_r(E \text{ and } F)$$

In our continuing poker saga, we wish to discover the probability that the card drawn from a deck of 47 will be either a 4 or a heart. The probability of drawing a heart (event E) is 9/47, the probability of drawing a 4 is 4/47, and the probability of drawing the 4 of hearts is 1/47. It follows that the chance of getting a straight, a flush, or a straight-flush is:

$$P_r(E \text{ or } F) = \frac{9}{47} + \frac{4}{47} - \frac{1}{47} = \frac{12}{47} = 0.255$$

Even mothers might approve of these odds.

Bayes's Rule

Our discussion of the laws of probability has led us to a reconciliation between the *a priori* and *subjective* views of probability. Suppose we hypothesize that event x_1 causes event E. For instance, suppose an increase in the money supply causes inflation. If we observed a situation where E occurred and x_1 did not occur, this would constitute strong evidence *against* the hypothesis. But should we take such evidence seriously? The answer depends on how strongly we felt about the hypothesis to begin with. Each investigator begins a study with some *prior* belief or subjective probability about the truth of a hypothesis. The probability of observing a "cause" given an effect is given by the *inverse probability rule*, which is also known as *Bayes's theorem*, in honor of Thomas Bayes, an English minister and mathematician who first proved the rule in 1763.

We begin by noting the symmetry of the multiplication rule for two events. The probability that both x_1 and E occur is the probability of x_1 given E times the probability of E, and also the probability of E given x_1 times the probability of x_1:

$$P_r(E \text{ and } x_1) = P_r(x_1) \cdot P_r(E \mid x_1) = P_r(E) \cdot P_r(x_1 \mid E)$$

Dividing both sides of the expression by $P_r(E)$ we obtain *Bayes's rule*:

$$P_r(x_1 \mid E) = \frac{P_r(E \mid x_1) \cdot P_r(x_1)}{P_r(E)}$$

The probability of observing event x_1, the purported cause of observed event E, is the conditional probability of E given "cause" x_1 times the probability of x_1, divided by the probability of event E.

As such, there is nothing especially controversial, or even exciting about this truism. However, if we interpret this equation in terms of *subjective* probabilities, we arrive at a method of revising *estimated* probabilities in light of new evidence. We can interpret the left-side term, $P_r(x_1 \mid E)$ as the subjective probability of observing "cause" x_1 in the presence of "effect" E. This is equal to the *prior likelihood function*, $P_r(E \mid x_1)$, times the estimated probability of x_1 divided by the estimated probability of outcome E. The prior likelihood function measures the investigator's degree of belief in a hypothesis prior to test. How likely does the investigator believe that a change in the money supply x_1 causes a change in the price level E? For a monetarist, a change in the money supply is the *only* cause of inflation, so a monetarist would have a very strong prior. To a Keynesian, other factors besides changes in the money supply might cause inflation, and not every change in the money supply would cause inflation. Hence, the Keynesian would have weaker prior probability estimates and would be more influenced by current evidence.

Bayes's rule helps to reconcile two types of uncertainty the investigator confronts. First, there are various attitudes about the validity of a hypothesis, ranging from (subjective) certainty that the hypothesis is false ($P_r(E \mid x_1) = 0$), to an unshakable conviction that the hypothesis is true ($P_r(E \mid x_1) = 1$). Secondly, there is uncertainty about the reliabilty of the data used to test the hypothesis. In Part III we will concentrate on the statistical procedures used to estimate econometric models. These provide probabilistic statements about the observed relation between the "cause" and the "effect." But it is important to understand why statistical results, by themselves, are never decisive in disproving or proving an economic hypothesis. The state of the investigators' own beliefs are at least as important as the (so-called) objective evidence.

PROBABILITY DISTRIBUTIONS

We are now in a position to alter our terminology to conform to that used in our discussions of econometric models. We have spoken of the probability of an event, but we may regard the event as the value of a variable. For instance, let the event be the occurrence of five "heads" in ten tosses of a coin. We can interpret this "5" as the value of some variable. In this case, the variable may assume the values of all integers from 0 to 10, inclusive. But we know that the event is not certain; it has a definite probability. Similarly, the value of "5" of the variable has a measurable probability of occurring. There is another probability that a "1" will occur, another probability that an "8" will occur, and so on.

Consequently, we say that the variable in question is a random variable. It is defined as a variable that can assume a number of values according to some probabilty rule, which may or may not be known. A random variable is sometimes called a *chance variable* or a *stochastic variable*. The outcome of ten tosses of a coin is a random variable, because it can assume the values of 0, 1, 2, 3, 4, 5, 6, 7, 8, 9, or 10 with definite probabilities. Furthermore, this variable is a discrete random variable, since it can assume only the values of the integers 0 through 10.

Discrete Random Variables

Let us define a random variable u that can assume the values u_i. With each value u_i, we associate a probability p_i. In the example of tossing a fair coin ten times, the values of the discrete random variable u_i, defined as the number of "heads," is given by the binomial formula introduced on page 300.

$$P_r(u) = {_{10}C_u} p^u q^{10-u} = \frac{10!}{u!\,(10-u)!} \cdot (0.5)^{10}$$

Performing these calculations generates the results presented in Table 15.1. These results conform to the rules of probability. Each p_i lies between 0 and 1 and the sum of all p_i's is 1.

Table 15.1

u_i	p_i
0	0.0009766
1	0.0097656
2	0.0439453
3	0.1171875
4	0.2050781
5	0.2460938
6	0.2050781
7	0.1171875
8	0.0439453
9	0.0097656
10	0.0009766

$$\sum_{i=0}^{10} p_i = 1.0000000$$

This entire array of the values the random variable can assume together with the corresponding probabilities of each of these values is called the *probability distribution* of the variable. In contrast to a systematic variable, whose value is known with certainty, a random variable is determined by its underlying probability distribution.

Let us investigate a diagram of a probability distribution. Figure 15.1 presents a *histogram* showing each possible value of the random variable, u, plotted on the horizontal axis and the probabilty of each value of u plotted

Figure 15.1

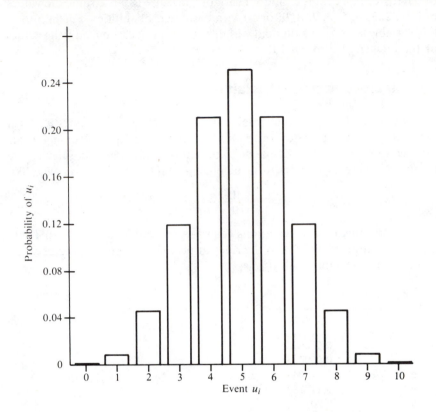

on the vertical axis. Because the values of u are discrete, the graph consists of vertical bars at each value of u. If we put all the bars "end-to-end," we would find that the total height of these bars is 1.

Figure 15.2 shows the *cumulative probability distribution* of u. The cumulative probability is the probability that u is less than or equal to some value. The probability that u is less than or equal to 0 is the same as the probability that u is equal to 0, since 0 is the lowest value that u can take. The probability that u is less than or equal to 1 is the equal to the sum of the probability that $u = 1$ and the probability that $u = 0$, that is:

$$P_r(u \le 1) = P_r(u = 0) + P_r(u = 1)$$
$$= 0.0009766 + 0.0097656 = 0.0107422$$

The cumulative probabilities for all values of u are given in Table 15.2. The cumulative probabilities are plotted in Figure 15.2. Note that since the probability distribution is a discrete one, the cumulative probability distribution is a series of eleven bars of progressively increasing height.

Table 15.2

u_i	p_i	$P_r(u \leq u_i)$
0	0.0009766	0.0009766
1	0.0097656	0.0107422
2	0.0439453	0.0546875
3	0.1171875	0.1718750
4	0.2050781	0.3769531
5	0.2460938	0.6230469
6	0.2050781	0.8281250
7	0.1171875	0.9453125
8	0.0439453	0.9892578
9	0.0097656	0.9990234
10	0.0009766	1.0000000

Figure 15.2

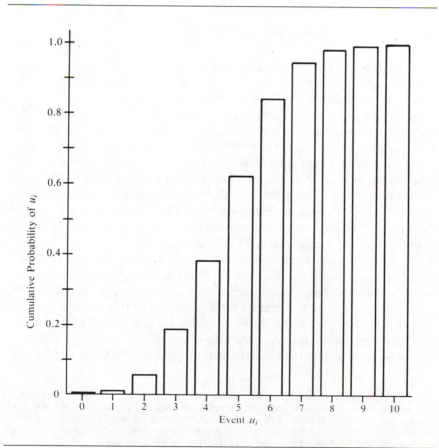

Continuous Random Variables

If a random variable is continuous, it can assume any value in an interval over which the variable is defined. For instance, a variable may take on any value greater than 0 and less than 10. Different *probability distributions* determine the likelihood of observing the value of a variable within some smaller range within the range of all possible values. The simplest continuous probability distribution is the *rectangular* distribution. Let x be a random variable that can take on any value within the range $a < x < b$. For a rectangular distribution, the probability of observing the value of x within some subinterval $a_1 < x < b_1$ (where $a_1 > a$ or $b_1 < b$) is equal to the ratio of the relative size of the two intervals:

$$P_r(a_1 < x < b_1) = \frac{b_1 - a_1}{b - a}$$

The chance that x takes on some precise value, is, according to this definition, 0. The probability that the value of x is exactly b_1 is given as:

$$P_r(b_1 < x < b_1) = \frac{b_1 - b_1}{b - a} = \frac{0}{b - a} = 0$$

Suppose the variable x is subject to a rectangular probability distribution over the range $0 \leq x \leq 10$. There is a 10 percent probability that x will have a value greater than 0 and less than 1, a 20 percent probability that x will have a value greater than 1 and less than 3, a 57 percent probability that x will have a value greater than 3.7 and less than 9.4, and so forth. However, the chance that x is exactly 2 or exactly 7.965 is 0.[2]

We saw in Figure 15.1 that the diagram for a discrete probability distribution is a histogram, a set of distinct bars whose height reflects the probability of observing a precise value of the random variable. Since the probability of observing a precise value of a continuous variable is 0, we cannot construct histograms for their distributions. The diagram of a continuous variable is, like the variable itself, continuous. In Figure 15.3, we see that the plot of a rectangular distribution is, indeed, a rectangle. The width of the rectangle is the range of the values of x, the height of the rectangle is the probability that x falls within a unit increment, e.g., between 1 and 2, or between 6.5 and 7.5, and so forth. The area of this rectangle is equal to its width (10) times its height (0.1), which is equal to 1. The probability that x falls in some subinterval is the area of the relevant rectangle. The probability that x is greater than 6 and less than 8 is equal to $0.1(8 - 6) = 0.2$.

---

[2]Only by introducing "rounding error" can we give finite probabilities to precise numbers. For instance, if we round each number observed to two decimal places, there are only 1,000 observations that could be made. Since this is a discrete probability distribution, the probability of recording a "2" is 1/1,000. However, this is precisely the same probability of observing a number between 1.995 and 2.015 drawn from a rectangular distribution.

Figure 15.3

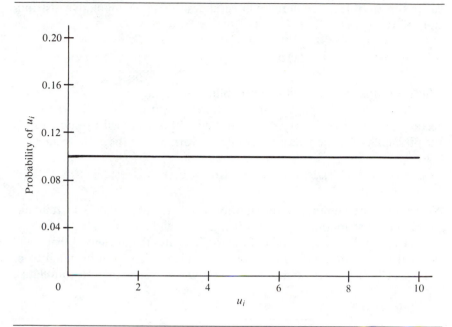

In Chapter 11 we learned how the definite integral of a function could be used to evaluate the area under a curve given by a continuous function. It follows that if we can describe the probability distribution of a continuous variable as a function, we can calculate the cumulative distribution of that function as a definite integral. In our example, the probability that x lies between a_1 and b_1, where $a_1 \geq 0$ and $b_1 \leq 10$ is:

$$P_r(a_1 < x < b_1) = \frac{b_1 - a_1}{10 - 0} = 0.1(b_1 - a_1)$$

Now suppose we divide the range of x into very small intervals. Then the area under the rectangular distribution between a_1 and b_1 is given by:

$$P_r(a < x < b) = \sum_{x=a}^{b}(0.1)\Delta x$$

By allowing the size of each interval to approach zero, we allow the number of intervals to approach infinity. Therefore, we can invoke the concept of the definite integral:

$$P_r(a < x < b) = \lim_{\Delta x \to 0}\sum_{x=a}^{b}(0.1)\Delta x = \int_{a}^{b}(0.1)\,dx$$
$$= 0.1(b) - 0.1(a) = 0.1(b - a)$$

If we set the lower end of the definite interval at the lower end of the range for variable x, the definite integral describes the cumulative distribution of x:

$$P_r(x < x_o) = \int_a^{x_o} p(x)\, dx = P(x_o)$$

where $P(x_o)$ is the cumulative probability function.

The cumulative probability function (shown in Figure 15.4) for the rectangular distribution of x between 0 and 10 is obtained by substituting the probability function $p(x) = 0.1$ into the formula for the definite integral:

$$P(x) = \int_0^x (0.1)\, dx = 0.1x - 0.1(0) = 0.1x$$

Notice that the cumulative distribution for a variable with a rectangular probability distribution is a straight line with a slope of 0.1.

The cumulative probability function indicates the likelihood that x will be smaller than or equal to the value x_o, which is less than or equal to b, the upper limit of the range. If we know the formula for the cumulative

Figure 15.4

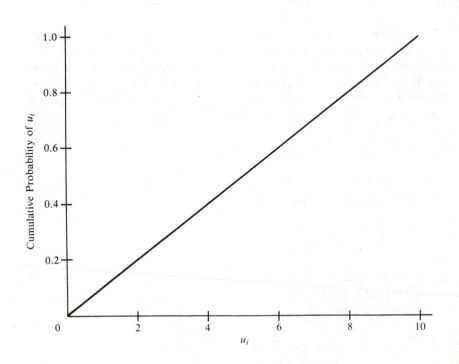

probability function, we can obtain the formula for the *probability density function* by taking the first derivative of the cumulative probability function. If we let $P(x)$ represent the cumulative probability function for the rectangular distribution between 0 and 10, then:

$$p(x) = \frac{dP(x)}{dx} = \frac{d(0.1x)}{dx} = 0.1$$

What is the probability that x will be smaller than six? We have:

$$\int_0^6 0.1\,dx = 0.1(6) - 0.1(0) = 0.6$$

The probability that x will be between two and four is given by:

$$\int_2^4 0.1\,dx = 0.1(4) - 0.1(2) = 0.2$$

CHARACTERISTICS OF THE PROBABILITY DISTRIBUTION

We have just seen that the probability functions can be distinguished by whether they are discrete or continuous. They can also be distinguished by the "average" value of the distribution and the degree of dispersion around that average. We now turn our attention to the discussion of the *mean* and the *standard deviation* of probability functions.

The Mathematical Expectation

We have seen that when a variable is random, the actual value observed in any "trial" is governed by the probability distribution for that variable. So even though many possible values might actually be observed, there is an average value that we *expect* to observe. The *mathematical expectation* of a variable is its arithmetic mean and is computed by multiplying all possible values of a random variable by their respective probabilities and summing these products.

Assume a discrete random variable u can assume the values of all integers from 0 through 10. Each value has a corresponding probability. The mathematical expectation of u, usually denoted by $E(u)$ or μ is computed as follows:

$$\mu = E(u) = 0 \cdot p_0 + 1 \cdot p_1 + 2 \cdot p_2 + \cdots + 10 \cdot p_{10}$$

In general, we let u assume the discrete values u_1, u_2, u_3, ..., u_n with the associated probabilities p_1, p_2, p_3, ..., p_n. The mathematical expectation of u is:

$$\mu = E(u) = \sum_{i=1}^{n} u_i p_i$$

Suppose the value of u corresponds to the number of "heads" resulting from ten random tosses of a fair coin. Applying the binomial formula, we generate the probability distribution for u reported in Table 15.3. The last column in Table 15.3 gives the *weighted* value of each outcome, whereby each possible value of u is multiplied by its respective probability. Summing these weighted values of u_i yields the mathematical expectation, $\mu = E(u_i) = 5$.

Table 15.3

u_i	p_i	$p_i \cdot u_i$
0	0.0009766	0
1	0.0097656	0.0097656
2	0.0439453	0.0878906
3	0.1171875	0.3515625
4	0.2050781	0.8203125
5	0.2460938	1.2304688
6	0.2050781	1.2304688
7	0.1171875	0.8203125
8	0.0439453	0.3515625
9	0.0097656	0.0878906
10	0.0009766	0.0097656
$\sum_{i=0}^{10}$	1.0000000	5.0000000

If u is continuous, varies between $u = a$ and $u = b$, and has the probability density function $p(u)$, then we merely replace the summation by integration:

$$\mu = E(u) = \int_{a}^{b} u p(u) \, du$$

In our example on page 308, the variable x is continuous, taking on values between 0 and 10 with equal probability. The probability density function is $p(x) = 0.1$. Applying the methods of integration, we obtain the mathematical expectation of x as:

$$\mu = E(x) = \int_{0}^{10} 0.1x \, dx = 0.05(10)^2 - 0.05(0)^2 = 5$$

There are some simple rules for the calculation of expectations that will prove useful for later applications.

1. The mathematical expectation of a constant is equal to that constant. Let $u = k$, a known constant. Then:

   $$E(u) = E(k) = k$$

2. The mathematical expectation of a random variable times a constant is equal to the constant times the mathematical expectation of the random variable.

   $$E(k \cdot u) = k \cdot E(u)$$

3. The mathematical expectation of a sum or a difference of random variables is the sum or difference of the mathematical expectations. Let u and v be random variables.

   $$E(u + v) = E(u) + E(v)$$
   $$E(u - v) = E(u) - E(v)$$

Variation Around the Mean

There is a paradox in the concept of the mathematical expectation that requires further elaboration. The mean is the expected value of a variable in the sense that the probability of observing values greater than the mean of the variable is identical to the probability of observing values less than the mean of the variable. If we perform a large number of trials, we would expect few, if any observations, to exactly equal the mean. For a finite distribution, the mean itself might not even be a possible value of the variable. For a continuous distribution, the probability of observing a precise value of the variable is literally zero; yet the mean is a precise value. Hence, we expect each observation to deviate or vary from the mean of a distribution. Some variations will be large, others small. So how are we to describe the expected deviation between an observation and the mean?

We might decide to calculate the average deviation between a set of observations and the expected values of the distribution. Such a measure is formally called *the first moment* about the mean. We calculate it as the expected difference between the mean and each observation.

The first moment about the mathematical expectation is zero. This means that for any distribution, the *average* difference between that value and the expected value of that variable is zero. In other words, when we add up the weighted differences between each value the variable can have and its mathematical expectation, the result is zero:

$$E(u - \mu)^1 = E(u) - E(\mu) = \mu - \mu = 0$$

The second moment about the mathematical expectation is called the *variance*. It is a measure of the dispersion of the probability distribution about the mean of the distribution. The variance is denoted by σ^2:

$$E(u - \mu)^2 = \sigma^2$$

A special symbol is given to the variance because it plays such an important role in statistical theory and applications. Because the square of any number is positive, the variance shows the relative deviation between a typical value of u and its mathematical expectation. When the weighted values of $(u - \mu)^2$ are added together, the result is a positive number. The smaller the computed value of the variance, the more closely the values of u cluster about the mean of u. Conversely, the larger the variance, the greater the (absolute) deviation between values of u and the average or mean value.

The square root of the variance is called the *standard deviation* and is represented by σ:

$$\sigma = \sqrt{E(u - \mu)^2}$$

The standard deviation measures the average (absolute) difference between a variable and its mean. Because it is measured in the same units as the mean (whereas the variance is measured in *squared* units), it is often the more convenient way to express the dispersion for a probability distribution. Consequently, it enters into many computations in statistical analysis.

We can illustrate the computation of the variance and the standard deviation for the two probability distributions that we used to calculate mathematical expectation. For the binomial distribution describing the number of "heads" in ten random tosses of a fair coin, we add a third column to measure the squared deviation between each value of u_i and the expected value, 5. (See Table 15.4.) In the fourth column we weight each squared term by p_i, the probability of u_i. Summing the entries in the fourth column yields the variance, which is reported in Table 15.4. The standard deviation is simply the square root of the variance:

$$\sigma = \sqrt{2.50} = 1.5811388$$

For the continuous variable v which takes on values between 0 and 10 with equal probability:

$$\sigma^2 = \int_0^{10} 0.1(v - \mu)^2 \, dv = (0.03\tfrac{1}{3})[(5)^3 - (-5)^3]$$

$$= \frac{25.0}{3} = 8.3333$$

Again, the standard deviation is obtained by taking the square root of the variance:

$$\sigma = \sqrt{8.3333} = 2.8867513$$

Table 15.4

u_i	p_i	$(u_i - \mu)^2$	$p_i \cdot (u_i - \mu)^2$
0	0.0009766	25	0.0244141
1	0.0097656	16	0.1562500
2	0.0439453	9	0.3955078
3	0.1171875	4	0.4687500
4	0.2050781	1	0.2050781
5	0.2460938	0	0.0000000
6	0.2050781	1	0.2050781
7	0.1171875	4	0.4687500
8	0.0439453	9	0.3955078
9	0.0097656	16	0.1562500
10	0.0009766	25	0.0244141

$$\sigma^2 = \sum_{i=0}^{10} E(u - \mu)^2 p_i = 2.50$$

Summary

We have defined the concept of probability and illustrated the methods of calculation. We then showed that the entire array of values of a random variable, together with the probability of each value, comprises the probability distribution of that variable. Furthermore, any given probability distribution has certain characteristics that may be used to describe the general form of the distribution. The two most important of these are (1) the mathematical expectation of the probability distribution or mean of the random variable, and (2) the variance or manner in which the various values of the variable are distributed around the mathematical expectation.

PARTICULAR DISTRIBUTIONS

In this section we shall discuss two types of probability distributions that have special importance for statistical analysis. The first, the binomial distribution, is a discrete distribution derived by fundamental probability processes. The other, the normal or Gaussian distribution, is a continuous distribution that is a limiting case of the binomial.

The Binomial Distribution

In the second section of this chapter, we discussed the calculation of the probability of obtaining x successes (occurrences of an event) in n

independent trials. According to the theory of combinations, this probability involving the binomial coefficient is:

$$P_r(E_x) = {}_nC_x \cdot p^x \cdot q^{n-x}$$

where p is the probability of a success in any one trial and $q = 1 - p$ is the probabilty of a failure. The factor ${}_nC_x$ is called the binomial coefficient because it may be obtained by expanding a binomial expression raised to the nth power. Like any other probability distribution, a binomial probability distribution can be constructed if the event in question is regarded as a value of a random variable.

Let us consider an example of tossing a die. Assume we make five trials, so $n = 5$. The probability of a particular number between one and six on any trial is $p = 1/6$. That is, the probability of a "one" is 1/6, the probability of a "two" is 1/6, etc., since the die has six sides. The probability of the nonoccurrence of each event is therefore $q = 1 - 1/6 = 5/6$. Let the event in question be the occurrence of a "four." We construct the entire probability distribution for the number of "fours" occurring in five trials: the probability of no "fours" in five trials, the probability of one "four" in five trials, and so on. In the calculation of each of these probabilities, the formula for $P_r(E_x)$ is used:

$$P_r(E_0) = {}_5C_0 \left(\frac{1}{6}\right)^0 \left(\frac{5}{6}\right)^5 = \frac{5!}{0!5!} \cdot 1 \cdot \frac{3{,}125}{7{,}776} = 0.4019$$

$$P_r(E_1) = {}_5C_1 \left(\frac{1}{6}\right)^1 \left(\frac{5}{6}\right)^4 = \frac{5!}{1!4!} \cdot \frac{1}{6} \cdot \frac{625}{1{,}296} = 0.4019$$

$$P_r(E_2) = {}_5C_2 \left(\frac{1}{6}\right)^2 \left(\frac{5}{6}\right)^3 = \frac{5!}{2!3!} \cdot \frac{1}{36} \cdot \frac{125}{216} = 0.1608$$

$$P_r(E_3) = {}_5C_3 \left(\frac{1}{6}\right)^3 \left(\frac{5}{6}\right)^2 = \frac{5!}{3!2!} \cdot \frac{1}{216} \cdot \frac{25}{36} = 0.0322$$

$$P_r(E_4) = {}_5C_4 \left(\frac{1}{6}\right)^4 \left(\frac{5}{6}\right)^1 = \frac{5!}{4!1!} \cdot \frac{1}{1{,}296} \cdot \frac{5}{6} = 0.0032$$

$$P_r(E_5) = {}_5C_5 \left(\frac{1}{6}\right)^5 \left(\frac{5}{6}\right)^0 = \frac{5!}{5!0!} \cdot \frac{1}{7{,}776} \cdot 1 = 0.0001$$

Note that, unlike our previous example involving the number of "heads" in ten tosses of a fair coin, the number of "fours" (or any other value of the die) in five tosses is not symmetrical. This is because the probability of a success is less than one-half, making low outcomes (e.g., $x = 0$ or 1) much more likely than high-valued outcomes (e.g., $x = 2, 3, 4,$ or 5). Nevertheless, the sum of these probabilities is equal to one. (Any small difference is due to rounding.) Furthermore, we could obtain the cumulative probability distribution by successively adding the probabilities.

There are some interesting and useful properties of the binomial distribution. The mathematical expectation is equal to $n \cdot p$, and the variance is $n \cdot p \cdot q = n \cdot p \cdot (1 - p)$:

$$\mu = E(x) = np$$
$$\sigma^2 = E(x - \mu)^2 = npq = np(1 - p)$$
$$\sigma = \sqrt{npq} = \sqrt{np(1 - p)}$$

Thus, considering the occurrences of a "four" as a random variable x, we have the expected outcomes for five trials to be:

$$\mu = 5 \cdot \frac{1}{6} = \frac{5}{6}$$

$$\sigma^2 = 5 \cdot \frac{1}{6} \cdot \frac{5}{6} = \frac{25}{36}$$

$$\sigma = \sqrt{\frac{25}{36}} = \frac{5}{6}$$

That is, in five tosses of the dice, we "expect" to see slightly less than one "four." The average difference between the observed number of "fours" and the expected number will be 5/6, the standard deviation.

It is a worthwhile exercise to obtain these same results by computing the mathematical expectation and variance by the formulas given in the preceding section. But it is also quite convenient to have the above formulas to shorten the calculation process.

The Normal Distribution

The binomial distribution is developed from a set of first principles, using probability theory and some specific experimental conditions. This basic distribution serves as a transition to another well-known and widely used, although somewhat more complex, distribution. This is the *normal* distribution. Although the normal distribution also can be derived from basic probability principles, it is a limiting form of the binomial that is approached as n becomes very large with both p and $q = 1 - p$ remaining finite. Whereas the binomial is a discrete distribution, the normal is a continuous distribution. From experience with the previous example, it is easy to see that the computation of the coefficient $_nC_x$ becomes extremely laborious and time-consuming if both x and n are very large. Consequently, it is convenient to have a continuous distribution at hand that closely approximates the binomial when the number of experiments is large.

The normal distribution is more than an approximation to the binomial, however. It also describes the distribution of the mean of a sample drawn from a rectangular distribution. As an example, we draw a series of ten numbers from a rectangular distribution with range $0 < u < 10$. We have already established the expected value and the variance of the distribution as:

$$\sigma = E(u) = \int_0^{10} 0.1u\,du = 0.05(10)^2 - 0.05(0)^2 = 0.05(100) = 5$$

$$\sigma^2 = E(u - \mu)^2 = \int_0^{10} 0.1(u - 5)^2\,du$$
$$= 0.03\tfrac{1}{3}(10 - 5)^3 - 0.03\tfrac{1}{3}(0 - 5)^3 = 8.33$$

However, as we will see in the next chapter, the process of sampling from a population with a known distribution does not produce the "expected" result on each trial. To demonstrate, the following set of experiments was performed. A computer was programmed to produce 10 numbers from the rectangular distribution described above. The mean, $\bar{u}$, and the sample variance, s^2 (described in the next chapter), for ten such experiments are reported in Table 15.5.

Table 15.5

Experiment	$\bar{u}$	s^2
1	6.30	5.15
2	6.19	8.76
3	3.50	4.58
4	4.30	6.05
5	4.34	10.43
6	4.34	7.18
7	6.69	10.05
8	3.69	5.76
9	5.34	7.73
10	4.34	7.18
average	4.903	7.287
variance	1.30	1.99

Remember that Table 15.5 was the result of a random process. The chance of getting exactly the same results again is, for all practical purposes, zero. Yet the results obtained were influenced by the characteristics of the probability density function programmed into the computer. The distribution of the means for the ten samples, however, was influenced by the probability density function for the sample means, which is different from the probability density function governing the values of individual experiments. For instance, the average value of $\bar{u}$ for all experiments is 4.903. This is closer to the expected value of u than is any particular sample mean. Also, the variance in the sample means equals 1.30. This is considerably smaller than the average variance of the individual samples, which is 7.287. Drawing observations from sample means causes those observations to cluster closer to the *population mean* than drawing observations from a rectangular distribution. The distribution of *means* from samples drawn from a rectangular distribution is, in fact, *normally* distributed, with an expected value equal to the mean of the rectangular distribution and a variance equal to the variance of the variable *divided by the sample size.*

Many empirical distributions of phenomena in the natural and social sciences follow a normal distribution. This is especially true of the distribution of errors of observations. In fact the mathematician Gauss developed the normal (or *Gaussian*) distribution to explain the distribution of errors made in astronomical observations. The normal distribution provides a standard pattern with which other distributions can be compared. In some important phases of statistical analysis, the distribution of the observations is assumed to approximate the normal distribution. If the data in the sample actually depart seriously from this assumed pattern, unsatisfactory and even nonsensical statistical inferences may be drawn. It should be obvious, therefore, that this distribution plays an important role in statistical estimation and the test of hypotheses embedded in econometric models.

Since the normal distribution is continuous, it can be expressed by an equation, and the curve corresponding to this equation is smooth. For a random variable u, normally distributed with mean μ and standard deviation σ, the equation for the cumulative probability distribution is:

$$P(u) = \frac{1}{\sigma\sqrt{2\pi}} \int_{-\infty}^{u} e^{-\frac{1}{2}\left(\frac{u-\mu}{\sigma}\right)^2} du$$

where π, pi, is the ratio of the circumference of a circle to its diameter (approximately 3.1416) and e is the exponential base (approximately 2.71828). The probability density function, obtained by differentiating the cumulative function with respect to u, is given by:

$$p(u) = \frac{1}{\sigma\sqrt{2\pi}} e^{-\frac{1}{2}\left(\frac{u-\mu}{\sigma}\right)^2}$$

These formulas no doubt present an intimidating appearance; who wants to calculate these equations every time a statistical analysis is called for? However, closer inspection may ease the mind of the troubled reader. Note that the variable u occurs only once in each expression. All the other terms are constants or parameters. The two parameters of the normal distribution are μ, the mathematical expectation for the distribution, and σ, the standard deviation for that distribution. It is very convenient for applications of the normal distribution to standardize it, that is, to reconstruct the variable to have a mean of zero and a standard deviation of one. To do this we define another random variable, z, in the following way:

$$z = \frac{u-\mu}{\sigma}$$

Then we can write the probability density function more simply as:

$$p(z) = \frac{1}{\sqrt{2\pi}} e^{-\frac{z^2}{2}}$$

The calculation of the mean and standard deviation of z is straightforward:

$$E(z) = E\left(\frac{u - \mu}{\sigma}\right) = E\left(\frac{0}{\sigma}\right) = 0$$

$$E(z - E(z))^2 = E\left(\frac{u - \mu}{\sigma} - 0\right)^2 = E\left(\frac{(u - \mu)^2}{\sigma^2}\right) = E\left(\frac{\sigma^2}{\sigma^2}\right) = 1$$

where $\mu = E(u)$ and $\sigma^2 = E(u - E(u))^2$.

Figures 15.5 and 15.6 depict the normal probability density function and the normal cumulative probability function, respectively. They are drawn with the variable z on the horizontal axis, so that the mean of the distribution is zero. The numerical value of the ordinate of the graph in Figure 15.6 at any one value of z, say z_o, is equal to the numerical value of the area under the curve in Figure 15.5 to the left of z_o (the shaded area in Figure 15.5).

Figure 15.5
Standard Normal Curve

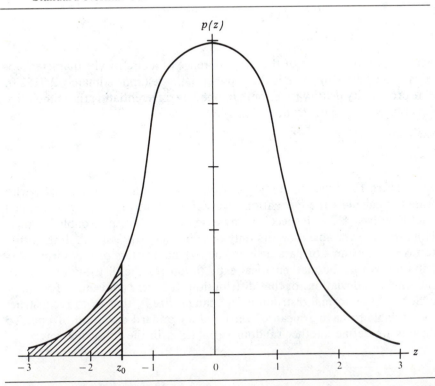

We can see in Figure 15.5 that the normal distribution is symmetrical about its mean. The value of z ranges from minus infinity to plus infinity. But for all practical purposes, nearly all the likely values of z are contained within three units of zero. Published tables (such as Table D in this text) exist that give the area under the probability density curve from zero to any value of z. From these one can find the probability of values within any interval of z, between z_1 and z_2, for example. We will have opportunities in later chapters to make practical use of "z-tables."

From the information in Table D we can determine another characteristic of the normal distribution that proves very useful in the interpretation of statistical measurement. If u is a random variable, normally distributed with mean μ and standard deviation σ, then:

1. 68.28 percent of the values of u deviate less than *one* standard deviation, σ, from the mean μ.
2. 95.44 percent of the values of u deviate less than *two* standard deviations, 2σ, from the mean μ.
3. 99.72 percent of the values of u deviate less than *three* standard deviations, 3σ, from the mean μ.

Figure 15.6
Cumulative Standard Normal Curve

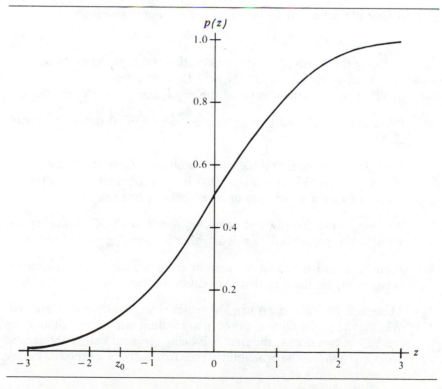

In terms of the variable z, which has $\mu = 0$ and $\sigma = 1$, this means that 68.28 percent of the values of z fall within $z = -1$ and $z = +1$; 95.44 percent fall within $z = -2$ and $z = +2$; 99.72 percent fall within $z = -3$ and $z = +3$. We shall see that these characteristics of the normal distribution are valuable in judging the reliability of empirical measurements.

PROBLEMS

Group I

1. An unbiased coin is tossed 10 times with the result of 3 "heads" and 7 "tails." The same coin is then tossed 30 times, yielding 17 "heads" and 13 "tails." Finally, the coin is tossed 100 times, yielding 48 "heads" and 52 "tails." What is the probability of "heads" and "tails" in each experiment using the relative frequency definition of probability? What is the limit of the relative frequency of "heads"? Of "tails"?

2. What is the probability of obtaining 3 "heads" in 10 tosses of an unbiased coin?

3. A true die is thrown 10 times with the following outcomes:

    3, 1, 6, 4, 6, 5, 4, 3, 2, 3

    a. Using the relative frequency definition, what is the probability of a 3 occurring among all throws? Of a 6? Of a 2?
    b. What is the limit of each of the preceding relative frequencies?

4. What is the probability of getting 3 "sixes" in 10 throws of a true die?

5. Suppose a box contains 100 colored chips, of which 20 are green, 50 are red, and 30 are white. What is the probability of drawing at random either a green chip or a red chip in one draw?

6. Assume a card is drawn at random from a deck of playing cards. What is the probability that it is either a "king" or a "queen"?

7. Assume a card is drawn at random from a deck of playing cards. What is the probability that it is either an "ace" or a "spade"?

8. There are 10 balls in an urn, of which 7 are white and 3 are red. What is the probability of drawing at random one white ball and one red ball in two draws, the first ball being replaced before the second is drawn? What is the probability if the first ball is *not* replaced before the second is drawn?

9. Assume a discrete random variable v that can assume the following values with the associated probabilities:

v_i	p_i
1	0.05
2	0.15
3	0.35
4	0.25
5	0.10
6	0.10
	1.00

a. Construct the histogram for this probability function.
b. Construct the graph of the cumulative probability distribution.

10. The following probability distribution of the discrete random variable u is given:

u_i	p_i
0	0.03
1	0.07
2	0.10
3	0.20
4	0.17
5	0.13
6	0.13
7	0.10
8	0.07
	1.00

a. Find the mathematical expectation and variance of the probability distribution.
b. Graph the distribution and indicate the mathematical expectation of u on the diagram.

11. If x, y, z, ... are a series of exclusive events that exhaust all possibilities, it follows that $P_r(x) + P_r(y) + P_r(z) + ... = 1$. Explain.

Group II

12. If x and y are two events that are not mutually exclusive, then $P_r(x \text{ or } y) = P_r(x) + P_r(y) - P_r(x \text{ and } y)$. Explain in common sense terms.

13. If x and y are dependent events, then $P_r(x \text{ and } y) = P_r(x) \cdot P_r(y \mid x)$. Explain in common sense terms.

14. Construct the probability distribution of the number of "heads" occurring in 5 tosses of an unbiased coin. From the probability distribution find the mathematical expectation and the variance.

15. Assume a continuous random variable u whose probability density function is given as:

$$p(u) = \frac{1}{5u}, \ u \geq 1$$

a. Graph the probability density function from $u = 1$ to $u = 10$.
b. Find $p(3)$, $p(5)$, $p(8)$, $p(10)$, $p(12)$.
c. Find the cumulative probability function, $P(u)$, from $u = 1$ to $u = u_0$.
d. Graph the cumulative function from $u = 1$ to $u = 10$, that is, let u_0 vary from 1 to 10.
e. Find $P(3)$, $P(5)$, $P(8)$, $P(10)$.

16. The following probability distribution of the discrete random variable v is given:

v_j	p_j
-4	0.04
-3	0.08
-2	0.12
-1	0.16
0	0.20
1	0.16
2	0.12
3	0.08
4	0.04

a. Find the mathematical expectation and variance of the probability distribution.
b. Explain the meaning of the expectation and variance in common sense terms.

16

Sampling
Theory and
Statistical
Inference

The theory of probability is the foundation for the statistical theory of sampling. In turn, the theory of sampling forms the basis for statistical estimation of econometric models. Having surveyed probability theory, we turn next to sampling theory and the general methods of statistical inference. This is the final preparatory step before discussing the actual methods of statistical measurement used in econometrics in Part III.

The central problem of analytical statistics is that of inductive inference. Theoretical propositions are generalizations; they refer to all conceivable observations on the subject matter to which the theory applies. For example, the theoretical economic proposition that unionization of an otherwise competitive labor market will increase wage rates at the expense of employment is meant to apply to all instances in which competitive conditions hold. To test this prediction we cannot, in general, observe all conceivable instances. Empirical tests are limited to data on events that actually occur. It is impossible to record data on circumstances that did not actually happen. The problem is to infer from the characteristics of the limited number of empirical observations, called a *sample*, the characteristics of all conceivable observations, called the *population*.

THE STATISTICAL POPULATION

As used in statistics, the term population means the total of all conceivable observations of some specified kind. The consumption expenditure of all human beings forms a statistical population, the consumption of all Americans forms another, the consumption of all New York households a third, and so forth. Notice that it is the expenditure on consumer goods, not the individuals or households, which comprises the observations that go to make up the population. This is made clear by consideration of another population, namely total consumer expenditure for the United States in 1985. If measurements were recorded on different days, or if the data were recorded by different people, it is unlikely that any two of the measurements would be exactly equal. The set of measurements (not aggregate consumption) forms a statistical population. Furthermore, the observations that form the population need not be measurements as in the preceding examples. They may be designations of the presence or absence of some specified characteristics. Thus, observations of different individuals at a particular time might involve categorizing individuals as "employed" vs. "unemployed," "retired" vs. "participating in the labor force," or "college graduate" vs. "high school dropout."

Populations may be *finite* or *infinite*, depending on whether there is a limit to the number of possible observations. In our previous example, the employment status of members of households is a finite population, because there are a limited number of possible outcomes for each person (e.g., "employed," "unemployed," and "not in the labor force") and there are a finite number of persons. The example of values of aggregate consumption, on the other hand, is one of an infinite population, since the number of possible different measurements is infinite.

As we have seen, sometimes populations are susceptible to only qualitative specification. A population consisting of employment status is such a population. Each observation would consist of information about whether the particular characteristic were present, e.g., Y if employed, N if unemployed. Or a "dummy variable," which takes on the value of 1 if the characteristic is present and 0 if it is not present, might be used to record individual observations. In such cases the statistics that describe these populations may be in terms of the proportion of the population that possesses that characteristic. For instance, the statistic may be that 6.8 percent of the participants in the labor force are unemployed. When the population consists of a characteristic that is amenable to numerical expression, however, the quantitative values of the measurements are regarded as values of a variable. The variable may be continuous or discrete, and it is very convenient to think of populations in this way.

The term "parameter" is familiar to us from our discussions in Parts I and II. It is a term used to indicate the constants in an equation. The purpose of such constants is to designate one particular quantitative relationship out of many similar equations. A linear equation in one variable has the general form:

$$y = a + bx$$

where x and y are variables and a and b are constants. All linear equations in two variables are qualitatively similar in that they have (or can be translated into) this form, but they have different numerical values for a and b. The particular values of the parameters tell us which one linear equation is relevant out of the family of all possible linear equations. Different values of a and b yield different straight lines when graphed, but the graphs of all linear equations show straight lines.

In statistics, the term parameter has a similar interpretation. The parameters of a population are those measures that differentiate a population quantitatively from all other populations of the same form. For instance, the population given by all possible tosses of a coin has several parameters, one being the probability of heads occurring. This characteristic (a constant) is given for this population but will differ from one population to another. All throws of an unfair or *biased* coin would have a different probability of heads—a different parameter. All possible observations on the price of wheat in the United States forms a population. A parameter of this population is the arithmetic mean or average value of wheat prices. The mean price of corn is a parameter of the population that consists of all observations on corn prices. In both cases, the average price is a constant characteristic of the population.

THE STATISTICAL SAMPLE

Ordinarily, the data we have to work with consist of a limited number of observations rather than all possible observations. Such a partial collection is called a *sample*. The statistical problem then becomes one of providing information about the unknown population characteristics from knowledge of the characteristics of the sample. When doing this, special importance is attached to *random samples*, so that we make inferences about a population from samples drawn at random from the population. When a given sample is random, it means that each member of the population has the same probability of being included in the sample. We shall treat only random samples, but it should be kept in mind that under some conditions other methods of sampling may be preferable. Such methods may be more effective in yielding information about a population.

Just as a population has certain characteristics that describe it, so a sample has such characteristics called *statistics*. A sample statistic has a meaning similar to the corresponding population parameter. Suppose we have observations on the consumption and income of 1,000 American families.

Assume we are interested in the ratio of consumption to income, so we record this ratio for each family. The arithmetic mean or average value of this ratio for all 1,000 observations is a sample statistic. It corresponds in meaning to the mean ratio in the population that consists of *all possible* observations on the ratio of consumption to income.

ELEMENTS OF SAMPLING THEORY

In the preceding chapter some of the elementary laws of probability were described. The laws of probability form the foundation for a theory of random sampling. The population mean, the degree of variation in the observations of the population, the range of observations, the largest value, the smallest value, etc., are parameters of the population. The sample mean, variance, standard deviation, etc., are statistics of the sample. In practical situations, we begin with a known sample and calculate the sample statistics. We then attempt to *infer* the population parameters from the calculated sample statistics. Sampling theory bases those inferences on the laws of probability. In sampling theory we deduce the likelihood of obtaining alternative statistics from samples drawn at random from a population of known parameters. Once these theoretical laws are established, the reliability of moving in the opposite direction (i.e., inferring population parameters from calculated sample statistics) is greatly enhanced.

The methods of statistical inference involve four elements: (1) the population as it actually is, (2) the relationship between the characteristics of this population and the characteristics of many samples drawn from the population, (3) the relationship between the characteristics of the many samples and the characteristics of one sample, and (4) the one sample that we do observe in practice. Now the problem is to infer from the statistics of one sample, element (4), the characteristics of the true but unknown population, element (1). To do this we use the laws provided by elements (2) and (3). We can never know the population parameter(s) precisely, but the object of the theory of sampling is to provide a stepping-stone from the one sample to the population.

Relation of Population
Parameters to Many Samples

Let us examine the several rules derived by statisticians that relate known parameters to the characteristics of a set of many samples drawn at random from the population. We shall show that experimental sampling yields results that can also be achieved by a purely mathematical approach founded on the theory of probability. The normal distribution plays an important role in this mathematical derivation, but we shall not go through the mathematical steps involved in the derivation itself. The interested reader can find proofs for the conclusions in most textbooks on mathematical statistics.

Finite Populations

Suppose we have a known finite population consisting of N observations on some variable x. The number of samples, each consisting of n observations, it is possible to draw from this population is $_NC_n$. We already know this from the theory of probability. For example, this population might be composed of the integers 1, 2, 3, 4, and 5, so $N = 5$. The mean of this population is $\mu = E(x) = (1 + 2 + 3 + 4 + 5)/5 = 15/5 = 3$. The standard deviation is:

$$\sigma = E(x - \mu)^2$$

$$= \sqrt{\frac{(1 - 3)^2 + (2 - 3)^2 + (3 - 3)^2 + (4 - 3)^2 + (5 - 3)^2}{5}}$$

$$= \sqrt{\frac{4 + 1 + 0 + 1 + 4}{5}} = \sqrt{2} \approx 1.4142$$

Suppose we decide to take samples of two numbers *without replacement*, meaning that any of the five members of the finite population can appear at most one time in any sample. The number of possible samples of 2 numbers, $n = 2$, is:

$$_5C_2 = \frac{5!}{2!3!} = \frac{120}{(2)(6)} = 10$$

Because the number of possible samples is small, we can list them for analytical purposes. This is done in Table 16.1.

Table 16.1

Sample #	Elements		Sample Mean	Standard Deviation
1	1	2	1.5	0.5
2	1	3	2.0	1.0
3	1	4	2.5	1.5
4	1	5	3.0	2.0
5	2	3	2.5	0.5
6	2	4	3.0	1.0
7	2	5	3.5	1.5
8	3	4	3.5	0.5
9	3	5	4.0	1.0
10	4	5	4.5	0.5
mean			3.0	1.0

Note that each sample is composed of two elements, listed with the smaller number first, although order is not important in this context. The mean value of x for the first sample, designated by $\overline{x}_1$, is calculated by adding up the values of the observations in the sample and dividing by the size of the sample:

$$\overline{x}_1 = \frac{1 + 2}{2} = \frac{3}{2} = 1.5$$

In general, for the ith sample consisting of n observations of a variable x, the mean has the formula:

$$\overline{x}_i = \frac{x_{1i} + x_{2i} + x_{3i} + \ldots + x_{ni}}{n} = \frac{1}{n} \sum_{j=1}^{n} x_{ji}$$

where x_{ji} is the value of the jth observation in the ith sample. In general, $\overline{x}_i$ designates the mean of the ith sample. The mean of each *possible* sample is recorded in the third column of Table 16.1. At the bottom of that column we have recorded the mean of all possible sample means, often designated as $\mu_{\overline{x}}$. Note that the expected value of all the sample means is the mean of the population:

$$E(\overline{x}) = \mu_{\overline{x}} = \mu = 3$$

In general, for a finite population of N elements or observations, we consider all possible samples of n observations each drawn from this population. There are $_N C_n$ such samples. The probability function that describes the likelihood of observing a particular sample mean is called the *sampling distribution of means*. The expected value of $\overline{x}_i$ is $\mu_{\overline{x}}$. The mean of the expected values of all possible samples of n observations each is equal to the population mean. This is true for any size n, as long as $0 < n < N$. Hence, it is also true for samples of size 1. Any number drawn randomly from a finite population of N elements will have as its expected value the mean of the population. Both the sample mean and the value of a single element drawn at random are *unbiased* estimates of the population mean. A sample statistic is said to be an *unbiased* estimate of a population parameter when the expected value of that sample statistic is the population parameter.

But if we can get an unbiased estimate of a population mean by sampling only one element, why bother with larger samples, let alone multiple samples? It turns out that the larger the sample size, the smaller will be the *standard deviation* of the estimates of the parameter. The *population standard deviation* is the average absolute difference between an element of the population and the population mean. It follows that the average difference between the population mean and any number randomly drawn from that population is the standard deviation of the population. However, as the number of elements in the sample (called the *sample size*) grows, the standard deviation for the sampling distribution of the sample means falls.

The standard deviation of the sample means is a measure of how the various sample means are distributed around the mean of the sample means (that is, the mean of the population). A general rule has been developed for this concept, namely: The standard deviation of means of all possible samples of n observations each is equal to the population standard deviation times the factor:

$$\frac{1}{\sqrt{n}}\sqrt{\frac{N-n}{N-1}}$$

Where N is the total number of observations in the population. We express this symbolically as follows:

$$\sigma_{\bar{x}} = \frac{\sigma}{\sqrt{n}}\sqrt{\frac{N-n}{N-1}}$$

where σ represents the population standard deviation. Note that if $n = 1$, the expression simplifies to $\sigma_{\bar{x}} = \sigma$. If N is very large relative to n, then $(N-n)/(N-1)$ is almost equal to one and so $\sigma_{\bar{x}}$ is nearly equal to $\sigma/\sqrt{n}$.

We have carried through the explanation for the mean and the standard deviation of the distribution of *sample means*. A similar type of argument can be made for statistics other than the sample means. For example, the argument can be applied to the distribution of sample sums: if x_j is the value of the jth observation in a sample, the sample of n observations has the sample sum $\sum\limits_{j=1}^{n} x_j$. The only difference here is that one deals with a sample distribution of sums rather than means. There are sample statistics that have very complicated sampling laws, and in such cases one often has to resort to experimental sampling based on random numbers generated by a computer or published in a table to discover characteristics of the sampling fluctuations.

Before discussing infinite populations it is worth noting the relation of the distribution of sample means to the normal distribution. Under a very broad set of conditions, when N and n are both large, with N much larger than n, the normal distribution gives a good approximation of the distribution of sample means. Even in some special cases where N and n are rather small, the normal distribution gives a fairly good estimate of the distribution of sample means.

Infinite Populations

Most of the data with which economists work are considered as random samples from a hypothetically infinite population. For instance, a series of automobile prices quoted or recorded on the market may be considered as a random sample of all possible automobile prices. These possible prices form a hypothetically infinite population of prices. Therefore, we shall consider the general theory of sampling from an infinite population. Here also statisticians have shown that by using mathematical probability theory, a relationship can be established between the population and samples drawn at random from the population. We shall continue to use the sample mean as our statistic.

Assume a population has a known probability distribution with mean μ and standard deviation σ. The population may represent either a discrete or continuous random variable. The results of successive observations from an infinite population are independent of one another, since the probability that a random variable x has a particular value on one observation is not affected by its value on any other observation. We state the following general maxim for the mean of sample means: The mean of the distribution of means of an infinitely large number of samples drawn from an infinite population is equal to the mean of the population. In symbolic notation, we write:

$$E(\overline{x}) = \mu_{\overline{x}} = \mu$$

This expresses the same result in the notation of the mathematical expectation of the probability distribution of sample means.

Furthermore, the standard deviation of the distribution of means of infinitely many samples, consisting of n observations each, from an infinite population is equal to the standard deviation divided by $\sqrt{n}$. Briefly, we write:

$$\sigma_{\overline{x}} = \frac{\sigma}{\sqrt{n}}$$

As in the case of theoretical sampling from a finite population, so the distribution of means from an infinite population can be approximated by the normal distribution under certain conditions. As a matter of fact, the following general rule can be demonstrated: For samples of large size the distribution of means of samples from an infinite population is approximately normal. Moreover, if n is the number of observations in each sample and n is large, then:

$$E(\overline{x}) = \mu \quad \text{and} \quad \sigma_{\overline{x}} = \frac{\sigma}{\sqrt{n}}$$

The closeness of the approximation to the normal distribution improves as the size of the sample increases. If the sample size were infinite, the fit between a normal distribution and the distribution of sample means would be perfect. Nevertheless, in some situations the approximation is sufficiently close for practical purposes for n as small as ten. If the population is exactly normally distributed with mean μ and standard deviation σ, then the sample means are exactly normally distributed with mean equal to μ and standard deviation equal to $\sigma/\sqrt{n}$.

This overview of sampling theory provides an insight into the general nature of the relations between a population and many samples drawn from the population. The results of a number of independent samples drawn at random from a known population can be determined from probability theory. As the size of each sample is allowed to become larger, the variation from sample to sample decreases and the samples possess more nearly the characteristics of the population from which they are taken.

Relation of One Sample
and Many Samples

With the connection between population parameters and the statistics of a set of many samples given to us, what can we say about the connection between the population parameters and the statistics of one sample? In practice research workers most often observe but one sample. This is practically always so in economics. The usual procedure is to calculate statistics (mean, variance, range, sum, etc.) from the sample frequency distribution, and then try to figure out from the values of these statistics what the values of the population parameters (mean, variance, range, sum, etc.) are likely to be. We have to consider the known sample, the theoretical distribution of the population values that we construct by inference from the sample, and the population as it actually is. Since we never know the true population precisely, we use sample statistics to generate a satisfactory description of the population parameters of interest. The distribution of many sample statistics (not actually observed) may be used in interpreting the results of one sample. Since the general statistical procedure of inference from samples has applicability to many fields, we shall illustrate here the general statistical principles for the sample mean. In the following two chapters, we shall examine particular methods of special importance to economics.

Let us suppose we have a sample that consists of 1,000 observations on some variable x. Our first step is to construct a frequency distribution of the observed values of x. No one observed value of x may be exactly the same as any other observed value. To simplify construction of the frequency distribution we group the observed values into classes and record each value of x as the midpoint of a class interval. Thus, in Table 16.2 the classes and the midpoints of x are shown in columns (1) and (2). For example, if a value of x between 4 and 6 is observed, say 4.4, it is recorded at the midpoint of this class interval and treated as if the observed value were 5. We have only one sample, so the letter i is used to designate the ith observation on x in the sample.

The third column shows the frequency with which a value of x occurred that fell inside each class interval. Naturally, the total number of frequencies, n, is equal to the total number of observations. If the relative frequency, f_i/n, is recorded for each class midpoint, we have the relative frequency distribution of the variable x. Columns (4) and (5) will be used to compute the statistics of the sample.

Table 16.2

(1)			(2)	(3)	(4)	(5)
Class Limits of x			Mid-point of Class	Frequency of Occurrence		
From	But Less Than		x_i	f_i	$x_i f_i$	$x_i^2 f_i$
0	–	2	1	50	50	50
2	–	4	3	90	270	810
4	–	6	5	150	750	3,750
6	–	8	7	225	1,575	11,025
8	–	10	9	200	1,800	16,200
10	–	12	11	160	1,760	19,360
12	–	14	13	85	1,105	14,365
14	–	16	15	40	600	9,000
Totals				$n = \sum_{i=1}^{8} f_i = 1,000$	$\sum_{i=1}^{8} x_i f_i = 7,910$	$\sum_{i=1}^{8} x_i^2 f_i = 74,560$

Our next step is to compute the sample statistics. We shall compute the sample mean and variance. Earlier we said that the mean of ungrouped data is defined as:

$$\bar{x} = \frac{1}{n} \sum_{i=1}^{n} x_i$$

where the variable x assumes the values $x_1, x_2, x_3, ..., x_n$.

For grouped data like that in Table 16.2, the sample mean has the formula:

$$\bar{x} = \frac{1}{n} \sum_{i=1}^{m} x_i f_i$$

where $n = \sum_{i=1}^{m} f_i$ and m is the total number of classes (in our sample $m = 8$). That is, the midpoints of all classes of x are multiplied by their respective frequencies and summed. Then the sum is divided by the total number of frequencies or observations.

In our example, we have:

$$\bar{x} = \frac{1}{1,000}(7,910) = 7.91$$

from the totals of columns (3) and (4) in the table.

The sample variance is a measure of the distribution of the values of x in the sample around the mean. The greater the variance the greater the dispersion of values of x around the mean. We use the symbol s^2 to denote the sample variance. For ungrouped data, the sample variance is given by:

$$s^2 = \frac{\sum_{i=1}^{n}(x_i - \bar{x})^2}{n-1}$$

We take the difference between the mean value of x and the observed value of x for each observed value of x in the sample. These differences are squared and then summed over all observations. The resulting sum is then divided by the number of observations in the sample minus one ($n - 1$). The quantity $n - 1$ is called the *degrees of freedom* used to compute the variance.[1] Note the similarity of this formula to that given for the population variance in Chapter 15, where $\bar{x}$ is replaced by the mathematical expectation of x in the population. For *grouped data* the formula becomes:

$$s^2 = \frac{\sum_{i=1}^{m}(x_i - \bar{x})^2 f_i}{n-1} = \frac{\sum_{i=1}^{m}x_i^2 f_i - n\bar{x}^2}{n-1}$$

In our example with the number of classes $m = 8$, the quantity $\sum_{i=1}^{8} x_i^2 f_i$ is given at the bottom of column (5) in Table 16.2. Substituting this quantity and the sample mean already computed, we have for the variance carried out to two decimal places:

$$s^2 = \frac{74,560 - (1,000)(7.91)^2}{1,000 - 1} = \frac{11,991.9}{999} = 12.00$$

Grouping the data leads to some inaccuracy in the computation of the variance. By substituting the midpoint of the class for the observed value of x some error is introduced. A formula known as Sheppard's correction is often applied to the result in order to rectify this error. By substituting from the variance the size of the class interval squared and dividing by twelve, we correct for the error introduced by grouping. In our example the

---

[1]We divide by $n - 1$ rather than n because some of the information contained in the sample was used to compute the sample mean. The so-called *degrees of freedom* decrease as the amount of information is used up. A sample of, say, 50 observations contains more information than samples of less than 50 observations. We use some of the information in the sample to compute the sample mean. This uses up one degree of freedom. If we know 49 observations and the sample mean, we are "forced" to infer the other observation; we have used up one degree of freedom. For a sample of 50 observations there are only 49 degrees of freedom left to compute the variance, since to compute the variance we need to know the mean.

size of the class interval is two. Hence, we square this quantity and divide by twelve. Sheppard's correction is:

$$\frac{(2)^2}{12} = \frac{4}{12} = 0.33$$

The computed variance is 12.00 so the corrected variance is:

$$s^2 = 12.00 - 0.33 = 11.67$$

The standard deviation is defined as the square root of the variance. Hence, we have as our sample standard deviation:

$$s = \sqrt{11.67} = 3.42$$

Having computed these sample statistics, let us concentrate attention on the sample mean, $\bar{x} = 7.91$. If we were to take another sample from the same population, it is almost certain that the second sample would not have the same mean. This is likewise true of a third, a fourth, and so on. Even if many additional samples were to be drawn, we probably would not obtain exactly the same value of the mean twice. But would these other sample means vary greatly from the one we have observed? Sample theory helps us to decide how all possible sample means are distributed around the population mean. We can see our sample mean fits into this distribution and we can thereby establish some grounds for an inference about the population mean.

The *standard error of the sample mean* is an estimate of the variability that would occur among the means of many samples if many samples were to be drawn at random from the same population. If we are to estimate the variation that would appear among the means of many samples, we must take into account the magnitude of the standard deviation of our observed sample and the size of the sample. The standard error of the mean is denoted by $s_{\bar{x}}$ and is given by the formula:

$$s_{\bar{x}} = \frac{s}{\sqrt{n}}$$

In the case of the sample illustrated in Table 16.2, the standard error of the mean rounded to two decimal places is:

$$s_{\bar{x}} = \frac{3.42}{\sqrt{1,000}} = \frac{3.42}{31.61} = 0.11$$

This is an estimate of the standard error of the mean that would have been secured had we (1) taken a large number of random samples from the population, (2) computed the mean of each sample, (3) arranged these means in a frequency distribution, and (4) calculated the standard deviation of these means. If this distribution of means is approximately normal, we know that about 68.27 percent of the sample means would lie within ±0.11 of the mean of this distribution of sample means, 95.45 percent would fall within ±0.22, and 99.73 percent would fall within ±0.33 of the mean of the sample means.

Let us pause now to check our bearings. Tracing our steps backwards we have seen that from knowledge of the sample mean and the sample standard deviation of the one observed sample, we can compute the standard error of the sample mean. This quantity tells us the degree to which our sample mean might be expected to differ from the mean value of the distribution of many sample means—without our having actually to draw many samples. The theory of sampling in the second section of this chapter establishes a relationship between the mean value of many sample means and the population mean. Therefore, we have a link between the mean of one observed sample and the unobserved population mean. The final problem, then, is to consider the conditions under which one can estimate population parameters directly from knowledge of the statistics of one sample.

STATISTICAL ESTIMATION

Confidence Intervals

We have seen that we cannot make statements about the population parameters with certainty; "errors" in sampling prevent our doing so. However, sampling theory permits us to make probabilistic statements about the population parameters based on sample statistics. As we have seen, subjective or Bayesian probability theory views the probability of an event as a *degree of confidence* that the event will occur (or has occurred). Hence, for some preassigned "degree of confidence," the statistician can establish a *confidence interval* or *confidence limits* on the basis of the information in the sample. We then say that with a given degree of probability the population parameter will be within these limits. We choose a probability in advance and refer to it as the *confidence coefficient*. Suppose this preassigned coefficient is 95 percent. The statistician combines the sample statistic, the standard error of that sample statistic, and the relevant range of the standard normal curve (or some other known probability density function) to calculate the *likely* range of the population parameter. In terms of subjective probability, the statistician is 95 percent certain (5 percent uncertain) that the value of the population parameter is within the calculated 95 percent confidence interval.

In the second section of this chapter, we presented the general rule that the mean of a sample of n observations has itself the mathematical expectation equal to the population mean:

$$E(\overline{x}) = \mu$$

We saw also that the variance of the sample means equals the population variance divided by the number of observations in the sample:

$$\sigma_{\overline{x}}^2 = \frac{\sigma^2}{n}$$

In our discussion of the normal distribution, we saw that we can define the variable:

$$z = \frac{x - \mu}{\sigma}$$

which has mean zero and variance one if x is normally distributed. If the sample comes from a normally distributed population, moreover, the variable:

$$z = \frac{\overline{x} - \mu}{\sigma_{\overline{x}}}$$

is distributed normally with a mean of zero and a variance of one. Even when the population is not normally distributed but the sample is large, z will be approximately normally distributed. Finally, we recall that the standard error of the sample mean is given by:

$$s_{\overline{x}} = \frac{s}{\sqrt{n}}$$

For large samples, the sample standard deviation s, is a reasonably good estimate of the unknown population standard deviation. Now we can compute $s_{\overline{x}}$ from our known sample, so we substitute $s_{\overline{x}}$ for $\sigma_{\overline{x}}$ in the definition of z:

$$z = \frac{\overline{x} - \mu}{s_{\overline{x}}}$$

where z is approximately normally distributed with mean zero and variance one. The larger the sample the closer will be the approximation.

Note that in the definition of z, the quantities $\overline{x}$ and $s_{\overline{x}}$ are computed from the data while the value of μ itself is generally unknown. By stipulating a value of z as the *confidence coefficient*, the only "unknown" is the population parameter, μ. With one equation and one unknown, we can solve for the "value" (in this case the confidence interval) of the unknown. In this case:

$$\mu = \overline{x} \pm z s_{\overline{x}}$$

Suppose we specify the confidence coefficient as 95 percent. We see, from Table D on the normal distribution at the end of the book,[2] the probability that z is between -1.96 and 1.96 is:

$$\mu = \overline{x} - 1.96 s_{\overline{x}} \quad \text{and} \quad \mu = \overline{x} + 1.96 s_{\overline{x}}$$

[2]The use of Table D is discussed in the next section on tests of hypotheses. We are looking for a value of z that yields a 95 percent probability of observing the true value of the population mean. Since the mean of z is equal to zero, Table D gives the probability (p) of z from zero to any of the values of z shown in the left margin. Since we want to know the deviation of z from its mean (zero) in *both* the positive and the negative directions, we must find the value of $2p$ that equals 0.95. When $p = 0.4750$, then $2p = 0.95$, the chosen probability level. Therefore, we read off the value of z corresponding to 0.4750 as 1.96. Since we are going in both directions from the mean of z (we have multiplied p by 2), we have $+1.96$ and -1.96 as the values of z corresponding to a probability level of 0.95.

We estimate that the unknown population mean, μ, will lie within these limits. In the long run following such a procedure, we would be correct in 95 cases out of 100.

Table 16.3 provides some examples of confidence intervals for four macroeconomic statistics: the average unemployment rate (*UE*), the average rate of inflation (*INF*, measured as the annual rate of change in the *GNP* implicit price deflator), the average propensity to save (*APS*, measured as household saving expressed as a percentage of disposable personal income), and the deficit in the federal budget (*DEF*, measured as a percentage of *GNP*). Quarterly data were used for the period between 1948 and 1984, yielding 148 observations. The mean, standard deviation, standard deviation of the sample means, and the 95 percent confidence interval for each variable are reported in Table 16.3.

Table 16.3

Variable	$\bar{x}$	s_x	$s_{\bar{x}}$	95% Confidence Interval
UE	5.52	1.73	0.142	$5.24 < \mu < 5.80$
INF	4.186	2.91	0.239	$3.72 < \mu < 4.65$
APS	6.149	1.147	0.094	$5.96 < \mu < 6.33$
DEF	1.095	2.469	0.203	$0.697 < \mu < 1.493$

For each variable, the standard deviation, s_x, measures the average deviation between a particular observation in the sample of 148 and the sample mean. The standard error for the sample mean, $s_{\bar{x}}$, is calculated by dividing the sample standard deviation by $\sqrt{148} = 12.166$, which makes $s_{\bar{x}}$ considerably smaller than s_x. If we assume that these variables had a stable distribution, we are 95 percent confident that the average unemployment rate for the period 1948 to 1984 was between 5.24 and 5.80 percent. It would be unlikely (less than one chance in twenty) that the true (unobserved) average unemployment rate was as low as 5 percent or as high as 6 percent. Similarly, the average percentage change in the price level (as measured by the implicit price deflator) was probably between 3.72 and 4.65 percent per year. The average propensity to save was clustered quite closely to the sample mean of 6.149 percent, although there is one chance in twenty that the *APS* is greater than 6.33 percent or less than 5.96 percent. Finally, the average deficit during 36 years of observation was probably not more than 1.5 percent of *GNP* and probably not less than 0.7 percent of *GNP*.

From our single sample of quarterly macroeconomic variables, we estimated a range for the population mean. We are not certain that the true mean lies in that range; our inference is probable. We make each statistical estimate with 95 percent confidence. We feel that if we were to make many such estimates, we would be correct about 95 times out of 100.

Point Estimation

Sometimes we wish to obtain a single figure for an estimate of the unknown population parameter rather than an interval. A number of methods have been developed by statisticians. The two most important are the method of maximum likelihood and the method of least squares.

The method of maximum likelihood chooses as the population estimate the value of the random variable that maximizes its probability of being observed. The estimate of the population parameter should be that value of the variable which, if it were correct, would maximize the probabilty of obtaining the sample actually observed. For every possible value of the population parameter, the probabilty of the observed sample's occurring in random sampling is calculated. The particular value that maximizes this probability is selected as the estimate of the parameter.

The method of least squares chooses the value that minimizes the sum of the squares of the deviations from the chosen value. This method is used extensively in econometrics, and we shall have more to say about it in the next chapter. Besides the methods of maximum likelihood and least squares, there are other methods available for point estimation. They are not very often used, however.

TESTS OF HYPOTHESES

A hypothesis is a theoretical proposition that is capable of empirical verification or disproof. It is an explanation of some event or events, and it may be a true or false explanation. The following statements are statistical hypotheses: "The average rate of inflation for countries in 1978 was greater than the average rate of inflation in 1977." "The average unemployment rate in the United States was greater between 1970 and 1984 than between 1948 and 1969." "An increase in the proportion of workers belonging to labor unions increases the average wage rate in a state, *ceteris paribus*." "An increase in the unemployment rate reduces the rate of inflation." Notice that these are statements about some statistical population. The problem is one of determining from a sample whether the hypothesis is probably true or probably false.

Often econometric problems are phrased in terms of a hypothesis. Empirical tests of hypotheses are called *tests of significance*. Such a test is a probability test based on sampling theory and is designed to determine whether a given sample could reasonably come from a specified population. Suppose we have a given hypothesis about a population and a sample drawn at random from that population. We intend to judge the truth or falsehood of the hypothesis on the basis of the evidence in the sample. To do this, we compute the probability that this particular sample would have arisen if the hypothesis were true. A so-called level of significance is specified in advance. This significance level is used to decide whether or not we reject the hypothesis as false. Rejection or nonrejection turns on the probability of an error we might commit in making that decision. If the probability of making the wrong decision is less than a preassigned value, we go ahead and make that decision.

A hypothesis can never be tested in a vacuum. If the hypothesis we stipulate appears to be false, there must be some opposite or *null hypothesis* that is true. The *significance level* is the calculated probability that the null hypothesis is true. It can also be interpreted as the probability that the hypothesis we believe in (called the *alternative hypothesis*) is false. We actually test the null hypothesis; that is, we seek to determine whether evidence warrants rejecting the null hypothesis in favor of the alternative hypothesis.

The convention in statistical analysis is to place the burden of proof on the alternative hypothesis. This is done by setting the preassigned significance level relatively low. One significance level that is commonly chosen is 5 percent; another is 1 percent. Suppose we chose a 5 percent level of significance. This means we will reject the null hypothesis only when the probability of its being true is less than 5 percent. If this probability is greater than 5 percent, the statistical evidence is considered inadequate to overturn the null hypothesis in favor of the alternative hypothesis. If the probability that the null hypothesis is true is greater than 5 percent, we do not reject it. The latter conclusion does not mean that we have proved the null hypothesis or disproved the alternative hypothesis. It merely means that we have insufficient evidence to overturn the null hypothesis in favor of the alternative hypothesis.

Two types of error may be made in testing hypotheses. One, called *type I* error, occurs if a true *null hypothesis* is rejected. The probability of this error is given by the level of significance chosen. *Type II* error occurs if a false *null hypothesis* is not rejected; that is, the null hypothesis is not overturned in favor of the alternative hypothesis, even though the latter is true. Statisticians use the concept of *level of confidence* to indicate their optimism that when they reject a null hypothesis they are *not* accepting a false alternative hypothesis. If statistical results are *significant* at the 0.05 level, we are *confident* at the 0.95 level that the alternative hypothesis is not false. By reducing the chance of *type I* error we increase the probability of *type II* error, and vice versa.

Before we proceed with examples of hypothesis testing, we will discuss the specification of the alternative and null hypothesis in more detail. An appropriate analogy might be the convention in criminal justice of *assuming* that an accused person is innocent until *proven* guilty. The judicial system operates in an uncertain environment; whether or not the accused actually committed a crime is unknown (although suspected) until evidence is presented. In considering evidence, a jury can make two types of errors: guilty persons can be acquitted or innocent persons can be convicted. If the goal of the criminal justice system is to deter would-be felons from committing crimes, the *conditional* probability of conviction for the guilty should be set considerably higher than the *conditional* probability of conviction for the innocent. Hence, trials begin with the *null hypothesis* that the accused is *not* guilty. Only when the risk of convicting an innocent person is acceptably small, will the jury (in theory) return a guilty verdict. The burden of proof rests on the prosecution.

Of course, the goal of the criminal justice system may be different than deterring would-be criminals. For instance, the goal may be to maximize the number of convicts available for slave labor or medical experiments. In such cases, the null hypothesis would be that the accused is *guilty* and only in the case of *overwhelming* evidence of innocence would the accused be acquitted.

The goals of econometrics, like those of criminal justice, can vary. We have argued so far that econometricians seek to discover the values of true population parameters by investigating the values and distributions of sample statistics. But there can be strongly held beliefs about the values of the population parameters, or compelling motives to "prove" one hypothesis or another. It is conceivable that one's own prejudices or biases might interfere with an objective evaluation of the statistical evidence. Econometricians attempt to minimize any distortions their own beliefs might cause by specifying the hypothesis that they believe as the *alternative* hypothesis and the hypothesis they wish to refute as the *null* hypothesis. Hence, before presenting evidence to their peers or clients, they attempt to gather overwhelming evidence in favor of their conclusions. That is, before rejecting a hypothesis they disagree with, they satisfy themselves that the chances of that hypothesis being true are less than 5 percent. Equivalently, before arguing for the acceptance of an alternative hypothesis, they assure themselves that they can have 95 percent confidence that the alternative hypothesis is true.

But not every econometric project necessarily involves the juxtaposition of two competing hypotheses. There are many instances when the econometrician seeks to estimate the parameters for a particular theory without seriously questioning whether the theory itself is valid. In this case, the chief concern is that the sample itself is a poor reflection of the underlying economic reality. Hence, if an estimated demand equation fails to reflect an inverse relation between price and quantity, it is not the theory of demand which is suspect, but the adequacy of the sample. The econometrician still looks for a *significant* inverse relation between price and quantity (that is, he or she seeks to reject the null hypothesis of a direct or random relation between price and quantity) not because the null hypothesis is seriously believed, but because the implications of an inadequate sample are considered costly.

In summary, then, the audience who receives the report of an econometric investigation can draw its own inferences about the strength of the evidence by noting whether the hypothesis being supported is the null hypothesis or the alternative hypothesis. Since the "odds" favor the null hypothesis, evidence is more impressive when it implies rejecting the null hypothesis in favor of the alternative hypothesis. Showing that the chance of one's hypothesis being false is less than 5 (or 1) percent is more likely to impress skeptics than arguing that the probability of the hypothesis being true is greater than 5 percent. Hence, when one makes one's own hypothesis the null hypothesis, the chances are quite good that the hypothesis will "stand up" to empirical scrutiny; after all, it has 20 to 1 odds in its favor. However, such evidence is not likely to impress those less enamored with that particular idea.

Tests of Hypotheses About the Value of a Population Mean

There are two types of tests that involve estimates of the population mean. The first of these, to be discussed in this section, concerns hypotheses that the population mean for some variable has some specific value. In terms of the evidence presented in Table 16.3, suppose that it is widely believed that the average propensity to save is *less than* 6 percent. Let us specify that general belief as the null hypothesis and ask whether there is *compelling evidence* to reject that belief. Recall that the 95 percent confidence interval for that average APS between 1948 and 1984 is $5.96 < \mu < 6.33$. Note that this confidence interval contains possible values for μ that support the null hypothesis. Hence, even though the sample mean of 6.149 appears to contradict the null hypothesis that $APS < 6$, the estimated standard error is great enough that the *difference* between the measured APS and the hypothetical APS is deemed *insignificant*.

So we see that one means of testing a hypothesis about the population mean for a variable is to calculate a confidence interval for the population mean and see whether that interval includes the value of the mean characterizing the null hypothesis. If so, we fail to reject the null hypothesis; our test is deemed *insignificant*. If the hypothetical value of the mean falls outside of the confidence interval, the significance of that result equals the difference between the confidence level that generated the interval and 100 percent. That is, if the hypothesized value of the mean lies outside of the 95 percent confidence interval, we reject the *null hypothesis* and our results are deemed to be significant at the 5 percent level. If the hypothesized value of the mean lies outside of the 99 percent confidence interval, we reject the null hypothesis and our results are deemed to be significant at the 1 percent level.

The problem of using the confidence interval to test a hypothesis about the population mean is that the confidence interval contains two extreme values or "tails," while the hypothesis often concerns only one of those "tails." In our example, we stipulate the alternative hypothesis that $\mu > 6$ for the APS between 1948 and 1984. This is symbolized by the notation,

H_a: $\mu > 6$. Since the null hypothesis is true if the alternative hypothesis is false, our null hypothesis is $\mu \leq 6$. This is symbolized by the notation H_o: $\mu \leq 6$. Our 95 percent confidence interval tells us that there is a 5 percent chance that the population mean of the *APS* is less than 5.96 *or greater than* 6.33. However, only if the population mean is 6 or less is the null hypothesis true; the "upper tail" of the confidence interval is irrelevant to the hypothesis being tested.

There is another method for testing a hypothesis about a population without calculating confidence intervals. To perform a one-tail test of our hypothesis, we compute the statistic:

$$z = \frac{\overline{x} - \mu_0}{s_{\overline{x}}}$$

where μ_0 is the extreme value of the population mean reflecting the null hypothesis. In this case, the hypothetical population mean is known, as are the sample mean, $\overline{x}$, and the sample standard deviation, $s_{\overline{x}}$, which is the estimate for the unknown parameter $\sigma_{\overline{x}}$. If the sample size is large (e.g., the 148 observations reflected in Table 16.3), then z will be approximately normally distributed with a zero mean and a variance equal to one. By looking up the calculated value of z in Table D or a similar table, we can determine whether the null hypothesis ought to be rejected.

Staying with our example of the average propensity to save, we calculate z as:

$$z = \frac{\overline{x} - \mu_0}{s_{\overline{x}}} = \frac{6.149 - 6}{0.094} = \frac{0.149}{0.094} = 1.585$$

Since we are interested in the value of z for one tail of the distribution, we look for that value of z corresponding to the significance level $p = 0.05$, where p is the probability that the null hypothesis is true. According to Table D the *critical value* of z for 5 percent significance with a one-tail test is 1.645. That is, 5 percent of the values of z will be greater than 1.645. Since the calculated value of z is less than the critical value of z, we fail to reject the null hypothesis.

The preceding test is valid for large samples. If the sample is small, say less than 30 observations, the test is not applicable. For samples from a normal population, however, *Student's t distribution* or simply the *t distribution* closely approximates the normal distribution, where:

$$t = \frac{\overline{x} - \mu_0}{s_{\overline{x}}}$$

Table C gives the *t* distribution for various degrees of freedom. The larger the number of degrees of freedom (the number of observations in the sample minus the number of statistics estimated from that sample), the closer the *t* distribution approximates the normal distribution.

For example, suppose we wish to argue that the average percent change in the *real* wage rate between 1970 and 1984 was less than zero. From Table 16.4 in the next section we see that there are 15 (annual) observations on the variable, leaving us 14 degrees of freedom. Since the hypothesis we wish to test is that $\mu < 0$, we specify our null hypothesis as $\mu \geq 0$. Our sample statistics are:

$$\bar{x} = -0.14 \quad \text{and} \quad s_{\bar{x}} = \frac{2.64}{\sqrt{14}} = \frac{2.64}{3.74} = 0.706$$

We calculate the relevant t statistic:

$$t = \frac{\bar{x} - \mu_0}{s_{\bar{x}}} = \frac{-0.14 - 0}{0.706} = \frac{-0.14}{0.706} = -0.198$$

For 14 degrees of freedom and a *one-tail* test, the critical value of t in this case would be -1.745. Notice the minus sign; this is because we are testing the hypothesis that the true sample mean is less than the value indicated by the null hypothesis. Now, despite the fact that the calculated t value has the correct sign, the value of the calculated t is considerably smaller (in absolute value) than the level necessary to imply 5 percent significance. Once again, we fail to reject the null hypothesis. Although the sample mean is negative for the period in question, the probability that the true mean is actually positive or zero is greater than 5 percent.

Tests About the Equality
of Two Sample Means

Another hypothesis that is frequently tested in econometric work is whether or not two different samples, drawn from hypothetically different sets of observations, actually belong to the same population. That is, we hypothesize that two groups, say of companies, states, time periods, etc., are different. Then we test this by determining whether or not there is a significant difference in the sample means for these groups. In other words, we specify the null hypothesis that the means for two samples are equal (presumably to a single population mean). We reject the null hypothesis in favor of the alternative hypothesis if the critical value of z or t (depending on sample size) indicates that there is a low probability that the null hypothesis is true.

Table 16.4 presents annual macroeconomic statistics on the unemployment rate (*UE*), the inflation rate (*INF*), the rate of change in the nominal wage rate (*DWAGE*), the rate of change in productivity (*DPROD*, measured as the percent change in real *GNP* per worker), and the rate of change in the real wage rate (*DRWAGE*). There are 37 observations. As we will see in Chapter 18, the inverse relation between inflation and unemployment appears to hold from 1948 to 1969, but not for the period 1970 to 1984. This

Table 16.4

Year	UE	INF	DWAGE	DPROD	DRWAGE
1948	3.8	1.6	7.5	4.3	−0.1
1949	5.9	−0.9	2.5	2.0	3.6
1950	5.3	1.9	5.8	6.0	4.7
1951	3.3	6.9	8.9	1.7	0.8
1952	3.0	1.2	4.8	2.3	2.7
1953	2.9	1.6	5.1	1.7	4.4
1954	5.5	1.4	1.2	1.4	0.5
1955	4.4	2.2	5.0	3.9	5.4
1956	4.1	3.1	4.5	0.3	3.1
1957	4.3	3.3	3.7	1.7	0.1
1958	6.8	1.7	2.4	2.4	−0.4
1959	5.5	2.1	4.9	3.4	4.1
1960	5.5	1.8	2.4	0.8	0.7
1961	6.7	0.9	2.4	2.9	1.4
1962	5.5	1.9	4.0	3.6	3.0
1963	5.7	1.4	3.0	3.2	1.7
1964	5.2	1.5	3.2	3.9	1.8
1965	4.5	2.2	4.5	3.1	2.7
1966	3.8	3.4	3.5	2.5	0.6
1967	3.8	2.9	3.1	1.9	0.2
1968	3.6	4.6	5.8	3.3	1.5
1969	3.5	5.0	6.4	−0.3	0.9
Mean ($\bar{x}_1$)	4.66	2.35	4.30	2.55	1.97
St. Dev. (s_1)	1.12	1.57	1.80	1.39	1.67
1970	4.9	5.4	4.6	0.3	−1.3
1971	5.9	5.0	6.2	3.3	1.9
1972	5.6	4.2	7.5	3.7	4.1
1973	4.9	5.7	6.2	2.4	0.0
1974	5.6	8.8	6.4	−2.5	−4.1
1975	8.5	9.2	5.7	2.0	3.1
1976	7.7	5.2	7.3	3.2	1.5
1977	7.1	5.8	7.7	2.2	1.2
1978	6.1	8.1	7.8	0.6	0.2
1979	5.8	7.7	8.0	−1.5	−3.1
1980	7.1	9.0	6.9	−0.7	−5.8
1981	6.6	9.1	8.5	1.9	−1.5
1982	9.7	6.9	4.6	−0.1	−1.3
1983	9.6	4.2	5.0	3.1	2.0
1984	7.5	3.2	4.2	3.2	1.0
Mean ($\bar{x}_2$)	6.84	6.50	6.44	1.41	−0.14
St. Dev. (s_2)	1.48	1.96	1.33	1.87	2.64
($\bar{x}_2 - \bar{x}_1$)	2.18	4.15	2.14	−1.14	−2.11
$s_{\bar{x}_2 - \bar{x}_1}$	0.46	0.62	0.52	0.58	0.79
t statistic	4.72	6.72	4.13	−1.97	−2.69

could be explained by a structural change in the underlying equations that explain macroeconomic behavior, specifically, that during the first era of relatively low inflation, expected inflation was zero, and such an inverse relation appeared to hold. However, during the 1970s and early 1980s, there was positive expected inflation, and the so-called "Phillips curve" did not apply.

For each of the five variables in Table 16.4, we first calculate the mean and standard deviation for the period 1948-1969 and for the period 1970-1984. Then we calculate the difference between the mean for the first period $(\overline{x}_1)$ and the mean for the second period $(\overline{x}_2)$. Then the standard error for the *difference of the means*, $s_{\overline{x}_1 - \overline{x}_2}$, is calculated according to the formula:

$$s_{\overline{x}_1 - \overline{x}_2} = \sqrt{\frac{s_1^2}{n_1} + \frac{s_2^2}{n_2}}$$

That is, the standard error for the difference in means for two groups equals the square root of the sum of the sample variance for each group divided by the number of observations on that group. The t statistic for the difference in the means is then calculated as:

$$t = \frac{\overline{x}_2 - \overline{x}_1}{s_{\overline{x}_1 - \overline{x}_2}}$$

Since two means were calculated for each variable, there are $37 - 2 = 35$ degrees of freedom for the t statistic. According to Table C the critical value of t with 30 degrees of freedom for a two-tail test and 5 percent significance is 2.042. We note in Table 16.4 that the difference in the means of four of the five variables is significantly different for the period 1948-1969 and the period 1970-1984. In each case we can reject the null hypothesis that the variables were drawn from the same population.

Note that we used a *two-tail t test* in drawing our inferences from Table 16.4. This is because we merely wished to test the hypothesis that the means of the two hypothetical populations (i.e., the period 1948-1969 and the period 1970-1984) are different, that is, that $\mu_2 - \mu_1 \neq 0$, without specifying whether the difference is positive or negative.

If we hypothesize relative sizes for the two means, for instance that the average rate of inflation in the latter period is greater than in the former, a one-tail test is more appropriate. In this case, we first check to see whether the calculated t statistic has the "correct" sign (that is, the sign predicted by the alternative hypothesis). If not, we automatically embrace the null hypothesis and the magnitude of the t statistic is irrelevant. If the calculated t statistic does have the predicted sign, we then determine whether the magnitude of the t statistic allows us to reject the null hypothesis. Since the t statistics in Table 16.4 justify rejecting the null hypothesis on the basis of a two-tail t test, we may also reject the null hypothesis on the basis of a one-tail t test, as long as the sign on the t statistic is appropriate. Hence, we may infer that the population means for the unemployment rate, the inflation rate, and the rate of change in the nominal wage rate were all significantly *greater* in 1970-1984 than in 1948-1969. Also, the population means for the rate of change in productivity and the rate of change in the real wage rate were significantly smaller in the 1970-1984 time period.

THE RELATIONSHIP OF ESTIMATION
TO TESTS OF HYPOTHESES

You may have realized by now that there is a close connection between statistical estimation and hypotheses testing. The error of rejecting a true null hypothesis really amounts to the error of excluding the correct value of a population parameter from the confidence interval. Likewise, accepting a false null hypothesis (rejecting a true alternative hypothesis) amounts to including the wrong value of the population parameter in the confidence interval. Indeed, testing the hypothesis that some parameter has a specified value is ordinarily equivalent to computing the confidence interval for that parameter. If the value specified by the null hypothesis is enclosed by the confidence interval, the null hypothesis is accepted and the alternative hypothesis is rejected. If not, the null hypothesis is rejected and the alternative hypothesis is accepted.

However, when the alternative hypothesis specifies a particular range for a parameter, then the two-tail test implied by the confidence interval is inappropriate and a one-tail test is used. This amounts to calculating a z or t statistic for the sample and hypothesized population parameter, checking whether the sign on that statistic is consistent with the alternative hypothesis, then determining whether the result is significant in terms of one tail of the appropriate distribution. Nevertheless, just as in the case of two-tail tests, there is a very close connection between statistical estimation and hypothesis testing in the case of one-tail tests. The primary reason for treating the two subjects separately is that sometimes hypotheses refer to more than population parameters. When this is the case, the methods of statistical estimation and hypothesis testing are not equivalent.

PROBLEMS

1.   Let the variable Y designate family income. Suppose the following sample of observations on Y has been obtained for a certain community, where family income is recorded in thousands of dollars per year.

24.6	31.4	37.5	28.4	17.7	36.0	28.5	33.0
18.0	18.9	26.4	60.1	42.4	24.4	11.7	20.8
15.3	18.3	14.9	24.1	33.3	30.2	51.2	27.0
23.7	21.2	22.6	39.3	30.7	49.6	14.9	17.8
14.4	17.7	19.5	21.2	16.8	14.6	22.5	30.7

    a. Compute the sample mean for the ungrouped data.

    b. Compute the sample standard deviation.

    c. Assume the population is normally distributed and use Table D at the end of the book to establish the 95 percent confidence limits for the population mean family income.

    d. How do you interpret the limits found in Part c?

2.   From the sample in Problem 1, test the hypothesis that the average family income is $27,000 per year. Test the null hypothesis that the average family income is $30,000 per year (i.e., the alternative hypothesis is that the average family income is *not* $30,000 per year). Test the null hypothesis that the average family income is *not less* than $30,000. Choose the 5 percent level of significance.

3.   A manufacturing firm wishes to test the quality of its product. From its weekly output, a statistician selects at random a sample of 30 finished product items. Using a quality index supplied by the engineers, the following measurements are recorded.

100	101	98	101	100	102
100	99	101	102	98	100
101	99	100	98	99	100
103	101	99	98	97	101
99	100	99	101	103	100

Assuming the population follows Student's t distribution and using the 1 percent level of significance, test the hypothesis that the average quality exceeds 99.

4.   Let the variable x represent scores on an aptitude test. The following sample of test scores is given:

33	72	27	28	36	72
45	84	87	83	82	79
52	91	41	61	75	39
76	88	56	68	65	58
64	13	77	66	48	75

Group the data in class intervals of 0-9.99 with a midpoint of 5, 10-19.99 with a midpoint of 15, ..., 90-99.99 with a midpoint of 95.

    a. Compute the sample mean for the grouped data.

    b. Compute the sample standard deviation.

    c. Assume the population is normally distributed and use Table D to establish the 95 percent confidence limits for the population mean.

5.   Using the sample given in Problem 4, test the hypothesis that the average test score is less than 85. Test the hypothesis that the average test score is greater than 65. Choose the 5 percent level of significance.

6. Listed below are data on per capita milk consumption (in quarts) for
    the United States for the years 1951 to 1981:

Year	PCMILK	Year	PCMILK	Year	PCMILK
1951	320	1961	298	1971	262
1952	321	1962	296	1972	265
1953	319	1963	295	1973	262
1954	321	1964	293	1974	254
1955	323	1965	292	1975	259
1956	325	1966	287	1976	252
1957	323	1967	276	1977	253
1958	318	1968	272	1978	251
1959	312	1969	264	1979	248
1960	307	1970	264	1980	245
				1981	246

a. Compute the mean and standard deviation for the entire sample.
   What is the 95 percent confidence interval for that mean?
b. Test the hypothesis that milk consumption between 1951 and 1965
   was higher than milk consumption from 1966 to 1981.
c. Test the hypothesis that milk consumption between 1971 and 1981
   was lower than milk consumption between 1951 and 1961.

7. Between 1977 and 1982, manufacturing employment grew by an aver-
    age of 9.05 percent for 22 sunbelt states (with a standard deviation of
    14.64). It declined by 2.34 percent for 38 snowbelt states (with a stan-
    dard deviation of 10.12). Test the hypothesis that "employment growth
    in manufacturing in the sunbelt exceeds employment growth in manu-
    facturing in the snowbelt."

8. An econometrician is doing preliminary research on the relation be-
    tween the proportion of workers in a state who belong to unions and
    the average wage rate for manufacturing workers in that state. The
    econometrician believes that states fall into distinct populations: those
    that allow mandatory union membership clauses in union contracts
    ("union shop states") and those that forbid such contracts ("right-to-
    work states"). In 1978, there were 30 states in the union shop category
    and 20 states in the right-to-work category. The sample means and
    sample standard deviations shown in the table on the next page were
    computed for the two groups of states.
    a. Compute the difference in the mean for each variable and the stan-
       dard error for that difference.
    b. Test the hypothesis that the population mean for each variable is
       greater for union shop states.

	Percent of Workers in Unions	Average Hourly Wage Rate	Value-Added per Hour
Union Shop:			
Mean	24.84	6.50	24.23
Standard Deviation	7.21	0.83	3.51
Right to Work:			
Mean	14.00	5.64	22.84
Standard Deviation	3.87	0.71	5.54

PART III

Econometrics

17

Simple

Regression and

Correlation

We have completed the groundwork for econometrics. In Part I we developed the mathematical tools necessary to translate economic relationships into mathematical models. In Part II we discussed the role of uncertainty and probability in the estimation of econometric models. In Part III we will develop the statistical techniques to translate general mathematical models into specific equations. In this chapter we introduce those statistical techniques by discussing simple regression.

SIMPLE LINEAR REGRESSION

Simple regression refers to methods of estimating equations with one exogenous and one endogenous variable using a sample of observations. When more than two variables are involved, the estimation technique is called *multiple regression*. In this chapter, we treat only simple regression. Assume that some dependent variable y is related to some independent systematic variable x in some unspecified way:

$$y = f(x)$$

This relationship merely stipulates that each value of x is associated with a unique value of y. This relationship is presumed to hold in a population of infinite size.

To discover the equation that describes the relationship between x and y, a sample of observations is taken. Each observation consists of one value of x and the associated value of y. The sample may have been obtained from observations at the same place at different times, yielding *time-series* data. Or the sample may have been obtained from observations obtained at different places at the same time, yielding *cross-section* data. Table 17.1 presents cross-sectional observations on the percent change of the money stock (M1) for forty-five countries between 1978 and 1979 and the associated percent change in the consumer price index. According to economic theory, an increase in the money stock is predicted to increase the price level, *ceteris paribus*. Hence, we stipulate that the independent variable, x, is the change in M1 while the dependent variable, y is the change in the CPI.

Figure 17.1 depicts a *scatter diagram* of the data reported in Table 17.1. Each point in Figure 17.1 relates the *observed* value of y to the *observed* value of x. Our goal is to use the scatter of points to discover the equation that describes the population. We might decide to "connect the dots," literally join all the points with a broken line. This is equivalent to assuming that the sample of observations is taken without error. Although such a broken line would "fit" the scatter of points perfectly, it would represent a very complex mathematical equation. The preferred approach is to stipulate a simple functional form, say a linear equation, and estimate that equation that gives the best fit to the scatter of points. This is equivalent to assuming that some error is encountered for some or all observations.

Figure 17.1

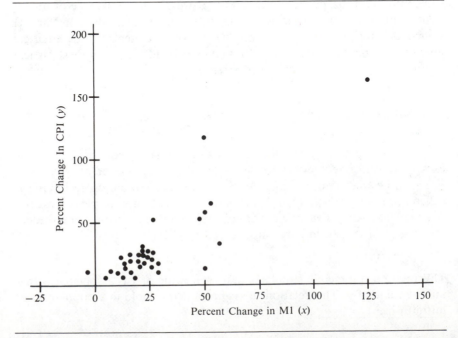

Table 17.1
Money Growth and Inflation for 45 Selected Countries, 1978-1979

Country	Percent Change in M1 (x)	Percent Change in CPI (y)
Austria	−6.1	3.7
Netherlands	2.7	4.2
Belgium	3.8	4.5
Canada	4.9	9.1
Germany, Fed Rep	7.2	4.1
Venezuela	7.6	12.4
Switzerland	7.8	3.6
United States	8.2	11.3
Kenya	9.3	8.0
Japan	9.9	3.6
Nigeria	10.3	11.1
Phillipines	11.9	18.8
United Kingdom	12.2	13.4
France	12.3	10.8
Sweden	12.6	7.3
Ethiopia	13.1	16.1
Burma	13.8	5.7
Spain	13.8	15.6
South Africa	15.3	13.1
Thailand	16.6	9.9
Morocco	17.0	8.4
Yugoslavia	17.4	21.3
Sri Lanka	17.8	10.8
Algeria	17.8	11.4
Korea, Rep of	18.0	18.3
Malaysia	18.0	3.6
Bangladesh	18.4	12.7
Portugal	18.4	23.8
India	19.6	6.4
Indonesia	19.6	21.9
Greece	19.7	19.0
Syria	19.8	4.8
Pakistan	22.5	9.4
Italy	23.9	14.7
Egypt	23.9	9.9
Columbia	25.0	24.7
Ghana	30.3	54.4
Mexico	31.4	18.2
Iran	48.1	10.5
Brazil	51.6	52.7
Zaire	54.1	108.6
Turkey	54.8	58.7
Peru	59.6	66.7
Chile	60.0	33.4
Argentina	125.4	159.5

Source: *Statistical Abstract of the United States, 1983-1984.*

Instead of a general equation of the form $y = f(x)$, we stipulate a precise form, $y = a + bx$, which is linear in the parameters a and b and which is *assumed* to hold for the population. But it should be obvious from Figure 17.1 that the scatter of points does not describe a line exactly. If the true equation is linear, some error is introduced into our observations. The convention then is to specify the equation governing our observations as:

$$y = a + bx + u$$

where u is the *random error term* describing deviations between our observed values of y and the values generated by the equation.

There are two ways we could proceed in our estimate of the parameters a and b. One is to begin with the scatter of points in Figure 17.1 and attempt to estimate the equation that provides the "best fit." As we will see presently, this procedure amounts to minimizing the sum of the squared vertical distances between the fitted line and the observed points. This technique is wholly mechanical and does not require any assumptions about the distribution of the error term. Another approach is to begin with the meaning of the parameters themselves and produce plausible estimates of those parameters based on assumptions about the error term. We will follow the latter procedure first, later showing that both techniques provide equivalent estimates of the parameters.

Consider the parameters we wish to estimate. Parameter b is the slope, which indicates how a change in x, the independent variable, is translated into the change in y, the dependent variable. Parameter a is the intercept, the value of y when the value of x is zero. If we assume that the sum of the errors is zero (i.e., the errors cancel over the set of observations), then it follows that the sum of the residuals should also equal zero. Using $\hat{a}$ to designate the *estimated* value of a and $\hat{b}$ to designate the estimated value of b, this condition translates into:

$$\sum_{i=1}^{n} \hat{u}_i = \sum_{i=1}^{n} (y_i - \hat{y}_i) = \sum_{i=1}^{n} (y_i - \hat{a} - \hat{b}x_i) = 0$$

where n is the number of observations in the sample.

If we distribute the summation sign over the terms in the last expression, we have:

$$\Sigma y - \Sigma \hat{a} - \Sigma \hat{b}x = \Sigma y - n\hat{a} - \hat{b}\Sigma x = 0$$

since $\hat{a}$ and $\hat{b}$ are constants. Solving for $\hat{a}$, we have:

$$\hat{a} = \frac{\Sigma y}{n} - \hat{b}\frac{\Sigma x}{n} = \bar{y} - \hat{b}\bar{x}$$

In order for the deviations between the fitted line and the data points to sum to zero, it is necessary for the line to pass through the point given by the means of x and y. This is assured if we select the value of the intercept equal to the mean of observed y, minus the mean of x times the slope coefficient, $\hat{b}$. If $x = \bar{x}$, we have:

$$\hat{y} = \hat{a} + \hat{b}\bar{x} = \bar{y} - \hat{b}\bar{x} + \hat{b}\bar{x} = \bar{y}$$

We are still without an estimate for b, the slope. However, since we now know that the fitted line must pass through the point $(\bar{x}, \bar{y})$ we can use this information to establish a point of reference from which to measure deviations in x and y. The deviation between any value of x and its mean is $(x_i - \bar{x})$ and the deviation between any value of y and its mean is $(y_i - \bar{y})$, where the subscript i designates a specific observation. Taking the product of $(x_i - \bar{x})$ and $(y_i - \bar{y})$ for each observation, summing for all observations, and dividing by the number of observations yields the *covariance* between x and y.

$$\text{cov}_{xy} = \frac{\Sigma(x_i - \bar{x})(y_i - \bar{y})}{n}$$

When we divide the covariance between x and y by the variance of x, we obtain an estimator for b, the slope coefficient. Recall from Chapter 16 that the variance in x is given by the sum of the squared deviations between x and its mean divided by the number of observations. Cancelling the n in the numerator and the denominator, we have:

$$\hat{b} = \frac{\Sigma(y - \bar{y})(x - \bar{x})/n}{\Sigma(x - \bar{x})^2/n} = \frac{\Sigma(y - \bar{y})(x - \bar{x})}{\Sigma(x - \bar{x})^2} = \frac{\text{cov}_{xy}}{\text{var}_x}$$

Since the variance is always positive, the sign of $\hat{b}$ depends on the sign of the numerator, the covariance. When y and x generally move in the same direction, as in Figure 17.1, the covariance is positive, and the slope coefficient is positive. When y and x generally move in opposite directions (i.e., when x is greater than its mean, y tends to be less than its mean), the covariance is negative and $\hat{b}$ is negative.

Table 17.2 shows the derivation of the coefficients $\hat{a}$ and $\hat{b}$ using the deviations between x and y and their respective sample means. The first three columns in Table 17.2 are the same as Table 17.1. In the last row we find that the mean for x is 22.65 and the mean for y is 21.56. The fourth and fifth columns give the deviations of x and y, respectively, for each observation. The sixth column is the product of $(x - \bar{x})$ and $(y - \bar{y})$ and the seventh column gives the square of $(x - \bar{x})$. For the present we can ignore the last column. With this information, the slope and intercept coefficients are easily calculated. Dividing the sum of the sixth column by the sum of the seventh column, we have:

$$\hat{b} = \frac{24,959.28}{21,245.65} = 1.175$$

Table 17.2

Country	x	y	$(x-\bar{x})$	$(y-\bar{y})$	$(x-\bar{x})(y-\bar{y})$	$(x-\bar{x})^2$	$(y-\bar{y})^2$
Austria	−6.1	3.7	−28.75	−17.86	513.43	826.63	318.90
Netherlands	2.7	4.2	−19.95	−17.36	346.31	398.05	301.29
Belgium	3.8	4.5	−18.85	−17.06	321.56	355.36	290.97
Canada	4.9	9.1	−17.75	−12.46	221.14	315.10	155.20
Germany, Fed Rep	7.2	4.1	−15.45	−17.46	269.74	238.74	304.77
Venezuela	7.6	12.4	−15.05	−9.16	137.83	226.54	83.86
Switzerland	7.8	3.6	−14.85	−17.96	266.69	220.56	322.48
United States	8.2	11.3	−14.45	−10.26	148.24	208.83	105.22
Kenya	9.3	8.0	−13.35	−13.56	181.01	178.25	183.81
Japan	9.9	3.6	−12.75	−17.96	228.98	162.59	322.48
Nigeria	10.3	11.1	−12.35	−10.46	129.17	152.55	109.37
Phillipines	11.9	18.8	−10.75	−2.76	29.65	115.59	7.61
United Kingdom	12.2	13.4	−10.45	−8.16	85.26	109.23	66.55
France	12.3	10.8	−10.35	−10.76	111.35	107.15	115.73
Sweden	12.6	7.3	−10.05	−14.26	143.31	101.02	203.28
Ethiopia	13.1	16.1	−9.55	−5.46	52.13	91.22	29.79
Burma	13.8	5.7	−8.85	−15.86	140.36	78.34	251.47
Spain	13.8	15.6	−8.85	−5.96	52.73	78.34	35.50
South Africa	15.3	13.1	−7.35	−8.46	62.17	54.04	71.53
Thailand	16.6	9.9	−6.05	−11.66	70.54	36.62	135.90
Morocco	17.0	8.4	−5.65	−13.16	74.36	31.94	173.13
Yugoslavia	17.4	21.3	−5.25	−0.26	1.35	27.57	0.07
Sri Lanka	17.8	10.8	−4.85	−10.76	52.19	23.53	115.73
Algeria	17.8	11.4	−4.85	−10.16	49.28	23.53	103.18
Korea, Rep of	18.0	18.3	−4.65	−3.26	15.15	21.63	10.61
Malaysia	18.0	3.6	−4.65	−17.96	83.52	21.63	322.48
Bangladesh	18.4	12.7	−4.25	−8.86	37.66	18.07	78.46
Portugal	18.4	23.8	−4.25	2.24	−9.53	18.07	5.03
India	19.6	6.4	−3.05	−15.16	46.25	9.31	229.76
Indonesia	19.6	21.9	−3.05	0.34	−1.04	9.31	0.12
Greece	19.7	19.0	−2.95	−2.56	7.55	8.71	6.54
Syria	19.8	4.8	−2.85	−16.76	47.78	8.13	280.82
Pakistan	22.5	9.4	−0.15	−12.16	1.84	0.02	147.81
Italy	23.9	14.7	1.25	−6.86	−8.56	1.56	47.03
Egypt	23.9	9.9	1.25	−11.66	−14.56	1.56	135.90
Columbia	25.0	24.7	2.35	3.14	7.38	5.52	9.87
Ghana	30.3	54.4	7.65	32.84	251.21	58.51	1,078.61
Mexico	31.4	18.2	8.75	−3.36	−29.38	76.54	11.27
Iran	48.1	10.5	25.45	−11.06	−281.41	647.65	122.27
Brazil	51.6	52.7	28.95	31.14	901.53	838.04	969.84
Zaire	54.1	108.6	31.45	87.04	2,737.38	989.03	7,576.35
Turkey	54.8	58.7	32.15	37.14	1,194.08	1,033.55	1,379.54
Peru	59.6	66.7	36.95	45.14	1,667.95	1,365.22	2,037.82
Chile	60.0	33.4	37.35	11.84	442.29	1,394.94	140.24
Argentina	125.4	159.5	102.75	137.94	14,173.41	10,557.33	19,028.06
Total	1,019.3	970.1	0.00	0.00	24,959.28	21,245.65	37,426.27
Mean	22.65	21.56					

Using this result in the formula for $\hat{a}$ we have:

$$\hat{a} = 21.56 - 1.175(22.65) = -5.05$$

Hence, our equation is:

$$\hat{y} = -5.05 + 1.175x$$

Now we turn our attention to the derivation of the least squares estimators of the simple regression equation. Ironically, it is easier to appreciate the least squares regression technique once the equation of the line is known. In Figure 17.2 we have fit the linear equation $y = -5.05 + 1.175x$ to the scatter of points depicted in Figure 17.1. The vertical distance between the line and each point is our estimate of the error term: $\hat{u}_i = y_i - \hat{y}_i$. Since any line that passes through the point $(\bar{x}, \bar{y}) = (22.65, 21.56)$ will guarantee that the sum of the $\hat{u}$'s equals zero, we seek to find that line that minimizes the sum of the squared deviations. This line corresponds to the "best fit" of all lines passing through the mean of the two variables.

The formulas for $\hat{a}$ and $\hat{b}$ are derived by minimizing the sum of the squared estimated errors:

$$\sum_{i=1}^{n} \hat{u}_i^2 = \sum_{i=1}^{n} (y_i - \hat{y}_i)^2 = \sum_{i=1}^{n} (y_i - \hat{a} - \hat{b}x_i)^2$$

Figure 17.2

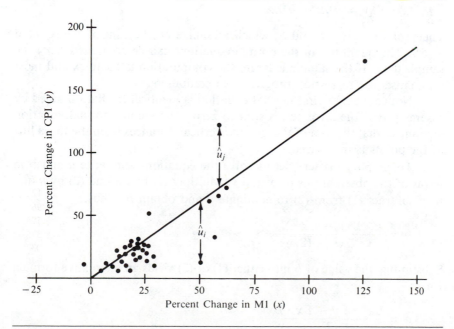

Let

$$D = \hat{u}_1{}^2 + \hat{u}_2{}^2 + \ldots + \hat{u}_n{}^2 = \sum_{i=1}^{n} (y_i - \hat{a} - \hat{b}x_i)^2$$

Quantity D is to be minimized with respect to $\hat{a}$ and $\hat{b}$. We have the necessary conditions:

(1) $\dfrac{\partial D}{\partial \hat{a}} = -2(y_1 - \hat{a} - \hat{b}x_1) - 2(y_2 - \hat{a} - \hat{b}x_2) - \ldots$
$$- 2(y_n - \hat{a} - \hat{b}x_n) = 0$$

(2) $\dfrac{\partial D}{\partial \hat{b}} = -2x_1(y_1 - \hat{a} - \hat{b}x_1) - 2x_2(y_2 - \hat{a} - \hat{b}x_2) - \ldots$
$$- 2x_n(y_n - \hat{a} - \hat{b}x_n) = 0$$

Dividing both sides of each equation by 2 and combining like terms gives:

(1) $\quad -\sum_{i=1}^{n} y_i + \hat{a}n + \hat{b}\sum_{i=1}^{n} x_i = 0$

(2) $\quad -\sum_{i=1}^{n} x_i y_i + \hat{a}\sum_{i=1}^{n} x_i + \hat{b}\sum_{i=1}^{n} x_i{}^2 = 0$

These results are called the *normal equations*. They can be rewritten as:

(1) $\Sigma y = \hat{a}n + \hat{b}\Sigma x$
(2) $\Sigma xy = \hat{a}\Sigma x + \hat{b}\Sigma x^2$

Their solution gives $\hat{a}$ and $\hat{b}$, which minimize D, the sum of the squared errors. The quantities in the normal equations can be computed from the sample data. If the sample is large, the computation is complex and most economists use regression programs on computers.

Notice that the first normal equation is identical to that obtained by assuming that the error terms sum to zero. The second normal equation guarantees that the sum of the *squared* vertical distances from the fitted line to the points is minimized.

To simplify matters, let us solve the equations and write $\hat{a}$ and $\hat{b}$ in terms of the observations on x and y. Multiply (1) by Σx and (2) by n and then subtract (1) from (2) to eliminate $\hat{a}$ and obtain $\hat{b}$. Thus:

$$\hat{b} = \frac{n \cdot \Sigma xy - \Sigma x \cdot \Sigma y}{n \cdot \Sigma x^2 - (\Sigma x)^2}$$

Substituting the value of $\hat{b}$ into either (1) or (2) yields an alternative formula for $\hat{a}$:

$$\hat{a} = \frac{\Sigma x^2 \cdot \Sigma y - \Sigma x \cdot \Sigma xy}{n \cdot \Sigma x^2 - (\Sigma x)^2}$$

To illustrate, let us return to the example of the forty-five observations given in Table 17.1. These are shown again in Table 17.3, where we have $n = 45$. The quantities other than n used to compute $\hat{a}$ and $\hat{b}$ are shown at the bottom of each column. For the present, we can ignore the last column. We substitute the computed values from the table into the formulas for $\hat{a}$ and $\hat{b}$, and obtain:

$$\hat{a} = \frac{(44,333.9)(970.1) - (1,019.3)(46,933.3)}{45(44,333.9) - (1,019.3)^2} = \frac{-4,830,592}{956,053} = -5.05$$

$$\hat{b} = \frac{45(46,933.1) - (1,019.3)(970.1)}{45(44,333.9) - (1,019.3)^2} = \frac{1,123,167}{956,053} = 1.175$$

Hence, our two approaches generate the same equation:

$$\hat{y} = -5.05 + 1.175x$$

This equation provides an estimate of the rate of inflation, that is, y, if the rate of change in M1, x, is given. On the average, each 1 percent increase in the money supply between 1978 and 1979 is predicted to generate an increase in the rate of inflation by 1.175 percent. Although the data were collected from the past (all data are), we still predict the value of the dependent variable in the sense that our sample contains only one possible set of observations.

Recall it is this equation that was used to fit the straight line to the sample of data in Figure 17.2. Hence, the problem of computing the regression of y on x is equivalent to the geometric problem of obtaining the best fit of a line to a scatter of points by means of least squares techniques. The size of the errors committed in fitting the line and predicting y from it are equivalent to the values of $\hat{u}$ as shown in Figure 17.2.

The formulas for minimizing the squared deviations about the regression line were used to compute the values of the sample statistics $\hat{a}$ and $\hat{b}$ in Table 17.3. Those computed in Table 17.2 were derived from assumptions about the error term. Although the estimates of a and b are identical in this case, we require a general proof.

From the second normal equation we have:

$$(2) \quad \Sigma xy - \frac{\Sigma x \Sigma y}{n} = \left(\Sigma x^2 - \frac{(\Sigma x)^2}{n} \right) \hat{b}$$

This can be equivalently (if redundantly) expressed as:

$$(2') \quad \Sigma xy - \frac{2\Sigma x \Sigma y}{n} + \frac{\Sigma x \Sigma y}{n} = \left(\Sigma x^2 - \frac{2(\Sigma x)^2}{n} + \frac{(\Sigma x)^2}{n} \right) \hat{b}$$

or

$$\Sigma(x - \bar{x})(y - \bar{y}) = \Sigma(x - \bar{x})^2 \hat{b}$$

This implies:

$$\hat{b} = \frac{\Sigma(x - \bar{x})(y - \bar{y})}{\Sigma(x - \bar{x})^2}$$

Table 17.3

Country	x	y	xy	x^2	y^2
Austria	−6.1	3.7	−22.57	37.21	13.69
Netherlands	2.7	4.2	11.34	7.29	17.64
Belgium	3.8	4.5	17.10	14.44	20.25
Canada	4.9	9.1	44.59	24.01	82.81
Germany, Fed Rep	7.2	4.1	29.52	51.84	16.81
Venezuela	7.6	12.4	94.24	57.76	153.76
Switzerland	7.8	3.6	28.08	60.84	12.96
United States	8.2	11.3	92.66	67.24	127.69
Kenya	9.3	8.0	74.40	86.49	64.00
Japan	9.9	3.6	35.64	98.01	12.96
Nigeria	10.3	11.1	114.33	106.09	123.21
Phillipines	11.9	18.8	223.72	141.61	353.44
United Kingdom	12.2	13.4	163.48	148.84	179.56
France	12.3	10.8	132.84	151.29	116.64
Sweden	12.6	7.3	91.98	158.76	53.29
Ethiopia	13.1	16.1	210.91	171.61	259.21
Burma	13.8	5.7	78.66	190.44	32.49
Spain	13.8	15.6	215.28	190.44	243.36
South Africa	15.3	13.1	200.43	234.09	171.61
Thailand	16.6	9.9	164.34	275.56	98.01
Morocco	17.0	8.4	142.8	289.00	70.56
Yugoslavia	17.4	21.3	370.62	302.76	453.69
Sri Lanka	17.8	10.8	192.24	316.84	116.64
Algeria	17.8	11.4	202.92	316.84	129.96
Korea, Rep of	18.0	18.3	329.40	324.00	334.89
Malaysia	18.0	3.6	64.80	324.00	12.96
Bangladesh	18.4	12.7	233.68	338.56	161.29
Portugal	18.4	23.8	437.92	338.56	566.44
India	19.6	6.4	125.44	384.16	40.96
Indonesia	19.6	21.9	429.24	384.16	479.61
Greece	19.7	19.0	374.30	388.09	361.00
Syria	19.8	4.8	95.04	392.04	23.04
Pakistan	22.5	9.4	211.50	506.25	88.36
Italy	23.9	14.7	351.33	571.21	216.09
Egypt	23.9	9.9	236.61	571.21	98.01
Columbia	25.0	24.7	617.50	625.00	610.09
Ghana	30.3	54.4	1,648.32	918.09	2,959.36
Mexico	31.4	18.2	571.48	985.96	331.24
Iran	48.1	10.5	505.05	2,313.61	110.25
Brazil	51.6	52.7	2,719.32	2,662.56	2,777.29
Zaire	54.1	108.6	5,875.26	2,926.81	11,793.96
Turkey	54.8	58.7	3,216.76	3,003.04	3,445.69
Peru	59.6	66.7	3,975.32	3,552.16	4,448.89
Chile	60.0	33.4	2,004.00	3,600.00	1,115.56
Argentina	125.4	159.5	20,001.30	15,725.16	25,440.25
Total	1,019.3	970.1	46,933.12	44,333.93	58,339.47

From the first normal equation:

(1) $n\hat{a} + \hat{b}\Sigma x = \Sigma y$

or

$$\hat{a} = \frac{\Sigma y}{n} - \hat{b}\left(\frac{\Sigma x}{n}\right)$$

Hence, we find that the estimator of the slope parameter can be calculated as the ratio of the sample covariance between x and y to the sample variance of x. The intercept parameter can be estimated as the mean of y minus the mean of x times the slope coefficient. These parameter estimates are equivalent to those obtained by minimizing the sum of the squared residuals of the regression equation. For this reason, this approach is also called *ordinary least squares regression*.

THE RELIABILITY OF
ORDINARY LEAST SQUARES

We have seen that the formulas for the least-squares coefficients can be derived as a straightforward minimization problem, based on a sample of observations on the dependent and independent variables. These estimated coefficients are sample statistics because different sets of observations would yield different values of those coefficients. Although most economists have at their disposal only one set of observations from which to estimate a regression equation, it is important to remember that those observations constitute but one sample of an infinite number of possible samples of observations. We can view the error term u as a random variable that distinguishes the sample of observations being used from the infinite population of observations from which it was drawn. It follows that the assumptions we make about the error term determine how confident we are about the accuracy of our calculated coefficients—that is, how closely our coefficients approximate the unknown population parameters.

The Gauss-Markov Theorem

The assumptions we make about the error term are as follows:

1. The expected value of the error term is zero: $E(u) = 0$. This is equivalent to invoking the *law of large numbers* which specifies that if an observed variable has many random independent causes, they will tend to cancel in the aggregate, yielding a zero expected value for that variable. As we will see in Chapter 19, this assumption is violated when *important* variables are omitted from the regression equation.

2. The value of u is independent of the value of x, the independent variable: $E(xu) = 0$. Violation of this assumption occurs when x, treated as an exogenous variable, is actually an endogenous variable, casting suspicion on ordinary least squares results.

3. The variance in the error term is constant over the observations. That is, the variance in u does not change *systematically* with the value of x.

4. The error terms for different observations are independent of each other. Violation of assumption 3 or assumption 4 would compromise the *reliability* of the regression estimate.

When these four assumptions are satisfied, the ordinary least squares estimators have some desirable qualities: They are *unbiased*, *consistent*, and *efficient*. Unbiasedness means that the expected values of $\hat{a}$ and $\hat{b}$ are equal to their "true" values. That is, if we estimated those coefficients from an infinite number of random samples of data, the average value of $\hat{a}$ would be its true value and the average value of $\hat{b}$ would be its true value. A set of least squares estimates would be *biased* if either of the first two assumptions about the error term were violated.

Suppose, for instance, that the "true" equation for y is given as:

$$y = a + bx + cz + u$$

where u conforms to our four assumptions. If we attempted to estimate an equation with x as the only systematic influence on y, our model would become:

$$y = a + bx + v$$

where $v = cz + u$. The expected value of v would equal zero only if $E(cz) = 0$; that is, only if $c = 0$ or if the influence of z cancelled in the aggregate (e.g., due to the law of large numbers). The least squares estimators for a and b would be derived under the assumption that $E(v) = 0$. If this assumption were false, those estimators would always be erroneous, regardless of the number of samples we used.

Similar results would occur if the (alleged) independent variable were really simultaneously determined with the (left-side) dependent variable. The least squares estimation technique attributes the joint variation between x and y to the influence of x on y and not to the influence of y on x. If x does depend on y, the least squares coefficients will have been calculated on a false premise. The calculated values of $\hat{b}$ and $\hat{a}$ would be biased.

Consistency means that as the sample size used to estimate the coefficients increases, the *standard error* of those estimates approaches zero. As we will see in later chapters, there are certain situations in which unbiased estimates of the parameters are unattainable because one or more of the assumptions about the error term are violated. In such cases researchers must content themselves with consistency: as the sample size grows, the degree of biasedness decreases.

Efficiency means that the ordinary least squares estimators have the minimum variance of all possible estimating techniques. Remember that least squares estimators are sample statistics whose distributional characteristics determine their reliability. When the four assumptions about the error term are true, then the least squares estimators have the smallest variance of all possible linear unbiased estimators. When one or more of these assumptions is false, there may be other estimating techniques that are more reliable than ordinary least squares.

The characteristics of the least squares estimators are summarized formally by the Gauss-Markov theorem,[1] which we will merely state here without proof. When all four assumptions about the error term are true, ordinary least squares estimates are said to be *BLUE*, meaning *best linear unbiased estimators*. We have already discussed unbiasedness as the characteristic that assures that the expected value of the estimated coefficients equals the respective population parameters. *Linear* means that the estimated equation is linear in its parameters, even though, as we will see in the last section of this chapter, the variables themselves may be nonlinear transformations of some other variables. The "best" estimating technique is the one that minimizes the expected difference between the "true" and fitted regression lines. This corresponds to the efficiency property.

We will see in subsequent chapters that violations of either of the first two assumptions about the error term (i.e., when important variables are omitted, or when the right-side variable is endogenous) cause the least squares results to become biased and inconsistent. On the other hand, violations of the third or fourth assumptions (i.e., when the variance in the error term is not constant or when different error terms are correlated) compromise the efficiency of least squares estimates.

The Standard Error of the
Slope Coefficient

We have seen that simple regression analysis involves the *estimation* of the relationship between two variables in a population using sample data. As in any statistical analysis involving samples, some error is bound to occur. Indeed, we make this explicit by the introduction of the error term u into the econometric model. Since the slope coefficient $\hat{b}$ is a random variable whose value would change from one sample to another, it will have an associated sampling distribution. We have already seen that the *expected value* of $\hat{b}$ will equal b, the true population parameter, when the Gauss-Markov assumptions are met. Nevertheless, it is virtually certain that the calculated value of $\hat{b}$ will be different from the true value of b. The *expected absolute*

---

[1] Interested readers can find a proof of this theorem in J. Johnston, *Econometric Methods*, third edition, McGraw-Hill, 1984, p. 173.

difference between b and $\hat{b}$ is called the *standard error of* $\hat{b}$ and is analogous to the standard deviation in the sampling distribution of a variable.

Although the standard error of $\hat{b}$ is routinely reported in the results of regressions fit by computer, it is important to understand how this statistic is measured so that we can use it appropriately.

The *variance in y given x* is defined as the sum of the squared deviations in y around the regression line, divided by the degrees of freedom, which in this case is $n - 2$ since one degree of freedom is used up in calculating each of $\hat{a}$ and $\hat{b}$:

$$s_{\hat{y}}^2 = \frac{\Sigma(y - \hat{y})^2}{n - 2} = \frac{\Sigma(y - \hat{a} - \hat{b}x)^2}{n - 2}$$

The statistic $s_{\hat{y}}$, which is the square root of $s_{\hat{y}}^2$, is called the *standard error of the regression* since it measures the average difference between the observed and predicted values of y. To get the standard error of the coefficient $\hat{b}$, we divide the standard error of the regression by the sum of the squared deviations about x:

$$s_{\hat{b}}^2 = \frac{s_{\hat{y}}^2}{\Sigma(x - \overline{x})^2} = \frac{\Sigma(y - \hat{y})^2}{(n - 2)\Sigma(x - \overline{x})^2} = \frac{\Sigma(y - \hat{a} - \hat{b}x)^2}{(n - 2)\Sigma(x - \overline{x})^2}$$

Table 17.4 presents information on x and y from Tables 17.1 through 17.3. In addition, it reports the predicted value of y for each observation (country), and uses this information to compute $\hat{u} = y - \hat{y}$ and $\hat{u}^2$. We see from Table 17.4 that $\Sigma\hat{u}^2 = \Sigma(y - \hat{y})^2 = 8,104.246$. Since $n = 45$, $n - 2 = 43$, and:

$$s_{\hat{y}}^2 = \frac{8,104.25}{43} = 188.47$$

From Table 17.2 we find that $\Sigma(x - \overline{x})^2 = 21,245.65$. It follows that:

$$s_{\hat{b}}^2 = \frac{188.47}{21,245.65} = 0.0089$$

Taking the square root of $s_{\hat{b}}^2$, we have the standard error of $\hat{b}$:

$$s_{\hat{b}} = \sqrt{0.0089} = 0.0942$$

The occasion may arise when we wish to compute the standard error of $\hat{b}$ without first calculating $\hat{u}$ for each observation. Substituting the formulas for $\hat{a}$ and $\hat{b}$ and doing some tedious algebra, we find:

$$s_{\hat{b}}^2 = \frac{n\Sigma y^2 - (\Sigma y)^2 - \left(\dfrac{(n\Sigma xy - \Sigma x\Sigma y)^2}{n\Sigma x^2 - (\Sigma x)^2}\right)}{(n - 2)[n\Sigma x^2 - (\Sigma x)^2]}$$

You may wish to demonstrate that an equivalent value of $s_{\hat{b}}$ can be obtained using only information available in Table 17.3.

Table 17.4

Country	x	y	$\hat{y}$	$\hat{u} = y - \hat{y}$	$\hat{u}^2$
Austria	−6.1	3.7	−12.22	15.92	253.33
Netherlands	2.7	4.2	−1.88	6.08	36.94
Belgium	3.8	4.5	−0.59	5.09	25.87
Canada	4.9	9.1	0.71	8.39	70.45
Germany, Fed Rep	7.2	4.1	3.41	0.69	0.48
Venezuela	7.6	12.4	3.88	8.52	72.62
Switzerland	7.8	3.6	4.11	−0.51	0.26
United States	8.2	11.3	4.58	6.72	45.12
Kenya	9.3	8.0	5.88	2.12	4.51
Japan	9.9	3.6	6.58	−2.98	8.88
Nigeria	10.3	11.1	7.05	4.05	16.40
Phillipines	11.9	18.8	8.93	9.87	97.42
United Kingdom	12.2	13.4	9.28	4.12	16.96
France	12.3	10.8	9.40	1.40	1.96
Sweden	12.6	7.3	9.75	−2.45	6.01
Ethiopia	13.1	16.1	10.34	5.76	33.18
Burma	13.8	5.7	11.16	−5.46	29.83
Spain	13.8	15.6	11.16	4.44	19.70
South Africa	15.3	13.1	12.92	0.18	0.03
Thailand	16.6	9.9	14.45	−4.55	20.71
Morocco	17.0	8.4	14.92	−6.52	42.53
Yugoslavia	17.4	21.3	15.39	5.91	34.92
Algeria	17.8	11.4	15.86	−4.46	19.90
Sri Lanka	17.8	10.8	15.86	−5.06	25.61
Malaysia	18.0	3.6	16.10	−12.50	156.15
Korea, Rep of	18.0	18.3	16.10	2.20	4.86
Portugal	18.4	23.8	16.57	7.23	52.33
Bangladesh	18.4	12.7	16.57	−3.87	14.95
Indonesia	19.6	21.9	17.98	3.92	15.40
India	19.6	6.4	17.98	−11.58	133.99
Greece	19.7	19.0	18.09	0.91	0.82
Syria	19.8	4.8	18.21	−13.41	179.84
Pakistan	22.5	9.4	21.38	−11.98	143.58
Italy	23.9	14.7	23.03	−8.33	69.34
Egypt	23.9	9.9	23.03	−13.13	172.32
Columbia	25.0	24.7	24.32	0.38	0.14
Ghana	30.3	54.4	30.55	23.85	569.02
Mexico	31.4	18.2	31.84	−13.64	186.00
Iran	48.1	10.5	51.46	−40.96	1,677.46
Brazil	51.6	52.7	55.57	−2.87	8.23
Zaire	54.1	108.6	58.51	50.09	2,509.46
Turkey	54.8	58.7	59.33	−0.63	0.39
Peru	59.6	66.7	64.97	1.73	3.00
Chile	60.0	33.4	65.44	−32.04	1,026.35
Argentina	125.4	159.5	142.27	17.23	296.96
Total	1,019.3	970.1	970.1999	−0.09999	8,104.246
Mean	22.65	21.56	21.56	0.00	180.09

The standard error of $\hat{b}$ can be interpreted as the expected deviation between the true but unknown value of b and the computed value $\hat{b}$. When the standard error of $\hat{b}$ is large relative to $\hat{b}$ itself, we generally infer that the estimate of b is unreliable. This inference is formalized in hypothesis testing.

Testing Hypotheses About the Slope Coefficient

Econometricians estimate regression equations to test hypotheses about the parameters of the true, but unknown equation. For instance, if we believe that there is a linear relationship between x and y, but we do not know whether the relationship is positive or negative, we stipulate the alternative hypothesis H_a: $b \neq 0$, which implies the null hypothesis H_o: $b = 0$. Since the probability of obtaining the result $\hat{b} = 0$ is zero, we would not be justified in rejecting the null hypothesis simply because the measured value of $\hat{b}$ is not precisely 0. Here is where the standard error of $\hat{b}$ comes into play. The value of $s_{\hat{b}}$ tells us how close to zero we would expect the computed value of $\hat{b}$ to be if the true value of b actually equals zero.

We have assumed that the errors u are randomly distributed and independent. These assumptions assure us that the ordinary least squares estimators are *BLUE*. If the distribution of errors is approximately normal, the quantity

$$t = \frac{\hat{b} - b}{s_{\hat{b}}}$$

follows the t distribution with $n - 2$ degrees of freedom. The number of degrees of freedom is two less than the number of observations because two coefficients ($\hat{a}$ and $\hat{b}$) have already been calculated from the sample data. We can see that t is a measure of the difference between the estimated coefficient and the hypothetical population parameter, taking account of sampling variability. It is useful for establishing confidence limits and tests of significance.

There are two ways we can test hypotheses about the slope coefficient. First, we can compute a confidence interval for b based on the estimated values of $\hat{b}$ and $s_{\hat{b}}$. If the value of b stipulated by the *null hypothesis*, say b_0, lies outside of the confidence interval for b (that is, if the confidence interval does not include b_0), we reject the null hypothesis ($b = b_0$) in favor of the alternative hypothesis ($b \neq b_0$). If the value of b stipulated by the null hypothesis lies within the confidence interval for b, we would *not* reject the null hypothesis with the appropriate level of confidence.

Let us first compute the 95 percent and the 99 percent confidence intervals for b, with $n - 2 = 43$ degrees of freedom. Since we are using two-tail tests, the critical values of t are 1.992 and 2.686 for 95 percent and

and 99 percent confidence, respectively. The 95 percent confidence interval for b is:

$$b = \hat{b} \pm (1.992)s_{\hat{b}} = 1.175 \pm (1.992)(0.0942)$$

or

$$0.987 < b < 1.363$$

Similarly, the 99 percent confidence interval for b is:

$$b = \hat{b} \pm (2.686)s_{\hat{b}} = 1.175 \pm (2.686)(0.0942)$$

or

$$0.922 < b < 1.428$$

Suppose we wish to test the null hypothesis that $b = 0$, that is, that a change in the money stock of individual countries has no impact on their rates of inflation. Since $b = 0$ falls outside of the 99 percent confidence interval, we may reject the null hypothesis with 99 percent confidence. The chance that changes in the money stock have no effect on the rate of inflation for countries in 1979 is less than 1 in 100.

On the other hand, suppose that we wished to test the widely held conviction that a stipulated change in the money stock will cause an equal percentage change in the CPI, that is, that $b_0 = 1$. In this case we note that the value $b = 1$ falls inside the 95 percent confidence interval. Hence, even though our estimate, $\hat{b}$, differs from the value stipulated by the null hypothesis, we cannot reject that null hypothesis with 95 percent confidence.

The advantage of the confidence interval in hypothesis testing is that we can test multiple null hypotheses about the value of the parameter by computing one confidence interval. In this case we found we could reject the null hypothesis that $b = 0$ but we could not reject the null hypothesis that $b = 1$. However, as discussed in Chapter 16, there is a distinct disadvantage to confidence intervals in hypothesis testing. The confidence interval involves two tails in testing the null hypothesis, which implies that the alternative hypothesis does not stipulate whether the true slope coefficient is greater than or less than the value embedded in the null hypothesis. In our example, the appropriate alternative hypothesis is H_a: $b > 0$, implying the null hypothesis H_o: $b \leq 0$. If the computed value of b were negative, we would accept the null hypothesis, regardless of whether $b = 0$ fell into the confidence interval.

For a one-tail t test, we first calculate the statistic:

$$t = \frac{\hat{b} - b_0}{s_{\hat{b}}}$$

where b_0 is the value of the slope parameter under the null hypothesis. Then the significance of the slope coefficient is obtained from a table of t values.

For the alternative hypothesis $b = dy/dx > 0$, we calculate t as:

$$t = \frac{1.175 - 0}{s_{\hat{b}}} = \frac{1.175}{0.0942} = 12.47$$

Since the critical value of t for 1 percent significance with 43 degrees of freedom is 2.39, we can clearly reject the null hypothesis that $b \leq 0$.

Suppose we wished to prove that $dy/dx < 1$. That is, our alternative hypothesis is H_a: $b < 1$ and the null hypothesis is H_o: $b \geq 1$. In this case the calculated value of t is $t = (1.175 - 1)/0.0942 = 0.175/0.0942 = 1.847$. We cannot reject the null hypothesis since the numerator of the t statistic, namely $\hat{b} - b_0$, is positive while the "expected" sign is negative. However, if our alternative hypothesis were $dy/dx > 1$, we calculate the same t statistic: $t = (1.175 - 1)/0.0942 = 1.847$. This t statistic has the "expected" sign and is greater than the critical value of 1.66 for 5 percent significance. We can reject the null hypothesis that $b \leq 1$ with more than 95 percent confidence, but with less than 99 percent confidence.

In summary, as long as the sign on $\hat{b} - b_0$ conforms to the prediction of the alternative hypothesis, using a two-tail test instead of a one-tail test increases the probability of type II error—the acceptance of a false null hypothesis. When t statistics are large in absolute value, the probability of type II error is low, regardless of whether a one-tail or two-tail test is used. However, when the t statistic is low, or when its sign is "wrong," one-tail tests are usually preferred.

Testing Hypotheses About the
Intercept Coefficient

Although econometricians most frequently test hypotheses about the value of the slope parameter, b, we occasionally wish to test hypotheses about the value of the intercept parameter, a. In our example, we may believe that the rate of inflation is proportional to the rate of change of the money stock, i.e., that $b = 1$ and $a = 0$. If the true value of a is zero, the true regression line passes through the origin and has equation $y = bx + u$. The mechanics of forcing a regression line through the origin are discussed in Chapter 18.

We have already tested the hypothesis that $b = 1$. To test the hypothesis that $a = 0$, we require a measure of the standard error of a, $s_{\hat{a}}$. The square of $s_{\hat{a}}$ is:

$$s_{\hat{a}}^2 = s_{\hat{y}}^2 \cdot \frac{\Sigma x^2}{n\Sigma(x - \overline{x})^2} = \frac{\Sigma(y - \hat{y})^2 \cdot \Sigma x^2}{n(n - 2)\Sigma(x - \overline{x})^2}$$

From Table 17.4 we have $\Sigma(y - \hat{y})^2 = 8,104.246$; from Table 17.3 we find $\Sigma x^2 = 44,333.93$; and from Table 17.2 we learn that $\Sigma(x - \overline{x})^2 = 21,245.65$. Using this information, we compute $s_{\hat{a}}^2$ as:

$$s_{\hat{a}}^2 = \frac{(3,104.246)(44,333.93)}{45(43)(21,245.65)} = \frac{359,293,074.9}{41,110,332.75} = 8.74$$

Therefore, $s_{\hat{a}} = \sqrt{s_{\hat{a}}^2} = \sqrt{8.74} = 2.96$.

Since $a = -5.05$, our t statistic is:

$$t = \frac{-5.05}{2.96} = -1.71$$

We are willing to reject the null hypothesis ($a = 0$) if t is significantly greater or significantly less than its critical value. Therefore, a *two-tail t* test is in order. With 43 degrees of freedom, the critical value for 5 percent significance is $t = \pm 1.99$. Since our value of t is smaller (in absolute value) than the critical value, we fail to reject the null hypothesis that $a = 0$.

While we have discussed how to calculate the standard errors and the t statistics "by hand" for the slope and intercept coefficients, many regression programs print these statistics as a matter of course in reporting regression results. Nevertheless, it is up to the researcher to determine whether a one-tail or two-tail test is more appropriate. Furthermore, the researcher will have to calculate the t statistics for null hypotheses other than the standard ones: $b \leq 0$ and $b \geq 0$.

SIMPLE CORRELATION

A measure of the degree to which two variables are related is given by the *sample correlation coefficient*, usually designated by r. If two variables x and y are linearly related, the value of r measures the extent to which observed changes in x are matched by changes in y, either in the same or in the opposite direction. It is a pure number, so that the units in which x and y are measured do not affect the value of r. The number r can range between -1 and $+1$. If r is positive, then y generally increases when x increases and generally decreases when x decreases. If r is negative, then y generally increases when x decreases and generally decreases when x increases. If r is zero, then we infer that there is neither a positive nor a negative relationship between x and y and the two variables are *statistically independent* of one another.

Suppose r turns out to be equal to $+1$. In this case, there is a perfect positive correlation between x and y in the sample. Diagrammatically, all the observed sample points (x, y) lie on a straight line running from lower left to upper right, as in Figure 17.3a. If r turns out to be -1, there is a

Figure 17.3a

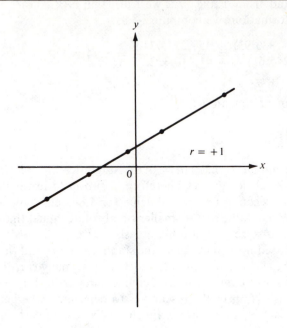

Figure 17.3b

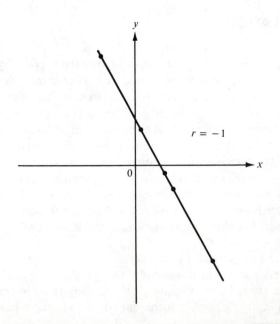

Figure 17.3c

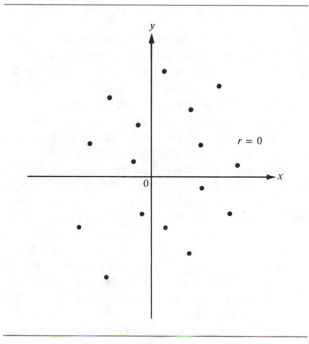

$r = 0$

perfect negative correlation between x and y. All sample points lie exactly on a line running from upper left to lower right, as in Figure 17.3b. When r is found to be zero, there is no distinguishable line formed by the sample scatter diagram. An example of zero correlation is depicted in Figure 17.3c.

In practice, we almost never observe either perfect correlation or zero correlation. Usually r is some (positive or negative) number whose absolute value lies between zero and one. But the closer the absolute value is to one, the greater is the degree of correlation—the closer will the scatter of points approximate a straight line. Naturally, the more the scatter of points diverge from a straight line, the closer r is to zero.[2]

Based on information in Table 17.2, the correlation coefficient can be computed as $r = 0.8851$; the change in the rate of inflation and the change in the money stock tend to move together. But although the positive correlation is close to $+1$, the relationship is not perfect.

The concepts of correlation and regression give different types of information, but there is a connection between them. If the correlation coefficient is positive, the slope of the fitted regression line is also positive. Conversely, if r is negative, $\hat{b}$ is also negative. Finally, it follows that if r

[2]If all the points lie on a line with zero slope, the correlation coefficient will be zero also. For variations in one variable are not associated with variations in the other. Changes in x, for example, are not correlated with changes in y.

is zero, then $\hat{b}$ is also zero. Nevertheless, the concepts of regression and correlation differ in two important ways:

1. A regression model selects one of the variables as the independent or predictor variable and the other variable as the dependent or predicted variable. That is, regression analysis assumes a causal relationship between the two variables. Correlation analysis does not imply a causal relationship. The same correlation coefficient for x and y would be consistent with a model that x causes y or that y causes x or that the two variables are mutually determined. Correlations are sometimes observed between quantities that could not conceivably be causally related (such as soil erosion in Alaska and the amount of alcohol consumed in South America). Such correlations are sometimes called spurious or nonsense correlations.

2. A given correlation coefficient is consistent with an infinite number of straight lines. If we were to shift every point in Figure 17.3a upward or downward by an equal amount, the correlation coefficient would still be equal to $+1$. The regression equation would have a different y-intercept, however. Likewise, if we rotate all the points around one given point in Figure 17.3b so that they fall exactly on a different straight line (with a different slope), the regression coefficient $\hat{b}$ would change (and perhaps $\hat{a}$) but the correlation coefficient would still equal -1. In other words, the correlation coefficient measures the degree to which the points scatter about a fitted straight line, but it does not give the equation for the fitted line.

Computation of the

Correlation Coefficient

To grasp the importance of the correlation coefficient, we shall first consider its statistical meaning. It is the ratio of the standard deviation of the predicted values of the dependent variable to the standard deviation of the observed values of the dependent variable. Let s_y represent the standard deviation of the actual values of y in the sample. Let $s_{\hat{y}}$ designate the standard deviation of the predicted values of y. Hence:

$$r = \frac{s_{\hat{y}}}{s_y}$$

This then is a measure of the closeness of the relationship between the two variables y and $\hat{y}$. It compares the variation in y that is associated with variations in x ($s_{\hat{y}}$) to the variation in y (s_y).

The formula for the practical computation of the numerical value of the simple correlation coefficient is:

$$r = \frac{\Sigma(x - \bar{x})(y - \bar{y})}{\sqrt{\Sigma(x - \bar{x})^2 \Sigma(y - \bar{y})^2}}$$

where $\bar{x}$ and $\bar{y}$ are the sample means of x and y. Note that the numerator of this expression is identical to the numerator of the estimator for the slope coefficient $\hat{b}$ expressed in deviation form. Indeed, if we have already calculated the value of $\hat{b}$ using the deviation formula, we can calculate the correlation coefficient from the transformation:

$$r = \hat{b} \cdot \frac{\sqrt{\Sigma(x - \bar{x})^2}}{\sqrt{\Sigma(y - \bar{y})^2}}$$

From Table 17.2 we have $\Sigma(x - \bar{x})^2 = 21{,}245.65$ and $\Sigma(y - \bar{y})^2 = 37{,}426.27$. Hence:

$$r = 1.175 \cdot \frac{145.76}{193.46} = 0.885$$

If we have not computed the slope coefficient and wish to compute r directly, the information in Table 17.2 provides the most straightforward computation:

$$r = \frac{24{,}959.28}{\sqrt{(21{,}245.65)(37{,}426.27)}} = \frac{24{,}959.28}{28{,}198.32} = 0.885$$

This value is positive, indicating that x and y are positively related. But we already knew this from the value of $\hat{b} = 1.175$. But the value of r reveals another valuable piece of information: The square of the correlation coefficient, r^2, gives the percentage of the variation of the dependent variable that can be attributed to the variation in the independent variable. This quantity is called the *coefficient of determination*.

If $r = +1$ or if $r = -1$, then $r^2 = 1$, and all the variation in y can be attributed to the variation in x. This implies that the errors $\hat{u}$ in the regression equation are all equal to zero; there are no deviations of points from the fitted line. At the other extreme if $r = 0$, then $r^2 = 0$, and none of the variation in y is attributed to the variation in x. All of the variation in y is due to the "unexplained" component $\hat{u}$. We say that there is no linear relationship between x and y (although there may be a nonlinear one). In our example, we found that $r = 0.885$; therefore, $r^2 = 0.783$. We may conclude that about 78 percent of the variation in y, in this sample, can be explained by the linear regression of y on x:

$$\hat{y} = -5.05 + 1.175x$$

The remaining 22 percent of the total variation in y is unaccounted for: the errors in the prediction of y amount to 22 percent.

Tests of Significance

Just as for other sample statistics, it is possible to test hypotheses about the value of r. One way of testing the hypothesis that there is a linear relation between variable y and variable x is to use the null hypothesis that $r = 0$.

The correlation coefficient is a proportion whose variance is given by $1 - r^2$. The standard deviation of the correlation coefficient for the underlying population is given by:

$$s_r = \frac{\sqrt{1 - r^2}}{\sqrt{n - 2}}$$

Notice that two degrees of freedom are used up in computing the correlation coefficient. As with other null hypothesis tests, we compute a t statistic, whose numerator is the difference between the computed r and that stipulated by the null hypothesis, $H_o: r_0 = 0$, and whose denominator is the standard error of r:

$$t = \frac{r - 0}{s_r} = \frac{r\sqrt{n - 2}}{\sqrt{1 - r^2}}$$

If we reject the null hypothesis, we say that r is significant; there is less than a 5 percent chance that variables x and y are statistically independent.

In our example, $r = 0.885$, $r^2 = 0.783$, and $n - 2 = 43$. Using this information, we compute:

$$t = \frac{(0.885)\sqrt{43}}{\sqrt{1 - 0.783}} = \frac{(0.885)(6.557)}{\sqrt{0.217}} = \frac{5.80}{0.465} = 12.47$$

This t statistic is identical to the one we computed for the null hypothesis that $b = 0$. The null hypothesis that $r = 0$ is equivalent to the null hypothesis that $b = 0$.

NONLINEAR FUNCTIONS AND
ORDINARY LEAST SQUARES

Up to this point we have assumed that the "true" equation describing the function $y = f(x)$ is linear, both in its parameters and in its variables. However, ordinary least squares techniques are also applicable to functional forms that are nonlinear in their variables, as long as they are linear in their parameters. In this section we will review how functions that generate nonlinear graphs may be estimated using ordinary least squares techniques.

Generally, theoretical considerations will enable us to judge whether a relationship between two variables should be positive or negative. For instance, in economics we expect an inverse relation between the quantity demanded of a commodity and its price. Often, however, theory does not permit us to infer the relation as linear or nonlinear, except in some special instances. One exception is the theory of cost, where the law of diminishing returns implies that marginal cost is an increasing function of output, so that the slope of the total cost function varies from one rate of output to another.

When theory does not provide a hint about the functional form of an equation, one procedure is to take a look at the sample data by plotting a scattergram. The general form of the scatter may suggest that a linear equation gives a good approximation of the plotted points. According to the principle of *Occam's razor* the simplest explanation for a phenomenon is the preferred explanation in the absence of any compelling evidence to the contrary. Hence, the assumption of a linear relationship between variables often serves as a null hypothesis against which the investigator can test an alternative specification.

The techniques of simple linear regression are easily extended to the case of nonlinear equations. Suppose we suspect that the relationship between total cost, C, and the rate of output, q, should be described by a parabola of the form:

$$C = a + bq^2 + u$$

This equation is nonlinear in the variables but linear in the parameters. Starting with observations on output and cost, the researcher computes a new variable for each observation, the square of output: $q^2 = q \cdot q$. Using the variable q^2 as the independent variable, and C as the dependent variable, the researcher fits the equation:

$$C = a + bq^2 + u$$

The coefficient b is the estimated impact of a change in q^2 on C. To obtain the formula for marginal cost, we take the derivative of C with respect to q, using the chain rule:

$$\frac{dC}{dq} = \frac{dC}{dq^2} \cdot \frac{dq^2}{dq} = \hat{b}(2q) = 2\hat{b}q$$

In this case the researcher would test the null hypothesis that $b > 0$ to verify that cost does increase as the rate of output increases.

There are other types of nonlinear equations that can be estimated with ordinary least squares. Suppose we wish to compute the coefficients in the equation:

$$y = ax^b e^u$$

In this case, the two parameters, a and b represent a multiplicative constant and an exponent, respectively. Furthermore, the error term is expressed as an exponent of the base of the natural logarithms, e. By taking logarithms to the base e of both sides of the equation, we obtain:

$$\log_e y = \log_e a + b \log_e x + u$$

If we set $\log_e y = z$, $\log_e x = w$, and $\log_e a = A$ (a constant), then we can rewrite the equation as:

$$z = A + bw + u$$

This is a linear equation, and a simple regression of z on w can be computed by the methods in the first section of this chapter. The practical procedure is first to compute $z = \log_e y$ and $w = \log_e x$ for each observation of the sample. (Most regression programs have subroutines for this task.) Then fit the regression:

$$\hat{z} = \hat{A} + \hat{b}w$$

using simple regression procedures. Since $A = \log_e a$, $a = e^A$. Hence, we reconvert the regression equation into its original form:

$$\hat{y} = \hat{a}x^{\hat{b}}$$

If $b = 0$, then our equation becomes $y = ax^0 = a$; the value of y is independent of the value of x. Hence, the null hypothesis that y is independent of x could be tested by calculating:

$$t = \frac{\hat{b} - 0}{s_{\hat{b}}} = \frac{\hat{b}}{s_{\hat{b}}}$$

where $s_{\hat{b}}$ is the standard error of $\hat{b}$.

If $b = 1$, the equation becomes $y = ax^1 = ax$, a linear relationship. We could test the null hypothesis that the relation between y and x is linear by computing the t statistic:

$$t = \frac{\hat{b} - 1}{s_{\hat{b}}}$$

If this test statistic is positive and significant, we accept the alternative hypothesis that $d^2y/dx^2 > 0$. If t is negative and significant we reject the null hypothesis that the relationship is linear and accept the alternative hypothesis that $d^2y/dx^2 < 0$.

Similarly, the exponential function:

$$y = ae^{bx+u} = e^{A+bx+u}$$

could be estimated by first taking the logarithm of both sides:

$$\log_e y = \log_e a + bx + u = A + bx + u$$

and estimating:

$$\log_e \hat{y} = \hat{A} + \hat{b}x$$

Again the null hypothesis that y is independent of x could be tested by determining whether b is significantly different from zero.

Thus, a nonlinear equation can be converted into a regression that is linear in parameters by defining new variables. From the original variables of the nonlinear equation, new variables are defined that result in an equation that is linear in its parameters. After the ordinary least squares coefficients of the transformed equation have been computed, the researcher reverses the transformation to obtain the desired functional form. In the estimation of nonlinear equations, the regression coefficients are least-squares estimates. Like the coefficients of linear equations, they are estimates of population parameters. Tests of significance, tests of hypotheses, and confidence limits can be established in a manner like that described for linear regression equations.

PROBLEMS

1.   The following sample of observations on price paid and quantity purchased of a commodity X by a household is given:

Month	Price of X	Quantity of X
January	10	110
February	8	98
March	20	75
April	16	100
May	24	80
June	30	58
July	36	54
August	40	40
September	35	55
October	25	60
November	28	55
December	30	65
January	35	80
February	40	30
March	45	40
April	40	40

a. Construct a scatter diagram from the observations and establish the form of the population demand equation for X.
b. Estimate the parameters of the demand equation by least squares.
c. Compute the coefficient of determination. How do you interpret it?
d. Is the regression coefficient statistically significant at the 5 percent level? How do you interpret this?

2.   The following sample of observations on price and quantity produced
     of a commodity Y by a competitive firm is given:

Month	Price of Y	Quantity of Y Produced
1	15	44
2	20	60
3	25	4
4	20	110
5	40	45
6	35	85
7	60	52
8	50	50
9	45	45
10	60	140
11	70	100
12	40	125
13	80	90

a. Construct a scatter diagram from the observations and establish
   the form of the population equation for Y.
b. Estimate the parameters of the supply equation by least squares.
c. Test the statistical significance of the regression coefficient at the 1
   percent level of significance and at the 5 percent level of significance.

3.   The following observations on the total money supply for the economy
     as a whole and the general price level are given:

Year	Money Supply (M1)	Price Level
1959	141.0	67.60
1960	141.8	68.70
1961	146.5	69.33
1962	149.2	70.61
1963	154.7	71.67
1964	161.8	72.77
1965	169.5	74.36
1966	173.7	76.76
1967	185.1	79.06
1968	199.4	82.54
1969	205.8	86.79

a. Compute the correlation coefficient. Is it significant at the 5 percent
   level of significance? How do you interpret this result?
b. Compute the percent change for the two variables (note that one
   observation is lost). Compute the correlation coefficient for these
   computed variables. Is it significant at the 5 percent level of significance? How do you interpret this result?

4.   The net investment function for a medium-size firm is assumed to be
      of the form:

$$I = ai^b$$

where I denotes net investment, i denotes the interest rate, and a and
b are the unknown parameters of the investment function. The following sample is given:

Investment (Million Dollars)	Interest Rate (Percent)
9.0	6
5.5	7
8.5	6
4.0	8
3.5	9
2.5	10
3.0	8
1.5	10
1.2	12
1.8	11
1.5	13

a. Construct a scatter diagram.
b. Estimate the parameters of the investment function by least squares
   (remember to transform the variables into natural logarithms first).
c. Test the significance of the regression coefficient at the 1 percent
   level of significance and at the 5 percent level of significance.
d. Establish the confidence limits of the regression coefficient for a
   95 percent confidence coefficient.

5.   The following observations on Gross National Product are given:

Year	GNP	Year	GNP	Year	GNP
1960	506.5	1970	992.7	1980	2,631.7
1961	524.6	1971	1,077.6	1981	2,954.1
1962	565.0	1972	1,185.9	1982	3,073.0
1963	596.7	1973	1,326.4	1983	3,309.5
1964	637.7	1974	1,434.2		
1965	691.1	1975	1,549.2		
1966	756.0	1976	1,718.0		
1967	799.6	1977	1,918.3		
1968	873.4	1978	2,163.9		
1969	944.0	1979	2,417.8		

a. Plot GNP over time.

b. With 1960 as the origin ($t = 0$ in 1960), estimate the trend equation for GNP by least squares.

c. What is the percentage of the total variation in GNP that can be attributed to the trend?

d. Compute the residual for each observation. Which years seem to depart most dramatically from the trend? How might these departures be explained by excluded variables?

6. Assume it is given from theoretical considerations that the total amount of inventories of a commodity X held in stock is an increasing linear function of the change in the price of X. In symbolic notation:

$$y_t = a + b(p_t - p_{t-1}) + u_t$$

where y_t denotes inventories in month t, p_t is the price in month t, and u_t is the error term. The following sample of observations is given:

Month t	y_t	p_t	Month t	y_t	p_t
0	15	10	8	55	13
1	20	9	9	50	16
2	15	6	10	60	19
3	25	4	11	55	21
4	30	4	12	40	21
5	40	5	13	35	20
6	50	7	14	25	19
7	45	9			

a. Estimate the parameters of the inventory function by least squares.

b. What percentage of the total variation in inventories is attributed to the price spread?

c. Test the significance of the regression coefficient at the 5 percent level of significance.

d. Find the confidence limits of the regression coefficient for a confidence coefficient of 95 percent.

7. Recompute the ordinary least squares coefficients for the data in Table 17.1 after dropping all observations for which x is greater than 50 percent. What happens to the values of the two coefficients and to the correlation coefficient? What does this tell you about the sensitivity of regression results to the exclusion of so-called *outliers* (observations much greater or much less than the average)?

18

Economic

Applications of

Simple

Regression

We have seen in the previous chapter that regression analysis uses sample data to relate the change in the dependent variable to the change in the independent variable. The reliability of the regression equation—that is, our confidence in the correspondence between the statistical results and the slope of the "true" equation—is based on crucial assumptions about the random error term.

We have made five assumptions: (1) the expected value of the error term is zero (there are no *important* excluded variables), (2) the error term and the independent variable are uncorrelated (the right-side variable is not caused by the left-side variable), (3) the variance in the error term is constant over the population, (4) the values of the error term for each observation are uncorrelated with the values of the error term for other observations, and (5) the error term is normally distributed. When the first four assumptions are true, the ordinary least squares regression techniques are said to be the *best, linear unbiased estimators* (BLUE), that is, the ordinary least squares estimates are unbiased, consistent, and efficient.

Unbiased means that the expected value of the error term is zero, implying that the expected value of each estimated coefficient is equal to the true parameter. *Consistent* means that the expected difference between the estimated coefficients and the true parameters gets smaller as the sample size gets larger. *Efficient* means that the standard errors of the coefficients are minimized. The last assumption is used in testing assumptions about the value of the population parameters from knowledge of the standard errors of the estimated coefficients.

In later chapters we will discuss how violations of these assumptions affect the reliability of regression results, how these departures can be diagnosed, and what modifications in ordinary least squares procedures will mitigate these problems. In this chapter, however, the assumptions about the error term constrain the number of economic applications we can consider. For instance, estimates of market supply and demand equations involve more than one endogenous variable. Hence, these examples must wait until we discuss how such models are estimated. Many other economic examples involve more than one exogenous variable in an equation, and must await our discussion of multiple regression analysis. We will not worry too much about violations of the third, fourth, and fifth assumptions, since such violations do not distort the estimates of the population equations as much as they compromise the tests of hypotheses about the population parameters.

In this chapter we will discuss five applications of simple regression analysis. We begin by showing how tests of hypotheses about the differences in the means of two populations, discussed in Chapter 16, can be performed using ordinary least squares regressions involving *dummy variables*.

UNION MEMBERSHIP AND
RIGHT-TO-WORK LAWS:[1]
DUMMY VARIABLES

We saw in Chapter 16 that economists can test hypotheses about allegedly different populations by computing a *t* statistic for the differences in the means of two samples. A similar test can be conducted with regression techniques using special dichotomous variables called *dummy variables* or *indicator variables*.

Table 18.1 shows the proportion of the nonagricultural labor force who belonged to unions by state for two years. *PU70* = the proportion of workers belonging to unions in 1970 and *PU80* = the proportion of workers belonging to unions in 1980. The states are divided into two groups: *union shop* states, in which unions are allowed to bargain for mandatory union membership contracts, and *right-to-work* states, in which mandatory union membership contracts are illegal. The Taft-Hartley amendments to the National Labor Relations Act make it illegal for a labor contract to require that workers belong to unions *prior to* employment. This same law allows

---

[1]Material in this section is based on Thomas M. Carroll, "Right-to-Work Laws Do Matter," *Southern Economic Journal*, (October 1983).

Table 18.1
Union Membership and Right-to-Work Laws

Union Shop States ($RTW = 0$)			Right-to-Work States ($RTW = 1$)		
State	*PU70*	*PU80*	State	*PU70*	*PU80*
Alaska	34.4	33.6	Alabama	22.6	21.8
California	35.7	27.0	Arizona	21.4	15.8
Colorado	25.0	18.1	Arkansas	19.4	16.0
Connecticut	27.5	22.9	Florida	16.2	11.7
Delaware	25.8	25.1	Georgia	17.5	15.0
Hawaii	30.3	27.9	Iowa	24.5	22.0
Idaho	22.1	18.5	Kansas	21.1	15.5
Illinois	37.3	30.6	Mississippi	14.9	16.3
Indiana	37.5	30.4	Nebraska	21.0	18.2
Kentucky	32.2	24.0	Nevada	36.5	23.8
Maine	22.0	24.1	North Carolina	9.4	9.6
Maryland/DC	24.5	22.6	North Dakota	21.4	17.1
Massachusetts	27.2	24.9	South Carolina	11.6	7.8
Michigan	43.5	37.4	South Dakota	14.9	14.7
Minnesota	31.9	26.2	Tennessee	23.5	19.1
Missouri	37.5	27.6	Texas	15.8	11.4
Montana	34.3	29.2	Utah	26.2	17.8
New Hampshire	21.2	15.8	Virginia	18.2	14.7
New Jersey	31.2	25.6	Wyoming	24.8	18.6
New Mexico	18.8	18.9	Louisiana*		16.4
New York	40.2	38.7			
Ohio	38.9	31.5			
Oklahoma	18.8	15.3			
Oregon	36.7	26.0			
Pennsylvania	40.0	34.6			
Rhode Island	27.9	28.4			
Vermont	21.0	18.0			
Washington	45.3	34.4			
West Virginia	46.8	34.4			
Wisconsin	33.3	28.6			
Louisiana*	19.4				
Number	31.0	30.0		19.0	20.0
Mean	31.23	26.68		20.05	16.17
Stnd Dev	8.12	6.25		6.04	4.03

$$PU70 = 31.23 - 11.18(RTW70); \ r^2 = 0.3589$$
$$(1.33) \quad (2.16)$$

$$PU80 = 26.68 - 10.51(RTW80); \ r^2 = 0.4790$$
$$(1.00) \quad (1.58)$$

*Passed Right-to-Work Law in 1976; $RTW70 = 0$, $RTW80 = 1$.

Data Source: *Statistical Abstract of the United States*, 1985, Table 709, page 424.

individual states to determine whether union contracts can require workers to join unions *after* employment. The hypothesis is that union membership will tend to be higher in states that allow union shop contracts than in states that forbid such contracts (right-to-work states). In 1970 there were 19 right-to-work states and in 1980 there were 20. (Louisiana passed its right-to-work law in 1976.)

Whether a state permits a union shop contract is a *qualitative* difference whose *quantitative effect* can be measured with a *t* test for a difference in the population means for some quantitative variable. Letting $\bar{y}_0$ stand for the average union membership in union shop states and $\bar{y}_1$ stand for the average union membership in states with right-to-work laws in effect, we have:

$$\bar{y}_0 = 31.23 \qquad\qquad \bar{y}_1 = 20.05$$
$$s_{\bar{y}_0} = 8.12 \qquad\qquad s_{\bar{y}_1} = 6.04$$

The difference in the means is $\bar{y}_1 - \bar{y}_0 = 20.05 - 31.23 = -11.18$. The standard error for this difference is:

$$s_{\bar{y}_1 - \bar{y}_0} = \sqrt{\frac{(8.12)^2}{31} + \frac{(6.04)^2}{19}} = \sqrt{4.293} = 2.072$$

This yields a *t* statistic for the difference of:

$$t = \frac{-11.18}{2.072} = -5.396$$

With 50 observations and two sample statistics ($\bar{y}_0$ and $\bar{y}_1$), the *t* statistic has 48 degrees of freedom. For a one-tail test, the critical value of *t* is 2.40 for 40 degrees of freedom at 1 percent significance. Since the value of our test statistic is considerably greater than -2.40 in absolute value, we can reject the null hypothesis with 99 percent confidence that right-to-work states do have a smaller proportion of workers in unions than union shop states.

We can find the same information and more by regressing the quantitative variable *PU70* against the independent variable *RTW70*. The variable *RTW70* is set equal to zero for the 31 union shop states in 1970, and is set equal to one for the 19 right-to-work states in 1970. The variable *RTW70* is a *dummy variable*. It takes on a value of one when the characteristic is present (i.e., the state does have a right-to-work law) and takes on the value of zero when the characteristic is not present (i.e., the state does *not* have a right-to-work law). The results of regressing the continuous variable *PU70* against the dichotomous variable *RTW70* are reported in Table 18.1 as:

$$PU70 = 31.23 - 11.18(RTW70); \ r^2 = 0.36$$
$$ (1.33) \quad (2.16)$$

The numbers in parentheses are the standard errors of the respective coefficients. This is a standard way of reporting regression results. (An alternative way is to report the *t* statistics in parentheses.)

Since the variable *RTW70* can take on only two values, the predicted value of the dependent variable can also take on only two values. For union shop states, $RTW70 = 0$, so the *predicted* value of *PU70* is $31.23 - 11.18(0) = 31.23$. Note that the intercept term is the average union membership for states where $RTW70 = 0$, that is $\bar{y}_0$. For right-to-work states, the predicted value of *PU70* is $31.23 - 11.18(1) = 20.05$. The slope coefficient is the difference in the means for the two groups. Hence, testing the hypothesis that the coefficient of *RTW70* is negative is equivalent to testing the hypothesis that average union membership for right-to-work states is less than average union membership for union shop states in 1970. Following the procedures outlined in Chapter 17, we calculate the *t* statistic for the slope coefficients as:

$$t = \frac{\hat{b} - b_0}{s_{\hat{b}}} = \frac{-11.18 - 0}{2.16} = -5.18$$

Regressing a quantitative variable against a dummy variable reflecting a qualitative difference between groups gives similar results as a *t* test for a difference in the mean of the dependent variable for those groups. However, the regression also gives us the coefficient of determination, $r^2 = 0.3589$. About 36 percent of the variation in union membership across 50 states in 1970 could be attributed to whether the state allowed union shop contracts.

We can repeat the test for 1980. In that year, the difference in union membership between right-to-work states and union shop states was -10.51, with a standard error of the difference equal to 1.58. This yields a *t* statistic of -6.65 for that difference, which is significant at the 1 percent level. Regressing *PU80* against *RTW80*, we find:

$$\widehat{PU80} = 26.68 - 10.51(RTW80); \quad r^2 = 0.4790; \quad t = -6.65$$
$$\phantom{\widehat{PU80} = }(1.00) \quad (1.58)$$

When $RTW80 = 0$, $\widehat{PU80} = 26.68 - 10.51(0) = 26.68$; when $RTW80 = 1$, $\widehat{PU80} = 26.68 - 10.51(1) = 16.17$. Union membership predicted by the regression equation is the mean of the dependent variable for each group. Furthermore, just under 48 percent of the variation in union membership in 1980 can be attributed to the absence or presence of right-to-work laws in that year.

THE CONSUMPTION FUNCTION:
LAGGED REGRESSION

We have seen in Chapter 13 that economic theory may postulate a *lagged* functional relationship between two economic variables. Study of institutions may lead the investigator to suspect that there are certain rigidities that cause changes in the dependent variable to lag in time behind changes in the independent variable. To take an example from macroeconomic theory, we may postulate that consumption observed in one period reflects income earned in the previous period.

Table 18.2 presents summary statistics on real consumer expenditure ($RCON_t$), real disposable personal income lagged one quarter (INC_{t-1}), the natural logarithm of real consumption ($LCON_t$), and the logarithm of lagged real disposable personal income ($LINC_{t-1}$). The table uses quarterly economic data from the second quarter 1947 to the fourth quarter 1984, yielding 151 observations. Also provided are the sample variances, the covariance between relevant pairs of variables, and the associated correlation coefficients. Following the procedures outlined in Chapter 17, we can convert these summary statistics into regression equations.

Recall that the slope coefficient for a regression equation can be computed as the ratio of the covariance between the dependent and independent variables to the variance in the independent variable. Letting $x = INC_{t-1}$ and $y = RCON_t$, we have:

$$\hat{b} = \frac{\Sigma(x - \bar{x})(y - \bar{y})/n}{\Sigma(x - \bar{x})^2/n} = \frac{56,852.331}{62,661.600} = 0.9073$$

From information on the means of the dependent and independent variables, we find:

$$\hat{a} = 608.94 - 0.9073(660.25) = 9.895$$

We note that the correlation coefficient is $r = 0.99915$, implying $r^2 = 0.9983$. Thus, more than 99.8 percent of the variation in current real consumption can be attributed to variations in real disposable personal income three months earlier.

With estimates of $\hat{b}$ and r we can proceed to test hypotheses about the marginal propensity to consume. Since Keynesian theory hypothesizes that $0 < b < 1$, we could calculate t statistics for the two null hypotheses, $b \leq 0$ and $b \geq 1$. Recall that the former hypothesis is equivalent to the null hypothesis $r \leq 0$, which we can test directly using our estimate of r. Hence:

$$t = \frac{0.99915\sqrt{149}}{\sqrt{1 - 0.9983}} = \frac{12.062}{0.04158} = 290.06$$

We hardly need a t table to assure ourselves that real aggregate consumer expenditure is indeed positively related to lagged real disposable personal income.

Testing the second null hypothesis, namely that $b \geq 1$, would seem to present a problem. In order to calculate the t statistic for this hypothesis, we need $s_{\hat{b}}$, which we have yet to calculate. However, because of the equivalence of t statistics for the null hypotheses $b \leq 0$ and $r \leq 0$, we have:

$$t = \frac{\hat{b} - 0}{s_{\hat{b}}} = \frac{\hat{b}}{s_{\hat{b}}} = 290.06$$

Table 18.2

Consumer Spending and Lagged Real Disposable Income
Quarterly Data, 1947 to 1984

Variable	Mean
$RCON_t$	608.94
INC_{t-1}	660.25
$LCON_t$	6.34
$LINC_{t-1}$	6.42

Variable(s)	Variance/Covariance	Correlation
$RCON_t$	51,669.765	
$RCON_t, INC_{t-1}$	56,752.331	0.99915
INC_{t-1}	62,661.600	
$LCON_t$	0.14466	
$LCON_t, LINC_{t-1}$	0.14787	0.99919
$LINC_{t-1}$	0.15140	

$$y = RCON_t; \quad x = INC_{t-1}$$

$$\hat{b} = \frac{\Sigma(x - \bar{x})(y - \bar{y})/n}{\Sigma(x - \bar{x})^2/n} = \frac{56,852.331}{62,661.600} = 0.9073$$

$$\hat{a} = 608.94 - 0.9073(660.25) = 9.895$$

$$y = LCON_t; \quad x = LINC_{t-1}$$

$$\hat{b} = \frac{\Sigma(x - \bar{x})(y - \bar{y})/n}{\Sigma(x - \bar{x})^2/n} = \frac{0.14787}{0.15140} = 0.9767$$

$$\hat{a} = 6.34 - 0.9767(6.42) = 0.0697$$

so that $s_{\hat{b}} = \hat{b}/t = 0.9082/290.06 = 0.00314$. Therefore, we can calculate the t statistic:

$$t = \frac{\hat{b} - 0}{s_{\hat{b}}} = \frac{0.9082 - 1}{0.00314} = \frac{-0.0918}{0.00314} = -29.27$$

This is also significant at the 1 percent level.

So far we have *assumed* a linear relation between real aggregate consumer expenditure and lagged real disposable personal income. Indeed, consumption functions are usually plotted as straight lines in textbooks, and so a linear specification makes a reasonable null hypothesis. However, we may suspect that the marginal propensity to consume (out of lagged income), $dRCON_t/dINC_{t-1}$, decreases as lagged real disposable personal income increases. We cannot test this hypothesis with a linear specification but we can test it by transforming our data into natural logarithms. Hence, we calculate:

$$x = LCON_t = \log_e(RCON_t) \text{ and } y = LINC_{t-1} = \log_e(INC_{t-1})$$

From the information in Table 18.2 we calculate:

$$\hat{b} = \frac{\Sigma(x - \bar{x})(y - \bar{y})/n}{\Sigma(x - \bar{x})^2/n} = \frac{0.14787}{0.15410} = 0.9767$$

and:

$$\hat{a} = 6.34 - 0.9767(6.42) = 0.0697$$

Since $\widehat{LCON_t} = 0.0711 + 0.9767LINC_{t-1}$, we have $\widehat{RCON_t} = 1.074(INC_{t-1})^{0.9767}$, with $r = 0.9992$. First we can test the reliability of our results by calculating the t statistic for the null hypothesis $r \le 0$:

$$t = \frac{0.9992(149)^{1/2}}{(1 - 0.9984)^{1/2}} = \frac{12.08}{0.0400} = 304.92$$

The null hypothesis that the (lagged) consumption function is linear is tested by stipulating $b_0 = 1$. First, we must compute:

$$s_{\hat{b}} = \frac{\hat{b}}{t} = \frac{0.9767}{304.92} = 0.0032$$

Next we compute the relevant t statistic:

$$t = \frac{\hat{b} - 1}{0.0032} = \frac{0.9767 - 1}{0.0032} = \frac{-0.0233}{0.0032} = -7.27$$

Apparently we can reject the hypothesis that real consumer expenditure is a linear function of *lagged* real disposable personal income, in favor of the alternative hypothesis that the marginal propensity to consume out of lagged income decreases as lagged income increases.

THE PHILLIPS CURVE:
NONLINEAR REGRESSION CURVES

In 1958 British economist A. W. Phillips hypothesized a nonlinear relationship between nominal wage changes and the unemployment rate:

> When the demand for labor is high and there are very few unemployed we should expect employers to bid wage rates up quite rapidly ... On the other hand ... when the demand for labor is low and unemployment is high ... wage rates fall only very slowly.[2]

[2]A. W. Phillips, "The Relation Between Unemployment and the Rate of Money Wage Changes in the United Kingdom, 1861-1957," *Economica* (November 1958), p. 283.

During the 1960s many economists took this relationship between wage rate changes and unemployment to imply an inverse relationship between the rate of price inflation and the unemployment rate. We will explore variations on this theme in future chapters. At this point we will limit our analysis of the Phillips curve to an investigation of the circumstantial evidence that led economists to suspect an inflation-unemployment trade-off.

Table 18.3 shows the results of three regressions run on annual data for unemployment and inflation for the period 1948 to 1968, reported in Table 16.4. The first regression relates the rate of change in the implicit price deflator (INF) to the average annual unemployment rate (UE). The fitted equation:

$$\widehat{INF} = 6.43 - 0.84UE$$

implies an expected rate of inflation of 6.43 percent when the unemployment rate is zero, and a decrease in the rate of inflation by 0.84 percent for

Table 18.3

Inflation and Unemployment, Annual Data: 1948-1968

Year	UE_t	INF_t
1948	3.8	1.6
1949	5.9	−0.9
1950	5.3	1.9
1951	3.3	6.9
1952	3.0	1.2
1953	2.9	1.6
1954	5.5	1.4
1955	4.4	2.2
1956	4.1	3.1
1957	4.3	3.3
1958	6.8	1.7
1959	5.5	2.1
1960	5.5	1.8
1961	6.7	0.9
1962	5.5	1.9
1963	5.7	1.4
1964	5.2	1.5
1965	4.5	2.2
1966	3.8	3.4
1967	3.8	2.9
1968	3.6	4.6

$$\widehat{INF_t} = 6.43 - 0.84UE_t; \quad r^2 = 0.3868$$
$$\qquad\quad (1.18) \quad (0.243)$$

$$\widehat{LINF_t} = 3.49 - 1.85LUE_t; \quad r^2 = 0.3048$$
$$\qquad\quad (0.99) \quad (0.642)$$

$$\widehat{INF_t} = -0.983 + 15.32/UE_t; \quad r^2 = 0.3262$$
$$\qquad\quad (1.17) \quad (5.05)$$

every 1 percent increase in the rate of inflation. The standard error of 0.243 for the slope coefficient yields a t statistic of -3.46. The null hypothesis that inflation does not decrease with increases in the unemployment rate can be rejected with 99 percent confidence. Nevertheless, the rather low coefficient of determination, $r^2 = 0.3868$, implies that other factors besides unemployment rate may have an important influence on the rate of inflation.

It is possible, of course, that the low explanatory power of the linear regression is due to a misspecification of the functional form of the inflation-unemployment relation. That is, a nonlinear curve may characterize the population equation, so that a nonlinear function may fit the data better than the linear function. Two nonlinear specifications (which are linear in parameters) are also fit and reported in Table 18.3. The log-linear specification, which we have investigated in the previous section, implies an *elasticity* of -1.85 for *INF* with respect to *UE*. The constant term for the log-linear regression is the natural logarithm for the multiplicative constant in the power function. Hence:

$$\widehat{INF} = e^{3.49} UE^{-1.85} = 32.6(UE)^{-1.85}$$

In this case, the curve depicting the relation between inflation and unemployment is asymptotic to the vertical axis. The multiplicative constant can be interpreted as the inflation rate that would prevail when the unemployment rate is 1 percent. The prediction that $INF = 32.6$ when $UE = 1$ is strikingly different from the linear regression implying $INF = 6.43 - 0.84UE = 5.59$ percent when $UE = 1$ percent. However, it is also worth noting that the lowest unemployment rate in the 1948-1968 period was 2.9 percent, and that the predicted rates of inflation for the two models are fairly similar:

$$\widehat{INF}(2.9) = 6.43 - 0.84(2.9) = 3.99$$
$$\widehat{INF}(2.9) = 32.6(2.9)^{-1.85} = 4.45$$

This result underscores an important lesson: over the range of data, a linear equation often provides a close approximation of a curvilinear equation. However, considerable care must be taken when making inferences outside of the range of observed data.

By testing the null hypothesis that $b = -1$ in the power function specification of the Phillips relation, we set the stage for another nonlinear equation, the inverse function. First, we note:

$$t = \frac{-1.86 - (-1)}{0.642} = \frac{-0.86}{0.642} = -1.34$$

which is insignificant at the 10 percent level (two-tail test with 19 degrees of freedom). On this evidence, we proceed to the third specification. By using the inverse of the unemployment rate ($INUE = 1/UE$), we fit the equation:

$$\widehat{INF} = -0.98 + 15.32INUE$$

Figure 18.1

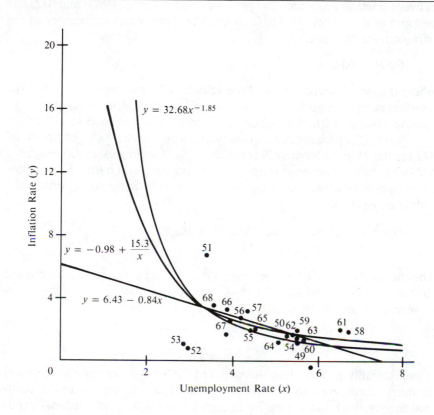

In the case of the inverse equation, $dINF/dUE = -15.32(UE)^{-2}$. As the unemployment rate increases, the inflation rate decreases at a decreasing rate. According to Table 18.4, the inverse of the unemployment rate has a significant positive effect on the rate of inflation. Furthermore, Figure 18.1 shows that the three fitted regressions lie close together over the range of observed points.

THE QUANTITY THEORY OF MONEY:
REGRESSION THROUGH THE ORIGIN

One of the fundamental equations of macroeconomic theory is the equation of exchange, $MV = PQ$, where M is the money stock, V is the velocity of money, Q is real output, and P is the price index. If we *assume* that the velocity of money, V, is an unknown constant of proportionality between *nominal* gross national product (our measure of PQ) and $M2$, our measure of the money stock, we can estimate the velocity of money as the parameter in the equation:

$$GNP = bM2 + u$$

where the slope parameter, b, is the velocity of circulation. Note that the constant term is suppressed in the above equation. This is equivalent to assuming that $a = 0$ in the conventional ordinary least squares specification.

Table 18.4 presents annual observations on nominal GNP and nominal $M2$ for the 25 years from 1959 through 1983. If we regressed GNP against $M2$ using the ordinary least squares estimators for a and b (that is, we allow for the possibility that the "true" intercept term is nonzero), we obtain the estimated equation:

$$\widehat{GNP} = -12.80 + 1.5675M2; \ r^2 = 0.9965$$
$$\phantom{\widehat{GNP} = } (20.51) \quad\ \ (0.01938)$$

The standard errors for the coefficients $\hat{a}$ and $\hat{b}$ are enclosed in parentheses, that is, $s_{\hat{a}} = 20.51$ and $s_{\hat{b}} = 0.01938$. It is obvious that a change in $M2$ has a significant impact on nominal GNP. The t statistic:

$$t = \frac{1.5675}{0.01938} = 80.86$$

is considerably greater than the required 2.50 for 1 percent significance. In other words, we can be virtually certain that an increase in the nominal money stock has a positive impact on nominal gross national product. However, we can also test the hypothesis that the intercept term, a, is different from zero. The t statistic for the null hypothesis $a = 0$ is given by:

$$t = \frac{\hat{a} - 0}{s_{\hat{a}}} = \frac{\hat{a}}{s_{\hat{a}}} = \frac{-12.80}{20.51} = -0.624$$

which is clearly insignificant. We cannot reject the null hypothesis that nominal GNP would equal zero if the money stock were also equal to zero.

If theory specifies that the intercept term is zero, there is only one parameter to estimate, the slope coefficient, $\hat{b}$. In this case the ordinary least squares regression requires minimizing the sum of the squared deviations:

$$\Sigma \hat{u}^2 = \Sigma(y - \hat{b}x)^2$$

Taking the derivative of $\Sigma \hat{u}^2$ with respect to $\hat{b}$ and solving for $\hat{b}$ we have:

$$\frac{d\Sigma \hat{u}^2}{d\hat{b}} = \frac{d\Sigma(y - \hat{b}x)^2}{d\hat{b}} = -2\Sigma x(y - \hat{b}x) = 0$$

This implies:

$$\Sigma xy = \hat{b}\Sigma x^2$$

or

$$\hat{b} = \frac{\Sigma xy}{\Sigma x^2}$$

When regressing through the origin, we first multiply the dependent variable by the independent variable for each observation. This is shown in the fourth column of Table 18.4. Also, we calculate the square of the independent variable for each observation (column 5). Next we sum xy for all observations and sum x^2 for all observations. Finally, we calculate the slope coefficient as the ratio of Σxy to Σx^2.

Recall that the slope coefficient, when the intercept term is nonzero, can be expressed as:

$$\hat{b} = \frac{\Sigma(x - \bar{x})(y - \bar{y})}{\Sigma(x - \bar{x})^2}$$

We have seen that this specification implies that the regression line passes through the point $(\bar{x}, \bar{y})$, given by the means of x and y, respectively. Now we see that the researcher can force the regression line through the origin by pretending that $\bar{x} = 0$ and $\bar{y} = 0$. In Table 18.4 we see that this approach yields the estimate $\hat{b} = 1.56$, which is quite close to the estimate we obtained using the ordinary least squares procedures. However, this will not usually be the case, since different formulas are involved.

One consequence of constraining the regression line through the origin is that the sum of the residuals no longer equals zero. The standard error of $\hat{b}$ can be calculated as the square root of the *mean square error* divided by the sum of the squared independent variable:

$$s_{\hat{b}} = \sqrt{\frac{\Sigma(y - \hat{b}x)^2/(n-1)}{\Sigma x^2}} = \sqrt{\frac{\Sigma\hat{u}^2/(n-1)}{\Sigma x^2}} = 0.010776$$

As indicated in Table 18.4, the resulting t statistic for the null hypothesis, $H_0: b = 0$, is $t = 1.56/0.010776 = 144.7$, which is clearly significant at the 1 percent level.

Note that the correlation coefficient now reflects the covariance of x and y about the origin:

$$r = \frac{\Sigma(y - 0)(x - 0)}{\sqrt{\Sigma(x - 0)^2\Sigma(y - 0)^2}} = \frac{\Sigma xy}{\sqrt{\Sigma x^2\Sigma y^2}}$$

Because of this change, the t statistic is no longer equivalent to the t statistic calculated to test the null hypothesis $r = 0$. Therefore, caution must be exercised when calculating the standard error of $\hat{b}$ from the t statistic calculated for r.

Table 18.4
Nominal *GNP* and Nominal *M2*: 1959 to 1983

Year	M2 (x)	GNP (y)	xy	x^2	y^2	u	u^2
1959	297.8	487.9	145,296.6	88,684.8	238,046.4	23.38	546.79
1960	312.3	506.5	158,180.0	97,531.3	256,542.3	19.37	375.05
1961	335.5	524.6	176,003.3	112,560.3	275,205.2	1.28	1.63
1962	362.7	565.0	204,925.5	131,551.3	319,225.0	−0.75	0.56
1963	393.2	596.7	234,622.4	154,606.2	356,050.9	−16.62	276.35
1964	424.7	637.7	270,831.2	180,370.1	406,661.3	−24.76	612.98
1965	459.1	691.1	317,284.0	210,772.8	477,619.2	−25.02	625.82
1966	480.2	756.0	363,031.2	230,592.0	571,536.0	6.97	48.60
1967	524.8	799.6	419,630.1	275,415.0	639,360.2	−19.00	360.89
1968	566.9	873.4	495,130.5	321,375.6	762,827.6	−10.87	118.07
1969	590.2	944.0	557,148.8	348,336.0	891,136.0	23.39	547.10
1970	627.9	992.7	623,316.3	394,258.4	985,453.3	13.28	176.49
1971	712.7	1,077.6	768,005.5	507,941.3	1,161,221.8	−34.09	1,162.03
1972	805.3	1,185.9	955,005.3	648,508.1	1,406,358.8	−70.23	4,932.04
1973	861.2	1,326.4	1,142,295.7	741,665.4	1,759,337.0	−16.92	286.38
1974	908.6	1,434.2	1,303,114.1	825,554.0	2,056,926.6	16.94	287.01
1975	1,023.0	1,549.2	1,584,831.6	1,046,529.0	2,400,020.6	−46.50	2,162.51
1976	1,163.5	1,718.0	1,998,893.0	1,353,732.3	2,951,524.0	−96.86	9,381.55
1977	1,286.4	1,918.3	2,467,701.1	1,654,825.0	3,679,874.9	−88.26	7,790.02
1978	1,388.5	2,163.9	3,004,575.2	1,927,932.3	4,682,463.2	−1.92	3.68
1979	1,497.5	2,417.8	3,620,655.5	2,242,506.3	5,845,756.8	81.96	6,717.35

1980	1,630.3	2,631.7	4,290,460.5	2,657,878.1	6,925,844.9	88.71	7,870.26
1981	1,794.9	2,954.1	5,302,314.1	3,221,666.0	8,726,706.8	154.37	23,829.17
1982	1,959.5	3,073.0	6,021,543.5	3,839,640.3	9,443,329.0	16.52	272.89
1983	2,184.6	3,309.5	7,229,933.7	4,772,477.2	10,952,790.3	−98.10	9,623.11
Sum	22,591.3	35,134.8	43,654,728.6	27,986,908.9	68,171,820.9	−103.71	78,008.34
Mean	903.65	1,405.39					

$$y = bx + u$$

$$\hat{b} = \frac{\Sigma xy}{\Sigma x^2} = \frac{43,654,728.6}{27,986,908.9} = 1.56$$

$$r = \frac{\Sigma xy}{\sqrt{\Sigma x^2 \, \Sigma y^2}} = \frac{43,654,728.6}{\sqrt{(27,986,909)(68,171,821)}} = \frac{43,654,728.6}{43,679,514.7} = 0.9994$$

$$s_{\hat{b}}^2 = \frac{\Sigma(y - \hat{y})^2/(n-1)}{\Sigma x^2} = \frac{78,008.34/24}{27,986,908.9} = \frac{3,250.35}{27,986,908.9} = 0.000116$$

$$s_{\hat{b}} = \sqrt{0.000116} = 0.0108$$

$$\text{For } b_0 \le 0: \; t = \frac{1.56 - 0}{0.0108} = 144.76$$

CAPITAL, OUTPUT, AND WAGE
RATES: RECURSIVE MODELS

Having explored several macroeconomic models, we conclude our applications with an example from microeconomic theory. According to the marginal productivity theory of distribution, equilibrium wage rates across industries reflect differences in the marginal productivity of labor. Furthermore, production theory implies that output per labor unit should increase as the ratio of capital to labor increases. Hence, we have a *recursive* model wherein output per hour is a positive function of capital per hour, and the hourly wage rate is a positive function of output per hour. Although output per hour is a dependent variable in one function, it is the independent variable in the other function. As long as we are confident that simultaneous causation does not occur between the dependent variable and the independent variable in either equation, we can use ordinary least squares to estimate each of the equations in the model.

Table 18.5 presents the average hourly wage rate, $WAGE = z$, value-added per production hour, $VAPH = y$, and capital per hour, $KPH = x$ (measured as the dollar value of assets divided by the number of production hours), for twenty manufacturing industries (identified by their Standard Industrial Classification numbers) for 1980.

On page 394 we found that linear regression equations sometimes closely approximate regression equations that are nonlinear in their variables. However, this is not always the case. First, if we regress the value-added per hour against capital per hour, we obtain the estimated equation:

$$VAPH = 16.31 + 0.649KPH; \ r^2 = 0.8211$$
$$\quad\quad\quad (3.22) \quad (0.071)$$

The standard errors for the two regression coefficients are in parentheses. Testing the null hypothesis that $b = 0$, we compute:

$$t = \frac{0.649}{0.071} = 9.09$$

This is clearly significant at the 1 percent level. We may reject the null hypothesis that increases in the capital-labor ratio do not increase output (value-added) per hour.

Microeconomics tells us that both labor and capital services should be subject to diminishing returns. As capital-per-labor hour increases, output-per-labor hour should increase *at a decreasing rate*. A linear regression equation implies that output per hour increases at a constant rate as capital per hour increases. It would seem appropriate to test our choice of a linear specification with a logarithmic regression.

Table 18.5

Wage Rates, Value-Added, and Capital per Worker
Twenty Manufacturing Industries, 1980

SIC	Wage Rate (z)	Value-Added per Hour (y)	Assets per Hour (x)
20	6.85	34.94	21.73
21	8.67	69.80	26.16
22	5.16	13.67	11.40
23	4.23	11.69	2.30
24	6.10	16.45	14.01
25	5.37	15.99	6.46
26	8.12	29.51	40.23
27	7.21	33.44	15.20
28	8.74	67.84	72.55
29	10.65	124.11	167.73
30	6.53	21.84	18.07
31	4.71	14.02	3.34
32	7.57	25.41	26.41
33	10.51	29.03	40.29
34	7.49	24.28	13.61
35	8.15	31.53	16.11
36	7.10	29.31	13.65
37	10.12	32.20	19.22
38	6.92	38.65	15.59
39	5.48	21.02	8.30

$$\hat{y} = 16.31 + 0.649x; \; r^2 = 0.8211$$
$$\quad\;\; (3.22) \quad (0.071)$$

$$\hat{z} = 5.66 + 0.047y; \; r^2 = 0.4523$$
$$\quad (0.526)\,(0.012)$$

$$\hat{z} = 6.38 + 0.032x; \; r^2 = 0.4180$$
$$\quad (0.412)\,(0.009)$$

$$\ln\hat{y} = 1.87 + 0.517\ln x; \; r^2 = 0.7186$$
$$\quad\;\; (0.228)\,(0.076)$$

$$\ln\hat{z} = 0.770 + 0.354\ln y; \; r^2 = 0.6411$$
$$\quad\;\; (0.212) \quad (0.062)$$

$$\ln\hat{z} = 1.29 + 0.233\ln x; \; r^2 = 0.7477$$
$$\quad\;\; (0.096)\,(0.032)$$

Regressing the logarithm of $VAPH$ ($LVAPH$) against the logarithm of KPH ($LKPH$), we find:

$$\widehat{LVAPH} = 1.87 + 0.517LKPH; \; r^2 = 0.7186$$
$$\phantom{\widehat{LVAPH} = }(0.228) \; (0.076)$$

To test the null hypothesis, H_o: $b = 1$, we compute:

$$t = \frac{0.517 - 1}{0.076} = \frac{-0.483}{0.076} = -6.36$$

The critical t statistic for 18 degrees of freedom and a one-tail test is -2.861. Apparently we should reject the null hypothesis that $b = 1$, in favor of the nonlinear specification implied by diminishing returns ($b < 1$). Yet the coefficient of determination is higher under the linear specification than under the log-linear specification. The typical econometrician does not allow goodness of fit to be the sole, or even the major, criterion in picking between statistical models. Since there is a theoretical reason for preferring the nonlinear specification, and since the test of the null hypothesis allows rejecting the linear specification, most econometricians would favor the nonlinear model obtained from a linear regression on logarithmic data:

$$\widehat{VAPH} = e^{1.876}KPH^{0.517} = 6.53KPH^{0.517}$$

This result states that if industry B has 10 percent more capital per worker than industry A, wage rates in industry B will tend to be 5.17 percent greater.

As mentioned, a variable may be dependent in one equation and be independent in another equation without violating the assumption that the error term is uncorrelated with the right-side variable. As long as we believe causation goes from output per hour to the hourly wage rate, and not in the opposite direction, we can relate $WAGE$ to $VPAH$ by means of ordinary least squares. First we try the linear specification:

$$WAGE = 5.66 + 0.0475VAPH; \; r^2 = 0.4523$$
$$(0.526) \; (0.0123)$$

This equation implies that an extra dollar of value-added per hour increases the average hourly wage rate by a paltry 4.75 cents. Furthermore, the coefficient of determination, r^2, implies that about 45 percent of the variation in the average hourly wage rate can be attributed to variations in value-added per hour. Perhaps the linear specification is not appropriate in this context.

Fitting a log-linear regression, we find:

$$LWAGE = 0.770 + 0.354LVAPH; \; r^2 = 0.6411$$
$$(0.212) \; (0.062)$$

This specification predicts that a 10 percent variation in value-added per hour would be associated with a 3.5 percent variation in the average hourly wage rate.

For the null hypothesis, H_o: $dLWAGE/dVAPH = 0$, we compute the t statistic:

$$t = \frac{0.354}{0.062} = 5.67$$

Furthermore, the null hypothesis H_o: $dLWAGE/dVAPH = 1$ is tested by computing:

$$t = \frac{0.354 - 1}{0.062} = \frac{-0.646}{0.062} = -10.35$$

Both null hypotheses can be rejected with 99 percent confidence.

We have just estimated a two-equation recursive model, which first relates value-added per hour to capital per hour, then relates the average hourly wage rate to value-added per hour. According to our findings, a 10 percent variation in capital per hour across industries would increase value-added per hour by 5.17 percent. Furthermore, an increase in value-added per hour would increase the average hourly wage rate by 0.354(5.17) = 1.83 percent. We can check this prediction by regressing $LWAGE$ against $LKPH$ directly. We find:

$$LWAGE = 1.29 + 0.233LKPH; \; r^2 = 0.7477$$
$$\quad\;\; (0.096) \; (0.032)$$

According to our regression results, a 10 percent variation in capital per hour is associated with a 2.33 percent variation in the average hourly wage rate. This estimate is about 13 percent greater than that predicted by the recursive model. It seems likely that in addition to its indirect impact on wage rates through value-added, an increasing capital-labor ratio may have a direct impact on wage rates, perhaps because a greater degree of capital intensity increases the propensity of industries to unionize. But such concerns imply that the dependent variable may be caused by several independent variables. And this leads us to multiple regression analysis, the topic of the next chapter.

SUMMARY

The last two chapters have introduced the methods of simple regression and correlation. The material in these chapters forms the foundation of the concepts to be introduced in subsequent chapters, so it is important that these concepts be well understood. Therefore, we will briefly summarize our findings here.

First, we derived the ordinary least squares estimators for a two-variable regression equation, $y = a + bx + u$. The estimates of the parameters, a and b, were derived by minimizing the squared vertical distances between the scatter of points reflecting empirical observations and the fitted line that depicts the hypothesized *true* relation. The validity of the estimated equation ultimately depends on the following assumptions about the error term, u:

1. The expected value of the error term is zero. There are no *important* variables omitted from the regression equation.
2. The error term is uncorrelated with the regressor, x. The right-side variable is *not caused* by the left-side variable.
3. The variance in the error term is constant over the range of the independent variable.
4. The error terms for different observations are independent of one another.

In addition, to test hypotheses about the population parameters, we made the additional assumption that the error term is normally distributed.

In the chapters that follow we will discover that violations of the first two assumptions introduce *bias* into the regression results so that the expected value of the estimator does not equal the *true* parameter it is purported to measure. Such bias can lead to serious errors of inference that may not be detected in significance tests. Violations of the third and fourth assumptions leave the regression results unbiased but distort the standard error of the coefficients. This can lead to inaccurate tests of hypotheses, although such distortions can often be diagnosed by analyzing the residuals of the regression.

We also calculated the correlation coefficient for two variables. The correlation coefficient measures the degree of association between two variables, but, unlike the regression equation itself, does not imply the direction of causation. We saw that the t statistic for the correlation coefficient generates another test of the null hypothesis that two variables are independent. We also saw that the square of the correlation coefficient yields the *coefficient of determination*, which measures the proportion of variation in the dependent variable attributed to the variation in the independent variable.

Next we saw that the simple regression techniques that were based on the assumption of a linear relationship between the dependent and independent variables could be extended to nonlinear equations. This is done by first transforming the data, then proceeding to apply simple regression techniques to the transformed data. Significance tests not only determine whether the (transformed) dependent variable is related to the (transformed) independent variable in a meaningful way, but also help determine whether sufficient evidence exists to warrant a nonlinear functional specification.

The examples in this chapter serve to illustrate how the method of least squares can be used to estimate the parameters of structural equations that comprise econometric models. When only two variables are assumed to be related in the population, simple regression can, under suitable conditions, yield the desired estimates. Which of the two variables is to be designated as the independent variable and which as the dependent variable cannot be decided on the basis of statistics. This decision requires knowledge of economic theory. A variety of applications are possible. If the independent variable chosen is a dichotomous or dummy variable, regression analysis yields a test of the difference between the means of two hypothetical populations. Institutional rigidities and behavioral inertia, such as a sluggish response of consumer expenditure to income changes, can be handled by regressing the current dependent variable (e.g., consumer expenditure) on a lagged independent variable (e.g., disposable personal income). Regression lines can be forced through the origin by modifying the formula for the least squares slope coefficient.

We found that linear and nonlinear equations may provide roughly equivalent fits to a range of observations. And finally, we found that multiple equation models can be estimated using ordinary least squares as long as the model is recursive, that no variable is both a "cause" and an "effect" *in the same equation.*

PROBLEMS

1.   Using the data in Table 18.1, fit three different equations to predict union membership in 1980 on the basis of union membership in 1970. The first model should be a linear equation with a nonzero intercept, the second should be a linear model with a zero intercept, and the third should be a log-linear model. Using these results, test the following null hypotheses: (1) Union membership in 1980 is the same as union membership in 1970; (2) Union membership in 1980 is proportional to union membership in 1980.

2.   Use the data in Table 18.4 to regress the natural log of nominal *GNP* against the natural log of *M2*. Use these results to test the appropriateness of the linear specification of the equation of exchange, $PQ = bM$.

3.   Median family income, y, was regressed against the proportion of the labor force who are high school graduates, x, using 1980 census data for 50 states. The results are:

$$y = 4,514.63 + 222.70x; \quad r = 0.6347$$
$$(2,651.56) \quad (39.14)$$

with standard errors in parentheses. What is the economic meaning of each of the estimated coefficients? Test the hypothesis that median family income increases as the proportion of the labor force with a high school education increases. Also test the null hypothesis that this regression line passes through the origin.

4. An interesting regularity observed in urban-regional economics is the "rank-size" correlation of urban areas. Variable y is the population (in thousands) of each of 170 "standard metropolitan statistical areas" (SMSA's) according to the 1980 Census of Population. Variable x is the population "rank" of that SMSA (e.g., $x = 1$ for New York, $x = 2$ for Los Angeles-Long Beach, etc.). The hypothesis to be tested is "Population times rank is a constant." Two regressions were fit:

(1) $y = 481.419 + 11{,}933.317\left(\dfrac{1}{x}\right); \; r = 0.906$

(2) $\log_e y = 9.898 - 0.854 \log_e x; \; r = -0.988$

Which regression provides the more appropriate test of the hypothesis? What are the results of that test?

5. The average annual wage rate for construction workers ($CWAGE$) is hypothesized to be a positive linear function of value-added per construction worker ($VACON$), with the regression line passing through the origin. To test these two hypotheses, a linear regression and a log-linear regression (the natural logs denoted by L) were fit using data for 48 states for 1978. The results were (with standard errors in parentheses):

$$CWAGE = 171.415 + 0.432 VACON; \; r^2 = 0.8386$$
$$\quad\quad (770.154) \quad (0.028)$$

$$LCWAGE = 0.379 + 0.882 LVACON; \; r^2 = 0.8048$$
$$\quad\quad (0.651) \quad (0.064)$$

Using these results, explain which equation is appropriate for testing the hypothesis that there is a positive linear relationship between $CWAGE$ and $VACON$. Which equation is appropriate for testing the hypothesis that the regression line passes through the origin? What can you infer from those two tests?

6. To determine if right-to-work laws influence the average wage rate received by manufacturing workers, the average hourly wage rate (AHW) in 1980 in each of 50 states was regressed against the right-to-work dummy variable, $RTW80$, reported on page 389. The results of the regression are:

$$AHW = 6.50 - 0.864 RTW; \; r^2 = 0.2253$$
$$\quad\quad (0.15) \quad (0.231)$$

a. How do you interpret the intercept and slope coefficients in the above equation?

b. Test the null hypothesis that workers in right-to-work states ($RTW = 1$) do not receive lower average hourly wage rates than workers in union shop states ($RTW = 0$). Standard errors are in parentheses.

c. What does the value of r^2 imply about the validity of the implicit assumption that right-to-work laws are the only *important* influence on average wage rates? What might some other factors be? Are these variables likely to be independently distributed with expected values of zero? What are the implications of your answer?

7. According to Irving Fisher's theory of interest, the *real* rate of interest equals the nominal rate of interest minus the *expected* rate of inflation. Since the expected rate of inflation is likely to be highly correlated with the actual rate of inflation, the latter is often used as a proxy for the former. To test this theory, the nominal rate of interest on three-month Treasury bills (*RTRS*) was regressed against the rate of change in the implicit price deflator (*INF*) using annual data for the period 1948 to 1983. The result of the regression is:

$$\widehat{RTRS} = 1.658 + 0.785INF; \ r^2 = 0.4121$$
$$\quad\quad (0.793) \quad (0.161)$$

Use these results to test the following hypotheses:

a. The nominal rate of interest increases as the rate of inflation increases.

b. The nominal rate of interest increases by 1 percent for each 1 percent increase in the rate of inflation.

c. The real rate of interest (i.e., the nominal rate of interest when *INF* = 0) is positive.

19

Multiple

Regression and

Correlation

In the two preceding chapters we have concentrated on simple regressions, models that assume that the dependent variable is influenced by only one systematic variable and the random error term. The slope coefficient in a simple linear regression model measures the derivative of the dependent variable with respect to the independent variable. Its estimate is based on the assumption that all influences on the dependent variable, other than the one regressor, are adequately represented by the error term, which is assumed to have an expected value of zero. If this assumption is inaccurate—if there is an *important* variable left out of the regression equation whose influence is not adequately represented by the error term—then the regression model is said to be *misspecified*.

Specification error—the mistake of estimating an equation different from the true (but unknown) population equation—renders the regression coefficients biased and inconsistent. The expected values of the slope and intercept coefficients do not equal the relevant parameters of the population equation, even though the estimated coefficients may appear to be significant. One of the most common forms of specification error is *omitted variable bias*, the mistake of omitting important regressors from a fitted equation. The remedy for omitted variable bias is multiple regression, whereby the influences of more than one independent variable are taken into account when generating the predicted value of the dependent variable. The slope coefficients produced with multiple regression are estimators of the *partial derivatives* of the dependent variable with respect to the relevant variables.

The method of multiple regression is an extension of simple regression to the case of two or more explanatory variables or predictors. We attempt to predict the value of an "explained" variable y from known values of two or more explanatory variables, say x and z, rather than from knowledge of the value of x or z alone. Suppose we formulate a regression equation as:

$$y = a + bx + cz + u$$

where a, b, and c are the population parameters and u is the deviation of the observed value of y from the one predicted by the "true" equation. Then from the multiple regression:

$$\hat{y} = \hat{a} + \hat{b}x + \hat{c}z$$

we obtain least squares estimates of $\hat{a}$, $\hat{b}$, and $\hat{c}$, which generate the predicted values, $\hat{y}$. We then generate the residual, $\hat{u}$, as the deviation between the observed y and the predicted $\hat{y}$: $\hat{u} = y - \hat{y}$.

As in the case of simple regression, the values of the coefficients $\hat{a}$, $\hat{b}$, and $\hat{c}$ can be derived in a mechanical way without making any assumptions about the error term u. However, in order to use these coefficients to test assumptions about the population parameters, we must be reasonably confident that the residual of the regression, $\hat{u}$, is an unbiased estimate of the error term, u. Accordingly, the following assumptions are typically made:

1. The expected value of the error term is zero. There are no important variables excluded from the equation (the influence of all excluded variables tends to cancel).
2. All right-side variables are uncorrelated with the error term (the value of the left-side variable does not influence the value of any right-side variable).
3. The correlation between each right-side variable and the other right-side variables, either individually or in combinations, is not perfect.
4. The error terms for different observations are statistically independent.
5. The variance in the error term is the same for all observations.

Note that assumptions 1, 2, 4, and 5 are approximately the same as the assumptions on which the simple regression coefficients are based. As we will see, assumption 3 must hold true in order for the computer to calculate the multiple regression coefficients. Violation of this assumption is easy to detect because the computer cannot perform the regression if there is perfect correlation among two or more regressors.

MULTIPLE LINEAR REGRESSION:
FUNCTIONS OF TWO VARIABLES

Suppose we wish to estimate a regression equation wherein dependent variable y is related to independent variables x and z so that:

$$y = a + bx + cz + u$$

We are given a sample of n observations, each of which consists of a value of x, a value of z, and a value of y: (x_1, z_1, y_1), (x_2, z_2, y_2), ... (x_n, z_n, y_n). We set up the estimated multiple regression equation:

$$\hat{y} = \hat{a} + \hat{b}x + \hat{c}z$$

As with simple regression the estimates of the population parameters a, b, and c are obtained by minimizing the sum of the squared errors:

$$SSE = \Sigma(y - \hat{y})^2 = \Sigma[y - (\hat{a} + \hat{b}x + \hat{c}z)]^2$$

$$\frac{\partial SSE}{\partial \hat{a}} = -2(\Sigma y - \Sigma\hat{a} - \Sigma\hat{b}x - \Sigma\hat{c}z) = 0$$

This implies that $\Sigma y = n\hat{a} + \hat{b}\Sigma x + \hat{c}\Sigma z$

$$\frac{\partial SSE}{\partial \hat{b}} = -2x(\Sigma y - \Sigma\hat{a} - \Sigma\hat{b}x - \Sigma\hat{c}z) = 0$$

This implies that $\Sigma xy = \hat{a}\Sigma x + \hat{b}\Sigma x^2 + \hat{c}\Sigma xz$

$$\frac{\partial SSE}{\partial \hat{c}} = -2z(\Sigma y - \Sigma\hat{a} - \Sigma\hat{b}x - \Sigma\hat{c}z) = 0$$

This implies that $\Sigma zy = \hat{a}\Sigma z + \hat{b}\Sigma xz + \hat{c}\Sigma z^2$

The three resulting equations are the normal equations for a regression with two independent variables. There are three unknowns ($\hat{a}$, $\hat{b}$, and $\hat{c}$), so these three equations can be solved simultaneously, as long as none of the normal equations is a linear transformation of either of the others. (This would occur if assumption 3 were violated.) The sums and products associated with $\hat{a}$, $\hat{b}$, and $\hat{c}$ in the normal equations can be computed from sample data. Once the sums and products have been computed, the three equations can be solved for $\hat{a}$, $\hat{b}$, and $\hat{c}$.

To be more concrete, let us consider a specific example. Suppose we hypothesize that the percent change in the average *real* wage rate (the average money wage rate adjusted for inflation), y, is linearly related to the unemployment rate, x, and the percent change in productivity, z. According to economic theory, we predict that $\partial y/\partial x < 0$ and $\partial y/\partial z > 0$. The sample data, taken from annual statistics for the U.S. economy between 1948 and 1984,[1] are given in columns (2), (3), and (4) of Table 19.1. Columns (5) through (9) are computed to solve the normal equations.

---

[1]Source of these data is *The Economic Report of the President*, 1985, Tables B-35 and B-41.

Table 19.1

Percent Change in Real Wage Rate (y), Unemployment Rate (x), and Percent Change in Productivity (z): 1948 to 1984

Year	y	x	z	xy	zy	xz	x^2	z^2
1948	0.8	3.8	4.3	3.04	3.44	16.34	14.4	18.5
1949	3.9	5.9	2.0	23.01	7.80	11.80	34.8	4.0
1950	4.8	5.3	6.0	25.44	28.80	31.80	28.1	36.0
1951	0.7	3.3	1.7	2.31	1.19	5.61	10.9	2.9
1952	3.2	3.0	2.3	9.60	7.36	6.90	9.0	5.3
1953	4.8	2.9	1.7	13.92	8.16	4.93	8.4	2.9
1954	2.7	5.5	1.4	14.85	3.78	7.70	30.3	2.0
1955	3.9	4.4	3.9	17.16	15.21	17.16	19.4	15.2
1956	4.4	4.1	0.3	18.04	1.32	1.23	16.8	0.1
1957	2.2	4.3	1.7	9.46	3.74	7.31	18.5	2.9
1958	1.0	6.8	2.4	6.80	2.40	16.32	46.2	5.8
1959	3.2	5.5	3.4	17.60	10.88	18.70	30.3	11.6
1960	2.7	5.5	0.8	14.85	2.16	4.40	30.3	0.6
1961	2.1	6.7	2.9	14.07	6.09	19.43	44.9	8.4
1962	2.8	5.5	3.6	15.40	10.08	19.80	30.3	13.0
1963	2.2	5.7	3.2	12.54	7.04	18.24	32.5	10.2
1964	3.2	5.2	3.9	16.64	12.48	20.28	27.0	15.2
1965	1.7	4.5	3.1	7.65	5.27	13.95	20.3	9.6
1966	3.0	3.8	2.5	11.40	7.50	9.50	14.4	6.3
1967	2.6	3.8	1.9	9.88	4.94	7.22	14.4	3.6
1968	3.2	3.6	3.3	11.52	10.56	11.88	13.0	10.9
1969	1.1	3.5	-0.3	3.85	-0.33	-1.05	12.3	0.1
1970	1.0	4.9	0.3	4.90	0.30	1.47	24.0	0.1
1971	2.2	5.9	3.3	12.98	7.26	19.47	34.8	10.9
1972	3.3	5.6	3.7	18.48	12.21	20.72	31.4	13.7
1973	1.3	4.9	2.4	6.37	3.12	11.76	24.0	5.8
1974	-1.4	5.6	-2.5	-7.84	3.50	-14.00	31.4	6.3
1975	0.4	8.5	2.0	3.40	0.80	17.00	72.3	4.0
1976	2.2	7.7	3.2	16.94	7.04	24.64	59.3	10.2
1977	1.0	7.1	2.2	7.10	2.20	15.62	50.4	4.8
1978	0.9	6.1	0.6	5.49	0.54	3.66	37.2	0.4
1979	-2.0	5.8	-1.5	-11.60	3.00	-8.70	33.6	2.3
1980	-2.8	7.1	-0.7	-19.88	1.96	-4.97	50.4	0.5
1981	-0.6	7.6	1.9	-4.56	-1.14	14.44	57.8	3.6
1982	1.6	9.7	-0.1	15.52	-0.16	-0.97	94.1	0.0
1983	2.3	9.6	3.1	22.08	7.13	29.76	92.2	9.6
1984	1.0	7.5	3.2	7.50	3.20	24.00	56.3	10.2
Sum	70.6	206.2	77.1	355.9	210.8	423.4	1,255.3	267.3
Mean	1.91	5.57	2.08					

Source: *Economic Report of the President*, 1985.

We form the regression equation:

$$y = \hat{a} + \hat{b}x + \hat{c}z + \hat{u}$$

Minimizing the sum of squares of $\hat{u}$ gives the following normal equations:

$$70.6 = 37\hat{a} + 206.2\hat{b} + 77.1\hat{c}$$
$$355.9 = 206.2\hat{a} + 1{,}255.3\hat{b} + 423.4\hat{c}$$
$$210.8 = 77.1\hat{a} + 423.4\hat{b} + 267.3\hat{c}$$

Solving these equations by the methods of Chapter 4 or Chapter 5, we obtain the following coefficients:

$$\hat{a} = 2.48$$
$$\hat{b} = -0.319$$
$$\hat{c} = 0.579$$

Therefore, our multiple regression is:

$$\hat{y} = 2.48 - 0.312x + 0.579z$$

If both the unemployment rate and the percent change in productivity are zero, the average real wage rate is predicted to increase by slightly less than 2.5 percent per year. If the unemployment rate increases by 1 percent, the predicted percent change in the real wage rate decreases by about 0.3 percent, *the percent change in productivity remaining constant*. For each 1 percent increase in productivity, the predicted percent change in the real wage rate increases by about 0.6 percent, *the unemployment rate remaining constant*. Multiple regression coefficients are the estimates of the *partial derivatives* of the dependent variable with respect to the respective regressors.

Multiple Regression and the Deviation of Variables About Their Means

In Chapter 17 we showed that simple regression techniques guarantee that the fitted regression line passes through the point corresponding to the means of the independent and the dependent variables. This observation led to convenient formulas for the regression coefficients, based on the deviations between the variables and their means. Similar formulas can be developed for multiple regression. According to the first normal equation:

$$n\hat{a} + \hat{b}\Sigma x + \hat{c}\Sigma z = \Sigma y$$

Dividing through by n and solving for $\hat{a}$, we have:

$$\hat{a} = \frac{\Sigma y}{n} - \frac{\hat{b}\Sigma x}{n} - \frac{\hat{c}\Sigma z}{n} = \bar{y} - \hat{b}\bar{x} - \hat{c}\bar{y}$$

For the regression equation, when $x = \bar{x}$ and $z = \bar{z}$, we have:

$$\hat{y} = \hat{a} + \hat{b}\bar{x} + \hat{c}\bar{z} = \bar{y} - \hat{b}\bar{x} - \hat{c}\bar{z} + \hat{b}\bar{x} + \hat{c}\bar{z} = \bar{y}$$

Recall from Chapter 17 that a simple regression generates the equation of a line in two dimensions. A multiple regression with two independent variables generates the equation for a plane in three dimensions. Ordinary least squares estimators for multiple regression guarantee that the regression plane passes through the point representing the means of all variables.

We can also derive the formulas for the two slope coefficients in terms of the deviations between each variable and its respective mean:

$$\hat{b} = \frac{\Sigma(x - \overline{x})(y - \overline{y})[\Sigma(z - \overline{z})^2] - \Sigma(z - \overline{z})(y - \overline{y})[\Sigma(x - \overline{x})(z - \overline{z})]}{[\Sigma(x - \overline{x})^2\Sigma(z - \overline{z})^2] - [\Sigma(x - \overline{x})(z - \overline{z})]^2}$$

$$\hat{c} = \frac{\Sigma(z - \overline{z})(y - \overline{y})[\Sigma(x - \overline{x})^2] - \Sigma(x - \overline{x})(y - \overline{y})[B(x - \overline{x})(z - \overline{z})]}{[\Sigma(x - \overline{x})^2\Sigma(z - \overline{z})^2] - [\Sigma(x - \overline{x})(z - \overline{z})]^2}$$

Notice the symmetry between the two slope coefficients. Each estimates the influence of one independent variable on the dependent variable, with the other independent variable held constant. If the two regressors, x and z, were truly uncorrelated, their correlation coefficient would be zero:

$$r_{xz} = \frac{\Sigma(x - \overline{x})(z - \overline{z})}{\sqrt{\Sigma(x - \overline{x})^2\Sigma(z - \overline{z})^2}} = 0$$

implying

$$\Sigma(x - \overline{x})(z - \overline{z}) = 0$$

If x and z were uncorrelated, the second term in the denominator and the numerator of the expressions for $\hat{b}$ and $\hat{c}$ would become zero. The two formulas would simplify to:

$$\hat{b} = \frac{\Sigma(x - \overline{x})(y - \overline{y})}{\Sigma(x - \overline{x})^2} \quad \text{and} \quad \hat{c} = \frac{\Sigma(z - \overline{z})(y - \overline{y})}{\Sigma(z - \overline{z})^2}$$

These are the same coefficients obtained with simple regression.

If variable z were uncorrelated with variable x, the coefficients estimated with simple regressions would be identical to the multiple regression coefficients. (Although, as we will see, the standard errors of those regression coefficients would be different.) When the correlation between x and z is not zero, the influence of each variable on the dependent variable must be separated from the influence of the other dependent variable(s). This is what distinguishes multiple regression from simple regression.

Table 19.2 presents the regression of the percent change in the real wage rate (y) against the unemployment rate (x) and the percent change in productivity (z). The equation generated,

$$\hat{y} = 2.48 - 0.319x + 0.579z$$

shows that coefficients estimated using the deviations of x, y, and z from their means are identical to those generated from the normal equations.

Table 19.2

Year	y	x	z	$(x-\bar{x})(y-\bar{y})$	$(z-\bar{z})(y-\bar{y})$	$(x-\bar{x})(z-\bar{z})$	$(x-\bar{x})^2$	$(z-\bar{z})^2$
1948	0.8	3.8	4.3	2.0	−2.5	−3.9	3.1	4.9
1949	3.9	5.9	2.0	0.7	−0.2	0.0	0.1	0.0
1950	4.8	5.3	6.0	−0.8	11.3	−1.1	0.1	15.4
1951	0.7	3.3	1.7	2.7	0.5	0.9	5.2	0.1
1952	3.2	3.0	2.3	−3.3	0.3	−0.6	6.6	0.0
1953	4.8	2.9	1.7	−7.7	−1.1	1.0	7.1	0.1
1954	2.7	5.5	1.4	−0.1	−0.5	0.0	0.0	0.5
1955	3.9	4.4	3.9	−2.3	3.6	−2.1	1.4	3.3
1956	4.4	4.1	0.3	−3.7	−4.4	2.6	2.2	3.2
1957	2.2	4.3	1.7	−0.4	−0.1	0.5	1.6	0.1
1958	1.0	6.8	2.4	−1.1	−0.3	0.4	1.5	0.1
1959	3.2	5.5	3.4	−0.1	1.7	−0.1	0.0	1.7
1960	2.7	5.5	0.8	−0.1	−1.0	0.1	0.0	1.6
1961	2.1	6.7	2.9	0.2	0.2	0.9	1.3	0.7
1962	2.8	5.5	3.6	−0.1	1.4	−0.1	0.0	2.3
1963	2.2	5.7	3.2	0.0	0.3	0.1	0.0	1.3
1964	3.2	5.2	3.9	−0.5	2.3	−0.7	0.1	3.3
1965	1.7	4.5	3.1	0.2	−0.2	−1.1	1.1	1.0
1966	3.0	3.8	2.5	−1.9	0.5	−0.7	3.1	0.2
1967	2.6	3.8	1.9	−1.2	−0.1	0.3	3.1	0.0
1968	3.2	3.6	3.3	−2.5	1.6	−2.4	3.9	1.5
1969	1.1	3.5	−0.3	1.7	1.9	4.9	4.3	5.7
1970	1.0	4.9	0.3	0.6	1.6	1.2	0.4	3.2
1971	2.2	5.9	3.3	0.1	0.4	0.4	0.1	1.5
1972	3.3	5.6	3.7	0.0	2.3	0.0	0.0	2.6
1973	1.3	4.9	2.4	0.4	−0.2	−0.2	0.4	0.1

Year								
1974	-1.4	5.6	-2.5	-0.1	15.2	-0.1	0.0	21.0
1975	0.4	8.5	2.0	-4.4	0.1	-0.2	8.6	0.0
1976	2.2	7.7	3.2	0.6	0.3	2.4	4.5	1.3
1977	1.0	7.1	2.2	-1.4	-0.1	0.2	2.3	0.0
1978	0.9	6.1	0.6	-0.5	1.5	-0.8	0.3	2.2
1979	-2.0	5.8	-1.5	-0.9	14.0	-0.8	0.1	12.8
1980	-2.8	7.1	-0.7	-7.2	13.1	-4.3	2.3	7.7
1981	-0.6	7.6	1.9	-5.1	0.5	-0.4	4.1	0.0
1982	1.6	9.7	-0.1	-1.3	0.7	-9.0	17.1	4.8
1983	2.3	9.6	3.1	1.6	0.4	4.1	16.2	1.0
1984	1.0	7.5	3.2	-1.8	-1.0	2.2	3.7	1.3
Sum	70.6	206.2	77.1	-37.5	63.7	-6.3	106.2	106.6
Mean	1.91	5.57	2.08	-1.01	1.72	-0.17	2.87	2.88

$$\hat{b} = \frac{(-37.5)(106.6) - (63.7)(-6.3)}{(106.2)(106.6) - (-6.3)^2} = \frac{-4{,}002.4 - (-403.0)}{11{,}319.2 - 39.7} = \frac{-3{,}599.4}{11{,}279.5} = -0.319$$

$$\hat{c} = \frac{(63.7)(106.2) - (-37.5)(-6.3)}{(106.2)(106.6) - (-6.3)^2} = \frac{6{,}764.9 - 236.3}{11{,}320.9 - 39.7} = \frac{6{,}528.7}{11{,}279.5} = 0.5786$$

$$\hat{a} = 1.91 - (-0.319)(5.57) - (0.5786)(2.08) = 2.481$$

It is informative to contrast multiple regression coefficients with simple regression coefficients. Using the data in Table 19.2, we regress y on x (ignoring z). This yields the estimated coefficients:

$$\hat{b} = \frac{\Sigma(x - \bar{x})(y - \bar{y})}{\Sigma(x - \bar{x})^2} = \frac{-37.5}{106.2} = -0.353$$

and

$$\hat{a} = 1.91 - (-0.353)(5.57) = 3.87$$

Our first simple regression equation is:

$$\hat{y} = 3.87 - 0.353x$$

Regressing y against z (ignoring x) generates the coefficients:

$$\hat{c} = \frac{\Sigma(z - \bar{z})(y - \bar{y})}{\Sigma(z - \bar{z})^2} = \frac{63.7}{106.2} = 0.5998$$

and

$$\hat{a} = 1.91 - (0.5998)(2.08) = 0.662$$

Our second simple regression is:

$$\hat{y} = 0.662 + 0.5998z$$

Excluding z from the regression caused the value of $\hat{b}$ to change from -0.319 to -0.353 and the value of $\hat{a}$ to increase from 2.48 to 3.87. If the variable z is omitted from the regression, the variation in y attributed to the joint variation between x and z is attributed to x. The variation of y due to z alone (that is, not shared with x) is absorbed by the constant term when z is omitted from the equation.

Similar results occur when x is excluded from the regression. The value of the slope coefficient increases slightly, from 0.579 to 0.5998, and the value of the intercept term decreases substantially, from 2.48 to 0.662. Again, the joint influence of x and z on y is wholly attributed to z when x is omitted from the regression. The influence of x on y which is independent of z distorts the value of the intercept when x is excluded from the regression.

In this example, the partial derivatives estimated by multiple regression analysis are close to the coefficients estimated through simple regression because the *interaction* between x and z is fairly small in this example. From Table 19.2, we can calculate the correlation coefficient for these two variables as:

$$r_{xz} = \frac{\Sigma(x - \bar{x})(z - \bar{z})}{\sqrt{\Sigma(x - \bar{x})^2\Sigma(z - \bar{z})^2}} = \frac{-6.3}{\sqrt{(106.2)(106.6)}} = \frac{-6.3}{106.40} = -0.059$$

Because little of the movement in x is reflected in a change in z (and vice versa), the simple regression coefficients approximate the multiple regression coefficients. However, because these variables are not perfectly independent, and each is thought to be an important *nonrandom* influence on the dependent variable, the multiple regression model is the preferred model.

Geometric Interpretation

In Chapter 2 we saw that there is a geometric counterpart to every equation with one or two independent variables. An equation in three variables (one dependent and two independent) corresponds to a plane. The purpose of the regression of y on x and z is to compute the values of the parameters in the linear equation. Once these values are determined, a plane in three-dimensional space is also determined. If y, x, and z are measured on three mutually perpendicular axes, a graph of the plane can be constructed. For a given value of x and a given value of z, a value of $\hat{y}$ is determined from the regression equation. These three values locate a point in the three-dimensional space. For all possible pairs of values of x and z, all possible values of $\hat{y}$ are determined by the regression equation—and these form a plane in the space.

The geometric interpretation of the least squares estimates of the regression coefficients is similar to that for simple regression. In problems of simple regression, each observation fixes a point in two-dimensional space, and the total of all observations forms a scatter diagram. The regression equation is such that the line corresponding to it minimizes the sum of the squared values of the deviations of the points from the line. Likewise, when the sample consists of observations on three variables, each observation fixes a point in three-dimensional space and the set of all observations forms a scatter in this space. The multiple regression equation is such that the sum of the squared deviations of the observed points from the plane is minimum.

When multiple regression involves functions of more than two variables, the limits of our perception make a geometric interpretation difficult. Nevertheless, an algebraic interpretation is possible. The residual $\hat{u}$ represents the difference between the observed value of y and the value of y predicted by the fitted regression ($\hat{y}$). Because we assume that the error term has an expected value of zero, we construct the residual to have a mean of zero. All that we require for $\Sigma\hat{u} = 0$ is that the predicted value of y equals its mean when all regressors are set equal to their means. There are an infinite number of estimators with this property. We define the *best* of those estimation techniques as the one that minimizes the squared residual, which (we hope) also minimizes the variance of the error term. It is these characteristics of unbiasedness and efficiency that provide the basis for hypothesis testing.

Significance Tests

If we are willing to make the assumption that the distribution of the error term is approximately normal, we can construct t statistics to test hypotheses about the population parameters of a multiple regression model. As in the case of simple regression, we stipulate an alternative hypothesis. This implies a null hypothesis we would accept if evidence in favor of the alternative hypothesis were weak. If our alternative hypothesis were that parameter b is less than zero, the null hypothesis would be that b is greater than or equal to zero. The t statistic for this test is computed as the ratio of the difference between the estimated value of b and the value given by the null hypothesis, to the standard error of that coefficient:

$$t = \frac{\hat{b} - b_0}{s_{\hat{b}}}$$

We state without proof that the formulas for the variance in the regression coefficients are given as:

$$\text{Var } \hat{b} = s_{\hat{b}}^2 = s_{\hat{u}}^2 \frac{\Sigma(z - \bar{z})^2}{\Sigma(x - \bar{x})^2\Sigma(z - \bar{z})^2 - [\Sigma(x - \bar{x})(z - \bar{z})]^2}$$

$$\text{Var } \hat{c} = s_{\hat{c}}^2 = s_{\hat{u}}^2 \frac{\Sigma(x - \bar{x})^2}{\Sigma(x - \bar{x})^2\Sigma(z - \bar{z})^2 - [\Sigma(x - \bar{x})(z - \bar{z})]^2}$$

Notice that the denominator of both variances is the same as the common denominator of the slope coefficients.

The sample variance for the residual, $s_{\hat{u}}^2$, is obtained by summing the squared residuals for all observations, then dividing by the degrees of freedom:

$$s_{\hat{u}}^2 = \frac{\Sigma\hat{u}^2}{n - k} = \frac{\Sigma(y - \hat{y})^2}{n - k}$$

where n is the number of observations and k is the number of parameters to be estimated.

The standard error of each regression coefficient is obtained by taking the square root of the respective variances:

$$s_{\hat{b}} = \sqrt{s_{\hat{b}}^2} \text{ and } s_{\hat{c}} = \sqrt{s_{\hat{c}}^2}$$

Earlier we concluded that if regressors x and z were uncorrelated, the coefficients estimated with multiple regression would be identical to the coefficients estimated with simple regression. We might wonder whether multiple regression is worth the trouble under such circumstances. One answer is suggested by comparing the variances of the simple and multiple regression coefficients.

If x and z were uncorrelated, we have:

$$r_{xz} = \frac{\Sigma(x - \bar{x})(z - \bar{z})}{\sqrt{\Sigma(x - \bar{x})^2\Sigma(z - \bar{z})^2}} = 0$$

implying

$$\Sigma(x - \bar{x})(z - \bar{z}) = 0$$

The variance for $\hat{b}$ would equal:

$$s_{\hat{b}}^2 = s_{\hat{u}}^2 \frac{\Sigma(z - \bar{z})^2}{\Sigma(x - \bar{x})^2 \Sigma(z - \bar{z})^2} = \frac{s_{\hat{u}}^2}{\Sigma(x - \bar{x})^2}$$

At first this formula looks identical to the one derived for a simple regression. However, as long as y is correlated with z, $s_{\hat{u}}^2$ would generally be lower for a multiple regression than for a simple regression.[2] Therefore, even when we believe that two regressors are uncorrelated, multiple regression tends to be more efficient than simple regression.

Table 19.3 presents the additional information necessary to compute the standard errors of our two slope coefficients. Column (5) presents the predicted value of y for each observation and column (6) shows the corresponding residual. Column (7) presents the squared residual for each observation, whose total is given at the bottom of that column as $\Sigma\hat{u}^2 = 60.0$. Hence, we have:

$$s_{\hat{u}}^2 = \frac{\Sigma(y - \hat{y})^2}{34} = \frac{60.0}{34} = 1.765$$

Using the information from Table 19.2, we can compute the two standard errors:

$$s_{\hat{b}}^2 = 1.765\left(\frac{106.6}{11,320.9}\right) = 0.0166; \ s_{\hat{b}} = \sqrt{0.0166} = 0.129$$

$$s_{\hat{c}}^2 = 1.765\left(\frac{106.2}{11,320.9}\right) = 0.0166; \ s_{\hat{c}} = \sqrt{0.0166} = 0.129$$

With our information about the standard errors, we can test various null hypotheses about the equation. According to economic theory, real wage rates should decrease as the unemployment rate increases ($\partial y/\partial x < 0$), and the null hypothesis is $b \geq 0$. We also predict that the faster productivity increases, the greater is the percent increase in the real wage rate ($\partial y/\partial z > 0$), and the null hypothesis is $c \leq 0$. The critical t statistics for 30 degrees of freedom and a one-tail test are 1.679 and 2.424 for 5 percent and 1 percent significance, respectively. (We have 34 degrees of freedom, but the corresponding critical values are not reported in the table. However, if we err, we err on the side of caution.) The corresponding t statistics are:

$$t_{\hat{b}} = \frac{-0.319 - 0}{0.129} = -2.47; \ t_{\hat{c}} = \frac{0.579 - 0}{0.129} = 4.49$$

In both cases, the t statistics have the expected sign. We can reject the null hypothesis that an increase in the unemployment rate does not reduce the change in the real wage rate with 99 percent confidence. We can also

---

[2] If the correlation between y and z were very small, it is possible that the reduction in $\Sigma(y - \hat{y})^2$ gained from adding z to the regression of y on x may be outweighed by the decrease in the degrees of freedom. This is most likely when the number of observations is small.

Table 19.3

Year	y	x	z	$\hat{y}$	$\hat{u} = (y - \hat{y})$	$\hat{u}^2$	$(y - \bar{y})^2$
1948	0.8	3.8	4.3	3.76	−2.96	8.73	1.23
1949	3.9	5.9	2.0	1.76	2.14	4.60	3.96
1950	4.8	5.3	6.0	4.26	0.54	0.29	8.35
1951	0.7	3.3	1.7	2.41	−1.71	2.92	1.46
1952	3.2	3.0	2.3	2.85	0.35	0.12	1.66
1953	4.8	2.9	1.7	2.54	2.26	5.12	8.35
1954	2.7	5.5	1.4	1.54	1.16	1.36	0.62
1955	3.9	4.4	3.9	3.33	0.57	0.32	3.96
1956	4.4	4.1	0.3	1.35	3.05	9.33	6.20
1957	2.2	4.3	1.7	2.09	0.11	0.01	0.08
1958	1.0	6.8	2.4	1.70	−0.70	0.49	0.83
1959	3.2	5.5	3.4	2.69	0.51	0.26	1.66
1960	2.7	5.5	0.8	1.19	1.51	2.28	0.62
1961	2.1	6.7	2.9	2.02	0.08	0.01	0.04
1962	2.8	5.5	3.6	2.81	−0.01	0.00	0.79
1963	2.2	5.7	3.2	2.51	−0.31	0.10	0.08
1964	3.2	5.2	3.9	3.08	0.12	0.01	1.66
1965	1.7	4.5	3.1	2.84	−1.14	1.29	0.04
1966	3.0	3.8	2.5	2.71	0.29	0.08	1.19
1967	2.6	3.8	1.9	2.37	0.23	0.05	0.48
1968	3.2	3.6	3.3	3.24	−0.04	0.00	1.66
1969	1.1	3.5	−0.3	1.19	−0.09	0.01	0.66
1970	1.0	4.9	0.3	1.09	−0.09	0.01	0.83
1971	2.2	5.9	3.3	2.51	−0.31	0.09	0.08
1972	3.3	5.6	3.7	2.83	0.47	0.22	1.93
1973	1.3	4.9	2.4	2.31	−1.01	1.01	0.37
1974	−1.4	5.6	−2.5	−0.75	−0.65	0.42	10.96
1975	0.4	8.5	2.0	0.93	−0.53	0.28	2.28
1976	2.2	7.7	3.2	1.88	0.32	0.10	0.08
1977	1.0	7.1	2.2	1.49	−0.49	0.24	0.83
1978	0.9	6.1	0.6	0.88	0.02	0.00	1.02
1979	−2.0	5.8	−1.5	−0.24	−1.76	3.11	15.29
1980	−2.8	7.1	−0.7	−0.19	−2.61	6.82	22.18
1981	−0.6	7.6	1.9	1.16	−1.76	3.08	6.30
1982	1.6	9.7	−0.1	−0.67	2.27	5.15	0.10
1983	2.3	9.6	3.1	1.21	1.09	1.18	0.15
1984	1.0	7.5	3.2	1.94	−0.94	0.88	0.83
Sum	70.6	206.2	77.1	70.6	0.00	60.0	108.8
Mean	1.91	5.57	2.08				

reject the null hypothesis that an increase in the percent change in productivity does not increase the change in the real wage rate with better than 99 percent confidence.

MULTIPLE CORRELATION

We have already seen that the simple correlation coefficient measures the degree of association between any two variables. We also found that in a simple regression, the coefficient of determination is given by the square of the correlation coefficient. The coefficient of determination, r^2, measures the proportion of variation in the dependent variable that is attributed to the variation in the independent variable. For a multiple regression, the *coefficient of multiple determination*, R^2, measures the proportion of the variation in the dependent variable that is attributed to two or more regressors. It is computed as the ratio of the *explained* variation to the total variation about $\bar{y}$:

$$R^2 = \frac{\Sigma(\hat{y} - \bar{y})^2}{\Sigma(y - \bar{y})^2} = 1 - \frac{\Sigma(y - \hat{y})^2}{\Sigma(y - \bar{y})^2}$$

In Table 19.3 we see that the total variation of y about its mean is 108.8 and the sum of the squared residuals is 60.0. Therefore, we have:

$$R^2 = 1 - \frac{60.0}{108.8} = 1 - 0.5515 = 0.4485$$

Slightly less than 45 percent of the variation in y is attributed to the variation of x and z.

We have argued that avoiding specification error requires that all important or systematic influences on the dependent variable be included in the model. The size of R^2 is not critical, *per se*. That is, it is possible for R^2 to be high and important variables still to have been omitted, or for R^2 to be relatively low, and yet all omitted influences be essentially random in character. The ultimate issue in estimating an econometric model is how well the variables included in the equation(s) reflect the theory being tested.

Adjusted R^2

There is sometimes a temptation to throw as many variables as possible into the right-hand side of the equation in an attempt to "improve" R^2. Since each variable entered picks up a portion of the variation in the dependent variable that was unexplained by the other regressors, such a strategy will almost always increase R^2. However, this could lead to an extreme case where the number of parameters being estimated equals the number of observations. In this case, $R^2 = 1$, but there would be no degrees of freedom left. The investigator would have merely forced a "good fit" by using up all the observations.

As a check against the overzealous inclusion of variables, researchers often calculate a coefficient of multiple determination which controls for the degrees of freedom. This coefficient is appropriately named the *adjusted* R^2, and is designated as $\overline{R}^2$. Its formula is:

$$\overline{R}^2 = 1 - (1 - R^2)\frac{n - 1}{n - k}$$

where n is the number of observations and k is the number of parameters being estimated. In our example, $n = 37$ and $k = 3$, so:

$$\overline{R}^2 = 1 - (1 - 0.4485)\frac{37}{34} = 1 - 0.6001 = 0.3999$$

If the change in R^2 is smaller than the percent change in the degrees of freedom when an additional variable is added to the regression equation, the adjusted R^2 will fall.

Partial Correlation Coefficients

The *partial correlation coefficient* between a dependent and an independent variable measures the net association between those two variables after excluding (holding constant) the common influence of other independent variables included in the regression equation. Recall that the correlation coefficient is measured as the ratio of the joint variation between two variables to the square root of the product of the variances of the variables. Hence, in our example:

$$r_{xy} = \frac{\Sigma(x - \overline{x})(y - \overline{y})}{\sqrt{\Sigma(x - \overline{x})^2\Sigma(y - \overline{y})^2}} = \frac{-37.5}{\sqrt{(106.2)(108.8)}} = \frac{-37.5}{107.49} = -0.349$$

$$r_{zy} = \frac{\Sigma(z - \overline{z})(y - \overline{y})}{\sqrt{\Sigma(z - \overline{z})^2\Sigma(y - \overline{y})^2}} = \frac{63.7}{\sqrt{(106.6)(108.8)}} = \frac{63.7}{107.69} = -0.5915$$

and $r_{xz} = -0.059$, as already calculated.

For the variables in question, we define:

$$r_{xy \cdot z} = \frac{r_{yx} - (r_{yz}r_{xz})}{\sqrt{1 - r_{xz}^2}\sqrt{1 - r_{yx}^2}}$$

$$= \frac{-0.349 - (0.5915)(-0.059)}{(0.9965)^{1/2}(0.6501)^{1/2}} = \frac{-0.3141}{0.8049} = -0.3902$$

$$r_{zy \cdot x} = \frac{r_{zy} - (r_{yx}r_{xz})}{\sqrt{1 - r_{xz}^2}\sqrt{1 - r_{yz}^2}}$$

$$= \frac{0.5915 - (-0.349)(-0.059)}{(0.9965)^{1/2}(0.6501)^{1/2}} = \frac{0.5709}{0.8049} = 0.7093$$

After isolating the effect of productivity changes, the relationship between real wage changes and unemployment is strengthened slightly. After removing the effect of unemployment, the relationship between real wage changes and productivity changes is strengthened substantially.

MATRIX NOTATION IN
MULTIPLE REGRESSION

Sometimes we find it necessary to relate a dependent variable y to three (or more) variables x, z, and w. The linear model is then written:

$$y = a + bx + cz + dw + u$$

where a, b, c, and d are the unknown population parameters and u is the difference between the observed values of y and those predicted by the (unknown) population equation. The estimated multiple regression equation is written:

$$\hat{y} = \hat{a} + \hat{b}x + \hat{c}z + \hat{d}w$$

with $\hat{u} = y - \hat{y} = y - \hat{a} - \hat{b}x - \hat{c}z - \hat{d}w$.

As in the case of one and two independent variables, the estimates of the coefficients are computed by minimizing the sum of the squares of $\hat{u}$. Just as in the case of functions of two variables, this minimization operation yields the normal equations that are solved for the least squares values of $\hat{a}$, $\hat{b}$, $\hat{c}$, and $\hat{d}$. For a function of three variables, the normal equations are:

$$\Sigma y = \hat{a}n + \hat{b}\Sigma x + \hat{c}\Sigma z + \hat{d}\Sigma w$$
$$\Sigma xy = \hat{a}\Sigma x + \hat{b}\Sigma x^2 + \hat{c}\Sigma xz + \hat{d}\Sigma xw$$
$$\Sigma zy = \hat{a}\Sigma z + \hat{b}\Sigma xz + \hat{c}\Sigma z^2 + \hat{d}\Sigma zw$$
$$\Sigma wy = \hat{a}\Sigma w + \hat{b}\Sigma xw + \hat{c}\Sigma zw + \hat{d}\Sigma w^2$$

All quantities in the equations except $\hat{a}$, $\hat{b}$, $\hat{c}$, and $\hat{d}$ can be computed from the sample data, so the four equations can be solved for the values of the four unknowns. Standard errors of the regression coefficients can be computed and tests of significance conducted. The coefficient of multiple determination is computed in the same way as that shown for the case of functions of two variables.

In general for a function of k variables, the same principles apply. Let the general multiple regression equations be written as:

$$y = b_0 + b_1x_1 + b_2x_2 + \ldots + b_kx_k + u$$

where the subscripts designate different explanatory variables and their corresponding coefficients.

Minimization of the sum of squares of $\hat{u}$ yields the normal equations:

$$\Sigma y = \hat{b}_0 n + \hat{b}_1 \Sigma x_1 + \hat{b}_2 \Sigma x_2 + \ldots + \hat{b}_k \Sigma x_k$$

$$\Sigma x_1 y = \hat{b}_0 \Sigma x_1 + \hat{b}_1 \Sigma x_1{}^2 + \hat{b}_2 \Sigma x_1 x_2 + \ldots + \hat{b}_k \Sigma x_1 x_k$$

$$\Sigma x_2 y = \hat{b}_0 \Sigma x_2 + \hat{b}_1 \Sigma x_1 x_2 + \hat{b}_2 \Sigma x_2{}^2 + \ldots + \hat{b}_k \Sigma x_2 x_k$$

$$\vdots$$

$$\Sigma x_k y = \hat{b}_0 \Sigma x_k + \hat{b}_1 \Sigma x_1 x_k + \hat{b}_2 \Sigma x_2 x_k + \ldots + \hat{b}_k \Sigma x_k{}^2$$

There are $k + 1$ unknowns $(\hat{b}_0, \hat{b}_1, \ldots, \hat{b}_k)$ and $k + 1$ normal equations that can be solved for values of the unknowns. When the number of unknowns or the number of observations is relatively large, the problem of estimation is given over to an electronic computer. The computer sets the problem in matrix form:

$$\mathbf{y} = \mathbf{Xb} + \mathbf{u}$$

where $\mathbf{y}$ is a vector of n observations on the dependent variable and $\mathbf{X}$ is a ($k + 1$ by n) matrix of observations on the k independent variables. The first column of $\mathbf{X}$ consists of "1's" to pick up the constant term. The vector $\mathbf{b}$ represents the $k + 1$ unknown coefficients, and $\mathbf{u}$ is a vector of error terms. The estimated regression equation is given by:

$$
\begin{bmatrix} \hat{y}_1 \\ \hat{y}_2 \\ \vdots \\ \vdots \\ \hat{y}_n \end{bmatrix}
=
\begin{bmatrix}
1 & x_{11} & x_{21} & x_{31} & \cdots & x_{k1} \\
1 & x_{12} & x_{22} & x_{32} & \cdots & x_{k2} \\
\vdots & \vdots & \vdots & \vdots & \cdots & \vdots \\
\vdots & \vdots & \vdots & \vdots & \cdots & \vdots \\
1 & x_{1n} & x_{2n} & x_{3n} & \cdots & x_{kn}
\end{bmatrix}
\begin{bmatrix} \hat{b}_0 \\ \hat{b}_1 \\ \vdots \\ \vdots \\ \hat{b}_k \end{bmatrix}
$$

Substituting $y_i - \hat{u}_i$ for $\hat{y}_i$ in each observation, and collecting the residuals on the right side we get:

$$\hat{\mathbf{y}} = \mathbf{X}\hat{\mathbf{b}} + \hat{\mathbf{u}}$$

where $\hat{\mathbf{b}}$ is the vector of estimated coefficients. The procedures for solving a matrix equation were outlined in Chapter 6. First, we recall that a matrix equation system is solved by finding the inverse of the coefficient matrix, in this case matrix $\mathbf{X}$. In order to have an inverse, a matrix must be square and nonsingular. Because the number of observations (n) is usually much greater than the number of unknowns ($k + 1$), it is clear that matrix $\mathbf{X}$ is not a square matrix.

We can multiply both sides of this equation by the transpose of $\mathbf{X}$, designated by $\mathbf{X}'$. (Recall from Chapter 5 that the transpose of a matrix is formed by switching the rows and columns of the matrix.) We obtain:

$$\mathbf{X}'\mathbf{y} = \mathbf{X}'\mathbf{Xb} + \mathbf{X}'\hat{\mathbf{u}}$$

The matrix $\mathbf{X'X}$ results from the multiplication of a ($k + 1$ by n) matrix ($\mathbf{X'}$) times an (n by $k + 1$) matrix ($\mathbf{X}$). Hence, $\mathbf{X'X}$ is a square matrix with ($k + 1$) rows and columns. The vector $\mathbf{X'\hat{u}}$ is set equal to zero by the assumption that the error term is independent of the regressors. As long as the $\mathbf{X'X}$ matrix is not singular (i.e., as long as no perfect correlation exists among any of the right-side variables), it has an inverse matrix of the form $(\mathbf{X'X})^{-1}$, yielding the result:

$$\hat{\mathbf{b}} = (\mathbf{X'X})^{-1}\mathbf{X'y}$$

When a computer solves a multiple regression problem, it first arranges the data in a matrix whose number of rows equals the number of observations and whose number of columns equals the number of parameters (the number of right-side variables plus one for the constant term). After forming the transpose, the resulting $\mathbf{X'X}$ matrix yields the normal equations for that number of independent variables. Multiplying both sides of the equation system by the inverse of the transpose yields the estimated coefficient vector $\hat{\mathbf{b}}$. In the process of generating the least squares estimates, the computer also generates the coefficient of determination and the standard errors of the estimated coefficients.

To keep the discussion simple, we shall trace through the estimation of our regression of real wage changes (y) against the unemployment rate (x) and the rate of change of productivity (z). The $\mathbf{X'X}$ matrix is given by:

$$\mathbf{X'X} = \begin{bmatrix} 37.00 & 206.20 & 77.10 \\ 206.20 & 1{,}255.32 & 423.35 \\ 77.10 & 423.35 & 267.27 \end{bmatrix}$$

The vector obtained from multiplying the transpose of matrix $\mathbf{X}$ times the vector $\mathbf{y}$ is:

$$\mathbf{X'y} = \begin{bmatrix} 70.60 \\ 355.91 \\ 210.83 \end{bmatrix}$$

Using procedures like those outlined in Chapter 5, we can find the inverse of the $\mathbf{X'X}$ matrix as:

$$(\mathbf{X'X})^{-1} = \begin{bmatrix} 0.374488 & -0.053845 & -0.022741 \\ -0.053845 & 0.009452 & 0.000561 \\ -0.022741 & 0.000561 & 0.009413 \end{bmatrix}$$

You may wish to verify that the above matrix really is the inverse of the $\mathbf{X'X}$ matrix by matrix multiplication. The vector of estimated coefficients is readily obtained by multiplying $\mathbf{X'y}$ by the inverse, $(\mathbf{X'X})^{-1}$:

$$\hat{\mathbf{b}} = (\mathbf{X'X})^{-1}\mathbf{X'y} = \begin{bmatrix} 2.481 \\ -0.319 \\ 0.579 \end{bmatrix}$$

These are the same results found using data in Tables 19.1, 19.2, and 19.3. In addition, many regression programs report the *variance-covariance* matrix for regression coefficients. In this case, the variance-covariance matrix is:

$$\mathbf{V} = \begin{bmatrix} 0.660811 & -0.095012 & -0.040128 \\ -0.095012 & 0.016679 & 0.000990 \\ -0.040128 & 0.000990 & 0.016610 \end{bmatrix}$$

The elements along the diagonal of matrix $\mathbf{V}$ indicate the variance of each coefficient: $s_{\hat{a}}^2 = 0.660811$, $s_{\hat{b}}^2 = 0.016679$, and $s_{\hat{c}}^2 = 0.016610$. The square roots of these variances can, of course, be used to test hypotheses about the respective coefficients.

MULTIPLE REGRESSION OF NONLINEAR EQUATIONS

Like simple regression techniques, the ordinary least squares procedures can be used to estimate nonlinear regression equations that are linear in their parameters. Recall that A. W. Phillips argued that the relation between nominal wage changes and unemployment is likely to be nonlinear. We might suspect a nonlinear relation between real wage rates and unemployment. Our choice of a linear equation between y (the rate of change in the real wage rate) and x (the unemployment rate) does not allow us to test that hypothesis. However, if we define a new variable $w = x^2$ (i.e., the square of the unemployment rate), we can test whether there is a *significant* deviation from a linear relationship between real wage changes and the unemployment rate.

We can write the regression equation as:

$$\hat{y} = \hat{a} + \hat{b}x + \hat{c}z + \hat{d}w$$

which is linear in all coefficients, so we have reduced the problem to one of multiple linear regression. Since most regression programs have routines for data transformation, the values of w can easily be calculated from the observations on x. Then the computer forms a matrix with the values of x, z, and the transformed variable w (along with 1's for the intercept), finds the inverse of the $\mathbf{X}'\mathbf{X}$ matrix, and generates the estimates of a, b, c, and d.

$$\hat{y} = 5.424 - 1.387x + 0.590z + 0.088w; \quad \overline{R}^2 = 0.4826$$
$$\quad (2.16) \quad (0.739) \quad (0.127) \quad (0.060)$$

By adding the variable $w = x^2$, the adjusted $\overline{R}^2$ increases slightly from 0.4164 to 0.4356, implying that a quadratic specification explains more of the variation in y than the linear model did. However, neither the coefficient $\hat{c}$ nor its standard error is changed by the addition of variable w. Holding unemployment constant is the same as holding unemployment and its square constant. The coefficient of x is modified, as is the standard error for $\hat{b}$. This coefficient is now significant at the 5 percent level $(t = -1.387/0.739 = -1.878)$.

We test the null hypothesis that the relationship between real wage changes and unemployment is linear by determining whether coefficient $\hat{d}$ is significantly different from zero. The critical value of t for 30 degrees of freedom and 5 percent significance is 2.017, since a two-tail test is involved. The t statistic for $\hat{d}$ is $t = 0.088/0.060 = 1.468$, which is insignificant. We fail to reject the null hypothesis, the probability at $d = 0$ is greater than 5 percent.

By transforming the variables used in a linear equation, we can use multiple regression to estimate many forms of nonlinear equations, as long as the equations remain linear in their parameters. For instance, we could transform either independent or dependent variables into logarithms, square roots, or inverses.

MULTICOLLINEARITY

In multiple regression problems, very often we wish to know the separate influences that each of two or more explanatory variables exerts on the explained variable. For example, suppose the regression equation is given by:

$$\hat{y} = \hat{a} + \hat{b}x + \hat{c}z$$

We can predict the direction and the amount of change in y in response to changes in x by the computed value of $\hat{b}$, and we can predict the direction and amount of change in y in response to changes in z by the computed value of $\hat{c}$. As we have noted, the multiple regression coefficients are estimates of the *partial derivatives* of the dependent variable with respect to each of the regressors. That is, $\hat{b}$ measures the effect of a change in x on y when the effect of z on y has been removed. Similarly, $\hat{c}$ measures the effect of a change in z on y when the effect of x on y has been removed.

In multiple regression there is a particularly bothersome problem that often arises, especially in economics. It is very often the case in economic data that observations on theoretically independent variables move together through time or across space. For the above linear multiple regression, we may find that a correlation exists between x and z. When such a linear relation exists among two or more of the explanatory variables, it is not possible to exactly separate their individual influences on the dependent variable. If two or more right-side variables in a regression equation are perfectly correlated, the matrix composed of observations will be singular, and the computer cannot perform the multiple regression. If the correlation between variables is high but not perfect, the computer can estimate the regression coefficients, and indeed, those estimates will be unbiased. However, the standard errors for those coefficients will be bloated, leading to low t statistics and generally insignificant results.[3] Furthermore, high correlation between regressors, dubbed *multicollinearity*, may sometimes cause the signs of the regression coefficients to be "wrong."

Diagnosing Multicollinearity

Simple multicollinearity involving only two regressors is most readily diagnosed by computing the simple correlation coefficient for that pair of regressors. For example, suppose we wish to modify our simple regression of price changes in 1979 (y) against money stock changes in 1979 (x) by introducing the rate of inflation in 1978 (z) as a separate regressor. The reasoning behind this involves the impact of previous inflation on current inflationary expectations. Countries that experienced greater inflation in 1978 should also experience higher inflation in 1979, even with the rate of change of money in 1979 taken into account.

Table 19.4 presents the simple correlation coefficients between the dependent variable, the rate of inflation in 1979 (y), and the two regressors, the rate of change of M1 in 1979 (x) and the rate of inflation in 1978 (z). Note that the correlation between z and x is quite high: $r_{xz} = 0.8807$. A plausible explanation is that monetary authorities often ratify previous inflation with monetary growth in an attempt to avoid a liquidity crisis (such as the one the United States experienced between 1979 and 1983). However, the recursive relationship between x, z, and y makes it difficult to trace individual influence of the regressors.

The first simple regression in Table 19.4 reprises the one presented in Chapter 17. If one country had a rate of money growth 1 percent greater than another country in 1979, we predict that the inflation rate of the latter will exceed that of the former by 1.175 percent. Note that the coefficient of determination, r^2, is 0.7835. Thus, a little over 78 percent of the variation in rate of inflation for 45 countries in 1979 could be attributed to variation in money growth among those countries. Variation in the inflation rate in 1978 appears to account for 86 percent of the variation in the inflation rate in 1979 across countries. If inflation in country A is 1 percent more than that of country B in 1978, country A is predicted to have an inflation rate 0.95 percent higher than country B's in 1979.

---

[3]Suppose that the correlation coefficient between x and z is close but not actually equal to one (in absolute value). Since their denominator is not equal to zero, $\hat{b}$ and $\hat{c}$ can be calculated. However, the standard errors become inflated by the presence of high correlation between regressors. Note that:

$$s_{\hat{b}}^2 = \frac{\Sigma(z - \overline{z})^2}{\Sigma(x - \overline{x})^2 \Sigma(z - \overline{z})^2 - [\Sigma(x - \overline{x})(z - \overline{z})]^2} s_{\hat{u}}^2 = \frac{s_{\hat{u}}^2}{\Sigma(x - \overline{x})^2(1 - r_{xz}^2)}$$

As r_{xz}^2 approaches 1, the denominator approaches 0, causing $s_{\hat{b}}$ (and $s_{\hat{c}}$) to approach infinity.

Table 19.4

Simple Correlation Coefficients:

	y	x	z
y	1.0000		
x	0.8851	1.0000	
z	0.9271	0.8807	1.0000

Simple Regressions:

$\hat{y} = -5.053 + 1.175x$; $r^2 = 0.7835$
    (2.96)   (0.094)

$\hat{y} = 3.630 + 0.9473z$; $r^2 = 0.8596$
    (1.98)   (0.058)

Multiple Regression:

$\hat{y} = -0.356 + 0.406x + 0.672z$; $R^2 = 0.8806$
    (2.36)   (0.149)   (0.115)

When two regressors are highly correlated there is little either regressor can add to the equation once the influence of the other regressor is accounted for. The multiple regression equation shows that both money growth (x) and the previous year's inflation (z) together account for about 88 percent of the variation in inflation in 1979 (y). Variable z accounts for only 10 percent of the variation in y not attributable to x. Variable x accounts for only 2 percent of the variation in y not attributable to z. Clearly, the influence of x on y overlaps with the influence of z on y. Nevertheless, each multiple regression coefficient is significant at the 1 percent level.

Table 19.4 shows two approaches to diagnosing multicollinearity. First, the correlation coefficient $r_{xz} = 0.8807$ reflects overlapping influences of these two variables. Second, the small change in the coefficient of determination when a second variable is entered is a useful method of diagnosing multicollinearity when more than two variables are involved (which may not be diagnosed by simple correlation coefficients).

Another means of diagnosing the presence of multicollinearity is through the use of the F statistic for the regression equation. The F statistic is routinely reported for multiple regression results by most computer regression software, and is an example of a *nonparametric statistic*, meaning that the computation of this statistic is not based on the estimated parameters of the equation (i.e., the calculated regression coefficients). The F statistic is calculated as:

$$F = \frac{\Sigma(\bar{y} - \hat{y})^2/(k+1)}{\Sigma(y - \hat{y})^2/(n-k)} = \frac{R^2/(k+1)}{(1-R^2)/(n-k)}$$

The F statistic measures the average of the deviation between the mean and the predicted value of y (the "explained" variation) divided by the average deviation between the observed value of y and the predicted value of y. F tables list critical values based on the number of degrees of freedom in the numerator (which equals the number of regression coefficients calculated) and the number of degrees of freedom in the denominator (the number of observations minus the number of parameters estimated). The F statistic is used to test the null hypothesis that none of the regressors has an effect on the dependent variable. When the t statistics for individual regressors are all insignificant, but the F statistic for the equation is significant, multicollinearity is suspected.

Remedial Measures

It is extremely important at the outset to emphasize that multicollinearity is usually a *data problem* as opposed to an econometric mistake. Multicollinearity occurs when two or more variables, treated as independent for theoretical purposes, tend to move together. Sometimes multicollinearity is useful for diagnosing a problem in the model itself.

For instance, two variables believed to be causally independent are actually linked together in a recursive or simultaneous way, as in our example of money stock changes and the previous year's inflation rate. A regression of y against x and z causes the coefficient of x to be considerably smaller than in the simple regression of y against x. Most of the effect of money changes on current inflation appears to be "captured" by the previous year's inflation. Nevertheless, the coefficient of x is statistically significant at the 1 percent level, even in the presence of multicollinearity.

Multicollinearity is the ally of the null hypothesis. If we test our models according to the procedures outlined in Chapter 16, namely making the model we believe in the alternative hypothesis and the model we wish to reject the null hypothesis, then multicollinearity represents an additional risk we take when we subject our own beliefs to the burden of proof. Since multicollinearity increases the likelihood that the null hypothesis will be accepted, it follows that results that are significant in the presence of multicollinearity would tend to be even stronger in the absence of multicollinearity. In such cases, no remedial measures are called for.

However, if we "cheat" by making our own hypothesis the null hypothesis, we can almost always rely on multicollinearity to destroy a model we wish to disprove. For instance, several equations in a recursive model may be collapsed into one so that the resulting independent variables are highly correlated. When the individual t statistics fail to be significant, we smugly proclaim that the hypothesis has failed a statistical test and that the null hypothesis must be true. Needless to say, such a strategy is not going to impress those who believe in the alternative hypothesis, which we kill with multicollinearity.

To summarize, multicollinearity is a problem that increases the probability of type II error, the acceptance of a false null hypothesis. We must take care when taking remedial action, because "corrections" may introduce bias into our results, increasing the probability of type I error, the rejection of a true null hypothesis. When the researcher is hostile to the alternative hypothesis, remedial steps to remove multicollinearity are appropriate since multicollinearity is a tempting means of "killing" the offending hypothesis. One way of introducing multicollinearity is to collapse a multi-equation model into a single equation. The appropriate remedy is to specify and estimate the model correctly as a multi-equation one.

One popular remedy for multicollinearity is particularly dangerous. Too often, one or more variables found to be highly correlated are simply dropped from an equation. If the two variables were in fact measuring the same phenomenon (e.g., including two different measures of income in the same regression), then it is appropriate to let one variable do the job of a pair. However, if the two variables have theoretically distinct influences but are highly correlated, then arbitrarily dropping one of them would introduce specification error into the equation. The influence of both variables (the one included and the one excluded) would be attributed to the included variable.

There are other remedies for multicollinearity that are less drastic than outright omission of an offending regressor. Since several of these techniques will be illustrated in the next chapter, we will simply mention them here:

1. Multicollinearity often occurs when several variables seem to be moving together, particularly in the case of nominal time-series data. For instance, both investment spending and government spending tend to move together as the price level rises. Translation of *nominal* variables into *real* magnitudes through the use of a price index may alleviate this joint movement.

2. Sometimes two variables may be highly correlated because they have roughly the same magnitude. For instance, suppose we wish to include the number of workers in unions and the number of workers in construction jobs to determine the effect of unionization on wage rates of construction workers. Across states the magnitude of the two variables is likely to run parallel, causing multicollinearity. We could achieve the same effect by dividing the number of workers in construction unions by the number of construction workers, creating a ratio. Perhaps we would also divide the number of construction workers by total employment. These two ratios are not likely to be as highly correlated as the original raw numbers are.

3. Variables may be highly correlated through time, but not across space, or vice versa. If data sources are available, multicollinearity can sometimes be lessened by using cross-section data instead of time-series, or in *pooling* time-series and cross-section observations.

4. A final way of avoiding multicollinearity is through the use of *instrumental variables*, which are discussed in the next chapter.

HETEROSCEDASTICITY

Another problem that is encountered in economic data is the problem of *heteroscedasticity*, which means a nonconstant variance in the error term. Although not as pervasive as multicollinearity, heteroscedasticity also undermines the reliability of significance tests. That is, regression estimates made in the presence of heteroscedasticity are unbiased, meaning that the expected values of the estimated coefficients equal the values of the true parameters, but the standard errors of the regression coefficients are biased. And, unlike the problem of multicollinearity which tends to bias the significance tests in favor of type II error (inappropriate acceptance of a false null hypothesis), heteroscedasticity tends to bias significance tests in favor of type I error (inappropriate rejection of a true null hypothesis). In other words, if we have made the hypothesis we wish to prove the alternative hypothesis, heteroscedasticity will make our results look better than is objectively warranted. Prudence dictates remedial measures if heteroscedasticity is suspected.

Because regression equations estimated in the presence of heteroscedasticity are unbiased, we can use the residual for each observation as a reliable estimator of the error term of the true regression equation. As long as the expected value of the error term is zero (as long as no important variables are omitted and the regressors are independent of the error term), the variance in the error term can be estimated by the squared residual. Therefore, the usual way of diagnosing heteroscedasticity involves an analysis of the residuals from the regression.

Table 19.5 presents the three variables, the predicted dependent variable, the residual, and the squared residual for the 45 countries investigated in Table 19.4. There seems a tendency for the squared residual to increase as the inflation rate increases. While a mere examination of the squared residual is an imprecise test of heteroscedasticity, such a pattern helps determine whether more precise tests are in order.

One approach that has had widespread use has been suggested by R. E. Park.[4] The "Park test" involves first computing the squared residual after a simple or multiple regression equation has been fit. This is often a simple matter in regression programs which automatically save the residuals after each regression. Next the logarithm of the squared residual is calculated, along with the logarithm of some variable (other than the dependent variable) which seems to parallel the squared residual. In Table 19.6, the logarithm of the squared residual (which must be positive) is regressed against the logarithm of z^2 (since z is negative for one country and the logarithm of a negative number is undefined).

Because corrections for heteroscedasticity may undermine the unbiasedness (although preserving the consistency) of the regression coefficients, we

---

[4]See Edward J. Kane, *Economic Statistics and Econometrics*, New York: Harper and Row, 1968, p. 376.

Table 19.5

Country	y	x	z	$\hat{y}$	$\hat{u}$	$\hat{u}^2$
Malaysia	3.6	18.0	4.9	10.24	6.64	44.13
Japan	3.6	9.9	3.8	6.22	2.62	6.84
Switzerland	3.6	7.8	0.8	3.35	−0.25	0.06
Austria	3.7	−6.1	3.6	−0.41	−4.11	16.91
Germany, Fed Rep	4.1	7.2	2.7	4.38	0.28	0.08
Netherlands	4.2	2.7	4.1	3.50	−0.70	0.50
Belgium	4.5	3.8	4.5	4.21	−0.29	0.08
Syria	4.8	19.8	5.1	11.11	6.31	39.79
Burma	5.7	13.8	−6.1	1.14	−4.56	20.75
India	6.4	19.6	2.5	9.28	2.88	8.29
Sweden	7.3	12.6	9.9	11.41	4.11	16.91
Kenya	8.0	9.3	16.9	14.78	6.78	45.94
Morocco	8.4	17.0	9.7	13.06	4.66	21.75
Canada	9.1	4.9	9.0	7.68	−1.42	2.01
Pakistan	9.4	22.5	6.7	13.28	3.88	15.05
Thailand	9.9	16.6	6.9	11.02	1.12	1.25
Egypt	9.9	23.9	11.1	16.81	6.91	47.68
Iran	10.5	48.1	11.7	27.03	16.53	273.27
Sri Lanka	10.8	17.8	12.1	15.00	4.20	17.65
France	10.8	12.3	9.1	10.75	−0.05	0.00
Nigeria	11.1	10.3	18.7	16.39	5.29	28.03
United States	11.3	8.2	7.6	8.08	−3.22	10.37
Algeria	11.4	17.8	17.2	18.43	7.03	49.42
Venezuela	12.4	7.6	7.1	7.50	−4.90	24.00
Bangladesh	12.7	18.4	13.2	15.98	3.28	10.79
South Africa	13.1	15.3	10.2	12.71	−0.39	0.15
United Kingdom	13.4	12.2	8.3	10.17	−3.23	10.40
Italy	14.7	23.9	12.1	17.48	2.78	7.71
Spain	15.6	13.8	19.8	18.55	2.95	8.73
Ethiopia	16.1	13.1	14.4	14.64	−1.46	2.13
Mexico	18.2	31.4	17.4	24.08	5.88	34.62
Korea, Rep of	18.3	18.0	14.4	16.63	−1.67	2.79
Phillipines	18.8	11.9	7.6	9.58	−9.22	84.97
Greece	19.0	19.7	12.6	16.11	−2.89	8.36
Yugoslavia	21.3	17.4	13.6	15.85	−5.45	29.73
Indonesia	21.9	19.6	8.1	13.04	−8.86	78.44
Portugal	23.8	18.4	22.5	22.24	−1.56	2.45
Columbia	24.7	25.0	17.8	21.76	−2.94	8.67
Chile	33.4	60.0	40.1	50.95	17.55	308.01
Brazil	52.7	51.6	38.7	46.60	−6.10	37.21
Ghana	54.4	30.3	73.1	61.08	6.68	44.59
Turkey	58.7	54.8	45.3	52.34	−6.36	40.51
Peru	66.7	59.6	57.8	62.69	−4.01	16.12
Zaire	108.6	54.1	48.5	54.20	−54.40	2,959.15
Argentina	159.5	125.4	175.5	168.51	9.01	81.12
Sum	970.1	1,019.3	850.6	969.4	−0.7	4,467.4
Mean	21.6	22.7	18.9	21.5	0.0	99.3

do not wish to correct for heteroscedasticity if it does not exist. Hence, we specify the *null* hypothesis of a constant variance in the error term (*homoscedasticity*). If the regression coefficient of the regressor is significant (as in Table 19.6), we reject the null hypothesis of homoscedasticity and accept the hypothesis of heteroscedasticity.

According to the Park test, the square of the residual is a positive function of the variable z: $\hat{u}^2 = \hat{\alpha} z^{2\hat{\beta}}$, where $\hat{\beta} = 0.627$. If we divide $\hat{u}^2$ by $z^{2\hat{\beta}}$, we get $\hat{u}^2/z^{2\hat{\beta}} = \hat{\alpha}$, a constant. To alleviate heteroscedasticity, we divide all variables in the regression equation by $z^{\hat{\beta}}$, so that when squared, the resulting residual will have a constant variance. The resulting *weighted least squares* regression is the third regression reported in Table 19.6. We note that correcting for heteroscedasticity between u^2 and z does indeed reduce the significance of that variable, although the latter remains statistically significant at the 1 percent level. However, the coefficient of x also becomes less significant. In fact, it is just barely significant at the 5 percent level for a one-tail test. (With 39 degrees of freedom, the critical t value is 1.685.) The moral of this story is that correction for heteroscedasticity tends to affect all variables more or less proportionally when those variables are highly correlated.

Table 19.6

$y = -0.356 + 0.406x + 0.672z;\ R^2 = 0.8806$
$(2.36)\quad\ (0.149)\quad (0.115)$

$\ln(\hat{u}^2) = -0.745 + 0.627 \ln(z^2);\ r^2 = 0.2402$
$\phantom{\ln(\hat{u}^2) = }(0.891)\quad\ (0.170)$

$w_z y = 1.94 w_z + 0.135 w_z x + 0.699 w_z z;\ R^2 = 0.8352$
$(0.451)\quad (0.051)\qquad (0.101)\qquad (w_z = 1/z^{0.627})$

$\ln(\hat{u}^2) = -2.94 + 0.9266 \ln(x^2);\ R^2 = 0.3248$
$\phantom{\ln(\hat{u}^2) = }(1.19)\quad\ (0.204)$

$w_x y = 1.117 w_x + 0.329 + 0.614 w_x z;\ R^2 = 0.5749$
$(0.754)\qquad (0.089)\ (0.100)\qquad (w_x = 1/x)$

Of course there is also the possibility that the heteroscedasticity is traceable to x. This prospect is investigated through the fourth regression in Table 19.6. When the squared residual is regressed against the logarithm of x^2, an elasticity of 0.9266 is estimated. This is significantly greater than 0, but not significantly different from 1. This latter result allows us to simplify the weight regression equation by dividing all terms by x. As a practical matter, this means we do not have to suppress the constant term in this equation. Not all regression software have this option. Instead, the inverse of x picks up the intercept term, and the intercept of the regression becomes the coefficient of x. In this case both the lagged inflation rate, z, and the constant term, x, remain significant, despite the lower R^2.

CONCLUSION

By applying the methods of multiple regression and correlation, we are able to determine the impact of several influences on the dependent variable within the same equation. Each slope coefficient in a multiple regression equation measures the *partial derivative* of the dependent variable with respect to the relevant independent variable. Multiple regression is called for when we believe that the error term in a simple regression does not have a zero expected value because of the nonrandom influence of important excluded variables.

There are two reasons for including a variable in a multiple regression equation: (1) We are directly interested in the influence of that variable on the dependent variable. That is, the variable in question is part of the hypothesis being tested. (2) Although we are not directly interested in the influence of that particular variable, we nevertheless include it because we wish to avoid specification error. It follows that a variable should not be excluded from a regression equation just because it is not statistically significant. If theory implies that the variable has a nonrandom influence on the dependent variable, it should be included to avoid specification bias.

In the next chapter we will explore several applications of the ideas introduced in this chapter. We will discover that our examples are still constrained by some of the topics that we have yet to explore. For instance, we must avoid regressions in which right-side variables are plausibly correlated with the error term, and we cannot fully explore time-series examples because of the prevalence of correlated error terms. Nevertheless, as we advance through the text, the number of legitimate examples from economic reality increase. This is called progress.

PROBLEMS

1. The quantity supplied of a commodity X by a competitive firm is assumed to be a linear function of the price of X and the wage rate of labor used in the production of X. The population supply equation is given as:

    $$x = a + bp_x + cw$$

    where x denotes the quantity produced by the firm, p_x denotes the price of X, w denotes the wage rate, and a, b, and c are the

unknown supply parameters. The sample data are given in the following table:

x	p_x	w
20	10	12
35	15	10
30	21	9
47	26	8
60	40	5
68	37	7
76	42	4
90	33	5
100	30	7
105	38	5
130	60	3
140	65	4
125	50	3
120	35	1
135	42	2

a. Estimate the supply parameters by least squares.
b. Test the following alternative hypotheses:
   (1) An increase in price increases quantity supplied, *ceteris paribus*.
   (2) An increase in the wage rate reduces quantity supplied, *ceteris paribus*.

2.   The production function of a firm is given as:

$$x = al^b k^c$$

where x denotes the quantity produced of the commodity X, l and k
denote the quantities of the factors of production L and K, respectively,
and a, b, and c are the unknown parameters of the production function. The sample data are given in the following table:

x	l	k
100	1.0	2.0
120	1.3	2.2
140	1.8	2.3
150	2.0	2.5
165	2.5	2.8
190	3.0	3.0
200	3.0	3.3
220	4.0	3.4

a. Estimate by least squares the parameters of the production function.

b. Find the marginal productivity functions of the two factors L and K.
c. Test the null hypotheses that both marginal products are positive but decreasing functions of the relevant input. (Hint: Take partial derivatives for the general formula of the production function, then test for the values of the parameters implied.)

3. The savings function for the Warbucks family is given as:

$$s_t = a + by_{t-1} + ci_t$$

where s_t denotes aggregate saving in year t, y_{t-1} denotes disposable income in year $t - 1$, and i_t denotes the real interest rate in year t. The symbols a, b, and c denote the unknown population parameters. The sample data are given in the following table.

Year	s	y	i
1965	20,000	100,000	2
1966	25,000	110,000	2
1967	25,000	130,000	3
1968	30,000	140,000	2
1969	33,000	160,000	3
1970	38,000	170,000	4
1971	35,000	170,000	3
1972	45,000	200,000	4
1973	43,000	240,000	4
1974	50,000	250,000	5
1975	55,000	260,000	5

a. Estimate by least squares the parameters of the savings function.
b. What percentage of the total variation in saving is explained by both income and the interest rate?
c. Compute the marginal propensity to save out of income. Is it significantly greater than zero?
d. Does an increase in the interest rate increase or decrease saving, *ceteris paribus*? Is the result significant?

4. Using the data in Table 19.1, estimate the impact of productivity changes and the *inverse* of the unemployment rate on the rate of change in the real wage rate. What inferences can be drawn from the resulting regression equation?

20

Economic

Applications of

Multiple

Regression

This chapter will present five economic applications of multiple regression analysis. As with the applications explored in Chapter 18, we are constrained to examples in which the variables on the right side of the equation are thought to be uncorrelated with the error term, and for which the error terms for different observations are thought to be independent. Examples involving violations of the latter assumption will be discussed in Chapter 21, and models with endogenous variables on the right side of the equation will be considered in Chapters 22 and 23.

PRE-OPEC DEMAND FOR OIL
IN EUROPEAN COUNTRIES

So far we have avoided discussions of supply and demand equations involving market equilibria because such models contain endogenous variables on the right side of the equation, violating the ordinary least squares requirement that regressors be independent of the error term. For fungible products like oil or gasoline, the market involved can reasonably be considered as global in scope. Hence, if we try to determine the demand or supply equations for the world oil market, we cannot use ordinary least squares to estimate the structural equations of the model because price (one of the right-side variables in each equation) is simultaneously determined with quantity exchanged. Instead, techniques designed for simultaneous equations models would have to be used. These techniques are explored in Chapters 22 and 23.

However, if we use submarket data, it is permissible to estimate supply or demand equations if the economic agents being observed can reasonably be considered as price-takers. In this example we will look at the demand for gasoline for six continental European countries (Belgium, France, West Germany, Italy, Luxemburg, and the Netherlands) for the period 1960-1970.[1] The prices paid for gasoline within a price-taking country reflect average refinery and transportation costs, assumed to be independent of quantity purchased, and local gasoline taxes, assumed to be independent of wholesale fuel prices. Hence, we are justified in assuming that price is *causally prior* to quantity demanded. That is, price determines quantity, but quantity does not determine price at the subaggregate level.

Figure 20.1a presents a scatter of points relating the price of gasoline, P, (measured in dollars per 100 liters and plotted on the horizontal axis) and the total quantity of gasoline, Q, (measured in thousands of tons per year and plotted on the vertical axis). Note that we depart from the usual economics convention of plotting price on the vertical axis to emphasize that price is the causal variable.

It is difficult to discern anything looking even vaguely like a demand curve in Figure 20.1a. Indeed, Table 20.1 shows that the simple correlation coefficient between P and Q is 0.349. In the simple regression of Q against P, we find a positive coefficient of 599.72. This means that through time and across countries, price and quantity demanded appear to be moving in the same direction.

This would seem to contradict the theory of demand that states that quantity demanded varies inversely with price, *ceteris paribus*. But there is the rub: in simple regression analysis "other factors" cannot be held constant unless they are explicitly included in the regression equation. It is likely that quantity is responding to factors other than price that vary through time or across space, and when these factors are taken into account, a negatively sloped demand curve will emerge. Or so we hope!

According to demand theory, the quantity of a product consumers are willing and able to purchase depends on the price of the product, the size of the market, the prices of substitutes and complements, income, and tastes.

---

[1]Data for this example are taken from Gilbert Jenkins, *Oil Economists' Handbook: 1985*, London and New York: Elsevier Applied Science Publishers Ltd., 1985, Tables 29, 112, 115, 116, 117, and 118.

Figure 20.1a

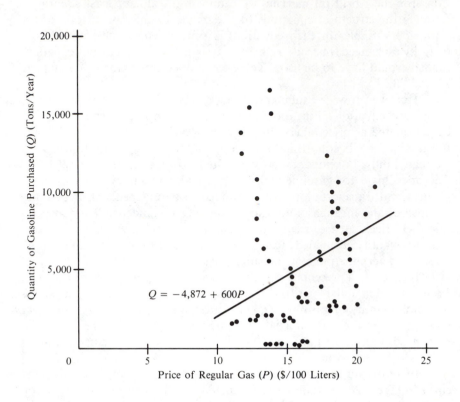

When these other factors are held constant, economists generate a demand curve showing an inverse relationship between price and quantity. However, when these other factors are ignored, as in the case of a *simple regression* of price against quantity, the inverse relationship between quantity demanded and price may not be evident.

In multiple regression analysis, we include variables in an equation in order to *isolate* their influence. Two major influences on gasoline consumption, besides price, are population, *POP*, and the number of automobiles in a country, *NCARS*. When both variables are added to the regression of gasoline consumption, Q, against the price of gasoline, P, all three variables are significant. The R^2 of 0.9899 seems to imply that most of the variation in the dependent variable is captured by the (joint and individual) influence of the three regressors. Figure 20.1b shows the pattern of observation on Q and P when the influences of *POP* and *NCARS* have been removed via

Table 20.1

Demand for Regular Gasoline: Six European Countries, 1960-1970
(Standard errors in parentheses)

Variable	Mean	Standard Deviation	Minimum	Maximum
Q	4,723.8	4,234.8	48	15,492
POP	30,857.4	24,734.5	314	96,163
$NCARS$	4,654.74	4,349.7	35.0	14,377
P	16.0	2.47	11.92	21.07

Correlation Coefficients:

	Q	P	POP	$NCARS$
Q	1.000	0.349	0.847	0.988
P		1.000	0.431	0.453
POP			1.000	0.851
$NCARS$				1.000

Simple Linear Regression:
$$Q = -4,872.09 + 599.72P; \quad R^2 = 0.1219$$
$$\quad (3,256.38) \quad (201.18)$$

Multiple Linear Regression:
$$Q = 3,399.05 + 0.981*NCARS + 0.0077**POP - 217.43*P; \quad R^2 = 0.9899$$
$$\quad (372.73) \quad (0.024) \quad (0.0042) \quad (24.73)$$

Simple Log-Linear Regression:
$$LQ = -5.57 + 4.78LP; \quad r^2 = 0.1756$$
$$\quad (3.58) \quad (1.30)$$

Multiple Log-Linear Regression:
$$LQ = 1.97* + 0.786*LNCARS + 0.207*LPOP - 0.804*LP; \quad R^2 = 0.9950$$
$$\quad (0.351) \quad (0.041) \quad (0.038) \quad (0.126)$$

*significant at 1 percent level
**significant at 5 percent level

multiple regression.[2] Unlike Figure 20.1a, the inverse relation between price and quantity is evident in Figure 20.1b.

Note that two other regressions are presented in Table 20.1: a simple log-linear regression (relating the logarithm of gasoline consumption, LQ, to the logarithm of the price of gasoline, LP), and a multiple log-linear

[2]Figure 20.1b was generated by first defining variable $Q^* = Q - (0.981NCARS - 0.0077POP)$, then plotting Q^* against P.

Figure 20.1b

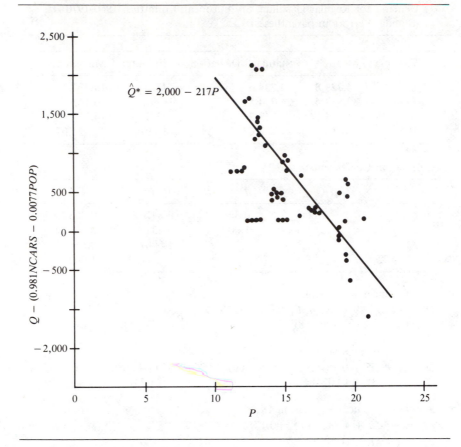

regression (in which the logarithm of population, *LPOP*, and the logarithm of the number of cars, *LNCARS*, are added to the equation). As in the simple linear model, gasoline consumption appears to increase with the price of gasoline in the simple log-linear regression. However, when the other two regressors are added, the coefficient of *LP* assumes the "correct" sign.

In the log-linear specification of the demand equation, the coefficient of *LP* is the estimated price elasticity of demand. Each 10 percent increase in the price of gasoline is predicted to decrease gasoline consumption by 8 percent, *the number of cars and population remaining constant*. The coefficient is significantly less than zero, as predicted by the law of demand ($t = -0.804/0.126 = -6.39$). However, this coefficient is *not* significantly greater than minus one ($t = [-0.804 - (-1)]/0.126 = 0.196/0.126 = 1.56$) at the 5 percent level. Although this estimate implies that the demand for gasoline is price inelastic, we do not reject the null hypothesis that the demand for gasoline is unit elastic or price elastic.

EXECUTIVE COMPENSATION, SALES, AND PROFIT: HETEROSCEDASTICITY REVISITED[3]

In the previous chapter we discussed two problems frequently encountered in regression based on cross-section data. Multicollinearity and heteroscedasticity are similar problems in that each reflects a characteristic of the data, rather than a flaw in the model being tested. Multicollinearity arises when two or more regressors are highly correlated, making it difficult to isolate the influence of each variable on the dependent variable. Heteroscedasticity results when the variance in the error term tends to change systematically over the data set. Positive heteroscedasticity results when the variance in the error term gets progressively larger as the independent variable gets larger. Negative heteroscedasticity occurs when the variance of the error term gets smaller as the independent variable gets larger.

Because neither multicollinearity nor heteroscedasticity biases the regression coefficients themselves, either can be diagnosed from the results of the regression analysis. Evidence of multicollinearity involves a large discrepancy between the change in the coefficient of determination when a variable is entered and the square of the simple correlation coefficient between that variable and the dependent variable. Another sign is a high correlation coefficient between allegedly independent variables. Heteroscedasticity can be discovered by investigating the pattern of the squared residual. If there is a significant relationship between the squared residual and the magnitude of the dependent variable (or an independent variable whose magnitude parallels the dependent variable), remedial measures are called for.

The most important distinction between multicollinearity and heteroscedasticity involves the effects of these conditions on inferences about the significance of the regression coefficient. Not only are coefficients estimated in the presence of multicollinearity unbiased, but multicollinearity tends to favor rejection of the alternative hypothesis in favor of the null hypothesis. It follows that if results are significant in the presence of multicollinearity, no remedial action is called for. Multicollinearity is most troublesome when one seeks to reject a hypothesis, actually making the "favored" hypothesis the null hypothesis. In this case it becomes all too tempting to load the regression equation with every conceivable variable, until there is so much shared influence among regressors that the hypothesis proves insignificant.

Heteroscedasticity is another matter. Positive heteroscedasticity tends to *reduce* the standard error of a regression coefficient, making a coefficient appear to be significant when it is not. Positive heteroscedasticity is the ally of the alternative hypothesis. When positive heteroscedasticity is diagnosed,

[3]This section is based on D. Ciscel and T. Carroll, "The Determinants of Executive Compensation: An Econometric Survey," *Review of Economics and Statistics* (February 1980), 7-13.

the careful researcher should correct for it. However, a word of caution is also in order. Overcorrection for positive heteroscedasticity can generate negative heteroscedasticity, which, like multicollinearity, increases the probability of type II error (incorrectly accepting a false null hypothesis). For this reason, we employ tests to detect the presence of heteroscedasticity, using the assumption of homoscedasticity (constant variance in the error term) as the null hypothesis.

One area of economic controversy where both multicollinearity and heteroscedasticity play a prominent role is in the issue of the determinants of executive compensation. It is a well-known assumption of the theory of the firm that producers attempt to maximize economic profit, the difference between total revenue and total (opportunity) cost. This assumption is usually justified for the small firm on two bases: (1) the proprietor making the decisions would receive any profit earned by the firm, so that maximizing profit is consistent with self-interest, and (2) the competitive market environment leads toward zero economic profit in long-run equilibrium so that competitive firms that do not maximize profit would not survive.

The controversy over the profit maximization assumption arises when economists analyze the decisions of corporations. The executives who make those decisions are minority stockholders, at best. Unless the corporation is closely held (has a few stockholders owning large blocks of stock), it may be difficult for stockholders to police managers, thereby forcing profit maximizing behavior. According to some commentators, most notably John Kenneth Galbraith, managers of large corporations pursue goals of stable growth in sales, rather than those of maximizing profits.

So the battle lines are drawn. The hypothesis to test is the following: "Are executives of major corporations rewarded for increasing sales (a measure of firm size) or for increasing profit (a measure of the firm's economic success)?" The easy answer to this question is "Yes." After all, firms report their "sales" as "revenue." When a firm's revenue increases (by more than cost) its profit also increases. However, if we really want an either/or sort of answer to this problem, then we end up trying to sort out the independent influences of these two variables. If executive compensation appears to increase with sales (revenue), profit remaining constant, we will accept the sales maximization hypothesis. If executive compensation tends to increase with profit, sales remaining constant, we will accept the profit maximization hypothesis.

Table 20.2 shows the extreme degree of multicollinearity between the two allegedly "independent" variables. In each year profit, P (measured as net revenue after taxes), and sales, S (measured as total revenue), are more highly correlated with each other than either is with executive compensation, E (measured as salary plus bonus of the chief executive officer).[4] In the six

---

[4]The data were obtained from the annual directories of *Fortune* and *Forbes*. The former published the data on profit and sales, the latter the data on executive pay. *Forbes* did not publish that data in 1972, which is why that year is missing from the analysis.

Table 20.2a

Determinants of Executive Compensation: Linear Model
(Standard errors in parentheses)

Linear Correlation Coefficients:

Year	r_{sp}	r_{sE}	r_{pE}
1970	0.795	0.397	0.361
1971	0.889	0.256	0.246
1973	0.894	0.493	0.440
1974	0.855	0.434	0.500
1975	0.827	0.388	0.428
1976	0.903	0.522	0.489

Multiple Linear Regressions:

Year	Intercept	Profit	Sales	R^2
1970	186,093*	0.0679	0.0112*	0.1637
	(6,775)	(0.0584)	(0.0039)	
1971	213,029*	0.0339	0.0061	0.0680
	(7,453)	(0.0635)	(0.0048)	
1973	262,820*	−0.0015	0.0154*	0.2426
	(8,259)	(0.0522)	(0.0041)	
1974	296,558*	0.1652*	0.0005	0.2506
	(7,550)	(0.0390)	(0.0026)	
1975	309,095*	0.1595*	0.0028	0.1866
	(9,231)	(0.0515)	(0.0028)	
1976	349,859*	0.0408	0.0110*	0.2742
	(10,067)	(0.0578)	(0.0034)	

Goldfeld-Quandt Test, Linear Model:

Year	SSE_1	SSE_3	F	Significance
1970	3.6×10^9	8.4×10^9	2.33	0.001
1971	10.3×10^9	8.1×10^9	0.786	0.164
1973	4.7×10^9	14.6×10^9	3.11	0.0001
1974	6.3×10^9	11.4×10^9	1.81	0.01
1975	8.0×10^9	13.0×10^9	1.63	0.024
1976	15.7×10^9	14.0×10^9	0.893	0.323

*significant at 1 percent level

years of multiple linear regression results, we generally find that the variable with the larger simple correlation coefficient with executive compensation is statistically significant, while the other variable is insignificant. Hence, sales are significant in three years and profits are significant in two years, with neither being significant in 1971. Of greater note is the fact that the coefficient of multiple determination is quite small in each year. While the debate rages over whether profit or sales are more influential in determining what chief executives make, it appears that both of them together explain less than 30 percent of the variation in the dependent variable.

When the significance of competing hypotheses vary from one data set to another, there is always the danger that researchers with axes to grind might selectively report regression results favorable to their pet hypotheses, while suppressing results that seem unfavorable. In this case, advocates of the profit maximization hypothesis might report the results for 1974 and 1975, while ignoring the results for 1970-1973 and 1976. Conversely, devotees of the sales maximization hypothesis might report results for 1970, 1973, or 1976, while ignoring the other years. Objectivity is best served by finding some pattern of results which is consistent over all available data.

Before abandoning the linear model reported in Table 20.2a, the possibility of heteroscedasticity should be investigated. Several researchers have discovered a positive relationship between the variance in the squared residual of executive compensation regressions and the book value of a firm's assets.[5] In Chapter 19 we introduced the Park test for heteroscedasticity. This test involves the regression of the logarithm of the squared residual against the logarithm of a scalar whose magnitude parallels that of the dependent variable. The Park test has been criticized on the basis that the regression of the log of the squared residual against the log of a scalar is probably heteroscedastic itself, and may even involve correlation between the regressor and the error term of that regression. The authors of that criticism, Stephen M. Goldfeld and Richard E. Quandt,[6] have suggested another test for the presence of heteroscedasticity. Their test is particularly well-suited to large data sets like those used in the executive compensation regressions.

The Goldfeld-Quandt test involves several steps. First, the observations are sorted in the order of the scalar presumed to parallel the variance in the error term. Second, about one-third of the observations are deleted from the middle of the data set. Third, separate regressions are run on the first and last third of the observations. Fourth, an F statistic is calculated, using

[5]W. Lewellen and B. Huntsman, "Managerial Pay and Corporate Performance," *American Economic Review*, (June 1970), 710-720, found heteroscedasticity involving the level of assets. Ciscel and Carroll (*op. cit.*) discovered heteroscedasticity involving the square root of assets. Ironically, in T. Carroll and D. Ciscel, "The Effects of Regulation on Executive Compensation," *Review of Economics and Statistics*, (August 1982), the same authors discovered that heteroscedasticity seems to disappear when regulated firms are added to the data set.

[6]S. M. Goldfeld and R. E. Quandt, *Nonlinear Methods of Econometrics*, North-Holland Publishing Company, Amsterdam, 1972.

the ratio of the mean square error (MSE) for the two regressions. If the ratio of the two average values of the absolute error is significantly greater than one (implying that the variance in the error term increases with the scalar), positive heteroscedasticity is diagnosed. If the ratio is significantly less than one, negative heteroscedasticity is inferred. And if the ratio is not significantly different from one, the null hypothesis of homoscedasticity is accepted.

In Table 20.2a, data for each year were first ranked according to the book value of assets, then divided into three groups. Groups 1 and 3, used for the Goldfeld-Quandt test, contained 70 observations each. Group 2, the middle omitted group, contained from 69 to 82 observations. For each group the mean square error for the regression was computed as $\Sigma(E - \hat{E})^2/67$ and the F statistic calculated. If the mean square error was approximately the same for both groups (implying homoscedasticity), the F statistic would be approximately one. Positive heteroscedasticity would be implied by an F statistic greater than one, whereas negative heteroscedasticity would be implied by an F statistic significantly less than one.

We see in Table 20.2a that positive heteroscedasticity is implied in four of the six years. In two of those years the sales variable was significant while the profit variable was not. Since sales tend to be of the same magnitude as assets (the scalar variable), the significance of sales is suspect due to positive heteroscedasticity. On the other hand, the heteroscedasticity in 1974 and 1975 would work to the disadvantage of the profit variable. As we have seen significance of a variable in the presence of negative heteroscedasticity requires no remedial changes.

One way that has been suggested to alleviate heteroscedasticity is the transformation of a linear model into a log-linear one.[7] Not only does transformation into logarithms reduce the range of the variance in the error term, it also smooths out that variance across observations. The results of the log-linear regression, reported in Table 20.2b, seem much more favorable to the profit maximization hypothesis. In all six years, the log of executive pay is positively and significantly related to the log of profit, *with the log of sales included in the regression*. By contrast, the log of sales is significant in only one year, 1970.

However, when a Goldfeld-Quandt test is performed on the log-linear model, we find that significant negative heteroscedasticity (working to the detriment of the sales maximization model) seems to exist in 1971 and 1976, precisely those years when the null hypothesis of homoscedasticity could not be rejected in Table 20.2a. We are only able to conclude that the profit maximization model is clearly supported in 1974 and 1975, while the sales maximization model seems to be supported unambiguously in 1970 and 1976. The significance of the profit variable in 1971 and 1976 seems to depend on the presence of negative heteroscedasticity, and the significance of the sales variable in 1973 seems to be due to positive heteroscedasticity.

[7]Damodar Gujarati, *Basic Econometrics*, New York: McGraw-Hill, 1978, pp. 210, 211.

Table 20.2b

Determinants of Executive Compensation: Log-Linear Model
(Standard errors in parentheses)

Log-Linear Correlation Coefficients:

Year	r_{sp}	r_{sE}	r_{pE}
1970	0.642	0.437	0.464
1971	0.612	0.325	0.405
1973	0.763	0.506	0.613
1974	0.788	0.495	0.578
1975	0.763	0.492	0.608
1976	0.810	0.513	0.582

Log-Linear Multiple Regressions:

Year	Intercept	Log (Profit)	Log (Sales)	R^2
1970	9.28* (0.456)	0.108* (0.027)	0.124* (0.042)	0.2483
1971	10.64* (0.373)	0.088* (0.022)	0.050 (0.033)	0.1733
1973	9.74* (0.391)	0.192* (0.029)	0.045 (0.040)	0.3791
1974	10.25* (0.369)	0.155* (0.028)	0.044 (0.039)	0.3386
1975	10.23* (0.372)	0.179* (0.027)	0.030 (0.038)	0.3719
1976	10.12* (0.379)	0.161* (0.031)	0.059 (0.041)	0.3445

Goldfeld-Quandt Test, Log-Linear Model:

Year	SSE_1	SSE_3	F	Significance
1970	0.124	0.096	0.779	0.155
1971	0.119	0.081	0.680	0.058
1973	0.094	0.085	0.989	0.482
1974	0.090	0.074	0.825	0.215
1975	0.095	0.070	0.737	0.108
1976	0.097	0.061	0.628	0.029

*Significant at 1 percent level

The moral of this story is that it is extremely difficult to decisively prove one model over another when the influence of the data used for the test is mired in both multicollinearily and heteroscedasticity. We must conclude that the influence of the sales variable probably works *through* the profit variable, which is consistent with the profit maximization and sales maximization models. However, we also must infer that the influence of both profit and sales is relatively small and neither variable seems to dominate the executive compensation equation.

WAGE RATES, PRODUCTIVITY, AND EMPLOYMENT BY GENDER

In Chapter 18 we investigated a recursive model that involved capital per worker, output per worker, and average wage rates for 20 manufacturing industries. We discovered that a recursive model could be used to relate the average wage rate in each industry to output (value-added) per worker, and that output could in turn be related to the capital-labor ratio. In this section we will employ a larger data set (337 observations covering 20 industries for 17 years[8]) in order to relate the average wage rate across industries to value-added per worker and the proportion of workers who are female.

According to the marginal productivity theory of distribution, the average wage rate in an industry should be proportional to marginal productivity and demographic factors should be irrelevant, *once productivity has been taken into account*. Hence, any simple negative correlation between the real average hourly wage rate ($RAHW$) and the percent of workers who are female (PCF) should be traceable to lower real value-added per hour ($RVAPH$) in those industries.

Table 20.3 presents summary statistics and correlation coefficients on logarithms for the real average hourly wage rate ($LRAHW$), real value-added per hour ($LRVAPH$), real value of capital per hour ($LRKPH$), the proportion of workers in white collar jobs ($LPWC$), the proportion of workers who are female ($LPCF$), and a trend variable ($Year = 0$ in 1962 to 18 in 1980).

As we found in Chapter 18, there is a strong positive correlation between $LRAHW$, $LRVAPH$, and $LRKPH$; $LPWC$ was also highly correlated with these variables. On the other hand, all variables, except the time trend $Year$, are negatively correlated with $LPCF$. That is, without taking the interaction among variables into account, there is a negative relationship between $LRAHW$ and $LPCF$, as might be consistent with discrimination. However, there is also a negative correlation between $LRVAPH$ and $LPCF$ suggesting that output per worker is smaller in industries with a higher proportion of

---

[8]Data for this section were taken from T. Carroll, "A Test of the Job Crowding Hypothesis," *Economic Journal*, 1986.

Table 20.3

Wage Rates, Productivity, and Female Employment Patterns
(Standard errors in parentheses)

Variable	Mean	Standard Deviation	Minimum	Maximum
LRAHW	1.307	0.269	0.131	3.696
LRVAPH	2.567	0.506	1.645	4.376
LRKPH	2.154	0.911	0.131	4.543
LPWC	3.101	0.402	2.103	4.394
LPCF	3.237	0.594	1.758	4.394
Year	9.656	5.448	0.000	18.000

Log-Linear Correlation Coefficients:

	LRAHW	LRVAPH	LRKPH	LPWC	LPCF	Year
LRAHW	1.000	0.718	0.720	0.610	−0.567	0.237
LRVAPH		1.000	0.798	0.648	−0.336	0.262
LRKPH			1.000	0.514	−0.636	0.094
LPWC				1.000	−0.256	0.137
LPCF					1.000	0.160
Year						1.000

Log-Linear Multiple Regressions:

$$LRVAPH = -0.170 + 0.011*Year + 0.428*LRKPH + 0.364*LPWC$$
$$ (0.157) \quad (0.0027) \qquad (0.022) \qquad\quad (0.040)$$
$$+ 0.179*LPCF; \ R^2 = 0.7632$$
$$(0.031)$$

$$LRAHW = 0.745* + 0.010*Year + 0.101*LRKPH + 0.220*LPWC$$
$$ (0.099) \quad (0.0016) \qquad (0.014) \qquad\quad (0.025)$$
$$- 0.135*LPCF; \ R^2 = 0.6656$$
$$(0.019)$$

$$LRAHW = 1.10* + 0.008*Year + 0.286*LRVAPH - 0.186*LPCF;$$
$$ (0.080) \quad (0.0017) \qquad (0.019) \qquad\qquad (0.016)$$
$$R^2 = 0.6583$$

*Significant at 1 percent level

female workers. We also find negative correlations between *LPCF* and *LRKPH*, and *LPWC*, all of which have a positive impact on *LRVAPH*. Ultimately we would like to know the impact of the proportion female on real value-added and on the real wage rate, once other factors have been taken into account.

The first regression in Table 20.3 shows a positive elasticity of real value-added per hour with respect to percent female, once other influences on *LRVAPH* have been accounted for. Real value-added per hour is predicted to increase by 0.428 percent for each 1 percent increase in real capital per labor hour, by 0.364 percent for each 1 percent increase in the proportion of workers in white collar jobs, and by 1.1 percent per year. Given the positive relation of *LRVAPH* to *LRKPH*, *LPWC*, and *Year* (time), output per worker tends to *increase* by about 0.18 percent for each 1 percent increase in the proportion of workers who are female.

The second equation in Table 20.3 relates the logarithm of the real average hourly wage rate (*LRAHW*) to the regressors in the first equation. As predicted by the marginal productivity theory, the real wage rate increases as capital per worker increases. Labor and capital are complementary inputs, as are blue collar workers (whose pay is the dependent variable) and white collar workers. The regression coefficient on *Year* implies an increase in the average wage rate of about 1 percent per year. With all these factors constant, the average real wage rate across industries is predicted to *decrease* by 0.135 percent per year for each 1 percent increase in the proportion of jobs held by women. Given our finding of a positive relationship between average productivity and the proportion of female workers, this is inconsistent with the marginal productivity theory of distribution.

The third regression implies that once all influences on *RVAPH* have been taken into account (by including that variable in the regression), the inverse relation between *LRVAPH* and *LPCF* appears to grow stronger. For every 1 percent increase in real value-added per hour, the real average hourly wage rate increases by 0.268 percent, *the proportion of female employees and time remaining constant*. By contrast, the real average hourly wage rate tends to *decrease* by 0.186 percent for each 1 percent increase in the proportion of female employees, *real value-added per hour and time remaining constant*. Because *PCF* seems to increase *RVAPH*, *ceteris paribus*, regressing *LRAHW* against the determinants of *LRVAPH*, instead of against *LRVAPH* and *LPCF* tends to understate the elasticity of *RAHW* with respect to *PCF* by about 28 percent.

The model in Table 20.3 does not allow us to test for the direction of causation between *LPCF* and *LRAHW*. We have merely assumed that average wage rates are influenced by the proportion of women in an industry, but that the proportion of women in an industry is not influenced by the average wage rate. This pattern is consistent with *wage discrimination* whereby women receive lower pay than men for jobs generating similar revenue for the firm. However, the inverse relation between *LRAHW* and *LPCF* might also be explained by *job discrimination*, whereby women have a lower probability than men of being hired in high wage industries, or by compensating wage differentials, whereby industries with low pay have desirable characteristics (such as low layoff rates) preferred by women.

If we admit the possibility that causation could run from *LRAHW* to *LPCF*, then ordinary least squares regression results become suspect. To explore this possibility further, we must first learn how to estimate simultaneous equations models in Chapter 22.

DETERMINANTS OF UNION
MEMBERSHIP: DUMMY VARIABLES

In Chapter 18 we discovered that qualitative distinctions between observations could be represented by dichotomous or *dummy* variables, which assume values of zero or one according to whether that qualitative distinction is "off" or "on," respectively. For instance, individual states of the United States can be distinguished by whether or not they allow mandatory union membership (union shop) contracts. In Chapter 18 we saw that regressing the continuous *quantitative* variable PU (the proportion of workers belonging to unions) against the dichotomous *qualitative* variable RTW (whether or not a state has a right-to-work law) provided the same test for a difference in the dependent variable as would a t test for a difference in the mean of PU for those groups. That is, the intercept term for the regression measures the average value of PU for states for which the dummy variable equals zero, and the slope coefficient measures the *difference* in the mean for the two groups. Hence, if the t test for the slope coefficient is significant, we may reject the null hypothesis that the mean of PU for those two groups is the same.

Frequently an investigator may wish to determine the influence of more than one dichotomous variable, particularly when testing a hypothesis involving the influence of one dummy variable. For instance, there is a clear pattern in the regional distribution of right-to-work states, states that forbid union shop contracts. There were no right-to-work states in the Northeast in 1980, while 11 of 14 Southern states had right-to-work laws. By contrast, the proportion of right-to-work states in the Midwest and the West was approximately the same as the proportion of right-to-work states in the country as a whole. In order to test the hypothesis that right-to-work laws reduce union membership, we must take other influences (in this case, regional tastes and preferences) into account.

For purposes of illustration, we define four regional dummy variables: NE equals 1 for 11 Northeastern states and 0 for the other 39 states; $S = 1$ for 14 Southern states and $S = 0$ for the other 36 states; $MW = 1$ for 12 Midwestern states and $MW = 0$ otherwise; $W = 1$ for 13 Western states and $W = 0$ for all other states. The regional dummy variables are mutually exclusive and exhaustive, meaning we have 3 *degrees of freedom* for the four regional dummy variables. Once any three regional dummy variables have been assigned, there is no more "freedom" to assign the fourth: any state not receiving a "1" for NE, S, or MW automatically receives a "1" for W.

To demonstrate how degrees of freedom can be exhausted by the overzealous assignment of dummy variable categories, we also define the dummy variable US, which takes on the value of 1 if the state allows union shop contracts and equals 0 if such contracts are not allowed. Note that this variable could be calculated as $US = 1 - RTW$. That is, when $RTW = 1$,

$US = 0$ and when $US = 1$, $RTW = 0$. When the variable RTW has been assigned, the variable US is also determined. We get no additional information from the second variable when the first is known.

Table 20.4 presents the summary statistics for the continuous variable PU, the six dummy variables (NE, S, MW, W, RTW, and US), and a "variable" C which always equals 1 and stands for the vector of "1's" the computer uses when estimating the intercept term using matrix methods. Note that the variable NE has a mean of 0.22. This is the percentage of observations for which $NE = 1$. Similar interpretations can be made for the other dummy variables. The "variable" C has a mean of 1 and a standard deviation of 0; C always takes the same value.

Recall that the intercept term of a regression equation is the estimated value of the dependent variable when all regressors equal zero. In order for a regression equation to have an intercept, it must be possible for all regressors to equal zero for the same observation. Such is not the case if we include all four regional dummies (when any three equal zero the fourth must equal one) or if we include both RTW and US (when $RTW = 1$, $US = 0$ and vice versa). Hence, we must suppress one dummy variable from each category or we must drop the constant term.

More formally, the vector of "1's," which picks up the constant term when the regression is written in matrix form, is perfectly correlated with the four regional dummy variables. For each observation, we have $NE + S + MW + W = 1$. If we try to include a nonzero intercept *and* all four regional dummies (or both RTW and US) in the same regression equation, the computer would be unable to perform the regression, and would tell us so!

However, if we suppress one of the regional dummies and if we suppress either RTW or US, we can include the intercept term. In the first regression equation reported in Table 20.4, we omit the dummy variables W and US, regressing PU against the other four indicator variables. We interpret the intercept term as the predicted union membership in a Western state that does not have a right-to-work law (i.e., $NE = S = MW = RTW = 0$). The coefficients of the three regional dummies measure the difference in union membership among non-right-to-work states between each region and the Western region. Hence, Northeastern states have an average of 1.38 percent less of the labor force in unions than union shop Western states. Southern states for which $RTW = 0$ have an average of 2.38 percent less of their labor force in unions, while Midwestern states that allow union shop contracts have an average of 2.23 percent more of their labor force in unions relative to comparable Western states. In all cases the standard errors of these regression coefficients (indicated in parentheses) are large relative to the coefficients themselves, implying that the differences in union membership between regions are statistically insignificant, *once variations in union membership due to right-to-work laws are taken into account.*

Table 20.4

Determinants of Union Membership, 1980
(Standard errors in parentheses)

Variable	Mean	Standard Deviation	Minimum	Maximum
PU	22.474	7.525	7.8	38.7
C	1.000	0.000	1.0	1.0
NE	0.22	0.418	0.0	1.0
S	0.28	0.454	0.0	1.0
MW	0.24	0.431	0.0	1.0
W	0.26	0.443	0.0	1.0
RTW	0.40	0.495	0.0	1.0
US	0.60	0.495	0.0	1.0

Correlation Coefficients:

	PU	C	NE	S	MW	W	RTW	US
PU	1.000	0.000	0.218	−0.486	0.189	0.108	−0.693	0.693
C		0.000	0.000	0.000	0.000	0.000	0.000	0.000
NE			1.000	−0.331	−0.298	−0.315	−0.434	0.434
S				1.000	−0.350	−0.370	0.491	−0.491
MW					1.000	−0.333	0.019	−0.019
W						1.000	−0.112	0.112
RTW							1.000	−1.000
US								1.000

Multiple Regressions:

$PU = 26.91* - 1.38NE - 2.38S + 2.23MW - 10.01*RTW;\ R^2 = 0.5328$
$\quad\ \ (1.60)\quad\ (2.27)\quad\ \ (2.26)\ \ (2.15)\quad\ \ (1.89)$

$PU = 25.53*NE + 24.53*S + 29.14*MW + 26.91*W - 10.01*RTW;$
$\quad\ \ (1.62)\quad\quad\ (2.07)\quad\ \ (1.74)\quad\quad (1.60)\quad\quad (1.89)$
$\quad\quad\quad\quad\quad\quad\quad\quad\quad\quad\quad\quad\quad\quad\quad\quad\quad\quad R^2 = 0.5328$

$PU = 16.90*RTW + 26.91*US - 1.38NE - 2.38S + 2.23MW;\ R^2 = 0.5328$
$\quad\ \ (1.98)\quad\quad\quad (1.60)\quad\quad (2.27)\quad\ (2.26)\ \ (2.16)$

*Significant at 1 percent level

The coefficient of *RTW* measures the difference in union membership due to right-to-work laws, with the influence of regional differences in union membership removed. The regression coefficient of −10.01 means that right-to-work states tend to have 10.01 percent fewer union members than states that permit union shop contracts. The t statistic ($t = (-10.01 - 0)/1.89 = -5.30$) implies that we can reject the null hypothesis that states with right-to-work laws have the same amount of union membership as states without them, once regional differences in union membership have been taken into account.

If we suppress the intercept term, it is possible to include all four regional dummies *or* both *US* and *RTW* in the regression equation. Since suppressing the intercept term forces the regression line through the point where all variables are zero, the coefficients of the dummy variables now measure the average value of the dependent variable when that dummy variable equals 1. In the second regression in Table 20.4, the intercept is suppressed and the four regional dummies are included in the regression. In this case, we see that the coefficient for dummy variable *W* is the same as the intercept in the first regression. However, the coefficients of *NE*, *S*, and *MW* now measure the average union membership for those regions in 1980. Note that the coefficient of *RTW* is identical in the first two regressions. Since *US* is excluded from the regression to avoid perfect multicollinearity, the coefficient of *RTW* estimates the average difference in union membership between right-to-work and union shop states.

In the first regression, t tests were used to verify significant differences in union membership across regions and between union shop and right-to-work states. Only the latter difference was statistically significant. In the second regression, we find that the ratio of each coefficient to its standard error is considerably greater than 2.42, the critical t value for 1 percent significance with a one-tail test and 45 degrees of freedom. This implies that the average union membership in each region is significantly greater than zero when $RTW = 0$. Since union membership cannot be negative, this result is really not unexpected.

The third regression equation again suppresses the Western dummy variable, *W*, and the intercept term, but includes both *RTW* and *US*. Note that the slope coefficients of the three included regional dummies are identical in the first and third regressions. However, the coefficients of *RTW* and *US* now measure the average union membership for states that prohibit and allow union shop contracts, respectively. Although the coefficient of *RTW* is less than the coefficient of *US* (indeed, the difference is 10.01), both coefficients are significantly greater than zero, for reasons explained above. Finally, note that the R^2 term in all three regressions is identical. Suppressing the constant term to include all the dummy variables in a category provides equivalent regression results.

The lesson of this section is simple but very important: do not use too many dummy variables, or you may introduce perfect correlation into your regression equation making it impossible to estimate.

INFLATION AND UNEMPLOYMENT:
SLOPE DUMMIES

In Chapter 18 we saw that three different models—a linear model, a log-linear model, and an inverse model—all provided roughly equivalent estimates of the alleged trade-off between inflation and unemployment for the period 1948 to 1968. What we did not explore was the stability of this relationship over time. In Table 20.5, which reprises the results of Table 18.3, we also include regressions of the rate of inflation against the unemployment rate for the period 1969 to 1984. In each of the three models we find a reversal of the sign of the coefficient for the (transformed) unemployment rate. In the linear and log-linear models, where a negative slope coefficient is hypothesized, the coefficient is positive. In the inverse model, wherein a positive coefficient is hypothesized, the estimated coefficient is negative. That the coefficients are insignificant is irrelevant; when the sign of the regression coefficient contradicts the alternative hypothesis, the null hypothesis must be accepted.

Much more than their colleagues in the physical and natural sciences, economists must contend with the prospect that a hypothesis that seems to be valid for one set of observations may be invalid for another. If the statistical model is a valid representation of the theory being tested (which advocates of the Phillips curve may dispute), then the universal validity of the trade-off between inflation and unemployment is called into question. Something about the relationship between inflation and unemployment apparently changed over the two periods being observed. But how is that change to be measured and tested statistically?

There are two ways that simple regression results can differ between samples of observations. One is that two regression lines have unequal intercepts. This difference can be detected by the use of *intercept dummy variables* of the kind discussed in the previous section. Accordingly, we define a new variable D, which takes on the value of zero from 1948 to 1968 and the value of one between 1969 and 1984. When included in the regression, the coefficient of D measures the difference in the intercept of the regression equation between 1948-1968 and 1969-1984. If statistically significant, we infer that the regression line has been displaced, either upward if the coefficient of D is positive and significant, or downward if the coefficient of D is negative and significant.

The second possible difference between regression results is a difference in the slope. Changes in the slope coefficient over alternative sets of observations can be diagnosed with the use of a *slope dummy variable*, which takes on the value of 0 in the first period and the value of the regressor in the second period. This slope dummy can be generated by multiplying the dummy variable D times the (transformed) variable UE. If the coefficient of the slope dummy is positive and significant, we infer that the

Table 20.5

Inflation and Unemployment: 1948-1983
(Standard errors in parentheses)

Linear Model: $(dp/p)_t = a + bUE_t + u_t$

1948-68 $(dp/p)_t = 6.43* - 0.84*UE_t; r^2 = 0.3262$
           $\quad\quad\;\;(1.18)\quad(0.243)$

1969-84 $(dp/p)_t = 5.99* + 0.066UE_t; r^2 = 0.0029$
           $\quad\quad\;\;(2.25)\quad(0.326)$

1948-84 $(dp/p)_t = 6.43* - 0.443D - 0.841*UE_t + 0.907*DUE_t;$
           $\quad\quad\;\;(1.61)\quad(2.39)\quad\;\;(0.332)\quad\quad\;(0.419)$
           $$R^2 = 0.6284$$

Log-Linear Model: $\log_e(dp/p)_t = \log_e a + b\log_e(UE_t) + \log_e u$

1948-68 $\log_e(dp/p)_t = 3.49* - 1.86*\log_e(UE_t); r^2 = 0.3052$
           $\quad\quad\quad\;\;\;(0.991)\quad(0.643)$

1969-84 $\log_e(dp/p)_t = 1.69* + 0.062\log_e(UE_t); r^2 = 0.0024$
           $\quad\quad\quad\;\;\;(0.630)\quad(0.334)$

1948-84 $\log_e(dp/p)_t = 3.49* - 1.80D - 1.86*\log_e(UE_t)$
           $\quad\quad\quad\;\;\;(0.814)\quad(1.35)\quad\;(0.528)$
           $$+ 1.92*D\log_e(UE_t); R^2 = 0.5833$$
           $$(0.776)$$

Inverse Model: $(dp/p)_t = a + b(1/UE)_t + u_t$

1948-68 $(dp/p)_t = -0.987 + 15.33*(1/UE)_t; r^2 = 0.3261$
           $\quad\quad\;\;(1.17)\quad\quad(5.06)$

1969-84 $(dp/p)_t = 7.40* - 6.08(1/UE)_t; r^2 = 0.0178$
           $\quad\quad\;\;(2.00)\quad(12.07)$

1948-84 $(dp/p)_t = -0.987 + 8.39*D + 15.33*(1/UE)_t$
           $\quad\quad\;\;(1.54)\quad\;(2.22)\quad\;\;(6.65)$
           $$- 21.41**D(1/UE)_t; R^2 = 0.6209$$
           $$(11.70)$$

---

*Significant at 1 percent level
**Significant at 5 percent level

---

slope has increased in the latter period. If the coefficient of the slope dummy is negative and significant, we infer that the slope has decreased in the latter period. Note that the t statistic for the slope dummy tests the hypothesis that the slopes are different between the two periods, not that the slope is different from zero in the latter period.

Although macroeconomic textbooks often depict the Phillips curve as shifting outward after the 1960s, implying an inverse relation between inflation and unemployment occurring at a higher rate of unemployment (or inflation), the evidence in Table 20.5 implies that the Phillips curve (if it exists anymore) actually rotated during the 1970s and early 1980s. Note first that the intercept and slope coefficients in the third regression for each model are identical to the regression coefficients for the 1948-1968 era. This is consistent with the fact that the intercept and slope dummies both equal zero during this period. In the linear and log-linear models, the coefficient of D is not statistically different from zero and we accept the null hypothesis that both regression equations have the same intercept. In contrast, the coefficient of D in the inverse model is positive and significant. Here we reject the null hypothesis and accept the alternative hypothesis that the Phillips curve shifted to the right.

In the linear model, we have $(dp/p)_t = 6.43 - 0.84UE_t$ for the 1948-1968 era and $(dp/p)_t = 5.99 + 0.066UE_t$ for the 1969-1984 period. We estimate the intercept for the later period by adding the coefficient of D to the intercept coefficient for the regression. The slope coefficient for the period when $D = 1$ is obtained by adding the coefficients of UE_t and DUE_t. The resulting equation is identical to the regression using data for the 1969-1984 period. Similar results can be seen for the log-linear and the inverse models.

You might be wondering why we would bother to introduce slope and intercept dummies if the results are consistent with the regressions done on smaller data sets. We can list two advantages to the dummy variable techniques. First, by pooling the two time periods, we obtain more degrees of freedom. This reduces the critical value of t necessary for a coefficient to be significant. Second, the slope and intercept dummies allow us to test hypotheses about the stability of the relationship through time (if time-series data are used, as in this example), or across space (if cross-section data are used). We also note that the coefficient of determination for the pooled data is about twice as great as for the regression using early data.

There is one caveat however. The use of intercept and slope dummies might lead us to an incorrect inference of significant relationships where none exist. In each specification, the significance of the slope dummy implies that the relationship between (transformed) inflation and (transformed) unemployment is *different* in the later period than in the earlier period. This does not contradict our findings from the simple regression during the 1969-1984 period that the null hypothesis (inflation does not decrease as unemployment increases) must be accepted. We will explore the inflation-unemployment relationship again in time in Chapters 22 and 23.

SUMMARY

In this chapter we have explored five different applications of multiple regression analysis. The example of the demand for gasoline for six European countries demonstrated how multiple regression analysis often uncovers patterns that are hidden or distorted by simple regression. Once variables accounting for *changes* in demand were taken into account, an inverse relationship between the quantity of gasoline demanded and the price of gasoline became evident. A similar lesson was learned using log-linear regression analysis.

In the second example, we found that both multicollinearity and heteroscedasticity tend to distort the simultaneous test of the profit maximization and sales maximization hypotheses about executive compensation. Although both profit and sales are positively correlated with executive pay, they tend to be more closely correlated with each other. Hence, when we attempt to measure the impact of sales on executive pay, with profit held constant, most of sales is also held constant, and vice versa. For this reason, the linear model that regresses executive pay against *both* sales and profit tends to give inconsistent results from year to year. Furthermore, at least in some years, positive heteroscedasticity seems to artificially inflate the importance of the sales variable.

A log-linear model seems to support the profit maximization hypothesis, but does so by introducing negative heteroscedasticity that works to the detriment of the sales maximization model. We concluded by noting the inherent danger in depending on multicollinearity to "prove" a null hypothesis.

The third example involved the relationship between average pay, productivity, and the proportion of women employed in different industries. Contrary to the marginal productivity theory of distribution, the real average hourly wage rate *decreases* as the proportion of females in an industry *increases, ceteris paribus*. However, because of the possibility that causation runs from real average hourly wage rates to the proportion of jobs held by women, the ordinary least squares results may be compromised by simultaneous equations bias.

The last two examples involved the role of dummy variables in multiple regression analysis. In the fourth example, we saw how regression equations can accommodate multiple dummy variables, as long as we take care to avoid perfect multicollinearity by including the exhaustive set of dichotomous variable categories. In the last example, we saw how dummy variables could be used to measure differences in slopes as well as differences in intercepts for equations fit for different data sets. The t tests for the coefficients of slope and intercept dummy variables allow us to determine whether regression equations estimated using samples from hypothetically distinct populations are significantly different from each other.

PROBLEMS

1. To the demand equation for gasoline, studied in the first section of this chapter, we introduced a time trend ($t = 0$ in 1960 to $t = 10$ in 1970), dummy variables for five of the countries F, G, I, L, and

N, and an index of industrial production (IQ). The resulting equation is:

$$Q = 1{,}732.85 + 31.78t + 681.0F + 1{,}441.17G + 15.70I - 452.9L$$
$$\quad (1{,}039.4) \quad (54.8) \quad (427.0) \quad (418.2) \quad\quad (352.9) \quad (155.2)$$
$$+ 260.9N + 0.004POP + 3.58IQ + 0.862NC - 126.6P$$
$$(153.8) \quad (0.006) \quad\quad (11.2) \quad\quad (0.003) \quad\quad (36.6)$$
$$R^2 = 0.9962, \; \overline{R}^2 = 0.9955$$

where Q is the quantity of gas, t is the time trend, $F = 1$ for France, $G = 1$ for Germany, $I = 1$ for Italy, $L = 1$ for Luxemburg, and $N = 1$ for the Netherlands, POP is population, IQ is the industrial production index, equal to 100 in 1963, NC is the number of cars, and P is the price of regular gasoline.

a. Interpret the coefficient on each dummy variable. Which countries have significantly different gasoline consumption than the reference country, Belgium?
b. Test the hypothesis that gasoline consumption falls as the price of gasoline rises, *ceteris paribus*.
c. Write the demand equation for each country.

2. To the set of unregulated corporations used to test the executive compensation hypotheses, we add 45 utility companies (which face maximum price regulation) and 21 transportation companies (which, in 1976, faced minimum price regulation). The utility companies are identified with the dummy variable U and the transportation firms with the dummy variable T. For 1976, the resulting regression is:

$$E = 349{,}858 - 180{,}070U - 60{,}052T + 0.011S + 0.050US$$
$$\quad (9{,}264) \quad\quad (21{,}478) \quad\quad (59{,}207) \quad (0.003) \quad (0.034)$$
$$- 0.066TS + 0.041P - 0.485UP + 1.10TP$$
$$(0.038) \quad\quad (0.053) \quad\quad (0.294) \quad\quad (0.443)$$
$$R^2 = 0.4598, \; F = 29.4$$

where E is the executive's compensation, S is the company's sales, and P is its profit. Use these results to test the following alternative hypotheses:

a. Maximum price regulation reduces the incentive for the executive to increase profits and increases the incentive to increase (sales) revenue (e.g., by obtaining a rate increase).
b. Minimum price regulation increases the incentive for the executive to increase profit and reduces the incentive to increase revenue (i.e., because price competition is precluded).
c. Both types of price regulation reduce the amount of executive compensation which is independent of profit and sales.

3.   You are given the following data on gross domestic product (*GDP*), gross investment (*GINV*), government consumption (*GOVT*), and injections (*INJ* = *GINV* + *GOVT*) for 63 countries in 1975 (all figures in billions of U.S. dollars).

	GDP	GINV	GOVT	INJ
Mean	77.60	14.22	11.70	25.92

Variables	Covariance	Correlation
GDP, GDP	46,945.064	1.0000
GDP, GINV	7,370.297	0.9032
GDP, GOVT	7,693.905	0.9229
GDP, INJ	15,064.20	0.9278
GINV, GINV	1,418.361	1.0000
GINV, GOVT	1,358.282	0.9373
GINV, INJ	2,776.643	0.9839
GOVT, GOVT	1,480.608	1.000
GOVT, INJ	2,838.891	0.9845
INJ, INJ	5,615.534	1.000

a. Calculate the simple regression of *GDP* against each of the other three variables. What happens to the size of the "multiplier" when either *GINV* or *GOVT* are excluded from the regression equation, compared to when both are included by aggregating them into *INJ*?

b. The multiple regression of *GDP* against *GOVT* and *GINV* yields the equation:

$$GDP = 10.49 + 3.53GOVT + 1.811GINV; \quad R^2 = 0.8637$$
$$(11.49) \quad (0.770) \qquad\quad (0.787)$$

Is it reasonable in terms of macroeconomic theory for the coefficient of *GOVT* to be greater than the coefficient of *GINV*? To what might this difference be attributed?

c. In light of your answers to parts a and b of this problem, what can you infer about the effect of aggregating highly correlated regressors whose impact on the dependent variable is theoretically the same?

4.   This problem reprises Problem 3, using a log-linear model instead of a linear model of gross domestic product, gross investment, and government consumption. The log-linear data are:

	LGDP	LGOVT	LGINV	LINJ
Mean	2.436	0.411	0.789	1.331

Variables	Covariance	Correlation
LGDP, LGDP	4.3975	1.0000
LGDP, LGOVT	4.0531	0.9005
LGDP, LGINV	4.0184	0.9090
LGDP, LINJ	4.0304	0.9094
LGOVT, LGOVT	4.6072	1.0000
LGOVT, LGINV	4.4435	0.9820
LGOVT, LINJ	4.5082	0.9938
LGINV, LGINV	4.4441	1.0000
LGINV, LINJ	4.4409	0.9968
LINJ, LINJ	4.4664	1.0000

a. Calculate the simple regression of *LDGP* against each of the other three variables. What happens to the size of the "multiplier" when either *LGINV* or *LGOVT* is excluded from the regression equation, compared to when both are included by aggregating them into *LINJ*?

b. The multiple regression of *LGDP* against *LGOVT* and *LGINV* yields the equation:

$$LGDP = 1.80 + 0.690 LGINV + 0.214 LGOVT; \quad R^2 = 0.8280$$
$$(0.159)\ (0.282) \qquad\qquad (0.227)$$

How has multicollinearity affected this equation? Explain.

c. What is the effect of omitting a highly correlated regressor from a log-linear regression equation, compared to including both variables through an aggregate "instrumental variable?" How does your answer reflect the meaning of the coefficient in a log-linear regression?

5. To determine the effects of right-to-work laws on average hourly wage rates (*AHW*), that variable was regressed against the four dummy variables, *NE*, *S*, *MW*, and *RTW*, and value-added per worker (*VAPH*):

$$AHW = 3.99 + 0.016 NE + 0.155 S + 0.609 MW - 0.843 RTW$$
$$(0.618)\ (0.296) \qquad (0.283) \quad (0.259) \qquad (0.224)$$
$$+ 0.099 VAPH; \quad R^2 = 0.5801$$
$$(0.022)$$

a. Write out the regression equation for union shop states and right-to-work states in each region. (Remember, there are no right-to-work states in the Northeast region.)

b. Test the hypothesis: "Lower average wage rates in right-to-work states are due to lower productivity in those states."

21

Problems of

Economic

Time Series

When economists make inferences about theoretical models, they use two types of data, cross-section data and time-series data. Cross-section data consist of observations on the values of economic variables at a given point in time or during a given interval of time. Each observation may be the measured value of x in a specified geographic locality, such as a country or state, or in a given institution, such as a firm or a household. An observation on x might be the percent change in the money stock in a given country in a given year. The total sample of observations might consist of the percent change in the money supply of 45 countries during 1979. Or the variable may be the proportion of workers belonging to unions, with the sample consisting of one observation per state for 50 states. The economic variable in question may be wage rates, and wage rates in various industries make up the cross-section sample. Thus, the primary reference of cross-section data is spatial or institutional. The factor that separates different observations is a difference in location or institutional membership at a given time.

Time-series data, on the other hand, consist of observations on a variable at different points in time or during different intervals of time. Each successive observation is separated from the others by its occurrence at a different time rather than its occurrence at a different place. A sample consisting of the total output of steel per month in the United States from 1960 to 1985 is a time series. So is the set of observations on national income per year in the United States for each year from 1929 to 1983. The sample data in Tables 19.1, 19.2, and 19.3 include three time series: one on the percent change in the real wage rate, one on the percent change in productivity, and one on the unemployment rate. Any economic variable (such as employment, saving, production, or cost) whose values are ordered with respect to time is called an economic time series.

Both cross-section and time-series data are used in regression analysis. In fact, some samples are composed of both types of data. The problem of multicollinearity may be encountered in either type of data used in multiple regression. The problem of heteroscedasticity can also occur in either cross-section or time-series data, although it is more frequently encountered in cross-section data. A common problem in time-series data is the mutual dependence among successive observations on a variable. The natural order of time-series data means that the change in one or more variables may be cumulative. The ordering of cross-section data (e.g., alphabetical, by industry number) is more or less arbitrary, so that the change in a variable across space or institutions is more likely to be random in character.

It is likely that a series of observations of some variable x (x_1, x_2, x_3, ..., x_n) that occur in successive time intervals are not independent of each other. As a matter of fact, most economic time series are characterized by mutual dependence. Indeed, this mutual dependence is the basis of econometric forecasting. Consider, for example, a price series. If successive observations from, say, one year to the next, were indeed independent of one another, we would be living in a chaotic economy. In such a world, changes in prices would occur as if generated by a random device, such as throws of a die or tosses of a coin. Knowledge of price in one time period would in no way permit us to predict the price in the next period, for in the succeeding time period any particular value for price would be as likely as any other.

While the mutual dependence of successive observations brings a certain amount of order into economic life, it also complicates the analysis of regressions estimated with time-series data. The Gauss-Markov theorem, introduced in Chapter 17, assures us that the method of least squares gives the best linear unbiased estimates of the population parameters in a regression equation, as long as the error term conforms to four assumptions: (1) the error term has an expected value of zero, (2) the error term is independent of all right-side regressors, (3) the error term is independent of the error terms of other observations, and (4) the error term has a constant variance over the population. In addition, we assume that the error term is normally distributed in order to draw inferences about the population parameters from the regression coefficients.

Note that the error term need not be normally distributed, have a constant variance, or even be independent from one observation to another in order for coefficients to be unbiased. The assumptions of constant variance (homoscedasticity) and mutual independence (zero autocorrelation) of errors are necessary for the least squares estimators to be efficient (i.e., to have the smallest variance of all possible linear unbiased estimators).

In order for significance tests of hypotheses to be reliable, the value of one deviation or error in prediction should in no way determine or influence the magnitude of any other error. The probability of obtaining a given size of error must not change as a result of the size of any other error. In a regression equation of the form $y = a + bx + u$, the analysis assumes that the variable y is a random variable (because u is random), but that x is not. That is, y has a systematic component (determined by x) and a random component (determined by u). The validity of traditional statistical tests is dependent on the randomness of u—more specifically, that successive values of u be independent of one another, as well as being normally distributed with a constant variance (homoscedastic). If such is not the case, the sample cannot be treated as the result of random sampling, and many of the usual statistical analyses may yield misleading results.

Now there is reason to believe that small deviations from normality will not seriously affect the results of significance tests, confidence limits, and hypotheses tests.[1] But if the successive errors are not independent—that is, if they are correlated—then the consequences are more serious. The ordinary least squares estimator is inefficient, because the number of degrees of freedom is greatly reduced. This occurs because the number of degrees of freedom is related to the number of independent observations. More importantly, the estimated standard errors of the coefficients are biased: upward in the case of negative autocorrelation (analogous to the effect of multicollinearity) and downward in the case of positive autocorrelation (analogous to the effect of positive heteroscedasticity). In the latter case, which is the more prevalent, hypothesis tests will be biased in favor of type I error, the inappropriate rejection of a true null hypothesis in favor of a false alternative hypothesis.

AUTOCORRELATION

Economic data ordered in a time sequence can seldom be regarded as random samples. An observation on price, production, inventory stocks, savings, and other economic variables in a given year is usually correlated with (not independent of) the value of that same variable in some previous year. The term *autocorrelation* is used to describe the correlation of a particular variable with the same variable lagged by a number of time units. A variable x observed in a time series is autocorrelated if the value of x in period t, x_t, is correlated with the value of x n periods earlier, x_{t-n}. The

---

[1]It has been shown that even the assumption of independence may be dropped under certain conditions. See A. C. Aitken, "On Least Squares and Linear Combinations of Observations," *Proceedings of the Royal Society of Edinburgh*, Vol. 55 (1934-1935), pp. 42ff.

most prevalent case of autocorrelation is *first degree autocorrelation*, when x_t is correlated with x_{t-1}, that is, when $n = 1$.

When the error term itself is autocorrelated, the assumption that the error terms for different observations are statistically independent is violated. As with the problems of multicollinearity and heteroscedasticity, the phenomenon of *autocorrelated error terms* compromises the tests of significance of economic hypotheses. *Positive autocorrelation*, in which the error term for one period is positively related to the error term of the previous period, tends to understate the standard error of the regression coefficient(s) and increases the probability of committing a type I error. *Negative autocorrelation*, in which the error term for one period is negatively related to the error term from the previous period, tends to overstate the standard error of the coefficients and increases the probability of making a type II error.[2]

The usual cause of autocorrelated errors is a sluggishness or inertia in the data. The estimated equation tends to underpredict the dependent variable for a while, then overpredict. The error term tends to change from positive to negative gradually, rather than changing between positive and negative in a random pattern. (If there were a regular pattern of sign reversals on the error term for each observation, negative autocorrelation would be indicated.) Formally, the presence of autocorrelated errors means that the error term in the current period is related to the error term in the previous period according to an equation of the form:

$$u_t = v_t + \rho u_{t-1}$$

where v_t is the noncorrelated component of the error term meeting the Gauss-Markov conditions: $E(v_t) = 0$ and $E(v_t v_{t-1}) = 0$. Similar to the value of the correlation coefficient, the value of ρ (rho) is assumed to take on values between -1 and $+1$: $-1 \leq \rho \leq 1$.[3] When ρ is close to zero, the

---

[2]Let λ be the autocorrelation coefficient for some variable x (i.e., the correlation coefficient between x_t and x_{t-1}), and let ρ be the autocorrelation coefficient for the error term (the correlation between u_t and u_{t-1}). The bias introduced into the measurement of the standard error of the regression coefficient for x is given by $-2\rho\lambda/(1 + \rho\lambda)$. When ρ and λ are both positive (the usual case), $s_{\hat{\beta}}$ approaches zero as ρ and λ approach one. See J. Johnston, *Econometric Methods*, 3rd Edition, New York: McGraw-Hill, 1984, pp. 310-313.

[3]Because of the assumption that the expected value of the error term is zero, the formula for rho can be written as:

$$\rho = \frac{\Sigma(u_t - 0)(u_{t-1} - 0)}{\Sigma(u_{t-1})^2} = \frac{\Sigma u_t u_{t-1}}{\Sigma u_{t-1}^2}$$

The correlation coefficient between successive error terms is defined as:

$$r_{u_t u_{t-1}} = \frac{\Sigma(u_t - 0)(u_{t-1} - 0)}{\sqrt{\Sigma(u_t - 0)^2 (u_{t-1} - 0)^2}} = \frac{\Sigma u_t u_{t-1}}{\sqrt{\Sigma u_t^2 \Sigma u_{t-1}^2}}$$

The correlation coefficient and the slope coefficient for ρ differ only in one observation: Σu_t^2 includes the error term for the last observation but omits the error term for the first observation (since u_{t-1} is undefined for that observation). Hence, we can think of ρ either as the derivative of u_t with respect to u_{t-1}, or as the square root of the proportion of u_t "explained by" u_{t-1}.

Gauss-Markov assumption is approximately true, and t tests are considered valid. When ρ is approximately equal to $+1$, we have positive autocorrelation, and significance tests are biased *in favor of the alternative hypothesis.* When ρ is approximately equal to -1, we have negative autocorrelation, and significance tests are biased *in favor of the null hypothesis.*

AUTOCORRELATION AND
OMITTED VARIABLE BIAS

We have just seen that autocorrelation tends to occur because of sluggishness in the data. Such inertia might be due to the exclusion of an important variable whose influence on the dependent variable is nonrandom. If the omitted variable is autocorrelated (i.e., it changes gradually through time), the residual of the regression equation is also likely to be autocorrelated. However, this problem is more serious than mere autocorrelation. Omission of such a variable would cause the regression coefficients to be biased and inconsistent. That is, the expected values of estimated regression coefficients do not equal the values of the true parameters, nor does the difference between estimated coefficients and the true parameters decrease as sample size increases.

Suppose we wish to test a simple economic hypothesis: aggregate household saving, measured in constant dollars, is a positive function of real disposable personal income. Economic theory tells us that there are many other economic influences on household saving behavior (e.g., the rate of interest, the rate of inflation, the rate of taxation, the unemployment rate, and the prevalence of social insurance programs). We learned in Chapters 19 and 20 that omitting important variables from a regression equation can cause ordinary least squares coefficients to diverge markedly from the true values of true parameters. Ordinary least squares requires that the average value of the residual be zero. If the expected value of the error term is not zero (because it reflects the influence of important excluded variables), the value of the estimated coefficients will be distorted.

In Table 21.1 we intentionally commit specification error to illustrate our point. In the table we present data on real disposable personal income ($RDPI = x$) and real household saving ($RSAVE = y$) for the years 1939 through 1984. Using procedures outlined in Chapter 18, we regress y on x and generate the regression equation:

$$y_t = 21.12 + 0.0376x_t; \ r^2 = 0.2531$$
$$\quad\ (6.45) \quad (0.0097)$$

where the standard errors are in parentheses.

The t statistic for the slope coefficient, $t = 0.0376/0.0097 = 3.88$, apparently allows us to reject the null hypothesis that real aggregate saving

Table 21.1

Year	RDPI (x)	RSAVE (y)	$\hat{y}$	$\hat{u}_t$	$\hat{u}_{t-1}$	$(\hat{u}_t - \hat{u}_{t-1})^2$	$\hat{u}_t^2$
1939	229.8	8.8	30.75	−21.95			481.75
1940	244.0	11.3	31.28	−19.98	−21.95	3.87	399.28
1941	277.9	31.9	32.56	−0.66	−19.98	373.53	0.43
1942	317.5	75.1	34.04	41.06	−0.66	1,739.97	1,685.75
1943	332.1	84.6	34.59	50.01	41.06	80.13	2,500.97
1944	343.6	92.0	35.02	56.98	50.01	48.56	3,246.47
1945	338.1	70.2	34.82	35.38	56.98	466.28	1,252.05
1946	332.7	31.1	34.61	−3.51	35.38	1,512.99	12.34
1947	318.8	10.5	34.09	−23.59	−3.51	403.13	556.53
1948	335.8	20.9	34.73	−13.83	−23.59	95.29	191.25
1949	336.8	14.3	34.77	−20.47	−13.83	44.06	418.89
1950	362.8	22.2	35.74	−13.54	−20.47	47.94	183.42
1951	372.6	28.1	36.11	−8.01	−13.54	30.60	64.18
1952	383.2	30.0	36.51	−6.51	−8.01	2.26	42.37
1953	399.1	31.4	37.11	−5.71	−6.51	0.64	32.56
1954	403.2	28.5	37.26	−8.76	−5.71	9.33	76.74
1955	426.8	26.9	38.15	−11.25	−8.76	6.18	126.48
1956	446.2	33.9	38.87	−4.97	−11.25	39.33	24.75
1957	455.5	34.3	39.22	−4.92	−4.97	0.00	24.25
1958	460.7	35.7	39.42	−3.72	−4.92	1.45	13.83
1959	479.7	31.8	40.13	−8.33	−3.72	21.28	69.44
1960	489.7	28.7	40.51	−11.81	−8.33	12.08	139.44
1961	503.8	33.2	41.04	−7.84	−11.81	15.77	61.43
1962	524.9	33.0	41.83	−8.83	−7.84	0.98	77.97
1963	542.3	30.6	42.48	−11.88	−8.83	9.32	141.22
1964	580.8	40.7	43.93	−3.23	−11.88	74.90	10.43
1965	616.3	45.4	45.26	0.14	−3.23	11.34	0.02
1966	646.8	46.9	46.41	0.49	0.14	0.13	0.24
1967	673.5	56.1	47.41	8.69	0.49	67.20	75.51
1968	701.3	50.7	48.45	2.25	8.69	41.52	5.04
1969	722.5	46.8	49.25	−2.45	2.25	22.05	6.00
1970	751.6	61.6	50.34	11.26	−2.45	187.89	126.72
1971	779.2	63.2	51.38	11.82	11.26	0.32	139.72
1972	810.3	52.6	52.55	0.05	11.82	138.48	0.00
1973	864.7	74.7	54.59	20.11	0.05	402.29	404.41
1974	857.5	74.1	54.32	19.78	20.11	0.11	391.26
1975	874.9	75.1	54.97	20.13	19.78	0.12	405.09
1976	906.8	62.5	56.17	6.33	20.13	190.38	40.06
1977	942.9	53.0	57.53	−4.53	6.33	117.84	20.49
1978	988.8	50.8	59.25	−8.45	−4.53	15.39	71.41
1979	1,015.7	52.9	60.26	−7.36	−8.45	1.19	54.17
1980	1,021.6	57.1	60.48	−3.38	−7.36	15.83	11.44
1981	1,054.7	55.1	61.72	−6.62	−3.38	10.52	43.89
1982	1,060.2	52.7	61.93	−9.23	−6.62	6.79	85.22
1983	1,094.3	53.2	63.21	−10.01	−9.23	0.61	100.24
1984	1,169.0	53.6	66.02	−12.42	−10.01	5.78	154.18
Sum	27,791.0	2,057.8	2,061.1	−3.3	9.1	6,275.7	13,969.3
Mean	604.15	44.73	44.81	−0.07	0.20	139.46	303.68

$$d = \frac{6,275.7}{13,969.3} = 0.456 < 1.48$$

does not increase with real disposable income. However, the validity of this test is dependent on the unbiasedness of the estimates of regression coefficients and the associated residual $\hat{u}$. Generating the predicted value of y, i.e., $\hat{y}$, from the estimated equation, we can compute the residual as $\hat{u} = y - \hat{y}$.

The pattern of the residual can be seen in the fifth column of Table 21.1 and in the scatter of points in Figure 21.1. We see very large errors for the years 1942 through 1945. During World War II a combination of patriotism and rationing of consumer goods caused household saving to increase substantially, coinciding with the sale of war bonds to finance the war effort. These "outliers" tend to pull the regression line up, generating a positive intercept. It also means that most of the other points (whose absolute error is smaller) tend to lie below the fitted line. All years between 1946 and 1967 have negative residuals. Over the entire data range, a negative residual one year predicts a negative residual the next and a positive residual one year implies a positive residual the next. This is the pattern of first-degree autocorrelated residuals that compromises hypothesis testing.

Figure 21.1

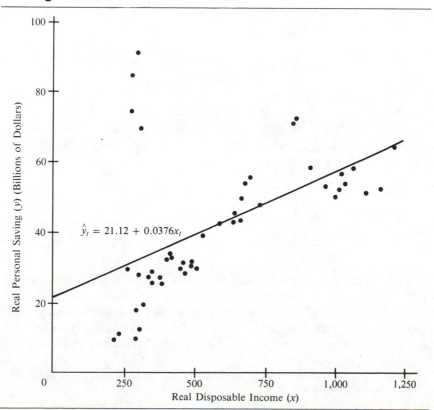

The Durbin-Watson Statistic

Plotting or "eyeballing" the residuals is one way of diagnosing patterns of autocorrelated error terms, although this approach lacks precision. One statistic that is relatively easy to calculate and routinely reported by regression software is the Durbin-Watson statistic.[4] This statistic, d, is calculated by summing the squared difference between successive residuals, then dividing by the sum of the squared residuals, that is:

$$d = \frac{\Sigma(\hat{u}_t - \hat{u}_{t-1})^2}{\Sigma \hat{u}_t^2}$$

Expanding the numerator, we have:

$$\Sigma(\hat{u}_t - \hat{u}_{t-1})^2 = \Sigma(\hat{u}_t^2 - 2\hat{u}_t\hat{u}_{t-1} + \hat{u}_{t-1}^2) \approx 2(\Sigma \hat{u}_t^2 - \Sigma \hat{u}_t\hat{u}_{t-1})$$

If there were no autocorrelation at all, $\Sigma \hat{u}_t\hat{u}_{t-1} = 0$, and the Durbin-Watson statistic simplifies to:

$$d \approx \frac{2\Sigma \hat{u}_t^2}{\Sigma \hat{u}_t^2} \approx 2$$

At another extreme, if successive error terms were perfectly positively correlated, we would have:

$$\hat{u}_t = \hat{u}_{t-1}$$

so that:

$$d \approx \frac{2(\Sigma \hat{u}_t^2 - \Sigma \hat{u}_t^2)}{\Sigma \hat{u}_t^2} = 0$$

Finally, in the case of perfect negative autocorrelation (positive and negative residuals alternate), we have:

$$\hat{u}_t = -\hat{u}_{t-1}$$

so that:

$$d \approx \frac{2(\Sigma \hat{u}_t^2 + \Sigma \hat{u}_t^2)}{\Sigma \hat{u}_t^2} = 4$$

In general, then, if the Durbin-Watson statistic is approximately equal to 2, we infer zero autocorrelation and accept the t tests of our OLS results (barring other violations of the Gauss-Markov assumptions). If the Durbin-Watson statistic is close to 0, we infer positive autocorrelation and become skeptical of our t statistics. This is because positive autocorrelation

[4]J. Durbin and G. S. Watson, "Testing for Serial Correlation in Least Squares Regression, II," *Biometrika* 38 (1951), pp. 159-78.

understates the standard error of regression coefficients, increasing the probability of a type I error. Results that look significant in the presence of positive autocorrelation might not be significant if the true variance of the error term were known. Finally, if the Durbin-Watson statistic is close to 4 we infer negative autocorrelation. This tends to overstate the standard error of coefficients, thereby overestimating the probability that the null hypothesis is true. Like multicollinearity and negative heteroscedasticity, negative autocorrelation may not be a problem if the coefficients appear to be significant. Removal of the negative autocorrelation would merely increase our confidence in the affected coefficients.

So far we have provided guidelines only for "extreme" values of the Durbin-Watson coefficient. How does one handle d values of 1.25 or 1.86 or 2.61? The answer is found in a table of Durbin-Watson statistics (Table F in the back of the book). The Durbin-Watson statistics depend on the number of observations (n) and the number of regressors (k). For each combination of n and k, two numbers are reported, a lower limit d_l and an upper limit d_u. If $2 > d > d_u$, we accept the null hypothesis of no *positive* autocorrelation because d is significantly close to 2. If $d < d_l$, we reject the null hypothesis of no autocorrelation in favor of the alternative hypothesis of positive autocorrelation. If $d_l < d < d_u$, the Durbin-Watson statistic is inconclusive, and some other test of autocorrelation (such as regressing the residual against the lagged residual) would be required. When negative autocorrelation is suspected (i.e., when $d > 2$), we subtract the critical values d_u and d_l from 4 and make the following inferences: (1) if $d > 4 - d_l$, then reject the null hypothesis in favor of the alternative hypothesis that negative autocorrelation exists, (2) if $4 - d_u > d$, then accept the null hypothesis of no negative autocorrelation, and (3) if $4 - d_l > d > 4 - d_u$, the test is inconclusive.

In our example, we have $n = 46$ observations and $k = 1$ regressor. We find that $d_l = 1.48$ and $d_u = 1.57$. In Table 21.2 we calculate the Durbin-Watson statistic as $d = 0.456$, which is considerably smaller than the lower limit of 1.48. We infer positive autocorrelation. Our t statistic is dubious because the standard error of the slope coefficient was underestimated.

Eliminating Autocorrelation by
Correct Specification

As we shall see later, there are several remedial measures for lessening the autocorrelated component of the error term, thus rendering significance tests more reliable. However, as we mentioned above, a *pattern* of autocorrelated residuals could be generated by the omission of slowly changing variables. The large error associated with the period 1942-1946 in Table 21.1 is apparently due to the failure to consider a higher average propensity to save during World War II. The second regression in Table 21.2 shows that including a dummy variable for that period ($WW2 = 1$ for 1942-1946 and

Table 21.2

Determinants of Real Household Saving: 1939-1984

(1) $\widehat{RSAVE}_t = 21.12 + 0.0376DPI_t; \ r^2 = 0.2531; \ d = 0.4563$
$\qquad\qquad$ (6.45)$\quad$ (0.0097)

$\quad \hat{u}_t = 0.279 + 0.757\hat{u}_{t-1}; \ r^2 = 0.5875$
$\qquad$ (1.69)$\quad$ (0.097)

(2) $\widehat{RSAVE}_t = 6.48 + 55.26WW2 + 0.055RDPI_t; \ R^2 = 0.7991; \ d = 0.9398$
$\qquad\qquad$ (3.68)$\quad$ (5.11)$\qquad\quad$ (0.0054)

$\quad \hat{u}_t = 0.029 + 0.517\hat{u}_{t-1}; \ r^2 = 0.2515$
$\qquad$ (1.18)$\quad$ (0.136)

(3) $\widehat{RSAVE}_t = -28.06 + 58.97WW2 + 0.1772RDPI_t - 0.00009RDPI_t^2$
$\qquad\qquad$ (7.99)$\qquad$ (4.27)$\qquad\qquad$ (0.026)$\qquad\qquad$ (0.000019)
$\qquad\qquad\qquad\qquad\qquad\qquad\qquad\qquad\qquad\quad R^2 = 0.8678; \ d = 1.48$

$\quad \hat{u}_t = -0.032 + 0.261\hat{u}_{t-1}; \ r^2 = 0.0679$
$\qquad$ (1.09)$\qquad$ (0.147)

(4) $\widehat{RSAVE}_t = -56.63 + 51.78WW2 + 0.3356RDPI_t - 0.00014RDPI_t^2$
$\qquad\qquad$ (9.93)$\qquad$ (4.46)$\qquad\qquad$ (0.040)$\qquad\qquad$ (0.000021)
$\qquad\qquad\quad - 2.24TRIN_t + 0.097UE_t + 0.956INF_t - 0.229RPTAX_t$
$\qquad\qquad\qquad$ (0.942)$\qquad\quad$ (0.467)$\qquad\quad$ (0.293)$\qquad\quad$ (0.138)
$\qquad\qquad\quad - 0.704RBSAVE_t - 1.42RTRS_t; \ R^2 = 0.9330; \ d = 2.17$
$\qquad\qquad\qquad$ (0.160)$\qquad\qquad$ (0.913)

$\quad \hat{u}_t = -0.0000003 - 0.106\hat{u}_{t-1}; \ r^2 = 0.0109$
$\qquad$ (0.796)$\qquad\qquad$ (0.154)

zero otherwise) increases the Durbin-Watson statistic from 0.462 to 0.9398. There is still significant positive autocorrelation, but we seem to be on the right track.

The next variable entered is the square of real disposable income, $RDPI_t^2$. This variable is included to test for a *nonlinear* relationship between real household saving and real disposable income. If the coefficient of $RDPI_t^2$ is positive, we infer that the marginal propensity to save tends to increase as income increases. A negative value of this term, as the one in Table 21.2, implies a decreasing *MRS*. Calculating t for this coefficient as $t = -0.000114/0.000026 = -4.74$, we reject the null hypothesis that *MRS* does not decrease as (real disposable personal) income increases. But is this result reliable? The Durbin-Watson statistic is 1.48, which equals d_u. A regression of the current residual $\hat{u}_t$ against the lagged residual $\hat{u}_{t-1}$ implies positive autocorrelation which is significant at the 5 percent level ($t = 0.261/0.147 = 1.78$).

The third equation in Table 21.2 may still suffer from specification error. There are still several variables left out of this equation which might imply omitted variable bias: (1) The incentive for precautionary saving may be reflected in the unemployment rate, UE_t, and the ratio of transfers to personal income, $TRIN_t$. (2) Increases in the rate of inflation, INF_t, and in the rate of taxation, $RPTAX_t$, both reduce the incentive to save on "supply side" grounds. (3) Martin Feldstein has suggested an inverse relation between real personal saving and real business saving (retained earnings $= RBSAVE_t$).[5] As firms retain more profits, presumably for investment motives, stockholders expect capital gains. This increases present consumption, thereby reducing present saving. (4) Classical economic theory predicts that saving will be a positive function of the interest rate. Microeconomic theory suggests that saving might change in the opposite direction to the rate of interest due to a perverse income effect.[6] If we suspect that a variable has a nonrandom effect on the dependent variable, that variable should be included in the regression to avoid specification error.

In the fourth equation in Table 21.2, real household saving ($RSAVE_t$) is regressed against the dummy variable for World War II ($WW2$), real disposable personal income ($RDPI_t$) and real disposable personal income squared ($RDPI_t^2$), the ratio of transfers to personal income ($TRIN_t$), the unemployment rate (UE_t), the rate of inflation (INF_t), real personal taxes ($RPTAX_t$), real business saving ($RBSAVE_t$), and the interest rate on three-month treasury bills ($RTRS_t$).

Admittedly, there is some multicollinearity among the regressors. The coefficients of UE_t, $RPTAX_t$, and $RTRS_t$ are insignificant, and the sign of INF_t is wrong (although this might be the effect of a money illusion). Nevertheless, the coefficients of interest, namely the ones for $RDPI_t$ and $RDPI_t^2$ are statistically significant. Although there is relatively small improvement in the R^2 term, the Durbin-Watson coefficient increases to 2.17. According to Table F, $d_l = 1.008$ and $d_u = 2.072$ for $n = 45$ and $k = 9$. Since $d > 2$, we compute $4 - d = 4 - 2.17 = 1.83 < 4 - d_u = 1.93$. Hence, we accept the null hypothesis of no autocorrelation. We check this result by regressing the residual of equation (4), $\hat{u}_t$, against the lagged residual, $\hat{u}_{t-1}$. Note that only 1 percent of the variation in $\hat{u}_t$ is attributed to the variation in $\hat{u}_{t-1}$. The t statistic of $t = 0.061/0.153 = 0.399$ also implies an insignificant amount of autocorrelation. Apparently the autocorrelation in the error term has been eliminated by improving the specification of the equation.

One point is worth repeating. Many regression programs have routines for "correcting" autocorrelation; these routines will be discussed in the next

[5]Feldstein, M., "Tax Incentives, Corporate Saving and Capital Accumulation in the United States," *Journal of Public Economics*, (2:1), 1973, 78-82.

[6]See Edgar K. Browning and Jacquelene M. Browning, *Microeconomic Theory and Applications*, Boston: Little-Brown, Inc., 1983, pp. 122-125.

section. If there is no reason to suspect that the autocorrelation in the error term does *not* appear to be due to misspecification of the equation (e.g., choosing the inappropriate functional form or omitting crucial variables), these routines may be appropriate. However, if the autocorrelated error term is really evidence of a misspecification in the equation, the appropriate (indeed, the only valid) remedial step is to specify the model correctly. If, as in our example, improved specification appears to remove the autocorrelation, no further steps are required. *Only when autocorrelation exists in an otherwise correctly specified model are transformations of the data appropriate as a means of correcting for autocorrelation.*

REMEDIAL MEASURES
FOR AUTOCORRELATION

Suppose there is evidence of autocorrelated residuals in a regression that otherwise appears to be correctly specified. In that case the ordinary least squares coefficients are unbiased and consistent, but may no longer be efficient. That is, there may be other unbiased linear estimators of the parameters which have a smaller variance. Of greater relevance, the standard errors of the regression coefficients will be biased, leading to inappropriate inferences or hypotheses tests. Hence, evidence of autocorrelation requires a double check of calculated t statistics.

Recall that autocorrelated error terms imply a relationship similar to:

$$u_t = v_t + \rho u_{t-1}$$

where u_t is the error term for a specified observation, v_t is the nonautocorrelated component of u_t (assumed to have an expected value of zero and a constant variance), u_{t-1} is the lagged error term, and ρ (rho) is the parameter linking a change in u_{t-1} to the change in u_t. If ρ were known, the best linear unbiased estimates of the model could be estimated by transforming the data.

Suppose our model has the form:

$$y_t = a + \Sigma b_i x_{it} + u_t$$

This model can be rewritten as:

$$y_t = a + \Sigma b_i x_{it} + v_t + \rho u_{t-1}$$

Now we lag the original equation by one period, multiply by ρ, and subtract the result from our transformed equation:

$$
\begin{array}{llll}
y_t = a & + \Sigma b_i x_{it} & + v_t + \rho u_{t-1} \\
- \rho y_{t-1} = \rho a & + \rho \Sigma b_i x_{it-1} & + \rho u_{t-1} \\
\hline
y_t - \rho y_{t-1} = a(1 - \rho) & + \Sigma b_i (x_{it} - \rho x_{it-1}) & + v_t
\end{array}
$$

If we define new variables, $y^* = y_t - \rho y_{t-1}$ and $x_i^* = x_{it} - \rho x_{it-1}$, an ordinary least squares regression of y^* on the x_i^* variables—a procedure known as *generalized least squares*—would provide a best linear unbiased estimator of the parameters a and the b_i's. The problem is that ρ is rarely known prior to estimation of the equation and must be estimated from analysis of the residuals. If we use an estimate of ρ instead of the true ρ, we can still obtain consistent and efficient estimators of the parameters. But unbiasedness would be sacrificed. For this reason, we make the absence of autocorrelation our null hypothesis, and reject that hypothesis only when the probability of its being true is less than 5 percent.

There are several techniques that can be used to estimate the auto-correlation coefficient, ρ. Table 21.3 presents a series of regressions relating real gross national product (GNP_t) to three types of "injections"—real gross investment (INV_t), real federal purchases of goods and services ($FGOVT_t$), and real exports ($EXPORT_t$)—and to the real money stock ($RM2_t$) using quarterly data for 1959 to 1984. According to the Keynesian model, GNP_t should be an increasing function of each of the three injections and should have coefficients greater than one (the multiplier effect). According to the monetarist model, real GNP should increase as the real money supply increases (the equation of exchange). Although there is considerable overlap between these two models, all four regressors are included in the first regression to avoid specification bias.

All regression coefficients are significantly greater than zero, consistent with both the Keynesian and monetarist models, but the coefficient of INV_t is smaller than one (probably due to multicollinearity with $RM2_t$ (much investment is financed with bank loans, which expand the money stock). However, the Durbin-Watson statistic is 0.631, which is smaller than the critical $d_u = 1.59$ for $n = 100$ and $k = 4$. This evidence of autocorrelation is reinforced by the regression of $\hat{u}_t$ against $\hat{u}_{t-1}$ ($t = 0.683/0.061 = 11.2$). However, since the value of ρ is unknown, we must use an estimated value of ρ. We will explore four alternative techniques.

First Differences

If the Durbin-Watson statistic is quite close to zero, we infer that the correlation between u_t and u_{t-1} is close to $+1$. In this case, the generalized least squares regression requires taking the difference between each variable and its lagged value. In other words, the regression equation becomes:

$$\Delta y_t = \Sigma b_i \Delta x_{it} + v_t$$

where delta (Δ) stands for "the change in." Notice that the constant term disappears, forcing the regression through the origin.

One clear advantage of the first difference equation approach is that the transformed equation is readily interpreted. In the second equation in

Table 21.3

Ordinary Least Squares:

(1) $GNP_t = 26.76 + 0.859INV_t + 1.421FGOVT_t + 1.628EXPORT_t + 0.924RM2_t$
$\qquad$ (14.60) (0.084) $\qquad$ (0.152) $\qquad\qquad$ (0.071) $\qquad\qquad$ (0.033)

$\qquad R^2 = 0.9973;\ d = 0.6308 < 1.59;\ \hat{u}_t = -0.142 + 0.683\hat{u}_{t-1}$
$\qquad\qquad\qquad\qquad\qquad\qquad\qquad\qquad$ (0.809) $\quad$ (0.061)

First Differences:

(2) $DGNP_t = 1.076DINV_t + 1.192DGOVT_t + 0.902DEXP_t + 0.746DM2_t$
$\qquad\qquad$ (0.081) $\qquad\qquad$ (0.260) $\qquad\qquad$ (0.170) $\qquad\qquad$ (0.086)

$\qquad R^2 = 0.6276;\ d = 2.41;\ \hat{u}_t = 1.11 - 0.218\hat{u}_{t-1}$
$\qquad\qquad\qquad\qquad\qquad\qquad$ (0.784) (0.098)

Durbin's Technique:

$\qquad \hat{\rho} = 1 - (d/2) = 1 - 0.6308/2 = 1 - 0.3154 = 0.6846$
$\qquad xc = 1 - 0.6846 = 0.3154$
$\qquad xGNP = GNP_t - 0.6846GNP_{t-1}$
$\qquad xINV = INV_t - 0.6846INV_{t-1}$
$\qquad xGOVT = FGOVT_t - 0.6846FGOVT_{t-1}$
$\qquad xEXP = EXPORT_t - 0.6846EXPORT_{t-1}$
$\qquad xRM2 = RM2_t - 0.6846RM2_{t-1}$

(3) $xGNP = 34.47 + 0.969xINV + 1.23xGOVT + 1.49xEXP + 0.932xRM2$
$\qquad\qquad$ (28.23) (0.103) $\qquad$ (0.273) $\qquad$ (0.126) $\qquad$ (0.050)

$\qquad R^2 = 0.9863;\ d = 2.10;\ \hat{u}_t = -0.032 - 0.052\hat{u}_{t-1};\ r^2 = 0.0027$
$\qquad\qquad\qquad\qquad\qquad\qquad\qquad$ (1.24) $\qquad$ (0.100)

Cochrane-Orcutt Technique:

(4) $GNP_t = 35.43 + 0.980INV_t + 1.21FGOVT_t + 1.46EXPORT_t + 0.936RM2_t$
$\qquad\qquad$ (31.29) (0.106) $\qquad$ (0.295) $\qquad\qquad$ (0.137) $\qquad\qquad$ (0.053)

$\qquad R^2 = 0.9985;\ \hat{\rho} = 0.7277;\ d = 2.18;\ \hat{u}_t = -0.025 - 0.093\hat{u}_{t-1}$
$\qquad\qquad\qquad\qquad$ (0.0714) $\qquad\qquad\qquad$ (1.02) $\qquad$ (0.0996)

Table 21.3, we see that the *change* in GNP ($DGNP_t$) from one quarter to the next is positively and significantly related to the change in gross investment ($DINV_t$), the change in federal government spending ($DGOVT_t$), the change in exports ($DEXP_t$), and the change in the money stock ($DM2_t$). Note that R^2 is reduced to 0.628, relative to its value of nearly 1 in regression (1). When the constant term is suppressed, R^2 can no longer be interpreted as the "percent variance explained" and is no longer bounded by 0 and 1.

$\qquad$ In this example, first difference regressions result in an overcorrection for autocorrelation. The Durbin-Watson statistic is greater than 2, and a regression of the residual against the lagged residual confirms the presence of negative autocorrelation. However, although the probability of a type I error may have been increased by negative autocorrelation, we can still reject the null hypothesis that real *GNP* does not increase with *INV*, *FGOVT*, *EXPORT*, or *RM2* with 99 percent confidence after correcting for autocorrelation by means of first difference regression.

If the true value of ρ is not close to zero, using first differences will generate residuals that are negatively autocorrelated, increasing the probability of a type II error (the inappropriate acceptance of a false null hypothesis). As in the case of multicollinearity, however, results that are significant in the presence of negative autocorrelation usually do not require remedial action to remove that autocorrelation.

Using the Durbin-Watson Statistic

We have seen that the Durbin-Watson statistic provides an approximation of the correlation between successive residuals by calculating the ratio of the sum of the squared differences between residuals to the sum of the squared residuals:

$$d = \frac{\Sigma(\hat{u}_t - \hat{u}_{t-1})^2}{\Sigma\hat{u}_t^2} \approx 2\left(1 - \frac{\Sigma\hat{u}_t\hat{u}_{t-1}}{\Sigma\hat{u}_t^2}\right) \approx 2(1 - \rho)$$

It follows that we can estimate the value of ρ as $\hat{\rho} = 1 - d/2$, where d is the Durbin-Watson statistic. In the first regression in Table 21.3 we have $d = 0.6308$, implying an estimated ρ of $1 - 0.6308/2 = 0.6846$. (Incidentally, this is quite close to the slope coefficient obtained by the regression of $\hat{u}_t$ against $\hat{u}_{t-1}$.) Using this estimate of ρ we define a new set of regressors (prefaced by x) in equation (3) of Table 21.3. Regressing the transformed dependent variable against the four transformed regressors (and the constant $xc = 1 - 0.6846$ used to estimate the intercept term), we obtain a regression apparently purged of autocorrelation. This is verified by the resulting value of d and the insignificant regression coefficient between $\hat{u}_t$ and $\hat{u}_{t-1}$ (after correction).

The Cochrane-Orcutt Technique

It sometimes happens that a significant amount of autocorrelation still exists after using Durbin's correction technique. There are two iterative techniques that attempt to find the value of ρ that provides the most efficient set of estimators for the parameters of the equation. Equation (4) in Table 21.3 illustrates the Cochrane-Orcutt technique for estimating the value of the autocorrelation coefficient. As long as the original equation is correctly specified, the residual of the equation represents an unbiased estimate of the error term for that equation, even in the presence of autocorrelated error terms. When the regression software saves the residual from a regression, it is a straightforward matter to regress the residual for each observation against the residual for the preceding period. The estimated slope coefficient in the second regression is the estimated value of ρ used to transform the variables for generalized least squares regressions.

Many canned regression programs have an easy to use Cochrane-Orcutt routine. In these programs, the computer automatically calculates the value of $\hat{\rho}$ from the original regression, uses this estimate to compute the generalized least squares results, then repeats the procedure, coming up with successive values of $\hat{\rho}$ until those estimated values converge on a single value. The final set of results is reported, either after the "tolerance" between two successive estimates of $\hat{\rho}$ is acceptably small or after a specified number of iterations have taken place.

In equation (4) in Table 21.3, we find an estimated value of ρ equal to 0.7277, which is close to the value of the autocorrelation coefficient estimated from the Durbin-Watson statistic. As with first differences, the Cochrane-Orcutt technique tends to overcorrect for autocorrelation although all coefficients remain significantly positive.

The Hildreth-Lu Scanning Procedure

We have seen that coefficients estimated in the presence of autocorrelated errors in an OLS regression that otherwise meets the Gauss-Markov assumptions are unbiased and consistent, although inefficient. This means that there may be some other technique, namely generalized least squares, that yields regression estimates with a lower standard error. It follows that we may wish to select our estimate of ρ on the basis of the most efficient estimator. That is, we may wish to select the value of $\hat{\rho}$ that minimizes the mean error (MSE) in the regression results. One procedure that performs this task is known as the Hildreth-Lu scanning procedure. It compares generalized least squares estimates with different values of $\hat{\rho}$ to identify the one with the minimum standard error for the regression.

A Hildreth-Lu scanning procedure is simulated in Table 21.4. Normally the computer does the "scanning" for us according to the instructions programmed into the computer. However, it is important to see that the best estimates in terms of the Hildreth-Lu procedure do not necessarily provide the preferred Durbin-Watson statistic.

To simplify, we combine the three injections into a single variable ($INJECT_t = INV_t + FGOVT_t + EXPORT_t$). In Table 21.4 we have estimated 11 regressions of GNP against $INJECT$ and $RM2$, using values of $\hat{\rho}$ ranging from 0 (the OLS equation) to 1 (first differences) in increments

Table 21.4

Hildreth-Lu Scanning Technique
(Standard errors in parentheses)

Rho	Intercept	*INJECT*	RM2	R^2	d	MSE
0.0	12.59	1.301	0.899	0.9957	0.390	331.90
	(7.94)	(0.072)	(0.041)			
0.1	11.77	1.29	0.904	0.9954	0.477	281.60
	(8.32)	(0.073)	(0.042)			
0.2	10.96	1.27	0.923	0.9954	0.675	218.77
	(8.26)	(0.073)	(0.042)			
0.3	12.17	1.27	0.914	0.9945	0.748	202.50
	(7.41)	(0.059)	(0.045)			
0.4	12.50	1.26	0.923	0.9945	0.949	173.74
	(9.76)	(0.078)	(0.045)			
0.5	13.09	1.23	0.934	0.9922	1.198	148.48
	(10.85)	(0.080)	(0.046)			
0.6	14.28	1.20	0.949	0.9894	1.43	130.67
	(12.69)	(0.083)	(0.049)			
0.7	17.21	1.16	0.964	0.9833	1.79	118.89
	(16.06)	(0.087)	(0.052)			
0.8	26.07	1.12	0.972	0.9663	2.07	113.07
	(23.23)	(0.090)	(0.057)			
0.9	66.93	1.09	0.937	0.8965	2.31	112.56
	(33.85)	(0.067)	(0.060)			
1.0	——	1.04	0.767	0.6255	2.54	114.94
		(0.091)	(0.104)			

of 0.1. For each regression, the dependent and independent variables are each transformed according to the formula:

$$x_t^* = x_t - \hat{\rho} x_{t-1}$$

where $\hat{\rho}$ is the value of ρ used in that iteration and x_t^* is the transformed variable x_t. Also, the vector of 1's used to pick up the constant term is set equal to $1 - \hat{\rho}$. Note that the smallest mean squared error is achieved when $\hat{\rho} = 0.9$. However, the "optimal" value of the Durbin-Watson statistic is achieved when $\hat{\rho} = 0.8$, which is very close to the result achieved with the Cochrane-Orcutt technique.

In economic forecasting, in which the researcher attempts to extrapolate regression results over nonobserved values of the dependent variable (usually into the future, using estimated or extrapolations of trends for independent variables), minimizing the variance of the residual may be the appropriate criterion for selecting the "best" equation. However, for the econometrician seeking to test one or more economic hypotheses, the trade-off between the efficiency of Hildreth-Lu and the unbiasedness of OLS results may select for the value of the Durbin-Watson closest to 2. In fact, correcting for auto-correlation may be used merely to double-check the accuracy of hypothesis tests. If, as in the example used in Tables 21.3 and 21.4, the *t* tests stand up to multiple corrections for autocorrelations, the researcher may still prefer the OLS results for reporting purposes.

LAGGED REGRESSORS IN
TIME-SERIES DATA

So far we have restricted our analysis of time-series data to exam-ples of regressions in which all observations are drawn from the same time period. That is, we have estimated static models even when employing time-series data. In order to estimate a dynamic model, the econometrician must relate the dependent variable for one period to one or more regressors drawn from earlier periods. The regressors, called *lagged variables*, represent delayed impact of a cause on the effect.

Distributed Lag Models

The typical reason for using lagged regressors is to allow for the pos-sibility of sluggishness in the adjustment process. For instance, it is widely believed that inflationary expectations incorporate a form of inertia in eco-nomic behavior. Table 21.5 investigates the relationship between inflation (INF_t), the percent change in the money stock ($DM1_t$), and the percent change in the producer price index for fuel ($PFUEL_t$), using annual data from 1948 to 1984. (Annual data are used to avoid autocorrelation, which would introduce more complications into the analysis than we wish to con-sider at this point.)

The first regression equation presented in Table 21.5 is a static model. Changes in the money supply and fuel prices account for about 70 percent of the current rate of inflation. In the second regression we introduce lagged values of *DM1* and *DPFUEL* for two periods (having dropped observa-tions for 1948 and 1949), which improves the R^2 but, ironically, reduces the Durbin-Watson statistic. We note that changes in the money supply *lagged one year* actually have a larger estimated impact on inflation than do current money supply changes. However, money supply changes two years previously appear to have an insignificant effect on inflation. Current and lagged fuel price changes have virtually identical coefficients and *t* sta-tistics, although fuel price changes lagged two years have a coefficient with the incorrect sign.

Table 21.5

Ordinary Least Squares, Annual Data, 1948-1984:

$INF_t = 1.867 + 0.324DMI_t + 0.159DPFUEL_t$
        (0.463)   (0.088)   (0.021)

$R^2 = 0.6930; d = 1.84$

Simple Two-Year Lag:

$INF_t = 1.071 + 0.150DMI_t + 0.257DMI_{t-1} + 0.088DMI_{t-2}$
        (0.096)   (0.083)   (0.087)   (0.096)

  $+ 0.085DPFUEL_t + 0.088DPFUEL_{t-1} - 0.003DPFUEL_{t-2}$
     (0.020)   (0.019)   (0.018)

$R^2 = 0.8690; d = 1.53; \hat{u}_t = -0.017 + 0.230\hat{u}_{t-1}$
                                  (0.164)   (0.173)

Koyck Lag Procedure:

$INF_t = 0.773 + 0.374INF_{t-1} + 0.249DMI_t + 0.121DPFUEL_t$
        (0.441)   (0.093)   (0.082)   (0.019)

$R^2 = 0.8124; d = 2.41; \hat{u}_t = 0.052 - 0.249\hat{u}_{t-1}; r^2 = 0.0662$
                                  (0.194)   (0.165)

Two-Year Linear Distributed Lag, Annual Data, 1950-1984:

$INF_t = 1.09 + 0.200\phi_0 - 0.040\phi_1 i + 0.105\Phi_0 - 0.046\Phi_1 j$
        (0.444) (0.075)   (0.075)   (0.016)   (0.013)

$R^2 = 0.8492; d = 1.52$

$INF_t = 1.09 + 0.196DMI_t + 0.160DMI_{t-1} + 0.120DMI_{t-2}$
        (0.444) (0.075)   (0.034)   (0.090)

  $+ 0.105DPFUEL_t + 0.059DPFUEL_{t-1} + 0.013DPFUEL_{t-2}$
     (0.016)   (0.008)   (0.013)

When a regressor is lagged several periods, and both the variable and its lagged values are used in the same regression, the problem of multicollinearity is often encountered. In the second regression in Table 21.5, we do not know whether the effects of money supply changes and fuel price changes are truly limited to one year, or if the high degree of correlation between those variables and their lagged counterparts make the regressors lagged two periods insignificant. To mitigate the problem of multicollinearity, economists use several procedures. The two most popular are the *Koyck lag* procedure and the *Almon lag* procedure.

Koyck Lags

In economics we typically assume that current values of exogenous variables determine the equilibrium values of endogenous variables. However, when expectations are an important influence on behavior, as in the case of *inflationary expectations*, previous values of exogenous variables, or even of endogenous variables, may have an important influence on equilibrium values of current endogenous variables. Assume, for instance, that the current rate of inflation depends on both current and lagged values of *DM1* and *DPFUEL*. Hypothetically, all previous values of the exogenous variables may influence inflationary expectations. Yet a regression cannot include more lags than there are observations. Some means must be found to limit the number of regressors that must be included in the equation.

An ingenious procedure was suggested by L. M. Koyck.[7] Each observation on a variable is given a weight that declines exponentially as the period between the occurrence of that variable and the current period increases. Further, we assume that all regressors have the same weight coefficient, which we shall dub as α. Letting $y_t = INF_t$, $x_t = DM1_t$, and $z_t = DPFUEL_t$, we can rewrite the first equation in Table 21.5 as:

$$y_t = a + b_1(x_t + \alpha x_{t-1} + \alpha^2 x_{t-2} + \ldots + \alpha^n x_{t-n})$$
$$+ b_2(z_t + \alpha z_{t-1} + \ldots + \alpha^n z_{t-n}) + u_t$$

Lagging this equation one period, multiplying by the parameter α, and subtracting from the original equation, we obtain:

$$y_t - \alpha y_{t-1} = a(1 - \alpha) + b_1(x_t - \alpha^{n+1} x_{t-n+1})$$
$$+ b_2(z_t - \alpha^{n+1} z_{t-n+1}) + u_t - \alpha u_{t-1}$$

As n approaches infinity, α^{n+1} approaches zero, as long as $\alpha < 1$. Simplifying, we have:

$$INF_t = a(1 - \alpha) + \alpha INF_{t-1} + b_1 DM1_t + b_2 DPFUEL_t + v_t$$

where $v_t = u_t - \alpha u_{t-1}$.

The mechanics of estimating a Koyck lag structure are relatively straightforward. In addition to the regressors $DM1_t$ and $DPFUEL_t$, we simply add the lagged dependent variable INF_{t-1}. Note that the coefficient of the lagged dependent variable is the estimate of the exponentially declining weight, α. In this case, we estimate $\hat{\alpha} = 0.374$. The standard error of 0.093 allows us to reject the null hypotheses that $\alpha \leq 0$ and that $\alpha \geq 1$ with t statistics of

[7]L. M. Koyck, *Distributed Lags and Investment Analysis*, North Holland, Amsterdam, 1954. A more advanced discussion can be found in J. Johnston, *Econometric Methods*, Third Edition, New York, McGraw-Hill, 1984, pp. 346-348.

$t = (0.374 - 0)/0.093 = 4.02$ and $t = (0.374 - 1)/0.093 = -0.628/0.093 = -6.76$, respectively. With this information, we may rewrite the equation as:

$$INF_t = 1.235 + 0.274DM1_t + 0.093DM1_{t-1} + 0.035DM1_{t-2} + \dots$$
$$+ 0.121DPFUEL_t + 0.045DPFUEL_{t-1} + 0.017DPFUEL_{t-2} + \dots$$

The relatively small estimated value of α implies a relatively rapid decay in the influence of the lagged values of DM1 and DPFUEL.

Before concluding the discussion of the Koyck lag model, a few caveats are in order. We have argued that a lagged endogenous variable can usually be considered as independent of the error term, since we imagine that the direction of causation runs from the past to the present and not in reverse. However, we know that the current error term, u_t, influences the current dependent variable, INF_t. If the error term is autocorrelated, the current error term is correlated with the lagged error term, implying that the current error term is also correlated with the *lagged* dependent variable. This violates the Gauss-Markov assumption of independence of the error term and the right-side variables. So it is particularly important to verify the absence of autocorrelation in the error term when using a Koyck model (or whenever a lagged dependent variable is used as a regressor).

Unfortunately, the Durbin-Watson test, which is our usual means of testing for autocorrelation, is biased *against* the finding of autocorrelated errors when lagged regressors are used. An alternative diagnostic tool has been developed by J. Durbin, called the h test. The h statistic is given by the formula:[8]

$$h = \hat{\rho} \sqrt{\frac{n}{1 - n \cdot \operatorname{var}(\hat{\alpha})}}$$

where n is the number of observations in the regression, $\hat{\rho}$ is the estimated value of ρ from the regression of $\hat{u}_t$ against $\hat{u}_{t-1}$, and $\operatorname{var}(\hat{\alpha}) = s_{\hat{\alpha}}^2$. That is, $\operatorname{var}(\hat{\alpha})$ is the square of the standard error for the coefficient of the lagged dependent variable in the Koyck regression. The h statistic is distributed like the t statistic, with a mean of zero and a variance of one.

In this example, we have $\hat{\rho} = -0.249$, $n = 35$, and $s_{\hat{\alpha}} = 0.093$, so that $\operatorname{var}(\hat{\alpha}) = s_{\hat{\alpha}}^2 = (0.093)^2 = 0.0086$. Computing the h statistic:

$$h = -0.249 \sqrt{\frac{35}{1 - 35(0.0086)}} = -0.249 \sqrt{\frac{35}{0.6990}}$$
$$= -0.249(50.0715)^{1/2} = -0.249(7.0761) = -1.76$$

Since a two-tail test is involved (the Koyck lag regression is unreliable if $\rho > 0$ or $\rho < 0$), we do not reject the null hypothesis that $\rho = 0$.

---

[8] J. Durbin, "Testing for Serial Correlation in Least Squares Regressions when Some of the Regressors are Lagged Dependent Variables," *Econometrica*, vol. 38, 1970, pp. 410-421.

In this case we see that an original regression (without lags) that had an insignificant amount of positive autocorrelation in the error term was transformed into a Koyck lag regression with an insignificant amount of negative autocorrelation. It should be clear that autocorrelation is endemic in the Koyck lag regression. Since the presence of lagged dependent variables renders the regression results biased and inconsistent in the presence of (either positive or negative) autocorrelation in the error, the Koyck lag model is used sparingly in econometric research.

Polynomial Distributed Lags

An alternative estimation strategy for models involving one lagged regressor has been suggested by Shirley Almon.[9] Unlike the Koyck lag model, which assumes that all regressors are subject to the same weighting factor that decays in influence at an exponential rate, the Almon approach to lagged regressors assumes a finite period of lags that decay according to some polynomial function. The last equation in Table 21.5 was estimated using a linear distributed lag model and a three-year lag for DMI_t and for $DPFUEL_t$.

First, we begin with a distributed lag model of the form:

$$y_t = a + \alpha_0 x_t + \alpha_1 x_{t-1} + \alpha_2 x_{t-2}$$
$$+ \beta_0 z_t + \beta_1 z_{t-1} + \beta_2 z_{t-2} + u_t$$

where $y = INF$, $x = DMI$, and $z = DPFUEL$. We could, of course, estimate the regression equation directly, since, unlike the Koyck model, the number of regressors is likely to be small relative to the number of observations. However, with an autocorrelated independent variable, such as the rate of change in the money supply, multicollinearity is likely to plague the results. Instead, we assume that each of the weights on the lagged regressors are given by some polynomial function of the form $\alpha_i \approx f(i)$ and $\beta_j \approx g(j)$. Alas, there is no way of determining empirically precisely what the degree of the polynomial should be. The intuition of the researcher is called into play. In this example we are assuming that each polynomial function is linear:

$$f(i) = \phi_0 + \phi_1 i \text{ and } g(j) = \Phi_0 + \Phi_1 j$$

where i is the lag for x and j is the lag for z.

By construction we have:

$$\alpha_0 \approx f(0) = \phi_0$$
$$\alpha_1 \approx f(1) = \phi_0 + \phi_1 i$$
$$\beta_0 \approx g(0) = \Phi_0$$
$$\beta_1 \approx g(1) = \Phi_0 + \Phi_1 j$$

[9]S. Almon, "The Distributed Lag between Capital Appropriations and Expenditures," *Econometrica*, vol. 30, 1962, pp. 407-423.

We require three steps from the computer. First, the polynomial functions $f(i)$ and $g(j)$ are estimated. Second, the *instrumental variables i* and *j* are used in place of the lagged regressors to estimate the equation. Third, the computer unravels the distributed lag regression, providing estimates of the coefficients for the lagged regressors. Note in Table 21.5 that both regressors are significant at the 1 percent level for the zero- and one-year lags, but insignificant for the two-year lag. This result is consistent with the Koyck lag model which implied that the effects of lagged regressors were virtually nil after a one-year lag.

Lagged Endogenous Variables
and Autocorrelation

In this section we will more closely examine the bias that results when a lagged endogenous variable is used in a regression equation that also suffers from autocorrelation. In Table 21.6 we regress the logarithm of real consumer expenditure ($LCON_t$) against the logarithm of real disposable personal income *lagged one quarter* ($LDPI_{t-1}$), using quarterly data for the United States from 1947 through 1984. The purpose of using lagged disposable income is to account for inertia in the consumption function, as well as to avoid simultaneous equations bias. It is well known from macroeconomic theory that consumer expenditure is a major determinant of national income, which in turn is used to compute disposable personal income. Hence, causation runs from income to consumption and from consumption to income. A simple regression of $LCON_t$ on $LDPI_t$ would violate the Gauss-Markov assumption that the error term is independent of the regressor, rendering the OLS results biased and inconsistent.

However, since last quarter's income is already determined, it is hard to imagine how lagged income would be caused by current consumption. Yet, if u_t is correlated with u_{t-1} and $LDPI_{t-1}$ is correlated with u_{t-1}, then u_t is also likely to be correlated with $LDPI_{t-1}$, foiling our attempt to avoid simultaneous equations bias. In the first regression of Table 21.6, the Durbin-Watson statistic implies significant positive autocorrelation. Since this statistic is biased against the finding of autocorrelation (because of the presence of a lagged endogenous variable), we must reject the null hypothesis of no autocorrelation. Not only is the standard error of the lagged regressors biased downward, but the slope coefficient (elasticity) of $LDPI_{t-1}$ may be biased as well.

At the outset of this chapter we discussed the prospect that evidence of autocorrelated errors may actually reflect misspecification of the model itself. One type of misspecification is an inappropriate lag structure. In equation (1) in Table 21.6 we are assuming that only last quarter's income influences current consumption. Yet theory tells us that the marginal propensity to consume out of *permanent* income is much higher than the marginal

Table 21.6

Autocorrelation With Lagged Endogenous Regressor

Ordinary Least Squares, Quarterly Data:

(1) $LCON_t = 0.048 + 0.980DPI_{t-1}$
         (0.021)   (0.0032)

   $R^2 = 0.9984;\ d = 0.746;\ \hat{u}_t = -0.0002 + 0.614\hat{u}_{t-1}$
                                      (0.0009)   (0.064)

Permanent Income (Koyck Lag) Model:

(2) $LCON_t = 0.013 + 0.867LCON_{t-1} + 0.130LDPI_{t-1}$
         (0.014)   (0.064)   (0.063)

   $R^2 = 0.9993;\ d = 1.85;\ \hat{u}_t = -0.00004 + 0.073\hat{u}_{t-1}$
                                      (0.0008)   (0.083)

Complete Equation With Koyck Lag:

(3) $LCON_t = 0.392 + 0.725LCON_{t-1} + 0.199LDPI_{t-1} - 0.0016LUE_{t-1}$
         (0.271)   (0.075)   (0.062)   (0.0047)

           $- 0.004LINF_{t-1} - 0.025LRINT_{t-1} + 0.0027LBSAVE_{t-1}$
             (0.0017)   (0.009)   (0.0035)

           $+ 0.028LTRIN_{t-1} + 0.00075\,Time$
             (0.009)   (0.0044)

   $R^2 = 0.9995;\ d = 1.92;\ \hat{u}_t = 0.00009 + 0.036\hat{u}_{t-1};\ r^2 = 0.0013$
                                      (0.0007)   (0.083)

propensity to consume out of *transitory* income. Consumers may take several quarters to adjust to a new standard of living in response to (unanticipated) changes in permanent income. Indeed, several quarters of experience may be required to determine whether a change in income is permanent. This suggests that a model with a one-quarter lag may be misspecified.

Because of its relative ease of estimation, we next fit a Koyck lag model. As we saw in the previous section, the Koyck lag model implies that autocorrelated errors may be introduced into a static model without autocorrelation. By the same logic, a Koyck lag model may remove autocorrelation from a static model. This appears to be the case in the second equation of Table 21.6. While the Durbin-Watson statistic is unreliable, regression of the residual against the lagged residual shows an insignificant positive coefficient. We cannot reject the null hypothesis of no autocorrelation. Rearranging the terms in the results of the second equation we have:

$$LCON_t = 0.392 + 0.199LDPI_{t-1} + 0.1725LDPI_{t-2} + 0.1496LDPI_{t-3}$$
$$+ 0.1297LDPI_{t-4} + 0.1124LDPI_{t-5} + 0.0975LDPI_{t-6} + \ldots$$

The influence of disposable personal income on real consumption appears to persist for more than a year and a half, a result quite consistent with the permanent income hypothesis.

As in the case of aggregate saving, there are other variables that might influence consumption, and these variables also could persist for several quarters. Accordingly we add the logarithm of the unemployment rate (LUE), the logarithm of the inflation rate ($LINF$), the logarithm of the real rate of interest ($LRINT$), the logarithm of real business saving ($LBSAVE$), and the logarithm of transfers relative to disposable income ($LTRIN$), all lagged one quarter, to obtain the third equation in Table 21.6. In the last equation all evidence of autocorrelation disappears, and the significance of $LCON_{t-1}$ and $LDPI_{t-1}$ are shown to be quite robust.

We close the chapter with the same moral that opened it: When there is evidence of autocorrelation, the first step to take is to examine the specification of the model and take corrective steps if it appears misspecified.

CONCLUSION

In this chapter we have addressed the special and often pernicious problems encountered in the use of time-series data. When observations are ordered in time, variables often change slowly, and values of variables in the current period are strongly related to values of those same variables in previous periods. This phenomenon of *autocorrelation* in the independent variables often creates special problems of multicollinearity: when two variables are moving parallel to each other through time, it may be hard to separate out the influence of the individual regressors. Ironically, that regularity in events that makes life predictable compounds the difficulty of time-series estimation.

A particularly perplexing and potentially serious problem is the presence of autocorrelation in the error term. When the current error term is correlated with the error term in the previous period(s), the number of independent observations is reduced, decreasing the number of degrees of freedom. Accordingly, significance tests conducted in the presence of autocorrelated errors are biased toward a *type I* error, the mistake of inappropriately rejecting a true null hypothesis because the standard error of the regression (and of the estimated coefficients) is biased downward.

Even more serious than biased or unreliable significance tests is the problem of biased and inconsistent regression equations that can occur in an environment of autocorrelated residuals (which is circumstantial evidence of autocorrelated error terms). First, if the model is misspecified, because of the omission of (slow-moving) variables or the specification of the incorrect functional form or the choice of the wrong lag structure, then the error term will not have an expected value of zero, and regression estimates will be erroneous. The appropriate remedial action is the correction of the model's specification. Second, if one of the regressors is a lagged endogenous variable, that regressor is likely to be correlated with the error term if the latter is autocorrelated. Furthermore, the Durbin-Watson test, usually employed to diagnose autocorrelation, is unreliable in that environment.

We reviewed several methods for mitigating autocorrelation in the error term when there is no reason to suspect omitted variable bias. But all these methods involve variations on a single theme. The researcher obtains an estimate of the autocorrelation coefficient ρ. He or she then lags the dependent variable and each regressor. Next, the estimated value of ρ is multiplied by each lagged variable and the "difference" is calculated. Then these transformed variables are used to reestimate the regression equation, thereby checking the reliability of the significance tests.

The chapter concluded with a discussion of the use of lagged regressors in time-series regressions. Lagged regressors allow the econometrician to estimate a dynamic economic model because the dependent variable is believed to react sluggishly to changes in one or more regressors. The most straightforward approach is simply to include the lagged regressors in the original regression equation. However, this strategy is prone to multicollinearity.

Two distributed lag approaches were briefly discussed. Both have potentially serious drawbacks. The Koyck lag approach uses the lagged dependent variable to estimate the exponentially decaying weighting factor for lagged regressors. This approach is prone to autocorrelation of the worst kind. The presence of the lagged regressor makes the regression results biased and inconsistent in the presence of autocorrelation. The Almon procedure uses a polynomial function to estimate the weights for the lagged regressors. However, the researcher must guess both the degree of the polynomial and the length of the lag.

We now turn our attention to the last complication of the regression process, the problem of how to estimate the parameters of structural equations with endogenous variables on the right side of the equal sign. After that important stop, our tour of econometrics will be at an end. However, you will likely discover that your fascination with econometrics has just begun.

PROBLEMS

1.   The table at the top of the next page presents quarterly observations on exports and imports from the first quarter 1976 to the last quarter 1984. All data are in constant 1972 dollars. Use the data to answer the questions that follow the table.

Date	Imports	Exports	Date	Imports	Exports
1976.1	110.72	124.71	1980.3	166.39	186.93
2	115.25	126.52	4	173.87	186.50
3	119.91	128.97	1981.1	187.05	193.32
4	122.79	129.66	2	180.18	191.10
1977.1	131.58	130.04	3	174.62	186.17
2	134.29	133.07	4	169.58	184.12
3	132.77	132.48	1982.1	161.27	175.95
4	134.80	126.54	2	160.78	176.94
1978.1	142.80	143.80	3	165.47	165.95
2	145.87	143.12	4	150.02	152.63
3	146.64	147.37	1983.1	145.61	153.60
4	149.29	155.79	2	156.42	152.45
1979.1	150.63	161.48	3	164.46	156.09
2	160.14	165.76	4	174.21	159.29
3	166.26	176.01	1984.1	153.20	144.90
4	178.57	184.82	2	156.20	144.70
1980.1	187.17	194.60	3	174.40	147.40
2	178.02	190.82	4	161.40	146.20

a. Regress current imports against current exports.
b. Calculate the slope and intercept coefficients, the standard errors, and the Durbin-Watson statistic.
c. On the basis of your results, can you reject the null hypothesis that imports do not respond positively to a change in exports? Explain your answer.

2. Using the data from Problem 1, calculate the "first differences" for imports (*DIMP*) and exports (*DEXP*) for each quarter.
a. Regress *DIMP* against *DEXP*. (Remember to suppress the constant term and to delete the first observation.)
b. What is the Durbin-Watson statistic for this regression, and what do you infer from it?
c. Comment on the use of first differences as a "cure" for autocorrelated errors in this context.

3. The following equation results from the regression of the natural logarithm of real disposable income (*LDPI*) against time ($T = 0$ for first quarter of 1947 and T increases by one unit for each observation) using data from the first quarter 1947 to the fourth quarter 1984:

$$LDPI_t = 5.74 + 0.0089T; \ R^2 = 0.9948; \ d = 0.1619$$
$$(3.37) \quad (0.025)$$

Standard errors are in parentheses and d stands for the Durbin-Watson statistic.

a. Can we infer that real disposable personal income was increasing at a significant rate between 1947 and 1984? Briefly explain why or why not.

b. First differences have been recommended as a means of eliminating any autocorrelation. Is this a good strategy? Explain your answer.

4. Donald Democrat is testing the hypothesis that increases in the federal deficit (DEF_t) increase the nominal rate of interest (r = AAA bond rate). He has included observations on the level of the money supply ($M1$, to pick up the effect of liquidity preference because Donald is a good Keynesian), the current rate of inflation (INF, he has also read Irving Fisher), and a dummy variable to pick up the effect of financial market deregulation ($DREG = 0$ from 1975 to 1979, $DREG = 1$ for 1980 and afterwards). Using quarterly data from the first quarter 1975 to the fourth quarter 1984, he produces the following results:

$$r_t = 4.38 + 3.07DREG_t + 0.0028DEF_t + 0.008M1_t + 0.239INF_t$$
$$\quad\;\;(1.65)\;\;(0.560)\qquad\;\;(0.0044)\qquad\;\;(0.0037)\qquad(0.082)$$

$$R^2 = 0.8687;\; d = 1.54$$

Donald suspects that there may be autocorrelation in the error term. Is this a relevant concern if he hopes to prove that r_t increases as DEF_t increases, *ceteris paribus*? Briefly explain.

5. Donald has decided that the results quoted in Problem 4 are wrong because all the regressors have a distributed lag effect on the nominal rate of interest. Choosing a Koyck lag structure, he fit the following equation:

$$r_t = 3.28 + 2.41DREG_t + 0.206r_{t-1} + 0.0023DEF_t$$
$$\quad\;\;(1.83)\;\;(0.740)\qquad\;\;(0.154)\qquad\;\;(0.004)$$
$$\qquad\qquad + 0.0068M1_t + 0.207INF_t$$
$$\qquad\qquad\;\;(0.0038)\qquad(0.084)$$

$$R^2 = 0.8753;\; d = 1.98$$

a. Is the Durbin-Watson statistic a good guide to accepting the null hypothesis of zero autocorrelation? Explain.

b. What does the coefficient of r_{t-1} imply about the hypothesis that deficits and other variables in the equation have a lagged influence on the nominal rate of interest?

c. All things considered, does this specification help or hurt the argument that large deficits increase the nominal rate of interest?

d. Do you think the evidence is "decisive?" Briefly explain.

22

Simultaneous Equations Models: Two Endogenous Variables

To this point we have limited the econometric equations we have estimated to those with only one endogenous variable. We have assumed that the dependent variable is caused by the exogenous variables on the right side of the equation and by the stochastic error term. We have assumed that regressors are independent of the error term. When the left-side variable is also a cause of a right-side variable, that right-side variable is no longer exogenous, but endogenous. This further implies that since the left-side variable is influenced by the error term, so is (are) the right-side endogenous variable(s). Ordinary least squares regression techniques would yield biased and inconsistent estimates of parameters in equations with endogenous variables on the right-side, since those regressors would not be independent of the error term. It follows that techniques other than ordinary least squares must be used to estimate simultaneous equations models. This chapter will concentrate on the relatively simple case of models with two endogenous variables. Chapter 23 will extend the analysis to models with three or more endogenous variables.

Although several different methods can be used to estimate the parameters of simultaneous equations systems, we will concentrate on the simplest and most practical of these procedures, the method of *two-stage least squares*. As the name implies, this procedure estimates the parameters of simultaneous equations in two steps or stages. In the first stage, each endogenous variable is regressed against *all* exogenous variables in the equation system. The values of the endogenous variables predicted by the first stage regressions are then used in place of the observed endogenous variables in the second stage regressions to estimate the parameters of the structural equations.

We will see that there are sometimes too few exogenous variables to estimate the coefficients of structural equations. In such cases the equation is said to be unidentified. Since it is possible to determine whether an equation is identified from the mathematical structure of the model, we can sometimes spare ourselves the effort of data collection and estimation by recognizing whether equation systems are identifiable before we begin the statistical phase of research.

SIMULTANEOUS EQUATIONS BIAS

Consider a simple econometric model of the form:

$$y_i = a + bx_i + cz_i + u_i$$

In order to estimate the model empirically, data are collected on the variables x_i, z_i, and y_i and assumptions are made about the model itself. These assumptions are:

1. The expected value of the error term is zero: $E(u_i) = 0$. This is equivalent to assuming that no important variables have been omitted from the equation.
2. All regressors are independent of the error term: $E(x_i u_i) = 0$ and $E(z_i u_i) = 0$. This is equivalent to assuming that the causation in the equation runs from the right-side variables to the left-side variable, *and not in the opposite direction*.
3. The right-side variables are not perfectly correlated. Violation of this assumption causes the matrix used to estimate the coefficients (the $\mathbf{X'X}$ matrix) to be singular. In this case, the matrix cannot be inverted and the coefficients cannot be estimated. When correlation between regressors is high but not perfect, the problem of multicollinearity is encountered. Although coefficients can be estimated, tests of significance tend to be biased against the alternative hypothesis.
4. The variance in the error term is constant across observations. Violation of this assumption (heteroscedasticity) distorts tests of significance in favor of the alternative hypothesis.
5. Error terms for different observations are uncorrelated. Violation of this assumption, autocorrelation, also distorts significance tests toward a type I error.

As we have seen, violations of any of the last three assumptions usually do not affect the unbiasedness and consistency properties of ordinary least squares, although, in the case of the fourth and fifth assumptions, OLS estimators may no longer be efficient. Generalized least squares may provide estimators with smaller standard errors, thereby yielding more reliable hypothesis tests. Violations of assumptions (1) and (2) are more serious. Specification error, violation of assumption (1), and simultaneous equations bias, violation of assumption (2), cause the residual of the regression equation to be an unreliable estimator of the error term in the regression equation. It is rarely possible to diagnose violations of these assumptions from regression results alone. For this reason, the econometrician must be guided by the theoretical and mathematical structure of the model being estimated.

As an example of the problem of simultaneous equations bias, consider a simple supply and demand model of the form:

(1) $Q_d = a_0 + a_1 p + a_2 p_j + u$
(2) $Q_s = b_0 + b_1 p + b_2 w + e$
(3) $Q_e = Q_d = Q_s$

where Q_d is the quantity demanded and p is the price of a commodity, p_j is the price of another commodity (i.e., a substitute or complement), Q_s is quantity supplied, w is a factor price (e.g., a wage rate), while u and e are random error terms assumed to follow the Gauss-Markov conditions. The first two equations are *behavioral equations*, implying that buyers and sellers each respond to a change in price by changing the quantity of a product demanded or supplied, respectively. We predict $a_1 < 0$ in accordance with the law of demand. Coefficient a_2 will be negative if the "other" good is a complement and will be positive if it is a substitute. In the supply equation, we expect that $b_1 > 0$ and $b_2 < 0$. The third equation is a definitional equation stipulating the conditions for equilibrium, namely that the quantity exchanged, Q_e, equals quantity demanded and equals quantity supplied.

If we had access to individual household data or individual firm data we could estimate either of the first two equations without fear of simultaneous equations bias. That is because both households and firms are assumed to be *price takers*: price influences individual quantity, but individual quantity does not affect price. Of course, if we were using individual data, the third equilibrium equation would not be present. There is no presumption that the quantity demanded by any particular household must correspond to the quantity supplied by any particular firm.

If we try to estimate simultaneous equations of market demand and market supply, the equilibrium equation becomes relevant. Using market data, we observe only one price and one quantity exchanged at each time and/or place. If, as is usually assumed, this price and quantity are equilibrium ones, the values of those variables are *mutually determined* by the equilibration process. The positions of the market demand curve and the market supply curve determine the observed quantity exchanged and the price. It is inappropriate in this context to treat price as an independent variable and quantity as the only dependent variable in the estimation of either structural equation.

To understand the problem of simultaneous equations bias formally, consider again our three equation statistical model of supply and demand. Substituting the equations for Q_d and Q_s into the third equation, we solve for the equilibrium values of p and Q_e:

$$Q_e = a_0 + a_1p + a_2p_j + u = b_0 + b_1p + b_2w + e$$

$$(4) \quad p = \frac{1}{b_1 - a_1}(a_0 - b_0 + a_2p_j - b_2w + u - e)$$

Substituting the equilibrium value for p into either the demand or the supply equation, we obtain the equilibrium value of Q_e. Using the demand equation:

$$Q_e = Q_d = a_0 + a_1\left[\frac{1}{b_1 - a_1}(a_0 - b_0 + a_2p_j - b_2w + u - e)\right]$$
$$+ a_2p_j + u$$

$$(5) \quad Q_e = \frac{1}{b_1 - a_1}(b_1a_0 - a_1b_0 + b_1a_2p_j - a_1b_2w + b_1u - a_1e)$$

You may wish to check this answer by substituting the formula for the equilibrium value of p into the supply equation.

According to the reduced form equations (4) and (5), the equilibrium values of price and quantity are determined by the parameters of the structural equations, the exogenous variables, and the stochastic error terms. The price-quantity pairs we observe are generated by shifts in the demand and/or supply curves, which are attributed to changes in the exogenous variables and changes in the error terms. Because the observed price is correlated with the error term in each structural equation, the assumption that error terms are independent of right-side variables is violated. Direct estimation of either structural equation price would violate an important assumption of the Gauss-Markov theorem. Estimated coefficients would be biased and inconsistent, and any inferences drawn from such regressions would be dubious, at best.

While we cannot estimate parameters directly from the structural equations in a simultaneous equations system, it is sometimes possible to estimate those parameters indirectly by estimating the parameters of the reduced form equations. In this era of low cost computers, the most practical approach to the estimation of simultaneous equations systems is *two-stage least squares* (TSLS). In order for this (or any other) estimation procedure to work, the individual equations must be *identified*. So before we address the procedures for estimating simultaneous equations, we must understand the identification problem.

THE IDENTIFICATION PROBLEM

The *identification problem* in econometrics concerns whether it is possible to estimate the structural equations of a simultaneous equations model from the estimation of the parameters of the reduced form equations (which is nearly always possible). The identification problem involving models with two endogenous variables is the easiest to visualize, so we will concentrate on these models in this chapter. Consider the three diagrams in Figure 22.1. In each diagram, the observed price-quantity pairs are generated by the intersection of a demand curve and a supply curve. The curves are drawn as discontinuous lines only when one price-quantity pair is observed on that line. This depicts the fact that too little information exists to estimate the slope of the line. As we recall from Chapter 2, at least two points are necessary to fix a straight line in two-dimensional space.

In Figure 22.1a, the demand curve D is drawn with a solid line. The first intersection of D and supply curve S_0 generates the equilibrium price p_0 and the associated equilibrium quantity Q_0. An increase in supply (a shift in the supply curve from S_0 to S_1, presumably caused by a change of an exogenous variable) causes a surplus at price p_0. This decreases price, which in turn increases quantity demanded along the demand curve D. When price reaches p_1, the market returns to equilibrium, with quantity equal to Q_1. The shift in the supply curve allowed us to observe two points on the stationary demand curve. In order for us to *predict* or *measure* the change in supply, there must be an exogenous variable that affects the supply curve but does not directly affect the demand curve. This is because the demand curve must remain stationary in order that this curve be "identified."

Figure 22.1a
Identification of Demand Curve

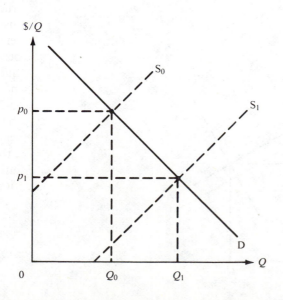

Figure 22.1b
Identification of Supply Curve

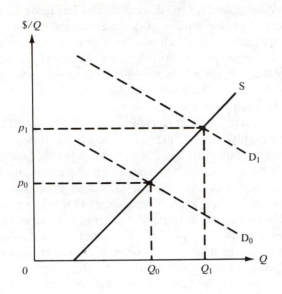

Figure 22.1c
Both Curves Shift

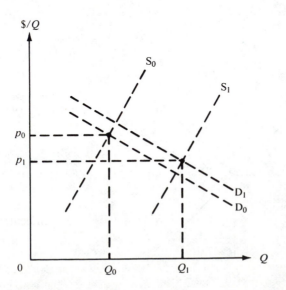

In Figure 22.1b, the supply curve S is drawn as a solid continuous line. The first observed price-quantity pair (p_0, Q_0) is generated by the intersection of demand curve D_0 and the supply curve S. An increase in demand (a shift in the demand curve from D_0 to D_1, caused by a change in an exogenous variable) generates a shortage at price p_0. This increases the price and quantity along the stationary supply curve. When price reaches p_1 and quantity reaches Q_1, equilibrium is restored. In this case the two observed points, (p_0, Q_0) and (p_1, Q_1), both lie on the stationary supply curve. In order to identify the supply curve, the demand curve must shift in response to some exogenous variable that does not influence the position of the supply curve.

If both the demand curve and the supply curve shift, a situation like that depicted in Figure 22.1c may occur. Observation (p_0, Q_0) is generated by the intersection of demand curve D_0 and supply curve S_0. Observation (p_1, Q_1) is produced at the intersection of demand curve D_1 and supply curve S_1. If the shifts in the two curves are caused by *different* exogenous variables, it is possible that *both* curves can be identified. However, if the two curves shift in response to the same exogenous variables (or in response to two highly-correlated exogenous variables), neither curve can be *identified*.

Each equation in our supply and demand example is said to be *exactly identified*, since each structural equation excludes exactly one variable that is contained in the other equation. If an equation excluded more than one variable appearing in the other equation, then that equation is said to be *overidentified*. Finally, if an equation excludes too few variables for identification (e.g., the supply curve in Figure 22.1a or the demand curve in Figure 22.1b), then that equation is said to be *underidentified* or *unidentified*.

TWO-STAGE LEAST SQUARES

Exactly Identified Models

To make this discussion more concrete, consider the data on annual per capita milk consumption (q), the annual average price of milk (p), the price index for food products (p_j), and an index of the wage rate for farm workers (w), reported for the United States for the years 1950 to 1981. (See Table 22.1.) Through time per capita milk consumption has tended to decline, whereas the *nominal* price of milk has tended to increase. A plot of q_t against p_t, presented in Figure 22.2, seems to suggest an inverse relation between quantity and price, although a nonlinear pattern also seems indicated.

Remember that the observations reported in Table 22.1 are market data: the average price and the quantity exchanged. Without taking into account the impact of exogenous variables (p_j and w) and the simultaneous determination of price and quantity, the scatter in Figure 22.2 might just as well reflect a supply curve as a demand curve.

Table 22.1

Year	Per Capita Milk Consumption (Quarts) (q)	Price of Milk (Cents/Half Gal) (p)	CPI Food (p_j)	Index of Farm Wage (w)
1950	319	37.0	0.745	0.22
1951	320	39.8	0.828	0.25
1952	321	41.6	0.843	0.26
1953	319	41.8	0.830	0.27
1954	321	41.2	0.828	0.27
1955	323	41.6	0.816	0.27
1956	325	42.0	0.822	0.28
1957	323	42.6	0.849	0.29
1958	318	42.6	0.885	0.30
1959	312	43.0	0.871	0.32
1960	307	43.4	0.880	0.33
1961	298	43.4	0.891	0.33
1962	296	43.8	0.899	0.34
1963	295	44.4	0.912	0.35
1964	293	47.7	0.924	0.36
1965	292	47.3	0.944	0.38
1966	287	49.8	0.991	0.41
1967	276	51.7	1.000	0.44
1968	272	53.7	1.036	0.48
1969	264	55.1	1.089	0.53
1970	264	57.4	1.149	0.57
1971	262	58.9	1.184	0.59
1972	265	59.8	1.235	0.63
1973	262	65.4	1.414	0.69
1974	254	78.4	1.617	0.79
1975	259	78.5	1.754	0.85
1976	252	82.7	1.808	0.93
1977	253	83.9	1.922	1.00
1978	251	88.7	2.114	1.07
1979	248	98.9	2.345	1.17
1980	245	104.9	2.546	1.26
1981	246	111.7	2.746	1.37

We have argued that the problem with direct estimation of either structural equation in our demand and supply model is that one of the right-side regressors, namely p, is correlated with the error term in each equation. One solution to this problem is to find another variable closely related to p but independent of the error term. The reduced form equation for p provides a method of obtaining such an *instrumental* variable. By regressing p against *all* the exogenous variables in the system, we obtain the *predicted value* of p ($\hat{p}$), which by construction, is independent of the residual in

Figure 22.2

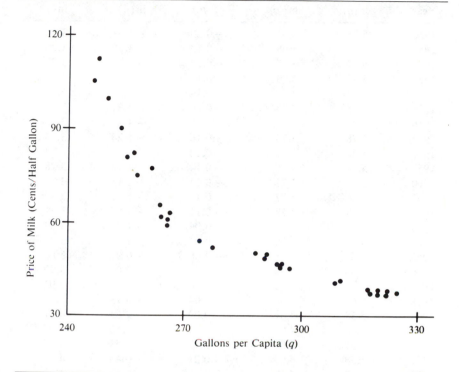

Gallons per Capita (q)

that equation. Using the computer to estimate the value of $\hat{p}$ for each observation, we substitute $\hat{p}$ for p in the estimation of the two structural equations.

Table 22.2 simulates the process of creating an instrumental variable for price. First, because a nonlinear model seems to be indicated by the pattern of data in Figure 22.2, all four variables are translated into logarithms. Next, a regression of $\ln(p)$ against $\ln(p_j)$ and $\ln(w)$, generates the equation:

$$\ln(p_i) = 4.095 + 0.542\ln(p_j) + 0.212\ln(w)$$
$$\quad\;\;(0.034)\quad(0.052)\qquad\quad(0.036)$$

$$R^2 = 0.9957;\; d = 1.559$$

where standard errors are in parentheses. This regression implies that the price of milk increases as the price of food goods in general increases (p_j reflects price changes of substitutes and complements for milk), and as the wage rate for farm labor increases (reflecting the cost of inputs for milk producers). Both regressors are statistically significant; the importance of this result will become apparent when the second stage results are discussed below. The R^2 of 0.9957 implies that the value of $\hat{p}$ is a good proxy for observed p.

Table 22.2

Year	ln(q)	ln(p)	ln(p_j)	ln(w)	ln($\hat{p}$)
1950	5.77	3.61	−0.29	−1.51	3.61
1951	5.77	3.68	−0.19	−1.39	3.70
1952	5.77	3.73	−0.17	−1.35	3.72
1953	5.77	3.73	−0.19	−1.31	3.72
1954	5.77	3.72	−0.19	−1.31	3.72
1955	5.78	3.73	−0.20	−1.31	3.71
1956	5.78	3.74	−0.20	−1.27	3.72
1957	5.78	3.75	−0.16	−1.24	3.74
1958	5.76	3.75	−0.12	−1.20	3.77
1959	5.74	3.76	−0.14	−1.14	3.78
1960	5.73	3.77	−0.13	−1.11	3.79
1961	5.70	3.77	−0.12	−1.11	3.80
1962	5.69	3.78	−0.11	−1.08	3.81
1963	5.69	3.79	−0.09	−1.05	3.82
1964	5.68	3.86	−0.08	−1.02	3.21
1965	5.68	3.86	−0.06	−0.97	3.86
1966	5.66	3.91	−0.01	−0.89	3.90
1967	5.62	3.95	0.00	−0.82	3.92
1968	5.61	3.98	0.04	−0.73	3.96
1969	5.58	4.01	0.09	−0.63	4.01
1970	5.58	4.05	0.14	−0.56	4.05
1971	5.57	4.08	0.17	−0.53	4.07
1972	5.58	4.09	0.21	−0.46	4.11
1973	5.57	4.18	0.35	−0.37	4.20
1974	5.54	4.36	0.48	−0.24	4.31
1975	5.56	4.36	0.56	−0.16	4.37
1976	5.53	4.42	0.59	−0.07	4.40
1977	5.53	4.43	0.65	0.00	4.45
1978	5.53	4.49	0.75	0.07	4.52
1979	5.51	4.59	0.85	0.16	4.59
1980	5.50	4.65	0.93	0.23	4.65
1981	5.51	4.72	1.01	0.31	4.71

Finally, the Durbin-Watson statistic implies that autocorrelation is not a problem in the first stage regression.

Using this first stage equation, we generate the variable ln($\hat{p}$), shown in the last column in Table 22.2. When the computer performs the second stage regression, the last column in Table 22.2 is used in place of the third column in that table in generating the **X** matrix. After the switch of variables is made, the computer proceeds to estimate the structural equations.

In Table 22.3 we present the second stage regression results for our example. The first equation reprises the first stage result presented above. Our estimate of the demand equation is presented as the second equation in Table 22.3. Note that the (logarithm of) quantity demanded decreases as

Table 22.3

Exactly Identified Model

First Stage (Reduced Form) Regressions:

$$\ln(\hat{p}_t) = 4.095 + 0.542 \ln(p_j) + 0.212 \ln(w)$$
$$\quad\quad\quad (0.034) \quad (0.052) \quad\quad\quad (0.036)$$

$R^2 = 0.9957; \ d = 1.559$

Second Stage Results (Uncorrected):

$$\ln(\hat{q}_{dt}) = 12.47 - 1.74 \ln(\hat{p}_t) + 1.23 \ln(p_{jt})$$
$$\quad\quad\quad (0.580) \quad (0.149) \quad\quad\quad (0.125)$$

$R^2 = 0.9662; \ d = 0.774$

$$\ln(\hat{q}_{st}) = 3.19 + 0.523 \ln(\hat{p}_t) - 0.481 \ln(w_t)$$
$$\quad\quad\quad (0.271) \quad (0.083) \quad\quad\quad (0.049)$$

$R^2 = 0.9662; \ d = 0.774$

Second Stage Results (Corrected):

$$\ln(\hat{q}_{dt}) = 12.25 - 1.69 \ln(\hat{p}_t) + 1.17 \ln(p_{jt})$$
$$\quad\quad\quad (0.888) \quad (0.228) \quad\quad\quad (0.188)$$

$R^2 = 0.9173; \ d = 2.07; \ \hat{\rho} = 0.541$
$$\quad\quad\quad\quad\quad\quad\quad\quad\quad (0.144)$$

$$\ln(\hat{q}_{st}) = 0.650 + 0.692 \ln(q_{st-1}) + 0.234 \ln(\hat{p}_t) - 0.194 \ln(w_t)$$
$$\quad\quad\quad (0.545) \quad (0.143) \quad\quad\quad\quad (0.090) \quad\quad (0.074)$$

$R^2 = 0.9851; \ d = 2.01; \ \hat{\rho} = -0.023$
$$\quad\quad\quad\quad\quad\quad\quad\quad\quad (0.189)$$

---

the (logarithm of) price increases. Indeed a price-elastic demand is predicted. In general, variable $\ln(p_{jt})$ behaves like the price of a substitute good in that as $\ln(p_{jt})$ increases, so does $\ln(q_{dt})$. The only problem with this result is the low value of d, implying positive autocorrelation. Tests of our hypotheses would be biased toward a type I error.

Before discussing the correction for autocorrelation in the demand curve, let us consider the (uncorrected) second stage equation for the supply curve. First, we note that both slope coefficients have the expected signs: the logarithm of quantity supplied is predicted to increase with the logarithm of price and to decrease with the logarithm of the farm wage. Again, a Durbin-Watson statistic ($d = 0.774$) implies significant positive autocorrelation. But note that both d and R^2 are identical in the two second stage regressions. This result is more than mere coincidence.

Remember that regressor $\ln(\hat{p})$ is an instrumental variable generated by a combination of the two exogenous variables, $\ln(p_j)$ and $\ln(w)$. In each second stage equation, the coefficient of the instrumental variable $\ln(\hat{p}_t)$ is calculated by accounting for the influence of the exogenous variable *included in that regression*. The influence of the instrumental variable is generated by the joint movement between that instrument and the *excluded* exogenous variable. Since one exogenous variable is excluded from each second stage regression, the proportion of the dependent variable "explained" by both exogenous variables (directly and indirectly) is the same in each equation. Also, the patterns of residuals are the same. Hence, when both equations are exactly identified and both structural equations have the same right-side endogenous variable, they will have the same R^2 and the same Durbin-Watson statistics.

Recall from Chapter 21 that evidence of an autocorrelated error term sometimes implies specification error. It is possible that an important variable has been omitted from the demand equation. We will discuss this possibility in the next section. For the present, to keep the model exactly identified, we use a Cochrane-Orcutt correction for autocorrelation. After correction, the slope coefficient of $\ln(p)$ is still negative and significant while the coefficient of $\ln(p_{jt})$ is still positive and significant.

To correct the supply equation, we consider the very real prospect of specification error in that equation. The ability of dairy farmers to supply milk depends on the size of their dairy herds. This in turn reflects decisions to purchase more cattle or to slaughter some cattle, depending on milk prices and farm wages prevailing in the past. To allow for a lagged adjustment model for milk supply, a Koyck lag model was fit. The coefficient of the lagged logarithm of quantity implies that the present output decision is influenced by the prices and farm wages of several previous years. Note, as we discovered in Chapter 21, the Koyck lag model eliminates autocorrelation, as the regression of the residual against the lagged residual attests.

Overidentified Equations

Table 22.4 presents the first and second stage regressions for a model of the milk market in which quantity demanded depends on the price of milk (p), the price index for other food products (p_j), and real disposable personal income (y). The supply equation remains the same as in our previous model:

$$Q_d = a_0 + a_1 p + a_2 p_j + a_3 y + u$$
$$Q_s = b_0 + b_1 p + b_2 w + e$$
$$Q_e = Q_d = Q_s$$

In this system there is one exogenous variable, w, excluded from the demand equation. That equation is still exactly identified. However, there are now two variables excluded from the supply equation, p_j and y. The supply equation is now overidentified.

Table 22.4

One Equation Exactly Identified, One Overidentified

First Stage Results:

$$\ln(\hat{p}_t) = 3.73 + 0.588 \ln(p_{jt}) + 0.152 \ln(w_t) + 0.049 \ln(y_t)$$
$$\quad\quad (0.622)\ (0.096) \quad\quad (0.111) \quad\quad\quad (0.082)$$

$R^2 = 0.9961; \ d = 1.65$

Second Stage Results (Uncorrected for Autocorrelation):

$$\ln(\hat{q}_{dt}) = 13.19 - 2.01 \ln(\hat{p}_t) + 1.41 \ln(p_{jt}) + 0.05 \ln(y_t)$$
$$\quad\quad (1.79) \quad (0.61) \quad\quad (0.44) \quad\quad\quad (0.098)$$

$R^2 = 0.9715; \ d = 0.607$

$$\ln(\hat{q}_{st}) = 3.21 + 0.518 \ln(\hat{p}_t) - 0.479 \ln(w_t)$$
$$\quad\quad (0.34) \quad (0.077) \quad\quad\quad (0.045)$$

$R^2 = 0.9703; \ d = 0.625$

Second Stage Results (Corrected for Autocorrelation):

$$\ln(\hat{q}_{dt}) = 13.45 - 2.05 \ln(\hat{p}_t) + 1.45 \ln(p_{jt}) + 0.034 \ln(y_t)$$
$$\quad\quad (1.59) \quad (0.54) \quad\quad (0.39) \quad\quad\quad (0.087)$$

$R^2 = 0.9840; \ d = 1.96; \ \hat{\rho} = 0.573$
$$\quad\quad\quad\quad\quad\quad\quad\quad\quad (0.129)$$

$$\ln(\hat{q}_{st}) = 0.898 + 0.613 \ln(q_{st-1}) + 0.277 \ln(\hat{p}_t) - 0.233 \ln(w_t)$$
$$\quad\quad (0.520) \quad (0.135) \quad\quad\quad (0.083) \quad\quad\quad (0.069)$$

$R^2 = 0.9868; \ d = 1.90$

As a practical matter, the estimation procedures for overidentified equations and exactly identified equations are the same when using two-stage least squares. However, we have included this example in Table 22.4 in order to illustrate the subtle differences between the second stage results for overidentified and exactly identified models.

Note in the estimation of the instrumental variable $\ln(\hat{p}_t)$ that $\ln(p_{jt})$ is the only significant variable; equilibrium price rises with p_{jt}, which acts like the price of a substitute. However, the coefficient of $\ln(y_t)$ is not significantly greater than zero ($t = 0.049/0.082 = 0.598$) and the coefficient of $\ln(w_t)$ is not significantly greater than zero ($t = 0.152/0.111 = 1.36$). This is probably traceable to multicollinearity between those two variables. Once the impact of inflation is taken into account (which is measured by p_{jt}), real disposable personal income and the nominal farm wage tend to move together. Nevertheless, multicollinearity between regressors that are excluded from different structural equations need not concern us in the estimation of the first stage regression. The purpose of the first stage regression is to obtain a good proxy for the endogenous variable $\ln(p_t)$, which is used to estimate the second stage regressions. As long as there are a sufficient number of exogenous variables excluded from the second stage equations, hypothesis testing should not be plagued by the multicollinearity in the first stage equation.

Notice in the second stage results in Table 22.4, $\ln(y_t)$ is not significantly greater than zero in the demand equation. The variable excluded from that structural equation, $\ln(w_t)$, is the cause of the independent change in the instrumental variable $\ln(\hat{p}_t)$. Since $\ln(w_t)$ is highly correlated with $\ln(y_t)$, there is little variance in $\ln(q_{st})$ not already attributed to $\ln(\hat{p}_t)$. Nevertheless, the coefficient of the instrumental variable $\ln(\hat{p}_t)$ is negative and significant at the 1 percent level, even after correction for autocorrelation. Because both $\ln(y_t)$ and $\ln(p_{jt})$ are excluded from the supply equation, there is no apparent multicollinearity between $\ln(\hat{p}_t)$ and $\ln(w_t)$ in the estimation of the second stage supply equation. The coefficient of the instrumental variable $\ln(\hat{p}_t)$ is positive and significant at the 1 percent level; the coefficient of the exogenous variable $\ln(w_t)$ is negative and significant at the 1 percent level.

As in Table 22.3, the second stage regression results are infected with autocorrelated residuals. Apparently the exclusion of income from the model in Table 22.3 was not the (sole) cause of the autocorrelated residuals. Correction for autocorrelation by means of the Cochrane-Orcutt approach does not materially affect the significance of the regressors in the demand equation. The use of a Koyck model again appears to alleviate the autocorrelation in the supply equation. Notice, however, that the R^2's and the Durbin-Watson statistics for the uncorrected second stage regressions are not identical in Table 22.4 the way they were in Table 22.3. Because two exogenous variables are excluded from the supply equation, while only one exogenous variable is excluded from the demand equation, we obtain a slightly higher R^2 in the second stage regression for the demand equation. The difference in the number of variables excluded from the structural equations also yields a different pattern for the residuals for the (uncorrected) second stage regression, producing different Durbin-Watson statistics.

THE IDENTIFICATION
PROBLEM REVISITED

The process of two-stage least squares presents another perspective on the identification problem. The instrumental variables used in the second stage of the estimation process are, by construction, linear combinations of all the exogenous variables in the model. Of course, if there were no exogenous variables in the model, there could be no instrumental variable estimates, and the second stage regression could not be performed. If one of the equations contained all the exogenous variables in the model, the instrumental variable in that equation would be perfectly correlated with those exogenous variables, and the regression could not be performed. However, if there were at least one (exogenous) variable that "determines" the value of the instrument, but which does not appear in the structural equation being estimated, then the coefficient of that instrument can be estimated. For all practical purposes, whether an equation in a two-equation model is exactly identified (has one excluded exogenous variable) or overidentified (has more than one excluded exogenous variable) is unimportant for two-stage least squares estimation.

Because of the relative simplicity of two-stage least squares regression techniques, a word of caution is in order. Ultimately the identifiability of a system of simultaneous equations is a feature of the mathematical structure of that model. If neither the supply equation nor the demand equation contains a variable not contained in the other, then neither equation can be estimated. Knowing this fact before the estimation stage of research can save the person much trouble. A case in point is the market for financial securities, such as stocks traded on the New York or American stock exchanges. We might think that with all the data available on financial markets, we should be able to estimate the demand and supply equations for any share of stock, including as exogenous variables observations on past stock prices, interest rates, various indexes of stock performance, etc. Yet there is a saying in economics and finance that the (financial) market takes a random walk, meaning that information on past market prices does not predict future market prices. One reason for this phenomenon is that the demand and supply equations are unidentified. Every variable that could conceivably affect the willingness of traders to buy a particular stock would also affect their willingness to sell. In other words, every time the demand curve for a stock shifts, so does its supply curve. Every observation of price and quantity exchanged involves a different demand curve and a different supply curve.

But surely it would not be hard to get a good-looking set of regression results! Suppose we arbitrarily exclude interest rates from the demand equation and stock indexes from the supply equation. Then each structural equation excludes a variable present in the other equation. Assuming that the excluded variables are not perfectly correlated, a two-stage regression procedure could be carried out. It might even show large R^2's and small standard errors. However, *two-stage regressions* performed on misspecified structural equations are fraught with *excluded variable bias*. It is better not to estimate a correctly specified but unidentified equation than to estimate an identified but knowingly misspecified equation. In the former case, the researcher is aware that accurate information is not available; if ignorance be not bliss, it can sometimes be reassuring to know that it is unavoidable. In the case of a misspecified model, the researcher knowingly perpetrates inaccurate information. Such a strategy is dishonest, and, potentially, disastrous.

If we suspect that a regressor in an ordinary least squares equation may be endogenous, prudence dictates using a procedure like two-stage least squares to avoid simultaneous equations bias. This means that we must be able to visualize the interaction between the left-side variable and this regressor, determining how the former influences the latter. The chain of causation maybe complex and may involve some third variable. (For example, variable y, the dependent variable, influences variable z, which is not in the equation. However, variable z is thought to cause variable x, a regressor in the equation being estimated.) As long as it is plausible that the regressor is correlated with the error term, remedial measures should be taken. That means the researcher must be able to stipulate at least one *exogenous* variable, not in the relevant equation, which also influences the endogenous regressor. If no such variable can be imagined, or if observations on that variable cannot be obtained, then the equation at hand is unidentified, and attempts at estimation must be abandoned. If exogenous variables not in the equation can be observed, two-stage least squares techniques serve as a validity check on the hypotheses tested with the OLS equation.

A final observation: The difficulties encountered with simultaneous equations models make it imperative that researchers follow the convention of making the hypothesis they wish to disprove the null hypothesis. If we wished to disprove the law of demand, it would be relatively easy to construct a plausible demand and supply model wherein the exogenous variables were very poor predictors of the product's price, the right-side endogenous variable in the structural equations. Using the first stage regressions to produce an instrumental variable for price which is poorly correlated with the observed price, we obtain second stage regression results with large standard errors for the price coefficients in the demand and supply equations. We then proclaim that we cannot reject the null hypothesis of no relation between quantity demanded and price. When we make our hypothesis the alternative hypothesis, we may sometimes be done in by our inability to identify the equations or by our inability to find good exogenous predictors of endogenous variables. But at least we would come on those problems honestly.

MORE ECONOMIC APPLICATIONS
OF TWO-EQUATION MODELS

In this section we will take a second look at some examples from earlier chapters now cast in terms of two-equation models.

Executive Compensation,
Sales, and Profit

In Chapter 20 we investigated the relationship between the compensation of chief executive officers of major corporations and the sales and profits of those firms. We found that the attempt to determine whether sales (revenue) or profit has the greater influence on executive pay is plagued by multicollinearity (profit equals sales minus cost) and heteroscedasticity. In this section we address the possibility that profit and executive compensation are mutually determined by the firm's sales and the market for executive talent. Given that running a major corporation requires abilities and experience possessed by a relatively few people, what a firm pays its executive may determine the caliber of executive talent it can attract. Firms that pay low salaries attract mediocre executives who inspire lackluster profits. Firms that pay high salaries attract very productive executives, who increase profit. Not only might a firm's profits determine the pay of its executive(s), but the pay of the executives may partly determine its profits. Hence, an ordinary least squares regression of executive compensation against profit could generate simultaneous equations bias.

We therefore hypothesize the following two-equation model:

$$E_{it} = a_0 + a_1 E_{it-1} + a_2 \pi_{it} + u_{it}$$
$$\pi_{it} = b_0 + b_1 S_{it} + b_2 E_{it} + e_{it}$$

The first structural equation states that the compensation of the chief executive officer of firm i in year t (E_{it}) depends on the compensation the firm paid in the previous year (E_{it-1}, meant to capture the payments for executive talents), and profit this year (π_{it}). We predict that both a_1 and a_2 will be positive. The second structural equation predicts that current profit reflects current sales (S_{it}) and current executive compensation (E_{it}). Consistent with the definition of profit as total revenue minus total cost, we predict a positive value for b_1. If executive talent were only useful at increasing the firm's sales (an extreme interpretation of the managerial hypothesis), then multicollinearity would probably render b_2 insignificantly different from zero. However, if executive pay increases the quality of executive talent, particularly for controlling costs, then coefficient b_2 would be positive. Alternatively, Armen Alchian[1] has suggested the possibility that executives for publicly held corporations might be overpaid to the detriment of profit, implying $b_2 < 0$. This gives us two interesting hypotheses to investigate.

Table 22.5a presents the first stage regression results using data for 202 firms for the years 1974-1976. The R^2's range from 0.52 to 0.62 for the executive compensation equations and exceed 0.70 in the profit equations, implying that the instrumental variables used in stage two of the regression will serve as good proxies for their respective endogenous variables.

Table 22.5b presents the second stage regressions. Note that the R^2's are identical to those reported in Table 22.5a for each equation. This reflects the fact that both structural equations are exactly identified. All the

[1] Armen A. Alchian, "The Basis of Some Recent Advancements in the Theory of Management of the Firm," *Journal of Industrial Economics*, (November 1965), pp. 30-41.

Table 22.5a

Executive Compensation, Sales, and Profit: 202 Firms
First Stage Regressions (Standard errors in parentheses)

$$\hat{E}_t = \hat{\alpha}_{0t} + \hat{\alpha}_{1t} E_{it-1} + \hat{\alpha}_{2t} S_{it}$$

Year	$\hat{\alpha}_0$	$\hat{\alpha}_1$	$\hat{\alpha}_2$	R^2
1974	113,966**	0.597*	0.0024**	0.5164
	(15,303)	(0.052)	(0.0012)	
1975	60,262*	0.836*	0.0024**	0.6055
	(18,082)	(0.056)	(0.0012)	
1976	115,163*	0.752*	0.0070*	0.6241
	(19,353)	(0.057)	(0.0011)	

$$\hat{\pi}_{it} = \hat{\beta}_{0t} + \hat{\beta}_{1t} E_{it-1} + \hat{\beta}_{2t} S_{it}$$

Year	$\hat{\beta}_0$	$\hat{\beta}_1$	$\hat{\beta}_2$	R^2
1974	25,714	−0.124	0.058*	0.7320
	(34,640)	(0.118)	(0.0028)	
1975	−140,792*	0.472*	0.040*	0.7099
	(35,548)	(0.111)	(0.002)	
1976	−76,261**	0.227*	0.051*	0.8213
	(32,622)	(0.097)	(0.002)	

*Significant at the 1 percent level
**Significant at the 5 percent level

information revealed in the first stage regression is repeated in the second stage regression for each endogenous variable.

The second stage regressions for the executive compensation regression consistently support our alternative hypotheses that managerial pay increases with last year's pay and this year's profit. In the structural equation for profit, all three years' results support the hypothesis that profit increases with sales. The results for coefficient b_2 are less decisive. In 1974, profit appears to decline as executive pay increases. This contradicts the "buying executive talent" hypothesis and seems to favor the "executives as embezzlers" hypothesis. However, since the coefficient is insignificant, the support for that hypothesis is minimal. During 1975 and 1976, the coefficient of E_{it} is positive and significant (at the 1 percent and 5 percent levels, respectively). This result supports the hypothesis that firms paying higher salaries attract more productive executives.

We discovered in Chapter 19 that the executive compensation equations are likely to be infected with heteroscedasticity. The last two columns in Table 22.5b report the results of a Park test. In this test, the logarithm of the squared residual is regressed against the logarithm of assets, A_{it},

Table 22.5b

Executive Compensation, Sales, and Profit: 202 Firms
Second Stage Regressions (Standard errors in parentheses)

$$E_{it} = a_{0t} + a_{1t}E_{it-1} + a_{2t}\hat{\pi}_{it} + u_{it}$$
Park Test: $\ln\hat{u}_t^2 = \hat{c} + \hat{d}\ln A_t$

Year	$\hat{a}_0$	$\hat{a}_1$	$\hat{a}_2$	R^2	$\hat{c}$	$\hat{d}$
1974	135,887*	0.602*	0.042**	0.5164	11.23	0.666*
	(15,163)	(0.051)	(0.021)		(2.63)	(0.184)
1975	68,706*	0.808*	0.060**	0.5548	12.88	0.541*
	(19,406)	(0.064)	(0.029)		(2.61)	(0.181)
1976	125,568*	0.721*	0.136*	0.5541	15.67	0.350
	(19,747)	(0.060)	(0.022)		(3.11)	(0.215)

$$\pi_{it} = b_{0t} + b_{1t}S_{it} + b_{2t}\hat{E}_{it} + e_{it}$$
Park Test: $\ln\hat{e}_t^2 = \hat{c} + \hat{d}\ln A_t$

Year	$\hat{b}_0$	$\hat{b}_1$	$\hat{b}_2$	R^2	$\hat{c}$	$\hat{d}$
1974	54,063	0.058*	-0.214	0.7320	-3.25	1.68*
	(60,446)	(0.003)	(0.198)		(3.04)	(0.213)
1975	$-174,838*$	0.039*	0.565*	0.7099	5.19	1.09*
	(43,149)	(0.002)	(0.133)		(3.03)	(0.210)
1976	$-111,103**$	0.049*	0.303**	0.8213	-3.46	1.68*
	(46,638)	(0.002)	(0.129)		(2.67)	(0.185)

*Significant at the 1 percent level
**Significant at the 5 percent level

which is suspected of paralleling the variance in the error term. The null hypothesis of a homoscedastic error term must be rejected in favor of the alternative hypothesis of positive heteroscedasticity in 1974 and 1975 for the executive compensation equation and in all years for the profit equation. Because the Park test is biased in favor of the finding of homoscedasticity, we correct all the second stage results for heteroscedasticity.

As shown in Chapter 18, a procedure for correcting heteroscedasticity is *weighted least squares*. The weight used in each equation is $w = A_{it}^{-c/2}$, where c is the coefficient of $\ln A_{it}$ estimated in the Park test regression. The weighted least squares regression equation for executive compensation is:

$$wE_{it} = a_{0t}w + a_{1t}wE_{it-1} + a_{2t}w\hat{\pi}_{it} + wu_{it}$$

For profit, the weighted least squares equation is:

$$w\pi_{it} = b_{0t}w + b_{1t}wS_{it} + b_{2t}w\hat{E}_{it} + we_{it}$$

To estimate the weighted least squares regressions, we simply multiply each variable, including the instrumental variable for the endogenous regressor and the vector of ones for the intercept term, by the weighting factor, w. Ordinary least squares procedures (with the intercept suppressed) are then used to estimate the weighted least squares equation. Ideally, the resulting equations have homoscedastic error terms.

Table 22.5c presents the weighted least squares regressions for the two structural equations. The R^2's for the regressions have not been reported because the intercept had to be suppressed. (The coefficient of w is the estimated value of the intercept parameter.) Correction for heteroscedasticity seems to undermine the significance of the instrumental variable for profit in the executive compensation equation. In 1975, the significance of that coefficient is 10 percent. On the other hand, the weighted least squares results strengthen the significance of the coefficient b_2. In 1974 (as in the other years), we may reject the null hypothesis that profit does not increase with the compensation of the executive officer with 99 percent confidence.

Table 22.5c

Executive Compensation, Sales, and Profit: 202 Firms
Second Stage Regressions (Corrected for Heteroscedasticity)
(Standard errors in parentheses)

$$wE_{it} = a_{0t}w + a_{1t}wE_{it-1} + a_{2t}w\hat{\pi}_{it} + wu_{it}$$

Year	w	$\hat{a}_0$	$\hat{a}_1$	$\hat{a}_2$
1974	$A_4^{-0.333}$	117,746* (14,009)	0.641* (0.050)	0.062** (0.037)
1975	$A_5^{-0.271}$	52,508* (19,209)	0.851* (0.069)	0.070*** (0.047)
1976	$A_6^{-0.175}$	110,512* (18,646)	0.765* (0.059)	0.137* (0.030)

$$w\pi_{it} = b_{0t}w + b_{1t}wS_{it} + b_{2t}w\hat{E}_{it} + we_{it}$$

Year	w	$\hat{b}_0$	$\hat{b}_1$	$\hat{b}_2$
1974	$A_4^{-0.843}$	−68,983* (34,640)	0.043* (0.118)	0.234* (0.062)
1975	$A_5^{-0.5}$	−84,318* (35,548)	0.036* (0.002)	0.290* (0.071)
1976	$A_6^{-0.84}$	−65,771* (13,373)	0.041* (0.003)	0.193* (0.040)

*Significant at the 1 percent level
**Significant at the 5 percent level
***Significant at the 10 percent level

The Phillips Curve: The Transmission
of Wage Changes into Inflation
and Inflation into Wage Changes

In Chapter 18 we introduced the Phillips model of price inflation and unemployment through a simple regression of the rate of change in the implicit price deflator against the unemployment rate. This relationship was found to be statistically reliable through a number of alternative specifications for the 1948-1968 period but statistically insignificant for the 1969-1984 period. In Chapter 19 we introduced multiple regression analysis by showing an inverse relationship between changes in real wage rates and the unemployment rate, once changes in productivity were taken into account. Apparently something goes astray in the translation of the effect of unemployment on real wage rates into an effect of unemployment on price changes.

Since workers and employers bargain over nominal wage rates, we are interested in how the rate of change in prices influences the change in nominal wage rates and vice versa. We hypothesize that nominal wage changes ($DWAGE$) are generated by factors that produce real wage changes—namely productivity changes ($DPROD$) and the unemployment rate (UE)—in addition to the rate of price inflation (INF). We also assume that the rate of inflation responds positively to increases in the nominal money stock (DMI), increases in fuel prices ($DPFUEL$), and nominal wage increases *in excess of productivity increases* ($EXWAGE = DWAGE - DPROD$). Our two-equation model is:

(1) $INF_t = a_0 + a_1 DMI_t + a_2 DPFUEL_t + a_3 EXWAGE_t + u_t$

(2) $DWAGE_t = b_0 + b_1 DPROD_t + b_2 UE_t + b_3 INF_t + e_t$

Annual data were used for the period 1948 to 1984 and were obtained from the *Economic Report of the President* as well as the *Monthly Labor Review*.

Because the last regressor in each equation is (or depends on) the dependent variable in the other equation, we have a simultaneous equations model that cannot be estimated accurately by ordinary least squares. Both INF_t and $DWAGE_t$ are correlated with the error terms in those equations where they appear as regressors. Specified in the Keynesian form the model has four exogenous variables (DMI_t, $DPFUEL_t$, $DPROD_t$, and UE_t). The nominal wage equation omits two variables included in the inflation equation, namely DMI_t and $DPFUEL_t$. The inflation equation omits two variables included in the nominal wage equation, namely UE_t and $DPROD_t$. Both factors are assumed to affect the inflation rate *indirectly* through their impact on the variable $EXWAGE$.

From the first stage regressions presented in Table 22.6, we can see that the instrumental variable for INF_t is a reasonably good proxy for its endogenous variable. The R^2 of 0.7266 implies that nearly 73 percent of

Table 22.6

First Stage Regressions:

$$\widehat{INF_t} = 1.79 + 0.174UE_t - 0.285DPROD_t + 0.289DMI_t + 0.134DPFUEL_t$$
$$\quad\;\; (0.951)\,(0.158) \qquad (0.175) \qquad\qquad (0.093) \qquad\quad (0.025)$$

$R^2 = 0.7266;\; d = 2.05$

$$\widehat{EXWAGE_t} = 5.62 - 0.167UE_t - 1.042DPROD_t + 0.270DMI_t$$
$$\qquad\qquad\; (1.03)\;\;(0.171) \qquad (0.189) \qquad\qquad (0.101)$$
$$+\, 0.119DPFUEL_t$$
$$(0.027)$$

$R^2 = 0.7970;\; d = 1.91$

Second Stage Regressions:

$$\widehat{INF_t} = 1.32 + 0.237\widehat{EXWAGE_t} + 0.274DMI_t + 0.111DPFUEL_t$$
$$\quad\;\; (0.491)\,(0.138) \qquad\qquad (0.077) \qquad\quad (0.033)$$

$R^2 = 0.8467;\; d = 1.93$

$$\widehat{DWAGE_t} = 3.99 + 0.902\widehat{INF_t} + 0.222DPROD_t - 0.319UE_t$$
$$\qquad\quad\; (1.12)\;\;(0.165) \qquad (0.204) \qquad\qquad (0.170)$$

$R^2 = 0.5576;\; d = 1.90$

Second Stage Regressions, Koyck Lag Model:

$$\widehat{INF_t} = -0.975 + 0.587\widehat{INF_{t-1}} + 0.452\widehat{EXWAGE_t} + 0.061DMI_t$$
$$\qquad\;\; (0.443) \quad\;\, (0.082) \qquad\quad (0.104) \qquad\qquad (0.061)$$
$$+\, 0.006DPFUEL_t$$
$$(0.026)$$

$R^2 = 0.9044;\; d = 2.11$

$$\widehat{DWAGE_t} = 1.85 + 0.553\widehat{DWAGE_{t-1}} + 0.633\widehat{INF_t} + 0.152DPROD_t$$
$$\qquad\quad\; (1.18)\;\;(0.181) \qquad\qquad (0.164) \qquad (0.153)$$
$$-\, 0.358UE_t$$
$$(0.154)$$

$R^2 = 0.6797;\; d = 1.85$

the observed variation in INF_t is captured by the four exogenous variables. Similarly, nearly 80 percent of the $EXWAGE_t$ is captured by the four exogenous variables.

According to the second stage regressions, the rate of change in the nominal wage rate increases with the rate of inflation and the rate of increase in productivity, while decreasing with the unemployment rate. The coefficient of the instrumental variable for inflation is 0.902, which is significantly greater than zero ($t = 5.47$) but is not significantly less than one ($t = (0.902 - 1)/0.165 = -0.594$). The coefficient of the unemployment rate is significant at the 5 percent level ($t = -1.86$), while the coefficient of $DPROD_t$, although having the expected positive sign, is not significant ($t = 1.09$). Accordingly, we support the hypothesis that the nominal wage rate increases with the rate of inflation (unemployment and productivity growth held constant), and that the nominal wage increase is dampened by increases in the unemployment rate (inflation and productivity growth constant).

In the other second stage regression we find that inflation increases with respect to all three regressors. The coefficients of DMI_t ($t = 3.56$) and $DPFUEL_t$ ($t = 3.36$) are significant at the 1 percent level, while the coefficient of the instrumental variable $EXWAGE_t$ is significant at the 5 percent level ($t = 1.71$).

The specification of nearly any econometric model can be criticized, and the model presented in Table 22.6 can be criticized on two different grounds. First, those who perceive changes in the unemployment rate as largely voluntary could argue that variations in the unemployment rate would reflect changes in the real wage rate, which equal the difference between nominal wage changes and inflation, our two endogenous variables. If UE_t is endogenous, then both the first and second stage regressions are biased and inconsistent since UE_t, and therefore the instrumental variables for $DWAGE_t$ and INF_t, would be correlated with the error terms of the equations in which it appears as a regressor. Since the prospect of three endogenous variables leads us beyond the confines of two-equation models, we will address this criticism in detail in the next chapter.

The second criticism of our two-equation model involves the unstated assumption that there are no lagged influences of either endogenous or exogenous variables on either the rate of inflation or the change in nominal wages. Yet we know from both theory and experience that inflationary expectations play a major role in the inflation process. Hence, money growth, oil price shocks, or "excessive" wage increases could have protracted influence on the inflation rate. Similarly, the inflation rate, productivity growth, and/or the unemployment rate could have lagged influence on the rate of change in nominal wage rates.

We saw in Chapter 21 that the Koyck lag model is one of the simplest methods for building a lag structure into an equation. We merely specify the lagged dependent variable as an additional regressor, interpreting the estimated coefficient of this regressor as the influence of all other regressors lagged one period. If this coefficient is significantly greater than zero, we reject the null hypothesis of a static model in favor of a dynamic one. If this coefficient is significantly less than one, we accept the alternative hypothesis that the influence of lagged regressors approaches zero as the length of the lag increases.

We also learned in Chapter 21 that the chief problem with the Koyck lag model lies in the possibility of an autocorrelated error term. Indeed, if the static model is generally free of autocorrelation (as our results seem to be), then the Koyck model is likely to suffer from negative autocorrelation.

If the error term is (positively or negatively) autocorrelated, then the error term in the equation is likely to be correlated with the lagged dependent variable. This problem is compounded by the fact that the Durbin-Watson statistic, the usual test for autocorrelation, is biased in favor of the finding of no autocorrelation in the presence of a lagged endogenous variable.

While there are several ways around this problem, the opportunity presents itself to illustrate another use of instrumental variables. Since both equations are overidentified, it is possible to add another endogenous variable to each equation without adding additional exogenous variables. We know that, by construction, each instrumental variable used in place of endogenous regressors is independent of the error term in the regression. It follows that using lagged *instrumental variables* in place of the lagged observations on *INF* and *DWAGE* would avoid the potential bias attributable to autocorrelation in the presence of lagged endogenous variables.

In the last two regressions in Table 22.6 we see the results for the Koyck lag model. The inflation equation seems to be better specified in dynamic terms rather than static ones. The coefficient of the lagged instrumental variable INF_{t-1} is significantly greater than zero ($t = 7.12$) and significantly less than one ($t = -5.04$). We predict that the inflationary impacts of changes in the nominal wage rate, the money stock, and fuel prices persist for several years. However, the lagged specification causes the coefficient of $DPFUEL_t$ to become insignificant ($t = 0.231$), a clear contradiction of structural theories of inflation. However, the coefficient of $EXWAGE_t$ continues to be positive and significant at the 1 percent level ($t = 4.35$) and the coefficient of DMI_t is significant at the 5 percent level ($t = 2.20$). Alas, mixed results once again may perpetuate controversy. Supporters of the "wage-price spiral" explanation of inflation are likely to embrace the lagged model, whereas supporters of fuel price theories of inflation will support the nonlagged regressions.

The Koyck lagged model of the wage change equation is less controversial. The coefficient of the lagged instrument, $DWAGE_{t-1}$ is positive and significantly greater than zero ($t = 3.06$). We reject the null hypothesis that changes in nominal wage rates are determined entirely by changes in productivity, the inflation rate, and the unemployment rate in the same year. Otherwise, there are no material differences in the lagged and nonlagged equations for $DWAGE_t$.

Money Growth, Output Growth, and
Inflation: A Cross-Sectional Analysis

Chapter 17 introduced the simple regression by relating the rate of change in the consumer price index for 45 countries to the rate of change in the money stock (M1) for each country. In this section we consider the possibility that increases in real output may mitigate the inflationary effect of monetary growth. We begin with the simple equation of exchange: $MV = PQ$, where M is the country's money stock, V is the velocity of money (defined as PQ/M), P is the relevant price index used to measure inflation, and Q is an index of real output. If we translate the expression into natural logarithms and take the derivative of $\ln P$ with respect to time (t), we obtain the following relation between the rates of change of the variables in the equation:

$$\ln P = \ln M + \ln V - \ln Q$$

$$\frac{d \ln P}{dt} = \frac{d \ln M}{dt} + \frac{d \ln V}{dt} - \frac{d \ln Q}{dt}$$

$$\frac{dP/dt}{P} = \frac{dM/dt}{M} + \frac{dV/dt}{V} - \frac{dQ/dt}{Q}$$

Using one year intervals to measure the change in time, we have $dt = 1$ and the equation simplifies to:

$$\frac{dP}{P} = \frac{dM}{M} + \frac{dV}{V} - \frac{dQ}{Q}$$

The percent change in the price level is predicted to increase with the money stock and velocity while decreasing with real output. For each country in our sample, we measure the percent change in *real* output as the percent change in its gross domestic product measured in dollars, minus the U.S. inflation rate for that year. Unfortunately, we do not have independent observations on the velocity of circulation (V) for individual countries, so we assume (perhaps heroically), that changes in velocity are adequately represented by the error term.

Because inflation can distort the behavior of economic agents and lead governments to adopt contractionary policies, the rate of inflation may also have an influence on the rate of change in real output. Hence, we treat inflation and real output growth as the *endogenous* variables, while the change in the money supply is treated as *exogenous*. Stated in these terms, the model is underidentified. If both real output growth and inflation depended on money stock changes, neither equation could be identified, since the instrumental variables for dP/P and dQ/Q would be perfectly correlated with dM/M, which would also be a regressor in each equation. However, since modern proponents of rational expectations seem to argue that predictable changes in the money stock will have no real influence on the economy, we will drop dM/M as an influence on real output, replacing it with the lagged value of real output. Our model becomes:

$$(dP/P)_t = f[(dM/M)_t, (dQ/Q)_t]$$
$$(dQ/Q)_t = g[(dQ/Q)_{t-1}, (dP/P)_t]$$

The estimation of our two-equation model is presented in Table 22.7a. The endogenous variables are the rate of inflation for 1978 (*DP78*) and the rate of real output growth for 1978 (*DQ78*). The exogenous variables are the percent change in the money stock for 1978 (*DM78*) and the percent change in real output for 1977 (*DQ77*). Note that the instrument for *DP78* is much better than the instrument for *DQ78*; a persistent problem for the quantity theory of money continues to be the explanation of real output changes. These results carry over into the second stage regressions. While the coefficient of *DQ78* is negative in the inflation equation, it is not statistically significant. By contrast, the coefficient of *DM78* is statistically greater than zero, although not statistically different from one. A Park test for heteroscedasticity also leads to an insignificant result. We can accept our significance tests as not being biased in favor of the *DM78* variable.

The second stage equation for real output growth reflects the expectation that current output growth responds to past output growth trends and that increasing inflation reduces real output. Although significant heteroscedasticity is detected by the Park test, the regression results remain significant after correction.

Since both Keynesian theory and monetarist theory predict that money changes can have *real* output effects, at least in the short run, the specification of the quantity theory presented in Table 22.7a is vulnerable to a charge of misspecification. Alas, if the rate of change in the money stock is included

Table 22.7a

First Stage Regressions, Model I:

$$\widehat{DP78} = -5.87 + 1.09DM78 - 0.515DQ77; \ R^2 = 0.8421$$
$$\quad\quad\quad (3.14) \quad (0.073) \quad\quad (0.518)$$

$$\widehat{DQ78} = 2.60 - 0.045DM78 + 0.657DQ77; \ R^2 = 0.2797$$
$$\quad\quad\quad (1.07) \quad (0.025) \quad\quad (0.176)$$

Second Stage Regressions, Model I:

$$\widehat{DP78} = -3.83 + 1.06DM78 - 0.784\widehat{DQ78}; \ R^2 = 0.8571$$
$$\quad\quad\quad (4.46) \quad (0.075) \quad\quad (0.750)$$

$$\ln(\hat{u}^2) = 1.08 + 0.335\ln(DM78^2); \ r^2 = 0.0507$$
$$\quad\quad\quad (1.33) \quad (0.221)$$

$$\widehat{DQ78} = 2.35 + 0.636DQ77 - 0.041\widehat{DP78}; \ R^2 = 0.3236$$
$$\quad\quad\quad (0.975) \ (0.170) \quad\quad (0.022)$$

$$\ln(\hat{u}^2) = -3.68 + 0.774\ln(DM78^2); \ r^2 = 0.3236$$
$$\quad\quad\quad (1.49) \quad\quad (0.248)$$

$$w\widehat{DQ78} = -0.365w + 0.719wDQ77 + 0.180w\widehat{DM78}$$
$$\quad\quad\quad (0.892) \quad\quad (0.124) \quad\quad\quad (0.099)$$

$$R^2 = 0.5378; \ w = 1/(DM78^2)^{0.774}$$

---

in the DQ equation, that equation becomes unidentified. However, if we also stipulate that lagged inflation has an impact on current inflation through an inflationary expectations effect, both equations become exactly identified again. In this case, $DM78$ is included in both structural equations, and accordingly plays no role in the identification of either equation. $DQ77$, which is excluded from the structural equation for $DP78$ identifies that equation, while $DP77$, which is excluded from the structural equation for $DQ78$, identifies that equation. The results for this second model are presented in Table 22.7b.

We notice that the first stage equation for $DP78$ has only a slightly higher R^2 than the equivalent equation in Table 22.7a. Thus, while lagged inflation has a significant influence on current inflation, it apparently takes the explanatory power away from $DM78$. However, including the lagged rate of inflation as an exogenous variable improves the R^2 in the first stage equation for $DQ78$ by nearly 17 percent. In the second stage regression for $DP78$ we find that the coefficient of $DM78$ is not statistically different

Table 22.7b

Money Growth, Real Output Growth, and Inflation
(45 Countries, 1977-1978)

First Stage Regressions, Model II:

$$\widehat{DP78} = -1.25 + 0.342DM78 + 0.582DP77 - 0.347DQ77; \ R^2 = 0.8794$$
$$\quad\quad (3.07) \quad (0.220) \quad\quad\ (0.163) \quad\quad\quad (0.460)$$

$$\widehat{DQ78} = 1.69 + 0.102DM78 - 0.115DP77 + 0.624DQ77; \ R^2 = 0.3367$$
$$\quad\quad (1.15) \quad (0.082) \quad\quad\ (0.061) \quad\quad\quad (0.624)$$

Second Stage Regressions, Model II:

$$\widehat{DP78} = -0.308 + 0.519DP77 + 0.399DM78 - 0.556\widehat{DQ78}; \ R^2 = 0.8847$$
$$\quad\quad (3.77) \quad\quad (0.187) \quad\quad\ (0.235) \quad\quad\quad (0.722)$$

$$\ln(\hat{u}^2) = -4.28 + 1.11 \ln(DM78)^2; \ r^2 = 0.2597$$
$$\quad\quad (1.71) \quad (0.285)$$

$$\widehat{wDP78} = -2.48w + 1.09wDP77 + 0.090wDM78 - 0.247w\widehat{DQ78}$$
$$\quad\quad\ (0.738) \quad\ (0.066) \quad\quad\ (0.125) \quad\quad\quad (0.217)$$

$$R^2 = 0.9295; \ w = 1/(DM78^2)$$

$$\widehat{DQ78} = 1.44 + 0.556DQ77 + 0.170DM78 - 0.197\widehat{DP78}; \ R^2 = 0.2988$$
$$\quad\quad (1.24) \quad (0.184) \quad\quad\ (0.120) \quad\quad\quad (0.108)$$

$$\ln(\hat{u}^2) = -1.76 + 0.494 \ln(DM78^2); \ r^2 = 0.0832$$
$$\quad\quad (1.51) \quad (0.250)$$

$$\widehat{wDQ78} = 0.800w + 0.576wDQ77 + 0.107wDM78 - 0.060w\widehat{DP78}$$
$$\quad\quad\ (0.720) \quad\ (0.068) \quad\quad\ (0.124) \quad\quad\quad (0.065)$$

$$R^2 = 0.4900; \ w = 1/\sqrt{DM78^2}$$

---

from zero (although that coefficient has the expected sign). The coefficient of *DM78* is barely significant ($t = 1.698$). This result is overturned once we correct for heteroscedasticity. In both the two-stage least squares results and the two-stage generalized least squares results, inflation in 1977 has a significant positive impact on inflation in 1978.

The second stage equation for the change in real output in 1978 implies a strong effect of the previous year's output ($t = 3.02$ for the coefficient of *DQ77* before correction and $t = 8.47$ for that coefficient after correction). The unweighted second stage equation implies that *DM78* has a positive effect on *DQ78* ($t = 1.42$, which is significant at the 10 percent level). However, this coefficient becomes insignificant in the weighted least squares second stage equation ($t = 0.863$). Furthermore, the instrumental variable for inflation in 1978 ceases to have a significant effect on real output once the results are corrected for heteroscedasticity.

CONCLUSION

This chapter has investigated the estimation procedures for simultaneous equations models with two endogenous variables. We learned that ordinary least squares regressions are unreliable when an endogenous variable is included on the right side of the equation, since this variable is predicted to be correlated with the error term. The procedures involved in estimating simultaneous equations rely on the use of ordinary least squares to estimate the *reduced form* equations. The researcher first regresses each endogenous variable against *all* the exogenous variables that appear in either equation. These first stage or reduced form regressions are then used to generate instrumental variables which are used in place of right-side endogenous variables in the estimation of the structural equations. Many regression programs (computer software) have built in two-stage least squares procedures. Because these programs use matrix procedures to simulate the first stage regressions, they sometimes produce strange results (e.g., negative R^2's). In such instances, you may find better results by performing the steps by hand. An added advantage of carrying out the first stage regressions yourself is that the descriptive statistics will give an indication of how good your instrumental variables are as proxies for the endogenous variables.

The *identification problem* arises when it is impossible to specify any variable excluded from the equation in question which can legitimately be included in the other equation. When an equation is unidentified, the instrumental variable for the endogenous variable on the right side of that equation is perfectly correlated with the other regressors (i.e., all the exogenous variables in the model). Underidentification does not lead to bad estimates; it leads to no estimates! Computer programs designed to carry out two-stage least squares regressions ordinarily report that the equation is not identified. However, by determining the identifiability of an equation (or model) prior to estimation (or data collection), the researcher can save time and effort.

It is important to reemphasize that identifiability is a feature of the model being estimated and is not subject to some easy fix. We might be tempted to arbitrarily omit one or more exogenous variables from an equation in order that it be identified. However, this step would trade the bias of specification error for the problem of nonidentification. If a model cannot be identified, we simply note that fact and go on about our business; perhaps someday a different theory will be developed that will allow for identification. If we purposefully distort a model by leaving important variables out of the structural equations, we may obtain a set of decent looking results. However, in the presence of specification error, parameter estimates, standard error estimates, and goodness of fit estimates are all biased and inconsistent. Results that appear good would only be found wanting when the model fails to predict or when policies implemented on the basis of the biased findings lead to cataclysmic outcomes.

We also found that all the problems that occur with ordinary least squares regressions can also occur with two-stage least squares regressions. However, when the problems compromise only the efficiency of the least squares estimates—e.g., when autocorrelated errors, heteroscedasticity, or multicollinearity are encountered—these are problems only in the *second stage* regressions. Typically a researcher hopes for unbiased instrumental variables in the first stage regressions and is unconcerned with hypothesis testing at that stage. So while he or she must be wary of specification error as well as correlation between alleged exogenous variables and the error term, the researcher is not usually troubled by multicollinearity, heteroscedasticity, or autocorrelation in the first stage results. Only when these problems occur in the second stage regressions are remedial measures called for.

Our final point involves the use of underidentified models or poor instrumental variables to "prove" a null hypothesis. General equilibrium theory could plausibly be used to argue that virtually all economic variables are endogenous, including even unpredictable variables like tastes or technological changes. By claiming that right-side variables are really endogenous, virtually any econometric result can be challenged. But there is an element of pragmatism in science that claims a theory can never be debunked except if it is replaced by a better one. If a researcher claims to have a better theory than the one being attacked on grounds of simultaneous equations bias, it is appropriate to make that preferred theory the alternative hypothesis. Otherwise, we end up placing the burden of proof on ideas toward which we are already hostile. When one has 20 to 1 or better odds in one's own favor, victory is easy, but rarely either deserved or convincing.

PROBLEMS

1. Tell whether the following models are identified. If a model is not identified, what adjustments would be necessary to identify it?

   a. (1) $q_d = a_0 + a_1 p + a_2 y + u$; $a_0 > 0$, $a_1 < 0$, $a_2 > 0$
      (2) $q_s = b_0 + b_1 p + v$; $b_0 < 0$, $b_1 > 0$
      (3) $q_d = q_s = q_e$ (equilibrium)

   where q_d and q_s denote quantities demanded and supplied, respectively, p denotes the price of the commodity, y denotes consumer income, and u and v are random variables.

   b. (1) $C = a_0 + b_0 Y + u$; $a_0 > 0$, $b_0 > 0$
      (2) $I = a_1 + b_1 Y + v$; $a_1 < 0$, $b_1 > 0$
      (3) $Y = C + I$

   where C denotes aggregate consumption, Y denotes national income, and I denotes aggregate net investment.

   c. (1) $x_d = f(p_x, p_o, y)$
      (2) $x_s = g(p_x)$
      (3) $x_d = x_s$

   where x_d and x_s equal quantity demanded and supplied, respectively, p is the price of good X, p_o is the price of a substitute good, and y is per capita income.

   d. (1) $C = a_0 + b_0(Y - T) + u$; $a_0 > 0$, $b_0 > 0$
      (2) $I = b_0 + b_1 Y + b_2(G - T) + v$; $b_0 < 0$, $b_1 > 0$, $b_2 < 0$
      (3) $Y = C + I + G$

   where C equals aggregate consumption, Y equals national income, T equals total tax collections, G equals government purchases of goods and services, and I equals aggregate net investment.

2. Suppose the plausible argument is made that p_j in Table 22.2 is simultaneously determined with p. What happens to the reliability of the milk demand and supply equations estimated in Tables 22.3 and 22.4? Is either equation identified? Explain.

3. Consider the following results:

   OLS: $w_i = 3.08 + 0.058PU + 0.080VAPH$; $R^2 = 0.5721$
              (0.468) (0.011)   (0.020)

   TSLS: $w_i = 2.56 + 0.079PU + 0.083VAPH$; $R^2 = 0.5651$
               (0.499) (0.015)   (0.020)

   where w_i is the average hourly wage rate in state i, PU is the proportion of the labor force in unions, and $VAPH$ is the value-added per production hour. Standard errors are in parentheses. Comment on the following: "Since the ordinary least squares (OLS) and two-stage least squares (TSLS) are practically identical, TSLS is meaningless."

4.   Below are three different specifications of the relationship between money changes (dM) and price changes (dP). The first two equations were estimated with ordinary least squares (in the second equation, the change in real output, dQ, was treated as an exogenous variable). The third equation was estimated with two-stage least squares, with lagged dM, dP, and dQ serving as predictors of current dQ. Standard errors are in parentheses; cross-section data were used.

(1) $dP = -7.78 + 1.086dM$; $R^2 = 0.8383$
        (2.49)   (0.0727)

(2) $dP = -3.33 + 1.052dM - 0.884dQ$; $R^2 = 0.8574$
        (3.02)   (0.0706)   (0.374)

(3) $dP = 1.026 + 1.019dM - 1.75dQ$; $R^2 = 0.8391$
        (4.34)   (0.0782)   (0.703)

Which model is most appropriate for testing the hypothesis: "The inflation rate is equal to the rate of change in the money supply, *ceteris paribus*?" Explain. How might we explain the lower R^2 in equation (3) relative to equation (2)?

23

Simultaneous

Equations Models:

Three or More

Endogenous Variables

This chapter extends our discussion of the estimation of simultaneous equations models to systems of equations containing more than two endogenous variables. The identification problem and simultaneous equation estimation procedures are different only in degree from those encountered with two-equation models. Nevertheless, more complex models are most easily addressed after all the aspects of two-equation estimation have been discussed. So having covered equation systems with two endogenous variables, we now turn our attention to models with three or more endogenous variables.

DEMAND, SUPPLY, AND ADVERTISING

In Chapter 22 we developed a supply and demand model of the milk market. The assumption that the milk market is competitive led us to use two-stage least squares estimation procedures, since price, a right-side variable, was considered to be correlated with the error terms in the supply and demand equations. In this section we study the supply and demand conditions in the automobile industry, using monthly data from June 1981 through September 1984. The auto industry is a hybrid of large oligopolistic manufacturers and small, monopolistically competitive retailers. Advertising plays an important role in this interface. Slick magazine advertising (the variety highlighted in this study) is generally financed by large auto manufacturers, yet may have a strong impact on the success of small retailers. An interesting issue is: "Does automobile advertising determine auto sales, or do automobile sales (or more precisely, price) determine advertising volume?" The answer, as we shall see, is "Yes."

If we treat advertising as an exogenous influence on automobile sales, we can develop a three-equation model of the type we stipulated for the milk market in Chapter 22. Let us assume that the quantity of cars demanded is a function of the price per car, per capita disposable income, and the amount of automobile advertising. Let us also assume that the quantity of automobiles supplied (by dealers) depends on the selling price of automobiles and the wage rate for automobile production workers (our proxy for the wholesale price the manufacturers charge dealers). Our model can be written formally as:

$$Q_d = a_0 + a_1 p + a_2 y + a_3 A + u$$
$$Q_s = b_0 + b_1 p + b_2 w + v$$
$$Q_d = Q_s = Q_e$$

where Q_d, Q_s, and Q_e are the quantity of cars demanded, supplied, and exchanged per month, respectively, p is the index of average new car prices, y is per capita disposable income, A is the expenditure on magazine advertising by the auto industry (in millions of dollars), w is the hourly wage rate for automobile workers, and u and v are random error terms.

Table 23.1a shows the regression results for the model with two endogenous variables (Q_e and p). Monthly data covering the period from June 1981 to September 1984 (40 observations) were obtained from the *Survey of Current Business* and the *Monthly Labor Review*. Note that we only need the first stage regression for the automobile price, since the other endogenous variable Q_e appears only on the left side of the demand and supply equations. The R^2 of 0.966 tells us we have a good instrument for automobile price in the second stage regression, although the low Durbin-Watson of 1.14 implies significant autocorrelation. Since we are not conducting significance tests in the first stage result, this autocorrelation is not troubling at this stage.

The second stage results generally support our expectations for the exogenous advertising model. In the demand equation, the coefficient of p_t is negative and significant ($t = -2.64$), the coefficient of y_t is positive and significant ($t = 3.43$), and the coefficient of A_t is also positive and significant ($t = 3.99$). After correction for autocorrelation, the significance of the price coefficient rises to 10 percent ($t = -1.36$), the coefficient of y_t rises to a significance of 5 percent ($t = 2.04$), while A_t retains significance at the 1 percent level ($t = 3.53$). In the supply equation, the coefficient of p_t is positive and significant at the 1 percent level ($t = 2.98$) and the coefficient of w_t is negative and significant at the 1 percent level ($t = 2.49$). After

Table 23.1a

First Stage Regressions, Two-Equation Model:
$$\hat{p}_t = 108.66 + 0.100y_t + 0.0029A_t + 6.05w_t; \; R^2 = 0.966; \; d = 1.14$$
$$\;\;\;\;\;\;(5.83)\;\;\;\;(0.0035)\;\;\;(0.019)\;\;\;\;\;\;(1.17)$$

Second Stage Regressions, Two-Equation Model:

Uncorrected:

$$\hat{Q}_{dt} = 4{,}983.81 - 37.62\hat{p}_t + 1.37y_t + 5.58A_t$$
$$\;\;\;\;\;\;\;(1{,}958.41)\;\;(14.27)\;\;\;\;(0.399)\;\;\;(1.40)$$
$$R^2 = 0.6413; \; d = 1.22; \; \hat{\rho} = 0$$

Corrected for Autocorrelation:

$$\hat{Q}_{dt} = 1{,}968.62 - 24.40\hat{p}_t + 1.02y_t + 4.87A_t$$
$$\;\;\;\;\;\;\;(1{,}546.72)\;\;(17.97)\;\;\;\;(0.501)\;\;\;(1.38)$$
$$R^2 = 0.489; \; d = 1.91; \; \hat{\rho} = 0.377$$
$$\;(0.153)$$

Uncorrected:

$$\hat{Q}_{st} = -9{,}390.48 + 89.79\hat{p}_t - 691.05w_t; \; R^2 = 0.5011; \; d = 1.09; \; \hat{\rho} = 0$$
$$\;\;\;\;\;\;\;(2{,}909.83)\;\;\;\;\;(30.15)\;\;\;\;(277.54)$$

Corrected for Autocorrelation:

$$\hat{Q}_{st} = -4{,}057.80 + 65.88\hat{p}_t - 465.37w_t; \; R^2 = 0.2805; \; d = 1.85; \; \hat{\rho} = 0.434$$
$$\;\;\;\;\;\;\;(2{,}124.19)\;\;\;\;\;(38.64)\;\;\;\;(355.46)\;(0.154)$$

correction for autocorrelation, the coefficient of p_t rises in significance to 5 percent ($t = 1.70$), while the coefficient of w_t is just barely significant at the 10 percent level ($t = -1.31$).

The major criticism of the model in Table 23.1a has already been noted: if the volume of automobile advertising depends either on the quantity of automobiles sold, or more plausibly, on the average price of automobiles, then variable A_t will be correlated with the error term in the *first stage* regression for p_t, thereby thwarting our attempt to obtain a reliable instrument for that variable. Furthermore, using the observed level of advertising instead of an instrumental variable in the *second stage* demand regression will thwart the consistency property of two-stage least squares. Obviously the fix for suspected simultaneous equations bias between A and p is to treat the former variable as endogenous. Alas, there is a rub.

Making A_t into an endogenous variable would require regressing A_t against y_t and w_t, generating a predicted instrumental variable, $\hat{A}_t$, and using this instrument in place of A_t in the second stage regression. However, we would also have to modify the instrument for p_t, since A_t is no longer assumed to be exogenous. So the instrument for p_t would also be a linear combination of variables y_t and w_t. Since y_t is included in the structural equation for Q_d, the only variable left out of that equation is w. This means that the instrumental variables for A_t and p would be perfectly correlated. The second stage demand equation could not be estimated.

In order for the demand equation (or any equation) to be identified, there must be at least as many variables excluded from that equation as there are *additional* equations in the model. Since there must be *two* additional equations (one for automobile advertising and one for the supply of automobiles by dealers), there must be at least *two* (endogenous or exogenous) variables excluded from every structural equation. As specified, the equation for automobile advertising would be overidentified, since it excludes y_t, w_t, and Q_t. The supply equation is exactly identified, since it excludes A_t and y_t. Hence, to identify the demand equation, we must add another variable to the advertising equation, the supply equation, or both.

Since the data used in Table 23.1a are all in nominal terms, suppose we make the plausible assumption that automobile advertising and the supply of automobiles are both influenced by the *real* price of automobiles rather than the nominal price. Merely substituting a deflated price of automobiles into those equations (e.g., dividing the price index for automobiles by some general price index) would not do the trick, however, since we would merely substitute one endogenous variable for another in each equation. Instead, we can add the consumer price index for all goods, P_t, as a separate regressor, treating it as an exogenous variable. Excluding this variable from the demand equation may make it seem that we are assuming that consumers suffer from a money illusion. However, since y_t and p_t are both in nominal terms, we actually assume that automobile demand is influenced by nominal income (which changes in part because of inflation) and automobile price changes independent of nominal income changes (that is, independent of inflation induced income changes). From this perspective, it may also be reasonable to exclude P_t from the supply equation, since nominal wage rates for automobile workers also pick up the influence of inflation. However, since the only other variable on the right side of the advertising equation is the nominal price, some proxy for "the cost of living" is required in that equation.

Our revised model becomes:

$$Q_d = a_0 + a_1 p + a_2 y + a_3 A + u$$
$$Q_s = b_0 + b_1 p + b_2 w + b_3 P + v$$
$$A = c_0 + c_1 p + c_2 P + e$$
$$Q_d = Q_s = Q_e$$

where all variables are the same as in the first model, with two new variables, P, the consumer price index, and e, the random error term in the advertising equation. Note that the fourth equation, which denotes the equilibrium condition that quantity demanded equals quantity supplied, is not materially changed by the addition of the third equation. However, the equilibrium process does have a new twist. In the revised model, when the price adjusts to reconcile the quantities demanded and supplied the volume of advertising will also adjust.

The estimation of the model with three endogenous variables is presented in Table 23.1b. Note that the variable P_t is insignificant in the first stage regression for p_t (since inflation effects may already have been captured by y_t and w_t), although the negative coefficient of P_t in the first stage

Table 23.1b

Automobile Sales and Advertising

First Stage Regressions, Three-Equation Model:

$$\hat{p}_t = 120.02 + 0.133y_t + 7.45w_t - 0.118CPI_t;\ R^2 = 0.967;\ d = 1.30$$
$$\quad\ \ (10.61)\quad (0.0043)\quad (1.53)\quad\ (0.093)$$

$$\hat{A}_t = 77.58 + 0.026y_t + 40.41w_t - 1.93CPI_t;\ R^2 = 0.3969;\ d = 1.56$$
$$\quad\ (88.73)\quad (0.036)\quad\ (12.72)\quad\ (0.775)$$

Second Stage Regressions, Three-Equation Model:
Uncorrected:

$$\hat{Q}_{dt} = 6{,}328.23 - 46.81\hat{p}_t + 8.64\hat{A}_t + 1.55y_t$$
$$\quad\ \ (3{,}502.66)\quad (24.79)\quad\ (5.32)\quad\ \ (0.601)$$

$$R^2 = 0.5126;\ d = 1.10;\ \hat{\rho} = 0$$

Corrected for Autocorrelation:

$$\hat{Q}_{dt} = 2{,}444.87 - 32.56\hat{p}_t + 6.73\hat{A}_t + 1.18y_t$$
$$\quad\ \ (3{,}348.55)\quad (41.81)\quad\ (8.39)\quad\ \ (0.969)$$

$$R^2 = 0.2739;\ d = 1.84;\ \hat{\rho} = 0.441$$
$$\qquad\qquad\qquad\qquad\ (0.154)$$

Uncorrected:

$$\hat{A}_t = -398.95 + 4.37\hat{p}_t - 1.52CPI_t;\ R^2 = 0.3796;\ d = 1.48;\ \hat{\rho} = 0$$
$$\quad\ \ (102.40)\quad\ (1.36)\quad\ (0.610)$$

$$\hat{u}_t = 0.238\hat{u}_{t-1};\ r^2 = 0.0522;\ d = 1.77$$
$$\quad\ (0.425)$$

Uncorrected:

$$\hat{Q}_t = -9{,}076.22 + 87.12\hat{p}_t - 648.49w_t - 0.893CPI_t$$
$$\quad\ \ (2{,}642.69)\quad\ (27.35)\quad\ (252.02)\quad\ (6.67)$$

$$R^2 = 0.5126;\ d = 1.10;\ \hat{\rho} = 0$$

Corrected for Autocorrelation:

$$\hat{Q}_t = -4{,}124.41 + 69.62\hat{p}_t - 489.44w_t - 0.937CPI_t$$
$$\quad\ \ (2{,}332.10)\quad\ (46.12)\quad\ (385.72)\quad\ (8.58)$$

$$R^2 = 0.2739;\ d = 1.84;\ \hat{\rho} = 0.441$$
$$\qquad\qquad\qquad\qquad\ (0.154)$$

regression for A_t is significant at the 1 percent level ($t = 2.49$). This evidence may vindicate our exclusion of this exogenous variable from the demand equation. However, the relatively low R^2 (0.3969) in the first stage equation for A_t may portend a poor instrument for this variable in the second stage regressions.

The second stage regressions in Table 23.1b present a theme all too prevalent in real world time-series data: beautiful results that are pulverized by correction for autocorrelation. In the uncorrected structural equation for demand, the coefficient of $\hat{p}_t$ is significant at the 5 percent level ($t = -1.89$), the coefficient of y_t is significant at the 1 percent level ($t = 2.58$), while the coefficient of $\hat{A}_t$ is significant at the 10 percent level ($t = 1.62$). Alas, the Durbin-Watson of 1.10 implies significant autocorrelation, whose correction cuts the R^2 by 47 percent and causes all regressors to become insignificant.

Luckily there is no significant autocorrelation in the second stage regression for A_t (the Durbin-Watson statistic of 1.48 is in the uncertain region, and the lack of significant autocorrelation is verified by regressing the residual against the lagged residual). As suspected, as the (instrumental) price of new cars increases, expenditures on automobile advertising also increases. The coefficient of $\hat{p}_t$ is significant at the 1 percent level ($t = 3.19$). This supports our alternative hypothesis that automobile advertising increases as the average price of automobiles increases. Furthermore, as the general price level increases, expenditures on automobile advertising in magazines decreases; this result is also significant at the 1 percent level ($t = 2.49$).

The results for the supply equation parallel those for the demand equation: significant uncorrected results that are rendered insignificant by correction for autocorrelation. In the uncorrected results, the quantity of automobiles supplied increases with the automobile price ($t = 3.19$, which is significant at the 1 percent level), and decreases as the wage rate paid to autoworkers increases ($t = 2.57$). As suspected, P_t does not appear to have an independent impact on the supply of new automobiles. After correction for autocorrelation, the (instrument for) new car price is significant at the 10 percent level ($t = 1.51$), while w_t ceases to be significant ($t = 1.27$).

There is a moral in all this: correctly specified models often give less support to an alternative hypothesis than incorrectly specified models. This is yet another example of the importance of honesty in hypothesis testing. By loading enough highly correlated variables into an equation, anyone can use econometrics as a weapon to destroy virtually any alternative hypothesis. However, if the model one seeks to destroy is always treated as the *null* hypothesis, there is less danger from the misuse of econometrics. We may still encounter underidentified models or good results may be destroyed by correction for autocorrelation. But at least those outcomes are part of the risk we take when we bear the burden of proof.

THE IDENTIFICATION
PROBLEM REVISITED

Having traced through a few examples in the last two chapters, we are now in a position to generalize the rules for establishing identification. Consider a model consisting of n equations in n endogenous variables and m exogenous variables. The ith equation is written:

$$(i) \quad \alpha_i + \sum_{j=1}^{n} \beta_{ij} \cdot x_j + \sum_{k=1}^{m} \gamma_{ik} \cdot y_k = u_i \quad (i = 1, 2, ..., n)$$

where

α_i = the intercept term in the ith equation.

x_j = endogenous variables (of which there are n).

y_k = exogenous variables (of which there are m).

u_i = random error terms (of which there are n).

β_{ij} = coefficient of the endogenous variable x_j in the ith equation (first subscript refers to the equation in which it appears and second to the variable of which it is the coefficient; note also that β_{ij} equals -1 on the left-side variable in the structural equation).

γ_{ik} = coefficient of the exogenous variable y_k in the ith equation.

Notice that all definitional equations have been eliminated from the system, so the number of endogenous variables equals the total number of equations. For instance, in the example of the automobile market, the last equation would not appear; instead, Q_e would be used in place of Q_d and Q_s in the first two equations. In terms of this notation the constant terms and the coefficients may be positive, negative, or zero. In fact, unless several coefficients are zero in an equation, that equation cannot be identified.

The necessary condition for identification of the ith equation is:

The number of variables excluded from the ith equation must be *at least* $(n - 1)$. To be exactly identified, the number excluded must equal $(n - 1)$. To be overidentified, the number excluded must be greater than $(n - 1)$.

The above condition is necessary for identification because, for two-stage least squares, the instruments used for endogenous variables are linear combinations of all the exogenous variables in the system. If the number of variables excluded from an equation is smaller than $(n - 1)$, the instrumental variable(s) in that equation will be perfectly correlated with the other variables in that equation, making estimation of that equation impossible.

The above condition is not *sufficient* for identification because of the possibility that the system of simultaneous equations cannot be solved because one or more of the equations is a linear transformation of some other equation(s). In this case the set of instrumental variables themselves would be perfectly correlated. Therefore, an equation meeting the necessary conditions for exact identification still could not be estimated.

As we have stated several times throughout the last two chapters, whether an equation is identifiable can be learned from the mathematical structure of the model. If we cannot legitimately exclude enough endogenous and/or exogenous variables from the equation to estimate that equation, the computer will tell us when we ask it to invert what turns out to be a singular matrix. However, if we can discern the "nonidentifiability" of an equation (or of an entire model) prior to the estimation stage, we will save ourselves some trouble and disappointment. Besides, we should understand the identification problem so that if the computer sends us an error message such as, "I cannot invert this matrix," we will know what it is talking about.

GENDER, PRODUCTIVITY, AND
WAGE RATES IN MANUFACTURING

In Chapter 20 we examined the relationship between employment patterns in manufacturing industries by gender and the impact of the percent of women employees on productivity and wage rates. Using ordinary least squares to estimate two log-linear regression equations, we found results that appear to contradict the marginal productivity theory of wage determination. As the proportion of female workers increases across industries, real value-added per hour (our measure of productivity) appears to increase, *ceteris paribus*. However, as the proportion of female workers increases, average wage rates decrease, also *ceteris paribus*.

In this section we will employ two-stage least squares techniques to determine if causation might run from average wage rates to the proportion of female employees, rather than in the opposite direction. That is, we will seek to determine whether the circumstantial evidence of wage discrimination (a higher proportion of female workers implies a lower average wage rate for all workers) might not actually reflect job discrimination (as the average wage rate in an industry increases, the proportion of jobs held by women in that industry decreases).

Recall the two-equation model from Chapter 20. First, real value-added per worker ($RVAPH$) was related to a time trend ($Year$), real capital per hour ($RKPH$), the proportion of workers in white collar jobs (PWC), and the proportion of workers who are female (PCF). The second equation related real average hourly wage rates ($RAHW$) to real value-added per hour, percent female, and the time trend. Using a log-linear model, the equations are:

$$(1) \quad LRVAPH = a_0 + a_1 Year + a_2 LRKPH + a_3 LPWC$$
$$+ a_4 LPCF + u$$
$$(2) \quad LRAHW = b_0 + b_1 Year + b_2 LRVAPH + b_3 LPCF + v$$

Under the assumptions of ordinary least squares, all right-side variables, including *LPCF*, are assumed to be nonrandom by virtue of their independence of the error term. However, if the real average hourly wage rate influences the proportion of workers who are female, the impact of *LPCF* on *LRAHW* and on *LRVAPH* could be overstated. Furthermore, if *LPCF* is simultaneously determined with *LRAHW*, then so is *LRVAPH* and we can no longer treat *LRVAPH* as *causally prior* to *LRAHW*.

Let us assume that the proportion of women employed in an industry increases with time (because of increasing labor force participation by women) and with the proportion of white collar jobs (given the high proportion of women in clerical jobs), while decreasing with the real average hourly wage rate. Then our system becomes:

$$\text{(1)} \quad LRVAPH = a_0 + a_1 Year + a_2 LRKPH + a_3 LPWC + a_4 LPCF + u$$

$$\text{(2)} \quad LRAHW = b_0 + b_1 Year + b_2 LRVAPH + b_3 LPCF + v$$

$$\text{(3)} \quad LPCF = c_0 + c_1 Year + c_2 LPWC + c_3 LRAHW + e$$

We note that there are three endogenous variables (*LRVAPH*, *LRAHW*, and *LPCF*) and three exogenous variables (*Year*, *LRKPH*, and *LPWC*). To be identified, each equation must exclude at least *two* variables that appear in the other equation. Note that equation (1) contains two endogenous variables (*LRVAPH* and *LPCF*) and all three exogenous variables (*Year*, *LRKPH*, and *LPWC*). Equation (1) is underidentified. There is no way to estimate this equation using two-stage least squares. Equation (2) and equation (3) are each exactly identified, since each excludes one endogenous variable and one exogenous variable. It follows that the last two equations can be estimated using two-stage least squares.

The hypotheses we wish to test are embedded in equations (2) and (3). Equation (2) hypothesizes that real average hourly wage rate falls as the proportion of female workers increases ($b_3 < 0$). Equation (3) hypothesizes that as the average hourly wage rate increases, the proportion of women employed in an industry falls ($c_3 < 0$). The reason for equation (1) was to determine whether real value-added per worker increased or decreased as the proportion of female workers increased, thereby testing the marginal productivity theory of distribution. However, that hypothesis can be tested with equation (2): Does the real average hourly wage rate increase as real value-added per worker increases? If so, the marginal productivity theory of distribution is supported. Hence, if the proportion of females does not have a significant negative effect on the real average hourly wage rate, once variations in productivity (*RVAPH*) are taken into account, the wage discrimination hypothesis is contradicted.

The first and second stage regressions are reported in Table 23.2. Note that the first stage regression for *LRVAPH* can be estimated. The reduced form equations can always be estimated, since by assumption the exogenous variables are not perfectly correlated with each other and are each independent

Table 23.2

Gender, Productivity, and Wage Rates in Manufacturing, 1962-1980

First Stage Regressions:

$$\widehat{LRAHW} = 0.287 + 0.0084\,Year + 0.153LRKPH + 0.193LPWC$$
$$\qquad\;\;(0.053)\;\;(0.0012)\qquad(0.0084)\qquad\quad(0.019)$$

$R^2 = 0.7407$

$$\widehat{LPCF} = 3.66 + 0.023\,Year - 0.412LRKPH + 0.104LPWC$$
$$\qquad\;(0.193)\,(0.0019)\qquad(0.031)\qquad\quad(0.070)$$

$R^2 = 0.4565$

$$\widehat{LRVAPH} = 0.487 + 0.015\,Year + 0.347LRKPH + 0.383LPWC$$
$$\qquad\quad(0.114)\;\;(0.0026)\qquad(0.018)\qquad\quad(0.041)$$

$R^2 = 0.7390$

Second Stage Regressions:

$$\widehat{LRAHW} = -0.115 - 0.00007\,Year + 0.044\widehat{LPCF} + 0.496\widehat{LRVAPH}$$
$$\qquad\;\;(0.313)\qquad(0.003)\qquad\quad(0.061)\qquad\quad(0.057)$$

$R^2 = 0.4482$

$$\widehat{LPCF} = 4.51 + 0.048\,Year - 2.96\widehat{LRAHW} + 0.680LPWC$$
$$\qquad\;(0.163)\,(0.0042)\qquad(0.175)\qquad\quad(0.083)$$

$R^2 = 0.5859$

of the error term in the equation. Hence, we can use an instrumental variable for $LRVAPH$ in the second stage equation for $LRAHW$. We also note that each of the exogenous variables in the reduced form equation for $LRVAPH$ is statistically significant. We would not be justified in arbitrarily excluding one of the exogenous variables from the structural equation for $LRVAPH$. If correctly specified, equation (1) cannot be estimated. If we try excluding variables to make that equation identifiable, we risk specification error.

Note that only $LRVAPH$ is statistically significant in the second stage equation for $LRAHW$. We cannot reject the null hypothesis that real average hourly wage rates do not decrease as the proportion of female workers increases, once productivity ($LRVAPH$) and time are taken into account. Yet we also note that the R^2 on $LPCF$ in the first stage equation is less than 0.5. The insignificance of the instrumental variable for $LPCF$ in the $LRVAPH$ equation may ultimately be explained by the simple fact that it is a bad proxy. If we could identify other influences on $LPCF$, we might get a better test of our hypothesis. As a bonus, if we find variables that influence $LPCF$ but do not directly influence $LRVAPH$, the second stage equation for the latter could be estimated.

The second stage regression for equation (3) offers strong evidence in support of the job discrimination hypothesis. If the wage rate in one industry is 1 percent greater in the same year (the proportion of white collar jobs constant), the proportion of women in that industry would be nearly 3 percent lower. Once the simultaneous relationship between *LPCF* and *LRAHW* is taken into account, causation seems to run from productivity to average wage rates, and from average wage rates to the proportion of women.

INFLATION, WAGE CHANGES, AND UNEMPLOYMENT: A FINAL LOOK

We next explore a topic that needs no further introduction: the macro-economic relationship between price inflation, wage changes, and the level of unemployment. In our third installment of this continuing drama, in Chapter 22, we found that nominal wages tend to increase with the rate of inflation and the rate of increase in productivity, while decreasing as the unemployment rate increases. In turn, the rate of inflation tends to increase with increases in nominal wage rates in excess of productivity increases, the rate of growth of the money stock, and the rate of increase of fuel prices. However, these results were derived from two-stage least squares regressions that treated the unemployment rate as an exogenous variable. That is, variations in the unemployment rate from one year to the next were assumed to be independent of both the rate of inflation and the change in nominal wage rates.

In this section we will test the hypothesis that the unemployment rate is an endogenous variable. Since both equations investigated in Chapter 22 were overidentified, we could make the unemployment rate endogenous without introducing new variables into the system. However, the three remaining exogenous variables generate a very poor instrument for the unemployment rate.[1] To enhance the viability of the model, we introduce an additional exogenous variable, $UEBEN_t$, the average weekly unemployment benefits. We now have the following three-equation system:

(1) $INF_t = a0 + a_1 EXWAGE_t + a_2 DM1_t + a_3 DPFUEL_t + u$

(2) $DWAGE_t = b_0 + b_1 INF_t + b_2 UE_t + b_3 DPROD_t + v$

(3) $UE_t = c_0 + c_1 UEBEN_t + c_2 DWAGE_t + c_3 INF_t + e$

---

[1]Regressing UE_t against the three endogenous variables $DM1_t$ (the percent change in the money stock), $DPFUEL_t$ (the percent change in the price index for fuel), and $DPROD_t$ (the percent change in productivity) yielded the following equation:

$$\widehat{UE_t} = 4.55 + 0.237DM1_t + 0.0067DPFUEL_t - 0.021DPROD_t; \; R^2 = 0.1698; \; d = 0.630$$
$$\quad\;\;(0.686)\;(0.094)\qquad\;(0.028)\qquad\qquad(0.193)$$

In equation (1), INF_t is the rate of inflation, $EXWAGE_t$ is the nominal wage rate change *minus* the change in productivity, DMI_t is the percent change in the money stock, and $DPFUEL_t$ is the percent change in fuel prices. All coefficients in equation (1) are predicted to be positive. In equation (2), $DWAGE_t$ is the percent change in the average nominal wage rate, INF_t is the inflation rate, UE_t is the civilian unemployment rate, and $DPROD_t$ is the rate of change in productivity. We predict $b_1 > 0$, $b_2 < 0$, and $b_3 > 0$. In the third equation, UE_t is the unemployment rate, $UEBEN_t$ is average weekly unemployment benefits, $DWAGE_t$ is the rate of change in the nominal wage rate, and INF_t is the rate of inflation. We predict that $c_1 > 0$, $c_2 < 0$, and $c_3 > 0$. That is, if unemployment is largely voluntary, the unemployment rate should increase with the level of unemployment benefits, while decreasing with the *real* wage rate (hence, decreasing with $DWAGE_t$ and increasing with INF_t).

The first and second stage regression results are reported in Table 23.3. We see that the addition of $UEBEN_t$ as an exogenous variable produces a relatively good instrument for the unemployment rate. Substitution of $UEBEN_t$ for UE_t also maintains good instrumental variables for the other two endogenous variables.

In the second stage results, we find that the assumption of endogenous unemployment does not materially affect the relationship between nominal wage changes and inflation produced by the two-equation model in Chapter 22. The inflation rate is positively related to $EXWAGE_t$ ($t = 5.76$), DMI_t ($t = 3.38$), and $DPFUEL_t$ ($t = 2.52$). The rate of change in nominal wage rates increases with the rate of inflation ($t = 7.26$ for the null hypothesis that $b_1 = 0$ and $t = -0.675$ for the null hypothesis that $b_1 = 1$), decreases with the unemployment rate ($t = -2.58$), and increases with productivity growth ($t = 1.82$).

It is in the third structural equation that we encounter difficulties with the treatment of UE_t as an endogenous variable. Unlike the other two equations, the second stage regression for UE_t shows a significant degree of autocorrelation. After correction, the coefficient of $UEBEN_t$ remains significantly positive ($t = 3.86$). However, the signs of the other two coefficients are contrary to our expectations: the unemployment rate allegedly increases with increases in the nominal wage rate while decreasing with the rate of inflation. This is not a viable reflection of worker behavior, although it may reflect employer behavior. Yet, because neither coefficient is significant, we cannot reject the null hypothesis that the unemployment rate is independent of both the change in the nominal wage rate and the rate of inflation.

Of course, it is conceivable that the insignificance of both instrumental variables is due to multicollinearity; we have already established a close link between inflation and nominal wage changes in equations (1) and (2). Hence, we reintroduce the variable $DRWAGE_t$, the rate of change in *real*

Table 23.3

Inflation, Nominal Wage Changes, and Unemployment

First Stage Regressions:

$\widehat{INF}_t = 1.83 - 0.179DPROD_t + 0.025UEBEN_t + 0.155DMI_t$
$\qquad (0.664)\ (0.171) \qquad\quad (0.011) \qquad\qquad (0.108)$
$\qquad\qquad\qquad\qquad\qquad\qquad\qquad\qquad + 0.129DPFUEL_t$
$\qquad\qquad\qquad\qquad\qquad\qquad\qquad\qquad\quad (0.024)$

$R^2 = 0.7592;\ d = 1.996$

$\widehat{EXWAGE}_t = 4.80 - 1.03DPROD_t + 0.002UEBEN_t + 0.218DMI_t$
$\qquad\qquad (0.775)\ (0.119) \qquad\quad (0.012) \qquad\qquad (0.127)$
$\qquad\qquad\qquad\qquad\qquad\qquad\qquad\qquad\quad + 0.118DPFUEL_t$
$\qquad\qquad\qquad\qquad\qquad\qquad\qquad\qquad\qquad (0.028)$

$R^2 = 0.7906;\ d = 1.86$

$\widehat{UE}_t = 2.96 + 0.210DPROD_t + 0.054UEBEN_t - 0.133DMI_t$
$\qquad (0.523)\ (0.134) \qquad\quad (0.008) \qquad\qquad (0.085)$
$\qquad\qquad\qquad\qquad\qquad\qquad\qquad\qquad - 0.006DPFUEL_t$
$\qquad\qquad\qquad\qquad\qquad\qquad\qquad\qquad\quad (0.019)$

$R^2 = 0.6372;\ d = 1.49$

Second Stage Regressions:

$\widehat{INF}_t = 0.728 + 0.495\widehat{EXWAGE}_t + 0.220DMI_t + 0.058DPFUEL_t$
$\qquad (0.387)\ \ (0.086) \qquad\qquad\qquad (0.065) \qquad\quad (0.023)$

$R^2 = 0.8467;\ d = 1.999$

$\widehat{DWAGE}_t = 4.24 + 0.915\widehat{INF}_t - 0.374\widehat{UE}_t + 0.229DPROD_t$
$\qquad\qquad (0.716)\ (0.126) \qquad (0.145) \qquad (0.126)$

$R^2 = 0.8411;\ d = 2.15$

$\widehat{UE}_t = 3.78 + 0.050UEBEN_t - 0.028\widehat{DWAGE}_t - 0.154\widehat{INF}_t$
$\qquad (2.49)\ \ (0.013) \qquad\quad (0.660) \qquad\qquad (0.564)$

$R^2 = 0.6177;\ d = 1.05$

Corrected for Autocorrelation, Cochrane-Orcutt:

$\widehat{UE}_t = 1.47 + 0.054UEBEN_t + 0.284\widehat{DWAGE}_t - 0.425\widehat{INF}_t$
$\qquad (1.23)\ \ (0.014) \qquad\qquad (0.572) \qquad\qquad (0.482)$

$R^2 = 0.3971;\ d = 1.62;\ \rho = 0.457$
$\qquad\qquad\qquad\qquad\qquad\quad (0.156)$

Substituting $\widehat{DRWAGE}_t$ for $\widehat{DWAGE}_t$ and $\widehat{INF}_t$:

$\widehat{UE}_t = 1.64 + 0.053UEBEN_t + 0.507\widehat{DRWAGE}_t$
$\qquad (2.04)\ \ (0.015) \qquad\qquad (0.571)$

$R^2 = 0.5352;\ d = 1.29;\ \hat{u}_t = 0.377\hat{u}_{t-1}$
$\qquad\qquad\qquad\qquad\qquad\qquad (0.220)$

wage rates. Substituting $DRWAGE_t$ for $DWAGE_t$ and INF_t is equivalent to assuming that $c_2 = -c_3$.[2] However, this substitution does not improve the case for an endogenous unemployment rate. The coefficient of $DRWAGE_t$ is positive and insignificant.

Before moving to the next example, we can use the results in Table 23.3 to reflect on the viability of an inflation-unemployment trade-off. Clearly the relationship between nominal wage changes and unemployment is considerably more complex than the simple model first reported by Phillips. Nominal wage rates increase with productivity increases and with inflation itself, while declining as the unemployment rate increases, *ceteris paribus*. However, only nominal wage increases in excess of productivity are inherently inflationary, so it would appear that wage increases are a "carrier" of inflation. Workers who wish to maintain constant or increasing real wage rates must obtain nominal wage gains in excess of productivity increases. However, this process may be self-defeating, since excessive wage increases also contribute to inflation (along with increases in the money stock and increases in fuel prices). Clearly, therefore, there is no simple, stable trade-off between price stability and employment. But, when subjected to the light of econometrics, there is support for a link between unemployment and inflation. When unemployment rates are high, nominal wage increases will not keep pace with price inflation, eventually lessening the wage pressure on prices. However, when inflation is being fed by growth in the money stock and increases in fuel prices, it is folly to expect increasing unemployment to cure inflation unless other causes of inflation also abate.

UNIONS, PRODUCTIVITY,
AND WAGE RATES

Our final application of estimating procedures to models with more than two endogenous variables takes us into the realm of labor economics. Economists have long been interested in the impact of labor unions on labor earnings. Yet there are many econometric pitfalls hidden in the underbrush of this topic. One approach is to compare the earnings of union workers with those of nonunion workers with similar characteristics. The problem with this approach is that union-nonunion wage differentials can overstate the impact of unionism on labor earnings if higher union wages imply lower nonunion earnings. Alternatively, if the specter of unionism (and its associated strike threat) causes employers of nonunion labor to increase wage

[2]The first stage regression for $DRWAGE_t$ is:

$$DRWAGE_t = 2.98 + 0.149DPROD_t - 0.012DPFUEL_t - 0.023UEBEN_t + 0.063DMI_t$$
$$ (0.469)\ (0.121) \qquad (0.017) \qquad\quad (0.0075) \qquad\quad (0.077)$$

with $R^2 = 0.4473$ and the Durbin-Watson statistic equal to 2.30.

payments to forestall unionization of that plant or industry, then union-nonunion wage differences would tend to understate the impact of unionism on the earnings of union workers.

Instead of determining the impact of unions on the earnings of individual workers, we will investigate the impact of statewide average union membership on average wage rates for all workers in a particular industry. In the first subsection we will investigate the relationship between wage rates, productivity, and union membership in the construction industry. Here we will find that a positive relation between average construction wages and the extent of union membership is essentially due to the impact of construction unions on worker productivity (partly by reducing employment, partly through job training). In the second subsection we will investigate the relationship between union membership, average wages, and productivity in manufacturing. Here evidence suggests that unions increase the proportion of value-added that goes into wages.

Construction Unions, Productivity, and Wage Rates

Most economists would investigate wage rates and employment in the construction industry through the use of a competitive market model. There are typically a large number of building contractors in any local labor market as well as a large number of persons with the aptitude and skills necessary to work in the building trades. In the absence of building trade unions, we predict that the equilibrium wage rate for construction workers would be set at the point of intersection between the supply and demand curves for that labor market. It follows that any increase in the wage rate above the competitive equilibrium would require a shift of the demand curve to the right (e.g., union apprenticeships may increase worker productivity more than would the on-the-job training with a nonunion firm), or a shift in the supply of labor to the left (e.g., unions effectively reduce the supply of *certified* labor through control over training or by negotiating mandatory union membership clauses in labor contracts).

Economist Gary S. Becker[3] has suggested that craft unions (like the building trade unions) may effectively use *union shop* contracts as *de facto closed shop* contracts. Closed shop contracts, nominally illegal in all states, would require union membership prior to employment. With such contracts, unions could control the number of jobs by limiting the number of union members. Union shop contracts, by contrast, are allowed in thirty states (those without right-to-work laws) and require union membership after a probationary period following employment. However, if unions refuse to

---

[3]Gary S. Becker, *The Economics of Discrimination*, 2nd Edition, Chicago: University of Chicago Press, 1971, p. 76ff.

admit workers after employment, the employer having a union shop contract could permanently employ only union members. If Becker is correct, we should find a smaller proportion of construction workers belonging to craft unions in right-to-work states than in union shop states, *ceteris paribus*.

Union membership is also predicted to increase with the wage rate for construction workers, since workers typically join unions because unionized jobs pay more. If unions are particularly adept at representing workers with less education, then union membership should decrease as the average educational level increases. Finally, as we will see, there is an incentive for craft unions to discriminate against minority workers. It follows that the higher the proportion of black construction workers, the lower the proportion of construction workers in unions.

If construction unions do function by reducing the number of construction jobs (i.e., a shift in the labor supply curve to the left), then we should find that the proportion of workers in construction falls as the proportion of construction workers in unions rises. However, shifts in the demand curve will also have an impact on the proportion of workers in construction. We predict that the proportion of workers in construction will increase with the average productivity of construction workers (measured as value-added per year) and with the rate of increase in total employment in the state.

According to the economic theory of production, output per worker should decrease as the number of workers increases, *ceteris paribus*. Hence, value-added per worker should decrease as the proportion of workers in construction increases, *ceteris paribus*. We should also find that value-added per worker increases with the amount of capital per worker, with the proportion of workers who have a high school education, and with the number of construction workers per firm (a proxy for the specialization of labor). Finally, since construction unions do provide labor training, we should find that output per worker increases with the proportion of workers who belong to construction unions.

Now we come to the relationship between unionism and average construction wages. We first predict that all influences on labor productivity, including increased unionism, will increase the average construction wage. Hence, construction wage rates should increase with the proportion of workers in unions, the number of construction workers per firm, capital per worker, and the extent of high school education. However, once productivity differences across states are taken into account, there should be no significant impact of unionism on the average construction wage. That is, after unionism, construction wages are still determined by the (modified) forces of market supply and demand.

Finally, we test the hypothesis that construction unions reduce the job opportunities for minority workers. We predict that the proportion of black construction workers will increase with the relative size of the black population, but decline with the proportion of construction workers in unions.

We have a five-equation model which, with modifications, gives us seven structural equations to estimate:

(1) $PU = a_0 + a_1 RTW + a_2 W + a_3 HSG + a_4 BC + u_1;$
$a_1, a_3, a_4 < 0;\ a_2 > 0$

(2) $PC = b_0 + b_1 PU + b_2 DTE + b_3 VA + u_2;$
$b_1 < 0;\ b_2, b_3 > 0$

(3a) $VA = c_0 + c_2 PC + c_3 CW + c_4 K + c_5 HSG + u_3;$
$c_2 < 0;\ c_3, c_4, c_5 > 0$

(3b) $VA = c_0 + c_1 PU + c_2 PC + c_3 CW + c_4 K + c_5 HSG + u_3;$
$c_1 > 0$

(4a) $W = d_0 + d_1 PU + d_2 CW + d_3 K + d_5 HSG + u_4;$
$d_1, d_2, d_3, d_5 > 0$

(4b) $W = d_0 + d_1 PU + d_4 VA + d_5 HSG + u_4;$
$d_1 = d_5 = 0;\ d_4 > 0$

(5) $BC = f_0 + f_1 PCB + f_2 PU + u_5;\ f_1 > 0;\ f_2 < 0$

The definitions of the variables are as follows:

PU = proportion of construction workers in unions (from *Construction Reports*, 1978).

PC = proportion of the nonagricultural labor force in construction (from *County Business Patterns*, 1978).

VA = value-added per construction worker (from 1977 *Census of Construction*).

W = average annual construction wage (*ibid*).

BC = proportion of craft jobs held by blacks (from *EEOC Reports*, 1978).

RTW = dummy variable, equal to one for right-to-work states, equal to zero for other states (see Chapter 19).

CW = construction workers per firm (*Census of Construction*).

DTE = percent change in nonagricultural employment from 1976 to 1978 (*County Business Patterns*).

K = dollar value of construction assets per worker (*Census*).

HSG = proportion of labor force with high school diploma (1979 *Statistical Abstract*).

PCB = proportion of labor force black (*ibid*).

Table 23.4 presents the first stage and second stage regressions for construction. With five endogenous variables and six exogenous variables, all equations are overidentified. According to the first stage regression, the only questionable instrumental variable is for union membership. However, since the results consistently support the alternative hypotheses, there seems little cause for concern.

In the first structural (second stage) regression, we find that the proportion of construction workers in unions is lower in right-to-work states, while increasing with the construction wage. Neither HSG nor BC appears to have a significant impact on union membership in construction. The

Table 23.4

Construction Unions, Productivity, and Wage Rates

First Stage Regressions:

$\widehat{PU} = 96.07 - 23.58RTW - 0.913HSG - 0.091PCB + 0.0024K$
     (56.29) (6.20)   (0.778)   (0.091)   (0.0010)
                            $- 0.547DTE - 0.156CW;$ $R^2 = 0.4052$
                              (0.587)   (1.74)

$\widehat{VA} = 2,415.1 - 5,283.5RTW + 179.79HSG - 85.35PCB + 0.995K$
      (13,141)   (1,447.5)   (181.7)   (109.1)   (0.250)
                            $- 420.1DTE + 1,112.9CW;$ $R^2 = 0.6377$
                              (137.2)   (406.4)

$\widehat{PC} = -2.45 + 1.06RTW + 0.049HSG - 0.045PCB + 0.00008K$
     (3.64)   (0.401)   (0.050)   (0.030)   (0.00007)
                            $+ 0.093DTE + 0.402CW;$ $R^2 = 0.5404$
                              (0.038)   (0.113)

$\widehat{W} = -6,487.6 - 2,660.1RTW + 167.17HSG + 0.215PCB + 0.446K$
     (5,462.5)   (601.7)   (75.54)   (45.3)   (0.104)
                            $- 230.77DTE + 713.14CW;$ $R^2 = 0.7191$
                              (54.01)   (168.94)

$\widehat{BC} = 1.28 + 2.13RTW + 0.026HSG + 0.700PCB + 0.00006K$
     (8.92) (0.933)   (0.123)   (0.074)   (0.00016)
                            $- 0.065DTE - 0.673CW;$ $R^2 = 0.8325$
                              (0.093)   (0.276)

Second Stage Regressions:

$\widehat{PU} = 83.21 - 14.85RTW + 0.0022\widehat{W} - 0.820HSG - 0.619BC;$ $R^2 = 0.4609$
     (47.30) (6.09)   (0.0011)   (0.691)   (0.535)

$\widehat{PC} = 0.365 - 0.097\widehat{PU} + 0.169DTE + 0.00029VA;$ $R^2 = 0.4853$
     (1.20)   (0.021)   (0.038)   (0.000056)

$\widehat{VA} = -19,500 - 4,701.3\widehat{PC} + 2,401.4CW + 1.68K + 533.29HSG$
     (13,780)   (935.61)   (497.8)   (0.289)   (197.81)
                                                         $R^2 = 0.5499$

$\widehat{VA} = -28,257 + 215.25\widehat{PU} - 1,612.2\widehat{PC} + 1,671.8CW + 0.714K$
     (13,348)   (82.05)   (1,468.50)   (543.44)   (0.459)
                                               $+ 507.47HSG;$ $R^2 = 0.6133$
                                                 (185.78)

$\widehat{W} = -21,017 + 138.01\widehat{PU} + 855.05CW + 0.043K + 294.33HSG;$ $R^2 = 0.6652$
     (5,757)   (21.28)   (159.69)   (0.099)   (79.38)

$\widehat{W} = 514.14 - 42.63\widehat{PU} + 0.591\widehat{VA} - 39.99HSG;$ $R^2 = 0.6978$
     (4,170.0) (30.07)   (0.085)   (66.61)

$\widehat{BC} = 3.23 + 0.610PCB - 0.072\widehat{PU};$ $R^2 = 0.7625$
     (1.92) (0.058)   (0.036)

second structural equation shows the proportion of workers in construction decreasing as the proportion of workers in construction unions increases. Also, the proportion of workers in construction increases as the change in employment increases and as value-added per worker increases.

Both versions of equation (3) support the alternative hypotheses, although some multicollinearity seems to infest equation (3b), as suspected. In equation (4a), value-added per worker decreases as the proportion of workers in construction increases, which is consistent with diminishing returns. Value-added per worker increases with the number of construction workers per firm, capital per construction worker, and the proportion of high school graduates. When the proportion of construction workers in unions is injected into the value-added equation, that variable has a significant positive influence, along with variables CW and HSG. As predicted, variable PC ceases to have a significant impact on VA, as apparently its explanatory power is captured by PU. The demise in the significance of variable K is more perplexing, apparently also due to correlation with PU.

Equations (4a) and (4b) ultimately make the case for the competitive theory of union wage rates. Equation (4a) contains all the influences on VA, except for PW. Note with other causes of labor productivity held constant the average annual wage rate for construction workers in a state is predicted to rise by $138 for each 1 percent increase in the proportion of workers in construction unions. Also having a significant positive influence are the number of construction workers per firm and the proportion of high school graduates. However, when value-added is substituted for CW and K, the coefficients of PU and HSG both become negative. The positive impact of unionism and high school graduation (human capital) on construction wages is captured by value-added per worker (labor productivity). The latter variable is highly significant; for each extra dollar of value-added, wage rates increase by 61 cents.

The last equation provides mixed evidence about the propensity of building trade unions to practice discrimination. *If* the proportion of workers in unions does depend on the proportion of black craft workers (which is *not* supported by the results for equation (1)), then there is a slight reduction in the proportion of black craft workers for each 1 percent increase in union membership. However, if the proportion of workers in construction unions is causally prior to the proportion of black construction workers, then the former has no significant impact on the latter. This result is something of an anomaly. Usually, making a variable endogenous decreases its significance; here, making union membership endogenous strengthens its impact.

Unionism, Productivity, and Manufacturing Wages

The results of the last subsection might leave the reader with the impression that economic theory and econometrics can support a strong antiunion case: construction unions increase the wage rate for members by reducing the proportion of workers in construction. Ultimately the apparent impact of unionism on wage rates could be attributed to enhanced labor productivity: productivity that might have been improved by increasing education or the degree of labor specialization. In this era of low popular approval of labor unions, there are assuredly many economists willing to generalize on these or similar results to condemn labor unions as impediments to otherwise competitive labor markets. But economists should always be wary of generalizing from evidence obtained from one time (1977-1978) and for one place or institution (the construction industry across states). It is possible that evidence on a different industry might yield different results. In fact, as you might imagine, that fact can be demonstrated.

In Table 23.5 we investigate a simplified model of the relationship between union membership, productivity, and wage rates in manufacturing across states. Many economists believe that the degree of total union membership determines whether states have right-to-work laws, rather than right-to-work laws having a dampening impact on union membership.[4] To avoid controversy, we use the proportion of workers who belong to unions in 1976 to predict the proportion of workers who belong to unions in 1978. Since we are using cross-section data, we do not incur the problem of autocorrelated errors. Other endogenous variables are AHW, the average hourly wage rate for manufacturing workers, and $VAPH$, value-added per hour in manufacturing. Other exogenous variables include KPH, capital per hour, and HSG, the proportion of high school graduates in the labor force.

Our three-equation model of the manufacturing labor market essentially parallels our model of the construction labor market:

(1) $PU78 = a_0 + a_1 PU76 + a_2 AHW + a_3 HSG; a_1, a_2 > 0; a_3 < 0$

(2) $VAPH = b_0 + b_1 KPH + b_2 PU78 + b_3 HSG; b_1, b_2, b_3 > 0$

(3) $AHW = c_0 + c_1 PU78 + c_2 VAPH + c_3 HSG; c_1, c_2, c_3 > 0$

where

$PU78$ = the proportion of nonagricultural workers in unions in 1978 (from the *Handbook of Labor Statistics, 1980*).

$VAPH$ = value-added per hour in manufacturing (from the 1978 *Survey of Manufacturing*).

AHW = average hourly wage rate in manufacturing in 1978 (*ibid*).

KPH = capital assets divided by production hours (*ibid*).

$PU76$ = the proportion of nonagricultural workers in unions in 1976 (*Handbook of Labor Statistics*).

HSG = the proportion of the labor force with high school diplomas in 1978 (*Statistical Abstract of United States*).

The results in Table 23.5 imply that the pattern between union membership, productivity, and wage rates established for construction does not

---

[4]See T. Carroll, "Right to Work Laws Do Matter," *Southern Economic Journal*, (October 1983).

Table 23.5

Unionism, Productivity, and Manufacturing Wages

First Stage Regressions:

$\widehat{PU78} = 3.37 + 0.924PU76 + 0.013KPH - 0.051HSG;\ R^2 = 0.9697$
$\qquad\ \ (3.84)\ \ (0.025)\qquad (0.022)\qquad\ (0.055)$

$\widehat{VAPH} = 22.51 + 0.165PU76 + 0.333KPH - 0.132HSG;\ R^2 = 0.6044$
$\qquad\ \ \ (7.85)\ \ \ (0.051)\qquad (0.046)\qquad\ (0.113)$

$\widehat{AHW} = 3.06 + 0.073PU76 + 0.033KPH + 0.012HSG;\ R^2 = 0.6295$
$\qquad\ \ (1.51)\ \ (0.010)\qquad (0.009)\qquad\ (0.022)$

Second Stage Regressions:

$\widehat{PU78} = 2.20 + 0.896PU76 + 0.322\widehat{AHW} - 0.055HSG;\ R^2 = 0.9685$
$\qquad\ \ (4.29)\ \ (0.058)\qquad (0.695)\qquad\ (0.059)$

$\widehat{PU78} = -16.37 + 9.999\widehat{AHW} - 0.363HSG;\ R^2 = 0.3186$
$\qquad\ \ \ (18.91)\qquad (1.39)\qquad\ (0.253)$

$\widehat{VAPH} = 22.87 + 0.332KPH + 0.152\widehat{PU} - 0.129HSG;\ R^2 = 0.5806$
$\qquad\ \ \ (8.12)\ \ \ (0.047)\qquad (0.056)\qquad (0.116)$

$\widehat{AHW} = 3.02 + 0.080\widehat{VAPH} + 0.063\widehat{PU};\ R^2 = 0.6192$
$\qquad\ \ (0.445)\ (0.019)\qquad (0.011)$

carry over to manufacturing. First, although the proportion of workers in unions in 1976 is a very good predictor of *PU78*, that variable so dominates the second stage regression for the first structural equation that neither *AHW* nor *HSG* is statistically significant. However, when *PU76* is removed from the second stage regression, *AHW* does become significant. As in the construction model, increases in union membership generate a significant increase in value-added per hour. In the third structural equation we find a different pattern. As value-added per hour increases, so does the average hourly wage rate. This is expected. However, as the proportion of workers in unions increases, the average hourly wage rate also increases, *value-added per hour remaining constant*.

In manufacturing we find that greater union membership, which increases the strength of unions in collective bargaining, increases the proportion of value-added paid in wages. This is difficult to reconcile with the competitive market model. Hence, it is entirely consistent that labor unions may improve the functioning of the labor market in some sectors of the economy (e.g., in manufacturing), while impeding the functioning of other markets. Ironically, right-to-work laws that make union shop contracts unenforceable in all industries, may have the effect of improving the efficiency of labor markets in construction while distorting the allocation of labor in manufacturing.

CONCLUSION

This chapter has looked at several simultaneous equations models involving more than two endogenous variables. While similar in kind to the types of models discussed in Chapter 22, the degree of difficulty of these models sometimes makes the whole topic seem too forbidding. This need not be. All we need to understand is that the exogenous variables in the system are used to create instrumental variables for the endogenous variables. If correct specification of an equation means that the instrumental variable(s) is (are) perfectly correlated with the exogenous variables in the equation, the parameters of that equation cannot be estimated. Often this represents a dead end. For example, economists have been forced to conclude that the demand and supply equations that might describe the behavior of speculators in financial markets are inherently unknowable; that is, the equations are unidentifiable. But in other cases, the inability of economists to identify one set of equations leads to the discovery of new theories that can be identified. This may be the case with future work on the Phillips curve.

Our formal work in this text is at an end. However, it is a good idea to end a text with a definitive summary. Hence, we include the next chapter, which we might title "Everything you are supposed to know about econometrics and are afraid might be asked on the final exam!" We hope you find it useful.

PROBLEMS

1.   Explain what happens to the identifiability of a simultaneous equation system if it is discovered that two or more exogenous variables are perfectly correlated.

2.   Evaluate the following quote: "A bad instrumental variable, like multicollinearity, is an ally of the null hypothesis."

3.   Consider the following structural model:

(1) $C_t = a_0 + a_1 Y_t + u_{1t}; \ a_1 > 0$
(2) $I_t = b_0 + b_1 Y_t + b_2 r_t + u_{2t}; \ b_1 > 0; \ b_2 < 0$
(3) $r_t = c_0 + c_1 M_t + u_{3t}; \ c_1 < 0$
(4) $G_t = d_0 + d_1 G_{t-1} + u_{4t}; \ d_1 > 0$
(5) $Y_t = C_t + I_t + G_t$

a.   Determine whether each equation is identified (variables not appearing on the left side of any equation may be considered exogenous).
b.   What happens to the identifiability of each equation if it is discovered that the reduced form (first stage) regression for G_t suffers from significant autocorrelation. Explain.

4.	Suppose the sex discrimination regressions on page 534 are criticized on the grounds that women are attracted to those industries in which high quit rates are tolerated. This leads to a *four*-equation model in which *LQUIT*, the logarithm of the quit rate in each industry is added as a regressor in the equation for *LPCF*, and *LLO*, the logarithm of the layoff rate, is added as a determinant of the quit rate. The following *second* stage regressions are reported:

(1)	$\widehat{LRVAPH} = -7.34 - 0.035\,Year + 1.31LRKPH$
	$\qquad\qquad\quad (3.16)\quad (0.020)\qquad (0.390)$
	$\qquad\qquad\qquad\qquad\qquad\qquad + 0.160LPWC + 2.14\widehat{LPCF}$
	$\qquad\qquad\qquad\qquad\qquad\qquad\quad (0.099)\qquad\quad (0.863)$

	$R^2 = 0.7438$

(2)	$\widehat{LRAHW} = 0.172 + 0.002\,Year + 0.445\widehat{LRVAPH}$
	$\qquad\qquad\quad (0.211)\ (0.002)\qquad (0.038)$
	$\qquad\qquad\qquad\qquad\qquad\qquad\qquad\quad - 0.010\widehat{LPCF}$
	$\qquad\qquad\qquad\qquad\qquad\qquad\qquad\quad\ \ (0.041)$

	$R^2 = 0.7287$

(3)	$\widehat{LPCF} = 2.91 + 0.030\,Year - 1.85\widehat{LRAHW} + 0.660\widehat{LQUIT}$
	$\qquad\qquad\ (1.65)\ (0.019)\qquad (1.12)\qquad\qquad (0.677)$
	$\qquad\qquad\qquad\qquad\qquad\qquad\qquad\qquad\quad + 0.665LPWC$
	$\qquad\qquad\qquad\qquad\qquad\qquad\qquad\qquad\qquad (0.096)$

	$R^2 = 0.4572$

(4)	$\widehat{LQUIT} = 0.300 - 0.035LLO - 0.807\widehat{LRAHW} + 0.418\widehat{LPCF}$
	$\qquad\qquad\quad (0.494)\ (0.074)\qquad (0.192)\qquad\qquad (0.088)$
	$R^2 = 0.3212$

As usual, standard errors are in parentheses. Use these results to test the following hypotheses:
a. As the proportion of women employees increases, real value-added per worker decreases, *ceteris paribus*.
b. As the proportion of women employees increases, the real average hourly wage rate decreases, *ceteris paribus*.
c. As the real average hourly wage rate increases, the proportion of female employees decreases, *ceteris paribus*.
d. As the quit rate in an industry increases, the proportion of female employees increases, *ceteris paribus*.
e. As the real average hourly wage rate increases, the quit rate decreases, *ceteris paribus*.
f. As the proportion of female employees increases, the quit rate increases, *ceteris paribus*.

5.	Using quarterly data from 1949 to 1984, the following *second stage* regressions were estimated, with *DPI*, *RINT*, and *BSAVE* as instrumental variables for disposable personal income, the real rate of interest, and real business saving, respectively:

(1) $\widehat{SAVE_t} = 4.07 + 0.098\widehat{DPI_t} - 2.54\widehat{RINT_t} - 0.572\widehat{BSAVE_t}$
       (2.58)   (0.016)   (0.670)   (0.151)
                                                    $- 0.589TRIN_t$
                                                       (0.762)

$R^2 = 0.7992$; $d = 0.7361$

(2) $\widehat{SAVE_t} = 1.31 + 0.664SAVE_{t-1} + 0.039\widehat{DPI_t} - 0.922\widehat{RINT_t}$
       (1.98)   (0.065)   (0.014)   (0.537)
                             $- 0.149\widehat{BSAVE_t} - 0.634TRIN_t$
                                (0.122)   (0.585)

$R^2 = 0.8842$; $d = 2.15$

a. Is either structural equation identified? How can you tell?
b. What is the potential problem with the Koyck lag equation, (2)? How do you test for this problem?

24

Postscript to

Econometrics

We have reached the end of the text and some summing up is in order. The title of this book is *Preface to Quantitative Economics and Econometrics*, which really means "everything you should know before attempting econometric research." By design a *preface* cannot be the last word on a subject; there are many excellent texts that can take the reader beyond the scope of this text. But it is a beginning.

In a typical econometrics course some sort of research project is required to be completed at the end of the semester. In that case you may be reading this chapter to get a hint on how to proceed on your project prior to mastering all the concepts in the text. For that reason this chapter is designed in roughly chronological order for one attempting to estimate an econometric model. It may be sufficient to cover the first few steps early in the term, referring to later material as the course and your econometric project develop.

An absolutely crucial preliminary to the estimation of an econometric model is a review of the relevant literature on the topic you wish to investigate. What have other researchers done? What problems have they encountered? How did they deal with those problems? What sort of data did they use? What were their estimation procedures? What did they find? Are there any "holes" or glaring biases in their findings? Do you want to replicate their findings or pursue a variation on that theme?

Another prerequisite to the estimation of an econometric model is a mastery of the mathematical underpinnings of econometric methods. You should be thoroughly familiar with the mathematical methods of Part I of this book. You should know enough conventional algebra and matrix algebra to be able to determine, at least in principle, whether the system of equations you seek to estimate has a unique solution. Are the number of equations and the number of endogenous variables equal? Can the computer "solve" for the unknown parameters; that is, are the number of parameters small relative to the size of the data set you intend to use? You should also understand the principles of differential calculus. Each parameter estimated is a measure of a partial derivative. Do you understand what a partial derivative is? The estimation procedures used in statistics and econometrics are based on minimizing the squared deviations around the fitted equation, or equivalently, maximizing the likelihood of finding the "true" parameter. Do you understand the necessary and sufficient conditions for a function to have a local maximum or a local minimum? Finally, the probability density functions used to test economic hypotheses by statistical means are based on the concepts of integral calculus. Do you understand these concepts?

There are many basic statistics books and even some econometrics books that bypass the requirements of mathematical analysis and go straight to the development of "rules of thumb" for estimating equations. This approach may be adequate if you want to "get by" and pass a statistics course. Alas, this approach will not work if you want to understand econometric and statistical results, let alone create them yourself.

SETTING UP THE MODEL

Econometrics, as we have seen, is a quest for the "true" parameters for a set of equations describing economic reality from a set of observations of actual economic events. Before starting on a quest, it is always prudent to have some idea of what you seek. If nothing else, Sir Gawain at least needed to know "The holy grail is a cup." In econometrics we rely on economic theory to generate a set of testable hypotheses. So the first step should be:

List the Hypotheses You Wish to Test

Always start an econometric project by making an itemized list of the hypotheses you wish to test. And remember, we place the burden of proof on our alternative hypothesis by also stipulating a viable null hypothesis. For instance, if you wish to estimate the demand and supply equations for, say, milk, you should remind yourself that quantity demanded should be inversely related to price while quantity supplied is positively related to price. Hence, the null hypotheses are: (1) quantity demanded rises or remains constant as price rises, *ceteris paribus*, and (2) quantity supplied falls or remains constant as price rises, *ceteris paribus*. In theory, each alternative hypothesis should be stated as a *ceteris paribus* condition. In mathematics, the *ceteris paribus* conditions should be stated as a series of *partial derivatives*. In econometrics, it is necessary to include observations on "other" variables in order to hold them constant. This brings us to the second step in setting up the model:

List the Other Variables that
Affect Your Hypothesis

Remember that your tests of your hypotheses will require using observations on economic variables that are responding to many stimuli. It is likely that simple tests of those hypotheses will fail because of omitted variable bias. If variables are omitted from your analysis, others who do not like your results will dismiss them out of hand. Hence, a good rule of thumb is: if a variable is "held constant" in theory (i.e., is subject to a *ceteris paribus* condition), it should be included in your data set. If observations on the variable are impossible, consider the use of *proxy* variables, particularly dummy variables. If proxies cannot be found or dummy variables cannot be defined, thank Providence for the random error term. This leads us to the third step:

How Will Information and
Time Be Handled?

We learned in Part II of this book that the statistical procedures used in econometrics are designed to transform the *uncertainty* of "the real world" into *probabilistic* or *risky* estimates. There is no way to avoid risk and uncertainty in our own work, but we may wish to abstract from information in our econometric models. That is, we assume that economic agents are well informed and that the market moves from one equilibrium to the next at a pace equal to or faster than the frequency of our data. Or we may wish to make the learning process an explicit feature of the model. In this case, a dynamic model, such as a distributed lag model, may be appropriate. This leads us to the fourth step:

Distinguish Between Endogenous
and Exogenous Variables

A crucial assumption in the estimation of econometric models is that causation runs in one direction only: from the independent variables to the dependent variable (that is, from the right side of the equation to the left side). Usually economic theory is based on the behavior of individual economic agents, so the structural equations that make up the econometric model collect all the "causes" on the right side of the equation and the single "effect" on the left side. However, when the model also includes one or more equilibrium conditions, variables on the right side of one equation may also appear on the left side of another. Or the equilibrium values of those variables (which we presumably observe), will be correlated with the error term in that structural equation. In such cases the structural equations cannot be directly estimated. Indirect methods, most likely two-stage least squares, must be used. Hence, it is important to determine which variables are exogenous and which are endogenous, which leads us to the last step in model construction:

Is the Model Identifiable?

If you are reading this chapter prior to completing Chapters 22 and 23, this step may confuse you. However, we will try to give you a feel for the "identification problem" as it involves the early stages of model construction. As we will see, recognition that a model is not identified at an early stage in the research process could spare you much time, trouble, and frustration.

When we actually estimate an econometric model, we cannot have any endogenous variables on the right side of the regression equation. Hence, either all the independent variables in an estimated equation must be exogenous, or they must be "instrumental variables"—proxies for endogenous variables created as linear combinations of the exogenous variables. It follows that for each instrumental variable we use in a regression equation, there must be at least one exogenous variable that was used to generate that instrument excluded from the equation, or perfect multicollinearity will result. Hence, by the use of the "counting rule" explained in Chapter 23, a researcher can determine if enough (endogenous and exogenous) variables have been excluded from a structural equation in order to estimate it. If the answer is yes, then the researcher can proceed to the next step, data collection. If the answer is no, the researcher must either find another *legitimate* specification of the model which allows the equation to be estimated, or give up on attempts to estimate it. However, as we said repeatedly in Chapters 22 and 23, if the researcher proceeds with attempts to estimate a non-identified equation, there is no lasting harm. The computer will inform the researcher that the task of estimation is impossible.

DATA COLLECTION

One of the most difficult, and often frustrating tasks in econometrics is data collection. If you or your instructor have access to a micro computer, you may find the data you need in the data disk that was provided to your instructor with the instructor's manual. On that disk are most of the data used in the examples in the third part of the text. So if your project involves a variation on one of the examples, your task should be fairly easy. However, you still may want to supplement these data with more recent observations or with additional variables or series. In which case, you will want to read on.

Data Sources

Good data are like lunches, they are never free. But sometimes they are cheap and once in a while you can get someone else to pick up the tab. One highly reliable and easily accessible source of data is the *Statistical Abstract of the United States*, which is published (roughly) annually by the Bureau of the Census, U.S. Department of Commerce. This is often an excellent source of cross-section data, although the time-series data is often limited. However, it is well documented, so if you find the series you want for several years, you can go back to the original sources quoted in the *Abstract* for the rest of the observations.

Excellent sources of aggregate time-series data are *The Survey of Current Business*, published monthly, *The Economic Report of the President*, and *The Manpower Report of the President*, both published annually. Other sources of cross-sectional data include the *Census of Population*, reported every decade, but updated frequently, as well as various economic censuses which are conducted every five years (e.g., *The Census of Manufacturing*, *The Census of Government*, ... *Construction*, *Service*, etc.). There are specialized sources like the *Handbook of Labor Statistics*, published annually, and *The Monthly Labor Review*. In general you will find the government documents section of your college or public library an excellent source of "free" (i.e., publicly-financed) data. However, always be wary when using data from several different sources that definitions are consistent.

Time-Series vs. Cross-Sectional Data

Frequently your topic will determine the "type" of data you use. For instance, if you are researching the determinants of national income for the United States, you will be forced to use *time-series* data, that is, data arranged in sequence over equal time intervals (e.g., monthly, quarterly, annually). After all, there is only one recorded level of national income each quarter, so cross-section data is out of the question. However, if you are willing to use data on different countries, then a cross-sectional study is within reason. However, try to obtain your data from a common source (e.g., the International Monetary Fund, the United Nations, or the Organization for Economic Cooperation and Development), or else you may have data incompatibility problems.

In Chapter 21 we learned that heteroscedasticity is a problem encountered more frequently in cross-sectional data than in time-series data. This problem can frequently be avoided by "scaling" your data so that the magnitudes of variables for large and small entities are roughly equivalent. For instance, international macroeconomic data could be transformed to per capita terms. Data for different (large and small) industries could be transformed into outputs or inputs per worker, etc.

The problem most frequently encountered with time-series data is autocorrelation: variables tend to move through time at a predictable pace. The problems created by autocorrelation can sometimes be reduced by translating *nominal* magnitudes like income and prices into *real* terms by the appropriate use of price indexes. Also, you may be able to find seasonally-adjusted data that control for predictable recurrent patterns in time-series data.

Most importantly, you should be aware that regression coefficients have a slightly different interpretation when time-series and cross-sectional data are used. We tend to think of events in terms of time: How does a change in cause x influence the response of variable y? Hence, we have little trouble in interpreting time-series results. However, when we use cross-sectional data, we do not observe *changes* in variables so much as *variations* (the true meaning of the concept *variable*). Hence, if we wish to explain the impact of unionization on wage rates, and we use cross-section data (since *changes* in union membership are reported only at two-year intervals), we are technically correct in saying that a *positive variation* in union membership is associated with a *positive variation* in wage rates.

Frequency of Data and the
Number of Observations

There is an understandable tendency to think of "more" data as "better" data, but this is not always so. As we saw in Chapter 21, autocorrelation is more prevalent in monthly data than in quarterly data, and more prevalent in quarterly data than in annual data. If one is attempting a *long-run* analysis of an economic model, it may be more prudent to use fewer observations and avoid the pitfalls of autocorrelation. On the other hand, with infrequent data there is a greater danger of definitional changes or even behavioral changes over the data set. Hence, picking the appropriate frequency of time-series data, like so many other economic choices, involves trade-offs. The careful researcher should be aware of what the trade-offs are for his or her particular data set.

In cross-sectional data, the problem is not so much the frequency of data as the number of observations. It is possible to get very large data sets from computer tapes on households, metropolitan areas, industries, or companies. Although mainframe and even micro computers can handle very large data sets, often time or cost constraints imply using a *sample* of the available data. You should keep in mind the fact that the original data were a sample of all possible observations and taking a sample of a sample may distort the observations used. Sometimes it is appropriate to use some random sampling techniques. The advisors in your university computer center may be able to help you with a sampling technique. Or you may wish to use some method of biased sampling (e.g., using only cities of over 1 million population, only unregulated industries, or only black households, etc.). In this case, make certain that you state the nature of your data set explicitly to avoid misleading the readers of your report.

The Level of Aggregation

Several times in the text we have mentioned that whether ordinary least squares or two-stage least squares is the appropriate estimating technique depends on the level of aggregation in the data. Economic theory predicts market or equilibrium outcomes from individual behavior. Hence, the structural equations in an econometric model usually consist of influences that are "given" to the individual economic agent (e.g., income in the consumption function, price in the demand or supply function, etc.). It follows that if your data consist of observations on individual households and firms, it is often appropriate to use ordinary least squares regression techniques to estimate the structural equations of the model. However, when individual data are used, there is no presumption of aggregate equilibrium, so be cautious about generalizing on regressions using individual data.

On the other hand, the use of aggregate or market level data does presume the operation of an equilibrium mechanism that turns right-side variables into endogenous variables. As discussed in Chapters 22 and 23, ordinary least squares cannot be used when there are endogenous variables on the right side of the equation; two-stage least squares or some other simultaneous equations technique must be used. So, when collecting your data, it is appropriate to understand the implications of the level of aggregation on the techniques that must be used to estimate your equations. Not surprisingly, most of the readily available data are aggregate in nature. Later in life, however, you may be an economic consultant or a research economist for a government or corporation and you may have more access to individual data. Better data sometimes make for easier estimation (but not always).

STATISTICAL PRELIMINARIES

As you collect your data (or after you come into the possession of a data set someone else has collected), it is generally a good idea to run some preliminary tests with your data. First, if your data set is small, print it out and proofread it for keypunch or transcription errors. A frequent data error is a misplaced decimal or a missing zero (sometimes caused by entering "fixed format" data in the wrong column). As you might imagine, if just one observation is off by an order of magnitude, your entire regression equation will be off. If your data set is large, you can sometimes detect serious data entry errors by checking the minimum and maximum entries, which are often reported on the "summary statistics" routines in statistical software packages. Also, by checking the mean and standard deviation, you can often determine if a particular series "looks" or "feels" right. If an error is indicated, more exhaustive data editing can take place.

Once you are reasonably sure of the accuracy of your data, you can proceed to calculate the correlation coefficients for those variables of interest. High correlations between dependent and independent variables is often a portent of a "good fit." However, this may not always be the case. If the correlation between your dependent variable and independent variable(s) seems much lower than you expected, you might think about changing the linear specification. Might not log-linear, inverse, or polynomial specifications give a more accurate rendering of the behavior your regression seeks to uncover? If so, refit your correlation coefficients with transformed data. However, be wary of letting "goodness of fit" determine the specification of your model. Usually, "bad" results backed up by economic theory are better than "good" results with no theory to explain them.

Another thing to commend correlation coefficients is the fact that the computation of correlation coefficients does not depend on a unidirectional line of causation as does regression analysis. So even if we suspect that two variables are simultaneously determined—in fact, even if we are unsure of the direction of causation—correlation coefficients still serve as a useful basis for preliminary statistical inferences. In particular, high correlation coefficients between allegedly independent regressors in the same equation can alert us to the problem of multicollinearity. However, we should proceed with the original specification of our model, even if multicollinearity is suspected, unless a superior specification occurs to us. This is because the results of the regression may turn out to be significant even though multicollinearity is present. More on this topic later.

A final preliminary step often undertaken by econometricians is the use of t tests or other tests for the difference between subgroups of data. These tests are particularly appropriate when dummy variables are being planned for the regression phase. By determining significant differences for subsamples of a series when the dummy is "on" and "off" often inspires the researcher in the respecification of the model. For instance, in the investigation of the "Phillips curve" we discovered that inflation, unemployment, and nominal wage changes were all significantly different before and after 1969. This led to the ultimate development of a three-equation model with these variables as the endogenous ones. In our exploration of the relationship between unions and wage rates, we discovered that manufacturing wage rates and union membership were significantly different for right-to-work and union shop states, although value-added per hour was not significantly different for these different states. This evidence inspired the link between wage rates, productivity, and union membership. The contrast was evident when not only construction wages and union membership were different for the two groups of states, but so was value-added per worker. As suspected, in construction, unions have no significant impact on wage rates *once productivity differences* traceable to differences in union membership are taken into account.

ORDINARY LEAST SQUARES (FIRST STAGE REGRESSIONS)

Whenever performing ordinary least squares regressions, it pays to remember the assumptions of the Gauss-Markov theorem:

The Expected Value of the Random Error Term Is Zero

This assumption is equivalent to assuming that the model is correctly specified. That is, there are no *important* regressors omitted from the equation. By "forcing" the regression equation through the point corresponding to the mean of all variables, the computer guarantees that the sum of the residuals will be zero. If the expected value of the error term is not zero because important variables have been omitted from the regression equation, the estimated coefficients will be biased and inconsistent, meaning that the significance tests will be unreliable, even if they look good. (Of course, significance tests could look bad, but this helps alert us to the presence of a problem). Usually it is not possible to diagnose specification error from the results of the regressions, although low coefficients of determination are sometimes a tip-off. We shall also see that sometimes a "bad" Durbin-Watson statistic may indicate a specification problem.

The correction for specification error is obvious: specify the model correctly. This, of course, is not always easy to do. The best we can hope for is that the model we fit is consistent with the hypothesis we seek to test. Those who disagree with us are likely to point out missing variables if we overlook them.

On the other hand, accusation of specification bias can sometimes constitute a "cheap shot" by someone wishing to make his or her own hypothesis the null hypothesis. There is no surer way to make a regression coefficient insignificant than to load the model with so many highly correlated variables that standard errors are blown sky high. So let prudence be your guide. This is usually accomplished by placing the burden of proof on your own hypothesis, not on the hypothesis you wish to debunk.

The Error Term Is Uncorrelated
with Right-Side Variables

The second assumption separates those situations in which ordinary least squares can legitimately be used from those requiring two-stage least squares or some other simultaneous equations technique. Like specification error, the problem of simultaneous equations bias makes the regression co-efficients biased and inconsistent estimators of the parameters of the true equation. The usual fix for simultaneous equations bias is two-stage least squares. First, each endogenous variable is regressed against all exogenous variables in the entire equation system. Then those *first stage* results are used to generate instrumental variables which are used in the *second stage* regressions to estimate the structural parameters. Note that the first stage of two-stage least squares constitutes a set of ordinary least squares regressions. Hence, it is important that all variables alleged or assumed to be exogenous are truly independent of the error term. If not, the first stage regressions are biased and inconsistent, making the instrumental variables used in the second stage poor proxies for the endogenous variables.

Another instance when this assumption can be violated is when the researcher uses *lagged* endogenous variables as regressors. Ordinarily, econometricians maintain that the future does not cause the past. Although economic agents attempt to anticipate the future, they are not clairvoyant. They cannot base their actions on the values of variables yet to be determined. Hence, if the right-side variable is from an earlier time than the dependent variable, the direction of causation does not run from the dependent variable. However, if there is positive or negative autocorrelation, the error term in this period is correlated with the error term from the previous period. It follows that the lagged endogenous variable, which is correlated with the lagged term, must also be correlated with the current error term. Hence, when lagged endogenous variables are present, autocorrelation makes regression results biased and inconsistent. In this case, it is appropriate to use an instrumental variable for the lagged endogenous variable, if there are sufficient degrees of freedom.

Two or More Regressors Are
Not Perfectly Correlated

As we showed in Chapter 19, computers use matrix inversion routines to estimate the set of parameters and the standard errors of those parameters. If two or more regressors are perfectly correlated, the computer cannot invert the $\mathbf{X'X}$ matrix and will report the problem to the operator. In ordinary least squares regressions, problems of perfect multicollinearity most frequently result from easily diagnosed mistakes. For instance, the programmer may have listed the same regressor twice or used a combination of dummy variables that are perfectly correlated with the vector of "1's" the computer uses to calculate the constant term. Such problems are embarrassing, but easy to fix.

In two-stage least squares, the problem of perfect multicollinearity is equivalent to underidentification of the structural equation. If the equation is correctly specified, there is little the researcher can do to legitimately fix the problem. Arbitrarily omitting exogenous or instrumental variables from the equation trades specification error for nonidentifiability. The results you get are bad, but they may look good! Better to be aware of a problem than to commit a catastrophic error, particularly on purpose. If the equation can be legitimately respecified, so much the better. But we often have to learn to live with our underidentified equations.

The problem usually referred to as "multicollinearity" exists when there is a high degree, but less than perfect, correlation between two or more regressors. Often multicollinearity can be diagnosed by large correlation coefficients between two regressors. The presence of multicollinearity does not prevent regression equations from being estimated. In fact, coefficients continue to be unbiased and consistent estimators of the "true" parameters. However, the standard error for infected regression coefficients becomes quite large, approaching infinity as the simple correlation coefficient between regressors approaches ± 1. This causes t tests to be biased toward type II error, the inappropriate acceptance of a false null hypothesis. Thus, one must be particularly wary of multicollinearity when seeking to debunk another hypothesis. Load in enough highly correlated variables, and any hypothesis can be rejected in favor of one's pet null hypothesis.

If we make our own hypothesis the alternative hypothesis, multicollinearity may not always be a problem. If a coefficient is significant in the presence of multicollinearity, we simply reject the null hypothesis. The suspicion that the probability that the null hypothesis is true was overestimated should not bother us. However, as so often happens, we may find that results we thought should be significant are not. Again, if this result is not central to the actual hypothesis being tested—that is, if we included a variable to avoid specification error—then again we do not let the results trouble us. Hence, only when multicollinearity infects the hypotheses we sought to test do we even seek out remedial measures.

When trying to correct for multicollinearity, we must avoid trading an *error* for a problem. If we have specified our model correctly, and multicollinearity appears, that's the chance we took by placing the burden of proof on our alternative hypothesis. If we simply throw out an offending variable, we run the risk of specification error. We now attribute to the included variable the joint influence of both the included and the excluded

variables. The danger, of course, is that since the two variables are not perfectly correlated, part of the influence of the excluded variable is now picked
up by the error term, which no longer has an expected value of zero.

Frequently, however, we can use theoretical or *a priori* information
to mitigate the influence of multicollinearity. For instance, instead of regressing national income changes against investment, government purchases,
and exports, we can regress national income against a composite variable,
injections. This substitution, which avoids the high degree of multicollinearity
between the original regressors, is equivalent to assuming that each type of
injection has the same "multiplier effect." Sometimes multicollinearity can
be avoided by transforming a linear model into a log-linear one, or through
the use of other equation forms. When the highly correlated regressors are
lagged terms for the same variable, various distributed lag systems, such as
the Koyck lag and the Almon lag, can be used. Finally, two variables may
be highly correlated through a time series but not highly correlated as a
cross-section (or vice versa). If both types of data sets are available, using
the one without a high degree of multicollinearity is recommended. Sometimes pooling time-series and cross-section data will mitigate the problem.
But sometimes nothing will work!

The Variance in the Error Term
Is Constant Across Observations

This is the assumption of *homoscedasticity*: the variance of the error
term does not change *systematically* across observations. When this assumption is violated, estimated coefficients are still unbiased and consistent,
but may no longer be efficient. That is, for small samples, the presence of
heteroscedasticity can cause estimated coefficients to vary greatly from
their true values. More importantly, the standard errors for effected coefficients will be downwardly biased in the case of positive autocorrelation
and upwardly biased in the case of negative autocorrelation. Positive heteroscedasticity is an ally of the alternative hypothesis, and it behooves the diligent
researcher to be wary of it.

Because the residual of the regression equation is still an unbiased
estimator of the true error term, even in the presence of heteroscedasticity,
we can use the residual to diagnose the presence of that problem. The simplest way, although it lacks precision, is to plot the residuals. It usually helps
to first arrange the observations in ascending or descending order in terms
of the variable (or scalar) suspected of "causing" the heteroscedasticity. If
the variance in the residual (positive or negative deviations from the mean
of zero) appear to increase with the scalar, positive heteroscedasticity is
implied. If that variance appears to get smaller, negative heteroscedasticity
may be present. More precise ways of diagnosis include the Goldfeld-Quandt
test and the Park test, both of which are discussed in the text.

If negative heteroscedasticity is present no remedial action will be necessary if the alternative hypotheses are significant. However, in the presence of positive heteroscedasticity, hypotheses tests should be double-checked. One simple approach is to transform a linear model into a log-linear one. A more complex procedure is *weighted least squares*, also discussed in the text.

Individual Error Terms Are
Uncorrelated with One Another

Violation of the fifth assumption implies an autocorrelated error term, the bane of time-series data. When the error term for one period is positively correlated with the error term from a previous period, estimated coefficients are generally unbiased and consistent. (The exception occurs in the case of lagged endogenous variables, when assumption (2) is also violated.) Hence, the residual can be used to diagnose the problem. The most frequently used diagnostic tool is the Durbin-Watson statistic, which is calculated as the sum of the squared first differences in residuals, divided by the sum of the squared residuals. By using a Durbin-Watson table (Table F), one can determine whether there is a significant probability that the subsequent error terms are positively (or negatively) correlated. In the case of negative autocorrelation, no remedial action may be necessary, since results are already biased in favor of the null hypothesis. If the null hypothesis can be rejected, why worry? However, if positive autocorrelation is diagnosed, remedial action is in order. In fact the problem may be more serious than an underestimation of the standard errors of one or more coefficients.

We saw in Chapter 21 that evidence of autocorrelation might actually be caused by misspecification of the model. In this case, of course, the appropriate action is to specify the model correctly. Also, if one of the regressors is a lagged endogenous variable, autocorrelation will generate biased and inconsistent results. Using a lagged instrumental variable will usually cure the inconsistency problem, although rarely the autocorrelation per se. However, because the Durbin-Watson statistic is also biased toward accepting the null hypothesis of no autocorrelation when a lagged endogenous variable is present, using a lagged instrumental variable is also preferred on diagnostic grounds. (Under certain circumstances, Durbin's h statistic will also find autocorrelation in the presence of a lagged endogenous variable. See Chapter 21.)

The "fix" for autocorrelation, aside from correct specification of the model, involves generalized least squares. First, the correlation coefficient ρ linking the current error term to the lagged error term is estimated. There are various techniques for this including "guessing" that $\rho = 1$ (first differences), the use of the Durbin-Watson statistic, the Hildreth Lu scanning technique, and the Cochrane-Orcutt regression technique. All are described in the text. Once ρ is estimated the variables are transformed according to the formula:

$$x_t^* = x_t - \hat{\rho}x_{t-1}$$

where x is the variable in question, $\hat{\rho}$ is the estimated value of ρ, and x_t^* is the transformed variable. Using the transformed variables in OLS regressions gives consistent estimators of the parameters of the equation and more reliable tests of the hypotheses. After correction for autocorrelation, coefficients typically have reduced significance (i.e., the probability that the null hypothesis is true rises) and the coefficient of determination (R^2) falls.

TWO-STAGE LEAST SQUARES

As mentioned several times, regression analysis requires that regressors (right-side variables) be uncorrelated with the random (error) term in the equation. If a structural equation contains endogenous variables, these variables must be replaced by instrumental variables before estimation can proceed. The simplest procedure is two-stage least squares, where the computer does the calculations. Typically the operator is asked for the structural equation, including endogenous variables, followed by a specification of the exogenous variables *in the system*. The computer then determines whether the equation is identified. This is a simple matter of comparing the list of exogenous variables with the number of regressors in the structural equation. If the latter is not smaller, the computer reports the equation is not identified, and the routine ends. If the model is identified, the computer proceeds with the estimation of the first and second stage regressions. Some programs report both stages of the regression, others report only the second stage.

There are several advantages to performing the first stage of the two-stage procedure "by hand." First, the operator typically has a clearer idea of what is going on. Since most ordinary least squares routines are faster than two-stage least squares routines, there may be little time lost. Second, "canned" two-stage least squares routines which do not report the first stage results do not provide the investigator with an understanding of how adequate the instrumental variables are. Doing the first stage regressions yourself solves this problem. The instrumental variables are fairly easy to generate, particularly when the regression program "saves" the residual from the last regression (e.g., the TSP, YSTAT, and RATS programs). The researcher simply defines the instrumental variable as the endogenous variable minus the residual from the first stage regression, for instance, with a command such as:

"Define yhat = y − residual"

The operator proceeds to use "yhat" in place of "y" when estimating the second stage regression using the OLS subroutine. Third, "bugs" in the software for two-stage least squares sometimes produce low (or even negative) R^2's and even incorrect standard errors. When the OLS subroutine is more reliable than the "2SLS" subroutine, it is best to estimate the first stage regression "by hand."

Once the second stage regressions have been estimated, we test our hypothesis in exactly the same fashion as we would with ordinary least squares. A t statistic is calculated by subtracting the value of a coefficient represented by the null hypothesis from the estimated coefficient, then dividing by the standard error of that coefficient. If the expected sign of the coefficient is known (which usually is the case, except possibly for the intercept term), then a one-tail test is used. Depending on the level of significance desired and the degrees of freedom in the equation (the number of observations minus the number of parameters estimated), the *critical value* of t is determined. If the t value for the coefficient is greater (in absolute value) than the critical value for the test, the null hypothesis is rejected in favor of the alternative hypothesis. If the calculated t value is smaller than the critical t value, the null hypothesis cannot be rejected, so the alternative hypothesis is not accepted.

AFTERWORD

There is no way that a single chapter, or even a single book, can make you into an econometric expert. Despite the technical character of quantitative economics and econometrics, empirical research is still as much of an art as a science. As often as not good econometric results come from inspiration and perseverance. Econometricians are stubborn, refusing to let either the computer or the data get the better of them. But we also have a stake in our econometric research, and we do not take kindly to being contradicted by others. After all, someone else's results can always be explained by sloppy procedure or questionable specification. Yet controversy is the food upon which curiosity thrives. And if we give pause, we can often find that the best results are the synthesis of two findings that at first seem irreconcilable.

Tables

Table A
Four-Place Natural Logarithms

n	$Log_e n$	n	$Log_e n$	n	$Log_e n$
1.0	0.0000	4.0	1.3863	7.0	1.9459
1.1	0.0953	4.1	1.4110	7.1	1.9601
1.2	0.1823	4.2	1.4351	7.2	1.9741
1.3	0.2624	4.3	1.4586	7.3	1.9879
1.4	0.3365	4.4	1.4816	7.4	2.0015
1.5	0.4055	4.5	1.5041	7.5	2.0149
1.6	0.4700	4.6	1.5261	7.6	2.0281
1.7	0.5306	4.7	1.5476	7.7	2.0412
1.8	0.5878	4.8	1.5686	7.8	2.0541
1.9	0.6419	4.9	1.5892	7.9	2.0669
2.0	0.6931	5.0	1.6094	8.0	2.0794
2.1	0.7419	5.1	1.6292	8.1	2.0919
2.2	0.7885	5.2	1.6487	8.2	2.1041
2.3	0.8329	5.3	1.6677	8.3	2.1163
2.4	0.8755	5.4	1.6864	8.4	2.1282
2.5	0.9163	5.5	1.7047	8.5	2.1401
2.6	0.9555	5.6	1.7228	8.6	2.1518
2.7	0.9933	5.7	1.7405	8.7	2.1633
2.8	1.0296	5.8	1.7579	8.8	2.1748
2.9	1.0647	5.9	1.7750	8.9	2.1861
3.0	1.0986	6.0	1.7918	9.0	2.1972
3.1	1.1314	6.1	1.8083	9.1	2.2083
3.2	1.1632	6.2	1.8245	9.2	2.2192
3.3	1.1939	6.3	1.8405	9.3	2.2300
3.4	1.2238	6.4	1.8563	9.4	2.2407
3.5	1.2528	6.5	1.8718	9.5	2.2513
3.6	1.2809	6.6	1.8871	9.6	2.2618
3.7	1.3083	6.7	1.9021	9.7	2.2721
3.8	1.3350	6.8	1.9169	9.8	2.2824
3.9	1.3610	6.9	1.9315	9.9	2.2925
				10.0	2.3026

Source: Generated with Lotus 1-2-3.

Table B
Square Roots

n	$\sqrt{n}$	$\sqrt{10n}$	n	$\sqrt{n}$	$\sqrt{10n}$	n	$\sqrt{n}$	$\sqrt{10n}$
1.0	1.00000	3.16228	4.0	2.00000	6.32456	7.0	2.64575	8.36660
1.1	1.04881	3.31662	4.1	2.02485	6.40312	7.1	2.66458	8.42615
1.2	1.09545	3.46410	4.2	2.04939	6.48074	7.2	2.68328	8.48528
1.3	1.14018	3.60555	4.3	2.07364	6.55744	7.3	2.70185	8.54400
1.4	1.18322	3.74166	4.4	2.09762	6.63325	7.4	2.72029	8.60233
1.5	1.22474	3.87298	4.5	2.12132	6.70820	7.5	2.73861	8.66025
1.6	1.26491	4.00000	4.6	2.14476	6.78233	7.6	2.75681	8.71780
1.7	1.30384	4.12311	4.7	2.16795	6.85565	7.7	2.77489	8.77496
1.8	1.34164	4.24264	4.8	2.19089	6.92820	7.8	2.79285	8.83176
1.9	1.37840	4.35890	4.9	2.21359	7.00000	7.9	2.81069	8.88819
2.0	1.41421	4.47214	5.0	2.23607	7.07107	8.0	2.82843	8.94427
2.1	1.44914	4.58258	5.1	2.25832	7.14143	8.1	2.84605	9.00000
2.2	1.48324	4.69042	5.2	2.28035	7.21110	8.2	2.86356	9.05539
2.3	1.51658	4.79583	5.3	2.30217	7.28011	8.3	2.88097	9.11043
2.4	1.54919	4.89898	5.4	2.32379	7.34847	8.4	2.89828	9.16515
2.5	1.58114	5.00000	5.5	2.34521	7.41620	8.5	2.91548	9.21954
2.6	1.61245	5.09902	5.6	2.36643	7.48331	8.6	2.93258	9.27362
2.7	1.64317	5.19615	5.7	2.38747	7.54983	8.7	2.94958	9.32738
2.8	1.67332	5.29150	5.8	2.40832	7.61577	8.8	2.96648	9.38083
2.9	1.70294	5.38516	5.9	2.42899	7.68115	8.9	2.98329	9.43398
3.0	1.73205	5.47723	6.0	2.44949	7.74597	9.0	3.00000	9.48683
3.1	1.76068	5.56776	6.1	2.46982	7.81025	9.1	3.01662	9.53939
3.2	1.78885	5.65685	6.2	2.48998	7.87401	9.2	3.03315	9.59166
3.3	1.81659	5.74456	6.3	2.50998	7.93725	9.3	3.04959	9.64365
3.4	1.84391	5.83095	6.4	2.52982	8.00000	9.4	3.06594	9.69536
3.5	1.87083	5.91608	6.5	2.54951	8.06226	9.5	3.08221	9.74679
3.6	1.89737	6.00000	6.6	2.56905	8.12404	9.6	3.09839	9.79796
3.7	1.92354	6.08276	6.7	2.58844	8.18535	9.7	3.11448	9.84886
3.8	1.94936	6.16441	6.8	2.60768	8.24621	9.8	3.13050	9.89949
3.9	1.97484	6.24500	6.9	2.62679	8.30662	9.9	3.14643	9.94987
						10.0	3.16228	10.00000

Table C

Student's *t* Distribution

Degrees of Freedom	One Tail: Two Tail:	0.05 0.10	0.025 0.05	0.01 0.02	0.005 0.01
1		6.544	12.505	32.5	93.9
2		2.913	3.993	6.385	8.665
3		2.345	3.143	4.397	5.558
4		2.128	2.779	3.804	4.79
5		2.006	2.559	3.372	4.092
6		1.931	2.429	3.132	3.727
7		1.881	2.345	2.981	3.503
8		1.845	2.285	2.877	3.351
9		1.818	2.240	2.799	3.241
10		1.797	2.205	2.740	3.159
11		1.780	2.178	2.694	3.094
12		1.766	2.155	2.657	3.042
13		1.755	2.137	2.626	3.000
14		1.745	2.121	2.600	2.964
15		1.736	2.107	2.578	2.934
16		1.729	2.096	2.559	2.908
17		1.722	2.086	2.543	2.885
18		1.717	2.077	2.528	2.866
19		1.712	2.069	2.515	2.848
20		1.707	2.061	2.504	2.833
21		1.703	2.055	2.494	2.819
22		1.700	2.049	2.484	2.806
23		1.696	2.043	2.476	2.793
24		1.693	2.039	2.468	2.785
25		1.690	2.035	2.461	2.775
26		1.688	2.031	2.456	2.767
27		1.685	2.027	2.449	2.759
28		1.683	2.023	2.443	2.751
29		1.681	2.020	2.438	2.745
30		1.679	2.017	2.434	2.738
40		1.666	1.996	2.400	2.694
50		1.657	1.983	2.380	2.667
60		1.652	1.975	2.367	2.650
70		1.648	1.969	2.358	2.638
80		1.645	1.964	2.351	2.629
90		1.643	1.961	2.346	2.622
100		1.641	1.960	2.342	2.616
∞		1.6405	1.96	2.327	2.575

Source: Computed using a program written in MS-DOS *Basic*.

Table D

Areas Under the Normal Distribution Curve

z	0.00	0.01	0.02	0.03	0.04	0.05	0.06	0.07	0.08	0.09
0.0	0.0000	0.0040	0.0080	0.0120	0.0160	0.0199	0.0239	0.0279	0.0319	0.0359
0.1	0.0398	0.0438	0.0478	0.0517	0.0557	0.0596	0.0636	0.0675	0.0714	0.0753
0.2	0.0793	0.0832	0.0871	0.0910	0.0948	0.0987	0.1026	0.1064	0.1103	0.1141
0.3	0.1179	0.1217	0.1255	0.1293	0.1331	0.1368	0.1406	0.1443	0.1480	0.1517
0.4	0.1554	0.1591	0.1627	0.1664	0.1700	0.1736	0.1772	0.1808	0.1844	0.1879
0.5	0.1915	0.1950	0.1985	0.2019	0.2054	0.2088	0.2123	0.2156	0.2190	0.2224
0.6	0.2257	0.2291	0.2324	0.2356	0.2389	0.2421	0.2454	0.2486	0.2517	0.2549
0.7	0.2580	0.2611	0.2642	0.2673	0.2703	0.2734	0.2764	0.2793	0.2823	0.2852
0.8	0.2881	0.2910	0.2939	0.2967	0.2995	0.3023	0.3051	0.3079	0.3106	0.3133
0.9	0.3159	0.3186	0.3212	0.3238	0.3264	0.3289	0.3315	0.3340	0.3365	0.3389
1.0	0.3414	0.3438	0.3461	0.3485	0.3508	0.3531	0.3554	0.3577	0.3599	0.3621
1.1	0.3643	0.3665	0.3687	0.3708	0.3729	0.3749	0.3770	0.3790	0.3810	0.3830
1.2	0.3849	0.3869	0.3888	0.3907	0.3925	0.3944	0.3962	0.3980	0.3997	0.4015
1.3	0.4032	0.4049	0.4066	0.4083	0.4099	0.4115	0.4131	0.4147	0.4162	0.4177
1.4	0.4193	0.4207	0.4222	0.4236	0.4251	0.4265	0.4279	0.4292	0.4306	0.4319
1.5	0.4332	0.4345	0.4357	0.4370	0.4382	0.4394	0.4406	0.4418	0.4429	0.4441
1.6	0.4452	0.4463	0.4474	0.4485	0.4495	0.4505	0.4515	0.4525	0.4535	0.4545
1.7	0.4554	0.4564	0.4573	0.4582	0.4591	0.4599	0.4608	0.4616	0.4625	0.4633
1.8	0.4641	0.4648	0.4656	0.4664	0.4671	0.4678	0.4686	0.4693	0.4699	0.4706
1.9	0.4713	0.4719	0.4726	0.4732	0.4738	0.4744	0.4750	0.4756	0.4761	0.4767
2.0	0.4772	0.4778	0.4783	0.4788	0.4793	0.4798	0.4803	0.4808	0.4812	0.4817
2.1	0.4821	0.4826	0.4830	0.4834	0.4838	0.4842	0.4846	0.4850	0.4854	0.4857
2.2	0.4861	0.4864	0.4868	0.4871	0.4874	0.4878	0.4881	0.4884	0.4887	0.4890
2.3	0.4893	0.4895	0.4898	0.4901	0.4903	0.4906	0.4909	0.4911	0.4913	0.4916
2.4	0.4918	0.4920	0.4922	0.4924	0.4926	0.4928	0.4930	0.4932	0.4934	0.4936
2.5	0.4938	0.4940	0.4941	0.4943	0.4944	0.4946	0.4948	0.4949	0.4951	0.4952
2.6	0.4953	0.4955	0.4956	0.4957	0.4958	0.4960	0.4961	0.4962	0.4963	0.4964
2.7	0.4965	0.4966	0.4967	0.4968	0.4969	0.4970	0.4971	0.4972	0.4973	0.4974
2.8	0.4974	0.4975	0.4976	0.4977	0.4977	0.4978	0.4979	0.4979	0.4980	0.4981
2.9	0.4981	0.4982	0.4982	0.4983	0.4984	0.4984	0.4985	0.4985	0.4986	0.4986
3.0	0.4986	0.4987	0.4987	0.4988	0.4988	0.4989	0.4989	0.4989	0.4990	0.4990
3.1	0.4990	0.4991	0.4991	0.4991	0.4992	0.4992	0.4992	0.4992	0.4993	0.4993
3.2	0.4993	0.4993	0.4994	0.4994	0.4994	0.4994	0.4994	0.4995	0.4995	0.4995
3.3	0.4995	0.4995	0.4995	0.4996	0.4996	0.4996	0.4996	0.4996	0.4996	0.4996
3.4	0.4997	0.4997	0.4997	0.4997	0.4997	0.4997	0.4997	0.4997	0.4997	0.4998
3.5	0.4998	0.4998	0.4998	0.4998	0.4998	0.4998	0.4998	0.4998	0.4998	0.4998
3.6	0.4998	0.4998	0.4999	0.4999	0.4999	0.4999	0.4999	0.4999	0.4999	0.4999
3.7	0.4999	0.4999	0.4999	0.4999	0.4999	0.4999	0.4999	0.4999	0.4999	0.4999
3.8	0.4999	0.4999	0.4999	0.4999	0.4999	0.4999	0.4999	0.4999	0.4999	0.4999
3.9	0.5000	0.5000	0.5000	0.5000	0.5000	0.5000	0.5000	0.5000	0.5000	0.5000

Source: Generated from Basic Program.

Table E

F Distribution (5 percent significance)

Degrees of Freedom Denominator (n_2)	Degrees of Freedom Numerator (n_1)									
	1	2	3	4	5	6	7	8	9	10
1	161	200	216	225	231	234	237	239	241	242
2	18.51	19.00	19.16	19.30	19.33	19.36	19.37	19.38	19.39	19.40
3	10.31	9.55	9.28	9.12	9.01	8.94	8.88	8.84	8.81	8.78
4	7.72	7.07	6.73	6.54	6.41	6.32	6.25	6.20	6.15	6.12
5	6.54	5.82	5.46	5.25	5.11	5.01	4.94	4.88	4.83	4.80
6	5.90	5.15	4.78	4.56	4.39	4.28	4.21	4.18	4.13	4.09
7	5.50	4.73	4.35	4.13	3.99	3.88	3.80	3.74	3.69	3.64
8	5.22	4.44	4.07	3.84	3.70	3.59	3.51	3.45	3.40	3.36
9	5.01	4.24	3.86	3.63	3.49	3.38	3.30	3.24	3.19	3.15
10	4.87	4.08	3.70	3.48	3.33	3.22	3.14	3.08	3.03	2.98
11	4.75	3.96	3.58	3.35	3.20	3.10	3.02	2.94	2.90	2.86
12	4.65	3.86	3.48	3.26	3.11	3.00	2.92	2.85	2.80	2.76
13	4.57	3.78	3.40	3.18	3.02	2.92	2.83	2.77	2.72	2.67
14	4.50	3.71	3.33	3.11	2.96	2.85	2.77	2.70	2.65	2.61
15	4.44	3.66	3.28	3.05	2.90	2.79	2.71	2.64	2.59	2.55
16	4.39	3.61	3.23	3.00	2.85	2.74	2.66	2.59	2.54	2.50
17	4.35	3.57	3.19	2.96	2.81	2.70	2.62	2.55	2.50	2.45
18	4.32	3.53	3.15	2.92	2.77	2.66	2.58	2.51	2.46	2.41
19	4.28	3.50	3.12	2.89	2.74	2.63	2.54	2.48	2.42	2.38
20	4.25	3.47	3.09	2.86	2.71	2.60	2.51	2.44	2.39	2.35
30	4.07	3.29	2.91	2.68	2.53	2.42	2.33	2.27	2.21	2.17
40	3.99	3.21	2.83	2.60	2.45	2.34	2.25	2.18	2.13	2.08
50	3.94	3.16	2.78	2.55	2.40	2.28	2.20	2.13	2.08	2.03
75	3.87	3.08	2.72	2.49	2.33	2.22	2.13	2.07	2.01	1.96
100	3.82	3.06	2.68	2.46	2.30	2.19	2.10	2.03	1.98	1.93

Source: Generated from Basic Program.

Table E
(continued)

	Degrees of Freedom Numerator (n_1)									
Degrees of Freedom Denominator (n_2)	11	12	14	16	20	30	40	50	75	100
1	243	244	245	246	248	250	251	252	253	253
2	19.40	19.41	19.42	19.43	19.44	19.46	19.47	19.47	19.48	19.49
3	8.76	8.74	8.71	8.69	8.66	8.62	8.60	8.58	8.57	8.56
4	6.09	6.07	6.03	6.00	5.98	5.90	5.88	5.86	5.83	5.82
5	4.77	4.74	4.70	4.67	4.62	4.56	4.53	4.51	4.48	4.47
6	4.06	4.03	3.99	3.95	3.91	3.84	3.81	3.79	3.76	3.74
7	3.62	3.59	3.55	3.51	3.46	3.40	3.36	3.34	3.31	3.29
8	3.32	3.30	3.25	3.21	3.16	3.09	3.06	3.03	3.00	2.99
9	3.11	3.08	3.03	3.00	2.95	2.87	2.84	2.81	2.78	2.77
10	2.95	2.92	2.87	2.83	2.78	2.71	2.67	2.64	2.61	2.60
11	2.82	2.79	2.74	2.71	2.65	2.58	2.54	2.51	2.48	2.46
12	2.72	2.69	2.64	2.60	2.55	2.47	2.43	2.41	2.37	2.36
13	2.64	2.61	2.56	2.52	2.46	2.39	2.34	2.32	2.28	2.27
14	2.57	2.54	2.49	2.45	2.39	2.31	2.27	2.25	2.21	2.19
15	2.51	2.49	2.43	2.39	2.33	2.25	2.21	2.18	2.15	2.13
16	2.46	2.43	2.38	2.34	2.28	2.20	2.16	2.13	2.09	2.07
17	2.42	2.39	2.33	2.29	2.23	2.15	2.11	2.08	2.04	2.02
18	2.38	2.35	2.29	2.25	2.19	2.11	2.07	2.04	2.00	1.98
19	2.34	2.31	2.26	2.22	2.16	2.08	2.03	2.00	1.96	1.94
20	2.31	2.28	2.23	2.19	2.13	2.04	2.00	1.97	1.93	1.91
30	2.13	2.09	2.04	2.00	1.94	1.84	1.80	1.76	1.72	1.70
40	2.04	2.01	1.95	1.91	1.84	1.75	1.70	1.66	1.62	1.59
50	1.99	1.95	1.90	1.85	1.79	1.69	1.64	1.60	1.56	1.53
75	1.92	1.89	1.83	1.78	1.72	1.61	1.56	1.52	1.46	1.44
100	1.89	1.85	1.80	1.75	1.68	1.58	1.52	1.48	1.43	1.40

Source: Generated from Basic Program.

Table F

Durbin-Watson Statistic: 5 percent Significance Points of dL and dU[a]

a	$k'=1$		$k'=2$		$k'=3$		$k'=4$		$k'=5$	
	dL	dU	dL	dU	dL	dU	dL	dU	dL	dU
6	0.670	1.400	-----	-----	-----	-----	-----	-----	-----	-----
7	0.700	1.356	0.467	1.896	-----	-----	-----	-----	-----	-----
8	0.763	1.332	0.559	1.777	0.368	2.287	-----	-----	-----	-----
9	0.824	1.320	0.629	1.699	0.455	2.128	0.296	2.588	-----	-----
10	0.879	1.320	0.697	1.641	0.525	2.016	0.376	2.414	0.243	2.822
11	0.927	1.324	0.758	1.604	0.595	1.928	0.444	2.283	0.316	2.645
12	0.971	1.331	0.812	1.579	0.658	1.864	0.512	2.177	0.379	2.506
13	1.010	1.340	0.861	1.562	0.715	1.816	0.574	2.094	0.445	2.390
14	1.045	1.350	0.905	1.551	0.767	1.779	0.632	2.030	0.505	2.296
15	1.077	1.361	0.946	1.543	0.814	1.750	0.685	1.977	0.562	2.220
16	1.106	1.371	0.982	1.539	0.857	1.728	0.734	1.935	0.615	2.157
17	1.133	1.381	1.015	1.536	0.897	1.710	0.779	1.900	0.664	2.104
18	1.158	1.391	1.046	1.535	0.933	1.696	0.820	1.872	0.710	2.060
19	1.180	1.401	1.074	1.536	0.967	1.685	0.859	1.848	0.752	2.023
20	1.201	1.411	1.100	1.537	0.998	1.676	0.894	1.828	0.792	1.991
21	1.221	1.420	1.125	1.538	1.026	1.669	0.927	1.812	0.829	1.964
22	1.239	1.429	1.147	1.541	1.053	1.664	0.958	1.797	0.863	1.940
23	1.257	1.437	1.168	1.543	1.078	1.660	0.986	1.785	0.895	1.920
24	1.273	1.446	1.188	1.546	1.101	1.656	1.013	1.775	0.925	1.902
25	1.288	1.454	1.206	1.550	1.123	1.654	1.038	1.767	0.953	1.886
26	1.302	1.461	1.224	1.553	1.143	1.652	1.062	1.759	0.979	1.873
27	1.316	1.469	1.240	1.556	1.162	1.651	1.084	1.753	1.004	1.861
28	1.328	1.476	1.255	1.560	1.181	1.650	1.104	1.747	1.028	1.850
29	1.341	1.483	1.270	1.563	1.198	1.650	1.124	1.743	1.050	1.841
30	1.352	1.489	1.284	1.567	1.214	1.650	1.143	1.739	1.071	1.833
31	1.363	1.496	1.297	1.570	1.229	1.650	1.160	1.735	1.090	1.825
32	1.373	1.502	1.309	1.574	1.244	1.650	1.177	1.732	1.109	1.819
33	1.383	1.508	1.321	1.577	1.258	1.651	1.193	1.730	1.127	1.813
34	1.393	1.514	1.333	1.580	1.271	1.652	1.208	1.728	1.144	1.808
35	1.402	1.519	1.343	1.584	1.283	1.653	1.222	1.726	1.160	1.803
36	1.411	1.525	1.354	1.587	1.295	1.654	1.236	1.724	1.175	1.799
37	1.419	1.530	1.364	1.590	1.307	1.655	1.249	1.723	1.190	1.795
38	1.427	1.535	1.373	1.594	1.318	1.656	1.261	1.722	1.204	1.792
39	1.435	1.540	1.382	1.597	1.328	1.658	1.273	1.722	1.218	1.789
40	1.442	1.544	1.391	1.600	1.338	1.659	1.285	1.721	1.230	1.786
45	1.475	1.566	1.430	1.615	1.383	1.666	1.336	1.720	1.287	1.776
50	1.503	1.585	1.462	1.628	1.421	1.674	1.378	1.721	1.335	1.771
55	1.528	1.601	1.490	1.641	1.452	1.681	1.414	1.724	1.374	1.768
60	1.549	1.616	1.514	1.652	1.480	1.689	1.444	1.727	1.408	1.767
65	1.567	1.629	1.536	1.662	1.503	1.696	1.471	1.731	1.438	1.767
70	1.583	1.641	1.554	1.672	1.525	1.703	1.494	1.735	1.464	1.768
75	1.598	1.652	1.571	1.680	1.543	1.709	1.515	1.739	1.487	1.770
80	1.611	1.662	1.586	1.688	1.560	1.715	1.534	1.743	1.507	1.772
85	1.624	1.671	1.600	1.696	1.575	1.721	1.550	1.747	1.525	1.774
90	1.635	1.679	1.612	1.703	1.589	1.726	1.566	1.751	1.542	1.776
95	1.645	1.687	1.623	1.709	1.602	1.732	1.579	1.755	1.557	1.778
100	1.654	1.694	1.634	1.715	1.613	1,736	1,592	1.758	1.571	1.780
150	1.720	1.746	1.706	1.760	1.693	1.774	1.679	1.788	1.665	1.802
200	1.758	1.778	1.748	1.789	1.738	1.799	1.728	1.810	1.718	1.820

Source: Reprinted from N. E. Savin and Kenneth D. White, "The Durbin-Watson Test for Serial Correlation with Extreme Sample Sizes or Many Regressors," *Econometrica* Vol. 45, No. 8 (November 1977), p. 1994. Reprinted with permission of the Econometrics Society.

Table F

(continued)

a	k' = 6 dL	k' = 6 dU	k' = 7 dL	k' = 7 dU	k' = 8 dL	k' = 8 dU	k' = 9 dL	k' = 9 dU	k' = 10 dL	k' = 10 dU
6	-----	-----	-----	-----	-----	-----	-----	-----	-----	-----
7	-----	-----	-----	-----	-----	-----	-----	-----	-----	-----
8	-----	-----	-----	-----	-----	-----	-----	-----	-----	-----
9	-----	-----	-----	-----	-----	-----	-----	-----	-----	-----
10	-----	-----	-----	-----	-----	-----	-----	-----	-----	-----
11	0.203	3.005	-----	-----	-----	-----	-----	-----	-----	-----
12	0.268	2.832	0.171	3.149	-----	-----	-----	-----	-----	-----
13	0.328	2.692	0.230	2.985	0.147	3.266	-----	-----	-----	-----
14	0.389	2.572	0.286	2.848	0.200	3.111	0.127	3.360	-----	-----
15	0.447	2.472	0.343	2.727	0.251	2.979	0.175	3.216	0.111	3.438
16	0.502	2.388	0.398	2.624	0.304	2.860	0.222	3.090	0.155	3.304
17	0.554	2.318	0.451	2.537	0.356	2.757	0.272	2.975	0.198	3.184
18	0.603	2.257	0.502	2.461	0.407	2.667	0.321	2.873	0.244	3.073
19	0.649	2.206	0.549	2.396	0.456	2.589	0.369	2.783	0.290	2.974
20	0.692	2.162	0.595	2.339	0.502	2.521	0.416	2.704	0.336	2.885
21	0.732	2.124	0.637	2.290	0.547	2.460	0.461	2.633	0.380	2.806
22	0.769	2.090	0.677	2.246	0.588	2.407	0.504	2.571	0.424	2.734
23	0.804	2.061	0.715	2.208	0.628	2.360	0.545	2.514	0.465	2.670
24	0.837	2.035	0.751	2.174	0.666	2.318	0.584	2.464	0.506	2.613
25	0.868	2.012	0.784	2.144	0.702	2.280	0.621	2.419	0.544	2.560
26	0.897	1.992	0.816	2.117	0.735	2.246	0.657	2.379	0.581	2.513
27	0.925	1.974	0.845	2.093	0.767	2.216	0.691	2.342	0.616	2.470
28	0.951	1.958	0.874	2.071	0.798	2.188	0.723	2.309	0.650	2.431
29	0.975	1.944	0.900	2.052	0.826	2.164	0.753	2.278	0.682	2.396
30	0.998	1.931	0.926	2.034	0.854	2.141	0.782	2.251	0.712	2.363
31	1.020	1.920	0.950	2.018	0.879	2.120	0.810	2.226	0.741	2.333
32	1.041	1.909	0.972	2.004	0.904	2.102	0.836	2.203	0.769	2.306
33	1.061	1.900	0.994	1.991	0.927	2.085	0.861	2.181	0.795	2.281
34	1.080	1.891	1.015	1.979	0.950	2.069	0.885	2.162	0.821	2.257
35	1.097	1.884	1.034	1.967	0.971	2.054	0.908	2.144	0.845	2.236
36	1.114	1.877	1.053	1.957	0.991	2.041	0.930	2.127	0.868	2.216
37	1.131	1.870	1.071	1.948	1.011	2.029	0.951	2.112	0.891	2.198
38	1.146	1.864	1.088	1.939	1.029	2.017	0.970	2.098	0.912	2.180
39	1.161	1.859	1.104	1.932	1.047	2.007	0.990	2.085	0.932	2.164
40	1.175	1.854	1.120	1.924	1.064	1.997	1.008	2.072	0.945	2.149
45	1.238	1.835	1.189	1.895	1.139	1.958	1.089	2.022	1.038	2.088
50	1.291	1.822	1.246	1.875	1.201	1.930	1.156	1.986	1.110	2.044
55	1.334	1.814	1.294	1.861	1.253	1.909	1.212	1.959	1.170	2.010
60	1.372	1.808	1.335	1.850	1.298	1.894	1.260	1.939	1.222	1.984
65	1.404	1.805	1.370	1.843	1.336	1.882	1.301	1.923	1.266	1.964
70	1.433	1.802	1.401	1.837	1.369	1.873	1.337	1.910	1.305	1.948
75	1.458	1.801	1.428	1.834	1.399	1.867	1.369	1.901	1.339	1.935
80	1.480	1.801	1.453	1.831	1.425	1.861	1.397	1.893	1.369	1.925
85	1.500	1.801	1.474	1.829	1.448	1.857	1.422	1.886	1.396	1.916
90	1.518	1.801	1.494	1.827	1.469	1.854	1.445	1.881	1.420	1.909
95	1.535	1.802	1.512	1.827	1.489	1.852	1.465	1.877	1.442	1.903
100	1.550	1.803	1.528	1.826	1.506	1.850	1.484	1.874	1.462	1.898
150	1.651	1.817	1.637	1.832	1.622	1.847	1.608	1.862	1.594	1.877
200	1.707	1.831	1.697	1.841	1.686	1.852	1.675	1.863	1.665	1.874

Source: Reprinted from N. E. Savin and Kenneth D. White, "The Durbin-Watson Test for Serial Correlation with Extreme Sample Sizes or Many Regressors," *Econometrica* Vol. 45, No. 8 (November 1977), p. 1994. Reprinted with permission of the Econometrics Society.

Index